Visit the **Essentials of Marketing, Second edition** Companion
Website with Grade Tracker at **www.pearsoned.co.uk/brassington**
to find valuable **student** learning material including:

- Multiple choice
  designed to hel
  strengths and w
  gradebook
- Annotated links   sites on the web
- Online glossary
- Flashcards to te   your knowledge of key terms and definitions
- Video interviews with top Marketing Managers, answering your
  questions on how they use the theories of marketing every day in
  their professional lives

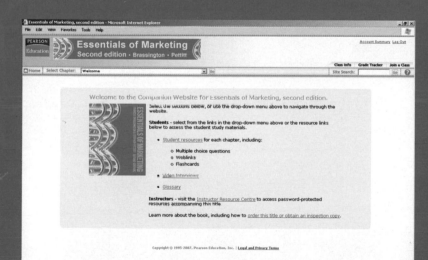

D0185369

We work with leading authors to develop the
strongest educational materials in marketing,
bringing cutting edge thinking and best
learning practice to a global market.

Under a range of well-known imprints, including
Financial Times Prentice Hall, we craft high-quality
print and electronic publications which help readers
to understand and apply their content, whether
studying or at work.

To find out more about the complete range of our
publishing please visit us on the World Wide Web at:
www.pearsoned.co.uk

second edition

ESSENTIALS OF MARKETING

Dr Frances Brassington
Senior Lecturer
Oxford Brookes University

Dr Stephen Pettitt
Deputy Vice Chancellor
University of Luton

FT Prentice Hall
FINANCIAL TIMES

An imprint of **Pearson Education**
Harlow, England • London • New York • Boston • San Francisco • Toronto
Sydney • Tokyo • Singapore • Hong Kong • Seoul • Taipei • New Delhi
Cape Town • Madrid • Mexico City • Amsterdam • Munich • Paris • Milan

Pearson Education Limited
Edinburgh Gate
Harlow
Essex CM20 2JE
England

and Associated Companies throughout the world

Visit us on the World Wide Web at:
www.pearsoned.co.uk

First published 2005
Second edition published 2007

ISBN: 978-0-273-70818-6

British Library Cataloguing-in-Publication Data
A catalogue record for this book is available from the British Library

Library of Congress Cataloging-in-Publication Data
Brassington, Frances,
    Essentials of marketing/Francis Brassington and Stephen Pettitt. -- 2nd ed.
        p. cm.
    Includes bibliographical references and indexes.
    ISBN-13: 978-0-273-70818-6
    ISBN-10: 0-273-70818-X
    1. Marketing. I. Pettitt, Stephen. II. Title.

 HF5415.B6336 2007
 658.8--dc22
                                                                    2006052469

10 9 8 7 6 5 4 3 2
11 10 09 08

Typeset by 30 in 10.25/11.5pt Minion
Printed and bound by Rotolito Lombarda, S.p.A., Milan, Italy

The publisher's policy is to use paper manufactured from sustainable forests.

contents

Supporting resources

Visit **www.pearsoned.co.uk/brassington** to find valuable online resources

Companion Website with Grade Tracker for students

- Multiple choice questions with instant feedback and results, designed to help you track your progress and diagnose your strengths and weaknesses through the use of an online gradebook
- Annotated links to relevant sites on the web
- Online glossary
- Flashcards to test your knowledge of key terms and definitions
- Video interviews with top Marketing Managers, answering your questions on how they use the theories of marketing every day in their professional lives

For instructors

- Media-rich PowerPoint slides, including animations, video clips and key figures from the book
- Extensive Instructor's Manual, including sample answers for all question material in the book
- TestGen testbank containing 500 multiple choice questions

Also: The Companion Website provides the following features:

- Search tool to help locate specific items of content
- Online help and support to assist with website usage and troubleshooting

For more information please contact your local Pearson Education sales representative or visit **www.pearsoned.co.uk/brassington**

guided tour

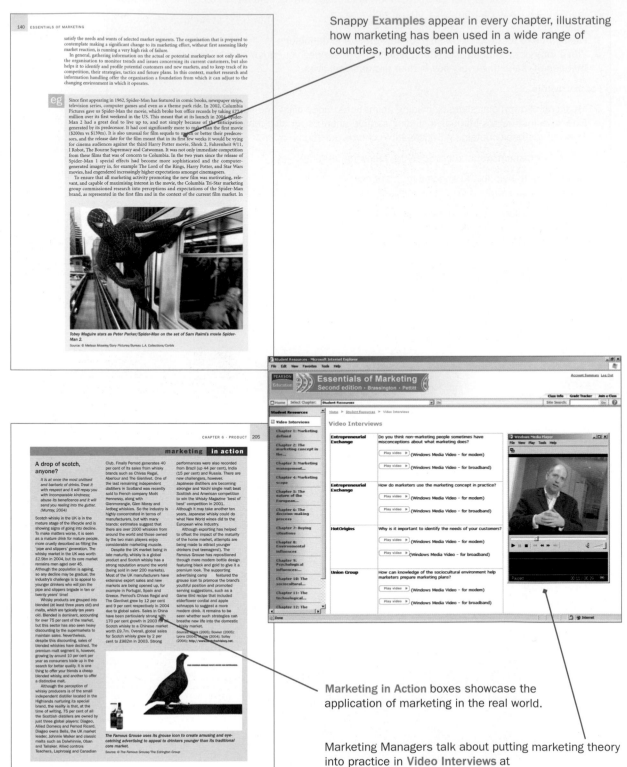

Snappy **Examples** appear in every chapter, illustrating how marketing has been used in a wide range of countries, products and industries.

Marketing in Action boxes showcase the application of marketing in the real world.

Marketing Managers talk about putting marketing theory into practice in **Video Interviews** at **www.pearsoned.co.uk/brassington**

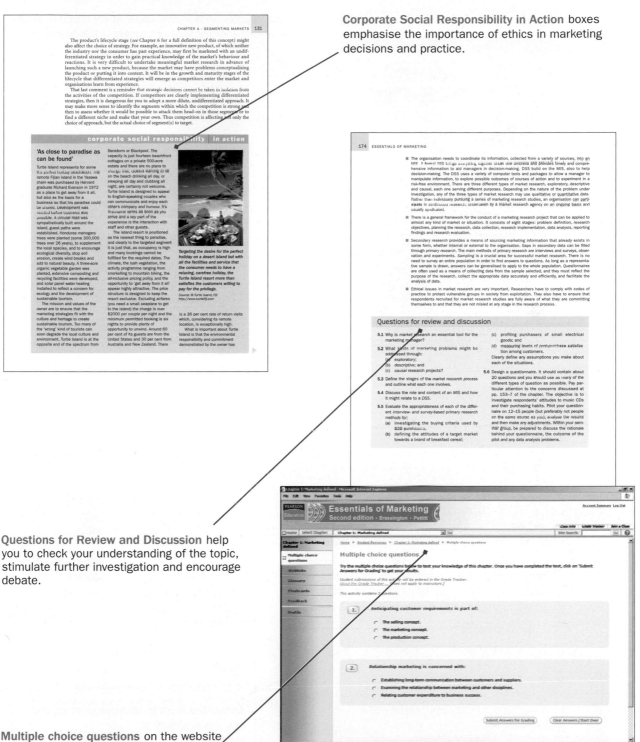

Corporate Social Responsibility in Action boxes emphasise the importance of ethics in marketing decisions and practice.

Questions for Review and Discussion help you to check your understanding of the topic, stimulate further investigation and encourage debate.

Multiple choice questions on the website help you monitor your progress.

guided tour

Each chapter ends with a **Case Study** that discusses notable marketing ideas by recognisable brands.

References are included for each chapter, to help you to take your studies further in the real world.

Annotated links to relevant sites on the web are available at
www.pearsoned.co.uk/brassington

---

218 ESSENTIALS OF MARKETING

case study 6

Small, but perfectly formed

The new version of the classic Mini Traveller, launched at the Tokyo Motor Show, reflects the Japanese appreciation of all things British. The car will feature new, experimental access and storage systems, including a cargo box which can be attached to the side window. When open this will create a table for serving tea and scones.
Source: © BMW AG http://www.mini.co.uk

110 ESSENTIALS OF MARKETING

References for chapter 3

preface

Essentials of Marketing is a concise, no-nonsense book, which shares its DNA with our *Principles of Marketing* text. It is designed to contain all the essential information that students need to understand when taking a short introductory course.

Like *Principles of Marketing*, our essentials text brings together theory and practice. It covers a wide range of applications, industries and markets, exploring the way marketers must respond to those situations that demand an innovative response.

Distinctive features

Written in a lively, elegant style, *Essentials of Marketing* features the following:

- Up-to-date vignettes and examples from a range of industries, organisations and countries.
- 'Corporate Social Responsibility in Action' vignettes highlighting recent corporate scandals and focusing on ethical issues.
- End-of-chapter questions to reinforce understanding.
- Real-world case studies designed for discussion drawn from a range of small, medium and large-sized companies.
- Vibrant and fresh text design and imagery offers a wide and provocative range of real-world marketing campaigns.

about the authors

Stephen Pettitt is Deputy Vice Chancellor at the University of Luton. Previously he was the Pro Vice Chancellor and Dean of Luton Business School, and before that he was Director of Corporate Affairs at the University of Teesside. He has had, therefore, the opportunity to practise and plan marketing as well as being a marketing educator. He also worked at the University of Limerick in Ireland for four years as a Lecturer in Marketing and was the Managing Director of The Marketing Centre for Small Business, a campus company specialising in research and consultancy for the small business sector.

He worked initially in various sales and marketing management posts for Olivetti, Plessey and SKF before taking up a career in higher education. He holds a bachelor's degree in geography and an MBA and PhD from Cranfield. In addition to a wide experience in marketing education at all levels, he has undertaken numerous in-company training, research and consultancy assignments. He has lectured in marketing and entrepreneurship in France, Poland, Bulgaria, Slovakia, South Africa, Switzerland, the USA and Kenya. He has published over 30 papers and articles along with major studies in tourism innovation strategies, large buyer–small firm seller relationships and small firm development.

Frances Brassington is a Senior Lecturer in Retail Management and Marketing at Oxford Brookes University Business School. She graduated from the University of Bradford Management Centre with a BSc (Hons) in business studies and a PhD. She has taught marketing at all levels and on a wide range of undergraduate marketing modules and programmes and has supervised a number of PhD research students. Her own research interests include retail marketing, international marketing and the use of project-based learning in marketing education. She has also designed and delivered marketing programmes for managers and academics in Poland and Bulgaria and has given guest lectures in China and South Africa.

acknowledgements

This is the second edition of *Essentials of Marketing* and there are many people who have helped, directly and indirectly, in its development. Without them it could not have been done.

Lorna Young's work on the examples, cases and vignettes for Chapters 5, 9 and 10 has been invaluable for this edition. Her extensive experience as a practitioner and consultant in the market research and advertising industries, as well as her teaching experience, have made a brilliant and insightful contribution. Once again, our most sincere thanks to you, Lorna.

Particular thanks are due to **Sue Williams** for her hard work and resourcefulness in yet again sourcing so many new photographs. Her diplomatic skills and patience have been tested to the full, and she's come through yet again with flying colours. Thank you so much for bearing with us, Sue.

Sylvia Rogan's case studies on the Bratz brand, co-written with Kathleen Rogan, and online dating, have added a lively and topical twist to this edition. The Bratz case has already provided the basis for some fascinating seminar discussions and looks set to become a firm favourite with tutors and students alike. Thank you Sylvia and Kathleen.

The evolution of this book would not have been possible without the support, understanding and constructive feedback that we have received from colleagues. They have offered constructive insights and feedback on various aspects of the book as well as continuing to supply coffee, comradeship and consolation as appropriate. Affectionate and heartfelt thanks, therefore, go to them all.

We are also grateful to the following for their courage in allowing us access to their brands and businesses for case study material and vignettes, and in some cases giving up so much of their valuable time for in-depth interviews:

Matt Allen: Voodoo Research
Lars Becker and Annabel Knight: Flytxt
Neil Dawson: Planning Director, TBWA London
Billy Franks: 'adhead'
Julie Hindmarch: Research Director, Leapfrog Research and Planning
Fiona Jack: Managing Director, Green Light Research International
Nina Jasinski: Partners Andrews Aldridge
Geraldine Jennings: ACNielsen
Roger Morris: Partners Andrews Aldridge
Deirdre Vanzyl: Wyeth

We would like to offer general thanks to all those other individuals and organisations who directly and indirectly helped to create the examples, case studies and 'Marketing in Action' profiles.

We would like to thank all those in the Pearson Education team who have helped to bring this second edition to fruition. In particular, we thank David Cox (Acquisitions Editor), Mary Lince (Desk Editor) and Maggie Wells (Designer). Their continuous encouragement, support and occasional nagging have been crucial in getting this edition finished. We also thank the unsung heroes behind the scenes: Patrick Bonham (freelance copy editor), Ellen Clarke (freelance permissions editor), Jenny Oates and Brian Burge (freelance proof readers), David Barraclough (freelance indexer), Sue Williams (freelance picture researcher) and all of those involved in design, production, marketing, distribution and sales who have made this book the polished, professional package that it is. They've obviously read it!

We were greatly encouraged by the enthusiasm with which the first edition was received and thank all of you who adopted it and used it. We hope you enjoyed the experience and that you will find the second edition even more stimulating. We have appreciated the reviews and feedback (both formal and informal) that we have had from lecturers and students alike and hope that you will stay in contact with us through our website http://www.pearsoned.co.uk/brassington.

Publisher's acknowledgements

We are grateful to the following for permission to reproduce copyright material:

Table 2.1 from *European Marketing Data and Statistics 2005*, 40th edn, (Euromonitor 2005) pp. 174–175; Table 4.2 © Experian Ltd, 2006. All rights reserved. The word "Experian" is a registered trademark in the EU and other countries and is owned by Experian Ltd. and/or its associated companies; Table 5.2 from *Admap*, December (Gray, R. 2000b) 'How to use existing channels to target customers', p. 255. © Roderick White, Editor; Table 6.2 © EUROMONITOR INTERNATIONAL; Figure 6.7 Reprinted and adapted with the permission of The Free Press, a Division of Simon & Schuster Adult Publishing Group, from DIFFUSION OF INNOVATIONS, 4th edition, by Everett M. Rogers. Copyright 1995 by Everett M. Rogers. Copyright 1962, 1971, 1983 by The Free Press. All rights reserved; Table 8.3 and Figure 8.7 from *Farmer's Market case study*, ACNielsen, New York; Figure 9.2 from *Marketing Communications: From Fundamentals to Strategies* (Rothschild, M.L. 1987), Houghton Mifflin Company, Boston, p. 640. Copyright © 1987 D.C. Heath and Company. Adapted with permission of Houghton Mifflin Company; Table 9.2 from *The Marketing Communications Process* (DeLozier, M.W. 1975) McGraw-Hill, New York. © Raymond L. DeLozier; Figure 12.7 reprinted by permission of Harvard Business Review [Exhibit 1 on p. 114]. From 'Strategies of Diversification by Ansoff, H.I., Sept/Oct/1957. Copyright © 1957 by the Harvard Business School Publishing Corporation, all rights reserved; Table 14.2 adapted from *Integrated Marketing Communications* (Pickton, D. and Broderick, A. 2001) Pearson Education Limited, Exhibit 11.3, p. 210. Copyright © 2001 David Pickton and Amanda Broderick.

National Farmers' Retail and Markets Association for two extracts from *www.farmersmarket.net*; Telegraph Group Limited for the headline 'Don't Drink and Drive and Don't Preach' taken from *Daily Telegraph Motoring Section*, 12 December 2001© Telegraph Group Limited 2001; The Department of Transport for the radio commercial 'Your Round' © Crown Copyright; Cadbury Schweppes plc for an extract from the *Cadbury Schweppes Policy Statement*; Biker Dating for an extract from *www.bikerdating.co.uk*; 'Crucial importance of clear business goals' from *The Financial Times Limited*, 5 June 2002, © Rod Newing; 'Handling the bad news' from *The Financial Times Limited*, 25 January 2002, © David Bowen.

We are grateful to the Financial Times Limited for permission to reprint the following material:

Cadbury's clean conscience, © *Financial Times*, 18 February 2002;

Photographs: p.3 Richard Cummins/Corbis; p.28 Help the Aged; p.30 Vivid Imaginations MGA; p.36 Kellogg Group Limited; p.44 Precious Woods Holding Ltd; p.55 The Fairtrade Foundation; p.66 Fleischman Europe; p.72 C&G; p.85 Harley-Davidson UK; p.97 Goodyear Dunlop Tyres Europe B.V.; p.102 Aker Yards; p.109 Tabooboo Ltd; p.118 Lorna Young; p.120 Experian Ltd; p.123 Quorn; p.131 Turtle Island, Fiji; p.140 Melissa Moseley/Sony Pictures/Bureau L.A. Collections/Corbis; p.143 hallornothing.com; p.157 Leapfrog Research and Planning Limited; p.175 SMA Nutrition; p.182 Dualit; p.186 The Advertising Archives; p.195 Mandy Haberman; p.200 Masterfoods, A Division of Mars UK Ltd; p.205 The Edrington Group; p.218 BMW AG; p.225 Olympus UK Ltd; p.227 easyHotel; p.235 KEF Audio (UK) Ltd; p.244 Kimberly-Clark Ltd; p.248 easyJet; p.265 Inter IKEA Systems BV; p.266 The Advertising Archives; p.275 Ferruccio/Alamy; p.289 Klemm Bohrtechnik/ Skelair International Ltd; p.298 Ocado Limited; p.304 Video Arts/Partners Andrews Aldridge; p.308 The Advertising Archives; p.313 The Advertising Archives; p.318 The Advertising Archives; p.321 The Advertising Archives; p.326 Nationwide Building Society; p.327 Greater London Authority; p.329 The Advertising Archives/Crown Copyright; p.347 Avon Cosmetics Ltd; p.358 Image Source/Alamy; p.362 Department for Transport; p.363 (top) The Advertising Archives; p.363 (bottom) Department for Transport; p.368 ORBIS/Matt Shonfeld; p.377 TNT Post (Doordrop Media) Ltd; p.381 (top) Chevron Ltd; p.381 (bottom left) Müller Dairy UK Ltd; p.381 (bottom right) Laurie Sparham/Universal Studies/ Bures L.A. Collections/Corbis; p.389 Slendertone Bio Medical Research Ltd; p.402 Dominic Burke/Alamy; p.409 Sue Williams; p.416 Linn Products; p.423 Sue Cunningham Photographic/Alamy; p.435 Eye Ubiquitous/Hutchison; p.437 Confiserie Teuscher AG; p.447 Cadbury Trebor Bassett; p.453 Jeff Morgan/Alamy; p.461 Hufton + Crow/VIEW Pictures Ltd/Alamy; p.463 Kirk Pflaum; p.471 Eye Ubiquitous/ Hutchison; p.476 eddy buttarelli/Alamy; p.483 Great Ormond Street Hospital Children's Charity; p.495 Friends Reunited; p.497 The Advertising Archives; p.512 The Fabulous Bakin' Boys; p.517 The EMAP Group: Kiss; p.522 Nomorefrogs Ltd.

In some instances we have been unable to trace the owners of copyright material, and we would appreciate any information that would enable us to do so.

chapter 1

marketing dynamics

learning objectives

This chapter will help you to:

1 define what marketing is;

2 trace the development of marketing as a way of doing business and consider the ways in which marketing is changing;

3 appreciate the importance and contribution of marketing as both a business function and an interface between the organisation and its customers; and

4 understand the scope of tasks undertaken in marketing, and the range of different organisational situations in which marketing is applied.

Introduction

You will have some sort of idea of what marketing is, since you are, after all, exposed to marketing in some form every day. Every time you buy or use a product, go window shopping, see an advertising hoarding, watch an advertisement, listen to friends telling you about a wonderful new product they've tried, or even when you surf the internet to research a market, company or product for an assignment, you are reaping the benefits (or being a victim) of marketing activities. When marketing's outputs are so familiar, it is easy to take it for granted and to judge and define it too narrowly by what you see of it close to home. It is a mistake, however, to dismiss marketing as 'just advertising' or 'just selling' or 'making people buy things they don't really want'.

What this book wants to show you is that marketing does, in fact, cover a very wide range of absolutely essential business activities that bring you the products you *do* want, when you want them, where you want them, but at prices you can afford, and with all the information you need to make informed and satisfying consumer choices. And that's only what marketing does for you! Widen your thinking to include what marketing can similarly do for organisations purchasing goods and services from other organisations, and you can begin to see why it is a mistake to be too cynical about professionally practised marketing. None of this is easy. The outputs of marketing, such as the packaging, the advertisements, the glossy brochures, the all-singing, all-dancing websites, the enticing retail outlets and the incredible bargain value prices, look slick and polished, but a great deal of management planning, analysis and decision-making has gone on behind the scenes in order to bring all this to you. By the time you have finished this book, you should appreciate the whole range of marketing activities, and the difficulties of managing them.

The humble olive tree is the start of a marketing and distribution process that blossoms into an industry employing 2.5 million people across the EU, roughly one-third of all EU farmers. The large producers are based in Spain, Italy and Greece. Their olives are sent to pressing mills and refineries and eventually end up in brands such as Bestfood's Napolina, available on supermarket shelves.

In the UK, there has traditionally never been the same consumer interest in using olive oil for cooking compared with other European countries. An Italian consumer, for example, typically purchases around 12 litres of olive oil per year compared with the average British consumer's miserly 2 litres. That is changing, however. Recent sales growth levels of around 8.5 per cent per annum have been recorded in the UK as consumers have became aware of the health benefits and the variety of cooking uses. Typical purchasers are ABC1 housewives, aged between 35 and 64.

The UK brand manager for Napolina must make a number of important marketing decisions. There is a need to inform sometimes confused consumers about the different oils and their cooking uses, as there is no tradition of olive oil usage for them to draw on. That in itself is not enough: for Napolina it is important that consumers are aware of its brand and its advantages over its competitors, and thus develop a predisposition to pick up and buy Napolina at the point of sale. The brand must compete with its rivals, so it has to remain fresh and innovative, exploiting the potential of various product variants such as light, mild, and flavoured oils, among others. The brand's distribution network has to be developed and managed through both wholesale and retail outlets to get the product to the mass market. In particular, that can mean persuading supermarkets to stock the Napolina brand rather than, or alongside, others, including the supermarket's own label. All of this, along with decisions on labelling, packaging, pricing, and promotion combine to form the marketing offer.

These marketing decisions are all made within the context of the wider social, business and legislative environment. For example, to improve consumer confidence, the EU has laid down specific olive oil quality and labelling standards to protect and inform the consumer. There are requirements for packaging and labelling covering things such as the list of ingredients, datemarks, the name and address of the manufacturer or packer, and any special information on storage. At the heart of all the brand marketing decisions, however, there must be a clear understanding of customer needs and what it takes to encourage greater consumption across an EU that is far from standard in its acceptance and use of the product (*The Grocer*, 2004; **http://www.defra.gov.uk**; **http://www.europa.eu.int**).

Before launching further into detailed descriptions, explanations and analyses of the operational tasks that make up the marketing function, however, it is important to lay a few foundations about what marketing really is, and to give you a more detailed overview of why it is so essential and precisely what it involves in practice.

This chapter defines and explores marketing as a philosophy of doing business which puts the customer first, and therefore casts the marketing department in the role of 'communicator' between the organisation and the outside world. Marketers have to tackle a surprising wide range of tasks on a daily basis to fulfil that function, and these too are defined. After you had read this section, marketing should mean a lot more to you than 'advertising', and you will appreciate that 'making people buy things they don't want' is the one thing that successful marketers do not do.

Marketing defined

This section is going to explore what marketing is and its evolution. First, we shall look at currently accepted definitions of marketing, then at the history behind those definitions. Linked with that history are the various business orientations outlined on pp. 8–13. These show how marketing is as much a philosophy of doing business as a business function in its own right. It is important to get this concept well established before moving on to the next section where we discuss philosophy and function in the context of the organisation.

What marketing means

Here are two popular and widely accepted definitions of marketing. The first is the definition preferred by the UK's Chartered Institute of Marketing (CIM), while the second is that offered by the American Marketing Association (AMA):

> *Marketing is the management process responsible for identifying, anticipating, and satisfying customer requirements profitably.* (CIM, 2001)

> *Marketing is the process of planning and executing the conception, pricing, promotion and distribution of ideas, goods and services to create exchange and satisfy individual and organisational objectives.* (AMA, 1985)

Both definitions make a good attempt at capturing concisely what is actually a wide and complex subject. Although they have a lot in common, each says something important that the other does not emphasise. Both agree on the following points.

Marketing is a management process

Marketing has just as much legitimacy as any other business function, and involves just as much management skill. It requires planning and analysis, resource allocation, control and investment in terms of money, appropriately skilled people and physical resources. It also, of course, requires implementation, monitoring and evaluation. As with any other management activity, it can be carried out efficiently and successfully – or it can be done poorly, resulting in failure.

Marketing is about giving customers what they want

All marketing activities should be geared towards this. It implies a focus towards the customer or end consumer of the product or service. If 'customer requirements' are not satisfactorily fulfilled, or if customers do not obtain what they want and need, then marketing has failed both the customer and the organisation.

The CIM definition adds a couple of extra insights.

Marketing identifies and anticipates customer requirements

This phrase has a subtle edge to it that does not come through strongly in the AMA definition. It is saying that the marketer creates some sort of offering only after researching the market and pinpointing exactly what the customer will want. The AMA definition is ambiguous because it begins with the 'planning' process, which may or may not be done with reference to the customer.

marketing · in action

Welcome aboard

The chances are that most of you will not yet be among the target market for cruise holidays. The general perception of cruises tends to be of formal dinners attended by well-off pensioners enjoying their moment of glory at the Captain's table. On board luxury, gluttony and an endless stream of activities appropriate for those of a typical average age of 55 are occasionally interrupted by brief, highly packaged on-shore visits with minimum interaction with the local culture. Typical passengers with Silversea Cruises, for example, which operates at the premium end of the market, are described as an affluent, sophisticated couple who enjoy the club-like atmosphere, exquisite cuisine and polished service.

Although the cruise ship vacation market has often experienced some stormy waters associated with international events, especially terrorism, it has still seen significant growth. The number of UK cruise bookings is around one million per annum and globally it was recently forecast that the 11.2 million passengers carried in 2002 will grow to 17 million by 2010. By way of comparison, the UK alone sells conventional package holidays to around 21 million people each year. That is the challenge for the cruise operators such as Silversea Cruises

Cruise ships now offer exciting experiences in locations that interest a different clientele. This ship docked in Seward, Alaska, boasts a large decktop swimming pool.

Source © Richard Cummins/Corbis

and Cunard. If the appeal can be broadened to stretch the age range down to those who are 45 and over, or even 35 and over, it will help to steer cruises out of a narrow niche into a more mainstream holiday package market.

So, here's the major marketing challenge: how do you make new cruise products more appealing to younger people who might well want a little more than tuxedos and ballroom dancing? The answer may lie in the concept of a floating holiday resort with a wider appeal. Now on offer are a wider range of holiday experiences reflected in different and distinctive brands. Island Cruises has targeted the top end of the package holiday market with cruise holidays starting at £750 per person. Out goes the formality, in come flexible dining times, a choice of restaurants and no fixed table plans. It seeks to reflect the elements of a better quality package holiday within a cruise experience. Action Ashore has gone even further with its range of on-shore activities such as water rafting, jeep safaris, mountain biking and even scuba diving.

Cruise ship offerings are evolving into three main groups:

■ Mainstream: First-time cruisers, repeat passengers, young and old alike. Mainstream cruise lines target singles, families, and groups – anyone who is looking for a fun and exhilarating holiday.
■ Premium: First-timers and experienced passengers who enjoy a more upmarket experience in lower-key surroundings. Premium lines attract families, singles, and groups. The average age tends to be higher on trips of more than 7–10 days.

■ Luxury: Well-heeled couples and singles accustomed to the best travel accommodation and service. Travelling in style to far-flung corners of the globe is the dream of luxury-minded passengers. These cruises are full of 'Enrichment Programs' with celebrity entertainers, scholarly guest speakers, and culinary classes all augmenting more traditional shipboard activities. Libraries are well stocked with books and videos. These adult-orientated luxury cruise lines are usually inappropriate for children and teens. The lack of organised activities makes them unappealing to young families.

Newer brands can position themselves to appeal to different lifestyle and demographic groups, but for established operators such as Cunard there is a need to balance the interests of its established, original target group with the demands of the younger, more active customer who needs to be tempted with more than the basic mainstream experience. Cunard has, for example, relaxed the formal dress code to two nights a week on some cruises. The communications appeal has been changed to focus on the experiences and feelings passengers can enjoy during the holiday rather than depicting just the product, the ship, on-board facilities and shore locations. Widening the target group is not without risk, if the more traditional, experienced cruisers have different expectations from the first timers who have been attracted perhaps by the novelty, lower prices and more informal activities. When

passengers on the Aurora suffered from an on-board stomach virus outbreak, some cruisers were accused of poor personal hygiene standards. Some of the traditional, experienced cruisers commented that there has been a 'massive degradation' of the type of people on board cruise ships.

So the marketing offer is evolving but some doubt whether it will really be possible to change the appeal sufficiently to attract a more youthful 35-year-old to cruising. Younger cruisers may make the sector look more appealing, but it is also important to retain customers who value the more traditional offers. New cruise liners, better facilities, interesting activities and new communication strategies may all help, but will the appeal really broaden? As people remain active for longer, perhaps it will only be the late 40s and 50s age groups that will appreciate and take full advantage of the potential for self-development through cruising. In that case, the age range appeal may change only a little, but the expectations may change a lot. Either way, many of us will become prime targets in the end, as an ageing population, the desire for more challenging and fulfilling experiences, and increasing affluence put the cruise experience within the reach of many more than just the original small niche. The smart cruise operators will need to understand the needs of the different customer groups and reflect that in what they offer. And after all what is wrong with a touch of premium luxury?

Sources: Johnson (2003); http://www.cruisediva.com.

Marketing fulfils customer requirements profitably

This pragmatic phrase warns the marketer against getting too carried away with the altruism of satisfying the customer! In the real world, an organisation cannot please all of the people all of the time, and sometimes even marketers have to make compromises. The marketer has to work within the resource capabilities of the organisation, and specifically work within the agreed budgets and performance targets set for the marketing function. Nevertheless, profitability can still be questionable. Marketing practice and, in part, marketing thinking, is now accepted within many non-profit organisations, from schools and universities to hospitals, voluntary organisations and activist groups such as Greenpeace and Friends of the Earth. Each must manage its dealings with its various publics and user groups and manage them efficiently and effectively, but not for profit. That important context aside, most commercial companies exist to make profits, and thus profitability is a legitimate concern. Even so, some organisations would occasionally accept the need to make a loss on a particular product or sector of a market in order to achieve wider strategic objectives. As long as those losses are planned and controlled, and in the longer run provide some other benefit to the organisation, then they are bearable. In general terms, however, if an organisation is consistently failing to make profits, then it will not survive, and thus marketing has a responsibility to sustain and increase profits.

The AMA definition goes further.

Marketing offers and exchanges ideas, goods and services

This statement is close to the CIM's 'profitably', but a little more subtle. The idea of marketing as an exchange process is an important one, and was first proposed by Alderson (1957). The basic idea is that I've got something you want, you've got something I want, so let's do a deal. For the most part, the exchange is a simple one. The organisation offers a product or service, and the customer offers a sum of money in return for it. Pepsi offers you a can of cola and you offer payment; you sign a contract to offer your services as an employee and the organisation pays you a salary; the hospital offers to provide healthcare and the individual, through taxes or insurance premiums, offers to fund it. A range of further examples is shown diagrammatically in Figure 1.1.

What all these examples have in common is the assumption that both parties value what the other has to offer. If they didn't, they would not be obliged to enter into the bargain. It is up to the marketer to make sure that customers value what the organisation is offering so highly that they are prepared to give the organisation what it wants in return. Whether the marketer is offering a product, a service or an idea (such as the environmental causes 'sold' by Greenpeace), the essence of the exchange is mutual value. From mutual value can come satisfaction and possible repeat purchases.

Pricing, promotion and distribution of ideas, goods and services

In saying that marketing involves the conception, pricing, promotion and distribution of ideas, goods and services, the AMA definition is a little more specific in describing the ways in which marketers can stimulate exchanges. It suggests a proactive seller as well as a willing buyer. By designing products, setting sensible, acceptable and justifiable prices, creating awareness and preferences, and ensuring availability and service, the marketer can influence the volume of exchanges. Marketing can be seen, therefore, as a demand management activity on the part of the selling organisation.

Both the CIM and the AMA definitions of marketing, despite their popular usage, are increasingly being criticised as failing to reflect the role and reality of marketing for the twenty-first century. Some criticism concerns the increasing importance of the globalisation of business and the focus on customer retention, relationship building and maintenance that characterises many markets (Christopher et al., 1991; Grönroos, 1997).

Relationship marketing

The traditional definitions of marketing tend to reflect a view that the transaction between buyer and seller is primarily seller-oriented, that each exchange is totally discrete, and thus lacking any of the personal and emotional overtones that emerge in a long-term relationship made up of a series of exchanges between the same buyer and seller. In B2B markets in particular, each of these exchanges could involve a complex web of interactions between the staff of both organisations, each seeking to work together for their mutual benefit against a history of previous exchanges. Dwyer et al. (1987), Gummesson (1987) and Turnbull and Valla (1986) particularly highlight the importance of enduring buyer–seller relationships as a major influence on decision-making in international B2B markets.

In some circumstances, however, the traditional non-relationship view is perfectly appropriate. A traveller on an unknown road passing through a foreign country may stop at a wayside café, never visited before and never to be visited again. The decision to purchase is thus going to be influenced by the ease of parking, the décor and the ambience rather than by any feeling of trust or commitment to the patron. The decision, in short, is based on the

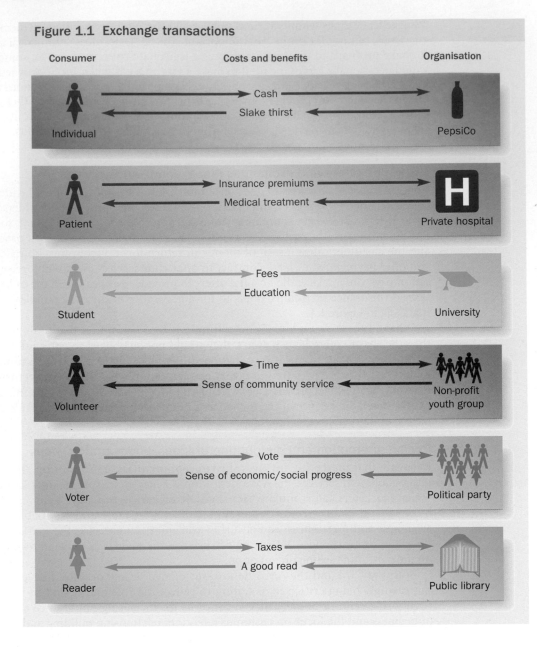

Figure 1.1 Exchange transactions

immediate and specific marketing offering. Well-lit signs, a menu in your own language and visibly high hygiene standards will all influence the decision to stop. This scenario describes an approach to marketing where the focus is on a single exchange or transaction between the buyer and the seller and that influences the seller to make the menu look good, the parking available and the décor attractive. The chances of your becoming a regular customer in this instance are, of course, unlikely unless you are a frequent traveller on that route. In contrast, a relationship-focused approach to marketing describes a network of communications and contacts between the buyer and the seller and a series of exchanges over time. Both parties have to be satisfied with the relationship and achieve their respective objectives from it. Marketing, therefore, is part of an interactive process between people, over time, of which relationship creation, building and management are vital cornerstones (Grönroos, 1997; Sheth *et al.*, 1988). Individual exchanges between buyer and seller are important and influenced by previous experiences, good and bad, but any seller that is concerned with the one-off sale and the immediate gain may find that the longer-term interests of both parties are not well served. Companies such as Volvo have supplier relationships that go back fifty years. Unlike the situation with the single exchange or transaction where profits are expected to follow from today's exchanges, in relationship marketing the time perspective can be very long indeed.

Relationship marketing is not just a B2B phenomenon, however. Internet and direct marketing are creating new opportunities for organisations in mass markets to become much closer to their customers. Consumers often stay loyal to familiar brands, retailers and suppliers for many years and with the enormous power of new technology, individual consumers can be identified and profiles developed, whether through loyalty schemes, monitoring internet shopping behaviour or other ways of capturing detailed information (see Chapter 5). It is now possible to track the purchase behaviour of individual shoppers and to create a database for directly targeted communication (see Chapter 11), and with such power it would be a foolish marketer who did not try to maintain customer loyalty and hence improve sales.

eg Fitness clubs have taken relationship marketing seriously in order to hang on to their customers. Over the past ten years membership of fitness clubs has grown significantly and operators such as Holmes Place, Fitness First, LA Fitness and David Lloyd Leisure have all established a share of the market. Mintel (2003) suggests that around 3.6 million Britons were members of private health and fitness clubs at the end of 2002, over 7 per cent of the UK population. Far from being the domain of bodybuilders, fitness is now a popular pastime for under 24s, and older age groups see club membership as a 'fashion and lifestyle statement'. Recruitment is not enough, however. Clubs have to retain their members too and build relationships with them. Holmes Place revamped its website to offer members exclusive health information and it will use a monthly newsletter to keep in touch. LA Fitness went further by launching a new customer relationship management package that uses detailed customer information to target retention campaigns more appropriately. By linking marketing communications with customer profiles the company will be able to track usage behaviours and tailor messages appropriately to particular groups of members (*Precision Marketing*, 2004).

Wider definition of marketing

So, definitions of marketing are moving away from the single exchange, seller-focused perspective adopted by the CIM and AMA definitions towards more socially relevant and relationship-oriented definitions that are considered to reflect the reality of modern marketing far better. Although relationship marketing over time focuses on customers' needs and attitudes as important points of concern, it can also embrace social and ethical concerns as well as issues more directly related to the series of transactions.

A definition that includes the important elements of both the AMA and CIM definitions, but still embraces the evolving relationship orientation, is offered by Grönroos (1997):

> *Marketing is to establish, maintain and enhance relationships with customers and other partners, at a profit, so that the objectives of the parties involved are met. This is achieved by mutual exchange and fulfillment of promises.*

Such relationships are usually, but not necessarily always, long-term. Some could be little more than a single episode but others could be very enduring. This definition still reflects a managerial orientation towards marketing, but emphasises the mutually active role that both partners in the exchange play. It does not list the activities that marketers undertake, but instead is more concerned with the partnership idea, the concept that marketing is about doing something *with* someone, not doing something *to* them. Of course, not all transactions between buyers and sellers can be considered to be part of a relationship, especially where the purchase does not involve much risk or commitment from the purchaser and thus there is little to gain from entering a relationship (Berry, 1983). This was clearly shown in the wayside café example cited earlier. Overall, however, marketing is increasingly about relationships in both B2B and consumer markets.

The idea of fulfilling promises is also an important one, as marketing is all about making promises to potential buyers. If the buyer decides, after the event, that the seller did not live up to those promises, the chances are that they will never buy again from that seller. If, on the other hand, the buyer decides that the seller has fulfilled their promises, then the seeds of trust are sown, and the buyer may be prepared to begin a long-term relationship with the seller.

Between them, therefore, the three definitions offered say just about everything there is to say about the substance and basic philosophy of marketing. Few would argue with any of that now, but marketing has not always been so readily accepted in that form, as the next two sub-sections show.

■ The development of marketing

The basic idea of marketing as an exchange process has its roots in very ancient history, when people began to produce crops or goods surplus to their own requirements and then to barter them for other things they wanted. Elements of marketing, particularly selling and advertising, have been around as long as trade itself, but it took the industrial revolution, the development of mass production techniques and the separation of buyers and sellers to sow the seeds of what we recognise as marketing today.

In the early days, the late nineteenth and early twentieth centuries, goods were sufficiently scarce and competition sufficiently underdeveloped that producers did not really need marketing. They could easily sell whatever they produced ('the production era' in which a 'production orientation' was adopted). As markets and technology developed, competition became more serious and companies began to produce more than they could easily sell. This led to 'the sales era', lasting into the 1950s and 1960s, in which organisations developed increasingly large and increasingly pushy sales forces, and more aggressive advertising approaches (the 'selling orientation').

It was not really until the 1960s and 1970s that marketing generally moved away from a heavy emphasis on post-production selling and advertising to become a more comprehensive and integrated field, earning its place as a major influence on corporate strategy ('marketing orientation'). This meant that organisations began to move away from a 'sell what we can make' type of thinking, in which 'marketing' was at best a peripheral activity, towards a 'find out what the customer wants and then we'll make it' type of market driven philosophy. Customers took their rightful place at the centre of the organisation's universe. This finally culminated, in the 1980s, in the wide acceptance of marketing as a strategic concept, and yet there is still room for further development of the marketing concept, as new applications and contexts emerge.

Historically, marketing has not developed uniformly across all markets or products. Retailers, along with many consumer goods organisations, have been at the forefront of implementing the marketing concept. Benetton, for instance, developed a strong, unique, international product and retail store image, but within the basic formula is prepared to adapt its merchandising and pricing strategies to suit the demands of different geographic markets. The financial services industry, however, has only very recently truly embraced a marketing orientation, some ten years or more behind most consumer goods. Knights *et al.* (1994), reviewing the development of a marketing orientation within the UK financial services industry, imply that the transition from a selling to a marketing orientation was 'recent and rapid'. They cite research by Clarke *et al.* (1988) showing that the retail banks were exceptionally early, compared with the rest of the sector, in becoming completely marketing driven. The rest have since followed.

■ Business orientations

We discuss below the more precise definitions of the alternative approaches to doing business that were outlined above. We then describe the characteristic management thinking behind them, and show how they are used today. Table 1.1 further summarises this information.

Table 1.1 Marketing history and business orientations – a summary

Orientation	Focus	Characteristics and aims	Eavesdropping	Main era (generalised)		
				USA	Western Europe	Eastern Europe
Production	Manufacturing	• Increase production • Cost reduction and control • Make profit through volume	'Any colour you want – as long as it's black'	Up to 1940s	Up to 1950s	Late 1980s
Product	Goods	• Quality is all that matters • Improve quality levels • Make profit through volume	'Just look at the quality of the paintwork'	Up to 1940s	Up to 1960s	Largely omitted
Selling	Selling what's produced – seller's needs	• Aggressive sales and promotion • Profit through quick turnover of high volume	'You're not keen on the black? What if I throw in a free sun-roof?'	1940–1950s	1950–1960s	Early 1990s
Marketing	Defining what customers want – buyer's needs	• Integrated marketing • Defining needs in advance of production • Profit through customer satisfaction and loyalty	'Let's find out if they want it in black, and if they would pay a bit more for it'	1960s onwards	1970s onwards	Mid-1990s onwards
Ethical and sustainable marketing	Serving the needs of the buyer with due respect for the welfare of society and the environment	• Integrated ethical marketing • Defining needs and designing and producing products to minimise harm/damage • Profit through customer satisfaction and loyalty, and through societal acceptance	'Let's find out if they want it in black, and then produce it as "greenly" as possible and think about what to do when its useful life ends'	Mid-1990s onwards	Mid-1990s onwards	Late 1990s onwards

Production orientation

The emphasis with a production orientation is on making products that are affordable and available, and thus the prime task of management is to ensure that the organisation is as efficient as possible in production and distribution techniques. The main assumption is that the market is completely price sensitive, which means that customers are only interested in price as the differentiating factor between competing products and will buy the cheapest. Customers are thus knowledgeable about relative prices, and if the organisation wants to bring prices down, then it must tightly control costs. This is the philosophy of the production era, and was predominant in Central and Eastern Europe in the early stages of the new market economies. Apart from that, it may be a legitimate approach, in the short term, where demand outstrips supply, and companies can put all their effort into improving production and increasing supply and worry about the niceties of marketing later.

A variation on that situation happens when a product is really too expensive for the market, and therefore the means have to be found to bring costs, and thus prices, down. This decision, however, is as likely to be marketing as production driven, and may involve technologically complex, totally new products that neither the producer nor the customer is sure of. Thus DVD players, videos, camcorders and home computers were all launched on to unsuspecting markets with limited supply and high prices, but the manufacturers envisaged that with extensive marketing and the benefits gained from progressing along the production and technology learning curve, high-volume markets could be opened up for lower-priced, more reliable products.

Product orientation

The product orientation assumes that consumers are primarily interested in the product itself, and buy on the basis of quality. Since consumers want the highest level of quality for their money, the organisation must work to increase and improve its quality levels. At first glance, this may seem like a reasonable proposition, but the problem is the assumption that consumers *want this product*. Consumers do not want products, they want solutions to problems, and if the organisation's product does not solve a problem, they will not buy it, however high the quality level is. An organisation may well produce the best ever record player, but the majority of consumers would rather buy a cheap CD player. In short, customer needs rather than the product should be the focus.

eg A modern form of production orientation can occur when an organisation becomes too focused on pursuing a low-cost strategy in order to achieve economies of scale, and loses sight of the real customer need. Tetra Pak, one of the market leaders in carton manufacture, ran into problems in the 1990s by concentrating on the interests of its direct customers rather than those of the end user. The focus was on production efficiency, i.e. how many cartons could be filled per hour, rather than on the problems of actually using a carton. Despite making nearly 90 billion cartons each year, the Swedish company did not fully address the problem that some of the cartons were difficult to open and tended to spill their contents rather easily all over the floor. It clearly had the know-how to solve the problem, but in the pursuit of a low-cost operator position, allowed its rival from Norway, Elo Pak, to develop a pack with a proper spout and a plastic cap that was more in tune with customer needs.

Tetra Pak learnt its lesson about listening to its immediate customers, the carton fillers, and those at next stage in the distribution channel, the grocery trade and ultimately the consumer. Only by understanding everyone's needs is it better able to innovate to deliver the specific solutions the carton fillers want. Thus the benefits claimed for the recently introduced Tetra Recart carton package include portability, easy opening and pouring, and convenient, space-saving stackability in kitchen cupboards. The focus has to be as much on making food safe, available and convenient to the end consumer, as on the cost effectiveness of the fillers' packaging solutions. That said, Tetra Pak still claims that the square shape of Tetra Recart offers efficiency gains throughout the distribution chain because up to 50 per cent more packages can be placed on a standard pallet and the shape also translates into superior on-shelf performance in supermarkets. So, avoiding a production orientation may not be as obvious as first imagined, as it requires close understanding of different levels of the distribution chain. For Tetra Pak it is even more of a challenge as it operates in 165 markets and produces 105 billion packages a year. In case you can't imagine that, all those packs standing end to end would cover a distance equivalent to 16 round trips to the moon (Mans, 2000; http://www.tetrapak.com).

In a review of the history of marketing thinking in China, Deng and Dart (1999) considered the market orientation of traditional state enterprises. From 1949 until economic reform began in 1979, Chinese organisations were part of a very rigid, planned economy. During that time denying marketing was a fundamental part of the political belief system and with a low GDP per capita and widespread scarcity of consumer goods, there was little, if any, incentive for the development of marketing activities (Gordon, 1991). The focus was on manufacturing output and all major marketing decisions such as product range, pricing and selection of distribution channels were controlled by government. The state set production targets for each enterprise, distributed their products, assigned personnel, allocated supplies and equipment, retained all profit and covered all losses (Zhuang and Whitehill, 1989; Gordon, 1991). The priority was production and virtually any product would do.

Since the reforms and the opening up of the economy, most enterprises, even if state-owned, have to now make marketing decisions as they are no longer allocated production inputs, nor are their outputs assigned to prearranged buyers. Price controls have been relaxed and distribution lists from the state ended. However, the transition process is not yet complete: many state-owned enterprises are being subsidised to retain employment levels and government power is still great. Most Chinese brands still have a long way to go before they can challenge European brands in consumer perception. Much of the growth has been based on Western multinationals benefiting from low-cost labour by contracting out the bulk of manufacturing while marketing is handled elsewhere. However, this may be transitory as once Chinese companies have gained experience of high-specification manufacturing, and learned some marketing and global branding skills, they may be better able to exploit the low-cost base themselves and create and establish their own seriously competitive brands (Prystay, 2003).

Sales orientation

The basis for the sales orientation way of thinking is that consumers are inherently reluctant to purchase, and need every encouragement to purchase sufficient quantities to satisfy the organisation's needs. This leads to a heavy emphasis on personal selling and other sales stimulating devices because products 'are sold, not bought', and thus the organisation puts its effort into building strong sales departments, with the focus very much on the needs of the seller, rather than on those of the buyer. Home improvement organisations, selling, for example, double glazing and cavity wall insulation, have tended to operate like this, as has the timeshare industry.

Schultz and Good (2000) proposed that a sales orientation can also emerge from commission-based reward and remuneration packages for sales people, even though the seller might actually want longer-term customer relationships to be established. When the pressure is on to make a sale and to achieve target sales volumes there is a danger that the sales person will focus on the one-off sale rather than the long-term relationship. There is a tension between the need to spend time on relationships and the urge to move on to the next sale.

Marketing orientation

The organisation that develops and performs its production and marketing activities with the needs of the buyer driving it all, and with the satisfaction of that buyer as the main aim, is marketing-oriented. The motivation is to 'find wants and fill them' rather than 'create products and sell them'. The assumption is that customers are not necessarily price driven, but are looking for the total offering that best fits their needs, and therefore the organisation has to define those needs and develop appropriate offerings. This is not just about the core product itself, but also about pricing, access to information, availability and peripheral benefits and services that add value to the product. Not all customers, however, necessarily want exactly the same things. They can be grouped according to common needs and wants, and the organisation can produce a specifically targeted marketing package that best suits the needs of one group, thus increasing the chances of satisfying that group and retaining its loyalty.

marketing **in action**

Crunch time for Apple?

Apple has had a tough time competing with Microsoft and its PC platform for computers. In the UK its share of the personal computer market for business and consumers slipped to just 1.7 per cent, a situation repeated in many other European markets. Although often the choice for users in the creative industries, Apple just lacked consumer acceptance among other, larger groups of computer users. Although Apple claimed to have a technically superior and easier to use product, its specialised, almost elitist branding did not make much impression on potential buyers.

All that may have been true before the launch of Apple's iPod, its digital music player. The iPod has established a 50 per cent share of the digital music player market despite competition from Microsoft, Virgin and Sony. iTunes, Apple's online music download service, covers 70 per cent of the legal download market, equating to 100 million downloads worldwide. By developing an innovative product that was well matched to a more mobile consumer demanding easy and instant gratification, Apple has become almost the Microsoft of the music download business (Stones, 2004). Not only has iPod been a major contributor to Apple's profits,

its success has had a positive effect on sales of Apple's iBook and PowerBook notebook computers through greater brand awareness and loyalty.

By spotting an opportunity and getting into the market first, Apple gained an early and significant lead. It deliberately reassessed its marketing strategy for distribution by opening 101 company-owned retail stores in addition to its online store. By being able to control its own retail space it has been able to give the product appropriate in-store attention to allow high degrees of customer interactivity and to offer over 400 accessories. Apple's pricing was deliberately aligned with a premium perception, at 79p per download in the UK and 68p elsewhere in Europe.

The key question, however, is how long iPod will retain its dominant position. Mobile phone companies keen to expand beyond voice and text messaging have entered the music download market as a way of recouping their huge investments in 3G technology. History is not on the side of iPod. Palm in PDAs (personal digital assistants), Nintendo in game consoles and indeed Apple in PCs are all examples of companies with technological and marketing leads that were subsequently eroded. Often, new competitors come in offering more features at lower prices, taking advantage of further advances. Korean iRiver introduced an MP3 player with a colour screen that also allowed the downloading of photos, and Archos, from France, launched various jukebox-cum-colour photo wallets. Both manufacturers, along with others, sell small, portable devices which play music and video. However, Apple is not standing idly by. Recently it launched the iPod Shuffle, a flash player that costs $99 (with a capacity of 120 songs) or $149 (240 songs). It is the size of a pack of chewing gum, although some commentators believe that Apple must be careful not to cannibalise the higher-priced, feature-packed iPod (Burrows and Park, 2005).

As the market grows and becomes more of a mass market than a niche, Apple might also have to look for new ways to promote iTunes. Currently the focus is on owning the download rather than 'renting' a favourite song on a subscription basis. Subscription services, where a regular monthly premium enables easy and frequent access, is a very low-cost way of exploring music alternatives and discovering new sounds without the need for ownership. Meledo is considering offering subscribers to particular bands early, and semi-exclusive access to new releases at a premium price. It has already launched a service to enable customers to send songs to friends and lovers that enables a free preview.

To give flexibility in pricing and profit management, Apple needs to ensure that economies of scale can be achieved in production, and that means gaining access to a wider cross-section of the market. In part this could be achieved by licensing the technology to other hardware suppliers such as Hewlett Packard and Motorola who will resell the iPod under their own brand names. If Apple could find more alliances such as with Amazon, Cisco and Nokia, it would be in a stronger position to establish a long-term industry standard and to achieve much wider distribution (Burrows and Lowry, 2004).

So Apple will need to be one beat ahead of the rest if it wants to maintain its early lead in a market still in its infancy. This will have implications for all of its marketing activities in an environment that will become more highly competitive as technologies and customer needs evolve.

Sources: Burrows (2004); Burrows and Lowry (2004); Burrows and Park (2005); Durman (2005); *The Economist* (2005); Morrison (2004); Rigby (2004); Stones (2004).

A marketing orientation is far more, however, than simply matching products and services to customers. It has to emerge from an organisational philosophy, an approach to doing business that naturally places customers and their needs at the heart of what the organisation does. Not all organisations do this to the same extent, although many are trying to move towards it.

Henderson (1998), however, urges caution in assuming that a marketing orientation is a guarantee of success in achieving above average performance. There are many internal and external factors at work in determining success, of which effective marketing thinking is but one. If marketing dominates the rest of the organisation it can help to diminish key competencies in other areas such as manufacturing productivity or technological innovation. Furthermore, the marketing department approach to organising the marketing function can isolate marketing from design, production, deliveries, technical service, complaints handling, invoicing and other customer-related activities. As a consequence, the rest of the organisation could be alienated from marketing, making the coordination of customer and market-oriented activities across the organisation more difficult (Piercy, 1992). This underlines the importance of Narver and Slater's (1990) three key factors that help the marketing function to achieve above average performance:

■ *Interfunctional orientation* enabling cooperation between the management functions to create superior value

- *Competitor orientation* to retain an edge
- *Customer orientation.*

Having established the importance of the marketing concept to an organisation, the chapter now turns to the issue of how it is developing further to meet the changing demands of society.

Emergent marketing philosophies

The marketing concept and the philosophy of a marketing orientation continue to evolve. In increasingly competitive global markets consisting of increasingly demanding customers, organisations are continually striving to find more effective ways of attracting and retaining customers, and sometimes that could mean refining further exactly what marketing means.

Corporate social responsibility: societal and ethical marketing. Corporate social responsibility suggests that organisations should not only consider their customers and their profitability, but also the good of the wider communities, local and global, within which they exist. As Smith and Higgins (2000) put it, consumers now are not only looking for environmentally sensitive and ethically considerate products, but also for businesses to demonstrate a wider set of ethical commitments to society, '[A business] must, as should we all, become a "good citizen"'. Carroll (1999) provides an excellent review of the history and evolution of the CSR concept, but it is his own 1991 paper which provides the basis for the most succinct definition of CSR which will underpin the coverage of CSR in this book:

> . . . *four kinds of social responsibilities constitute total CSR: economic, legal, ethical and philanthropic . . . [B]usiness should not fulfill these in sequential fashion but . . . each is to be fulfilled at all times . . . The CSR firm should strive to make a profit, obey the law, be ethical, and be a good corporate citizen.* (Carroll, 1991, pp. 40–3, as summarised by Carroll, 1999)

Marketing within a CSR context is concerned with ensuring that organisations handle marketing responsibly, and in a way that contributes to the well-being of society. Consumers have become increasingly aware of the social and ethical issues involved in marketing, such as the ethics of marketing to children, fair trade with third-world suppliers, the ecological impact of business, and the extent of good 'corporate citizenship' displayed by companies, for example. Companies looking to establish a reputable and trustworthy image as a foundation for building long-term relationships with their customers thus need to consider the philosophy of CSR seriously if they are to meet their customers' wider expectations, and create and maintain competitive advantage (Balestrini, 2001). Indeed, some companies, such as Body Shop, have adopted a very proactive approach to societal marketing and have made CSR a central pillar of their whole business philosophy (see Hartman and Beck-Dudley, 1999 for a detailed discussion of marketing ethics within Body Shop International).

The Responsible Century?, a survey published in 2000 by Burson-Marsteller and the Prince of Wales' Business Leaders' Forum, gathered opinions from 100 leading business opinion-formers and decision-makers from France, Germany and the UK. Two-thirds 'agreed strongly' that CSR will be important in the future and 89 per cent said that their future decisions would be influenced by CSR (CSR Forum, 2001). Interestingly, the survey points to a shift away from defining CSR purely in terms of hard, quantifiable issues such as environmental performance, charitable donations to an emphasis on softer issues such as treatment of employees, commitment to local communities and ethical business conduct. Internal as well as external behaviour now matters.

CSR is rapidly changing from being a 'would like' to a 'must have' feature of business. Although at the time of writing businesses are under no obligation to report on their CSR activities in the UK, many already do and it is likely that pressure for transparency on CSR will only increase. The latest buzzword in corporate accountability is '360 degree reporting' which acknowledges the need to produce annual reports that take a much more holistic view of a company's activities to meet the information needs of pressure groups, those looking for ethical investments, and the wider audience interested in CSR, rather than just shareholders and traditional bankers. Companies in potentially sensitive sectors, such as utilities and transport, have begun to produce separate reports on their CSR performance, for example utility company Kelda Group's annual *Corporate Social Responsibility Review*, water company Severn Trent's

Corporate Responsibility Report, Network Rail's *Corporate Responsibility Report*, and British Nuclear Fuel's *Corporate Responsibility Report*. These documents may not have the most imaginative titles, but they do represent an important step in the evolution of corporate reporting.

corporate social responsibility   in action

Consumers behaving badly?

While we are all so busy demanding that organisations take their CSR seriously, it is perhaps easy to forget that responsibilities and obligations of 'good citizenship' extend to us as consumers as well. Don't organisations also have the right to ask just how ethical their customers are? Babakus *et al.* (2004) undertook a survey across six different countries to explore the nature of consumer ethical beliefs and the influences on them. Eleven behavioural scenarios were presented to respondents who were then asked to indicate their degree of (dis)approval of that behaviour on a 1 to 5 scale, where 1 represented 'wrong' and 5 represented 'not wrong'. Across the whole sample, for instance, respondents tended to regard behaviours such as 'taking towels from hotels and blankets from aircraft as souvenirs' as far less wrong than 'drinking a can of soda in a supermarket and not buying it'. Age and nationality both appeared to be significant influencers. Thus in general,

respondents from Brunei, Hong Kong and the USA were more disapproving of the behaviours than respondents from Austria, France and the UK. Younger consumers (aged under 35) from the USA, France and the UK tended to be more tolerant of unethical consumer behaviour than older people. Young French consumers think that there is nothing wrong with 'cutting in when there is a long line' while young Austrians found this the least acceptable of all the scenarios. Interestingly, the Austrian respondents, regardless of age, were far more tolerant of 'reporting a lost item as stolen to an insurance company to collect the money' than any other nationality.

For marketers, it is perhaps a case of 'caveat vendor' and an indication of the need to make clear to customers what is expected of them and the consequences that will follow unethical behaviour on their part. It is a fine line for organisations to tread, however. Undoubtedly, record companies are well within their legal and ethical rights to take legal action against

individuals caught with illegal music downloads, but the publicity given to what are perceived as heavy-handed tactics does not reflect well on corporate reputations. An article in *The Daily Mail* (Poulter, 2005) is a typically emotive report, in that it highlights a couple of individual cases of children as young as 12 receiving demands to pay thousands of pounds in compensation or face legal action. There is an interesting phrase in this article, 'many of those being hit by music industry bosses are ordinary families, rather than criminal gangs', implying that context makes a difference to how behaviour is perceived and judged. However, at least one of the so-called pirates has seen the error of his ways: 'When you compare that with slogging about a music store to buy an album that costs £12 and has only two or three tunes that you like, it's not hard to see why so many people do it. I know it is stealing. I am stealing from someone what they have rightfully earned' (as quoted by Poulter, 2005).

Sources: Babakus *et al.* (2004); Poulter (2005).

eg Severn Trent plc, based in the UK Midlands, has a turnover of some £1.6 billion and employs over 14,000 people across the UK, US and Europe. With its strapline 'The Environment is Our Business', Severn Trent takes CSR very seriously. As an environmental services company, concerned with water treatment, waste disposal and utilities, it has always been focused on 'green' issues, but its commitment to CSR goes much further than that. In its *Corporate Responsibility Report: Stewardship 2004* it states 'Every business needs ideals above those of simply making money. And no business can operate in isolation from society ... We believe that business is part of the process of achieving a sustainable future for society as a whole. Business must practice stewardship of natural resources, recognise its role as an integral part of the communities within which it operates, and be accountable for its activities ... As a business we are both a corporate citizen, with opportunities to shape the lives of the communities where we operate, and an employer, with significant responsibilities for the working environment we provide for our people.' (Severn Trent, 2004, p. 8).

The Stewardship report thus covers many areas of CSR, relating not only to the Group's approach to the protection of the natural environment, biodiversity and the efficient use of natural resources within its operations, but also to its role within society and local communities, its perceived CSR leadership role among its suppliers and customers in improving the performance of the entire supply chain, and its internal application of ethical principles in its HRM policies, for example. All of this is very much in line with Carroll's (1999) ideas of CSR, mentioned earlier.

Towards 'sustainable marketing'. Inextricably tied in with the concept and best practice of CSR in its widest sense is the idea of sustainable development. Sustainability was defined in the Brundtland Report of 1987 as:

> *development that meets the needs of the present without compromising the ability of future generations to meet their own needs.* (WCED, 1987)

Sustainability is not just concerned with environmental and ecological issues, as important as these are, but also with the social, economic and cultural development of society. The wider 'softer agenda' includes, therefore, the fair distribution of economic benefits, human rights, community involvement and product responsibility. This is taken seriously by business. Echoing the sentiments expressed in the Severn Trent example above, Jürgen Strube, the chairman of BASF, the large German chemical company, said that sustainable development in the areas of the economy, ecology and society will be the key to the success in the twenty-first century (as reported by Challener, 2001). Society cannot continue to enjoy economic growth without reference to the consequences for environmental protection and social stability (*OECD Observer, 2001*).

In the light of the whole CSR/sustainability debate, sustainable marketing is likely to become the next stage in the conceptual development of marketing as it focuses on some of the significant long-term challenges facing society in the twenty-first century. The challenge to marketing thinking is to broaden the concept of exchange to incorporate the longer-term needs of society at large rather than the short-term pursuit of individual gratification and consumption. It is not about marketers revising strategies to exploit new societal opportunities, it is about what society can afford to allow marketers to exploit and over what timescale. This sounds very idealistic: in a competitive world in which the customer is free to choose and, moreover, in which business operates on the principle of meeting customers' needs and wants, it sometimes requires courage for a business to change those principles if those changes precede customer concern and government legislation. Consumers within society will have to travel up a learning curve and that process is only just beginning.

We would, therefore, like to define sustainable marketing as:

> *the establishment, maintenance and enhancement of customer relationships so that the objectives of the parties involved are met without compromising the ability of future generations to achieve their own objectives.*

In short, consumers today, whatever the market imperative, cannot be allowed to destroy the opportunities for society tomorrow by taking out more than is being put back in. This not only embraces environmental and ecological issues but also the social and cultural consequences of a consumer society that equates 'more' with 'better'.

How does all this impact on the marketing process? The internalisation of costs (making the polluters pay), green taxes, legislation, support for cleaner technology, redesigned products to minimise resources and waste streams, reverse distribution channels to receive products for recycling and consumer education on sustainability are all an essential part of a new marketing agenda for the twenty-first century. To some it is not a choice, but a mandate that cannot be ignored (Fuller, 1999). Ecological and environmental agendas to date have had an impact on marketing strategy, but it has been patchy. The old adage 'reduce, recycle and reuse' has, for example, influenced the type of packaging materials used to ensure recyclability. Clothing manufacturers have produced plastic outdoor clothing that can be recycled; glue manufacturers have reduced the toxic emissions from their products; car manufacturers, in accordance with the EU's End-of-Life Vehicle Directive, now have to consider the recycling or other means of disposal of old cars. However, research often indicates that consumers given a free choice are reluctant to pay more for environmentally friendly products such as organic food and many find it hard to establish the link between their individual buying decision and its global impact. It will require a societal balance and adjustment period, but evidence is mounting that if change does not take place, the negative long-term impact on the environment and society could be irreversible.

The marketing concept in the organisation

What does the philosophy of marketing as a way of doing business mean to a real organisation? In this section we explore the practicalities of implementing the marketing concept, showing just how fundamentally marketing can influence the structure and management of the whole organisation. First, we look at the complexity of the organisational environment, and then think about how marketing can help to manage and make sense of the relationship between the organisation and the outside world. Second, we examine the relationship between marketing and the internal world of the organisation, looking, for example, at the potential conflicts between marketing and other business functions. To bring the external and the internal environments together, this section is summarised by looking at marketing as an interface, i.e. as a linking mechanism between the organisation and various external elements.

■ The external organisational environment

Figure 1.2 summarises the complexity of the external world in which an organisation has to operate. There are many people, groups, elements and forces that have the power to influence, directly or indirectly, the way in which the organisation conducts its business. The organisational environment includes both the immediate operating environment and the broader issues and trends that affect business in the longer term.

Current and potential customers

Customers are obviously vital to the continued health of the organisation. It is essential, therefore, that it is able to locate customers, find out what they want and then communicate its promises to them. Those promises have to be delivered (i.e. the right product at the right time at the right price in the right place) and followed up to ensure that customers are satisfied.

Figure 1.2 The organisation's environment

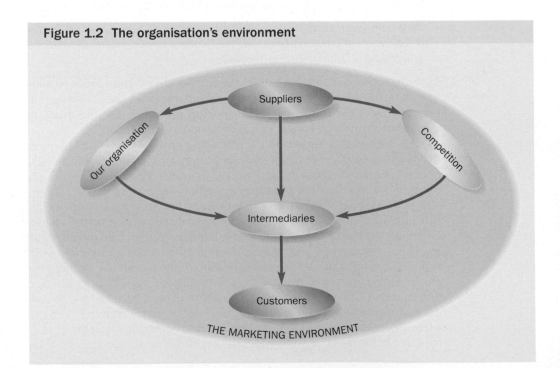

Competitors

Competitors, however, make the organisation's liaison with customer groups a little more difficult, since by definition they are largely pursuing the same set of customers. Customers will make comparisons between different offerings, and will listen to competitors' messages. The organisation, therefore, has not only to monitor what its competitors are actually doing now, but also to try to anticipate what they will do in the future in order to develop counter-measures in advance. European giants Nestlé and Unilever, for example, compete fiercely with each other in several fast moving consumer goods (fmcg) markets.

Intermediaries

Intermediaries often provide invaluable services in getting goods from manufacturers to the end buyer. Without the cooperation of a network of wholesalers and/or retailers, many manufacturers would have immense problems in getting their goods to the end customer at the right time in the right place. The organisation must, therefore, think carefully about how best to distribute goods, and build appropriate relationships with intermediaries. Again, this is an area in which competition can interfere, and organisations cannot always obtain access to the channels of distribution that they want, or trade on the terms that they want.

Suppliers

Another crucial link in the chain is the supplier. Losing a key supplier of components or raw materials can mean that production flow is interrupted, or that a lower-quality or more expensive substitution has to be made. This means that there is a danger that the organisation will fail in its promises to the customer, for example by not providing the right product at the right time at the right price. Choice of suppliers, negotiation of terms and relationship building therefore all become important tasks.

The wider marketing environment, which will be discussed in further detail in Chapter 2, covers all the other influences that might provide opportunities or threats to the organisation. These include technological development, legal and regulatory constraints, the economic environment and sociocultural changes. It is essential for the organisation to keep track of all these factors, and to incorporate them into decision-making as early as possible if it is to keep ahead of the competition.

This overview of the organisation's world has implied that there are many relationships that matter and that need to be managed if the organisation is to conduct its business successfully. The main responsibility for creating and managing these relationships lies with the marketing function.

■ The internal organisational environment

As well as fostering and maintaining relationships with external groups and forces, the marketing function has to interact with other functions within the organisation. Not all organisations have formal marketing departments, and even if they do they can be set up in different ways, but wherever the responsibility for the planning and implementation of marketing lies, close interaction with other areas of the organisation is essential. Not all business functions, however, operate with the same kind of focus, and sometimes there can be potential conflict where perspectives and concerns do not match up. This subsection looks at just a few other functions typically found in all but the smallest organisations and some of the points of conflict between them and the marketers.

Finance

The finance function, for example, sets budgets, perhaps early in the financial year, and expects other functions to stick to them. It wants hard evidence to justify expenditure, and it usually wants pricing to cover costs and to contribute towards profit. Marketing, on the other hand, tends to want the flexibility to act intuitively, according to fast changing needs. Marketing also takes a longer, strategic view of pricing, and may be prepared to make a short-term financial loss in order to develop the market or to further wider strategic objectives.

In terms of accounting and credit, i.e. where finance comes into contact with customers, the finance function would want pricing and procedures to be as standardised as possible, for administrative ease. An accountant would want to impose tough credit terms and short credit periods, preferably only dealing with customers with proven credit records. Marketing, however, would again want some flexibility to allow credit terms to be used as part of a negotiation procedure, and to use pricing discounts as a marketing tool.

Purchasing

The purchasing function can also become somewhat bureaucratic, with too high a priority given to price. A focus on economical purchase quantities, standardisation and the price of materials, along with the desire to purchase as infrequently as possible, can all reduce the flexibility and responsiveness of the organisation. Marketing prefers to think of the quality of the components and raw materials rather than the price, and to go for non-standard parts, to increase its ability to differentiate its product from that of the competition. To be fair to purchasing, this is a somewhat traditional view. The rise of relationship marketing (pp. 5–7) and the increasing acceptance of just-in-time (JIT) systems (Chapter 8) mean that marketing and purchasing are now working more closely than ever in building long-term, flexible, co-operative relationships with suppliers.

Production

Production has perhaps the greatest potential to clash with marketing. It may be in production's interests to operate long, large production runs with as few variations on the basic product as possible, and with changes to the product as infrequently as possible, at least where mass production is concerned. This also means that production would prefer to deal with standard, rather than customised, orders. If new products are necessary, then the longer the lead time they are given to get production up to speed and running consistently, the better. Marketing has a greater sense of urgency and a greater demand for flexibility. Marketing may look for short production runs of many varied models in order to serve a range of needs in the market. Similarly, changes to the product may be frequent in order to keep the market interested. Marketing, particularly when serving B2B customers, may also be concerned with customisation as a means of better meeting the buyer's needs.

Research and development and engineering

Like production, research and development (R&D) and engineering prefer long lead times. If they are to develop a new product from scratch, then the longer they have to do it, the better. The problem is, however, that marketing will want the new product available as soon as possible, for fear of the competition launching their versions first. Being first into a market can allow the organisation to establish market share and customer loyalty, and to set prices freely, before the effects of competition make customers harder to gain and lead to downward pressure on prices. There is also the danger that R&D and engineering may become focused on the product for the product's sake, and lose sight of what the eventual customer is looking for. Marketing, in contrast, will be concentrating on the benefits and selling points of the product rather than purely on its functionality.

■ Marketing as an integrative business function

The previous subsection took a pretty negative view, highlighting the potential for conflict and clashes of culture between marketing and other internal functions. It need not necessarily be like that, and this subsection will seek to redress the balance a little, by showing how marketing can work with other functions. Many successful organisations such as Sony, Nestlé and Unilever ensure that all functions within their organisation are focused on their customers. These organisations have embraced a marketing philosophy that permeates the whole enterprise and places the customer firmly at the centre of their universe.

What must be remembered is that organisations do not exist for their own sake. They exist primarily to serve the needs of the purchasers and users of their goods and services. If they cannot successfully sell their goods and services, if they cannot create and hold customers (or clients, or passengers, or patients or whomever), then they undermine their reason for existing. All functions within an organisation, whether they have direct contact with customers or not, contribute in some way towards that fundamental purpose. Finance, for example, helps the organisation to be more cost effective; personnel helps to recruit appropriate staff and make sure they are properly trained and remunerated so that they are more productive or serve the customer better; R&D provides better products; and production obviously churns out the product to the required quality and quantity specifications to meet market needs.

All of these functions and tasks are interdependent, i.e. none of them can exist without the others, and none of them has any purpose without customers and markets to serve. Marketing can help to supply all of those functions with the information they need to fulfil their specific tasks better, within a market-oriented framework. Those interdependencies, and the role of marketing in bringing functions together and emphasising the customer focus, are summarised in a simplified example in Figure 1.3.

Although the lists of items in the boxes in Figure 1.3 are far from comprehensive, they do show clearly how marketing can act as a kind of buffer or filter, both collecting information from the outside world then distributing it within the organisation, and presenting the combined efforts of the various internal functions to the external world. Taking, for example, two core issues from the 'customers' box:

Current product needs. To satisfy current needs, production has to know how much is required, when and to what quality specification. Production, perhaps with the help of the purchasing function, has to have access to the right raw materials or components at the right

Figure 1.3 Marketing as an interface

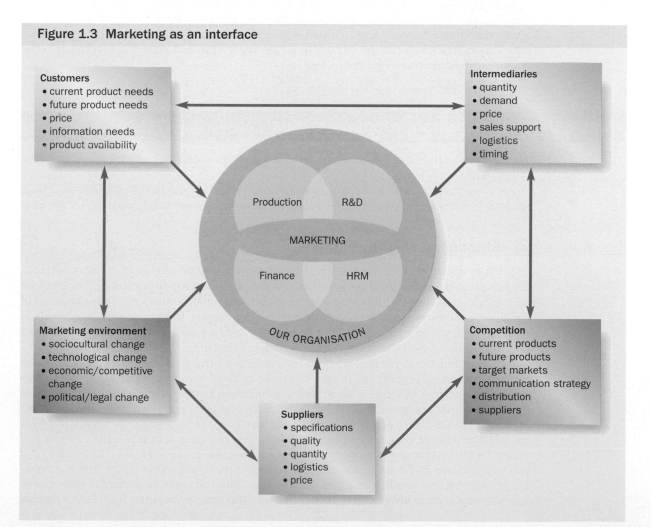

price. Keeping current products within an acceptable price band for the customer involves production, purchasing, finance and perhaps even R&D. A sales function might take orders from customers and make sure that the right quantity of goods is dispatched quickly to the right place. Marketing brings in those customers, monitoring their satisfaction levels, and brings any problems to the attention of the relevant functions as soon as possible so that they can be rectified with the minimum of disruption.

Future needs. Marketing, perhaps with the help of R&D, needs to monitor what is happening now and to try to predict what needs to happen in the future. This can be through talking to customers and finding out how their needs are evolving, or working out how new technology can be commercially exploited, or through monitoring competitors' activities and thinking about how they can be imitated, adapted or improved upon. Inevitably, there is a planning lead time, so marketing needs to bring in ideas early, then work with other functions to turn them into reality at the right time. Finance may have to sanction investment in a new product; R&D might have to refine the product or its technology; production may have to invest in new plant, machinery or manufacturing techniques; purchasing may have to start looking for new suppliers; and personnel may have to recruit new staff to help with the development, manufacture or sales of the new product.

When R&D and marketing do share common goals and objectives, it can be a very powerful combination. Marketing can feed ideas from the market that can stimulate innovation, while R&D can work closely with marketing to find and refine commercial applications for its apparently pointless discoveries.

These examples show briefly how marketing can be the eyes and ears of the organisation, and can provide the inputs and support to help each function to do its job more efficiently. Provided that all employees remember that they are ultimately there to serve the customers' needs, then the truly marketing-oriented organisation has no problem in accepting marketing as an interface between the internal and external worlds, and involving marketing in the day-to-day operation of its functions.

Marketing management responsibilities

This section outlines specifically what marketing does, and identifies where each of the areas is dealt with in this book.

All of marketing's tasks boil down to one of two things: identifying or satisfying customer needs in such a way as to achieve the organisation's objectives for profitability, survival or growth.

■ Identifying customer needs

Implicit in this is the idea of identifying the customer. The development of mass markets, more aggressive international competition and the increasing sophistication of the customer have taught marketers that it is unrealistic to expect to be able to satisfy all of the people all of the time. Customers have become more demanding, largely, it must be said, as a result of marketers' efforts, and want products that not only fulfil a basic functional purpose, but also provide positive benefits, sometimes of a psychological nature.

The basic functional purpose of a product, in fact, is often irrelevant as a choice criterion between competing brands – all fridges keep food cold, all brands of cola slake thirst, all cars move people from A to B, regardless of which organisation supplies them. The crucial questions for the customer are how does it fulfil its function, and what extra does it do for me in the process? Thus the choice of a BMW over a Lada may be made because the purchaser feels that the BMW is a better designed and engineered car, gets you from A to B in more comfort and with a lot more style, gives you the power and performance to zip aggressively from A to B if you want, and the BMW name is well respected and its status will reflect on the driver, enhancing self-esteem and standing in other people's eyes. The Lada may be preferred by someone who does not want to invest a lot of money in a car, who is happy to potter from A to B steadily without the blaze of glory, who values economy in terms of insurance, running and servicing costs, and who does not feel the need for a car that is an overt status symbol. These profiles of contrasting car buyers point to a mixture of product and psychological benefits, over and above the basic function of the cars, that are influential in the purchasing decision.

This has two enormous implications for the marketer. The first is that if buyers and their motives are so varied, it is important to identify the criteria and variables that distinguish one group of buyers from another. Once that is done, the marketer can then make sure that a product offering is created that matches the needs of one group as closely as possible. If the marketer's organisation does not do this, then someone else's will, and any 'generic' type of product that tries to please most of the people most of the time will sooner or later be pushed out by something better tailored to a narrower group. The second implication is that by grouping customers according to characteristics and benefits sought, the marketer has a better chance of spotting lucrative gaps in the market than if the market is treated as a homogeneous mass.

Identifying customer needs is not, however, just a question of working out what they want now. The marketer has to try to predict what they will want tomorrow, and identify the influences that are changing customer needs. The environmental factors that affect customer needs and wants, as well as the means by which organisations can fulfil them, are discussed further in Chapter 2. The nature of customers, and the motivations and attitudes that affect their buying behaviour, are covered in Chapter 3, while the idea of grouping customers according to common characteristics and/or desired product features and benefits is discussed in Chapter 4. The techniques of market research, as a prime means of discovering what customers are thinking and what they want now and in the future, is the subject of Chapter 5.

■ Satisfying customer needs

Understanding the nature of customers and their needs and wants is only the first step, however. The organisation needs to act on that information, in order to develop and implement marketing activities that actually deliver something of value to the customer. The means by which such ideas are turned into reality is the marketing mix. Figure 1.4 summarises the areas of responsibility within each element of the mix.

The concept of the marketing mix as the combination of the major tools of marketing was first developed by Borden in the 1950s (Borden, 1964), and the mnemonic '4Ps' (product, price, promotion and place) describing those tools was coined by McCarthy (1960). The marketing mix creates an offering for the customer. The use of the words *mix* and *combination* are important here, because successful marketing relies as much on interaction and synergy between marketing mix elements as it does on good decisions within those elements themselves. Häagen Dazs ice cream, for example, is a perfectly good, quality product, but its phenomenal success only came after an innovative and daring advertising campaign that emphasised certain adult-oriented product benefits. A good product with bad communication will not work, and similarly a bad product with the glossiest advertising will not work either. This is because the elements of the marketing mix all depend on each other, and if they are not consistent with each other in what they are saying about the product, then the customer, who is not stupid, will reject it all.

We now look more closely at each element of the marketing mix.

Product

This area, discussed in Chapter 6, covers everything to do with the creation, development and management of products. It is about not only what to make, but when to make it, how to make it, and how to ensure that it has a long and profitable life.

Furthermore, a product is not just a physical thing. In marketing terms, it includes peripheral but important elements, such as after-sales service, guarantees, installation and fitting – anything that helps to distinguish the product from its competition and make the customer more likely to buy it.

Particularly with fast moving consumer goods (fmcg), part of a product's attractiveness is, of course, its brand imagery and its packaging. Both of these are likely to emphasise the psychological benefits offered by the product. With B2B purchases, however, the emphasis is

Figure 1.4 The marketing mix

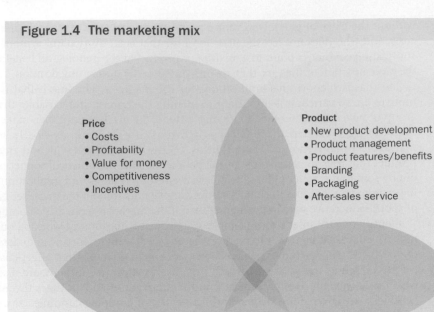

more likely to be on fitness for functional purpose, quality and peripheral services (technical support, delivery, customisation, etc.). As well as featuring in the product chapters, echoes of these concerns will come through strongly in the chapters on buyer behaviour and segmentation (Chapters 3 and 4).

Although much of the emphasis is on physical products, it must also be remembered that service markets are an increasingly important growth area of many European economies. The product chapters do cover some aspects of services, but the main discussion of the service product is in Chapter 13, which deals with services marketing.

Price

Price is not perhaps as clear cut as it might seem at first glance, since price is not necessarily a straightforward calculation of costs and profit margins. As Chapter 7 will show, price has to reflect issues of buyer behaviour, because people judge 'value' in terms of their perceptions of what they are getting for their money, what else they could have had for that money and how much that money meant to them in the first place.

Pricing also has a strategic dimension, in that it gives messages to all sorts of people in the market. Customers, for example, may use price as an indicator of quality and desirability for a particular product, and thus price can reinforce or destroy the work of other elements of the marketing mix. Competitors, on the other hand, may see price as a challenge, because if an organisation prices its products very low it may be signalling its intention to start a price war to the death, whereas very high (premium) prices may signal that there are high profits to be made or that there is room for a competitor to undercut and take market share away.

Overall, price is a very flexible element of the marketing mix, being very easy to tinker with. It is also, however, a dangerous element to play around with, because of its very direct link with revenues and profits, unless management think very carefully and clearly about how they are using it. The focus of the pricing chapter, therefore, is on the factors that influence price setting, the short-term tactical uses of pricing in various kinds of market and the strategic implications of a variety of pricing policies.

Place

Place is a very dynamic and fast moving area of marketing. It covers a wide variety of fascinating topics largely concerned with the movement of goods from A to B and what happens at the point of sale. Chapter 8 therefore looks at the structure of channels of distribution, from mail order companies that deal direct with the end consumer, to long and complex chains that involve goods passing between several intermediaries before they get to a retailer. The chapters explore the range of different intermediaries, and the roles they play in getting goods to the right place at the right time for the end buyer, as well as the physical distribution issues involved in making it all happen.

For consumer goods, the most visible player in the channel of distribution is the retailer. Manufacturers and consumers alike have to put a lot of trust in the retailer to do justice to the product, to maintain stocks and to provide a satisfying purchasing experience. Retailers face many of the same marketing decisions as other types of organisation, and use the same marketing mix tools, but with a slightly different perspective. They also face unique marketing problems, for example store location, layout and the creation of store image and atmosphere. Retailing has therefore been given a strong emphasis in this chapter.

Promotion

Chapters 9–11 are basically about communication, which is often seen as the most glamorous and sexy end of marketing. This does not mean, however, that marketing communication is purely an 'artistic' endeavour, or that it can be used to wallpaper over cracks in the rest of the marketing mix. Communication, because it is so pervasive and high profile, can certainly make or break a marketing mix, and thus it needs wise and constant analysis, planning and management.

These chapters look at the whole range of marketing communication techniques, not just advertising, but also sales promotions, personal selling, public relations and direct marketing. The activities undertaken within each area, the objectives each can best achieve, their relative strengths and weaknesses, and the kinds of management and planning processes that have to support them are discussed. To put all that into perspective, however, Chapter 9 first looks at the promotional mix as a whole, thinking about the factors that will influence the relative emphasis put on each individual communications area.

That, then, is the traditional 4Ps approach to marketing that has served very well for many years. More recently, however, it has become apparent that the 4Ps as they stand are not always sufficient. In the services sector in particular, they cannot fully describe the marketing activities that are going on, and so an extended marketing mix, the 7Ps, was proposed by Booms and Bitner (1981), adding people, processes and physical evidence to the traditional 4Ps.

People

Services often depend on people to perform them, creating and delivering the product as the customer waits. A customer's satisfaction with hairdressing and dentistry services, for example, has as much to do with the quality and nature of the interaction between the customer and the service provider as with the end result. If the customer feels comfortable with a particular service provider, trusts them and has a rapport with them, that is a relationship that a competitor would find hard to break into. Even where the service is not quite so personal, sullen assistance in a shop or a fast-food outlet, for example, does not encourage the customer to come back for more. Thus people add value and a dimension to the marketing package way beyond the basic product offering.

Processes

Manufacturing processes, once they are set up, are consistent and predictable and can be left to the production management team, and since they go on out of sight of the customer, any mistakes can be weeded out before distribution. Services, however, are 'manufactured' and consumed live, on the spot, and because they do involve people and the performance of their skills, consistency can be rather more difficult than with normal manufacturing. The marketer, therefore, has to think carefully about how the service is delivered, and what quality controls can be built in so that the customer can be confident that they know what to expect each time they consume the service product. This applies, for example, to banks and other retailers of financial services, fast-food outlets, hairdressers and other personal service providers, and even to professionals such as solicitors and management consultants.

Process can also involve queueing mechanisms, preventing waiting customers from getting so impatient that they leave without purchase; processing customer details and payment; as well as ensuring the high professional quality of whatever service they are buying.

Physical evidence

This final area is of particular relevance to retailers (of any type of product), or those who maintain premises from which a service is sold or delivered. It singles out some of the factors already mentioned when talking about retailers within the place element of the traditional 4Ps approach, such as atmosphere, ambience, image and design of premises. In other service situations, physical evidence would relate to the aircraft in which you fly, the hotel in which you stay, the stadium in which you watch the big match, or the lecture theatre in which you learn.

Other than in the services arena, the 4Ps are still widely accepted as defining the marketing mix. It has never been suggested, however, that the same mix is applicable in all situations or even for the same organisation at different times, so the task of the marketing manager is to review and change the mix to suit emerging circumstances. The marketing mix is simply therefore a set of categories of marketing variables that has become standard in marketing education and is the foundation for the structure of this book. As you read the subsections on the four elements of the marketing mix, look to see where aspects of people, process and physical evidence are being incorporated or implied within that traditional structure. Relationship marketing, in any type of market for any type of product, is increasingly throwing the emphasis on adding value to products through service. Inevitably, the extra 3Ps are going to impinge on that, and will be reflected in discussing applications of the original 4Ps.

The particular combination of the 4Ps used by any one organisation needs to give it competitive edge, or differential advantage. This means that the marketer is creating something unique, that the potential customer will recognise and value, that distinguishes one organisation's products from another's. In highly competitive, crowded markets, this is absolutely essential for drawing customers towards your product. The edge or advantage may be created mainly through one element of the mix, or through a combination of them. A product may have a combination of high quality and good value (price and product) that a competitor cannot match; an organisation may have established a 24-hour telephone ordering and home delivery service (place) that cannot easily be imitated; an effective and unique communications campaign combined with an excellent product living up to all its promises (promotion and product) can make an organisation's offering stand out above the crowd.

■ Strategic vision

It is clear that individual marketing activities must be looked at within the context of a coherent and consistent marketing mix, but achieving that mix has to be an outcome of a wider framework of strategic marketing planning, implementation and control. Chapter 12 looks at these wider issues.

Strategy is concerned with looking into the future and developing and implementing the plans that will drive the organisation in the desired direction. Implicit in that is the need for strategy to inform (and be informed by) marketing. Strategic marketing thinking also needs a certain amount of unblinkered creativity, and can only be really successful if the marketer thinks not in terms of product, but rather in terms of benefits or solutions delivered to the customer. The organisation that answers the question 'What business are you in?' with the reply 'We are in the business of making gloss paint' is in danger of becoming too inwardly focused on the product itself and improving its manufacture (the production orientation). A more correct reply would have been: 'We are in the business of helping people to create beautiful rooms' (the identification of customer needs). The cosmetics executive who said that in the factory they made cosmetics but in the chemist's shop they sold hope, and the power tool manufacturer who said that they did not make drills, they made quarter-inch holes, were both underlining a more creative, outward-looking, problem-solving way of marketing thinking. Products are bought by customers to solve problems, and if the product does not solve the problem, or if something else solves it better, then the customer will turn away.

marketing in action

Nederman: creating a better workplace

Nederman is not a name that many readers will be familiar with, but it is typical of many engineering companies that have adopted marketing principles in order to build international business in B2B markets. Based in Helsingborg, Sweden, it is a medium-sized company with a turnover of €82m in 2003 (www.eqt.se). The underlying theme for the company is 'improving your workspace' and it has built a successful international business helping customers to solve their workstation problems. This is achieved by removing air pollution, reducing noise levels, screening out unwanted light, and making a workstation easier to operate in through greater efficiency in providing liquids, power, light, lifting equipment, etc. In short, the company provides a total solution for a workstation environment tailored to meet the customer's requirements.

At the heart of the marketing proposition is the ability to solve customers' problems. Nederman has to listen to the customer then design, manufacture and install solutions either for individual workstations or across a factory area. To be innovative Nederman has to invest in research and development to ensure that its products are at the cutting edge in design and performance. This requires a commitment to R&D and the sourcing of components that meet the specifications required. It

is vital that Nederman is then able to listen to its customers and tailor solutions to meet the need. For that reason it must have direct contact both before and after the sale has been made, and if sales agents are used in less important markets, they must be fully trained and skilled in matching customer needs with system solutions. Technical support is available to help in that task, although as in many other B2B markets, the sales person with appropriate technical knowledge and support is at the forefront of the promotional effort. Nederman sells through 13 owned sales companies across Europe as well as the USA. It also sells through independent distributors in countries such as Australia, Brazil, India, Japan, Malaysia, Singapore, South Korea, and Thailand.

The approach to customers is made either by responding to enquiries generated by advertising in trade publications, directory listings, web and print based media, or by participation in trade fairs throughout the main markets. There is always the opportunity for repeat business, thus the importance of satisfied customers. Contact can also be initiated by the sales team, and this is sometimes achieved by offering a free health and safety assessment examining such matters as risk assessment, safety standards, signage, work practice, etc. Experience has indicated that this can often lead to the opportunity to open dialogue about production system improvement. Most of the sales

subsidiaries have installed 'working environments' that visitors can inspect to compare with the systems currently used.

An experience with Hamlin Electronics is indicative of the sales and marketing challenge facing Nederman. When Hamlin decided to become involved in developing sensors for air bags destined for the motor industry, it needed new workstations to extract fumes from gluing, printing and varnishing processes. Nederman was approached along with other potential suppliers to consider the specification options prior to a detailed quote. Quotations were prepared on the proposed systems and presentations and site visits to other users were organised so that the buyer could be assured of the benefits of the Nederman offering. Although some time elapsed before the evaluation was complete, Nederman was awarded the contract, but that was not the end of the process, as installing and operationalising the workstations is also an important part of creating a satisfied customer. During all that time and subsequently 'a very good relationship was established with Nederman's contract engineers so that the installation was completed to a high standard. To date we have a maintenance-free system and all the units are popular with the operators who use them on a daily basis,' said the engineer at Hamlin. This forms the basis of further referrals and repeat business.

Source: **http://www.nederman.com.**

The organisation that cannot see this and defines itself in product rather than market terms could be said to be suffering from *marketing myopia*, a term coined by Levitt (1960). Such an organisation may well be missing out on significant marketing opportunities, and thus may leave itself open to new or more innovative competitors which more closely match customer needs. A classic example of this is slide rule manufacturers. Their definition of the business they were in was 'making slide rules'. Perhaps if they had defined their business as 'taking the pain out of calculation' they would still exist today and be manufacturing electronic calculators. Green (1995) discusses how the pharmaceutical companies are thinking about what business they are in. The realisation that patients are buying 'good health' rather than 'drugs' is broadening the horizons of companies such as Sandoz in Switzerland, GlaxoSmithKline in the UK and Merck in the USA, all of which have diversified into areas of healthcare other than research and development of drugs. GlaxoSmithKline in particular wants to spread its efforts across what it sees as the four core elements of healthcare: prevention, diagnosis, treatment and cure.

Therefore the distinction between the product and the problem it solves matters, because marketing strategy is about managing the organisation's activities within the real world in which it has to survive. In that turbulent and dynamically changing world, a marketing mix that works today may not work tomorrow. If your organisation is too product-focused to remember to monitor how customer needs and wants are changing, then it will get left behind by competitors who do have their fingers on the customer's pulse. If your organisation forgets why it is making a particular product and why the consumer buys it, how can it develop marketing strategies that strike a chord with the customers and defend against the competition?

Think about a drill manufacturer that is product-focused and invests vast amounts of time and money in developing a better version of the traditional electric drill. How do you think it would feel if a competitor then launched a hand-held, cordless, laser gun that could instantly zap quarter-inch holes (controllably) through any material with no physical effort on the part of the operator, and with no mess because it vaporises the residue? The laser company was thinking ahead, looking at the consumer's problem, looking at the weaknesses in the currently available solutions, and developing a marketing package that would deliver a better solution.

What we are saying here is that it is not enough to formulate a cosy marketing mix that suits the product and is entirely consistent with itself. That marketing mix is only working properly if it has been thought through with due respect to the external environment within which it is to be implemented. As well as justifying the existence of that marketing mix in the light of current internal and external influences, the strategic marketer has to go further by justifying how that mix helps to achieve wider corporate objectives; explaining how it is helping to propel the organisation in its longer-term desired direction, and finally, how it contributes to achieving competitive edge.

Ultimately, competitive edge is the name of the game. If marketers can create and sustain competitive edge, by thinking creatively and strategically about the internal and external marketing environments, then they are well on the way to implementing the marketing concept and fulfilling all the promise of the definitions of marketing with which this chapter began.

Marketing scope

Marketing plays a part in a wide range of organisations and applications. Some of these are discussed specifically in Chapters 13 and 14 and elsewhere in this book, while others are implicit throughout the text.

■ Consumer goods

The consumer goods field, because it involves potentially large and lucrative markets of so many individuals, has embraced marketing wholeheartedly, and indeed has been at the root of the development and testing of many marketing theories and concepts. Consumer goods and markets will be a major focus of this text, but certainly not to the exclusion of anything else.

Since we are all consumers, it is easy to relate our own experience to the theories and concepts presented here, but it is equally important to try to understand the wider applications.

■ B2B goods

Industrial or B2B goods ultimately end up serving consumers in some way, directly or indirectly. The cleaned wool that the woolcomber sells to the spinner to make into yarn to sell to the weaver to make into cloth eventually ends up in the shops as clothing; the rubber that Dunlop, Goodyear or Firestone buys to make into tyres to sell to car manufacturers ends up being bought by consumers; the girders sold by British Steel to a civil engineering contractor for a new bridge end up serving the needs of individuals. If these organisations are going to continue to feed the voracious appetite of consumer markets successfully (the right product in the right place at the right time at the right price – remember?), then they also have to manage their relationships with other organisations, in a marketing-oriented way. A study by Avlonitis *et al.* (1997) found that companies in B2B markets that had developed a marketing orientation were a lot more successful than those that had not. The buying of goods, raw materials and components by organisations is a crucial influence on what can be promised and offered, especially in terms of price, place and product, to the next buyer down the line. If these inter-organisational relationships fail, then ultimately the consumer, who props up the whole chain, loses out, which is not in the interests of any organisation, however far removed from the end consumer. As Chapter 3 in particular will show, the concerns and emphases in B2B markets are rather different from those of consumer markets, and thus need to be addressed specifically.

■ Service goods

Service goods, to be discussed in Chapter 13, include personal services (hairdressing, other beauty treatments or medical services, for example) and professional skills (accountancy, management consultancy or legal advice, for example), and are found in all sorts of markets, whether consumer or B2B. As already mentioned on pp. 23–4, services have differentiated themselves somewhat from the traditional approach to marketing because of their particular characteristics. These require an extended marketing mix, and cause different kinds of management headaches from physical products. Many marketing managers concerned with physical products are finding that service elements are becoming increasingly important to augment their products and to differentiate them further from the competition. This means that some of the concepts and concerns of services marketing are spreading far wider than their own relatively narrow field, and this is reflected throughout this book. In between the two extremes of a largely service product (a haircut, for instance) and a largely physical product (a machine tool, for instance), are products that have significant elements of both. A fast-food outlet, for example, is selling physical products – food and drink – and that is primarily what the customer is there for. Service elements, such as speed and friendliness of service, atmosphere and ambience, are nevertheless inextricably linked with those physical products to create an overall package of satisfaction (or otherwise) in the customer's mind. This mixture of physical and service products is common throughout the retail trade, and thus services marketing not only features in its own chapter, but also permeates those chapters dealing with distribution (Chapter 8).

■ Non-profit marketing

Non-profit marketing is an area that increasingly asserted itself in the economic and political climate of the 1980s and 1990s. Hospitals, schools, universities, the arts and charities are all having to compete within their own sectors to obtain, protect and justify their funding and even their existence. The environment within which such organisations exist is increasingly subject to market forces, and altruism is no longer enough. This means that non-profit organisations need to think not only about efficiency and cost effectiveness, but also about their market orientation – defining what their 'customers' need and want and how they can provide it better than their rivals.

Chapter 13 looks in more detail at the particular marketing problems and situations facing non-profit organisations.

eg The international charity Help the Aged adopts marketing methods to help serve its core mission: to secure and uphold the rights of disadvantaged older people in the UK and around the world. However high the ideals, in order to deliver the services it must attract funds to enable it to run campaigns to assist older people. The scale of the challenge is great when it is claimed that 2 million pensioners in the UK live below the poverty line, and at least 20,000 older people die each year as a result of the cold. Funds are therefore needed for advice and helplines, lobbying, research publications and direct support for older disadvantaged people.

In order to generate revenue, Help the Aged must attract donations, gifts and legacies as well as running its network of shops. It organises special events such as treks and golf tournaments, campaigns to recruit volunteers (it has over 104,000) and runs the Sponsor a Grandparent programme. Corporate sponsorship and partnerships are especially important and organisations such as Tesco, Saga, the BBC, BT, Barclays, Reebok, Lloyd's of London, Marks & Spencer, Makro, Patak Foods and Safeway have been pleased to be associated with this worthwhile cause. Mention is given on the charity's website and a link is created back to the sponsor's own site.

Eye-catching images combined with a thought-provoking headline ensure that people give this ad a second look.

Source: © http://www.helptheaged.org.uk

Marketing thinking enables the non-profit-making charity to fulfil its mission. The exchange offering has to be designed (see Figure 1.1) so that givers feel rewarded, and the messages are communicated in the right way to attract funds, to lobby and to reach older people. Recent annual advertising spend has been around £4m, with 85 per cent being spent on direct marketing, nearly 10 per cent on press advertising and the balance on television and radio, according to Nielsen Media Research. The mission may be non-profit orientated but the marketing methods and culture are as professional and focused as those found in many a commercial organisation (http://www.helptheaged.org.uk).

■ Small business marketing

Small business marketing also creates its own perspectives, as discussed in Chapter 12. Many of the marketing theories and concepts laid out in this book have been developed with respect to larger organisations, relatively rich in management resources. Many small businesses, however, simply cannot live up to this. They often have only one or two managers who have to carry out a variety of managerial and operational functions and who often have very limited financial resources for investment in researching new markets and developing new products ahead of the rest. Throughout this book we therefore include examples that show more pragmatically how marketing theories and practice can be adapted to serve the needs of the small business.

■ International marketing

International marketing is a well-established field, and with the opening up of Europe as well as the technological improvements that mean it is now easier and cheaper to transfer goods around the world, it has become an increasingly important area of marketing theory and practice. Throughout the book, examples will be found of organisations dealing with issues of market entry strategies, whether to adapt marketing mixes for different markets and how, and the logistics of serving geographically dispersed markets, all providing an interesting perspective on marketing decision-making.

■ e-marketing

The development, strategic integration and implementation of e-marketing techniques, along with the adoption of new marketing communications media, was a rapid and startling phenomenon of the late 1990s and early 2000s. These techniques and media have pushed the boundaries of creativity as well as extending organisations' abilities to develop one-to-one relationships with consumers through better targeted and customised interactive communication. Again, this is an area that is given its own chapter, Chapter 14, to show how it has permeated all aspects of marketing decision-making.

Chapter summary

■ Marketing is about exchange processes, i.e. identifying what potential customers need and want now, or what they are likely to want in the future, and then offering them something that will fulfil those needs and wants. You thus offer them something that they value and, in return, they offer you something that you value, usually money. Most (but not all) organisations are in business to make profits, and so it is important that customers' needs and wants are fulfilled cost effectively, efficiently and profitably. This implies that the marketing function has to be properly planned, managed and controlled.

■ Marketing in some shape or form has been around for a very long time, but it was during the course of the twentieth century that it made its most rapid developments and consolidated itself as an important business function and as a philosophy of doing business. By the late 1990s, all types of organisations in the USA and Western Europe had adopted a marketing orientation and were looking for ways to become even more customer-focused, for example through relationship marketing.

■ The marketing orientation has been a necessary response to an increasingly dynamic and difficult world. Externally, the organisation has to take into account the needs, demands and influences of several different groups such as customers, competitors, suppliers and intermediaries, who all exist within a dynamic business environment. Internally, the organisation has to coordinate the efforts of different functions, acting as an interface between them and the customer. When the whole organisation accepts that the customer is absolutely paramount and that all functions within the organisation contribute towards customer satisfaction, then a marketing philosophy has been adopted.

■ Marketing's main tasks, therefore, are centred around identifying and satisfying customers' needs and wants, in order to offer something to the market that has a *competitive edge* or *differential advantage*, making it more attractive than the competing product(s). These tasks are achieved through the use of the *marketing mix*, a combination of elements that actually create the offering. For most physical goods, the marketing mix consists of four elements, product, price, place and promotion. For service-based products, the mix can be extended to seven elements with the addition of people, processes and physical evidence. The marketer has to ensure that the marketing mix meets the customer's needs and wants, and that all its elements are consistent with each other, otherwise customers will turn away and competitors will exploit the weakness. Additionally, the marketer has to ensure that the marketing mix fits in with the strategic vision of the organisation, that it is contributing to the achievement of longer-term objectives, or that it is helping to drive the organisation in the desired future direction. These marketing principles are generally applicable to any kind of organisation operating in any kind of market. But whatever the application, the basic philosophy remains: if marketers can deliver the right product in the right place at the right time at the right price, then they are making a crucial contribution towards creating satisfied customers and successful, efficient and profitable organisations.

Questions for review and discussion

1.1 What is meant by the description of marketing as an *exchange process*?

1.2 Distinguish between the four main *business orientations*.

1.3 What is *competitive edge* and why is it so important?

1.4 Choose a product that you have purchased recently and show how the elements of the marketing mix came together to create the overall offering.

1.5 Why is the question, 'What business are we in?' so important? How might
(a) a fast-food retailer,
(b) a national airline,
(c) a car manufacturer, and
(d) a hairdresser
answer that question if they were properly *marketing-oriented*?

case study 1

Tween queens

By Sylvia Rogan and Kathleen Rogan

The tastes of young children have changed dramatically in the past decade. Influenced by the media and advertising, girls as young as six are now deciding to put their doll-playing years behind them and focus instead on the preoccupations of their older siblings: shopping and fashion. Girls from a young age are thus now very fashion conscious and are greatly influenced by, and certainly wish to emulate, their pop star idols. Eight- to ten-year-olds aspire to be 16 and so will reject toys their younger sisters might play with. They want to be seen as independent, have fun, wear trendy clothes and most importantly have 'street cred'. Children, especially girls, are buying into the values and products of adulthood at a much younger age. As part of this, most children these days have access to mobile phones, the internet and other forms of electronic entertainment, again encouraging them to put aside traditional toys. As a result of 'kids growing older younger' (kgoy), the toy market as a whole has become incredibly volatile.

Dolls have always had a place in the hearts and imaginations of girls, and despite changing fashions,

Bratz Rock Angelz give pre-teen girls, who often model themselves on pop stars, an opportunity to play out their fantasies.

Source: © Vivid Imaginations http://www.evivid.co.uk

will probably continue to do so. The difference is, however, that as a result of kgoy, dolls have to find new ways of capturing girls' attention. They also have to appeal to the 'tween' market of 7–12-year-olds, which is currently the most attractive group.

For more than 40 years, Barbie has dominated the global toy market. The brand stood for fashion, career and inspiration. Indeed, Barbie has led a very worthy life, adopting almost 100 careers over time, such as astronaut, rock star, teacher and vet. It is easy for a girl to understand what role Barbie plays and to fantasise around this. Mothers feel safe with Barbie, even if her disproportionate figure (which is often criticised) still makes dad feel distinctly queasy! Parents and grand-parents grew up with Barbie and remain her strongest supporters. As they have a deep-seated affection for classic toy brands, they continue to consider her the best doll for their child.

Coming back to the idea of kgoy, however, whereas Barbie used to appeal to girls as old as 12, it is now three- and four-year-olds who are the dominant market. Mattel, Barbie's manufacturer, has realised that for many of its young customers, Barbie is over the hill and is increasingly seen as too mumsy by little girls looking for a more streetwise role model. The three- and four-year-olds like the 'pretty pink' image Barbie portrays (just look at Fairytopia) but the older child's attention has perhaps been distracted by other, trendier dolls.

Bratz dolls appeared on the scene in 2001. They are produced by MGA Entertainment and were created by Paula Treantafelles who joined MGA from Mattel in 1999. She realised that Mattel was failing to reach 7–10-year-olds and felt that this age group was about self-expression and self-identity. Her answer was not simply a doll but a 'self-expression' piece. The idea of Bratz is to reflect the latest trends in fashion and appeal to the 'tweens'. They are characterised by an oversized head with multi-ethnic features, large almond-shaped eyes, pouty lips and a small body. They are hipper, trendier and more outrageous than Barbie, and with their funky fash-ions and heavy make-up, they are all about fun. Unlike other fashion dolls, Bratz dolls are meant to be young girls rather than grown women, so the real girls who play with them can identify with them more easily and are more likely to envy their fashionable wardrobe.

Interestingly, the style of play encouraged by Bratz is appropriate to the target age group as their lives are beginning to be all about fashion, interacting with friends and socialising. Bratz, unlike Barbie, have no 'back story', i.e. they don't have careers or clearly defined roles so that the child can make them whatever they want them to be. Another difference from Barbie is the introduction of 'Bratz Boyz'. While Barbie did have a boyfriend, Ken, he was very much in Barbie's shadow and was never really developed. The Bratz Boyz product range offers a selection of potential boyfriends each with his own distinctive character. This further encour-ages realistic role play on more grown-up social interac-tion themes.

Bratz's provocative image is disliked by many par-ents. There has been a certain level of opposition from some adults, who claim that their make-up, facial expressions and clothing styles are rather slut-like. This impression isn't helped by Bratz's accessories: there's none of the tea sets and fairytale horse-drawn chariots that epitomise Barbie's 1970s glamour. In their place are motor bikes, sea scooters, party planes, concert stages and the wild west horse and carriage. Kay Hymowitz, who has written widely on the commercial-isation of children, believes that the marketing industry is deliberately sexualising girls for profit: 'Marketers make it sound like kgoy is just a fact of nature. The truth is, they have played a central role in making it happen. They know that the way you seize kids' atten-tion is make them feel older and more glamorous – and sexier.' MGA's view is that it is not making a deliberate effort to sexualise the dolls. The dolls are fashionable and fashions these days are coincidentally rather sexy. Why is it inappropriate to put a sexy outfit on a doll when the truth is, the celebrities these girls aspire to are far more inappropriate than Bratz? MGA's research further suggests that children like Bratz primarily because they are fashionable, not because they are sexy. MGA's President is unrepentant: 'We are going to make toys that the kids will like, not the parents. They're the customers. The world has changed.'

And make toys that kids want is what MGA has done. The company runs focus groups and gathers feedback from its Bratz-related websites. Nearly half the ideas for lifestyle merchandise are generated by girls. Bratz has developed beyond the core doll range into clothing, footwear, music, videogames and more, through 350 licensees worldwide. There are Bratz tele-vision shows and a DVD series as well as the full-length Bratz Rock Angelz (with a 1970s theme) music album. Innovation with the doll range is nevertheless still important to retain interest and freshness. In January 2005, for example, Punkz (boys only) and Pretty n' Punk were launched. The British-themed boy and girl dolls are dressed in tartan, chains and leather, with punk-inspired haircuts and bulldogs! Each punk doll, which comes with a change of clothes, some accessories, stickers and a dog, sells for around £18.

Vivid Imaginations took over the UK marketing and distribution rights to the Bratz doll brand in December 2003. The primary objective for Vivid's 2004 UK cam-paign for Bratz was to double market share from 16 per cent. The secondary aim was to build a lifestyle brand for tweens using the slogan 'Dolls with a passion for fashion' to mark them out as toys for a girl with atti-tude. As well as a £2m advertising campaign, targeting programmes with trendy tween appeal, such as

'Sabrina the Teenage Witch', a PR campaign concentrated on getting coverage in key tween girls' magazines. Sponsorship was also arranged with satellite channel Nickelodeon, concentrating on an on-air competition for girls to design clothes for Bratz. The results showed the strategy worked with 10,000 children entering the competition, the biggest response Nickelodeon had ever attracted for this type of activity. In parallel with this, the sales team worked to increase listings in key retailers, aiming for prominent gondola-end displays. By August 2004, Argos had devoted more catalogue space to Bratz than to Barbie. Hamleys was a particular success story. The weekend after a dedicated Bratz area was created in its London store, sales of dolls and other related merchandise rose by 149 per cent. The brand was also reinforced by licensed merchandise, such as mini-fridges, in-line skates and karaoke machines. These products helped build the brand, provided extra sources of revenue, and convinced retailers to back the brand. By early September 2004, Bratz had achieved a market share of 41 per cent, more than doubling its sales in less than a year, and had elbowed Barbie into second place.

Barbie, of course, is not too happy about this and has started to revamp her image. She has dumped Ken and taken up with new boyfriend Blaine as well as acquiring a motorcycle and a surfboard, among other 'cooler' accessories. There is Cali Girl (and her horse) at £24.99, Pop Idol dolls who really sing at £19.99, Fashion Fever dolls at £7.99, Wee 3 Friends, and My Scene, Club Birthday and Day & Night doll assortments (these last three items have an uncanny facial resemblance to Bratz). In 2003 the Flava range was launched in an effort to compete directly with Bratz, but this was scrapped early in 2004 because it failed to meet sales expectations. In addition, a 'My Scene Goes to Hollywood' film was released in 2005 and there is also a My Scene video targeting tweens. Barbie's film career has also developed further, with animated video movies aimed at younger girls: 'Fairytopia' and 'Barbie and the Magic of Pegasus'.

Marketing battles may go on between the two companies but at the end of the day it will be the consumer who decides their fates. One eight-year-old child is reported to have said that although she owns dozens of Barbies (and the car and the house), she hasn't played with them in ages as they are not teenagers like Bratz. Another, also aged eight, has one Bratz doll and all her Barbies had been stowed away in the loft. She asked her mother one day if she could have the Barbies again but added 'don't tell my friends that I am playing with Barbie again'. Bratz may have rejuvenated the doll industry and raised the age to which girls will be seen to be still playing with dolls. But in secret, perhaps, the Barbie doll is still loved and played with by tweens – but shhh, not a word, or their street cred is under threat.

Sources: *Brand Strategy* (2004); Fenton (2004); Foster (2005); Furman (2005); Griffiths (2004); King and Kelly (2005); *Marketing Week* (2005); Marsh (2004); Murphy (2004); Rowan (2004); Sook Kim (2004); Wray (2005).

Questions

1 Why do you think that Bratz has been so successful in competing against Barbie?

2 Why do you think Bratz has introduced so many variants within its range? Using the marketing mix to structure your thinking, what issues, risks and challenges do you think the Bratz marketers face whenever they launch a new variant?

3 To what extent and why do you think Mattel should be worried by Bratz? If you were advising Mattel, what would your recommendations be?

4 Some commentators have expressed concern about the extent to which toys such as Bratz are 'sexualising' children too early and accelerating the kgoy phenomenon. Do you believe that this is the case? Where do the marketers' responsibilities begin and end?

References for chapter 1

Alderson, W. (1957), *Marketing Behaviour and Executive Action: A Functionalist Approach to Marketing*, Homewood, IL: Irwin.

AMA (1985), 'AMA Board Approves New Marketing Definition', *Marketing News*, 1 March, p. 1.

Avlonitis, G. *et al.* (1997), 'Marketing Orientation and Company Performance: Industrial vs Consumer Goods Companies', *Industrial Marketing Management*, 26 (5), pp. 385–402.

Babakus, E., Cornwell, T., Mitchell, V., and Schlegelmilch, B. (2004), 'Reactions to Unethical Consumer Behaviour Across Six Countries', *Journal of Consumer Marketing*, 21 (4), pp. 254–63.

Balestrini, P. (2001), 'Amidst the Digital Economy, Philanthropy in Business as a Source of Competitive Advantage', *Journal of International Marketing and Marketing Research*, 26 (1), pp. 13–34.

Berry, L.L. (1983), 'Relationship Marketing', in L.L. Berry *et al.* (eds), *Emerging Perspectives of Services Marketing*, Chicago: American Marketing Association.

Booms, B.H. and Bitner, M.J. (1981), 'Marketing Strategies and Organisation Structures for Service Firms', in J. Donnelly and W.R. George (eds), *Marketing of Services*, Chicago: American Marketing Association.

Borden, N. (1964), 'The Concept of the Marketing Mix', *Journal of Advertising Research*, June, pp. 2–7.

Brand Strategy (2004), 'Barbie: Barbie's Mid-life Crisis', *Brand Strategy*, May, p. 20.

Burrows, P. (2004), 'Can the iPod Keep Leading the Band?', *Business Week*, 8 November, p. 54.

Burrows, P. and Lowry, T. (2004), 'Rock On, iPod', *Business Week*, 7 June, p. 130.

Burrows, P. and Park, A. (2005), 'Apple's Bold Swim Downstream', *Business Week*, 24 January, p. 32.

Carroll, A. (1991), 'The Pyramid of Corporate Social Responsibility: Toward the Moral Management of Organizational Stakeholders', *Business Horizons*, 34 (July/August), pp. 39–48.

Carroll, A. (1999), 'Corporate Social Responsibility', *Business and Society*, 38 (3), pp. 268–95.

Challener, C. (2001), 'Sustainable Development at a Crossroads', *Chemical Market Reporter*, 16 July, pp. 3–4.

Christopher, M., Payne, A. and Ballantyne, D. (1991), *Relationship Marketing: Bringing Quality, Customer Service and Marketing Together*, London: Butterworth.

CIM (2001), accessed via **http://www.cim.co.uk**.

Clarke, P.D. *et al.* (1988), 'The Genesis of Strategic Marketing Control in British Retail Banking', *International Journal of Bank Marketing*, 6 (2), pp. 5–19.

CSR Forum (2001), 'The Responsible Century?', accessed via http://www.csrforum.com, August 2001.

Deng, S. and Dart, J. (1999), 'The Market Orientation of Chinese Enterprises During a Time of Transition', *European Journal of Marketing*, 33 (5), pp. 631–54.

Durman, P. (2005), 'Hunt for Easy Profits Hits the Wrong Note', *Sunday Times*, 20 February, p. 9.

Dwyer, F., Shurr, P. and Oh, S. (1987), 'Developing Buyer and Seller Relationships', *Journal of Marketing*, 51 (2), pp. 11–27.

The Economist (2005), 'Crunch Time for Apple: Consumer Electronics', *The Economist*, 15 January, p. 60.

Fenton, B. (2004), 'Brash Bratz Gang Leave Barbie Feeling Her Age', *Daily Telegraph*, 7 October, p. 11.

Foster, L. (2005), 'Mattel Hit as Barbie Loses out to Bratz', *Financial Times*, 16 April, p. 6.

Fuller, D. (1999), *Sustainable Marketing: Managerial–Ecological Issues*, Sage Publications.

Furman, P. (2005), 'Bratz/Barbie in Dolls Duel', *New York Daily News*, 18 April.

Gordon, M. (1991), *Market Socialism in China*, Working Paper, University of Toronto.

Green, D. (1995), 'Healthcare Vies with Research', *Financial Times*, 25 April 1995, p. 34.

Griffiths, K. (2004), 'Battle of the Barbies Knocks Stuffing out of Mattel', *The Independent*, 19 October, p. 44.

The Grocer (2004), 'The Grocer Fact File: Italian Foods', *The Grocer*, 13 November.

Grönroos, C. (1997), 'From Marketing Mix to Relationship Marketing – Towards a Paradigm Shift in Marketing', *Management Decision*, 35 (4), pp. 322–39.

Gummesson, E. (1987), 'The New Marketing: Developing Long term Interactive Relationships', *Long Range Planning*, 20 (4), pp. 10–20.

Hartman, C. and Beck-Dudley, C. (1999), 'Marketing Strategies and the Search for Virtue: a Case Analysis of the Body Shop International', *Journal of Business Ethics*, 20 (3), pp. 249–63.

Henderson, S. (1998), 'No Such Thing as Market Orientation – A Call for No More Papers', *Management Decision*, 36 (9), pp. 598–609.

Johnson, B. (2003), 'Berth of Success?', *Marketing Week*, 13 November, p. 28.

King, S. and Kelly, K. (2005), 'Doll Face Off', *Wall Street Journal*, 17 February, p. B1.

Knights, D. *et al.* (1994), 'The Consumer Rules? An Examination of the Rhetoric and "Reality" of Marketing in Financial Services', *European Journal of Marketing*, 28 (3), pp. 42–54.

Levitt, T. (1960), 'Marketing Myopia', *Harvard Business Review*, July/August, pp. 45–56.

Mans, J. (2000), 'The European View of Future Packaging', *Dairy Foods*, 101 (6), pp. 42–3.

Marketing Week (2005), 'MediaVest Manchester Scoops Bratz Launch', *Marketing Week*, 14 July, p. 17.

Marsh, S. (2004), 'Barbie Left on the Shelf by Younger Sexier Challenger', *The Times*, 24 April, p. 15.

McCarthy, E. (1960), *Basic Marketing*, Homewood, IL: Irwin.

Mintel (2003), 'Health and Fitness Clubs', *Mintel UK Horizons*, May, accessed via **http://www.mintel.com**.

Morrison, S. (2004), 'Apple Leaps on Strong iPod Sales', *Financial Times*, 13 October, p. 1.

Murphy, C. (2004), 'Bratz', *Marketing*, 22 September, p. 29.

Narver, J. and Slater, S. (1990), 'The Effect of a Market Orientation on Business Profitability', *Journal of Marketing*, 54 (4), pp. 20–35.

OECD Observer (2001), 'Rising to the Global Development Challenges', *OECD Observer*, Issue 226/7 (Summer), p. 41.

Piercy, N. (1992), *Marketing-led Strategic Change*, Oxford: Butterworth-Heinemann.

Poulter, S. (2005), 'We Had to Pay £2,500 Because our Children Are Music Pirates', *Daily Mail*, 8 June, p. 7.

Precision Marketing (2004), 'Fitness Clubs Flex their Marketing Muscles', *Precision Marketing*, 16 January, p. 11.

Prystay, C. (2003), 'Made, and Branded, in China: Chinese Manufacturers Move to Market Under Their Own Names', *Wall Street Journal*, 22 August, p. A7.

Rigby, R. (2004), 'The iPod and its Ilk Will Not Stop at Music', *Financial Times*, 17 August, p. 1.

Rowan, D. (2004), 'Valley of the Dolls', *The Times*, 4 December, p. 21.

Schultz, R. and Good, D. (2000), 'Impact of the Consideration of Future Sales Consequences and Customer-oriented Selling on Long-term Buyer–Seller Relationships', *Journal of Business and Industrial Marketing*, 15 (4), pp. 200–15.

Severn Trent (2004), 'Corporate Responsibility Report: Stewardship 2004', accessed via **http://www.severntrent.com**, July 2005.

Sheth, J., Gardner, D. and Garrett, D. (1988), *Marketing Theory: Evolution and Evaluation*, New York: Wiley.

Smith, W. and Higgins, M. (2000), 'Cause-related Marketing: Ethics and the Ecstatic', *Business and Society*, 39 (3), pp. 304–22.

Sook Kim, Q. (2004), 'Toy Makers Outgrow Toys', *Wall Street Journal*, 19 October, p. B1.

Stones, J. (2004), 'Putting the Bite Back On', *Marketing Week*, 7 October, pp. 26–9.

Turnbull, P.W. and Valla, J.P. (1986), *Strategies for International Industrial Marketing*, Croom Helm.

WCED (1987), *Our Common Future*, Oxford: Oxford University Press.

Wray, R. (2005), 'Bratz Pack Dolls up Eggs for Easter', *The Guardian*, 26 March, p. 24.

Zhuang, S. and Whitehill, A. (1989), 'Will China Adopt Western Management Practices?', *Business Horizons*, 32 (2), pp. 58–64.

chapter 2

the European marketing environment

learning objectives

This chapter will help you to:

1. understand the importance of the external environment to marketing decision-making;

2. assess the role and importance of scanning the environment as a means of early identification of opportunities and threats;

3. appreciate the evolving and diverse nature of the European marketing environment;

4. define the broad categories of factors that affect the marketing environment; and

5. understand the influences at work within each of those categories and their implications for marketing.

Introduction

Marketing, by its very nature, is an outward-looking discipline. As the interface between the organisation and the outside world, it has to balance internal capabilities and resources with the opportunities offered externally. Chapter 1 has already shown, however, that the outside world can be a complex and difficult place to understand. Although the definition and understanding of the customer's needs and wants are at the heart of the marketing philosophy, there are many factors influencing how those customer needs evolve, and affecting or constraining the organisation's ability to meet those needs in a competitive environment. Thus in order to reach an adequate understanding of the customer's future needs and to develop marketing mixes that will satisfy the customer, the marketer has to be able to analyse the external environment and clarify which influences and their implications are most important.

This chapter will dissect the external environment and look closely at the variety of factors and influences that help to shape the direction of marketing thinking. First, the chapter clarifies the nature of the external environment, underlining why it needs to be understood, and what opportunities that understanding offers to the marketer.

Although the environment consists of a wide variety of factors and influences, it is possible to group them under four broad headings: sociocultural, technological, economic and competitive, and political and legal influences. Each will be examined in turn, discussing the various issues they cover and their implications for marketing decision-making.

eg Health and food processing issues have featured strongly in the media in recent years as consumers have become more critical about how food is processed, sources of ingredients, the extent and nature of additives, and the consequences of eating processed foods. Although memories may be short, various scares, such as BSE/CJD ('mad cow' disease and its human variant), foot and mouth disease, salmonella in eggs, and genetically modified foodstuffs have all raised concerns about the European food chain, the integrity of some of the providers and the wisdom of intensive farming. Then there are issues such as animal welfare, the impact of chemical additives and the lack of sustainable farming methods. The debate goes on. Some of France's top winemakers are challenging plans to introduce genetically modified vines in the Alsace even though the proposal was only for plant tests, not production. In direct response to the public's request for clearer nutritional information, a new easy-to-read nutritional counter now appears on all Kellogg's packs. It displays information based on Guideline Daily Amounts (GDA) to help people in their daily struggle to achieve a healthy, balanced lifestyle. The company is the first to include GDA on packs in the format of a GDA Counter. Work is also going on to harmonise across Europe the way suppliers describe their products and their nutritional and health benefits. Particular concerns have been expressed about misleading claims over products promoting general well-being, those offering psychological and behavioural effects, and slimming aids, along with partial, unrepresentative advice from health practitioners.

Research by Taylor Nelson Sofres suggests that fewer than 30 per cent of shoppers actually check food labels for the calorie, preservative and additive content, let alone worry about the farming method or the traceability of ingredients: as long as it is perceived as 'safe', many don't care. This means that many farmers are now in a trap. The consumer will not pay more for the food; retailers and processors want cheaper supplies, and yet the demand for sustainable and environmentally friendly farming methods grows. At the same time, trade restrictions are being lifted across the EU, and thus cheap supplies are coming in from developing countries with far fewer regulatory and welfare pressures on food processing, which is all very nice for the retailers and the consumers in terms of cheaper prices, but not so good for European food producers. (Doult, 2004; *The Grocer*, 2004b, 2004c)

GUIDELINE DAILY AMOUNTS (GDAs) Guideline amounts suitable for the majority of people SEE SIDE OF PACK FOR DETAILS		PER 30g SERVING WITHOUT MILK		25%	50%	75%	100%		GDA
CALORIES			112					2000	
FAT			0.3g					70g	
SAT. FAT			0.05g					20g	
SALT			0.55g					6g	
TOTAL SUGARS			2.5g					100g	
FIBRE			0.9g					24g	
IRON			2.4mg					14mg	

Customers are more aware of the nutritional value of foods and Kellogg's guidelines for daily amounts help individuals to monitor their daily intake.

Source: © http://www.kelloggs.co.uk

The nature of the European marketing environment

This section will first define the broad groupings of environmental influences, and then go on to look at the technique of environmental scanning as a means of identifying the threats and opportunities that will affect marketing planning and implementation within the organisation.

■ Elements of the marketing environment

Figure 2.1 shows the elements of the external environment in relation to the organisation and its immediate surroundings.

As the figure shows, the elements can be divided into four main groupings, known by the acronym STEP: Sociocultural, Technological, Economic and competitive, and Political and regulatory environments.

Sociocultural environment

The sociocultural environment is of particular concern to marketers as it has a direct effect on their understanding of customers and what drives them. Not only does it address the demographic structure of markets, but it also looks at the way in which attitudes and opinions are being formed and how they are evolving. A general increase in health consciousness, for instance, has stimulated the launch of a wide variety of products with low levels of fat and sugar, fewer artificial ingredients and no additives.

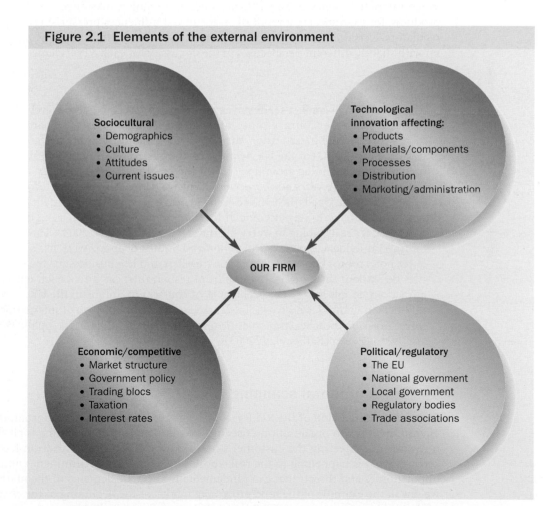

Figure 2.1 Elements of the external environment

Technological environment

Technological innovation and technological improvement have had a profound effect in all areas of marketing. Computer technology, for instance, has revolutionised product design, quality control, materials and inventory management, the production of advertising and other promotional materials, and the management and analysis of customer information. The internet has opened up new channels of communication and distribution. Technology also affects the development of new processes and materials, as well as the invention of completely new products or applications.

Economic and competitive environment

The economic and competitive environment covers both macro- and micro-economic conditions which affect the structure of competition in a market, the cost and availability of money for marketing investment in stock and new products, for example, and the economic conditions affecting a customer's propensity to buy.

Political and regulatory environment

The political and regulatory environment covers the external forces controlled by governments, both national and European, local authorities, or other trade or activity-oriented regulatory bodies. Some of the rules and regulations developed and implemented by bodies under this heading have the force of law, while others are voluntary, such as advertising codes of practice.

Each of the STEP areas will be looked at in more detail on pp. 39 *et seq*. There is, of course, much interdependence between them. Rules and regulations concerning 'green' aspects of products, for example, are a result of sociocultural influences pressurising the legislators and regulators. Certain issues, therefore, such as international, ethical and green issues, will crop up with slightly different perspectives in the discussion of each STEP element.

eg Any international conflict sends shivers down the spines of Western travel industry operators, anxious to encourage more of us to travel even when the perceived risks are increased. After the Iraq invasion, the number of American visitors to the UK plummeted by over 40 per cent. For the UK before 9/11, the US market represented about 20 per cent of all visitors, spending around £3bn, but this has now fallen to 13 per cent. Since then, terrorist attacks, SARS and the weak dollar have dented any serious recovery. The continued fear of al-Qaeda is believed to be generating a 'bunker mentality' with Western tourists preferring to stay at home. If this becomes a longer-term, more deep-seated attitude, then it's really going to worry the travel industry (Pitcher, 2004). The knock-on effect on travel providers, especially in London and Stratford-upon-Avon, has already been felt: fewer hotel rooms booked, fewer airline travellers and less business for the myriad companies dependent on tourists, ranging from restaurants, car hire, coach trips and visitor attractions, to gift shops. The problem is, of course, not unique to the UK. Foreign visitor numbers to France have also declined, based upon a combination of international tension, forest fires, oily beaches, transatlantic tensions, contagious diseases, public sector strikes and a strong euro (Barber *et al.*, 2003).

■ Environmental scanning

Even a brief discussion of the STEP factors begins to show just how important the marketing environment is. No organisation exists in a vacuum, and since marketing is all about looking outwards and meeting the customer's needs and wants, the organisation has to take into account what is happening in the real world. The marketing environment will present many opportunities and threats that can fundamentally affect all elements of the marketing mix, as we saw in the example of the food processing market at the beginning of the chapter. In terms of the product, for example, STEP factors help to define exactly what customers want, what it is possible (and legal) to provide them with, and how it should be packaged and presented.

Pricing is also influenced by external factors, such as the competition's pricing policies, government taxation and what consumers can afford. STEP factors also affect promotion, constraining it through regulation, but also inspiring the creativity that develops appropriate messages to capture the mood of the times and the target audience. Finally, the strength of relationships between manufacturers and retailers or other intermediaries is also affected by the external environment. Competitive pressures at all levels of the distribution channel; technology encouraging joint development and commitment in terms of both products and logistics; shifts in where and how people want to buy: all help to shape the quality and direction of inter-organisational relationships.

Thus the marketing mix is very dependent on the external environment, but the problem is that the environment is very dynamic, changing all the time. The organisation therefore has to keep pace with change and even anticipate it. It is not enough to understand what is happening today: by the time the organisation has acted on that information and implemented decisions based on it, it will be too late. The organisation has either to pick up the earliest indicators of change and then act on them very quickly, or try to predict change so that tomorrow's marketing offerings can be appropriately planned.

In order to achieve this successfully, the organisation needs to undertake environmental scanning, which is the collection and evaluation of information from the wider marketing environment that might affect the organisation and its strategic marketing activities. Such information may come from a variety of sources, such as experience, personal contacts, published market research studies, government statistics, trade sources or even through specially commissioned market research.

The approach to scanning can vary from being extremely organised and purposeful to being random and informal. As Aguilar (1967) pointed out, formal scanning can be very expensive and time consuming as it has to cast its net very wide to catch all the possible influences that might affect the organisation. The key is knowing what is important and should be acted upon, and what can wait.

eg There is a great deal of skill and perceptiveness involved in assessing the significance of any piece of information and whether it should be acted upon. Volvo, for example, failed to pick up the early signs indicating the emergence of markets for 'people carriers' and four-wheel-drive vehicles, and thus missed out on the growth stages of both markets. Organisations that supply components to the motor industry also have to be alert to changing tastes and trends, in order to plan production. Motor industry analysts predicted that airbags would not be as readily accepted by motorists in Europe as they were in the United States. What actually happened was that motorists quickly warmed to the idea and began to demand airbags as standard. The motor manufacturers were caught somewhat unprepared, and consequently put a lot of pressure on suppliers to fulfil demand immediately.

Environmental scanning is therefore an important task, but often a difficult one, particularly in terms of interpretation and implementation of the information gained. The following looks in more detail at each of the STEP factors, and gives a further indication of the range and complexity of the influences and information that can affect the marketing activities of the organisation.

The sociocultural environment

It is absolutely essential for organisations serving consumer markets, directly or indirectly, to understand the sociocultural environment, since these factors fundamentally influence the customer's needs and wants. Many of the factors discussed here will be looked at again in Chapters 3 and 4, and so this is a brief overview of the demographic and sociocultural influences on marketing thinking and activities.

■ The demographic environment

Demographics is the study of the measurable aspects of population structures and profiles, including factors such as age, size, gender, race, occupation and location. As the birth rate fluctuates and as life expectancy increases, the breakdown of the population changes, creating challenges and opportunities for marketers, particularly if that information is taken in conjunction with data on family structure and income.

One demographic group of great interest to marketers is what is known as the 'grey market', consisting of the over-55 age group. The over-55s represent between 20 and 30 per cent of the population of many EU countries. Their numbers are increasing, and because of better healthcare and financial planning, a significant proportion are able to indulge in high levels of leisure-oriented consumption, especially as they are likely to have paid off any mortgage or similar long-term debt, and are not likely to have dependent children. 'Generational marketing', for organisations seeking to appeal to this target age group, requires a fundamentally different perspective on the part of advertisers, according to Shannon (1998). Attitudes are changing. For example, research into the over-50s in Germany revealed that rather than thrift and self-denial, the growing emphasis is on enjoyment through consumption. To communicate effectively to this age group, the focus now has to reflect attitude and lifestyle rather than reinforcing an age-based stereotype.

eg Saga Holidays found that it had to redefine its idea of the most appropriate market to target and its notions of what potential customers want. In the 1990s, Saga shifted its focus from the over-60 to over-50 age group, as people retire earlier and want to have fun for longer. At the same time, Saga diversified from being purely a tour operator to using the brand name to launch publishing and financial services products for the same target market. However, it also found that age alone was not a good indicator of holiday preferences. Over 90 per cent of customers now want holidays abroad compared with 50 per cent ten years ago. They also want anything but two weeks in Benidorm or beach resorts. River rafting, jungle trekking, mountain hiking and elephant safaris are on the agenda as the age group becomes more diverse in outlook and aspirations.

Having identified its target market, Saga is keen to keep good customer relations and a high level of awareness among the over-50s. Cross-selling is now an important part of its marketing. It sells insurance of all kinds: home, car, travel, medical, boat, caravan, etc. It has three regional radio stations attracting a total of 855,000 listeners each week, and offers a credit card and a discount telephone service. It has Britain's second largest subscription magazine with a following of 1.25 million, with approximately half of this coming from subscriptions. Fundamental to this cross-selling is its database of 6.5 million households. This is carefully managed so that Saga can understand individual customer behaviour in order to predict responses to particular offerings.

The core of the business, however, remains its holiday offerings. In 1996, Saga purchased the cruise ship *Saga Rose*, a cruise ship exclusively for the over-50s: children and students are definitely not welcome! A further ship, *Saga Ruby*, began sailing for Saga in 2005, again offering facilities for the over-50s with plenty of space and room to relax and socialise.

Overall, the market looks set to grow as the number of over-50s will grow by over 20 per cent over the next ten years. This, combined with greater affluence, means the ship is set on a fair course! Whatever business lines are added, the proposition remains the same: worry-free, well-organised, well-designed services for those who are 'mature in years, but young at heart'. (Ashworth, 2003; Chesshyre, 2001; Milne, 2003; *Precision Marketing*, 2003; http://www.sagaholidays.co.uk).

Clearly, the size of a household combined with its income is going to be a fundamental determinant of its needs and wants, and its ability to fulfil them.

As data from Euromonitor (2005) shows, most European countries are experiencing a pattern of decline in the average household size. Again, marketers need to be mindful of these

Table 2.1 Consumer expenditure by object 2003 (% analysis)

Selected EU member states

	Food & non-alcoholic beverages	Alcoholic beverages & tobacco	Clothing & footwear	Housing	Household goods & services	Health goods & medical services	Transport	Communications	Leisure & recreation	Education	Hotels & catering	Miscellaneous goods & services
Czech Republic	18.9	8.7	5.5	20.8	6.1	1.7	10.7	3.9	10.2	0.6	7.6	5.4
Denmark	12.6	4.5	5.0	28.8	5.9	2.8	11.9	2.2	10.3	0.8	5.5	9.7
Finland	12.8	5.9	4.6	25.2	4.9	3.9	12.4	3.4	11.1	0.5	6.5	8.9
France	14.6	3.4	4.6	23.4	5.9	3.7	15.1	2.3	9.1	0.6	7.6	9.7
Germany	12.2	4.0	5.9	25.4	6.7	4.2	14.3	2.9	9.2	0.7	4.4	10.0
Hungary	18.8	8.0	4.3	17.5	6.7	4.0	15.7	5.5	7.9	1.1	5.4	5.1
Ireland	7.6	6.2	6.3	22.4	7.3	3.2	10.2	2.7	7.1	0.9	17.2	9.1
Netherlands	10.9	3.2	6.1	20.5	7.0	4.2	11.8	4.0	11.5	0.5	5.7	14.6
Poland	20.8	7.0	4.3	25.3	4.5	4.6	13.1	1.7	6.6	1.5	2.9	7.7
Portugal	18.8	4.2	7.6	11.0	7.0	4.6	16.8	2.6	6.6	1.4	9.7	9.7
Slovakia	22.2	5.4	4.5	26.9	4.5	1.5	9.2	3.9	8.8	0.9	6.6	5.6
Spain	15.9	3.1	6.3	14.4	5.8	3.4	12.1	2.6	8.3	1.6	19.4	7.0
Sweden	12.5	4.1	5.6	28.5	5.0	2.7	13.1	3.3	12.2	0.1	5.2	7.7
UK	9.4	4.0	5.8	18.1	6.4	1.7	15.0	2.3	12.1	1.4	11.7	12.2

Row totals may not equal 100 due to rounding.

Source: Adapted from Euromonitor (2005) *European Marketing Data and Statistics 2005*, 40th edition, London: Euromonitor, Table 6.2, pp. 174–5.

changes and to adapt their offerings accordingly. A significant increase in the proportion of single-person households will affect a whole range of marketing offerings, for example solo holidays, smaller apartments, pack sizes and advertising approaches and family stereotypes.

What is also important is the level of disposable income available (i.e. what is left after taxes have been paid), and the choices the household makes about saving and/or spending it. Table 2.1 shows how the spending of disposable income varies across Europe.

Clearly, housing is a fundamental cost, but the proportion of income it takes varies widely across Europe, with the Hungarians, Portuguese, Spanish and British spending the lowest percentage on housing. Looking at the food column, however, it is in the Eastern European economies, the newest members of the EU, that people are spending relatively more on food as a percentage of their total expenditure. In some of the other categories, the Hungarians like to communicate, the Swedes and British like to have a good time, Poles and Spaniards take their education seriously, the Portuguese are possibly Europe's best dressed nation, while the Czechs seem to enjoy their alcohol! Of course, patterns of expenditure will be dictated to some extent by national income levels and relative prices.

Such spending patterns are not fixed: they will vary not only because of changes in the demographic and economic structure of the household, but also because of sociocultural influences, discussed in the next subsection. A further factor which cuts across both demographic and sociocultural issues is employment patterns, specifically the number of working women in a community and the rate of unemployment. This influences not only household income, but also shopping and consumption patterns.

■ Sociocultural influences

Demographic information only paints a very broad picture of what is happening. If the marketer wants a really three-dimensional feel, then some analysis of sociocultural factors is essential. These factors involve much more qualitative assessment, can be much harder to measure and interpret than the hard facts of demographics and may be subject to unpredictable change, but the effort is worthwhile for a truly marketing-oriented organisation.

One thing that does evolve over time is people's lifestyle expectations. Products that at one time were considered upmarket luxuries, such as televisions and fridges, are now considered to be necessities. Turning a luxury into a necessity obviously broadens the potential market, and widens the marketer's scope for creating a variety of products and offerings to suit a spectrum of income levels and usage needs. Televisions, for example, come in a variety of shapes, sizes and prices, from the pocket-sized portable to the cheap, small set that will do for the children's bedroom, to the very large, technically advanced, state-of-the-art status symbol with flat screen and digital connectivity. This variety has the bonus of encouraging households to own more than one set, further fuelling the volume of the market, particularly as improvements in technology and production processes along with economies of scale further reduce prices.

Broadening tastes and demands are another sociocultural influence, partly fuelled by the marketers themselves, and partly emanating from consumers. Marketers, by constant innovation and through their marketing communications, encourage consumers to become bored with the same old standard, familiar products and thus to demand more convenience, variety and variation.

eg   Deli counter sales are falling all across Europe and in the United States. It has been suggested that the younger generation prefers to pay for pre-packed foods as it is more convenient and there is no need for counter queuing. Time is becoming increasingly precious to many consumers and queuing can be a real turn-off. Madrange, the French cooked meat and charcuterie producer, is attempting to address the loss of supermarket sales by introducing 'deli express' which means pre-slicing popular meats and cheeses and wrapping them in deli packaging, branded as 'Ultra fresh' so they can be sold in the 'ready to go' section of the deli counter. It looks like a deli package but has product information, weight and price displayed. It is hoped that the pre-packed option will become attractive to shoppers, combining the deli choice and freshness with the speed and convenience of self-selection. It will also clear some space on the deli counter to offer more exotic premium and regional speciality items which are still popular with shoppers (Hardcastle, 2001). This concept has now been adopted in some stores by UK chain Tesco (*The Grocer*, 2004d) and, indeed, in a recent store expansion and refurbishment in Aylesbury, the deli counter was greatly reduced in size with the introduction of a dedicated 'grab and go' deli area.

Fashions and fads are also linked with consumer boredom and a desire for new stimulation. The clothing market in particular has an interest in making consumers sufficiently discontented with the perfectly serviceable clothes already in the wardrobe that they go out to buy new ones every season. For some consumers, it is important for their social integration and their status to be seen to have the latest products and the latest fashions, whether it be in clothing, music or alcoholic drinks. Nevertheless, linking a product with fashion may create marketing problems. Fashions, by definition, are short lived, and as soon as they become widespread, the fashion leaders are moving on to something new and different. Marketers therefore have to reap rewards while they can, or find a means of shifting the product away from its fashionable associations.

More deeply ingrained in society than the fripperies of fashion are underlying attitudes. These change much more slowly than fashion trends and are much more difficult for the marketer to influence. It is more likely, in fact, that the marketer will assess existing or emerging attitudes and then adapt or develop to fit them. As can be seen in Figure 2.2, there are a number of areas in which changes in societal attitudes have influenced marketing approaches. Each is discussed below.

Environmental issues

Environmental issues have been of major concern in recent years, and this area has caused consumers to think more critically about the origins, content and manufacturing processes of the products they buy. Consumers, for example, want products made with the minimum of pollution and are looking for the reassurance, where applicable, that they come of renewable

Figure 2.2 The impact of societal attitudes on marketing strategy

Saving the trees to preserve the woods

Precious Woods Amazon is proud of its record in sustainable logging in tropical regions. The Swiss-owned company was founded in 1994 to show that commercial logging and sustainability could go together. Other loggers have followed, such as Gethal, adopting a planned forest management approach to ensure that rainforest is protected despite commercial interest. Forest management means undertaking proper timber inventories (location, species, measurement), harvesting plans and long harvesting cycles. This is backed up by certification and labelling which clearly communicates to consumers that responsible logging has taken place. The formation of the Forest Stewardship Council (FSC) was regarded even by pressure groups such as Greenpeace as a vital step in making the industry more responsible. Achieving FSC certification means that demanding social, economic and environmental standards have been met. Thus Precious Woods Amazon manages selective logging over a 25-year cycle and always seeks to preserve watercourses and to avoid soil erosion. Part of the deal also includes the principles that 25 per cent of the forest area remain permanently protected and that no pesticides or chemicals should be used.

The Amazon rainforest is one of the last frontiers on earth. Covering 2.3 million square miles, it has been called the earth's lungs as massive amounts of carbon dioxide are absorbed from the atmosphere each year and converted back into oxygen. However, land clearance, often by burning, and indiscriminate logging has meant that 40 per cent of the forest has already been destroyed. It has been estimated that 10,000 square miles of the forest is disappearing each year despite efforts to restrain deforestation. Since 1990, loggers have illegally harvested timber

For Precious Woods, Amazon forest management and sustainability are essential factors when it selects logging companies to work with. Here an inventory of the trees is carefully made before decisions are made as to which ones to harvest.

Source: © Precious Woods Holding Ltd
http://www.preciouswoods.com

worth £204m, some of which is sold outside Brazil, and it has been suggested that local officials often turn a blind eye and sometimes take bribes (Usborne, 2005). In a crackdown in 2005, 89 people were arrested of whom half were government officials. It is a priority to get things under control. Scientists have estimated that if the rate of illegal logging does not slow down, the tropical rainforest ecosystem will be destroyed by 2030. That's bad news for the lungs of the world. So what has all this to do with marketing and the consumer? It is demand for tropical wood that sets a chain of activities going that can be traced back to the forest. Wood consumption is closely related to per capita income: the higher the income the higher the wood consumption so the more trees get cut.

If consumers were more environmentally oriented they would read labels to make informed decisions on the best woods to buy. Reputable manufacturers offer

wood products from well-managed forests. Although ecofriendly wood may not be a great selling point, it is increasing in popularity as long as it is turned into well-designed and affordable products. This is where the FSC label gives increased reassurance to environmentally aware consumers. Nevertheless, despite all the measures, it has been estimated that 80 per cent of wood exported from Brazil has been cut illegally.

One of the UK's biggest FSC stockists is B&Q. It pioneered the sales of FSC products in the 1990s and yet has still maintained competitive pricing on its wood for the handyman and garden furniture. Unfortunately, many other manufacturers and retailers have not followed the B&Q lead. It is always worth remembering that the illegal trade is fuelled by the demand for wood in Europe and America, and the desire for more pasture land is to raise the cattle for North America's dinner tables and supermarkets around the world. Manage that more responsibly, and the demand for more land from the rainforest recedes.

There are two diametrically opposed views over the future of the rainforest. The FSC scheme, founded in 1993, enabled the environmentalists to negotiate with, rather than protest against, the commercial loggers. Certification and well-managed forests gave the loggers a way of continuing operations with far less pressure from the WWF, Greenpeace and Friends of the Earth. Ecological management, community involvement and good employment practice are all part of the guidelines. In the past, tropical timber markets in Europe and the US were closed by the boycotting campaigns in the 1990s, but the FSC scheme may allow them to reopen and thus stimulate more cutting in Brazil. The FSC labelling scheme operates worldwide and enables 'ethical buying' to take place, according to the loggers.

The alternative view, expressed by Laschefski and Freris (2001), questions the whole basis of continued logging before the rainforest has recovered from the ravages of the past thirty years. To them, the FSC has given an unwarranted legitimacy to logging under the ecologically sensitive label that allows commercial loggers to continue. At present, 96 per cent of certified forests are owned by either industrial-scale loggers or governments. However, by shifting the ethical buying responsibility to the consumer, it assumes that the buyer in Germany or the UK is conscious of green products, values the FSC scheme and is prepared to pay a little more rather than buy wood that may have been logged outside FSC guidelines. They argue that the FSC marketing certification legitimises logging when the priority should be preservation and reafforestation. Many of these views are strongly contested by Precious Woods.

The issue really comes back to the consumer in developed and developing countries. Pressure will grow in future years for Brazil to export more. The destruction of forests in SE Asia, the emergence of strong timber demand to fuel growth in China, along with the insatiable appetite for quality wood in Europe and North America, will create increasing pressure on the loggers to consume more forests albeit on a managed basis. So next time you buy wood from a stockist, perhaps you should play your part and ask whether it is FSC certified. You might just be helping to save a small part of one of the last great ecosystems in the world.

Sources: Barr (2004); Laschefski and Freris (2001); Montgomery (2003); Munk (2004); Usborne (2005); http://www.disasterrelief.org; http://www.preciouswoods.com.

resources. Many paper products now carry notices stating that they are made of wood from managed forests that are replanted after harvesting. In the same spirit, consumers are also demanding that unnecessary packaging is eliminated and that packaging should be recyclable.

Animal welfare

The issue of animal welfare is linked with environmental concerns, and shows itself in a number of ways. Product testing on animals has become increasingly unacceptable to a large number of vocal consumers, and thus there has been a proliferation of cosmetics and toiletries, for example, which proclaim that they have not been tested on animals. Cosmetics retailer The Body Shop has, for example, been at the forefront of positioning itself overtly on this issue, reassuring concerned customers about its own products and publicising the worst excesses of animal testing.

Another area of animal welfare which has captured the public imagination is that of intensive farm production methods. Public outcry against battery egg production, for example, opened new marketing opportunities for free-range eggs, since consumers wanted the alternative and were prepared to pay for it. Similarly, outdoor-reared pork and organic beef are starting to appear in supermarkets. Pressure groups are becoming more adept at using advertising and promotional techniques to activate public opinion.

Health concerns

Health consciousness has played a major role in the thinking behind consumer markets. The tobacco market has been particularly hard hit by increased awareness of the risks of smoking, and pressure from health lobbyists and the public has led to increased regulation of that industry. Food products have also been reappraised in the light of health concerns, with more natural ingredients, fewer artificial additives, less salt and less sugar content demanded. Linked with this, the market for low calorie products has also expanded, serving a market that wants to enjoy tasty food in quantity, but lose weight or at least feel that they are eating healthily.

eg Princes thought it was on to a winner after a study found that vitamin B3 and zinc could be found in its corned beef, as both have been linked with male fertility. Heinz, with a long tradition of nutrition, decided a few years ago to focus on the health agenda, reducing the salt in its baked beans by 20 per cent and pursuing salt reduction within its other products. By re-emphasising wholesomeness and nutritional values in its promotion, along with the launch of new chilled and healthy products and a more detailed labelling system, it hoped to demonstrate a commitment to healthy eating. Maybe it's a case of 'greenz meanz Heinz'! (*The Grocer*, 2000; Harrison, 2004).

Health concerns also led to a boom in products and services linked with fitness. Health clubs, aerobics classes, exercise videos, sportswear of all kinds and trainers are just some of the things that profited from the fitness boom.

Personal ethics

Apart from concern about the environment, animal welfare and health, all of which might be seen as ethical issues, there has been a subtle shift in people's attitudes to what is acceptable in other areas of their lives. In Western societies, a manageable level of personal debt is now considered normal. Hire purchase agreements, various types of loans and credit cards provide means of achieving a desirable lifestyle now and paying for it later. Previous generations might have been more inclined to take the view that if you want something, you save up for it and buy it outright when you can afford it. Consumers today are also more inclined towards self-indulgence and gratification, without too much guilt, through their consumption. This, it must be said, is openly encouraged by marketers, who want us to believe that we as individuals are special enough to deserve only the best. Indeed, a study by Dittmar and Pepper (1994) showed that adolescents, regardless of their own social background, generally formed better impressions of people who own rather than lack expensive possessions. In other words, materialism still seems to play a big part in influencing perceptions and attitudes towards others.

Business ethics

Encouraged by various pressure groups and inquisitive media, consumers now want to see greater levels of corporate responsibility, and more transparency in terms of the openness of companies. Bad publicity about employee relations, environmental records, marketing practices or customer care and welfare now has the potential to move consumers to vote with their pockets and shun an organisation and its products. McDonald's, for example, felt sufficiently concerned about stories circulating about its beef and about its record in the South American rainforests to invest in a considerable marketing communications campaign to re-establish its reputation. The Body Shop again features business ethics strongly in its marketing, emphasising, for example, its 'trade not aid' policy with developing countries and native tribes.

eg Chocolate manufacturers are generally regarded as upholding high standards of corporate citizenship. Companies such as Nestlé, Cadbury and Hershey buy cocoa in large quantities through the international commodity markets, and so have little contact with the thousands of small farms, especially in West Africa, that grow cocoa beans. It came as a shock, therefore, when accusations were made by UNICEF and Channel 4 in the UK that many migrant workers in West Africa, and the Ivory Coast in particular, were working in conditions not far removed from slavery on some of the one million cocoa and coffee farms. The confectionery industry immediately commissioned the independent Natural Resources Institute (NRI) to investigate and the subsequent findings found little evidence for the allegations but proposed that the wider socioeconomic dimensions of cocoa production should be examined. Given the sheer number of small independent farms involved, it is difficult to police, but just how can the chocolate manufacturers defend themselves against such accusations? The effect of an emotive issue such as child slavery on corporate image could be disastrous. The manufacturers' focus is thus now shifting to traceability, which means that the source of particular cocoa or coffee beans can be pinpointed and immediate action taken if any worker abuse is detected. To some, like Anti Slavery International, it is the only way that the confectionery giants can give 100 per cent guarantees to the consumer that offending farms have not been used by them. Up to this point, there had been little interest in tracing the origin of coffee, as much responsibility was delegated to intermediaries, but the NRI argues that true corporate social responsibility means taking a fundamental look at the whole supply chain. Ultimately, traceability will add to costs and that can only be at the expense of the consumer or the chocolate manufacturer (Watson, 2001).

■ Consumerism and consumer forces

Many of the influences discussed above might never have taken hold and become significant had it not been for the efforts of organised groups. They themselves often use marketing techniques as well as generating publicity through the media, quickly raising awareness of issues and providing a focal point for public opinion to form around and helping it to gather momentum.

The UK's Consumers' Association has long campaigned for legislation to protect consumers' rights, such as the right to safe products and the right to full and accurate information about the products we buy. As well as lobbying government and organisations about specific issues, the Consumers' Association also provides independent information to consumers, testing and comparing the features, performance and value for money of competing products in various categories. This information is published in *Which?* magazine. In a similar vein, specialist magazines, in fields such as computing and hi-fi, also undertake comparative testing of products of interest to their readership.

eg Tuna fishing is an activity that has been affected by campaigning leading to the exercise of 'consumer power'. The UK public had been happily buying canned tuna for many years without thinking of anything other than the price, the flavour and the quality of the can's contents. Green pressure groups, with the help of the media, then publicised the fact that the nets that were used to catch tuna also caught dolphins, which could not escape and so died pointlessly. A change in the net design would allow the dolphins to be freed without harm. Public outcry was such that the tuna canners had to take action to preserve sales. The USA-based Earth Island Institute was formed to monitor the harvesting of tuna to ensure that accidental killing of dolphins does not happen. This institute is supported by all the major tuna brands as it provides consumers with the reassurances that they seek, and the registered logo can only be used on cans deriving from approved canners. The canners are in turn monitored to ensure that their supplies are caught only in designated areas and using recommended fishing methods (*The Grocer*, 2001). The activities of such groups have not only served to change business practices on specific issues, such as tuna fishing, but also accelerated a general cultural change which has awakened the social conscience of organisations (only partly due to the fear of poor publicity and the loss of customers) and has raised the standards of corporate citizenship that consumers expect from business.

So far none of this activity has reduced consumption of tuna, and consumption by children in particular grew by 6 per cent in 2003–04, showing that responsible harvesting does not need to conflict with responsible consumption (*The Grocer*, 2004e).

High-profile and sometimes militant pressure has been brought to bear on organisations by green groups such as Friends of the Earth and Greenpeace. Although their interest is a wider, altruistic concern with ecology rather than consumer rights, they recognise that corporate practices that are harmful to the environment, wildlife and ecology can be partly discouraged by 'bottom-up' pressure. This means raising awareness, changing attitudes and altering purchasing habits among organisations' core customers.

Consumers have also been encouraged to think about their personal health as well as that of the planet. Sometimes sponsored by government (for example through the UK government's Department of Health) and sometimes through independent groups with a specific interest such as Action on Smoking and Health (ASH) or the British Heart Foundation, the public are urged to change their lifestyles and diets. Once it is generally known and accepted that too much of this, that or the other is unhealthy, food manufacturers are anxious to jump on the bandwagon and provide products to suit the emerging demand.

Awareness that full fat milk is high in cholesterol has been responsible for a significant shift towards semi-skimmed milk which retains most the vitamin and mineral content but cuts down the fat. Sometimes, a health issue does not even need the support of an organised group to capture the public imagination. A flurry of media coverage about research findings which indicated that eating sugar can actually help weight loss had many of us reaching hopefully for the biscuit tin, purely on medical grounds, of course.

Pressure groups and consumer bodies are not there just to criticise organisations, of course. They also encourage and endorse good practice, and such an endorsement can be very valuable to the organisation that earns it. A consumer who is inexperienced in buying a particular type of product, or for whom that purchase represents a substantial investment, may well look for independent expert advice, and thus the manufacturer whose product is cited as Which? magazine's best buy in that category has a head start over the competition. Organisations may also commission product tests from independent bodies such as the Consumers' Association or the Good Housekeeping Institute as a means of verifying their product claims and adding the bonus of 'independent expert opinion' to their marketing.

The technological environment

In an increasingly dynamic world, where the creation, launch and maintenance of a new product are more expensive and difficult than ever, no organisation can afford to ignore the technological environment and its trends.

The costs and the risks involved can be very high, since there is no guarantee that an R&D project will be successful in delivering a solution that can be commercially implemented. Nevertheless, many organisations feel the need to invest in R&D, recognising that they will get left behind if they do not, and are optimistic that they will come up with something with an unbeatable differential advantage that will make it all worthwhile.

IBM takes R&D very seriously in its desire to be at the head of the innovation curve and to remain competitive. It has learned that lesson the hard way, though. Originally, the world ran on IBM mainframes and databases but the trend towards smaller networked computers meant that competitors took market share away from IBM. In the 1990s IBM sought to regain a dominant position in a fast-moving technologically based industry. The search for technological leadership means developing an understanding of how the market is moving and spotting the areas that are likely to offer opportunities. IBM has eight research labs, employing 3000 researchers, and has 40,000 patents.

The research developed by IBM has been high grade. It has traditionally delivered the greatest number of patents in the US each year: its labs have invented magnetic storage, the first computer language (Fortran), relational databases and the scanning tunnelling microscope. Priorities within the R&D have evolved for IBM, however. Although it is working on Millipede, a nanomechanical device for data storage, it will not be made by IBM as it sold its storage division. IBM is in transition from being primarily a goods company to being primarily a service company concerned with innovative solutions to routine and complex applications (Fitzgerald, 2005).

To get the best out of the commercial exploitation of technology, R&D and marketers have to work closely together. R&D can provide the technical know-how, problem-solving skills and creativity, while the marketer can help guide and refine that process through research or knowledge of what the market needs and wants, or through finding ways of creating a market position for a completely innovative product. A lot of this comes back to the question 'What business are we in?'. Any organisations holding the attitude that they exist to solve customers' problems and that they have to strive constantly to find better solutions through higher-quality, lower-cost or more user-friendly product packages will be active participants in, and observers of, the technological environment. A striking example of this is the Italian firm Olivetti, which began by making manual typewriters, then moved into computers as it saw the likely takeover of the word processor as a means of producing business documentation.

The technological environment is a fast-changing one, with far-reaching effects on organisations and their products. Technological advances can affect many aspects of business and some of these areas will now be looked at briefly, to give just a flavour of the immense impact that technology has had on marketing practice.

■ Materials, components and products

Consumers tend to take products, and the materials and components that go into them, for granted as long as they work and live up to the marketers' promises. Technology does, however, improve and increase the benefits that consumers derive from products, and raise expectations about what a product should be. Some technological applications are invisible to the consumer, affecting raw materials and components hidden within an existing product, for example car engines which produce less harmful emissions, while others create completely new products, for example DVD players that offer 'record' as well as 'playback' functions.

One innovation that has revolutionised many product markets is the microchip. Not only are microchips the heart and soul of our home computers, but they also program our washing machines, DVD players and video recorders, among many things. The incorporation of microchips into products has increased their reliability, their efficiency in operation and the range of sophisticated functions that they can perform, all very cost-effectively. This in turn has raised consumers' expectations of what products can do, and revised their attitudes towards cost, quality and value for money.

Technology is not just about the physical product itself. It can also affect its packaging. Lightweight plastics and glass, recycled and recyclable materials, and cans that incorporate a device to give canned beer the character and quality of draught are examples of packaging innovations that have helped to make products more appealing, enhance their image or keep their cost down.

■ Production processes

The fulfilment of marketing promises can be helped or hindered by what happens in the production process. More efficient production can, for instance, increase the volume of product available, thus potentially meeting a bigger demand, or it can reduce the cost of the product, thus giving more scope to the pricing decision. Production can also contribute to better and more consistent product quality, again increasing customer satisfaction. Here are some examples where technology has influenced production processes and indirectly affected marketing activities.

Computer aided design (CAD) and computer aided manufacturing (CAM) systems have revolutionised product design/formulation, testing and production. In terms of design, technology allows ideas to be visualised, tested and accepted or rejected much more quickly than if paper plans and calculations had to be updated. Similarly, computer-controlled production systems can undertake tasks faster than human operatives, with more consistency and fewer errors. When this is all integrated with sophisticated quality assurance and control techniques, the outcome for the customer is that products get to the market more quickly, and in a more refined state, and may be cheaper and more reliable.

Materials handling and waste minimisation are also of concern for efficient, cost-effective production management. Stocks of materials need to be closely monitored; in a large operation, the location of materials needs to be planned so that they can be accessed quickly and spend the minimum amount of time being transported around the site; the packaging and bundling of materials need to be planned to balance out the sometimes conflicting concerns of adequately protecting and identifying the goods, and making sure that they can be unwrapped and put into the production line quickly. Computerised planning models and advances in packaging technology can both help to increase efficiency in these areas.

■ Administration and distribution

There is little point in using technology to streamline the production of goods if the support systems are inefficient or if distribution causes a bottleneck between factory and customer. Distribution has benefited from technology, as has materials handling, through systems for locating and tracking goods in and out. Integrated ordering and dispatch functions mean theoretically that as soon as an order is entered into the computer, goods availability can be checked and the warehouse can get on with the job of fulfilling it, while the computer handles all the paperwork, printing off packing slips and invoices, for example, and updating customer records. All of this speeds up the sending of orders to customers and reduces labour involvement, costs and risks of errors.

Telecommunications linking into computer systems can extend the administration efficiencies even further. Large retail chains, for example, can be linked with their major suppliers, so that as the retailer's stocks reduce, an order can be sent from computer to computer. Similarly, large organisations with sites and depots spread over a wide geographic area can use such technology to link sites, managing and tracking the flow of goods.

■ Marketing and customers

Much of the technology discussed above has implied benefits for the customer, in producing the right product at the right time in the right place at the right price, but technology also plays a part in the marketing processes that form the interface between buyer and seller. Increased and cheaper computer power, which means that large, complex sets of data can be input and analysed quickly and easily, has benefited both market research data collection and analysis, and relationship marketing initiatives, establishing and maintaining a one-to-one dialogue between buyer and seller. Organisations such as Heinz see this as an exciting development in consumer marketing, and it is only possible because of database technology that permits the storage, retrieval and maintenance of detailed profiles of many thousands, or even hundreds of thousands, of customers. The technology also allows the creation of tailored, personalised marketing offers to be made to subsets of those customers as appropriate.

Advertising media too have improved and proliferated through technology. The internet, interactive television and text messaging have become alternative media for many organisations. These media allow them not only to disseminate information about their products, services, news and corporate philosophy, but also to set up interactive dialogue with customers and potential customers. A website can be an exciting communications medium as it can feature sound and video clips and, if the site is well structured, visitors can select the topics that interest them. Also, the information can be updated easily and regularly. In addition, both the internet and interactive digital television allow potential customers to browse through product information, check availability and place an order, all in the comfort of their own armchairs.

Another area that can also be enhanced through computer technology is sales force support. Supplying a sales representative with a laptop computer can give access to current information about products, their availability and prices; it can store customer profiles and relevant information; the representative can update records and write reports while the information is still fresh in their mind; and it can store appropriate graphics to enhance a sales presentation. All of this is easily portable and accessible whether the representative is working in Scotland or Poland.

The economic and competitive environment

The effects of the economic and competitive environment are felt by organisations and consumers alike, and it has a profound effect on their behaviour. In the next few pages we look first at the macroeconomic environment, which provides the overall backdrop against which marketing activities take place. As well as issues of national interest, such as the effects of government economic policy on commerce, we cover the influence of international trading blocs and trade agreements. All of these things may provide opportunities or threats for an individual organisation. We then turn to the microeconomic environment. This is rather closer to home for the organisation, looking at the extent to which different market structures constrain or widen the organisation's freedom of action in its marketing activities and its ability to influence the nature of the market.

■ The macroeconomic environment

Figure 2.3 shows the basic economic concept of the circular flow of goods and income that makes a market economy go round. Marketing, as an exchange process and indeed as a force that actively encourages more exchanges, is an essential fuel to keep that flow going. The world is not, however, a closed, self-sustaining loop such as that depicted in Figure 2.3. Its operation is severely affected by the macroeconomic influences generated by government economic policy and by membership of international trading blocs and trade agreements.

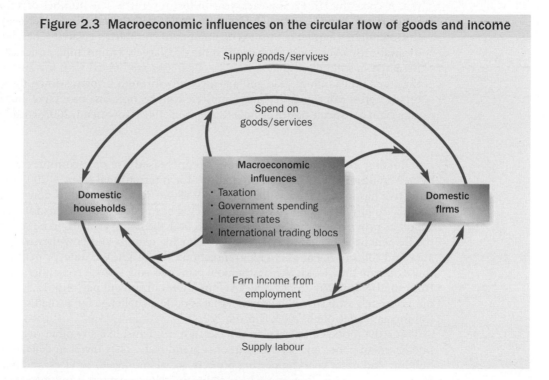

Figure 2.3 Macroeconomic influences on the circular flow of goods and income

Governments can develop and implement policies in relation to several macroeconomic influences, which in turn affect markets, organisations and customers. Just a few of these are discussed below.

Taxation and government spending

Taxes may be direct or indirect. Direct taxation, such as income tax and national insurance contributions, reduces the amount of money, or disposable income, that a household has available to spend on the goods and services that organisations provide. Indirect taxation, such as purchase tax or value added tax (VAT), is collected for the government by the seller, who is obliged to add a percentage to the basic price of the product. Thus a PC sold in the UK may be advertised with two prices: a basic price of £499, then £586 including VAT at $17\frac{1}{2}$ per cent.

Some products, such as alcohol, tobacco and petrol, have duty imposed on them, again collected by the seller. Both VAT and duties serve to increase the prices of products for the customer, and marketers need to think about the effect of the tax-inclusive price on the customer's attitude and buying habits. When rates of duty increase, marketers sometimes choose to absorb some of the increase themselves to keep prices competitive, rather than pass on the entire rise to the buyer.

Rates of VAT and duties vary across Europe and, despite over thirty years of trying, there is still no significant progress in persuading member states to move to a common VAT system based upon harmonised rates and structures. It is compulsory for membership of the EU for VAT rates to be between 15 and 25 per cent, but that still gives a lot of scope for variation (*Wall Street Journal*, 2005). The EU is looking to narrow the band to 16 to 19 per cent, but that seems some way off. Many national governments would regard a centrally imposed VAT rate as further evidence of creeping federalism.

eg The cigarette industry has been hard hit by a combination of the elimination of duty-free sales and by smuggling. The EU shopper can now bring around 3000 cigarettes into the UK without being stopped by Customs. This reflects the large differential between typical prices in the mainland EU and those in the UK, where higher duties sometimes double the price of a packet. Smuggling cigarettes for resale is illegal and it is claimed that it costs the UK £2.5bn each year in lost revenues. The number of smuggled cigarettes has dropped in recent years from around 30 per cent to 15 per cent of all sales through tighter border controls. The number of counterfeit cigarettes has, however, risen dramatically over the same period, smuggled largely from China and Eastern Europe. Research has indicated that at best the cigarettes are bulked with sawdust, but at worst they contain cadmium, lead and arsenic. Only through bringing down the level of duty on cigarettes can smuggling and counterfeiting become less profitable, but that in turn cuts right across the health agenda (Stevenson, 2005; Townsend, 2005; Urquhart, 2004).

A further challenge has come from the increased use of e-commerce, as this tends to bypass traditional VAT collection methods for international sales. A 2003 EU E-commerce Directive has taken the view that the EU VAT net should extend to non-EU suppliers who trade with any EU-based end-consumer. This has major implications for non-EU software suppliers providing games, music and video over the net. It remains to be seen how successful the EU will be in extending its tax laws to non-EU nations and how they will enforce compliance and collection. For EU to EU transactions, the 'origin VAT rate' principle applies, but for those outside the EU it is the 'destination' principle, so a Danish consumer buying downloads from the US may pay 25 per cent VAT but a UK citizen will pay only 17.5 per cent. Working out accurately who should be paying what is quite a challenge for a small software supplier in California (Coleclough, 2003; Ivinson, 2003)!

Using the money they 'earn' from taxes, governments, like any other organisations, are the purchasers of goods and services, but on a grand scale. They invest in defence industries, road building and other civil engineering projects, social and health services, and many other areas. Such large purchasing power can be used to stimulate or depress economic development, but if a government decides as a matter of policy to cut back on its spending, industry can be very badly hit. Defence, for example, is an area which many governments are reviewing in the aftermath of the ending of the 'cold war'.

eg The shipbuilding industry in the UK is just about hanging on in the fight against strong international competitors, a far cry from the days of Empire and the large shipyards in Glasgow, Newcastle, Birkenhead and so on. Despite Trafalgar, the recent government decision to offer to share the work on two new UK aircraft carriers, ironically with France, was assumed to be as much about politics as economics. A large Anglo-French defence project could demonstrate that the UK is not completely reliant on US defence technology and also act as a signal that the *entente cordiale* is not dead. A decision is awaited from the French government which is also planning to build one carrier (O'Connell, 2005).

The cost of money

Government economic policy affects interest rates, which have an impact on both consumers and business. For many consumers, the most serious effect of a rise in interest rates is on their monthly mortgage repayments. Paying £20 or more per month extra to the mortgage lender means that there is that much less cash available for buying other things, and across the country retail sales can be significantly reduced. Interest rate rises can also affect the attractiveness of credit to the consumer, either when buying large expensive items through instalments, or when using credit cards. A consumer thinking about buying a brand new car, for example, may need a loan, and will look at the repayment levels, determined by interest rates, when deciding how expensive a model can be afforded. To try to reduce this potential barrier to purchasing, many car dealers have entered into arrangements with credit companies to offer 0 per cent financing deals to car buyers.

A country's exchange rate is rather like the price of a share for a company; it is a sign of confidence in the continued prosperity, or otherwise, of an individual nation. Fluctuating exchange rates between different currencies can have a major impact on the prosperity of companies and individual consumers. If a currency is strong, imports become cheaper which is good news for businesses and consumers, but exports become more expensive which is bad news for manufacturers. The strength of sterling in the period after the launch of the euro has been blamed by some for precipitating a manufacturing recession in the UK as prices in the prime continental markets become less competitive.

eg The fall in the relative value of the dollar against a number of major currencies in 2005 had major implications for US trading partners around the world. Nippon Steel in Japan had particular reason to watch the rise of the yen against the dollar. In 2004, the price of steel was $400 per ton, fetching around 50,000 yen, but by the spring of 2005, $400 fetched only 44,000 yen, the equivalent of a price decline of around 10 per cent. Nippon Steel has had to meet similar fluctuations in the past, and its response is constant restructuring, changing capacity and rapid repositioning for survival. This is the challenge that will face European exporters to the US, should the dollar remain weak, and even in China any revaluation of the RMB could put pressure for the first time on some parts of the economy (Sapsford, 2005).

International trading blocs

Governments also negotiate membership of international trading blocs, and the scope, terms and conditions of international trade agreements. Membership of the EU, for example, and particularly the advent of the single European market (SEM), has had a profound effect on the wider commercial dealings of organisations operating within the EU, as well as on the economic and competitive environment. Organisations which exist in countries outside the EU have found it increasingly difficult to sell into the EU, since there are now many more EU-based potential suppliers for purchasers to turn to, and also the logistics of purchasing within the EU are easier.

The enlargement of the EU to 25 countries in 2004 created a market of 455 million people. Although the recent entrants into the EU in Central Europe are poorer than the long-established members, there is optimism that free access to trade with all the other EU states will allow significant growth and modernisation. Further expansion is possible with Bulgaria, Romania and some of the Baltic States along with Turkey at various stages of access negotiation and compliance. There is even the possibility of the Ukraine joining after the 'orange revolution'. However, the pace of change may slow down as the EU constitution is in difficulty; some nations are wary of opening their borders to potential terrorism threats; there are fears that the EU will become unmanageable; and most of the new entrants will need considerable financial support in the short term and may pose a threat to jobs within existing member states. The outcome of Turkey's application to join the EU will be the benchmark to assess whether further expansion really is still on the political agenda. Turkey is a large, relatively poor country whose population is 99 per cent Muslim, so its integration into the EU would be an interesting challenge. Nevertheless, it is clear that EU enlargement has moved beyond mere considerations of free trade to ensuring peace, preserving democracy and strengthening liberal values, all well beyond the scope of this book (*The Economist*, 2005; Watson, 2005).

Beyond the confines of formalised trading blocs, business is often affected by the existence of trade agreements. Some of these are protectionist, in that they are trying to cushion domestic producers from the effects of an influx of imports, while others are trying to liberalise trade between nations. For many years, for example, the UK's textile industry benefited from the multi fibre arrangement (MFA), which protected jobs and businesses by basically restricting the imports of low-priced clothing from various Far Eastern countries. Similarly, Japan agreed to implement voluntary export restraint (VER) with regard to its car industry's sales to Western Europe and the US. This helped to protect domestic car producers and jobs by imposing quotas on Japanese imports. One way of overcoming the restrictions of this VER was international direct investment, i.e. setting up factories within the EU (taking full advantage, by the way, of various EU investment incentives) to produce cars with sufficient local content to be labelled 'European'. Thus those people owning either a Nissan (built in Washington, Tyne and Wear), a Honda (built in Swindon) or a Toyota (built in Derby), for example, are technically driving a British car. From their British manufacturing bases, the companies can legitimately export, without quota constraints, to the rest of the EU under the terms of the SEM.

The protectionist stance of agreements like the MFA is, however, being overshadowed by wider moves towards trade liberalisation, through the General Agreement on Tariffs and Trade (GATT), for example. The broad aim of GATT is to get rid of export subsidies and import tariffs (effectively taxes on imports that push their prices up to make them less competitive compared with the domestically produced equivalent product) to make international trade a great deal fairer. This means that negotiated VERs, which do not depend on tariffs to control imports, are becoming an increasingly important tool.

■ The microeconomic environment

The general discussion in Chapter 1 of what marketing is, and its main tools, did not pay particular attention to the structure of markets. It is nevertheless important to think about market structures, because these will influence what sort of competition the organisation is up against, what scope the organisation has to manipulate the 4Ps and how broad an impact the organisation's marketing activities could have on the market as a whole.

Market structures can be defined in four broad categories, based on the number and size of competitors in the market.

marketing in action

Helping the rich at the expense of the poor

The management of large international trade blocs can be a challenge, not just in terms of trade bloc to trade bloc negotiation, but also in dealings with less developed nations. Whether running a farm in Zambia or a textile mill in India, marketing options can be severely constrained by trade agreements. It is when we consider the wider implications of these deals that

issues of values and morality come to the fore.

Consider a few statistics. It has been estimated that 2.5bn people live on $2bn a day between them, and 90m of them live on less than $1 a day, according to Oxfam. Some 96 per cent of the world's farmers, 1.3bn people, live in developing countries. Trade is one alternative to aid that developing countries can benefit from, but that is where the problems start. Poor countries face high tariffs, stiff quotas and subsidised competition from the rich nations, especially in

food processing, textiles and agriculture. Some tariffs are as high as 350 per cent for manufactured goods, thus making them uncompetitively expensive in EU markets. The World Bank estimates that if these barriers could be dismantled, it would be worth $350bn to the developing world over the next ten years, and help to lift 144m people out of poverty.

Yet trade protection in the US, Europe and Japan in agriculture alone is equivalent to $1bn a day. The EU has developed a particular reputation for protecting its agriculture through high tariffs. It pays €43bn a year to its farmers to over-produce, thus lowering world prices and thus reducing export revenue for those developing nations lucky enough to be able to supply (although the Common Agricultural Policy which provides these EU subsidies is being reformed).

Let's consider the case of bananas. After a ten-year debate over the rules for bananas, the EU eventually agreed in 2002 to offer the Caribbean and Latin American nations banana quotas to allow them access to the EU states. Quotas directly limit trade flows whereas tariffs restrict trade less, as there can be some competition. The reason why the EU has taken such an interest is that the Spanish produce bananas in the Canary Islands and France has some interests in some of its former colonies. These countries want a high tariff to keep other competitors out while they negotiate tariff-free access. As part of a renegotiation in 2005, the EU proposed a tariff of €230 per ton whereas most Caribbean and Latin American producers believe that they would be uncompetitive even at a tariff of €150 per tonne. The continuing banana wars may be passed to the WTO to sort out.

What is the solution to a problem where something grown

A worker with bananas at the Juliana Jaramillo Co-operative in the Dominican Republic, which supplies the fruit to supermarkets where it is sold in packaging with the Fairtrade Foundation logo.

Source: © Fairtrade Foundation 2002
http://www.fairtrade.org.uk

cheaply in poor countries either is denied entry to the EU or ends up at such a high price that it is uncompetitive? The easy answer would be to eliminate all tariffs, quotas and restrictions to allow poor nations to sell in the EU. That would be politically unacceptable to the majority of the EU population and even then, there is no guarantee that the beneficiaries would be the poor African countries

rather than the fast-developing nations of China and India. Even Oxfam doesn't argue for that; it is calling for fair trade so that the most deserving people gain the greatest access, as a means of wealth redistribution and of avoiding excessive aid and handouts. In reality, Oxfam is calling for a controlled market so that the poor countries get a bigger slice of the market than they could win on their own merits. But who decides who is the most needy? This hardly represents fair trade!

Dr Rowan Williams, the Archbishop of Canterbury, goes further and questions the morality of a system that allows procrastination in the wealthy nations as people starve elsewhere. To him, the paradox is that the rich protect their markets while promoting free and liberal trade regimes in the developing world. Ultimately, it is only through reforming EU agriculture policy to avoid market distortion that the key can be found to freer trade. If agriculture changes, the other sectors will soon fall into line. What is clear is that trading blocs have a major impact on the marketing environment for buyer and seller alike.

Sources: Daneshkhu (2005); Garten (2005); McGregor (2005); Miller (2004); Mortished (2005a, 2005b); Thornton (2004).

Monopoly

Technically, a monopoly exists where one supplier has sole control over a market, and there is no competition. The lack of competition may be because the monopolist is state-owned and/or has a statutory right to be the sole supplier to the market. Traditionally in the EU, this applied to public utilities, such as gas, water, electricity, telephone and postal services, and some key industries such as the railways, steel and coal. Government policy in member states over the past twenty years, however, was to privatise and open up some of these industries to competition, with the idea that if they were exposed to market forces and were answerable to shareholders, they would operate more efficiently and cost effectively. By 2000, the OECD reported that over one trillion dollars had been transferred worldwide from state to private enterprise. Manufacturing, banking, transportation, energy and public utilities have all been privatised in a significant number of countries. Some countries such as Hungary and Portugal have raised a quarter of GDP from privatisation sales. More recently, the telecommunications industry has the been the focus of attention. Privatisation in telecoms reflects the changing competitive structure facing the industry that organisations must operate within. With the internationalisation of telecoms, global competitiveness has increased while the pace of technological development requires significant investment to keep up to date.

eg The EU has also taken an interest in some state-owned monopolies. In Sweden, as in other Scandinavian countries, there is a state monopoly for retailing alcohol. The EU rejected the Swedish government's claim that it was better able to control retail sales and thus restrict the potential for Swedes to consume too much liquor. The EU considered that Systembolaget's state monopoly to sell wine, spirits and strong beer was a disproportionate measure for preventing alcohol abuse, and that the protected arrangement contravened the EU ruling on the free flow of goods. Currently 70 per cent of alcohol sold in Sweden comes from its stores or through restaurants. The grocery trade, for example, was not able to sell in competition with Systembolaget. In addition, Sweden, as part of its EU accession in 1995, negotiated a special five-year arrangement that restricted the amount of alcohol that could be brought into the country by returning Swedish travellers. Part of the argument is that the government wants to protect its people from the worst excesses of alcohol by restricting purchases and keeping prices high. There have also been complaints of long queues, poor service and restricted opening times in the state-owned retail alcohol outlets, which further frustrates the consumer.

Systembolaget is, however, slowly losing its stranglehold. The Danish government had to cut taxes on alcohol as, in a borderless Europe, Danes were crossing the border into Germany in huge numbers to buy more cheaply. The 45 per cent cut was deep, and the consequences inevitable: Swedes started to flood into Denmark as the Swedish government refused to cut its taxes. Bells Whisky cost Dkr 290 in Sweden and just Dkr 169 in Denmark. From the start of 2004, Swedes could import 10 litres of spirits, 20 litres of fortified wines, 90 litres of wine and 110 litres of beer, more than enough for even the most serious drinker. Drink consumption is increasing in Sweden, and the rationale for the monopoly is in tatters, as high taxes and high prices can be circumvented so easily. Systembolaget, however, continues as normal, although opening hours have lengthened (but forget trying to buy after 7 p.m. or on a Sunday). How long will all this last? Despite calls for change and tax cuts as in Denmark and Finland, to date alcohol control seems more important than tax revenue generation (Brown-Humes and MacCarthy, 2004; *The Economist*, 2000; George, 2004).

In practice, although the privatised companies have restructured themselves internally and revised their business philosophies to suit their new status, they still face limited competition as yet. This is mainly because of the barriers to entry faced by potential competitors, such as the massive capital investment required, or the monopolist's domination of essential resources or infrastructure.

The implication of all this is that a true monopoly is hard to find in a modern market economy, although several near-monopolies are operating. In the UK, a monopoly is deemed to exist where an organisation or a group of collaborating organisations control 25 per cent of a market. Where this occurs, or where a proposed or threatened takeover raises the possibility of its happening, the Competition Commission may undertake an inquiry to establish whether the situation is operating in the public interest and whether there is any unfair competition involved.

This discussion so far has been rather parochial in that it has concentrated on national or regional monopolies. In global markets, however, it is even more difficult, if not impossible, to establish and sustain a monopoly.

As a final thought, the concept of monopoly depends on how 'market' is defined. While it is true that currently SNCF, for example, holds a monopoly on passenger rail travel in France, it does not have a monopoly on moving people from Paris to Lyon. To travellers, rail is only one option, and they might also consider travelling to their destinations by air, by coach or by car. In that sense, the traveller's perception of rail, in terms of its cost, reliability and convenience, is developed in a very competitive context.

Oligopoly

Well-developed market economies are far more likely to see the emergence of oligopolies than monopolies. In an oligopoly, a small number of firms account for a very large share of the market, and a number of the privatised ex-monopolies discussed above are moving into this category. The oligopoly creates a certain amount of interdependence between the key players, each of which is large enough for its actions to have a big impact on the market and on the behaviour of its competitors. This certainly occurs in large-scale, worldwide industrial markets, such as chemicals, oil and pharmaceuticals, because the amount of capital investment required, the levels of production needed to achieve economies of scale and the geographic dispersion of large customers demanding large quantities make this the most efficient way for these markets to be structured.

Other consumer oligopolies are less visible to the casual observer. In the supermarket, the shopper may see a wide variety of brands of clothes-washing detergents, and thus imagine that there is healthy, widespread competition in that sector. Most brands are, however, owned and managed by either Procter & Gamble (P&G) (Ariel, Daz, Bold, etc.) or Unilever (Persil, Radion, Surf, etc.), and the proliferation of brands is more to do with fragmented demand and the creation of discrete segments (see Chapter 4) than the fragmentation of supply. Again, the supermarkets are the biggest threat to this oligopoly, with their own-brands, such as retailer Sainsbury's own brand Novon.

In marketing terms, it is nevertheless still very difficult for a new brand from a new competitor to enter an oligopolistic market, other than in a small niche. This is because the oligopolists have spent many years and vast amounts of marketing money establishing their brands and shares. The threat from a supermarket's own-brand is more serious, however, because of the retailers' inherent control over a major channel of distribution which neither of the oligopolists can afford to lose. All of this really leaves only very small gaps in the market for the smaller competitor, such as that filled by products such as Ark and Ecover, two detergent brands that positioned themselves as more environmentally friendly than anything else available, appealing to the 'dark green' consumer.

Oligopolists therefore spend their time watching each other, and developing their marketing strategies and tactics on the basis of what the other main players are doing or are likely to do. If, for example, Unilever launches a new brand, or implements a major new marketing communications strategy, P&G would prefer to anticipate it, thus either pre-empting Unilever or at least having a calculated response ready when needed. From P&G's point of view this is essential, even if it is only to maintain the delicate status quo of the two companies' relative market shares.

Monopolistic and perfect competition

Good marketing practice and the emphasis on differential advantage have created a market structure that might seem a little paradoxical at first sight: monopolistic competition. The idea is that although there are many competitors in the market (with the emphasis on smaller competitors without enough individual influence to create either an oligopoly or a monopoly, as discussed above), each has a product sufficiently differentiated from the rest to create its own monopoly, because to the customer it is unique, or at least any potential substitutes are considered to be inferior. The concept forms the basis of much of the rest of this book.

Perfect competition is at the opposite end of the spectrum from monopoly, and is about as likely to be found in practice. It involves many small producers, all supplying identical products that can be directly substituted for each other. No producer has the power to influence or determine price, and the market consists of many small buyers, who similarly cannot influence the market individually. There are no barriers to market entry or exit, and all buyers and sellers have complete information about what is happening in the market. All of this is clearly unrealistic. The influence of marketing concepts on even the smallest organisations, along with the development of powerful buyers and sellers in all kinds of markets, consumer and B2B, mean that these conditions cannot hold, and some kind of monopolistic competition or oligopoly soon emerges.

eg   Farm produce, such as vegetables, is often cited as an example of near-perfect competition. While it is true that the market does consist of many small suppliers, i.e. individual farms, the nature of the buyer is more complex, ranging from a family buying a few kilos of carrots from a farm shop, to the fruit and vegetable wholesalers and supermarket chains that buy such quantities that they can influence price and other supply variables. Even the product itself can be differentiated, for example organic and non-organic, or class I and class II quality. The farmer can also differentiate the offering through grading and packaging the produce to suit the retail customer. Even carrots, therefore, can be seen to be moving towards monopolistic competition.

The political and regulatory environment

Organisations have to exist in and operate according to the laws of the societies within which they do business, and thus in addition to the more general laws of contract and commerce, products have to conform to safety laws; manufacturing processes are subject to pollution controls; copyright and patents protect innovation; and retailers' opening hours are restricted in Germany, for example, by the *Ladenschlussgesetz*, and in the UK by the Sunday trading laws. We look below at the role and influence of national governments and the European Parliament in making rules that have a direct effect on the marketing mix.

Regulation is not only defined through legislation from national governments or the European Parliament, however. Organisations are also subject to rules passed by regulatory bodies, some of which have statutory powers delegated to them from government, while others are voluntary groupings, such as trade associations, with codes of practice to which the organisation chooses to adhere. We examine the nature and influence of such bodies on pp. 61 *et seq*. Inevitably, governments and other regulatory bodies are influenced in their policy making by other sources, such as lobbyists and pressure groups, and on p. 64 we take a wider view of the influences that drive the legislators and rule makers towards their policies.

■ National and local government

The obvious responsibility of national governments is to determine and maintain the legislative framework within which organisations do business. This will cover areas such as contract law, consumer protection, financial legislation, competition and trading practices, for example. There are variations in approaches across Europe but increasingly, as European integration proceeds and the internal market is fully liberalised, national governments are working within EU guidelines and directives, with the longer-term aim of achieving consistency across member states.

Within the UK, although Parliament passes legislation and puts it on the statute books, the responsibility for implementing and enforcing it is often delegated to specialist bodies, such as the Office of Fair Trading (OFT), Competition Commission, or Ofcom. The role of such bodies is discussed further on pp. 61 *et seq*.

As well as the legislation they pass that affects the day-to-day business practices of organisations, governments can also have profound effects on the competitive environment. The widespread privatisation of publicly owned utilities and other state-controlled national industries in the 1980s and 1990s, as has already been discussed, presented opportunities for new competitors to enter these markets, as well as profoundly changing the culture and business orientation of the newly privatised companies themselves.

Local government also carries some responsibility for implementing and enforcing laws made at a national level. In Germany, local government has responsibility for implementing pollution and noise control legislation. In the UK, local trading standards officers may well be the first to investigate claims of shady or illegal business practices. Christmas often heralds a flurry of warnings from trading standards officers about dangerous toys, usually cheap imports from the Far East, that do not conform to EU safety standards. Officers can prosecute the retailer and prevent further sales of the offending goods, but by then, significant numbers of the product may already have been sold. Trading Standards offices play an important role in ensuring consumer safety and that fair trading and quality standards are maintained. They are provided by over 200 local authorities in the United Kingdom.

eg Trading Standards officials undertook tests on children's sun creams to assess the validity of the claims made by the manufacturers. Of the eight sun creams targeted at children, seven failed to give the protection claimed. Three of the products did not live up to their UVA ratings and four did not achieve the Sun Protection factor. This means that children are being exposed to the harmful effects of the sun, despite parents thinking they are providing protection. Unlike in the US and Australia where there is greater regulation, in the EU sun creams are considered in the same category as lipsticks so have lighter controls. By raising the issue, the Trading Standards Institute acts as a force lobbying government for regulation and encouraging manufacturers to ensure that their products protect the consumer and are described accurately on the packs. Of particular concern to the TSI is that sunscreen manufacturers focus more on higher and higher levels of UVB protection, thus leading consumers to believe they can stay in the sun longer, and so increasing their exposure to the more harmful UVA rays (*The Grocer*, 2004a; http://www.tsi.org.uk).

Local authorities in the UK also have responsibility for granting planning permission. For businesses, this means that if they want to build a factory or supermarket, or change the usage of a commercial building, then the local authority has to vet the plans and grant permission before anything can be done. Local authorities are under pressure from small retailers who are worried about the major shift towards out-of-town superstore shopping. The argument is that town centres and small local businesses are dying because people would rather go to the out-of-town retail park or shopping mall. This means that local authorities are increasingly reluctant to grant planning permission for further out-of-town developments, seriously affecting the growth plans of many large retailers.

eg In the 1990s, supermarkets were criticised by some for changing the face of the High Street by attracting shoppers to out-of-town hypermarkets, superstores and malls. A number of countries, including France and the UK, introduced tough planning regimes to limit growth. Now, supermarkets are starting to play a part in urban renewal schemes using brownfield sites largely as a response to the ease and favour given to planning permission for redeveloping sites (Bedington, 2001). Even these schemes attract criticism, however. A planned Tesco development in Birmingham caused a public outcry as it involved building on playing fields to cater for a 400-space car park ('we are depriving future generations of these playing pitches'). This was despite the plans for the scheme including the development of new sports and youth facilities in the area (Elkes, 2005). Similarly in Dartford, London, a major deal between Tesco and developers featured a £94m redevelopment covering a rejuvenated town square, 450 homes and of course a supermarket. Although planning was granted, a petition of 13,000 signatures was presented objecting again to encroachment on an adjacent park for access (Gillman, 2005). It is perhaps not surprising, therefore, that a number of the supermarkets are targeting the takeover of local convenience outlets rather than planning the grand supermarket developments which are becoming harder and harder to get permission for (Barnes, 2004a).

Although the EU is making considerable progress towards eliminating national regulations that are contrary to fair and free trade, the scale of the task is great. National environmental laws in Germany and Denmark, for example, have been criticised as favouring local rather than international suppliers. The extent to which regulations affect business, therefore, varies between countries and industries. There is a slow move towards standardisation, which generally means that the advanced industrialised northern European nations are tending to deregulate, whereas the southern nations are tending to tighten up controls. Moves towards deregulation have been accompanied by increased self-regulation within industries.

■ The European Union

It is unfortunate that the pronouncements from Brussels that make the headlines tend to be the offbeat or trivial ones, such as the proposal to regulate the curve on a cucumber, the redesignation of the carrot as a fruit to allow the Portuguese to carry on their trade in carrot jam, and questions as to whether Cheddar cheese and Swiss rolls can continue to bear those names if they are not made in those places. Despite these delightful eccentricities, the EU works hard towards ensuring free trade and fair competition across member states' boundaries.

The SEM, which officially came into being on 1 January 1993, was the culmination of many years of work in breaking down trade barriers and harmonising legislation across the member states. One area that directly affects marketing is the abolition of frontier controls, so that goods can be transferred from state to state, or carried in transit through states, without lots of paperwork and customs checks. Additionally, road haulage has been freed from restrictions and quotas so that a haulier with a licence to operate in one EU member state can operate in any other. Further European integration is sought through EMU (European Monetary Union) and the introduction of the euro as a replacement for national currencies. This has made cross-border price comparisons a lot easier for customers and created more transparent pan-European competition. The euro has also eliminated problems caused by fluctuating exchange rates, thus reducing the costs of the cross-border movement of goods and encouraging more imports and exports between the countries of the EU.

In terms of products themselves, a set of European standards have been implemented through a series of directives, ensuring common criteria for safety, public health and environmental protection. Any product adhering to these directives and to the laws of its own country of origin will be acceptable in any member state. Look for the stylised CE symbol on products as the sign that they do conform to European standards.

In other areas of marketing, harmonisation of regulations and codes of practice across member states has not been so easy. Over the next few years, the EU intends to bring a series of separate legislation together into an overarching EU Communications Act, which would be wide ranging in terms of promotional and media types, including press and TV, direct marketing and sales promotion, online marketing and e-commerce (Simms, 2001). The problem with marketing communications is that the European law makers have to reconcile commercial freedom with consumer protection across 25 different countries, each with its own customs, laws, codes and practices. Sometimes, best practice is followed and harmonisation across all states can be achieved, but in other cases, the law of the country in which a transaction originates applies, by mutual recognition. There are wide variations in best practice across Europe, so finding a common approach will be difficult. The threats are, however, real for UK advertisers. Sweden, despite an initial rebuff, would still like to see a blanket ban across Europe on television advertising to children and the advertising of alcohol. Other lobbies exist to constrain advertising on 'unhealthy foods', financial services, and even cars (Smith, 2001).

eg   Defining just what chocolate actually is or is not has caused controversy in Europe among both politicians and chocolate manufacturers. The argument has been going on for over 30 years, since the UK and Ireland joined the EU with chocolate that included cheaper vegetable fats rather than a higher proportion of cocoa fats. The chocolate wars have been fought between an alliance of France and Belgium and a number of others against the UK, Ireland and five other states. An EU directive favouring one side over the other would create an unfair competitive advantage and would be a far cry from a single European market in chocolate. In 1997, the European Parliament ruled in favour of the France–Belgium alliance, overturning a previous compromise EU directive. This meant that the term 'milk chocolate' could not be used by the UK and the other states on its side. That meant that products from the UK and Ireland and some other member states would have to be renamed 'chocolate with milk and non-cocoa vegetable fats' or at least 'milk chocolate with high milk content'. Product labels would also need to show clearly that the product contains vegetable fats.

That was not acceptable to the UK chocolate producers and a further compromise was realised in 2000 with directive 2000/36 which agreed to two definitions of chocolate: 'milk chocolate' and 'family milk chocolate', the latter replacing the 'milk chocolate with high milk content' designation for the UK and Irish markets. Although the terminology was subsequently refined to 'chocolate substitute', it was eventually ruled in 2003 that it infringed Community law on free trade. Common sense at last prevailed, in that the ruling recognised that different chocolate traditions should exist in a marketplace to allow consumers a choice. So, at least in theory, Cadbury's Dairy Milk should be appearing on Italian supermarket shelves. By insisting on the term 'chocolate substitute' the Italians had effectively created an obstruction for those wishing to enter its market. Effectively, prior to the ruling, the Italians were asking some Community traders to modify their products or presentation and to incur additional packaging costs in the process. There was even the possibility that the consumer might regard a product with the word 'substitute' as inferior. So the 2003 ruling may mean at last that chocolate traditions can be retained and barriers removed for its free movement (Bremner, 1997; Morley, 2003; *The Times*, 2003; Tucker, 1997; **http://www.europa.eu.int**).

Direct marketing is a relatively new area which has great potential for the marketing of goods across Europe, and yet here too, a variety of national codes are in operation. In the UK, for example, 'cold calling' telephone selling (i.e. an organisation phoning a consumer for sales purposes without the consumer's prior permission) is permitted, but in Germany it is almost totally banned. Data protection laws (i.e. what information organisations are permitted to hold on databases and what they are allowed to do with it) and regulations on list broking (i.e. the sale of lists of names and addresses to other organisations) also vary widely across the EU. The relevant EU directives include the Data Protection Directive, the Distance Selling Directive and the Integrated Digital Services Network Directive. The current area for EU interest in regulation is in the taste, decency, accuracy and impartiality of internet broadcasting. In the UK, television delivered via the internet is unregulated, but rather than derive a new set of regulations specifically for internet broadcasting the EU intends to draft a directive based upon the 1989 Directive for 'Television without Frontiers' (Sabbagh, 2005).

■ Regulatory bodies

Within the UK, there are many regulatory bodies with greater or lesser powers of regulation over marketing practice. Quasi-governmental bodies such as the Office of Fair Trading (OFT) and the Competition Commission have had statutory duties and powers delegated to them directly by government to ensure the maintenance of free and fair commerce.

The Office of Fair Trading (OFT) in the UK aims to ensure that markets are working effectively. This is achieved by ensuring that competition and consumer protection laws and guidelines are followed in the public interest. It is the OFT that refers mergers to the Competition Commission. Being accountable to parliament, it is able to play a powerful role in shaping an organisation's marketing behaviour. One of its recent activities includes a clampdown on what it perceived as unfair flight pricing. Cheap airline seats offered over the internet sometimes failed to include airport taxes, insurance levies, credit card charges and handling fees, boosting the actual ticket price far beyond the figures advertised. One promotion offered one million seats at 99p, but five screens later, after the addition of taxes, etc., the price was over £60! The Competition Commission ruled that it should be clear to customers what the price of the ticket was going to be before, not after they had purchased. Only then could sensible price comparisons be made.

Slightly more remote from central government, quasi-autonomous non-governmental organisations (quangos) have a specific remit and can act much more quickly than a government department. Quangos such as Oftel, Ofgem and Ofwat, for instance, exist to regulate the privatised telephone, gas and electricity, and water industries respectively in the UK. The prime aim for the quangos is to protect consumer interests by ensuring appropriate levels of competition.

The scope of the work of quangos is clearly extensive and offers necessary protection for the consumer in markets that have been privatised. Suppliers in the industry must also consider the likely public and legislative impact of acting outside the public interest in the development of their marketing strategy and its implementation.

Voluntary codes of practice emerge from associations and trade bodies, with which their members agree to comply. The Advertising Standards Authority (ASA), for example, oversees the British Code of Advertising, Sales Promotion, and Direct Marketing (the CAP Code) which covers print, cinema, video, posters, internet, SMS text message advertising and leaflet media. The philosophy of the ASA is that advertisements should be:

- Legal, decent, honest and truthful
- Prepared with a sense of responsibility to consumers and society
- In line with the principles of fair competition accepted in business.

The ASA is not a statutory body, and can only *request* an advertiser to amend or withdraw an advertisement that is in breach of the code. Nevertheless, the ASA believes that 96 per cent of press advertisements, 99 per cent of posters and 91 per cent of direct marketing comply with the CAP Codes. However, if the ASA's Council of twelve people decides that an advertisement contravenes the code, then it does have remedies other than persuasion. It can *request* media owners to refuse to accept or repeat the offending advertisement, generate adverse publicity, and/or *recommend* that the OFT should take proceedings to apply for a legal injunction to prevent publication.

Most advertisers conform to requests from the ASA to withdraw an advertisement and some avoid any possible problems by voluntarily using the pre-publication vetting service. However, the ASA can now ask for vetting for up to two years if a particular advertiser has proven troublesome in the past. Previously, offending campaigns attracted a lot of publicity because of their sensational nature. Then, when the ASA makes a ruling, further publicity is generated, for instance through opinion articles in newspapers discussing advertising standards which include a picture of an offending advertisement so that the readers know what sort of thing they're talking about. Indirectly, therefore, in some cases, ASA involvement rather defeats its own objectives.

With the development of the SEM and transnational advertising campaigns, marketers not only need to consider national laws, self-regulatory rules and systems across the member states. The European Advertising Standards Alliance (EASA) represents the various advertising regulatory bodies, such as the ASA, across Europe. Although it has no direct powers it can intervene on behalf of complainants by asking the various national regulators to act. For example, when a Luxembourgois consumer complained about a French chewing gum manufacturer's health claims, the case was referred back to the French for investigation and action.

Although Ofcom (Office of Communications) is ultimately responsible for the policing of broadcast television and radio advertising, in November 2004 the day-to-day regulation of both these media was contracted out to the ASA. This means that consumers have a one-stop shop for complaints and that there can be consistency in the decisions made about problematic advertisements in different media. Ofcom is a statutory body, and carries a great deal of weight, since it has the power to issue and control broadcasting licences, and compliance with the advertising codes of practice is effectively part of the licence. The frequency and duration of advertising breaks are restricted and it is Ofcom that ensures that there is a distinct break between programmes and advertisements. Pharmaceuticals, alcohol, tobacco and diet products, to name but a few, are subject to tight restrictions under the code of practice and in addition EU directives specify what is and is not allowed. Thus in terms of broadcast advertising, ASA (B) (The Advertising Standards Authority (Broadcast) which is a body set up within the ASA to handle the regulation of broadcast advertising subcontracted by Ofcom) has wide concerns, covering the timing of advertisements, making sure that the advertisements are suitably differentiated from the programmes, protecting children from unsuitable advertising, prohibiting political advertising and regulating programme sponsorship, among other things. Its powers are similarly sweeping: ASA (B) can require an advertisement to be changed before further broadcast, instruct a broadcaster to restrict the transmission of an advertisement as directed, or instruct a broadcaster to stop broadcasting an advertisement altogether.

eg An advertisement for Garnier Nutrisse, a hair colourant, was shown on Channel 4 in an advertising break in the Saturday edition of Big Brother. There's nothing wrong with that, except the advertisement featured Davina McCall, who is also very closely associated with Big Brother as a presenter. A complaint was made because the CAP Code does not allow the same person to feature in both a programme and the advertising that surrounds it. In their defence, Channel 4 argued that the Saturday Big Brother programmes did not actually feature Davina McCall and thus the regulation was not breached. While the ASA acknowledged that Davina did not feature in the programme in question, it did feel that she was so closely associated with the whole Big Brother 'brand' that the public would make a connection between the advertisement and the programme and thus the complaint was upheld.

Another complaint that was upheld concerned the loudness of advertisements screened during a film on Channel 5. The CAP Code requires the sound level of advertisements to be consistent with that of the surrounding programme(s) so that there aren't any excessive changes in volume. In the case of advertisements screened during a showing of the film *Groundhog Day* in March 2005, the broadcaster was judged to have set the sound threshold too high, and thus to have breached the CAP Code.

There are no hard and fast rules about how far an advertiser can go before running foul of regulatory bodies and this becomes even more complex once you start advertising across European boundaries (*see* Chapter 10). A naked couple can kiss in a shower in an advertisement for condoms, but a woman's naked buttocks on a poster are 'unnecessarily shocking' in the words of the ASA.

eg Whether an advertisement causes complaints depends on the medium, the product and the audience likely to see it, so an advertisement that is 'slightly sexist' is fine in men's publications but would be banned in more family-orientated media. In 2004, the ASA adjudicated on complaints about an advertisement published in Sky TV magazine for an 'adult' television channel. The advertisement showed a woman on her hands and knees with strings attached, like a puppet. A man's hand was seen to be controlling the strings and the headline was 'You pull the strings'. According to the advertiser, the advertisement was meant to emphasise that the viewer had the choice of three alternative channels. While the ASA felt that the image was not particularly explicit or provocative, it did feel that the element of male control over a female could be interpreted as demeaning, and the fact that Sky TV magazine is essentially of interest to the whole family meant that the advertisement was not appropriate for that publication. The complaints were thus upheld and the advertisers were advised to take advice from the ASA's CAP Copy Advice team before publishing any more advertisements (**http://www.asa.org.uk**).

The Institute of Sales Promotion (ISP), the Institute of Practitioners in Advertising (IPA), the Institute of Public Relations (IPR) and the Direct Marketing Association (DMA) are effectively trade associations. All these areas are, of course, subject to prevailing commercial legislation generally, but, in addition, these particular bodies provide detailed voluntary codes of practice setting industry standards for fair dealing with customers. They are not statutory bodies, and only have jurisdiction over their members, with the ultimate sanction of suspending or expelling organisations that breach the code of practice. All of the bodies mentioned here represent organisations with interests in various areas of marketing communications, but trade associations can exist in any industry with similar objectives of regulating the professional practice of their members. There are, for example, the Fencing Contractors Association, the Glass and Glazing Federation, the Association of British Insurers, the British Association of Landscape Industries, and the National House Builders Confederation, to name but a few! As well as regulating business practice, such bodies can also provide other services for members, such as legal indemnities and representation, training and professional development services, and acting as the voice of the industry to government and the media.

■ Influences on the political and regulatory environment

The political and regulatory environment is clearly influenced by sociocultural factors, and particularly the pressure of public opinion, the media and pressure groups. Greenpeace and Friends of the Earth, for example, have educated consumers to become more aware of the content, origins and after-effects of the products they buy and use, and this led to the phasing out of chlorofluorocarbons (CFCs) as an aerosol propellant and as a refrigerant. The green movement has also spurred the drafting of regulations on the acceptable emissions from car exhausts, which has had a major impact on the product development plans of motor manufacturers for the next few years. Similarly, the consumer movement, through organisations such as the Consumers' Association, has also played an important role in promoting the rights of the consumer and thus in driving the regulators and legislators towards laws and codes of practice regarding product safety, selling techniques and marketing communications, for instance.

Not all pressure on legislators and regulators originates from pressure groups or consumer-based organisations, of course. Trade associations or groupings lobby the legislators to try to influence regulation in their members' favour. Sometimes, the lobbying is designed to slow the pace of change, influence the nature of any planned legislation, and to delay legislation perceived as potentially harmful to the industry's interests. In the case of tobacco, for instance, government must balance public health concerns against the employment and export potential from manufacturers. It is important, therefore, for the marketer to read the changing political environment, within Europe, in export markets and from international organisations such as the WTO and OECD who are influential in guiding change. Most industries face new legislation that affects them one way or another during the course of a year and an early appreciation gives companies more time to exploit an opportunity or to counter a threat. However, it could take between three and five years for legislation to come into effect in Europe, so a longer-term perspective must be taken (Smith, 2001). A failure to get involved early on in lobbying and putting across arguments can have knock-on effects down the line with policies that constrain marketing activity too much without enabling a more open internal market. Some policies could even favour particular member states who have lobbied harder. The Directives on online trading and e-commerce, for example, are topical within the EU, so internet marketers cannot afford to miss out on discussions concerning the legislative framework.

With increasing public concern for sustainability, competitiveness of markets, fair trading, product safety and quality and consumer rights, it is a very brave politician that can ignore the pressures for change. However, lobbying and participating in the legislative discussion can help steer outcomes towards those preferred by an organisation. Organisations such as Greenpeace have become very effective at lobbying key decision-makers, but tracking the legislative process can be a long and tortuous process. The Commission in Strasbourg frames EU legislation which is then debated and amended by the European parliament before the legislation is endorsed by the Council of Ministers and then implemented though European Directives. Even then it is not over, as individual member states may have to pass legislation to implement at a local level (Simms, 2001). The greater the understanding of the EU and national political processes, the more an organisation can move with change rather than risk being left behind.

Chapter summary

■ This chapter has explored the importance of the external marketing environment as an influence on the way in which organisations do business and make their decisions. Ways in which customers, markets, competitors, technology and regulation are changing are all important pointers to future strategy. Thus failure to understand the environment fully could mean missing out on opportunities or ignoring threats which in turn could lead to lost revenue or, more seriously, loss of competitive advantage.

■ Using environmental scanning, a technique for monitoring and evaluating information, organisations can understand their environment more thoroughly, pick up early signs of emerging trends, and thus plan their future activities appropriately. Such information may come from secondary sources, such as trade publications or published research data, or an organisation can commission research to increase their knowledge of the environment. Care must be taken, however, to ensure that all appropriate sources are constantly monitored (but avoiding information overload), and that internal mechanisms exist for disseminating information and acting on it.

■ The main framework for the chapter is the categorisation of the marketing environment into STEP factors: sociocultural, technological, economic/competitive and political/regulatory.

■ The first of the STEP factors is the sociocultural environment. This deals with 'hard' information, such as demographic trends, and with less tangible issues, such as changing tastes, attitudes and cultures. Knowledge of demographic trends gives the marketer a basic feel for how broad market segments are likely to change in the future. To gain the fullest picture, however, the marketer needs to combine demographic information with 'softer' data on how attitudes are changing.

■ The second STEP factor is technology. An organisation's technological advances may arise from the exploitation of breakthroughs from other organisations, or may be the result of long-term investment in R&D in-house to solve a specific problem. Either way, technology can present the opportunity to create a clear differential advantage that cannot be easily copied by the competition.

■ The economic and competitive environment constitutes the third STEP factor, and can be further divided into macro- and microeconomic environments. The macroeconomic environment analyses the effects of the broader economic picture, looking at issues such as taxation, government spending and interest rates. It also takes account of the threats, opportunities and barriers arising from membership of international trading blocs. The microeconomic environment is a little closer to the individual organisation, and is concerned with the structure of the market(s) in which it operates.

■ The final STEP factor is the political and regulatory environment. Laws, regulations and codes of practice emanate from national governments, the EU, local government, statutory bodies and trade associations to affect the way in which organisations do business. Consumer groups and other pressure groups, such as those representing the ecological movement, health issues and animal rights, are active in trying to persuade government to deregulate or legislate, or to influence the scope and content of new legislation.

Questions for review and discussion

2.1 What is *environmental scanning*, why is it important, and what are the potential problems of implementing it?

2.2 Differentiate between the *macro- and microeconomic environments*.

2.3 What sources of published demographic data are available in your own university or college library?

2.4 Find and discuss examples of products that are particularly vulnerable to changing consumer tastes.

2.5 Find and discuss recent examples of adjudications by the ASA (or the equivalent regulatory body in your own country) of advertisements in a variety of media. Do you agree with its judgement?

2.6 Using Figure 2.1 as a framework, choose a product and list under each of the *STEP factors* the relevant influences that have helped to make that product what it is.

case study 2

Does the muffin herald a new ice age?

The UK frozen food market, worth around £4bn per year (according to the British Frozen Food Federation), has been a market in meltdown for a while. Consumer perception is that it is 'food of last resort', something to have as a back-up when the rest of the kitchen cupboards, and the fridge, are bare. Frozen ready meals in particular are perceived as inferior in quality to their chilled counterparts and less adventurous in their recipes. This perception is not helped at the point of sale. For one thing, this is a very competitive market and price promotions are dominant. Mintel (2004) estimates that 40–50 per cent of sales of frozen meals are made at promotional prices. In addition, it is difficult to display frozen merchandise imaginatively and attractively; the old-style chest freezers in stores require the shopper to take an active role in bending over to see what's in them, while the newer upright cabinet freezers place a big heavy door between the goods and the shopper. Either type of freezer inhibits browsing and interaction with products, and neither of them makes it easy for shoppers to spot a brand or package from a distance to draw them to it. Chilled merchandise also benefits from the fact that it requires only refrigerator storage and almost 99 per cent of UK households own a fridge. Freezer penetration is a lot lower at around 60 per cent of households.

From the retailer's point of view, freezers take up a lot of floor space relative to the amount of merchandise they can display, and are expensive to run and maintain. This, coupled with the investment in the development of own-label chilled ready meals which carry much more attractive profit margins for retailers, and which are perceived as healthier and fresher by consumers, means that there has been very little impetus to encourage the frozen food market to evolve. Some retailers are even running promotions offering discounts on bulk purchases of chilled meals with the explicit suggestion that the consumer can eat one now and freeze the other(s) for another day! Of course, there is something of a self-fulfilling prophecy here: the more frozen food 'stands still', the less attention retailers will give it, and the less inclined shoppers will be to reassess its relevance to them (especially if they are filling their freezers with chilled ready meals!).

None of this is good news for the frozen food manufacturers who are going to have to respond in some way to this changing environment if they are going to survive. McCain, the originator of the frozen oven chip, seems to have decided to go down a 'fast comfort food snack' track, particularly with the launch of a range of frozen muffins and doughnuts with chocolate sauce. This fits with the repositioning of McCain chips as a comforting response to all the stresses that daily life throws at you. Life looks a lot more manageable over the top of a chip butty. The desserts tune in to a similar impulsive need for comfort or for a treat, and while it's not always possible to have fresh muffins in the cupboard, they can always be available in the freezer, zapped in the microwave and ready to eat, warm and fresh, within a couple of minutes. Snacking is also a core theme with McCain's frozen filled baguettes, and again thanks to the microwave, a warm fresh sausage and onion baguette can be yours within a couple of minutes. This seems to fit well with modern family lifestyles that have led to fragmented family eating with individuals demanding quick food to eat on the move. These product innovations are also important to McCain to reduce its dependence on potato products which are seen as something of a commodity product and not easy to differentiate. Analysts estimated that over 85 per cent of McCain's sales in 2004 came from potato products (Benady, 2004).

McCain is very keen to address the concerns of consumers and is working hard to improve its products in the light of those concerns. A spokesman for McCain told us, 'To claim McCain isn't addressing "healthy eating" is simply untrue. McCain is conscious of the consumer's need for convenience but today consumers

McCain is conscious of the consumer's need for convenience, but taste and health are now of paramount importance. They constantly add innovations to the product ranges though they still offer sweet treats for those who need them.

Source: © McCain Foods (GB) Ltd http://www.mccain.co.uk

are more demanding and the offer of convenience alone will not appeal as it used to. Taste and health are now of paramount importance and McCain is constantly innovating its existing and future product ranges to improve its offering.

'McCain has reformulated many products in order to reduce the salt and fat content and is constantly working to further enhance the nutritional content of its products. McCain is also trialling new methods of production in order to address the concerns of consumers, for example, Potato Smiles that are supplied to schools and caterers, are now being pre-cooked in sunflower oil which helps reduce levels of cholesterol and polyunsaturated fat. The nutritional benefits of food are an issue that will not disappear and one that McCain takes seriously.'

Birds Eye's approach is about fresh 'natural' healthiness. In 2004, Birds Eye spent £60m on a brand relaunch, emphasising the healthiness of food that has been frozen without additives. Even the humble fish finger, the mainstay of many a mum's freezer, and traditionally advertised by Captain Birds Eye rampaging round the high seas with his crew of lively kids, has been made the subject of a far more sober, adult-oriented advertising campaign. The advertisements based in a classroom offer an 'ABC' of food additives with Captain Birds Eye quietly telling us that 'N' is for 'Not in my food'.

Like McCain, Birds Eye is conscious of the consumer's need for speed and convenience in food preparation. The Steamfresh range, which includes meals as well as portions of vegetables, gives all the nutritional benefits of steamed food without the hassle of preparation, setting up a steamer and then washing it up afterwards: it just goes from freezer to microwave to the plate in disposable packaging. Across the Birds Eye range, packaging has been redesigned to give it a warmer, more contemporary character. As well as looking at brand positioning and product range innovation, Birds Eye's owner, Unilever, has also been thinking about the problems of in-store display. In spring 2004, it began to unroll Unilever-branded zones within frozen food departments in ASDA, although it was expected to be two years before the newly designed freezers would be actually installed. In the meantime, Unilever is adapting existing freezers, using graphics and signage to overcome shopper apathy about frozen foods. Within its branded zone, Unilever plans to offer a 'one-stop shop' of complete meal solutions to the shopper. So there will be frozen meals, desserts and ice-cream alongside the more traditional frozen meats and frozen vegetables, as well as a children's meals area.

Sources: Barnes (2004b); Benady (2004); Dowdy (2004); Euromonitor (2005); *Marketing Week* (2004); Mintel (2004); **http://www.bfff.co.uk**.

Questions

1 Summarise the ways in which the STEP factors affect this market.

2 Compare and contrast McCain's and Birds Eye's responses to this environment. Which is most likely to succeed and why?

3 Is there a future for frozen foods? What do you think are the main marketing priorities for frozen food manufacturers?

4 Choose another category within the food market (for example canned vegetables or breakfast cereals). Investigate the STEP factors affecting this category and present your findings.

References for chapter 2

Aguilar, F.J. (1967), *Scanning the Business Environment*, Macmillan.

Ashworth, J. (2003), 'The Saga that Became a Success Story', *The Times*, 27 November, p. 37.

Barber, T., Benoit, B., Guthrie, J., Johnson, J., Levitt, J. and Nicholson, M. (2003), 'Wish You Were Here', *Financial Times*, 9 August, p. 5.

Barnes, R. (2004a), 'Supermarkets Spy Local Attraction', *Marketing*, 5 February, p. 15.

Barnes, R. (2004b), 'Unilever Leads Freezer Fightback', *Marketing*, 28 April, p. 15.

Barr, D. (2004), 'A Green Piece of Furniture', *The Times*, 30 April, p. 15.

Bedington, E. (2001), 'The Regeneration Game', *The Grocer*, 19 May, pp. 36–8.

Benady, D. (2004), 'McCain Thaws Heart with Frozen Comfort', *Marketing Week*, 23 September, p. 25.

Bremner, C. (1997), 'All Because the Belgians Do Not Like Milk Tray', *The Times*, 24 October, p. 5.

Brown-Humes, C. and MacCarthy, C. (2004), 'EU Calls Time on Nordic Nations' Long Battle Against Alcohol', *Financial Times*, 10 January, p. 6.

Chesshyre, T. (2001), 'Over 50 But Not up the Creek', *The Times*, 5 May.

Coleclough, S. (2003), 'The Future of VAT in Europe', *International Tax Review*, July, p. 1.

Daneshkhu, S. (2005), 'Archbishop Criticises Cost of Free Trade to Poor Countries', *Financial Times*, 27 April, p. 4.

Dittmar, H. and Pepper, L. (1994), 'To Have is to Be: Materialism and Person Perception in Working Class and Middle Class British Adolescents', *Journal of Economic Psychology*, 15 (2), pp. 233–51.

Doult, B. (2004), 'Johnson Calls for Labelling Flexibility', *The Grocer*, 15 May.

Dowdy, C. (2004), 'A Fresh Look Inside the Shop Freezer', *Financial Times*, 25 March, p. 13.

The Economist (2000), 'Europe: Sweden Bottles Up', *The Economist*, 26 February, p. 62.

The Economist (2005), 'Europe: the End of Enlargement?', *The Economist*, 16 July, p. 38.

Elkes, N. (2005), 'Hands Off our Playing Fields', *Evening Mail*, 16 July, p. 4.

Euromonitor (2005), *European Marketing Data and Statistics*, 40th edn, Euromonitor Publications.

Fitzgerald, M. (2005), 'Research in Development', *Technology Review*, May, pp. 32–5.

Garten, J. (2005), 'Don't Just Throw Money at the World's Poor', *Business Week*, 7 March, p. 30.

George, N. (2004), 'Sweden is Advised to Cut Taxes on Alcohol', *Financial Times*, 10 January, p. 8.

Gillman, S. (2005), ' Dartford Renewal Faces Inquiry Test', *Planning*, 10 June, p. 5.

The Grocer (2000), 'Corned Beef Boosts Your Sperm Count', *The Grocer*, 9 September.

The Grocer (2001), 'Reassuring Consumers', *The Grocer*, 5 May, p. 23.

The Grocer (2004a), 'Children's Sun Creams', *The Grocer*, 23 June.

The Grocer (2004b), 'Kellogg Aims to Boost Health Credibility with Fact Panel', *The Grocer*, 17 July.

The Grocer (2004c), 'French Fight GM Vine', *The Grocer*, 17 July.

The Grocer (2004d), 'Tesco Running Trials to See if Customers Will Go for a Grab and Go Deli Operation', *The Grocer*, 7 August.

The Grocer (2004e), 'When Canned Tuna is Consumed', *The Grocer*, 21 August.

Hardcastle, S. (2001), 'Deli and Food to Go', *The Grocer*, 26 May, pp. 49–50.

Harrison, E. (2004), 'Greens Mean Heinz', *The Grocer*, 19 June.

Ivinson, J. (2003), 'Why the EU VAT and E-commerce Directive Does Not Work', *International Tax Review*, October, p. 1.

Laschefski, K. and Freris, N. (2001), 'Saving the Wood', *The Ecologist*, July/August, pp. 40–3.

Marketing Week (2004), 'McCain in Major Extension with Desserts', *Marketing Week*, 16 September, p. 7.

McGregor, D. (2005), 'Glimmer of Hope for New Global Trade Deal', *Financial Times*, 14 July, p. 8.

Miller, S. (2004), 'Why Not to Cut Farm Aid', *Wall Street Journal*, 16 December, p. A14.

Milne, R. (2003), 'Saga Buys Last Ship Built on Tyne from Cunard', *Financial Times*, 28 May, p. 6.

Mintel (2004), 'Frozen Ready Meals', *Mintel Market Intelligence: UK*, March, accessed via **http://www.mintel.com**.

Montgomery, D. (2003), 'Eco Fashion: Precious Wood', *In Business*, May/June, p. 30.

Morley, C. (2003), 'Choc Horror!', *Evening Mail*, 6 August, p. 13.

Mortished, C. (2005a), 'Why Europe Need Not Get Shirty', *The Times*, 27 April, p. 57.

Mortished, C. (2005b), 'Nothing Fair in War of Poor v Poorest', *The Times*, 25 May, p. 48.

Munk, D. (2004), 'Forces of Nature', *The Guardian*, 17 March, p. 12.

O'Connell, D. (2005), 'As We Hail Trafalgar, French Will Build Our Ships', *Sunday Times*, 26 June, p. 7.

Pitcher, G. (2004), 'Travel Industry Prepares to Count Cost of Iraq War', *Marketing Week*, 27 May, p. 25.

Precision Marketing (2003), 'Saga Holidays Builds Insight through Behaviour Analysis', *Precision Marketing*, 15 August, p. 6.

Sabbagh, D. (2005), 'EU Seeks to Regulate Television on the Net', *The Times*, 12 July, p. 36.

Sapsford, J. (2005), 'Dealing with the Dollar', *Wall Street Journal*, 1 March, p. A16.

Shannon, J. (1998), 'Seniors Convert to Consumerism', *Marketing Week*, 10 September, p. 22.

Simms, J. (2001), 'EU Rules, OK?', *Marketing*, 25 January, pp. 23–5.

Smith, C. (2001), 'Think Long Term or be Left Behind by EU Legislation', *Marketing*, 25 January, p. 19.

Stevenson, R. (2005), 'Excise', *The Independent*, 17 March, p. 6.

Thornton, P. (2004), 'Deal to Slash Farm Subsidies', *The Independent*, 30 July, p. 34.

The Times (2003), 'Restrictive "Chocolate" Law Breaches EU Free Trade', *The Times*, 21 January, p. 33.

Townsend, A. (2005), 'Duty Calls for Tobacco Giants', *The Independent on Sunday*, 26 June, p. 4.

Tucker, E. (1997), 'MEPs Reject Chocolate Compromise', *Financial Times*, 24 October, p. 20.

Urquhart, L. (2004), 'Smuggled Tobacco Makes Smoking More Dangerous', *Financial Times*, 16 December, p. 5.

Usborne, D. (2005), 'Brazil Arrests Civil Servants in Crackdown on Amazonian Logging', *The Independent*, 4 June, p. 26.

Wall Street Journal (2005), 'The Tax that France Built', *Wall Street Journal*, 4 March, p. A14.

Watson, E. (2001), 'Blind Tasting', *The Grocer*, 9 June, pp. 38–9.

Watson, R. (2005), 'Turkey Faces Fresh Obstacle on Rocky Road to Joining EU', *The Times*, 30 June, p. 40.

chapter 3

buyer behaviour

learning objectives

This chapter will help you to:

1 understand the decision-making processes that consumers go through as they make a purchase;

2 appreciate how those processes differ between different buying situations;

3 understand the influences that affect decision-making, whether environmental, psychological or sociocultural, and appreciate the implications of those processes and influences for marketing strategies;

4 understand the nature and structure of B2B buying and the differences between B2B and consumer buying; and

5 analyse the B2B buying process and the factors that influence its outcomes.

Introduction

In contrast to Chapter 2, which looked at the broad backdrop against which marketers have to do business, this chapter focuses closely on consumers and B2B customers who are at the centre of many a marketer's universe. While the customer is part of the marketing environment, and is shaped to some extent by the influences already discussed in Chapter 2, it is also very important to understand the more personal and specific influences affecting consumers and the nature of the decision-making processes through which they go.

This chapter, therefore, begins by looking at consumers as buyers and analysing the factors, both internal and external, that determine how and why they make their choices. The later part of the chapter examines B2B buyer behaviour. Having considered some of the differences between consumers and B2B customers in terms of how and why they purchase goods and services, we shall then analyse the B2B buying process and the pressures that shape the decisions that are made within an organisational context.

The decision-making process

Figure 3.1 offers a deceptively simple model of consumer buyer behaviour, presented as a logical flow of activities, working through from problem recognition to purchase to post-purchase evaluation. This section of the chapter deals with this core process.

Figure 3.1 The consumer buying decision-making process and its influencing factors

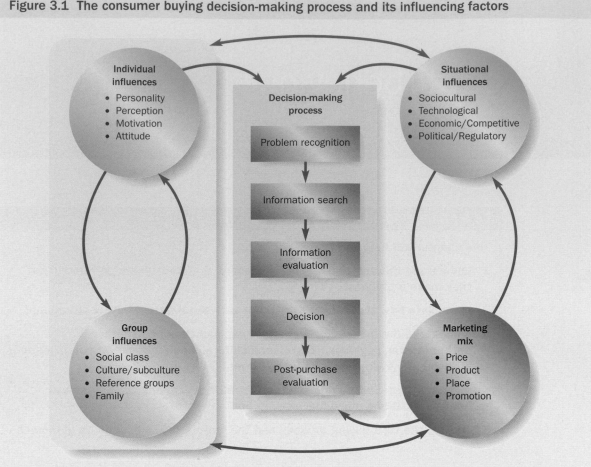

Baby food marketers have to pay particular attention to consumer behaviour patterns before deciding their marketing strategy. Research has indicated that consumers are highly brand loyal, with sometimes as many as 85 per cent always buying the same brand. They also have a clear idea of what they want before entering the store, so there isn't much impulse purchasing, and if there is no on-shelf availability they will either go elsewhere or delay purchasing until the next visit rather than buying an alternative. Research has shown that the average number of packs picked up is 3.3 and the average number of buys is 3, meaning that consumers are not doing much examination and evaluation of alternative brands.

The mother's decision as to which brand is appropriate for her child is a complex one. It is often based on careful evaluation of available information, using advice from friends, family and health professionals, and not least checking out the information on labels. As the child develops, the brands and products required also change. To help the mother make this transition easily, suppliers must ensure that in-store displays are meaningful, so that different categories are communicated clearly, with packaging labels that are clear and informative so that brand loyalty evolves and is retained as the child grows. To reinforce this, considerable effort must be made to ensure on-shelf availability and to reward brand loyalty (*The Grocer*, 2005).

The decision-making process is affected by a number of other more complex influences, as can be seen in Figure 3.1. Some of these influences relate to the wider marketing environment in which the decision is being made (*see* pp. 73–4). Others, however, relate to the individual purchaser and therefore pp. 75–80 will consider those influences emanating from within the individual such as personality, attitudes and learning. Similarly, pp. 80–94 will look at how the individual's decisions are affected by their social context, especially family and cultural groupings.

There have been many attempts to create models of consumer decision-making of greater or lesser complexity and detail that try to capture the richness of the experience. The Engel, Blackwell and Miniard (1990) model presented here, although concise and simple in its outline, provides a framework that still allows us to consider, through discussion, many of the more complex elements. It traces the progress of a purchasing event stage by stage from the buyer's point of view, including the definition of likely information needs and a discussion of the level of rationality and analytical behaviour leading to the eventual decision.

We now look at each stage in turn.

■ Problem recognition

In trying to rationalise the decision-making process, this is a good place to begin. After all, if you are not aware that you have a 'problem', how can you decide to purchase something to solve it? More functional purchases, such as replenishing stocks of washing powder or petrol, may be initiated by a casual glance at current stock levels. Other purchases may be triggered by a definable event. If, for example, the exhaust falls off your car, you will soon become aware of the nature of the problem and the kind of purchase that will provide the remedy.

Where psychological needs are involved, the problem recognition may be a slow dawning or may lead to a sudden impulse, when the consumer, realising that the current position or feeling is not the desired one, decides to do something to change it through a purchase (Bruner and Pomazal, 1988). Imagine, for instance, that you are wandering round the supermarket after a tough day at work. You're tired, listless and a bit depressed. You've filled your trolley with the potatoes, bread and milk you intended to buy, but you also slip a bar of chocolate (or worse!) in there on the basis that it will cheer you up as you drive home. The 'problem' here is less definable, based on a vague psychological feeling, and it follows that the solution is also less definable – it could be chocolate, cream buns, wine or clothing, whatever takes the purchaser's fancy.

What the examples given so far do have in common, however, is that the impetus to go into a purchasing decision-making routine comes from the consumer. The consumer identifies or recognises the problem, independently from the marketer, and looks for a solution. As will be seen in the following sections, marketers can then use the marketing mix elements to influence the choice of solution. It is also possible, however, for marketers to trigger the process by using the marketing mix to bring a problem to the consumer's attention.

eg The manufacturers of Radion laundry products ran an advertising campaign in the UK featuring a housewife who suddenly realised that even though the shirt she was ironing had just been washed, there was still a sweaty smell clinging to its armpits. Radion, of course, has the power to eliminate this in the wash. Housewives across the country supposedly became racked with fear and guilt, asking themselves: 'Do I have this problem? Should I switch to Radion?' A problem had been created in the consumer's mind, and a decision-making process initiated, largely through the marketer's efforts.

There is, of course, a significant difference between being aware of a need or problem and being able to do something about it. Many needs are latent and remain unfulfilled, either because consumers decide not to do anything about it now, or because they are unable to do anything. We might all feel the need for a three-week holiday in some exotic part of the world, but we must not only be willing, but also financially able, to disappear over the horizon. Problem recognition, if it is to lead anywhere, therefore requires both the willingness and the ability to fulfil the emerging need.

■ Information search

Defining the problem is one thing, but defining and implementing the solution is something else. The questions to be answered include what kind of purchase will solve the problem, where and how it can be obtained, what information is needed to arrive at a decision and where that information is available. In some cases, consumers will actively search out relevant information with a view to using it in making a decision, but they can also acquire information passively, storing it away until it is needed. Daily, consumers are exposed to a wide range of media all designed to influence awareness and recall of particular products and services. Thus they 'know' that Radion eliminates sweaty smells before they get anywhere near a conscious choice of laundry product in the supermarket. When they do get to the point of purchasing, the manufacturers hope that they will recall that knowledge and use it in making the brand choice.

Similarly, the Cheltenham & Gloucester mortgage advertisement is designed to appeal to someone who is already considering house purchase. It is hardly likely to inspire consumers to move house, but it could be useful if consumers are worried about finding the right mortgage for their circumstances before they start looking seriously. In some cases, a consumer might not be planning to move immediately, but the C&G would hope that they will recall the advertisement when the time does come.

Finding a mortgage to suit you is easy with freefone and online access, as well as the face-to-face advice available in branches.

Source: Cheltenham and Gloucester

Not all external sources of information are controlled by the marketer – don't forget the power of word of mouth as a marketing tool. Friends, family and colleagues, for example, may all give advice, whether based on experience, knowledge or opinion, to the would-be decision-maker in this phase. People are more likely to trust information given through word of mouth, because the source is generally assumed to be unbiased and trustworthy, and the information itself often derives from first-hand experience.

In other situations, the consumer might seek out information from the internet, specialist publications, retailers or even from marketing literature. For example, when buying a car, potential buyers will probably visit competing dealerships to talk to sales staff, look closely at the merchandise and collect brochures. Additionally, they might consult what they consider to be unbiased expert sources of advice such as *What Car?* magazine, and begin to take more notice of car advertisements in all media.

Hauser *et al.* (1993) emphasise the fact that time pressure can interfere with the information search. They found that consumers spend less time searching for different sources as pressure increases. At the other end of the spectrum, however, information overload may cause problems for the potential purchaser. There is evidence to suggest that consumers cannot cope with too much information at product level (Keller and Staelin, 1987). Thus the greater the relevance of the information to consumers, such as the key benefits and applications of the product, the easier it is for them to assimilate and process that information as part of their decision making. In other words, better and more extensive information may actually lead to poorer buying decisions!

■ Information evaluation

On what criteria do you evaluate the information gathered? If you are looking for a new car exhaust system, an online search could generate over 1000 entries to sift through and even a typical *Yellow Pages* could provide up to ten pages of exhaust system dealerships, featuring over 100 potential outlets within reasonable travelling distance. If you have had no previous experience of any of them, then you have to find a means of differentiating between them. You are unlikely to investigate all of them, since that would take too long, and so you may draw up a shortlist on the basis of those with the biggest feature entries in *Yellow Pages*, those whose names pop up first in an internet search, or those who also advertise prominently in the local press or on television. Such advertising may emphasise the advantages of using a particular outlet, pointing out to the consumer what the appropriate evaluative criteria are (speed, friendliness or price, for example). Location may also be an important factor; some outlets are closer to home or work than others.

In contrast, looking for chocolate in the supermarket, your information evaluation is likely to be less time consuming and less systematic. Faced with a set of brands of chocolate that are known and liked, the evaluation is cursory: 'What do I feel like eating?' The nearest to systematic thinking might be (in desperation) the evaluation of which one really represents the most chocolate for the price. Of course, if a new brand has appeared on the chocolate shelf, then that might break the habitual, unconscious grabbing at the familiar wrapper, and make a consumer stop and look closely to evaluate what the new product has to offer in comparison with the old ones.

What has been happening to varying degrees in the above examples is that the consumer has started to narrow down from a wide list of potential options to an evoked set (Howard and Sheth, 1969), a final shortlist for serious appraisal. Being a part of the consumer's evoked set, and staying there, is clearly important to the marketer, although it is not always easy. To make a choice from within the evoked set, the consumer needs either a formal or an informal means of selecting from the small number of choices available. This, therefore, implies some definition of evaluative or choice criteria.

Again, marketers will be trying to influence this stage. This can be done, for example, through their communications campaigns which may implant images of products in the consumer's mind so that they seem familiar (and therefore less threatening) at the point of sale. They may also stress particular product attributes, both to increase the importance of that attribute in the consumer's mind, i.e. to make sure that the attribute is number one on the list of evaluative criteria, and to ensure that the consumer believes that a particular brand is unsurpassed in terms of that attribute. Point-of-sale material can also reinforce these things, for example through displays, leaflets, the wording on packaging and on-pack promotions.

Generally, therefore, what is happening is that without necessarily being conscious of it, the potential buyer is constructing a list of performance criteria, then assessing each supplier or available brand against it. This assessment can be based on objective criteria, related to the attributes of the product and its use (price, specification, service, etc.), or subjective criteria such as status, fit with self-image or trust of the supplier.

To make the decision easier the consumer often adopts mental 'rules of thumb' that cut corners and lead to a faster decision. The consumer is especially prepared to compromise on the quality and thoroughness of assessment when the problem-solving situation is less risky and complicated. They may focus on brand, store choice, pricing, promotion or packaging, and will serve to limit the size of the evoked set and to eliminate some of the options.

■ Decision

The decision may be a natural outcome of the evaluation stage, if one of the options is noticeably more impressive on all the important criteria than the rest. If the choice is not as clear cut as this, the consumer may have to prioritise the criteria further, perhaps deciding that price or convenience is the one overriding factor. In the car exhaust example, the decision-making is a conscious act, whereas with the impulse purchase of chocolate, the decision may be made almost unconsciously.

In any case, at this stage the consumer must finalise the proposed deal, and this may take place in a retail store, over the telephone, by mail or in the consumer's own home. In the supermarket, finalising the deal may be as simple as putting the bar of chocolate into the trolley with the rest of the shopping and then paying for it at the checkout. With more complex purchases, however, the consumer may have the discretion to negotiate the fine details of cash or credit, any trade-in, order quantity and delivery dates, for example. If the outcome of the negotiation is not satisfactory, then the consumer may regretfully decide not to go ahead with the purchase after all, or rethink the decision in favour of another supplier – you cannot be certain of your customer until they have either handed over their money or signed the contract!

Suppliers can, of course, make it easy or difficult for potential customers to make their purchases. Lack of sales assistants on the shopfloor, long queues or bureaucratic purchasing procedures may all tax the patience of consumers, giving them time either to decide to shop elsewhere or not to bother buying at all. Even if they do persist and make the purchase (eventually), their impression of the supplier's service and efficiency is going to be damaged and this may influence their repeat purchasing behaviour negatively.

eg Vending machines make it easy for the consumer to make a decision and take action almost immediately, as long as they have some loose change in their pockets. Despite the sometimes infuriating ability of machines to gobble up coins faster than they are able to dispense goods, the vending industry in the UK alone is worth £2.5bn of which £1bn is generated from refreshment sales. Where impulse purchases are important, such as the confectionery sector in which up to 70 per cent of sales are impulse-led, what is presented, the familiarity of the brand names and how they are presented can be vital to the sale, hence the growth of chilled and glass-fronted cabinets.

New product sectors are now being targeted. Although 8 million cups of coffee and 2 million cups of tea are consumed each day from vending machines, much more exciting products are now being offered too, such as hot or chilled foods and ambient goods. Vending machines for pizzas are now being set up in the UK, offering a hot pizza in 90 seconds, albeit on a paper plate. The Wonder Pizza UK company is importing the machines from the USA and plans to install 2000 of them in the UK over the next three years. Fully automated shops such as those found in Tokyo and Petit Casino in France are likely to challenge the convenience store in the future in the UK. Generally, vending machine customers are not price sensitive, valuing speed of delivery, ease of self-service, and the knowledge that what you see on display is what you will get (Fleming, 2004; *In-Store*, 2003; **http://www.ukvending.co.uk**).

■ Post-purchase evaluation

The consumer's involvement with the product does not finish when cash changes hands, nor should the marketer's involvement with the customer. Whatever the purchase, there is likely to be some level of post-purchase evaluation to assess whether the product or its supplier lived up to the expectations raised in the earlier stages of the process. Particularly if the decision process has been difficult, or if the consumer has invested a lot of time, effort and money in it, then there may be doubt as to whether the right decision has actually been made. This is what Festinger (1957) labelled cognitive dissonance, meaning that consumers are 'psychologically uncomfortable', trying to balance the choice made against the doubts still held about it. Such dissonance may be aggravated where consumers are exposed to marketing communication that sings the praises of the features and benefits of the rejected alternatives. Generally speaking, the more alternatives that have been rejected, and the more comparatively attractive those alternatives appear to be, the greater the dissonance. Conversely, the more similar to the chosen product the rejected alternatives are, the less the dissonance. It is also likely that dissonance will occur with more significant purchases, such as extended problem-solving items like cars and houses, because the buyer is far more likely to review and assess the decision consciously afterwards.

Clearly, such psychological discomfort is not pleasant and the consumer will work towards reducing it, perhaps by trying to filter out the messages that undermine the choice made (for example advertising for a product that was a rejected alternative) and paying extra attention to supportive messages (for example advertising for the chosen alternative). This all underlines the need for post-purchase reassurance, whether through advertising, after-sales follow-up calls and even the tone of an instruction manual ('Congratulations on choosing the Acme Home Nuclear Reactor Kit, we know it will give you many years' faithful service . . .'). Consumers like to be reminded and reassured that they have made a wise choice, that they have made the best choice for them. From the marketer's point of view, as well as offering post-purchase reassurance, they can minimise the risk of dissonance by making sure that potential buyers have a realistic picture of the product, its capabilities and its characteristics.

Thus the post-purchase evaluation stage is important for a number of reasons. Primarily, it will affect whether the consumer ever buys this product again. If expectations have not been met, then the product may not even make the shortlist next time. If, on the other hand, expectations have been met or even exceeded, then a strong possibility of lasting loyalty has been created. The next shortlist may be a shortlist of one!

Monitoring of post-purchase feelings is an important task of marketing, not only to identify areas in which the product (or its associated marketing mix) falls short of expectations, but also to identify any unexpectedly pleasant surprises the purchaser may have had. The product may, for instance, have strengths that are being undersold. This is a natural part of the cycle of product and service development, improvement and evolution.

There are some points to note about the process as presented here. First, the consumer may choose to end the process at any stage. Perhaps the information search reveals that there is no obvious acceptable solution to the problem, or the information evaluation demonstrates that the cost of solving the problem is too high. It is, of course, the marketer's job to sustain the consumer's interest throughout this process and to prevent them from opting out of it. Second, the process does not necessarily have to run from stage 1 to stage 5 in an unbroken flow. The consumer may backtrack at any point to an earlier stage and reiterate the process. Even on the verge of a decision, it may be felt necessary to go back and get more information, just to make sure. Finally, the time taken over the process may vary enormously, depending on the nature of the purchase and the nature of the purchaser. Many months of agonising may go into making an expensive, important purchase, while only a few seconds may be invested in choosing a bar of chocolate. The next section looks more closely at this issue.

Buying situations

In the discussion of the decision-making process, it has been made clear that both the flow and the formality of the process, and the emphasis that is put on each stage, will vary from situation to situation. Some of these variations are to do with the particular environment relevant to the transaction (see pp. 78 *et seq.*), while others emanate from the consumer (pp. 79 *et seq.*) or from the consumer's immediate social surroundings (pp. 86 *et seq.*). The current section, however, will look more closely at the effect of the type of purchasing situation on the extent and formality of the decision-making process.

■ Routine problem solving

As the heading of this section implies, a routine problem solving purchasing situation is one that the consumer is likely to experience on a regular basis. Most grocery shopping falls into this category, where particular brands are purchased habitually without recourse to any lengthy decision-making process. As with the chocolate-buying example above, there is virtually no information search and evaluation, and the buying decision is made simultaneously with (if not in advance of) the problem recognition stage. This explains why many fmcg manufacturers spend so much time and effort trying to generate such loyalty and why it is so difficult for new products to break into an established market. When the consumer thinks 'We've run out of Colgate' rather than 'We've run out of toothpaste', or when beans really does mean Heinz, then the competition has an uphill marketing task on its hands.

As well as building regular shopping habits, i.e. brand loyalty, the manufacturer is also trying to capitalise on impulse purchasing of many products within this category. While toothpaste and beans can be the objective of a planned shopping trip ('When I go to the supermarket, I need to get . . .'), some other products may be purchased as the result of a sudden impulse. The impulse may be triggered, as mentioned in the previous section, by a realisation of need ('I'm depressed and this chocolate is just what I need to cheer me up'), or by external stimuli, for example eye-catching packaging attracting the shopper's attention. The trigger need not even be inside the store: the smell of coffee or freshly baked bread wafting into the street may draw a customer into a café on impulse, or an attractive shop window display may attract a potential customer into a clothing store that they otherwise had no intention of visiting (even though clothing is not necessarily a routine problem-solving purchase). Whatever the trigger, there is no conscious preplanning or information search, but a sudden surge of desire that can only be fulfilled by a purchase that the shopper may or may not later regret.

eg Elior, the French catering company, has built a solid business on serving routine but last-minute purchases. It runs commercial concession catering operations at airports, motorway service areas, railway stations and even museums, all under contract with the infrastructure providers. In France, it is market leader in many categories and now further expansion is planned in the UK and Spain with the Netherlands, Italy and Belgium also on the agenda for market development. In the UK it has teamed up with Hachette to run multi-service stores on 40 railway station forecourts in the south of England, selling train tickets, food, coffee, snacks, magazines and newspapers (Bruce, 2001). The experience from France and elsewhere is that travellers, having purchased their tickets, are vulnerable to a host of other items if they are effectively displayed and even to the smell of fresh coffee. Research suggests that by raising the quality of ambient stimuli, impulse buying can be stimulated (Matilla and Wirtz, 2001).

The items that fall into the routine problem-solving category do tend to be low-risk, low-priced, frequently purchased products. The consumer is happy that a particular brand satisfies their requirements, and there is not enough benefit to be gained from switching brands to make the effort of information search and evaluation of alternatives worthwhile. These so-called low involvement purchases simply do not carry enough risk, whether measured in terms of financial loss, personal disappointment or damage to social status, for the consumer to get excited about the importance of 'making the right decision'.

■ Limited problem solving

Limited problem solving is a little more interesting for the consumer. This is a buying situation that occurs less frequently and probably involves more deliberate decision-making than routine problems do. The goods will be moderately expensive (in the eyes of the individual consumer) and perhaps will be expected to last a long time. Thus the risks inherent in a 'wrong' decision are that much higher. There will, therefore, be some element of information search and evaluation, but this is still unlikely to absorb too much time and effort.

An example of this could be a consumer's purchase of a new piece of hi-fi equipment. If it is some years since they last bought one, they might feel that they need to update their knowledge of who makes what, who sells what, and the price brackets in this market. The information search is likely to include talking to any friends with recent hi-fi buying experience, and a trip round locally accessible electrical goods retailers. To this particular consumer, this is an important decision, but not a crucial one. If they make a 'wrong' choice (as defined in the post-purchase evaluation stage), they will be disappointed, but will feel that they have spent too much money to allow them simply to discard the offending product. Having said that, provided that the hi-fi fulfils its primary function of producing music on demand, they can learn to live with it and the damage is limited.

Limited problem solving is also likely to occur in the choice of service products. In purchasing a holiday or choosing a dentist (word-of-mouth recommendation?) the consumer has one chance to make the right choice. Once you are on the plane or in the dentist's chair, it is too late and the wrong choice could turn out to be expensive and painful. The necessity to get it right first time is thus likely to lead to a conscious and detailed information search, perhaps even going as far as extended problem solving, to which we now turn.

■ Extended problem solving

Extended problem solving represents a much more serious investment of money, time and effort from the consumer and, consequently, a much higher risk. Purchases of major capital items such as houses or cars fall into this category. These purchases occur extremely infrequently for most people and, given that they often require some kind of a loan, involve a serious long-term commitment. This means that the purchaser is motivated to gather as much information as possible, and to think quite consciously and systematically about what the decision-making criteria should be. That is not to say that the final decision will necessarily be made on purely functional, conscious or rational grounds. If, for example, two different makes of car have similar technical specifications, price, delivery and after-sales service terms, then final differentiation may be in terms of 'which one will most impress the neighbours?'.

■ The significance of buying situations

So what? Why categorise purchases in this way? After all, one consumer's limited problem-solving situation may be another's extended problem. This matters because it may add another dimension to help marketers develop more efficient and appropriate marketing strategies. If a significant group of potential buyers can be defined who clearly regard the purchase of a hi-fi as a limited problem-solving situation, then that has implications for the manufacturers in terms of both how and what to communicate, and where and how to distribute. If consumers are thought to regard a product as a limited problem-solving purchase, then perhaps the marketer will prefer to distribute it through specialist outlets, where the potential buyer can get expert advice, and can spend time making detailed product comparisons. Communication may contain a lot of factual information about technical specifications and product features (i.e. what the product can do), as well as selling product benefits (i.e. what all that means to you). In contrast, the same product as a routine problem-solving exercise may be distributed as widely as possible, to ensure availability, regardless of retailer specialism or expertise, and the communication might centre on product image and benefits, ignoring the detailed information.

Environmental influences

This section is about the wider context in which the decision-making is taking place. All of these environmental influences have already been covered in some depth in Chapter 2, so their treatment here will be brief. What is important is to recognise that decision-making is not completely divorced from the environment in which it is happening, whether the consumer is conscious of it or not.

■ Sociocultural influences

There are many pressures in this category and pp. 86 *et seq.* looks at them more closely. Individuals are influenced both by current trends in society as a whole and by a need to conform with the norms of the various social groups to which they belong, as well as to enhance their status within those groups.

In wider society, for example, there has been a move in recent years towards demanding more environmentally friendly products, and many consumers who are not necessarily 'deep green' have allowed this to influence their decision-making, looking more favourably on fair trade, CFC-free, recycled or non-animal-tested products. Examples of social group pressures can be seen in children's markets. Many parents feel unfairly pressured into buying particular goods or brands because the children's friends all have them. There is a fear of the child being marginalised or bullied because they don't possess the 'right' things, whether those are trainers, mountain bikes or computer games.

■ Technological influences

Technology affects many aspects of consumer decision-making. Database technology, for example, as discussed in Chapter 11, allows organisations to create (almost) personal relationships with customers. At its extreme, this means that consumers receive better-tailored personalised offerings, and thus that their expectations are raised in terms of the quality of the product, communication and service.

In its wider sense, technology applied to product development and innovation has created whole categories of fast evolving, increasingly cheap consumer 'toys' such as DVDs, hi-fi formats, camcorders and computer games. Many of these products used to be extended problem-solving goods, but they have moved rapidly towards the limited problem-solving area. As they become cheaper and more widely available, the amount of risk inherent in the purchase reduces for the consumer, who does not, therefore, need to spend quite so much time searching for and evaluating alternative options.

■ Economic and competitive influences

The 1990s saw recession and economic hardship across Europe and this inevitably affected consumers' attitudes, as well as their ability and willingness to spend. With uncertainty about employment prospects, many consumers postponed purchasing decisions, adjusted their decision-making criteria or cut out certain types of spending altogether. Price, value for money and a conscious assessment of the need to buy become prevalent influences in such circumstances.

Retailers, in turn, had to respond to the slowdown in trade caused by the economic environment. Money-off sales became prevalent in the High Street throughout the year, not just in the traditional post-Christmas period. While this did stimulate sales in the short term, it had one unfortunate effect for retailers. Consumers began to see the lower sale price as 'normal' and resented paying full prices, preferring to wait for the next sale that they were confident would come along soon.

In terms of competition, very few purchases, mainly low-involvement decisions, are made without any consideration of the competition. The definition of what constitutes competition, however, is in the mind of the consumer. The supplier of car exhaust systems can be fairly sure that the competition consists of other exhaust dealers and garages. The supplier of chocolate, however, may be in competition not only with other chocolate suppliers but also with cream buns, biscuits and potato crisps. The consumer's consideration of the competition, however it is defined, may be extensive, formal and time consuming, or it may be a cursory glance across the supermarket shelf, just to check. Competitors are vying for the consumer's attention through their packaging, their promotional mix and their mailshots, as well as trying to influence or interrupt the decision-making process. This proliferation of products and communication can either confuse the consumer, leading to brand switching and even less rational decision-making, or provide the consumer with the information and comparators to allow more discerning decision-making.

Political and regulatory influences

Political and regulatory influences, emanating either from the EU or from national bodies, can also affect the consumer. Legislation on minimum levels of product safety and performance, for example, means that the consumer does not need to spend time getting technical information, worrying about analysing it and comparing competing products on those criteria. Legislation and regulation, whether they relate to product descriptions, consumer rights or advertising, also reduce the inherent risks of making a decision. This takes some of the pressure off the customer, leading to better-informed and easier decisions and less risk of post-purchase dissonance.

This discussion of the STEP factors is not exhaustive, but simply acts as a reminder that an individual makes decisions within a wider context, created either by society's own dynamics or by the efforts of the market. Having set that context, it is now appropriate to look more closely at the particular influences, internal and external, that affect the individual's buying behaviour and decision-making.

Psychological influences: the individual

Although marketers try to define groups of potential customers with common attributes or interests, as a useful unit for the formulation of marketing strategies, it should not be forgotten that such groups or market segments are still made up of individuals who are different from each other. This section, therefore, looks at aspects that will affect an individual's perceptions and handling of the decision-making process, such as personality, perception, learning, motivation and the impact of attitudes.

Personality

Personality, consisting of all the features, traits, behaviours and experiences that make each of us distinctive and unique, is a very extensive and deep area of study. Our personalities lie at the heart of all our behaviour as consumers, and thus marketers try to define the particular personality traits or characteristics prevalent among a target group of consumers, which can then be reflected in the product itself and the marketing effort around it.

In the mid- to late 1980s, advertising in particular was full of images reflecting the personality traits associated with successful lifestyle stereotypes such as the 'yuppie'. Independent, level-headed, ruthless, ambitious, self-centred, materialistic traits were seen as positive characteristics, and thus marketers were anxious to have them associated with users of their products. The 1990s saw a softening of this approach, featuring images oriented more towards caring, concern, family and sharing as the route to self-fulfilment.

With high-involvement products, where there is a strong emotional and psychological link between the product and the consumer, it is relatively easy to see how personality might affect choice and decision-making. In choosing clothing, for instance, an extrovert self-confident achiever with an extravagant streak might select something deliberately *avant garde*, stylishly daring, vibrantly coloured and expensive, as a personality statement. A quiet, insecure character, with underdeveloped social skills, might prefer to wear something more sober, more conservative, with less attention-seeking potential.

Overall, however, the link between personality and purchasing, and thus the ability to predict purchasing patterns from personality traits, is at best tenuous. Chisnall (1985) takes the more cautious line that personality may influence the decision to buy a certain product type, but not the final brand choice.

■ Perception

Perception represents the way in which individuals analyse, interpret and make sense of incoming information, and is affected by personality, experience and mood. No two people will interpret the same stimulus (whether it is a product's packaging, taste, smell, texture or its promotional messages) in exactly the same way. Even the same individual might perceive the stimulus differently at different times. For example, seeing an advertisement for food when you are hungry is more likely to produce a positive response than seeing the same advertisement just after a heavy meal. Immediate needs are affecting the interpretation of the message. Alternatively, relaxing at home on a Sunday afternoon, an individual is more likely to spend time reading a detailed and lengthy print advertisement than they would if they were flicking through the same magazine during a short coffee break in the working day. Naturally, marketers hope that their messages reach target audiences when they are relaxed, at leisure and at ease with the world, because then the individual is more likely to place a positive interpretation on the message and is less likely to be distracted by other pressures and needs.

Selective attention

Consumers do not pay attention to everything that is going on at once. Attention filters allow the unconscious selection of what incoming information to concentrate on. In daily life we filter out the irrelevant background noise: the hum of the computer, the birds in the garden, the cars in the street, the footsteps in the corridor. As consumers we filter out the irrelevant marketing messages. In reading the newspaper, for instance, a split-second glance spots an advertisement, decides that it is irrelevant and allows the eye to read around it.

This means that marketers have to overcome these filters, either by creating messages that we will decide are relevant or by building attention-grabbing devices into the message. A print advertisement, for example, might use its position on the page, intense colour or startling images to draw the eye, and more importantly the brain, to it.

Selective perception

The problems do not stop once the marketer has got the consumer's attention, since people are infinitely creative in interpreting information in ways that suit them. It is less threatening to interpret things so that they fit nicely and consistently with whatever you already think and feel than to cope with the discomfort of clashes and inconsistency.

One way of creating this consistency or harmony is to allow perception to be coloured by previous experience and existing attitudes. A particularly bad experience with an organisation's offering creates a prejudice that may never be overcome. Whatever positive messages that organisation transmits, the consumer will always be thinking 'Yes, but . . .'. Similarly, a negative attitude towards a subject will make the consumer interpret messages differently. For example, someone who is deeply opposed to nuclear power will try to read between the lines of the industry's advertising and PR, looking for cover-ups and counter-arguments. This can distort the intended message and even reinforce the negative feelings. Conversely, a good experience makes it a lot easier to form positive perceptions. The good experience from the past creates a solid foundation from which to look for the best in the new experience.

Selective retention

Not all stimuli that make it through the attention filters and the machinery of perception and understanding are remembered. Many stimuli are only transitory, hence one of the reasons for the repetition of advertising: if you did not notice it or remember it the first time round, you might pick it up on subsequent occasions. Jogging the memory, by repeating messages or by producing familiar stimuli that the consumer can recognise (such as brand names, packaging design, logos or colour schemes), is therefore an important marketing task to reduce the reliance on the consumer's memory.

People have the capacity to remember what they want to remember and to filter out anything else. The reasons for retaining a particular message may be because it touched them emotionally, or it was of immediate relevance, or it was especially entertaining, or it reinforced previously held views. The reasons are many, but the consumer is under no obligation to remember anything.

■ Learning

Perception and memory are closely linked with learning. Marketers want consumers to learn from promotional material, so that they know which product to buy and why, and to learn from experience of the product, so that they will buy it again and pass on the message to others.

Learning has been defined by Hilgard and Marquis (1961) as:

> . . . the more or less permanent change in behaviour which occurs as a result of practice.

This implies, from a marketing perspective, that the objective must not only be for the consumer to learn something, but also for them to remember what has been learned and to act on it. Therefore advertising materials, for instance, are carefully designed to maximise the learning opportunity. A 30-second television advertisement selling car insurance over the phone repeats the freephone number four times and has it written across the bottom of the screen so that the viewer is likely to remember it. Demonstrating a product benefit in an advertisement also helps consumers to learn what they are supposed to notice about the product when they use it. Demonstrating a product in a particular usage context, or associating it with certain types of people or situations, gives the consumer guidelines about what attitudes to develop towards the product.

Humour, and other methods of provoking an emotional response to an advertisement, can also help a message to stick because the recipient immediately becomes more involved in the process. Similarly, associating a product with something familiar that itself evokes certain emotions can allow those feelings to be transferred to the product. Thus the advertisements for Andrex that feature puppies have helped the British public to learn to think of toilet paper as warm, soft, cuddly and harmless rather than embarrassing.

■ Motivation

One definition of marketing puts the emphasis on the satisfaction of customers' needs and wants, but what triggers those needs and wants, and what drives consumers towards their fulfilment? Motives for action, the driving forces, are complex and changeable and can be difficult to research, since individuals themselves often cannot define why they act the way they do. An additional problem is that at different times, different motivations might take priority and have more influence over the individual's behaviour.

Maslow's (1954) *hierarchy of needs* has long been used as a framework for classifying basic motivations. Five groups of needs, as shown in Figure 3.2, are stacked one on top of another and form a progression. Having achieved satisfaction on the lowest level, the individual can progress to strive to achieve the goals of the next level up. This model does have a certain logic behind it, and the idea, for instance, that true self-actualisation can only grow from solid

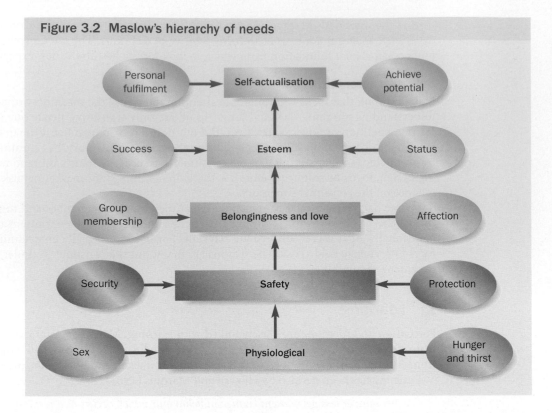

Figure 3.2 Maslow's hierarchy of needs

foundations of security and social acceptance seems reasonable. However, the model was developed in the context of US capitalist culture, where achievement and self-actualisation are often ends in themselves. It is questionable how far these motives can be extended to other cultural contexts.

Examples of consumer behaviour and marketing activity can be found to fit all five levels.

Physiological needs

Basic feelings such as hunger and thirst can be potent driving forces. After a strenuous game of squash, the immediate craving for liquid overrides normal considerations of brand preference. If the sports centre shop only has one type of soft drink in stock, then it will do. Similarly, seasoned shoppers are well aware of the dangers of visiting a supermarket when they are hungry: so much more seems to go into the trolley.

Marketers can capitalise on such feelings. The soft drink manufacturer can ensure that the sports centre stocks that brand and that the product image reflects refreshment and thirst-quenching properties. The food manufacturer can advertise at a time of day when the audience is likely to be feeling hungry so that they are more likely to pay attention to the message and remember it.

Safety needs

Once the individual has taken care of the basic necessities of life, food, drink and warmth, the need for self-protection and long-term survival emerges. In modern Western societies this may be interpreted as the desire for a secure home, protected against intrusion and other dangers (floods and fire, for example). It might also cover the desire for healthcare, insurance services and consumer protection legislation.

The car market in particular has focused on safety needs as a marketing platform. Driving is an inherently dangerous activity, so the manufacturers try to reassure us that their cars are as safe as possible. Various manufacturers have featured side impact bars, airbags and/or anti-lock braking systems in their advertising, showing how these either protect you or help to prevent accidents.

Safety needs in terms of health protection feature strongly in the marketing strategies of products such as bleaches and toilet cleaners. The kind of approach used often appeals to the mother who takes responsibility for safeguarding the health and well-being of the whole family. The threat from bacteria can be eliminated by choosing the right cleanser.

Belongingness and love needs

This is about emotional security, wanting to feel accepted and valued by those closest to you. Marketers again play on this need through the portrayal of the family in particular. Over many years, advertising told women that they would be better appreciated and loved as wives and mothers if they did their washing in Persil, cooked with Oxo or fed their husbands corn-flakes for breakfast.

Fear of loneliness or personal rejection can be a powerful motivator and features strongly in many marketing campaigns. Toiletries such as deodorants, toothpastes and mouthwashes have all advertised on the basis that you will be more lovable if you use these products, and showing the dire consequences of rejection if you don't. Even anti-smoking campaigns aimed at teenagers have tried this approach, implying that the smell of tobacco on your breath will put off prospective boy/girlfriends.

Esteem needs

This extends outwards from the previous stage to cover the individual's need for success, status and good opinion within wider society. This may include professional status and respect, standing within social groups, such as sports clubs and societies, or 'what the neighbours think'.

These needs are reflected in a wide variety of product and services marketing. Most car advertising, for example, contains some kind of message implying that if you drive this car it will somehow enhance your status and gain the respect of others. This even applies to the smaller, less expensive models, where the esteem arises from notions of 'wise choice' or 'a car that reflects the positive elements of my character'. More overtly, esteem can derive from the individual's sheer ability to afford the most expensive and exclusive items. Perfumes and other luxury products play heavily on the implication that you are a discerning and élite buyer, a cut above the rest, and that using these products makes a statement about who you are and the status you hold. Brand names such as Rolls-Royce, Gucci and Rolex have acquired such a cachet that simply saying 'she owns a genuine Rolex' speaks volumes about a person's social status.

Self-actualisation needs

This is the ultimate goal, the achievement of complete satisfaction through successfully ful-filling one's potential. That may mean anything, depending on who you are and what you want out of life. Some will only achieve self-actualisation through becoming the head of a multi-national organisation, while others will find it through the successful raising of a happy and healthy family. This is a difficult stage for the marketer to handle, because it is so individ-ual, and thus the hope is that by fulfilling the other needs discussed above, the marketer can help to propel the individual towards self-actualisation. Only the individual can tell, however, when this stage has been reached.

Generally in Western economies the fulfilment of the very basic needs can be taken for granted, however. Real physiological hunger, thirst and lack of safety do not exist for most people. Manufacturers of food products, for instance, cannot therefore assume that just because their product alleviates hunger it will be purchased and accepted. Any one of hun-dreds of food brands can do that, and thus the consumer is looking to see how a particular product can fulfil a higher-order need, such as love or esteem. Consequently, foods are often marketed on the basis that your family will enjoy it and love you more for providing it (Oxo, for example) or because your dinner party guests will be pleased (Viennetta or After Eight, for example). The emphasis, therefore, is largely on the higher-order needs (belongingness and love, esteem and self-actualisation).

■ Attitudes

As implied at p. 80 above, an attitude is a stance that an individual takes on a subject that predisposes them to react in a certain way to that subject. More formally, an attitude has been defined by Hilgard *et al.* (1975) as:

> . . . *an orientation towards or away from some object, concept or situation and a readiness to respond in a predetermined manner to these related objects, concepts or situations.*

Thus in marketing terms, consumers can develop attitudes to any kind of product or service, or indeed to any aspect of the marketing mix, and these attitudes will affect behaviour. All of this implies that attitudes play an important part in influencing consumer judgement, whether through perception, evaluation, information processing or decision-making. Attitudes play a key role in shaping learning and while they are fluid, evolving over time, they are nevertheless often difficult to change.

Williams (1981), in summarising the literature, describes attitudes as having three different components.

Cognitive

Cognitive attitudes relate to beliefs or disbeliefs, thus: 'I believe that margarine is healthier than butter'. This is a component that the marketer can work on through fairly straightforward advertising. Repeating the message that your product is healthy, or that it represents the best value for money, may well establish an initial belief in those qualities.

Affective

Affective attitudes relate to feelings of a positive or negative nature, involving some emotional content, thus: 'I *like* this product' or 'This product makes me *feel* . . .' Again, advertising can help the marketer to signal to the consumer why they should like it, or how they should feel when they use it. For some consumers, of course, affective attitudes can overcome cognitive ones. For example, I may believe that margarine is healthier than butter, but I buy butter because I like the taste better. Similarly, I believe that snacking on chocolate is 'bad', but it cheers me up so I do it anyway.

Conative

Conative attitudes relate to the link with behaviour, thus attitude *x* is considered likely to lead to behaviour *y*. This is the hardest one for marketers to predict or control, because so many things can prevent behaviour from taking place, even if the cognitive and affective attitudes are positive: 'I believe that BMWs are excellent quality, reliable cars, and I feel that owning one would enhance my status and provide me with many hours of pleasurable driving, but I simply cannot afford it', or it may even be that 'Audi made me a better offer'.

It is this last link between attitude and behaviour that is of most interest to marketers. Fishbein (1975) developed a model based on the proposition that in order to predict a specific behaviour, such as a brand purchase, it is important to measure the individual's attitude towards performing that behaviour, rather than just the attitude towards the product in question. This fits with the BMW example above, where the most important thing is not the attitude to the car itself, but the attitude towards *purchasing* the car. As long as the attitude to purchasing is negative, the marketer still has work to do.

Attitudes can thus involve feelings (positive or negative), knowledge (complete or partial) and beliefs. A particular female consumer might believe that she is overweight. She knows that cream cakes are fattening, but she likes them. All these things come together to form her attitude towards cream cakes (wicked, but seductive) and her behaviour when confronted by one (five minutes wrestling with her conscience before giving in completely and buying two, knowing that she will regret it later). An advertising campaign for cream cakes, centred around the slogan 'naughty but nice', capitalised brilliantly on what is a common attitude, almost legitimising the guilt and establishing an empathy with the hopeless addict. The really admirable thing about that campaign was that the advertiser did not even attempt to overturn the attitude.

It is possible, but very difficult, to change attitudes, particularly when they are well established and deeply ingrained. Companies like Lada and Aeroflot have been trying for years with varying degrees of success. The nuclear industry has also been trying to overcome hostile and suspicious attitudes with an integrated campaign of advertising, PR and site visits (**http://www.bnfl.co.uk**). Many people have indeed been responsive to this openness, and have been prepared to revise attitudes to a greater or lesser extent. There will, however, always be a hard core who will remain entrenched and interpret any 'positive' messages in a negative way.

There is a difference between attitudes that relate to an organisation's philosophy, business ethics or market and those that centre around experience of an organisation's specific product or service. An organisation that has a bad reputation for its employment practices, its environmental record or its dealings with suspect foreign regimes will have created negative attitudes that will be extremely difficult to overturn. Similarly, companies operating in certain markets, such as nuclear power, tobacco and alcohol, will never redeem themselves in the eyes of significant groups of the public. People care too much about such things to be easily persuaded to change their outlook. In contrast, negative feelings about a specific product or brand are more amenable to change through skilful marketing.

marketing in action

The open road to success

The Harley-Davidson brand is all about authority and prestige. It is not a bike for the sports motorcyclist: it seems to attract an awful lot of men in their late thirties and early forties, usually professionals seeking a bit of escapism by cruising the highways. For many of them, ownership of a product that could not be afforded in their dim and distant youth is a symbol of their achievement and success in life. Harley-Davidson dominates the cruiser/touring market, one of four market segments in the motorbike industry. It believes in what it describes as 360-degree marketing whereby it surrounds the customer to build a relationship that communicates the brand values and what ownership of a Harley-Davidson means. Wherever the customer has contact, through the product itself, its distribution channels, sales, customer service, design, communications, or brand extensions, etc., there is a consistent and integrated approach to enhancing the relationship.

Harley-Davidson is, however, having to appeal to a wider

Harley-Davidson has traditionally targeted the marketing of its motorbikes at men who dream of the open road as a way to forget the treadmill of work and rediscover their lost youth. Now that younger people have enough money to own such a prestige product, advertisements such as this one aim to attract their interest.

Source: © Harley-Davidson UK http://www.harley-davidson.com

audience despite its dominance in the tradional male sector. Its products and communication strategies are starting to target women and younger riders. They are still thought to be part of the 'dreamer group', wanting to ride and enjoy the Harley experience, and aspiring to join the Harley community. This status is demonstrated through clever promotional appeals, for example by showing a lone Harley rider near a mountain at the edge of the highway in the US with the tagline 'This country wasn't founded on the declaration of blending in' (Buss, 2004; Speros, 2004).

As the cream cake example quoted earlier shows, defining attitudes can provide valuable insights into target groups of customers and give a basis for communication with them. Measuring feelings, beliefs and knowledge about an organisation's products and those of its competitors is an essential part of market research (see Chapter 5), leading to a more effective and appealing marketing mix. Identifying changes in wider social or cultural attitudes can also provide the marketer with new opportunities, either for products or marketing approaches.

In summary, the individual is a complex entity, under pressure to take in, analyse and remember many marketing messages in addition to the other burdens of daily life. Marketers need to understand how individuals think and why they respond in particular ways, if they are going to develop marketing offerings that cut through defence mechanisms and create loyal customers. Individuals' behaviour, however, is not only shaped in accordance with their personalities, abilities, analytical skills, etc., as discussed above, but also affected by wider considerations, such as the sociocultural influences that will be discussed next.

Sociocultural influences: the group

Individuals are influenced, to a greater or lesser extent, by the social and cultural climate in which they live. Individuals have membership of many social groups, whether these are formally recognised social units such as the family, or informal intangible groupings such as reference groups (*see* pp. 89 *et seq.*). Inevitably, purchasing decisions will be affected by group membership, as these sociocultural influences may help the individual to:

1 differentiate between essential and non-essential purchases;
2 prioritise purchases where resources are limited;
3 define the meaning of the product and its benefits in the context of their own lives; and thus to
4 foresee the post-purchase implications of this decision.

All of these things imply that the individual's decision has as much to do with 'What other people will think' and 'How I will look if I buy this' as with the intrinsic benefits of the product itself. Marketers have, of course, capitalised on this natural wish to express oneself and gain social acceptance through one's consumption habits, both as a basis for psychographic or lifestyle segmentation (which will be discussed later on pp. 121 *et seq.*) and for many years as a basis of fear appeals in advertising.

The following subsections look more closely at some of these sociocultural influences.

■ Social class

Social class is a form of stratification that attempts to structure and divide a society. Some argue that egalitarianism has become far more pronounced in the modern Europe, making any attempts at social distinction ill-founded, if not meaningless. Nevertheless, today social class is established largely according to occupation, and for many years, British marketers have used the grading system outlined in Table 3.1. It has been widely used to group consumers, whether for research or for analysing media readership.

However, more fundamental problems can be found in attempting to link consumer behaviour with social class. The usefulness of such systems is limited. They rely on the occupation of the head of the household (more correctly called the main income earner), but fail to put that into the context of the rest of the household. Dual income households are becoming increasingly common, with the second income having a profound effect on the buying behaviour of both parties, yet most of these systems fail to recognise this. They tell very little about the consumption patterns or attitudes that are of such great use to the marketer. The disposable income of a C2 class household may be just as high as that of an A or B household, and they may have certain upmarket tastes in common. Furthermore, two households in the A or B cat-

Table 3.1 UK socioeconomic groupings

% of population	Group	Social status	Occupation of head of household
3	A	Upper middle	Higher managerial, administrative or professional
14	B	Middle	Intermediate managerial, administrative or professional
27	C1	Lower middle	Supervisory or clerical, junior managerial, administrative or professional
25	C2	Skilled working	Skilled manual workers
19	D	Working	Semi-skilled and unskilled manual workers
12	E	Those at lowest level of subsistence	State pensioners or widows, casual or lowest-grade workers

egories could easily behave very differently. One household might consider status symbols to be important and indulge in conspicuous consumption, whereas the other might have rejected materialistic values and be seeking a cleaner, less cluttered lifestyle. These contrasting outlooks on life make an enormous difference to buying behaviour and choices, hence the necessity for psychographic segmentation (*see* pp. 121 *et seq.*) to provide marketers with more meaningful frameworks for grouping customers.

eg Effectively the 'mass affluent' society in Western markets represents both the traditional middle class and an increasing percentage of the higher-earning working classes. Luxury goods are a good example of how the traditional classifications are becoming increasingly irrelevant. Real disposable incomes have risen by over 20 per cent in the UK since 1995 and it has been estimated that 10 million households can now afford what used to be exclusive to the richest 1 per cent. Two or three holidays per year, second homes, two or three cars, expanded use of professional services including private healthcare and education, are all indicators of the changes taking place. Having groceries delivered to your home or having someone to cook for you were once the luxuries of the rich, but now eating out, fast food and home delivery are considered normal in the UK. Mass affluence cuts across social class. The premium and luxury sectors have been growing by 10 per cent per annum compared with 2–3 per cent in other categories. The propensity to make buying decisions on quality and prestige rather than on price reflects these shifts (*Marketing*, 2004; *Marketing Week*, 2004).

■ Culture and subculture

Culture can be described as the personality of the society within which an individual lives. It manifests itself through the built environment, art, language, literature, music and the products that society consumes, as well as through its prevalent beliefs, value systems and government. Rice (1993, p. 242) defines culture as:

> *The values, attitudes, beliefs, ideas, artefacts and other meaningful symbols represented in the pattern of life adopted by people that help them interpret, evaluate and communicate as members of society.*

Breaking that definition down further, Figure 3.3 shows diagrammatically the influences that create culture.

Cultural differences show themselves in very different ways. Although eating, for example, is a basic natural instinct, what we eat and when is heavily influenced by the culture in which we are brought up. Thus in Spain it is normal to begin lunch at 4 p.m. and then have dinner after 10 p.m., while in Poland most restaurants would be closing down at those times.

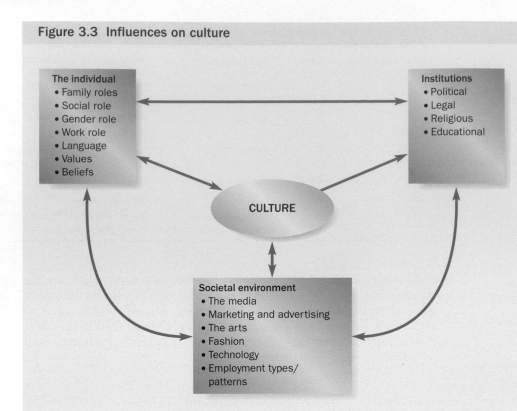

Figure 3.3 Influences on culture

Similarly, lunch in Central Europe would almost certainly include sauerkraut, but little fish compared with the wide variety offered on a typical Spanish menu. Even the propensity for eating out may be a cultural factor.

Of course, culture goes much further in prescribing and describing the values and beliefs of a society. It influences shopping hours, with many Mediterranean supermarkets open for far longer hours in the evening than some of their Northern European counterparts; the beliefs associated with advertising messages and symbols; the lifestyles of the inhabitants; and the products that are more or less acceptable and available in that culture – for example, try purchasing an electric kettle in Spain or Italy.

Culture is thus very important for the marketer to understand, first because marketing can only exist within a culture that is prepared to allow it and support it, and second, it has to act within boundaries set by society and culture. Over the past 10 years or so, for example, it has become more and more socially unacceptable in Europe for organisations to use animals for testing cosmetics. Society has informally rewritten one of the rules and marketers have had to respond. Changing attitudes to tobacco, alcohol and marketing to children are also examples of areas within which cultural change is altering organisations' approaches to business. In the UK, for instance, food marketers have been criticised for aiming too much advertising of products such as sweets, soft drinks, sugary cereals, crisps and fast foods at children. These kinds of product are thought to be of dubious nutritional value, if consumed in excess, and are also thought to be contributing to an increase in dental decay among children.

Any culture can be divided into a number of subcultures, each with its own specific characteristics, yet existing within the whole. It depends on the onlooker's perspective just how detailed a division is required. An American exporter might say that Europe represents a culture (as distinct from the US culture), with British, French, German and other national subcultures existing within it. Dealing with the home market, however, a German marketer would define Germany, or increasingly the German-speaking territories of Europe, as the dominant culture, with significant subcultures held within it. These subcultures could be based on ethnic origin (Turkish, Polish, Asian or whatever), religious beliefs, or more lifestyle-oriented groupings, defined by the values and attitudes held. Language may also be an important determinant of subculture. In Switzerland, for example, the three main languages reflect different customs, architecture and even external orientations. The Ticino region (Italian speaking) probably identifies itself more closely with Milan than Zurich or Basle as a point of cultural reference.

In many ways, the tension within ethnic-based subcultures is between cultural assimilation into the main, dominant culture and the preservation of cultural diversity in language, dress, food, family behaviour, etc. This tension can be seen even on a European scale, where increased emphasis on travel, rapid communication and pan-European marketing is slowly breaking down barriers at the same time as there is a strong movement towards the preservation of distinct national and regional identities.

As far as the immediate future is concerned, even within a united Europe, people are still celebrating and defending their own cultures and subcultures, and marketers need to recognise and empathise with this. One of the reasons (among many) cited for Disneyland Paris's poor start was that the organisation had underestimated French resistance, in particular, to an undiluted all-American cultural concept in the heart of Europe. Europeans are happy, and indeed eager, to experience Disney on US soil as part of 'the American experience', but cannot accept it, it would appear, within their own culture (**http://www.disney.go.com**).

Subculture need not only be an ethnic phenomenon, however. The existence of a youth subculture, spanning international boundaries, is widely accepted by marketers, and media such as MTV that reach right across Europe allow marketers to communicate efficiently and cost effectively with that subculture. Brands such as Coca-Cola, Pepsi and Pepe Jeans can create messages that capitalise on the common concerns, interests and attitudes that define this subculture. The core messages strike at something different from, and perhaps deeper than, national or ethnic culture, and thus may have pan-European currency without necessarily becoming bland in the process. That is not to say that all 16–25-year-olds across Europe should be stereotyped as belonging to a homogeneous 'yoof market'. What it does say is that there are certain attitudes and feelings with which this age group are likely to sympathise, and that these can therefore be used as a foundation for more targeted communication that manages to celebrate both commonalities and differences.

eg   Some advertising agencies deliberately try to appeal to 15–25-year-olds with themes that older people could find offensive and shocking. French Connection UK, or FCUK for short, had an outstanding success in the clothing retail sector with the full frontal use of the FCUK acronym, which meant that any advertising, especially on posters, was going to get noticed. Since 1997, FCUK had a few run-ins with the ASA, with some of its advertisements approved and some condemned. Poster themes such as 'fcuk fashion' and 'fcuk advertising' met with disapproval, while T-shirts with such themes as 'French Connection me' and 'my place now' along with the FCUK trademark slipped through. To French Connection, it was all meant to be a bit of fun, worth a smile. It could be claimed it was pure coincidence, but the reader was left in no doubt as to the innuendo and FCUK had effectively taken ownership of the f-word (Broadbent, 2001). Nevertheless, it didn't take too long for the novelty to wear off. By 2005, French Connection was reporting falling sales and falling profits. Analysts were of the opinion that the market viewed the whole 'fcuk' thing as tired and tacky, that product ranges lacked innovation, and that the clothes were overpriced compared with the competition (Grande, 2005; Mesure, 2005). It just goes to show that you cannot sit back and bask in the glory of one good advertising campaign!

■ Reference groups

Reference groups are any groups, whether formally or informally constituted, to which an individual either belongs or aspires to belong, for example professional bodies, social or hobby-oriented societies, or informal, vaguely defined lifestyle groups ('I want to be a yuppie'). There are three main types of reference group, each of which affects buying behaviour, and these are discussed in turn below.

Membership groups

These are the groups to which the individual already belongs. These groups provide parameters within which individuals make purchasing decisions, whether they are conscious of it or not. In buying clothing, for example, the purchaser might think about the occasion for which it is going to be worn and consider whether a particular item is 'suitable'. There is great concern here about what other people will think.

Buying clothes for work is severely limited by the norms and expectations imposed by colleagues (a membership group) and bosses (an aspirant group?), as well as by the practicalities of the workplace. Similarly, choosing clothes for a party will be influenced by the predicted impact on the social group who will be present: whether they will be impressed; whether the wearer will fit in; whether the wearer will seem to be overdressed or underdressed; or whether anyone else is likely to turn up in the same outfit.

Thus the influence of membership groups on buying behaviour is to set standards to which individuals can conform, thus consolidating their position as group members. Of course, some individuals with a strong sense of opinion leadership will seek to extend those standards by exceeding them and challenging the norms with the expectation that others will follow.

Aspirant groups

These are the groups to which the individual would like to belong, and some of these aspirations are more realistic than others. An amateur athlete or musician might aspire to professional status in their dreams, even if they have little talent. An independent professional single female might aspire to become a full-time housewife with a husband and three children; the housewife might aspire to the career and independent lifestyle. A young, junior manager might aspire to the middle management ranks.

People's desire for change, development and growth in their lives is natural, and marketers frequently exploit this in the positioning of their products and the subtle promises they make. Birds Eye frozen meals will not stop you being a bored housewife, but will give you a little more independence to 'be yourself'; buying Nike, Reebok or Adidas sports gear will not make you into Ronaldo, Beckham or Zidane, but you can feel a little closer to them.

The existence of aspirant groups, therefore, attracts consumers towards products that are strongly associated with those groups and will either make it appear that the buyer actually belongs to the group or signal the individual's aspirations to the wider world.

Dissociative groups

These are groups to which the individual does not want to belong or to be seen to belong. A supporter of the England soccer team would not wish to be associated with its notorious hooligan element, for example. Someone who had a violent aversion to 'yuppies' and their values might avoid buying products that are closely associated with them, through fear of being thought to belong to that group. An upmarket shopper might prefer not to be seen in a discount store such as Aldi or Netto just in case anyone thinks they are penny pinching.

Clearly, these dissociations are closely related to the positive influences of both membership and aspirational groups. They are simply the other side of the coin, an attempt to draw closer to the 'desirable' groups, while differentiating oneself from the 'undesirable'.

■ Family

The family, whether two parent or single parent, nuclear or extended, with or without dependent children, remains a key influence on the buying behaviour of individuals. The needs of the family affect what can be afforded, where the spending priorities lie and how a purchasing decision is made. All of this evolves as the family matures and moves through the various stages of its lifecycle. Over time, the structure of a family changes, for example as children grow older and eventually leave home, or as events break up families or create new ones.

This means that a family's resources and needs also change over time, and that the marketer must understand and respond to these changes.

Traditionally, marketers have looked to the family lifecycle as proposed by Wells and Gubar (1966), and shown in Table 3.2. Over the years, however, this has become less and less appropriate, as it reflects a path through life that is becoming less common in the West. It does not, for example, allow for single parent families, created either voluntarily or through divorce, or for remarriage after divorce which may create new families with children coming together from previous marriages, and/or second families. Other trends too undermine the assumptions of the traditional model of the family lifecycle. According to Lightfoot and Wavell (1995), estimates from the Office of Population Censuses and Surveys (OPCS) in the UK forecast that 20 per cent of women born in the 1960s, 1970s and 1980s may never have children. Those who do currently elect to have children are tending to leave childbearing until later in their lives, so that they can establish their careers first. OPCS has noted that the birth rate among women in their twenties has dropped, while it has increased rapidly for women in their thirties and forties. At the other end of the spectrum, the number of single, teenage mothers has increased alarmingly in the UK to 3 per cent of girls aged 15–19, the highest figure in the EU. Overall, however, European birth rates are falling, leading to 'ageing populations' throughout the EU as the proportion of children in the population falls.

Table 3.2 The family lifecycle

Stage	Title	Characteristics
1	Bachelor	Young, single, not living at home
2	Newly married	Young, no children
3	Full nest I	Youngest child under 6
4	Full nest II	Youngest child 6 or over
5	Full nest III	Older, married with dependent children
6	Empty nest I	Older married, no children living at home
7	Empty nest II	Older married, retired, no children living at home
8	Solitary survivor I	In labour force
9	Solitary survivor II	Retired

Source: Wells and Gubar (1966).

All of these trends have major implications for consumers' needs and wants at various stages in their lives, as well as for their disposable incomes. The marketer cannot make trite assumptions based on traditional stereotypes of the nuclear family, and something more complex than the Wells and Gubar model is needed to reflect properly the various routes that people's lives can now take. Figure 3.4 offers a revised family lifecycle for the way people live today.

Regardless of the structure of the family unit, members of a household can participate in each other's purchasing decision-making. In some cases, members may be making decisions that affect the whole family, and thus Figure 3.5 shows how a family can act as a decision-making unit where individual members play different roles in reaching the final decision. The roles that any one member takes on will vary from purchase to purchase, as will the length, complexity and formality of the process. The obvious manifestation of the family decision-making unit is in the ordinary week-to-week grocery shopping. The main shopper is not acting as an individual, pleasing only themselves by their choices, but is reflecting the tastes and requirements of a group of people. In a stereotypical family, Mother may be the ultimate decider and purchaser in the supermarket, but the rest of the family may have acted as initiators ('When you go shopping, will you get me some . . .?' or 'Do you know that we've run out of . . .?' or 'Can we try that new brand of . . .?') or influencers ('If you buy THAT, don't expect ME to eat it'), either before the shopping trip or at the point of sale.

Figure 3.4 A modern family lifecycle model

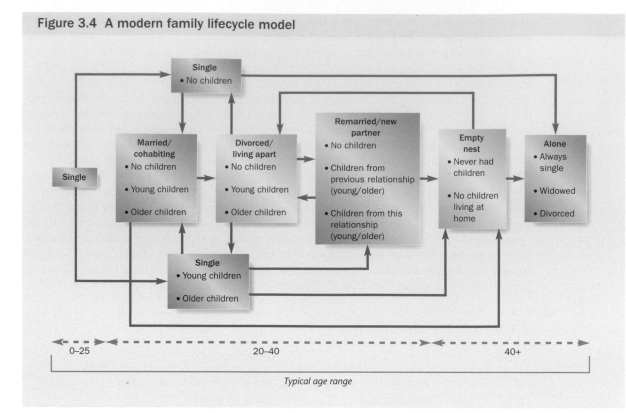

The buying roles may be undertaken by different family members for different purchases at different times. Thus in the example of purchasing a bicycle, a child may well be the user and influencer, but the parents may be the principal deciders and buyers.

Figure 3.5 The family as a decision-making unit

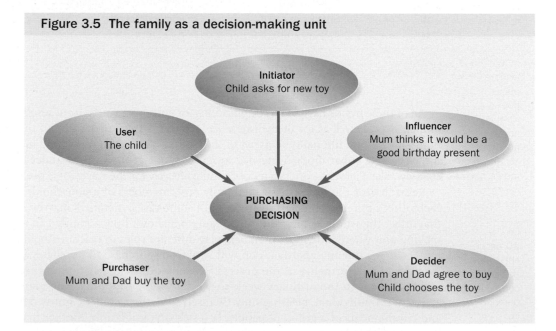

Do we know what's good for our kids?

Are children fair game for marketers? There is no doubt that children not only influence their parents' purchasing processes directly but also that they have their own spending power. With average pocket money of around £5 per week plus gift money, they have disposable income that can be usefully spent on categories such as confectionery, magazines, computer games, etc. However, there is a serious ethical and moral debate among advertisers, legislators and lobby groups as to whether there should be regulation to curb the power of marketing to kids. This has come to the fore again in the debate over obesity in children.

According to the Chief Medical Officer in the UK, the next generation is expected to suffer the first fall in average life expectancy in 100 years due to childhood obesity and the fatal diseases that go with a lack of exercise. Around 4 million children in the UK are considered overweight or obese, thus one in ten six-year-olds and one in six 15-year-olds are at risk. The key question for the food industry and the legislators is whether this situation has arisen because of changing lifestyles and poor eating and exercise habits or whether it is a result of the manipulative behaviours of advertisers seeking to influence children's choices through various media such as television, text messaging, the internet and in schools promotions.

Clearly, parents are in the front line. Surveys have shown that over 40 per cent of parents buy what the child wants. That means canned pasta, pot noodles and confectionery are high on the list of demands, with pizza and frozen chips not far behind. Fresh food

rarely makes it into the top 15 categories while ambient, long shelf-life, cupboard stock often proves most popular. Fish fingers and chips, beans and chips, beans on toast, pizza and chips have become the staples of many children's diets. It's a fast, convenient and unquestioning approach to children's meal planning by busy and overstretched parents. The popular choices indicate a lack of imagination, easy preparation and informal, sometimes child-only eating experiences, a long way from the sit-down family dinner so often featured in Hollywood classics.

Research indicates that obese children consume far more processed, convenient and highly branded foods. This raises the issue as to what manufacturers should do, if anything. There is a lot of pressure on them to reduce the fat and salt content of processed foods Health education and the development of healthier options are also possibilities, Some go further and argue that advertising to children should be more highly regulated to reduce the impact of 'pester power'.

The views are polarised on restricting advertising that is clearly targeted at kids, such as the advertising of snack foods and sugary cereals on Cartoon Network designed to get children to influence mum's shopping choices. Regulator Ofcom is considering whether new rules should be drawn up on the scheduling and content of food advertising on television. Sweden has gone further and has banned all commercial influences on children under 12. The interpretation is strict: one advertisement was banned as it featured a child running across the bathroom in a toilet cleaner ad! The European Union has been lobbied to declare confectionery a public health issue, like tobacco, and to

regulate it accordingly.

Central to the arguments against advertising to children is the use of pester power. Some claim that the way advertisements are designed and presented, for example often using cartoon characters, means that children are unable to separate the advertising from the programming. Wotsits, the snack from Walkers, ran into trouble when it was revealed that the brief given to the advertising agency was to generate a campaign that would make children think, 'I'm going to buy them when I get a chance and pester mum for them when she next goes shopping'. This was regarded by the House of Commons Health Select Committee as a deliberate attempt to undermine parental power over children's nutrition.

Kellogg's denies that its advertising makes children pester parents and states that it would never encourage such behaviour. However, Kellogg's and others spend a lot of time trying to understand children, their interests, the brands they identify with, and why and how children interact with parents in brand decision-making. In reality, children are being bombarded with advertising messages and are surrounded by attempts to influence their spend directly or indirectly and yet many advertisers and the government are in denial. They argue that in some countries where bans on food advertising to children exist, there is no marked difference in children's health. Furthermore, the advertising industry argues that advertising only reflects what is already prevalent in society and that the roots of the problem lie elsewhere.

The exercise of parental power over pester power is central to the debate. Is it up to parents to encourage their children to adopt healthier lifestyles, in terms of both diet and exercise? Should parents be preparing more nutritious food to inculcate the values and attitudes of healthy living, or should the children be protected from pester power and the techniques of advertisers? Often parents are complicit in allowing pester power to win. Family values often revolve around the welfare of the children, and money-rich, time-poor parents are eager to indulge their little ones as a form of emotional compensation. How many parents realise that it would take the average child 45 minutes to run off a bag of crisps, one hour and four minutes to run off a chocolate bar, and a marathon to run off a burger and fries?

Meanwhile, as the debate continues, the kids get more obese. After all, not many manufacturers' profits get fat by selling more fresh fruit and vegetables!

Sources: Brand Strategy (2003, 2004); Grimshaw (2004); Malkani (2004); O'Connell (2003); Roberts (2004); Silverman (2004).

Children are an important target group for the marketer, partly because of their ability to pester their parents and influence family purchasing, and partly because of the marketer's desire to create brand loyalty as early as possible in consumers' lives. For instance, Kellogg's gave away 800,000 sample packs of Choco Krispies, while McDonald's provides free meal vouchers to be used as prizes by schools. Not surprisingly, many teachers, parents and consumer groups are concerned that the young and vulnerable may be exposed to unreasonable marketing pressures.

Defining B2B marketing

So far, this chapter has looked exclusively at consumer buyer behaviour. We now turn our attention to organisational buyer behaviour, or B2B marketing. This is the management process responsible for the facilitation of exchange between producers of goods and services and their organisational customers. This might involve, for example, a clothing manufacturer selling uniforms to the army, a component manufacturer selling microchips to IBM, an advertising agency selling its expertise to Kellogg's, Kellogg's selling its breakfast cereals to a large supermarket chain, or a university selling short management training courses to local firms.

B2B marketing and purchasing is a complex and risky business. An organisation may buy many thousands of products and services, costing anything from a few pennies to many mil-

Table 3.3 Differences between B2B and consumer marketing

B2B customers often/usually . . .	Consumer customers often/usually . . .
• purchase goods and services that meet specific business needs	• purchase goods and services to meet individual or family needs
• need emphasis on economic benefits	• need emphasis on psychological benefits
• use formalised, lengthy purchasing policies and processes	• buy on impulse or with minimal processes
• involve large groups in purchasing decisions	• purchase as individuals or as a family unit
• buy large quantities and buy infrequently	• buy small quantities and buy frequently
• want a customised product package	• are content with a standardised product package targeted at a specific market segment
• experience major problems if supply fails	• experience minor irritation if supply fails
• find switching to another supplier difficult	• find switching to another supplier easy
• negotiate on price	• accept the stated price
• purchase direct from suppliers	• purchase from intermediaries
• justify an emphasis on personal selling	• justify an emphasis on mass media communication

lions of pounds per item. The risks are high in these markets where a bad decision, even on a minor component, can bring manufacturing to a halt or cause entire production runs to be scrapped as substandard.

There are several differences between B2B and consumer marketing, as Table 3.3 shows. If a consumer goes to the supermarket and finds that their preferred brand of baked beans is not there, then it is disappointing, but not a disaster. The consumer can easily substitute an alternative brand, or go to another supermarket, or the family can have something else for lunch. If, however, a supplier fails to deliver as promised on a component, then the purchasing organisation has a big problem, especially if there are no easily accessible alternative sources of supply, and runs the risk of letting its own customers down with all the commercial damage that implies. Any failure by any link in this chain has a severe impact on the others.

Thus the links have to be forged carefully, and relationships managed over time to minimise the potential problems or to diagnose them early enough for action to be taken.

B2B customers

While many B2B buying situations involve a profit-making organisation doing business with other similarly oriented concerns, there are other kinds of organisation that have different philosophies and approaches to purchasing. Overall, there are three main classes: commercial enterprises, government bodies and institutions, each of which represents a lot of buying power.

Commercial enterprises consist of profit-making organisations that produce and/or re-sell goods and services for a profit. Some are *users* who purchase goods and services to facilitate their own production, although the item purchased does not enter directly into the finished product. Examples of this are CAD/CAM systems, office equipment and management consultancy services. In contrast, *original equipment manufacturers* (OEMs) incorporate their purchases into their own product, as a car manufacturer does with electrical components, fabrics, plastics, paint, tyres, etc. *Re-sellers*, such as retailers, purchase goods for re-sale, usually making no physical changes to them and thus the value added stems largely from service elements. Government bodies are also very large, important purchasers of goods and services. This group of B2B buyers includes both local and national government, as well as European Commission purchasing. The range of purchasing is wide, from office supplies to public buildings, from army bootlaces to battleships, from airline tickets to motorways, from refuse collection to management consultancy. Finally, institutions include (largely) non-profit-making organisations such as universities, churches and independent schools. These institutions may have an element of government funding, but in purchasing terms they are autonomous. They are likely to follow some of the same procedures as government bodies, but with a greater degree of flexibility of choice.

Characteristics of B2B markets

The differences between consumer and B2B markets do not lie so much in the products themselves as in the context in which those products are exchanged, that is, the use of the marketing mix and the interaction between buyer and seller. The same model of personal computer, for example, can be bought as a one-off by an individual for private use, or in bulk to equip an entire office. The basic product is identical in specification but the ways in which it is bought and sold will differ.

The following subsections look at some of the characteristics of B2B markets that generate these different approaches.

■ Nature of demand

Derived demand

All demand in B2B markets is derived demand – derived from some kind of consumer demand. So, for example, washing machine manufacturers demand electric motors from an engineering factory, and that is a B2B market. The numbers of electric motors demanded, however, depend on predictions of future consumer demand for washing machines. If, as has happened, there is a recession and consumers stop buying the end product, then demand for the component parts of it will also dry up.

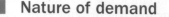

Some retailers are trying to achieve a competitive advantage by cutting the lead times involved in getting garments from the drawing board to the retail outlet. A pioneer of so-called 'fast fashion' is the Spanish retailer Zara which can get this lead time down to as little as 14 days. It can do this because there is a high degree of vertical integration within the design and production process. One of Zara's sister companies produces 40 per cent of its fabric needs and between 50 and 60 per cent of its manufacturing is done in-house. Fabric can be held in stock and then cut and dyed at the last minute to suit a fresh design. For a company producing some 11,000 new products per year (competing companies such as H&M and Gap produce up to 4000 products per year), and with sales of €5bn in 2004, its close relationship to suppliers makes life a lot easier. Zara has started to outsource some of its simpler, less high-fashion garments to low-cost producing countries, such as China, but it is questionable just how far this can be done while maintaining the flexibility and responsiveness.

Zara and its customers are happy to operate on a 'when it's gone, it's gone' philosophy, so that designs are produced in small batches, and stock-outs in stores are filled with a new product rather than more of the same. This gives designs a scarcity value that customers are prepared to pay for, and keeps customers coming back to the stores regularly with a strong sense of excitement and anticipation to see what's new. The founder of Zara, Amancio Ortega, has been quoted as saying that the key to successful retailing is to 'keep five fingers on the factory and five fingers on the customer' (as quoted by Saini, 2005) and that certainly seems to be at the core of Zara's operations. There's a strong communications link between the shop floor and the designers so that they can react quickly to what customers are buying and what they say they want. As well as this bottom-up approach, designers also gain inspiration from the catwalk fashion shows, and much of the success of chains like Zara is down to their ability to produce affordable mass-market versions of the latest designer couture before designers have even got the full-priced originals into their own stores (Carruthers, 2003; *The Economist*, 2005; Saini, 2005).

Joint demand

It is also important to note that B2B is often joint demand. That is, it is often closely linked with demand for other B2B products. For example, demand for casings for computers is linked with the availability of disk drives. If there are problems or delays with the supply of disk drives, then the firm assembling the computer might have to stop buying casings temporarily. This emphasises that there is often a need to plan and coordinate production schedules between the buyer and a number of suppliers, not just one.

Inelastic demand

Elasticity of demand refers to the extent to which the quantity of a product demanded changes when its price changes. Elastic demand, therefore, means that there is a great deal of price sensitivity in the market. A small increase in price will lead to a relatively large decrease in demand. Conversely, inelastic demand means that an increase in price will make no difference to the quantity demanded.

It's dark, it's raining, you've a flat tyre and you're 20 km from the nearest motorway exit

If you have ever had a flat tyre on a motorway you will know what a nuisance it is, especially if the spare tyre is also flat! Michelin, the French multinational tyre maker, wants to make flat tyres a thing of the past but the problem it faces is convincing car manufacturers. Michelin has developed a tyre that can still be run while deflated. One of its designs, the Pax system, has an inner plastic ring and a new method of attaching tyre rubber to the wheel frame which means it can be used on larger vehicles. So the Audi 8, for example, with the Pax system can travel at 55 mph on a fully deflated tyre. Audi found that the Pax wheel retained agility and passenger comfort, thus enabling the driver to get home without changing the wheel. Although launched in the late 1990s, it has only been adopted on some car models such as the Audi and the Rolls Royce Phaeton as standard. Michelin found it especially difficult to penetrate the Japanese car manufacturers and it wasn't until 2004 that was it adopted by Honda. Nissan was soon expected to follow.

Goodyear has launched a similar tyre, which uses RunOnFlat tyre technology and can be run for 80 km at 80 kph. Like Michelin, Goodyear has been working hard to get the new tyre system adopted by car manufacturers, and a number of them, such as BMW, Ferrari, Land Rover, Maserati, Mercedes and Mini

Goodyear RunOnFlat tyres are constructed with special reinforced sidewall inserts that use new compound technology. The increased stiffness means the tyre can bear the weight of the whole vehicle, even if totally deflated.

Source: © Goodyear Dunlop Tyres Europe B.V. http://eu.goodyear.com

(among others), offer it as either standard or optional on some of their models. From spring 2005, it was fitted as standard on the BMW 3-series.

On the face of it, the new tyres are great for drivers, as they spell an end to those miserable episodes of roadside tyre changing, and they're great for car manufacturers as the need to include a spare tyre takes up space and adds to costs. The problem for manufacturers, however, is that it is not just a case of fitting new tyres. The adoption requires joint development as it must work with a tyre monitoring system built into the car with a dashboard warning so that drivers actually know that they have a flat tyre and can adjust

their driving accordingly. However useful the tyre, Michelin and Goodyear cannot just sell it straight to tyre retailers, as without the accompanying tyre pressure monitoring system there is the danger that drivers will have accidents with a less stable, albeit functional, flat tyre. Perhaps the manufacturers will be encouraged by Goodyear's own market research that suggests that 84 per cent of drivers would prefer to have this type of tyre technology offered as an option with their new vehicle than things like satellite navigation systems or rear parking assistance systems, and that interest and demand for these tyres is spread across drivers of all kinds of cars, not just the high performance expensive models. Interestingly, in summer 2005, Goodyear was using television advertising to generate awareness and understanding of its RunOnFlat brand concept.

Technology continues to move on, however, and both Goodyear and Michelin work closely with the car manufacturers. The airless tyre is being developed to last as long as the vehicle, which is bad news for the tyre retailers. The Active Wheel project is also being developed by Michelin. This is a conventional tyre with active electric suspension, small disc brakes and electric motor in the rim to assist tracking and braking. Such cars could switch from front to rear to four-wheel drive as required and this innovation even opens up the possibility of eliminating conventional transmission systems. Talk about reinventing the wheel!

Sources: Carty (2004); Mound (2002); Stewart (2005); http://eu.goodyear.com; http://www.michelin.co.uk.

A car battery, for instance, is just one component of a car. A fall in the price of batteries is not going to have an impact on the quantity of cars demanded, and the car manufacturer will demand neither more nor fewer batteries than before the price change.

■ Structure of demand

One of the characteristics of consumer markets is that for the most part they comprise many potential buyers spread over a wide geographic area, that is, they are diffuse, mass markets. Think of the market for fast food, for example, which McDonald's has shown to have world-wide appeal to many millions of customers. B2B markets, in contrast, differ in both respects.

Industrial concentration

B2B markets tend to have a small number of easily identifiable customers, so that it is relatively easy to define who is or is not a potential customer. McDonald's can persuade non-customers to try its product and become customers; in that sense, the boundaries of the market are fuzzy and malleable, whereas a manufacturer of kilns to the brick and roofing tile industry would have problems in trying to extend its customer base beyond very specific types of customer.

Considerable knowledge, experience and trust can build up between buyers and suppliers. Where there is a finite number of known customers, most organisations in the trade know what the others are doing, and although negotiations may be private, the outcomes are very public.

Geographic concentration

Some industries have a strong geographic bias. Such geographic concentration might develop because of resource availability (both raw materials and labour), available infrastructure or national and EU government incentives. Traditionally, heavy industry and large mass producers, such as shipbuilders, the coal and steel industries and the motor industry, have acted as catalysts for the development of a range of allied suppliers. More recently, airports and sea-ports have given impetus to organisations concerned with freight storage, movement, insurance and other related services.

■ Buying process complexity

Consumers purchase primarily for themselves and their families. For the most part, these are relatively low-risk, low-involvement decisions that are made quickly, although there may be some economic and psychological influences affecting or constraining them. In contrast, B2B purchasers are always buying on behalf of other people (i.e. the organisation), which implies certain differences from the consumer situation. These differences give rise to much more complexity in the buying process, and the marketer must appreciate them when designing strategies for encouraging trial and reordering. The various dimensions of complexity are as follows.

B2B purchasing policy

Certain systems and procedures for purchasing are likely to be imposed on the B2B buyer. There may be guidelines on favoured suppliers, or rules on single/multiple sourcing or on the number of quotes required for comparison before a decision can be sanctioned. Further restraints might also be imposed relating to how much an individual is allowed to spend under particular budget headings on behalf of the organisation before a second or more senior signature is required.

In addition to the formal requirements associated with purchasing, guidelines are often produced on ethical codes of practice. These do not just cover the obvious concerns of remaining within the law and not abusing authority for personal gain, but also address issues such as confidentiality, business gifts and hospitality, fair competition and the declaration of vested interests.

Professional purchasing

The risk and accountability aspects of B2B purchasing mean that it needs to be done professionally. Much negotiation is required where complex customised technical products are concerned and, even for small components used in manufacturing, defining the terms of supply so that they are consistent and compatible with production requirements (for example performance specification, delivery schedules and quality standards) is a significant job. Most consumer purchasing does not involve so great a degree of flexibility: the product is standard and on the shop shelf, with clearly defined price, usage and function; take it or leave it.

eg BA decided to use an e-auction to help reduce its European public relations spend by 25 per cent. Originally, BA worked with three PR agencies across Europe but cut this to two agencies working on a three-year basis rather than on an annual rolling contract. The auction lasted two hours compared with the five days it would have normally taken by traditional methods, but due to the loss of face-to-face contact, BA was very careful to ensure that the specifications for the contract were very tightly defined in the first place. Using e-auctions is part of the strategy employed by BA to reduce its procurement bill by over 7.5 per cent. On a turnover of £8bn and a procurement expenditure budget of £4bn, every saving matters. In addition, the number of suppliers has been cut from 14,000 to 2000, streamlining costs and helping the procurement function to make a direct contribution to BA's profitability (Arminas, 2005).

Group decision-making

The need for full information, adherence to procedures and accountability tends to lead towards groups rather than individuals being responsible for purchasing decisions (Johnson and Bonoma, 1981). While there are group influences in consumer buying, for example the family unit, they are likely to be less formally constituted than in the B2B purchasing situation. It is rare, other than in the smallest organisations or for the most minor purchases, to find individuals given absolute autonomy in organisational spending.

Purchase significance

The complexity of the process is also dictated by the importance of the purchase and the level of experience the organisation has of that buying situation (Robinson *et al.*, 1967).

For instance, in the case of a routine re-buy, the organisation has bought this product before and has already established suppliers. These products may be relatively low-risk, frequently purchased, inexpensive supplies such as office stationery or utilities (water, electricity, gas, etc.). The decision-making process here is likely to involve very few people and be more a matter of paperwork than anything else. Increasingly, these types of purchase form part of computer-based automatic reordering systems from approved suppliers. A blanket contract may cover a specific period and a schedule of deliveries over that time is agreed. Bearings for the car and electrical motor industries are sold in this way. The schedule may be regarded as definite and binding for one month ahead, for example, but as provisional for the following three months. Precise dates and quantities can then be adjusted and agreed month by month nearer the time. Increasingly, with JIT systems, schedules may even be day or hour specific!

A modified re-buy implies that there is some experience of buying this product, but there is also a need to review current practice. Perhaps there have been significant technological developments since the organisation last purchased this item, or a feeling that the current supplier is not the best, or a desire to renegotiate the parameters of the purchase. An example of this is the purchase of a fleet of cars, where new models and price changes make review necessary, as does the fierce competition between suppliers who will therefore be prepared to negotiate hard for the business. The decision-making here will be a longer, more formal and involved process, but with the benefit of drawing on past experience.

New task purchasing is the most complex category. The organisation has no previous experience of this kind of purchase, and therefore needs a great deal of information and wide participation in the process, especially where it involves a high-risk or high-cost product. One example of this might be the sourcing of raw materials for a completely new product. This represents a big opportunity for a supplier, as it could lead to regular future business (i.e. routine or modified re-buys). It is a big decision for the purchaser who will want to take the time and effort to make sure it is the right one. Another situation, which happens less frequently in an organisation's life, is the commissioning of new plant or buildings. This too involves a detailed, many-faceted decision-making process with wide involvement from both internal members of staff and external consultants, and high levels of negotiation.

Laws and regulations

As we saw in Chapter 2, regulations affect all areas of business, but in B2B markets, some regulations specifically influence the sourcing of products and services. An obvious example would be the sourcing of goods from nations under various international trade embargoes, such as Iraq in the 1990s. More specifically, governments may seek to regulate sourcing within certain industrial sectors, such as utilities.

The buying decision-making process

It is just as important for marketers to understand the processes that make up the buying decision in B2B markets as it is in consumer markets. The formulation of marketing strategies that will succeed in implementation depends on this understanding. The processes involved are similar to those presented in the model of consumer decision-making described earlier, in that information search, analysis, choice and post-purchase evaluation also exist here, but the interaction of human and organisational elements makes the B2B model more complex.

There are many models of organisational decision-making behaviour, with different levels of detail, for example Sheth (1973), Webster and Wind (1972) and Robinson *et al.* (1967). How the model is formulated depends on the type of organisations and products involved; the level of their experience in purchasing; organisational purchasing policies; the individuals involved; and the formal and informal influences on marketing. Figure 3.6 shows two models of organisational decision-making and, on the basis of these, the following subsections discuss the constituent stages.

■ Precipitation

Clearly, the start of the process has to be the realisation that there is a need, a problem that a purchase can solve. The stimulation could be internal and entirely routine: it is the time of year to renew the photocopier maintenance contract. It could be a planned new buy precipitated, for example, by the implementation of expansion plans or the imminent production of a new product. It could also be something more sudden and dramatic than that, such as the failure of a piece of plant or machinery, or a lack of stock.

External influences can also stimulate a need. If the competition has invested in new technology, then other organisations will have to consider their response. Attending trade exhibitions, talking to visiting sales representatives or reading the trade press might also generate awareness of opportunities, whether based on new technology, cost reduction or quality improvements, which would stimulate the buying process.

Changes in the wider business environment can also trigger a need. The privatisation of electricity supply in the UK created a competitive market for supplying large industrial users. Organisations such as Ford, Tesco and Abbey National have appointed energy buyers with responsibility for undertaking a modified re-buy review of the electricity supply market. The energy buyers ensure that what was always considered a routine repurchase in the past can now be bought with the most advantageous long-term supply contracts from the most appropriate supplier. Thus changes in the energy environment have precipitated changes in purchasing decisions and processes.

Not all needs can or will be fulfilled and it is possible for the decision-making process to stop here, or be postponed until the organisational or environmental conditions are better. Nevertheless, some opportunities will be followed through and these move on to the next stage, product specification.

Figure 3.6 Models of organisational buying decision-making

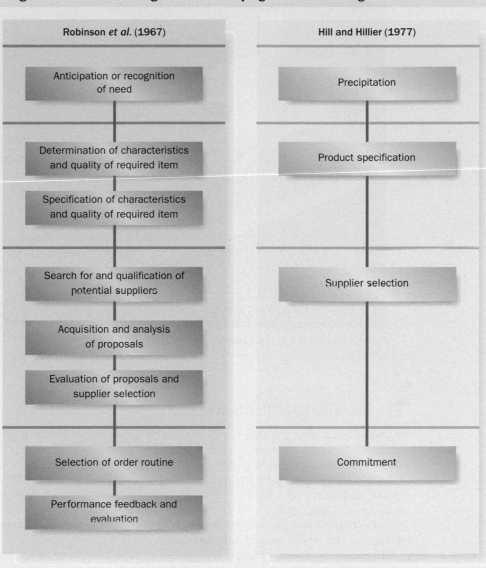

When there is a disaster at sea involving a significant oil spillage, there's usually an accompanying PR spillage too and the critical attention of the media and various 'green' groups turn to the site. It is very much in the interests of the company responsible and the relevant authorities to ensure a rapid clean-up that minimises the impact of the spillage on marine life, birds and beaches. Aker Yards (ex Alstom Marine) has been working on this problem and has developed a troubleshooting trimaran called the Oil Sea Harvester. It can operate in extreme conditions and travel quickly to a disaster zone. Through its innovative design and its equipment, it can work its way through the zone, stabilising the sea surface and collecting up to 6000 tonnes of oil while spreading a dispersant to break up any remaining pollutant into harmless droplets (**http://www.akeryards.com** or **http://osh-project.org**).

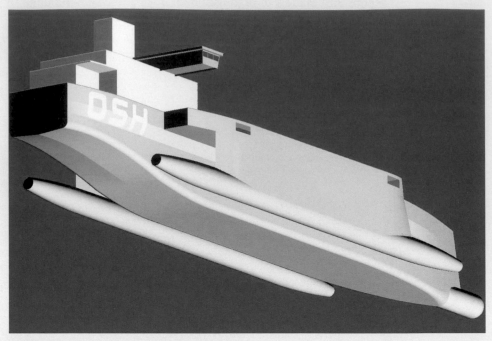

Artist's impression of the Alstom oil harvester.

Source: Aker Yards

Product specification

Unlike a consumer, for whom half the fun of shopping is often not quite knowing exactly what is wanted, an organisation must determine in some detail precisely what is required, and the greater the strategic significance of the purchase, the more true this is. Think about buying a component to be incorporated into another end product. The physical characteristics of that component must be specified, in terms of its function, its design, expected quality and performance levels, its relationship and compatibility with other components, but there are also the less tangible but no less important considerations of quantity required, delivery schedules and service backup, among others.

These specifications will need the combined expertise of engineers, production managers, purchasing specialists and marketers (representing the interests of the end customer), balancing ideals against cost and practicality. Even external consultants and suppliers could be involved in particularly complex situations. In the first instance, a general specification will be issued to potential suppliers, but a more detailed one would follow later, perhaps after a shortlist of two or three suppliers has been drawn up.

It is also worthwhile at this stage to define the criteria or priorities for choice. It may not necessarily be cost. If a machine has suddenly broken down, then speed of delivery and installation may be of the essence. In the case of new technology, the choice may hinge on compatibility with existing facilities, the future prospects for upgrading it or the service support offered.

Supplier selection

The next stage involves the search for a suitable supplier who can best meet all the specified criteria. Sometimes, the inclination to search for potential suppliers can be quite low, and the purchasing department will keep files on who can do what. If existing suppliers can do the job, then they are likely to be favoured. On other occasions, it may be necessary for buyers to be proactive by openly seeking new suppliers and encouraging quotations from those who could meet their requirements. Nevertheless, there is often a bias towards existing suppliers who are known and trusted.

Much depends, of course, on the nature of the purchasing task. A low-risk, frequent purchase might not warrant that kind of search effort, and the existing supplier might simply be asked to tender a price for resupply. One or two other known suppliers might also be requested to quote for the job, just as a checking procedure to make sure that the existing supplier is not taking advantage of the established relationship.

In a high-risk, infrequent purchase (i.e. the new task situation), a more serious, lengthy selection procedure is likely to be implemented. There will be complex discussion, negotiation, revision and reiteration at a high level with a number of potential suppliers before a final decision is made. Additional problems may be caused where different suppliers will be expected to work closely together, such as on the building of a new manufacturing plant, for instance. Their compatibility with each other, their reliability and their ability to complete their part within strict time limits dictated by the overall project schedule may all affect the decision-making.

■ Commitment

The decision has been made, the contract signed, the order and delivery schedules set. The process does not, however, end here. The situation has to be monitored as it unfolds, in case there are problems with the supplier. Is the supplier fulfilling promises? Is the purchased item living up to expectations? Are deliveries turning up on time?

Some buyers adopt formal appraisal procedures for their suppliers, covering key elements of performance. The results of this appraisal will be discussed with the supplier concerned in the interests of improving their performance and allowing the existing buyer–seller relationship to be maintained.

In concluding this discussion of the buying process as a whole, we can say that the Hill and Hillier (1977) model has provided a useful framework for discussing the complexities and influences on B2B buying. It is difficult, however, to generalise about such a process, especially where technical and commercial complexity exists. Stages may be compressed or merge into each other, depending on circumstances; the process may end at any stage; there may have to be reiteration: for example if negotiations with a chosen supplier break down at a late stage the search process may have to begin again.

The buying centre

A potential supplier attempting to gain an order from a purchasing firm needs to know just who is involved in the decision-making process, at what point in the process each person is most influential and how they all interact with each other. Then, the supplier's marketers can deal most effectively with the situation, utilising both the group and individual dynamics to the best of their advantage, for example tailoring specific communication packages to appeal at the right time to the right people, and getting a range of feedback from within the purchasing organisation to allow a comprehensive product offering to be designed.

Clearly, the amount of time and effort the supplier is prepared to devote to this will vary with the importance and complexity of the order. A routine re-buy may consist of a telephone conversation between two individuals to confirm the availability of the product and the fine detail of the transaction in terms of exact price and delivery. A new task situation, however, with the promise of either a large contract or substantial future business, provides much more scope and incentive for the supplier to research and influence the buying decision.

This section, therefore, looks at the different roles that can be played by individuals within the buying organisation, and how they interact to form a buying centre or decision-making unit (DMU).

Table 3.4 compares buying centres in consumer and B2B markets, indicating the membership, the roles they play and the functional areas that may be involved.

■ *Users*: Users are the people who will use the end product, for example an operator who will use production machinery, or a secretary who will use a word processor. These people may

Table 3.4 Comparison of DMUs in consumer and B2B markets

Consumer	Example	B2B	Example
Initiator	Child pesters parents for a new bike.	User	Machine breaks down; the operator reports it, thus initiating the process. May also be asked to help with specs for replacement.
Influencer	Mother thinks about it and says, 'Well, perhaps he has grown out of the old one.'	Influencer	User may influence; may also involve R&D staff, accountants, suppliers, sales reps, external consultants.
Decider	Father agrees and they all go to Toys 'Я' Us where the final decision is the child's, but under restraints imposed by parents' credit card limit.	Decider	May be a senior manager with either an active or a passive role in the whole process. May also be the buyer and/or influencer.
Purchaser	Parents pay the bill.	Buyer	Handles the search for and negotiations with suppliers.
User	The child.	Gatekeeper	Secretarial staff preventing influencers reaching the decision-maker; R&D staff withholding information.

trigger the purchasing process through reporting a need, and may also be consulted in setting the specifications for whatever is to be bought.

■ *Influencers*: Influencers can affect the outcome of the decision-making process through their influence on others. Influence could stem formally from expertise, for example the advice of an accountant on the return on investment from a piece of capital machinery or that of an engineer on a supplier's technical capability, or it could be an informal, personal influence. Their prime role is in specification, information gathering and assessment.

■ *Deciders*: Deciders have the formal or informal authority to make the decision. For routine re-buys, this may be the purchasing officer or someone in a functional role, but organisational structures may dictate that the final decision rests with top management, who are fed information and recommendations from below. The decider's role and level of involvement, therefore, will vary widely, depending on individual circumstances.

■ *Buyers*: Buyers have the authority to select and negotiate with suppliers. Buyers with different levels of seniority may exist to handle different types of transaction, for example a routine re-buy could be handled by a relatively junior clerical worker, whereas the high-cost, high-risk new buy might require a senior purchasing manager of many years' experience. Where devolved budgeting exists, the buyer may not belong to a formal purchasing department at all, but be someone who also has a functional role such as R&D or marketing.

■ *Gatekeepers*: Gatekeepers have some control over the decision-making process, in that they can control the flow of information by denying access to key members of the buying centre. For example, a secretary or purchasing manager may prevent a sales representative from talking directly to an executive, or intercept brochures and mailshots and throw them in the wastepaper basket before they reach the decision-maker. Technical staff can also act as gatekeepers in the way in which they choose to gather, present and interpret information to other members of the buying centre.

Bear in mind that the buying centre is not necessarily a fixed entity from transaction to transaction or even within a single transaction. It can be fluid and dynamic, evolving to meet the changing demands of the unfolding situation; it can be either formally constituted (for a major capital project, for instance) or loosely informal (a chance chat over coffee in the canteen between the purchasing manager and an R&D scientist); it can consist of two or three or many people. In other words, it is what it needs to be to do the job in hand.

When analysing the make-up of the buying centre, we should look not only at the allocation of roles between the different functional areas of the organisation, but also at the seniority of the members. Higher expenditure levels or purchases that have a critical impact on the organisation may involve much more senior management. Of course, input from the lower levels of the hierarchy will help to shape the decision, but the eventual authority may rest at board level. Thus, for example, a bank's decision to introduce a new account control system may be taken at a very senior level.

Also, an individual's contribution to it may not be limited to one role. In a small business, the owner/manager may be influencer and buyer as well as decider. Similarly, in a larger organisation, where routine re-buys are concerned, the buyer may also be the decider, with very little call for influencers. Whatever the structure, however fluid the buying centre is, it is still important for the aspiring supplier to attempt to identify the pattern within the target organisation in order to create effective communication links.

Having thus established decision-making structures, the next step is to examine the criteria applied during the process.

Buying criteria

In the previous sections, the emphasis in terms of decision-making has largely been on rational, functionally oriented criteria. These task-related or economic criteria are certainly important and reinforce the view of the organisation as a rational thinking entity. It is dangerous, however, to fall into the trap of forgetting that behind every job title lurks an individual whose motives and goals are not necessarily geared towards the greater good of the organisation. Such motives and goals may not form a direct, formally recognised part of the decision-making process, but nevertheless, they can certainly cause friction and influence the outcomes of it.

Economic influences

As has already been stressed, it is not always a matter of finding the lowest priced supplier. If the purchasing organisation can make the best use of increased reliability, superior performance, better customer service and other technical or logistical supports from its suppliers, then it can offer a better package to its own customers, with the rewards that brings. This route can also result in lower total costs, since it reduces production delays due to substandard components or delivery failures, and also improves the quality consistency of the purchaser's own end product, thus reducing the costs of handling complaints and replacing goods.

The main criteria are:

- *Appropriate prices*: The appropriate price is not necessarily the lowest, but one representing good value for money taking into account the whole service package on offer.
- *Product specification*: Product specification involves finding the right product to meet the purchaser's specified needs, neither more nor less. There are, of course, various trade-offs between specification and price. The main point is the closeness of the match and the certainty that it will be maintained throughout the order cycle.
- *Quality consistency*: It is important to find a supplier with adequate quality controls to minimise defects so that the purchaser can use the product with confidence. This is especially true for JIT systems, where there is little room for failure.
- *Supply reliability and continuity*: The purchaser needs to be sure that adequate supplies of the product will be available as and when needed.
- *Customer service*: Buyers require reassurance that the supplier is prepared to take responsibility for its product by providing fast and flexible backup service in case of problems.

■ Non-economic influences

Powers (1991) summarises non-economic influences under four main headings:

- *Prestige*: Organisations, or more specifically the individuals who make up organisations, hanker after 'status'. So, for example, they may be prepared to spend a little more when the office accommodation is refurbished on better-quality furnishings, decor and facilities to impress, instil confidence or even intimidate visitors to the site.
- *Career security*: Few people involved in the decision-making process are truly objective about it; at the back of the mind there is always the question, 'What does this mean for my job?' First, there is the risk element. A problem may have two alternative solutions, one which is safe, predictable and unspectacular, and one which is high risk, but promises a high return. If the high-risk decision is made and it all goes wrong, what are the consequences? The individual may not want to be associated with such an outcome and thus will push for the safe route. Second, there is the awareness of how others are judging the individual's behaviour in the decision-making process: 'Am I prepared to go against the main body of opinion on a particular issue that I feel strongly about or will that brand me as a trouble-maker and jeopardise my promotion prospects?'
- *Friendship and social needs*: Needs such as friendship can be dangerous and can sometimes stray very close to ethical boundaries. It is necessary, however, to value trust, confidence and respect built on a personal level between individuals in the buying and selling organisations. It does help to reduce the perceived risk of the buyer–seller relationship.
- *Other personal needs*: The individual's own personality and profile, such as demographic characteristics, attitudes and beliefs, coupled with factors like self-confidence and communication skills, can all shape the extent to which that individual is allowed to participate in and influence the outcome of the decision-making process.

A further dimension of non-economic forces is trust. Trust is the belief that another organisation will act in such a way that the outcomes will be beneficial to both parties and that it will not act in such a way as to bring about negative effects (Anderson and Narus, 1986). Trust can be built at an organisational level, but can also stem from a series of personal relationships between employees.

Chapter summary

This chapter has centred on consumer and B2B buying behaviour, in terms of both the processes through which potential buyers pass in deciding whether to make a purchase and which product to choose, and the factors that influence the decision-making itself.

- The consumer decision-making process was presented as a number of stages: problem recognition, information search, information evaluation, decision and, finally, post-purchase evaluation.

- The length of time taken over the process as a whole or over individual stages will vary according to the type of product purchased and the particular consumer concerned. An experienced buyer with past knowledge of the market making a low-risk, low-priced routine purchase will pass through the decision-making process very quickly, almost without realising that it has happened. This is a routine problem-solving situation. In contrast, a nervous buyer, lacking knowledge but facing the purchase of a one-off, high-risk, expensive purchase, will prolong the process and consciously seek and analyse information to aid the decision. This is extended problem solving.

- Decision-making is influenced by many factors apart from the type of purchase. Some of these factors are external to the consumer, such as social, economic, legal and technological issues existing within the wider environment. Closer to home, the consumer influences the decision-making process through psychological factors. The type of personality involved; the individual's perceptions of the world and ability to interpret information; the ability to retain and learn from both experience and marketing communication; the driving motivations behind behaviour; and finally the individual's attitudes and beliefs all shape their responses to the marketing offering and ultimately their acceptance or rejection of it. In addition to that, the individual's choices and behaviour are affected by sociocultural influences defined by the groups to which the individual either belongs or wishes to belong. Social class as traditionally defined is of limited help to the marketer, but cultural or subcultural groups provide clearly differentiated groups of potential customers. Other membership groups, formed through work, hobbies and leisure pursuits, provide the individual with norms that act as reference points to aid decision-making. Similarly, aspirations fuel people's needs and wants and marketers can attract customers through reflecting those dreams and promising products that can help fulfill them or at least visibly associate the individual with the aspirant group for a while. One of the strongest group influences comes from the family, affecting decisions on what is purchased, how that decision is made and how the individual feels about that purchase.

■ B2B marketing is about exchanges between organisations, whether they are commercial enterprises, government bodies or institutions. B2B markets have a number of distinct characteristics, including the nature of demand (derived, joint and inelastic), the structure of demand (concentrated in size and in geography), the complexity of the buying process and the risks inherent in it. The decision-making process that B2B purchasers go through has elements in common with consumer decision-making, but is likely to be formalised, to take longer and to involve more people. B2B buying is likely to involve higher value, less frequently placed orders for products that are more likely to be customised than in consumer markets. Staff with various functional backgrounds, such as purchasing, marketing, accounting, engineering, production and R&D, will be involved in the process and form a buying centre. The membership of the buying centre, the roles played and who takes the lead may vary from transaction to transaction or even from stage to stage within a single process.

■ The stages in the decision-making process include precipitation, product specification, supplier selection, and commitment to a long-term relationship. The decision-making process is affected not only by rational, measurable economic criteria (price, specification, quality, service, etc.), but also by non-economic influences (prestige, security, social needs, personality) emanating from the individuals involved.

Questions for review and discussion

3.1 Why is *post-purchase evaluation* important for:
(a) the consumer; and
(b) the marketer?

3.2 How do *perception*, *learning* and *attitudes* affect consumer decision-making, and how can the marketer influence these processes?

3.3 Define the three main types of *reference group*. Within each type, think of examples that relate to you as a consumer, and analyse how this might affect your own buying behaviour.

3.4 What are the main differences between *B2B* and *consumer buying behaviour*?

3.5 Define the main *economic* and *non-economic* influences on B2B decision-making.

3.6 How might the *roles* undertaken by various members of a two-parent family vary between the buying decisions for:
(a) a house;
(b) something for tonight's dinner; and
(c) a birthday present for a 10-year-old child?

How would your answer change if it was a one-parent family?

case study 3

'Vend me your leers'

It's an interesting question for debate: does marketing encourage cultural change or does it just reflect what's going on in society? The recent history of the market for sex toys perhaps suggests that there is a more complex synergy going on. In the early 1990s, against a backdrop of increasingly liberal attitudes towards sex, and an increasing proportion of independently minded working women, Jacqueline Gold took over as Chief Executive of Ann Summers, the UK's largest chain of sex shops. At that time, sex shops were mainly dimly lit, seedy backstreet stores catering for male fantasies. Jacqueline

Gold's idea was to move away from that and target the female consumer who wouldn't dream of going into a store like that. One of her first moves was to introduce party-based selling. A group of women are invited to someone's house and the merchandise is explained, displayed and passed around in a spirit of fun, playfulness and girly giggles. The women tend to encourage each other to be more daring, buy things that they could not imagine asking for in a store and, perhaps subconsciously, to redefine their perception of what's 'normal' or 'acceptable'. Some 4000 Ann Summers parties now take place in the UK every week. In parallel with this, Ann Summers' chain of 'bricks and mortar' stores is also expanding (currently there are over 120 stores in the UK). The stores are being revamped and brought out of the back streets to make them sexier (in a witty, playful way) and more female-friendly.

Following further this idea of making these products accessible, and perhaps thinking of those women who either can't wait for the next party opportunity or are too embarrassed to go to that sort of party or a retail store, Ann Summers successfully went into online retailing in 1999. The online presence is not only important for making sales, it is also a vital means of communication for an industry sector whose ability to use more traditional mainstream media is highly constrained in terms of both media and content. The launch in 2005 of Ann Summers' own independent WAP mobile internet site further enhances the company's ability to build relationships with customers and communicate discreetly with them.

Ann Summers' turnover in 2003 broke the £100m barrier, and by 2004 it had hit £130m, but perhaps the brand's biggest achievement (although some might argue that it is detrimental rather than beneficial) has been its contribution to legitimising the sex toy market for the benefit of many very happy women. Eighty per cent of Ann Summers' customers are women. There's no doubt too that popular culture, such as television series *Sex and the City*, has also done a lot to liberalise young women's attitudes to sex and thus to legitimise this market and the companies that operate within it. Featuring the Rampant Rabbit (we hesitate to call it product placement) in *Sex and the City* did wonders for sales of vibrators. A survey (as quoted by Godson, 2004) suggests that one-third of women in the UK owns a vibrator and one-fifth owns more than three sex toys, although as Godson goes on to comment, 'It is difficult to establish whether the enormous volume of internet sex toy shopping demonstrates how much women have always wanted sex toys, or whether internet accessibility has created a demand that didn't exist previously'.

Either way, others have sensed a profitable opportunity in sensuality and sexuality, with retailers such as Coco de Mer and Myla offering a more upmarket, design-led approach than Ann Summers. For those who are still unconvinced about this sort of shopping, Tabooboo, set up in 2003, has taken a slightly different approach to retailing from the stand-alone boutique. What could be more respectable and upmarket than a sex toys and accessories concession area within Selfridges among the other designer labels such as Miu Miu? Tabooboo also sells online and in addition, has set up around 60 vibrant pink sex toy vending machines in bars, clubs and hotels. Alan Lucas, the founder of Tabooboo, takes the view that 'People are put off sex toys because they associate them with porn. But if you take away the porn, there is no problem' (as quoted by Small, 2005). Targeting design-conscious women in their twenties, Tabooboo sees itself as cheeky and playful and about 'get stuck-in, down-to-earth fun' and is clearly doing something right as an entry in its visitor's book in Selfridges testifies: 'I have bought every single Tabooboo product and now I never need to leave the house'.

Foreign operators too see a lucrative market developing in the UK. The US chain Hustler Hollywood, for example, spent £8m on its first two UK stores in Birmingham and Nottingham, and had budgeted some £25m more for another six stores to follow. With an open frontage, a coffee shop with leather sofas, and a strong emphasis on lingerie in the merchandise mix, there's nothing that is embarrassing or seedy to deter female potential customers. Meanwhile, both Ann Summers and Tabooboo are themselves expanding into foreign markets. Ann Summers is targeting Spain and even thinking about Russia and China, while Tabooboo is considering the US, the Netherlands and Italy. Italy is seen as particularly attractive by Tabooboo, as according to Alan Lucas, 'The younger generation does not have any baggage around this subject, and while it is a design-literate country, there is no sophisticated shop environment for these products' (as quoted by Dowdy, 2004).

Back in the UK, it's not all about specialist niche retailers. These products are becoming so much a part of the cultural mainstream, and the profit margins on them are so high, that established high street names are also toying with the idea of cashing in on them. But maybe it's still a bit too early for that. When Boots, the high street pharmacy chain, announced in autumn 2004 that it was considering launching a range of sex toys, there was a largely negative flurry of comment in the mass media. In some ways, it is a natural extension of Boots' existing health and beauty merchandise and as Boots' own spokesman said, 'In reality, this is

Taking sex toys, corsets and whips out of the dark and into the pink, Tabooboo concession fuses sex, fashion and forward-thinking design.

Source: © Tabooboo Ltd http://www.tabooboo.co.uk

becoming a much more common thing on the high street. A healthy sex life is considered to be everybody's right these days' (as quoted by Hall, 2004). Many felt, however, that this was just too much for the more clinical atmosphere of a family store, and Jacqueline Gold of Ann Summers agreed. Her view is that 'We have more than 30 years' history of building a business with our customers to make them feel comfortable about coming into our stores and buying lingerie and sex toys. I can't see anyone going into Boots and buying their haemorrhoid cream and a sex toy' (as quoted by Hall, 2004). In the event, Boots took heed of the public reaction and dropped its plans. So, it appears that while the British public's attitudes have been revolutionised, there are still some boundaries that it is not yet ready to cross, and the marketers are not going to risk trying to shift them.

Sources: Dowdy (2004); Godson (2004); Hall (2004); *In-Store* (2005); *Marketing* (2005); *New Media Age* (2005a, 2005b); Small (2005).

Questions

1 Summarise the factors within the marketing environment that are affecting the development of this market.

2 Give an overview of how the buying decision-making process might work for purchasing an item in an Ann Summers shop. How might that process differ if the consumer is buying the same item at an Ann Summers party at a friend's home?

3 Was Boots right to decide to drop its plans to enter this market? Why?

4 What issues are likely to have affected both Ann Summers and Tabooboo in deciding to internationalise and in deciding which countries to enter?

References for chapter 3

Anderson, J.C. and Narus, J.A. (1986), 'Towards a Better Understanding of Distribution Channel Working Relationships', in K. Backhaus and D. Wilson (eds), *Industrial Marketing: A German–American Perspective*, Springer-Verlag.

Arminas, D. (2005), 'BA Goes Online to Net 25% Saving on PR Contracts', *Supply Management*, 26 May, p. 8.

Brand Strategy (2003), 'Kids Need to Eat their Greens', *Brand Strategy*, October, p. 26.

Brand Strategy (2004), 'Happy Families', *Brand Strategy*, October, p. 36.

Broadbent, G. (2001), 'Design Choice: FCUK', *Marketing*, 10 May, p. 15.

Bruce, A. (2001), 'Connex Stations Set for 40 Stores', *The Grocer*, 11 August, p. 5.

Bruner, G.C. and Pomazal, R.J. (1988), 'Problem Recognition: the Crucial First Stage of the Consumer Decision Process', *Journal of Consumer Marketing*, 5 (1), pp. 53–63.

Buss, D. (2004), 'Can Harley Ride the New Wave?', *Brandweek*, 25 October, pp. 20–2.

Carruthers, R. (2003), 'Rapid Response Retail', *Marketing*, 3 April, pp. 20–1.

Carty, S. (2004), 'Michelin Sets Pitch for New Technology', *Wall Street Journal*, 29 September, p. 1.

Chisnall, P.M. (1985), *Marketing: A Behavioural Analysis*, McGraw-Hill.

Dowdy, C. (2004), 'Sex Shops Set to Move Out of UK Side Streets', *Financial Times*, 29 September, p. 1.

The Economist (2005), 'The Future of Fast Fashion: Inditex', *The Economist*, 18 June, p. 63.

Engel, J.F., Blackwell, R.D. and Miniard, P.W. (1990), *Consumer Behaviour*, Dryden.

Festinger, L. (1957), *A Theory of Cognitive Dissonance*, Stanford University Press.

Fishbein, M. (1975), 'Attitude, Attitude Change and Behaviour: a Theoretical Overview', in P. Levine (ed.), *Attitude Research Bridges the Atlantic*, Chicago: American Marketing Association.

Fleming, N. (2004), '90-second Pizza from a Vending Machine', *The Daily Telegraph*, 14 April, p. 9.

Godson, S. (2004), 'Let's Go Sex Shopping', *The Times*, 13 March, p. 6.

Grande, C. (2005), 'FCUK in Search of a New Style', *Financial Times*, 2 July, p. 2.

Grimshaw, C. (2004), 'Wotsits Defended in "Pester Power" Spat', *Marketing*, 3 June, p. 10.

The Grocer (2005), 'Baby Love's a Branded Thing', *The Grocer*, 5 February, p. 21.

Hall, J. (2004), 'The Gentrification of Sex Toys', *The Sunday Telegraph*, 21 November, p. 10.

Hauser, J. *et al.* (1993), 'How Consumers Allocate their Time when Searching for Information', *Journal of Marketing Research*, November, pp. 452–66.

Hilgard, E.R. and Marquis, D.G. (1961), *Conditioning and Learning*, Appleton Century Crofts.

Hilgard, E.R. *et al.* (1975), *Introduction to Psychology*, 6th edn, Harcourt Brace Jovanovich.

Hill, R.W. and Hillier, T.J. (1977), *Organisational Buying Behaviour*, Macmillan.

Howard, J.A. and Sheth, J.N. (1969), *The Theory of Buyer Behaviour*, Wiley.

In-Store (2003), 'Hey Big Vendor', *In-Store*, October, p. 21.

In-Store (2005), 'Ann Summers Enjoys £60mn Sales Rise', *In-Store*, 14 March, p. 19.

Johnson, W.J. and Bonoma, T.V. (1981), 'The Buying Centre: Structure and Interaction Patterns', *Journal of Marketing*, 45 (Summer), pp. 143–56.

Keller, K.L. and Staelin, R. (1987), 'Effects of Quality and Quantity of Information on Decision Effectiveness', *Journal of Consumer Research*, 14 (September), pp. 200–13.

Lightfoot, L. and Wavell, S. (1995), 'Mum's Not the Word', *Sunday Times*, 16 April.

Malkani, G. (2004), 'Industry Served Up with an Image Problem', *Financial Times*, 28 May, p. 4.

Marketing (2004), 'Almost Rich', *Marketing* (Toronto), 26 April, pp. 9–10.

Marketing (2005), 'Ann Summers to Redesign Stores', *Marketing*, 16 March, p. 3.

Marketing Week (2004), 'Marketers Must Mine the Rich Seam of Our Affluence', *Marketing Week*, 8 July, p. 32.

Maslow, A.H. (1954), *Motivation and Personality*, Harper and Row.

Matilla, A. and Wirtz, J. (2001), 'Congruency of Scent and Music as a Driver of In-store Evaluations and Behaviour', *Journal of Retailing*, 77 (2), pp. 273–89.

Mesure, S. (2005), 'Fresh Crisis Hits French Connection', *The Independent*, 2 July, p. 42.

Mound, H. (2002), 'The Smarter Czar Could Save Your Life', *Sunday Times*, 20 October, p. 6.

New Media Age (2005a), 'Adult Retailers Enjoy Limitless Possibilities by Being Online', *New Media Age*, 20 January, p. 15.

New Media Age (2005b), 'Ann Summers Launches Own Independent WAP Presence', *New Media Age*, 28 April, p. 2.

O'Connell, S. (2003), 'Parents Have Fat Chance as Pester Power Adds Up', *The Sunday Times*, 9 February, p. 17.

Powers, T.L. (1991), *Modern Business Marketing: A Strategic Planning Approach to Business and Industrial Markets*, St Paul, MN: West.

Rice, C. (1993), *Consumer Behaviour: Behavioural Aspects of Marketing*, Oxford: Butterworth-Heinemann.

Roberts, Y. (2004), 'Junk the Food Ads', *The Observer*, 2 May, p. 29.

Robinson, P.J. *et al.* (1967), *Industrial Buying and Creative Marketing*, Allyn and Bacon.

Saini, A. (2005), 'New Kids on the High Street Cut a Dash with Fast Fashions', *The Observer*, 5 June, p. 6.

Sheth, J. (1973), 'A Model of Industrial Buying Behaviour', *Journal of Marketing*, 37 (October), pp. 50–6.

Silverman, G. (2004), 'The Standard Bearer', *Financial Times*, 14 December, p. 2.

Small, J. (2005), 'Tabooboo', *Marketing*, 2 February, p. 23.

Speros, J. (2004), 'Why the Harley Brand's So Hot', *Advertising Age*, 15 March, p. 26.

Stewart, T. (2005), 'The Tyres of Tomorrow', *The Independent*, 14 June, p. 10.

Webster, F.E. and Wind, Y. (1972), *Organisational Buyer Behaviour*, Prentice-Hall.

Wells, W.D. and Gubar, R.G. (1966), 'Life Cycle Concepts in Marketing Research', *Journal of Marketing Research*, 3 (November), pp. 355–63.

Williams, K.C. (1981), *Behavioural Aspects of Marketing*, Heinemann Professional Publishing.

chapter 4

segmenting markets

learning objectives

This chapter will help you to:

1 **explain how both B2B and consumer markets can be broken down into smaller, more manageable groups of similar customers;**

2 **understand the effects on the marketing mix of pursuing specific segments;**

3 **understand the potential benefits and risks of segmentation; and**

4 **appreciate the role of segmentation in strategic marketing thinking.**

Introduction

Building on the understanding of buyer behaviour and decision-making processes outlined in Chapter 3, this chapter concerns a question that should be very close to any true marketer's heart: 'How do we define and profile our customer?' Until an answer is found, no meaningful marketing decisions of any kind can be made. It is not usually enough to define your customer as 'anyone who wants to buy our product' because this implies a product-oriented approach: the product comes first, the customer second. If marketing is everything we have claimed it to be, then the product is only a small part of a total integrated package offered to a customer. Potential customers must, therefore, be defined in terms of what they want, or will accept, in terms of price, what kind of distribution will be most convenient for them and through what communication channels they can best be reached, as well as what they want from the product itself.

Remember too that in a consumer-based society, possession of 'things' can take on a symbolic meaning. A person's possessions and consumption habits make a statement about the kind of person they are, or the kind of person they want you to think they are. The organisation that takes the trouble to understand this and produces a product that not only serves its functional purpose well, but also appears to reflect those less tangible properties of a product in the purchaser's eyes, will gain that purchaser's custom. Thus sport shoe manufacturers such as Reebok and Nike not only developed shoes for a wide range of specific sports (tennis, soccer, athletics, etc.), but also realised that a significant group of customers would never go near a sports facility and just wanted trainers as fashion statements. This meant that they served three distinctly different groups of customers: the professional/serious sports player, the amateur/casual sports player and the fashion victim. The R&D invested in state-of-the-art quality products, combined with the status connected with the first group and endorsement from leading sports icons, helped these companies to build an upmarket image that allowed them to exploit the fashion market to the full with premium-priced products. This in turn led to the expansion of product ranges to include branded sports and leisure clothing.

eg

The business traveller is an important market segment for travel industry operators, such as airlines, hotel chains and car rental companies. Although business travellers expect better service, as frequent travellers they tend to spend more money, more often. This group of customers, therefore, differs significantly from leisure- and economy-class customers. Business travellers sometimes need to book at short notice, travel to tight schedules, travel frequently and could need to change arrangements at the last minute. Airlines have adapted their service provision to meet the needs of this group. Fast check-in facilities, first- or business-class travel options and lounges, special boarding arrangements and loyalty schemes are all important for attracting these customers. Airlines also advertise specifically to the business traveller and keep their pricing competitive within the business flyer segment on competitive routes such as London–Brussels.

As time pressures become greater, the business traveller is demanding satellite airports with good connections and direct flights, better airport services and better on-board services. Those things alone are no guarantee of success, however, as Primeflight found. The price of private hire small (up to ten seats) jets opens up the possibility of targeted services from regional airports. Primeflight introduced a twice-daily non-stop service between Belfast International and Brussels. The service was direct, had fast-track check-in, access to the business lounge and first-class service for £695 return, compared with the average business-class price of about £670. The seven-seater aircraft were ideal for the loads expected. Within five months, however, flights were suspended due to, it was claimed, technical and operational hitches, although some experts argued that the aircraft's small capacity and lack of scale could not operate cost-effectively. Such setbacks have not deterred other airlines from focusing on the business traveller. Swiss International launched a Zurich to Geneva service, business class only, in a Boeing 737 with just over 50 seats that convert to beds. The price of a ticket was $2374. Lufthansa has launched three routes between Germany and the US that cost about $2245 one way and Air France has launched flights from Paris to oil-industry destinations such as Angola, Iran and Uzbekistan. Airlines with a focus on the business travel segment realise that this kind of service is limited to unusual routes with heavy business traffic and limited tourism. Often they land at smaller airports where there are no delays and the passenger can be in a taxi within fifteen minutes. All of this is in contrast to the low-cost, no-frills operators at the other end of the market forcing prices down to attract large numbers of leisure customers, and offering minimum service (Garrahan, 2004; Johnson, 2005; McGill, 2004; Sarsfield, 2004).

All this forms the basis of the concept of segmentation, first developed by Smith (1957). Segmentation can be viewed as the art of discerning and defining meaningful differences between groups of customers to form the foundations of a more focused marketing effort. The following section looks at this concept in a little more depth, while the rest of the chapter will examine how the concept can be implemented and its implications for the organisation.

The concept of segmentation

The introductory section of this chapter has presented the customer-oriented argument for the adoption of the segmentation concept. There is, however, also a practical rationale for adopting it. Mass production, mass communication, increasingly sophisticated technology and increasingly efficient global transportation have all helped in the creation of larger, more temptingly lucrative potential markets. Few organisations, however, have either the resources or the inclination to be a significant force within a loosely defined market. The sensible option, therefore, is to look more closely at the market and find ways of breaking it down into manageable parts, or groups of customers with similar characteristics, and then to concentrate effort on serving the needs of one or two groups really well, rather than trying to be all things to all people. This makes segmentation a proactive part of developing a marketing strategy and involves the application of techniques to identify these segments (Wind, 1978).

It may help you to understand this concept better if you think of an orange. It appears to be a single entity, yet when you peel off the skin you find that it is made up of a number of discrete segments, each of which happily exists within the whole. Eating an orange is much easier (and much less wasteful and messy) if you eat it systematically, segment by segment, rather than by attacking the whole fruit at once. Marketers, being creative folk, have adopted this analogy and thus refer to the separate groups of customers that make up a market as market segments.

The analogy is misleading, however, in that each segment of an orange is more or less identical in size, shape and taste, whereas in a market, segments may be very different from each other in terms of size and character. To determine these things, each segment has its own distinct profile, defined in terms of a number of criteria, referred to as *bases* or *variables*, set by the marketer. The choice of appropriate criteria for subdividing the market is very important (Moriarty and Reibstein, 1986) and thus a significant proportion of this chapter is devoted to thinking about the bases by which segments might be defined in both consumer and B2B markets. Leading on from this, there is also the question of influences that might affect an organisation's choice of segmentation variables. Then, once an organisation has defined its market segments, what is it supposed to do with the information? This too is addressed in this chapter.

B2B and consumer markets, in general, tend to be segmented differently and will, therefore, be discussed separately, beginning with B2B markets.

Segmenting B2B markets

One major feature of B2B segmentation is that it can focus on both the organisation and the individual buyers within it. Additionally, there is the need to reflect group buying, that is, the involvement of more than one person in the purchasing decision (Abratt, 1993). All of this can be compared with a family buying situation in a consumer market, but operating on a much larger scale, usually within a more formalised process.

Wind and Cardozo (1974) suggest that segmenting a B2B market can involve two stages:

1 *Identify subgroups* within the whole market that share common general characteristics. These are called macro segments and will be discussed further below.
2 *Select target segments* from within the macro segments based on differences in specific buying characteristics. These are called micro segments and are discussed at p. 116.

■ Macro segmentation bases

Macro segments are based on the characteristics of organisations and the broader purchasing context within which they operate. Defining a macro segment assumes that the organisations within it will exhibit similar patterns and needs, which will be reflected in similar buying behaviour and responses to marketing stimuli.

The bases used for macro segmentation tend to be observable or readily obtained from secondary information (i.e. published or existing sources) and can be grouped into two main categories, each of which will now be discussed.

Organisational characteristics

There are three organisational characteristics: size, location and usage rate.

1 *Size.* The size of an organisation will make a difference to the way in which it views its suppliers and goes about its purchasing. A large organisation, for instance, may well have many people involved in decision-making; its decision-making may be very complex and formalised (because of the risks and level of investment involved), and it may require special treatment in terms of service or technical cooperation. In contrast, a small organisation may operate on a more centralised decision-making structure, involving one or two people and with simpler buying routines.

eg Similar segmentation strategies are now being employed in the modernising economies of Central Europe. Corporate banking hardly existed in Poland in the 1980s, but following economic reform, the number of companies in Poland has grown from 500,000 in 1990 to over 3 million in 2001. As well as this increase in the potential corporate customer base, the banks have been privatised and many have been taken over or have gone into partnership with Western European and US banks. This has led to a much more marketing-oriented attitude within the Polish banks and has started the process of client segmentation. Small and medium-sized enterprises, defined as those with a turnover of between Zloty 5–250m (€1.26–63.3m) have been targeted, initially for savings and loans products, but increasingly with cross-selling of factoring, leasing, trade finance and investment banking. This is changing the role of the banks from being simply lenders and deposit-takers to being financial advisers, and this has far-reaching implications for the type and level of communication required by existing and new customers. The next stage of development, internet banking, is still some way off, however, because of the need to create a stronger and more secure IT infrastructure for Polish businesses (Smorszczewski, 2001).

2 *Location.* Organisations may focus their selling effort according to the geographic concentration of the industries they serve. Such specialisation is, however, slowly breaking down as the old, heavy, geographically based industries, such as shipbuilding, mining and chemical production, become less predominant. Additionally, there is the emergence of smaller more flexible manufacturers, geographically dispersed in new technology parks, industrial estates and enterprise zones. Nevertheless, there are still examples of geographic segmentation, such as that of computer hardware and software sales, or in the financial sector, which is concentrated in London, Frankfurt, Zurich and the major capitals of the world. Organisations providing certain kinds of services might also look to geographic segments. A haulage company might specialise in certain routes and thus look for customers at specific points to make collection, delivery and capacity utilisation as efficient as possible.

3 *Usage rate.* The quantity of product purchased may be a legitimate means of categorising potential customers. A purchasing organisation defined as a 'heavy user' will have different needs from a 'light user', perhaps demanding (and deserving) different treatment in terms of special delivery or prices, for example. A supplier may define a threshold point, so that when a customer's usage rate rises above it, their status changes. The customer's account may be handed over to a more senior manager and the supplier may become more flexible in terms of cooperation, pricing and relationship building. It is generally a better investment to make concessions in order to cultivate a relationship with a single heavy user than to try to attract a number of light users, as implied in Chapter 3.

Product or service application

This second group of segmentation bases acknowledges that the same good can be used in many different ways. This approach looks for customer groupings, either within specific industries as defined by standard industrial classification (SIC) codes, each with its own requirements, or by defining a specific application and grouping customers around that.

The SIC code may help to identify sectors with a greater propensity to use particular products for particular applications. Glass, for example, has many industrial uses, ranging from packaging to architecture to the motor industry. Each of these application sectors behaves differently in terms of price sensitivity, ease of substitution, quality and performance requirements, for instance. Similarly, cash-and-carry wholesalers serve three broad segments: independent grocers, caterers and pubs. Each segment will purchase different types of goods, in different quantities and for different purposes.

The macro level is a useful starting point for defining some broad boundaries to markets and segments, but it is not sufficient in itself, even if such segmentation does happen too often in practice. Further customer-oriented analysis on the micro level is necessary.

■ Micro segmentation bases

Within a macro segment, a number of smaller micro segments may exist. To focus on these, the organisation needs to have a detailed understanding of individual members of the macro segment, in terms of their management philosophy, decision-making structures, purchasing policies and strategies, as well as their needs and wants. Such information can come from published sources, past experience of the potential buyer, sales force knowledge and experience, word of mouth within the industry, or at first hand from the potential buyer.

An overview of common bases for micro segmentation is given in Table 4.1.

Table 4.1 Bases for micro segmentation in B2B markets

- Product
- Applications
- Technology
- Purchasing policies
- DMU structure
- Decision-making process
- Buyer–seller relationships

Gathering, collating and analysing such depth of information is, of course, a time-consuming and sometimes difficult task, and there is always the question of whether it is either feasible or worthwhile. However, there are benefits in defining such small segments (even segments of one!) if it enables fine tuning of the marketing offering to suit specific needs. Given the volumes of goods and levels of financial investment involved in some B2B markets, the effort is not wasted. An organisation that has a small number of very important customers would almost certainly treat each as a segment of one, particularly in a market such as the supply of organisation-wide computer systems where individual customer needs vary so much. In contrast, in a market such as office stationery, where standard products are sold to perhaps thousands of B2B customers, any segmentation is likely to centre around groups aggregating many tens of customers on the macro level.

Segmenting consumer markets

Segmenting consumer markets does have some similarities with B2B segmentation, as this section indicates. The main difference is that consumer segments are usually very much larger in terms of the number of potential buyers, and it is much more difficult, therefore, to get close to the individual buyer. Consumer segmentation bases also put more emphasis on the buyer's lifestyle and context, because most consumer purchases fulfil higher-order needs (see, for example, Maslow's hierarchy of needs, discussed at pp. 81 *et seq.*) rather than simply functional ones. The danger is, however, that the more abstract the segments become, the less easily understood they may become by those designing marketing strategies (Wedel and Kamakura, 1999). Each of the commonly used bases is now discussed in turn.

■ Geographic segmentation

Geographic segmentation defines customers according to their location. This can often be a useful starting point. A small business, for example, particularly in the retail or service sector, operating on limited resources, may look initially for custom within its immediate locale. Even multinationals, such as Heinz, often tend to segment geographically by dividing their global organisation into operating units built around specific geographic markets.

In neither case, however, is this the end of the story. For the small business, simply being there on the High Street is not enough. It has to offer something further that a significant group of customers want, whether it is attractively low prices or a high level of customer service. The multinational organisation segments geographically, partly for the sake of creating a manageable organisational structure, and partly in recognition that on a global scale, geographic boundaries herald other, more significant differences in taste, culture, lifestyle and demand. The Single European Market (SEM) may have created a market of some 450 million potential customers, yet the first thing that most organisations are likely to do is to segment the SEM into its constituent nations.

eg Take the marketing of an instant hot chocolate drink, made with boiling water. In the UK, virtually every household owns a kettle, and hot chocolate is viewed either as a bedtime drink or as a substitute through the day for tea or coffee. In France, however, kettles are not common, and hot chocolate is most often made with milk as a nourishing children's breakfast. Thus the benefits of speed, convenience and versatility that would impress the UK market would be less applicable in the French market. France would require a very different marketing strategy at best or, at worst, a completely different product.

Geographic segments are at least easy to define and measure, and information is often freely available from public sources. This kind of segmentation also has an operational advantage, particularly in developing efficient systems for distribution and customer contact, for example. However, in a marketing-oriented organisation, this is not sufficient. Douglas and Craig (1983), for example, emphasise the dangers of being too geographically focused and making assumptions about what customers in a region might have in common. Even within a small geographic area, there is a wide variety of needs and wants, and this method on its own tells you nothing about them. Heinz divides its global operation into geographically based subdivisions because it does recognise the effects of cultural diversity and believes in 'local marketing' as the best means of fully understanding and serving its various markets. It is also important to note that any organisation segmenting purely on geographic grounds would be vulnerable to competition coming in with a more customer-focused segmentation strategy.

■ Demographic segmentation

Demographic segmentation tells you a little more about the customer and the customer's household on measurable criteria that are largely descriptive, such as age, sex, race, income, occupation, socioeconomic status and family structure.

Demographics might even extend into classifications of body size and shape! It has been suggested that any male with a waist over 102 cm or female with a waist over 88 cm should consider it a warning of obesity. That amounts to an awful lot of people, especially in the UK, Germany and the USA, where the working classes are relatively affluent (Stuttaford, 2001). Over 9 million people in the UK alone are classified as clinically obese and are at risk of weight-related illness. That could be good news for some pharmaceutical and diet food manufacturers, but it presents a challenge to some other business sectors. Clothing retailers such as High and Mighty and Evans primarily target larger men and women respectively. Other retailers have to get their mix of stock sizes right to meet seasonal demand. Marks and Spencer, for example, undertook a survey of 2500 women and found that the average dress size is now a 14 whereas in 1980 it was a 12. Transport operators such as airlines and railways have even bigger problems. Economy-class seats on many aircraft are around 26 inches wide which is pretty cramped, even for those of us who are not built along the lines of a Sumo wrestler! The increasing size of travellers as well as the bad publicity about deep vein thrombosis being associated with sitting in cramped aircraft on long-haul flights is making airlines rethink their seating arrangements. Train operators are less concerned, however. In a push to cram more passengers into a carriage, modern rolling stock actually offers 6 inches less seatroom for commuters than carriages built in the 1970s (Bale, 2001).

An uplifting tale of a developing market

So, how do you segment the bra market? Clearly manufacturers are primarily (but not exclusively) (don't ask!) targeting women, but that is only the beginning. The British bra and lingerie company Gossard has found that a geographic approach to market segmentation can have some validity. The types of product that sell best in various countries are different, partly for the practical reason that women vary in average size across Europe, and partly because of cultural and lifestyle factors. Italian women want to be seductive and thus buy a lot of basques; the Germans are practical and look for support and quality; the French want to be fashionable and impress other women; and the Scandinavians want natural fibres. This is, of course, a grossly generalised survey, but the basic trends are there and give Gossard a basis for developing appropriate new products and strategies for different markets.

You might think that bra size is a useful segmentation variable that cuts across geographic boundaries, and indeed it is: the needs and priorities of larger women perhaps wanting to minimise the impact of their assets are very different from those of smaller women wanting to maximise them. The Wonderbra, for instance, was designed to target younger women, aged between 15 and 25, wanting a fashionable, fun,

sexy bra that allows them to make the most of their assets. This appeal was reinforced by advertising slogans such as 'Hello, Boys', 'Mind If I Bring a Couple of Friends?' and 'In Your Dreams' alongside scantily clad, beautiful models. Even so, the marketers have to take into account more complex lifestyle issues as fashions change. Wonderbra's success is not just about the proportion of smaller-breasted women within the population but also the trend towards more revealing clothes and the desirability of cleavage. The Deep Plunge range from Wonderbra launched in 2005 capitalises on that by being specifically designed to enhance current clothing fashions. Aiming at a slightly older, more sophisticated consumer, Gossard has launched the Super Smooth which, it claims, gives all the uplift of the Wonderbra but is unique because it has no seams, stitching or elastic. It is designed to be invisible under clothing so that the emphasis is on the effect of the bra rather than on the bra as a garment in its own right.

Marketing managers within this market do, however, need to keep an eye on how the consumer profile is changing. Industry research has indicated that over the last ten years or so, the average British bust size has increased from 34B to 36C or D, and nearly one-third of British women wear a D cup or larger. This is perhaps less than good news for

Lorna and her friends air their customised bras after undertaking the Playtex Moonwalk in London to raise money for breast cancer charities.

Source: © Lorna Young

Wonderbra, but excellent for companies like Bravissimo that specialise in larger sizes.

Nevertheless, underlying (or should that be underwiring?) all this is a remarkable consensus about the core features and benefits that women want from their bras. According to Gossard, 98 per cent want comfort (so what do the other 2 per cent want?!); 83 per cent consider underwear 'as a pleasure and enjoy the fancy and refined side of it'; 78 per cent want silhouette enhancement and 77 per cent want underwear that is invisible under clothing. So whatever you are looking for, whether it's frills, thrills, or functionality, the right bra is out there somewhere.

Sources: Baker (2004); Broadhead (1995); *Marketing Week* (2004a; 2004b); **http://www.gossard.co.uk.**

As with the geographic variable, demographics are relatively easy to define and measure, and the necessary information is often freely available from public sources. The main advantage, however, is that demographics offer a clear profile of the customer on criteria that can be worked into marketing strategies. For example, an age profile can provide a foundation for choice of advertising media and creative approach. Magazines, for instance, tend to have readerships that are clearly defined in terms of gender, age bands and socioeconomic groups. The under-35 female reader, for example, is more likely to go for magazines such as *Marie Claire*, *Bella* and *Cosmopolitan* than the over-35s who are more likely to read *Prima*, *Good Housekeeping* and *Family Circle*.

On the negative side, demographics are purely descriptive and, used alone, assume that all people in the same demographic group have similar needs and wants. This is not necessarily true (just think about the variety of people you know within your own age group).

Additionally, as with the geographic method, it is still vulnerable to competition coming in with an even more customer-focused segmentation strategy. It is best used, then, for products that have a clear bias towards a particular demographic group. For instance, cosmetics are initially segmented into male/female; baby products are primarily aimed at females aged between 20 and 35; school fee endowment policies appeal to households within a higher income bracket at a particular stage of the family lifecycle. In most of these cases, however, again as with the geographic method, the main use of demographic segmentation is as a foundation for other more customer-focused segmentation methods.

■ Geodemographic segmentation

Geodemographics can be defined as 'the analysis of people by where they live' (Sleight, 1997, p. 16) as it combines geographic information with demographic and sometimes even lifestyle data (see below) about neighbourhoods. This helps organisations to understand where their customers are, to develop more detailed profiles of how those customers live, and to locate and target similar potential customers elsewhere. A geodemographic system, therefore, will define types of neighbourhood and types of consumer within a neighbourhood according to their demographic and lifestyle characteristics. Table 4.2 gives an example of how Experian's Mosaic UK™ profiles one of its neighbourhood types.

Table 4.2 Mosaic UK™ Group E: Urban Intelligence, Type E34: Town Gown Transition

- Older areas of large provincial cities close to universities, likely to consist of better quality early twentieth-century terraced housing with front gardens.
- Likely to be close to parks and strips of older shops, now including convenience stores, cheap restaurants and takeaways.
- Likely to be on bus routes and within easy cycling or walking distance of university campuses.
- Residents mainly aged around mid-20s and likely to be mature students, postgraduate or research students, or young lecturers. May also be young graduates working in professional jobs outside academia.
- Residents tend to be single and sociable, enjoying drinking, clubbing, cinema and generally 'hanging out' with their friends.
- They are idealistic and headstrong; concerned with international issues; sceptical of global corporations and brands; likely to sympathise with organisations such as Greenpeace and Friends of the Earth.
- They are likely to be *Guardian* readers.
- They are willing to recognise other cultures and are tolerant of immigrants.
- They are short of money, but not especially materialistic. They are not confident about financial management and they are not good at managing what money they do have.
- They are adventurous risk-takers who enjoy travel, and they are ambitious for their careers.
- They are at a transition stage of their lives and are likely to mature into lifestyles similar to those of their parents.

Source: © Experian Ltd, 2006. All rights reserved. The word '*Experian*' is a registered trademark in the EU and other countries and is owned by Experian Ltd and/or its associated companies.

A number of specialist companies, including Experian, offer geodemographic databases. Most of them are generally applicable to a range of consumer markets, although some are designed for specific industries, and others have developed a range of variations on the main database to suit different industries or geographic regions.

Geodemographic systems are increasingly becoming available as multimedia packages. Mosaic™ is available on CD-ROM, giving the manager access to colour maps, spoken commentary on how to use the system, photographs and text. Experian and other providers are also working on customised geodemographic packages, tailored to suit a particular client's needs.

eg   Door-to-door marketing has evolved still further in its ability to target individual homes. Blanket drops of product samples or sales literature have been used for some time by consumer goods marketers, but the increasing refinement of databases has led to more sophisticated targeting. TNT Post (Doordrop Media) Ltd, a leading door-to-door drop company, has launched its *Personal Placement* service which can match a purchased or client-provided database with geodemographic neighbourhoods from ACORN, Mosaic™, etc. to identify those areas with a reasonable proportion of target households. Within each neighbourhood postcode there are around 2500 homes, and there are 8900 postcodes in the UK. By adopting a micro-targeting system, units as small as 700 households can be identified to reflect differences in housing types even within a neighbourhood. This, matched with mailing lists and databases, enables cost-effective, better targeted door-to-door delivery.

Experian's Mosaic™ geodemographic system is available on CD-ROM, thus enhancing its user-friendliness and flexibility.

Such systems are invaluable to the marketer across all aspects of consumer marketing, for example in planning sampling areas for major market research studies, or assessing locations for new retail outlets, or finding appropriate areas for a direct mail campaign or door-to-door leaflet drop.

■ Psychographic segmentation

Psychographics, or lifestyle segmentation, is an altogether more difficult area to define, as it involves intangible variables such as the beliefs, attitudes and opinions of the potential customer. It has evolved in answer to some of the shortcomings of the methods described above as a means of getting further under the skin of the customer as a thinking being. The idea is that defining the lifestyle of the consumer allows the marketer to sell the product not on superficial, functional features, but on benefits that can be seen to enhance that lifestyle on a much more emotional level. The term *lifestyle* is used in its widest sense to cover not only demographic characteristics, but also attitudes to life, beliefs and aspirations.

---

marketing **in action**

C'est la vie!

Mazzoli (2004) reports extensive market research that was undertaken in France to define and describe various lifestyle segments within the French youth market (aged 15–25). Six distinct 'tribes' emerged:

■ *TV Addicts*: accounting for 39 per cent of the respondents, just over half the members of this tribe are female. They tend to live in small towns of fewer than 2000 inhabitants. As the label suggests, they like to watch television and they particularly enjoy series such as Charmed, Buffy the Vampire Slayer and Smallville. Not surprisingly, they identify with celebrities from the audio-visual world, such as Ben Affleck, Johnny Depp, Madonna, Robbie Williams, Tom Cruise, Brad Pitt and Steven Spielberg. Their favourite brands are Levis, Celio, Etam, Adidas and Hugo Boss.

■ *Lolita Spirit*: accounting for 16 per cent of the respondents, 81 per cent of this tribe are female, and mostly aged between 20 and 25. They have mainly left the parental home and are living either alone or within a couple. Their favourite celebrities include Evelyne Thomas, Laura Pausini, Nolwenn and Séverinne Ferrer. Like the TV Addicts, Levis, Adidas and Etam are among their favourite brands along with Camaieu and Agnés B.

■ *Electro Party*: comprising 8 per cent of the respondents, this tribe likes electronic music and its icons, such as Daft Punk, Carl Cox, Jeff Mills and Laurent Garnier. Members of this tribe are aged between 20 and 25, tend to live alone and are predominantly male. They tend to live in and around Paris. Their favoured brands are Mango, H&M, Dior, Diesel and Zara.

■ *Noisy Provocation*: this tribe (5 per cent of respondents) is a little younger in profile, between 15 and 19 years old, and thus live in the parental home and are still in full-time education. Mostly male, this tribe likes provocative and/or strong celebrities such as Johnny Knoxville, Marilyn Manson, Bjork and Kurt Kobain. Brands they like include Oxbow, Adidas, Decathlon, Quiksilver and Hugo Boss.

■ *Hip Hop Fiction*: again young in profile, between 15 and 19 years old, this tribe (14 per cent of respondents) likes its Hip Hop. Artists and celebrities such as Eminem, Puff Daddy, Saian Supa Crew, Halle Berry, Will Smith and Djamel Debouzze appeal to them. Just over half this tribe is female, and their favoured brands include Levis, Adidas, Puma, Hugo Boss and Nike.

■ *French Pride*: this tribe, 18 per cent of respondents, has a strong social conscience and a strong pride in 'Frenchness'. They admire the Dalai Lama, and French personalities such as Matthieu Kassovitz, Vincent Cassel and Olivier Besancenot. They live in large towns and cities (more than 100,000 inhabitants) and tend to be the oldest among the total sample surveyed. Their favoured brands include Zara, Levis, Dim, Hugo Boss and Diesel.

Plummer (1974) was an early exponent of lifestyle segmentation, breaking it down into four main categories: activities, interests, opinions and demographics.

Activities

The activities category includes all the things people do in the course of their lives. It therefore covers work, shopping, holidays and social life. Within that, the marketer will be interested in people's hobbies and their preferred forms of entertainment, as well as sports interests, club memberships and their activities within the community (voluntary work, for instance).

Interests

Interests refers to what is important to the consumer and where their priorities lie. It may include the things very close to them, such as family, home and work, or their interest and involvement in the wider community. It may also include elements of leisure and recreation, and Plummer particularly mentions areas such as fashion, food and media.

Opinions

The category of opinions comes very close to the individual's innermost thoughts, by probing attitudes and feelings about such things as themselves, social and cultural issues and politics. Opinion may also be sought about other influences on society, such as education, economics and business. Closer to home for the marketer, this category will also investigate opinions about products and the individual's view of the future, indicating how their needs and wants are likely to change.

Demographics

Demographic descriptors have already been extensively covered, and this category includes the kinds of demographic elements you would expect, such as age, education, income and occupation, as well as family size, lifecycle stage and geographic location.

By researching each of these categories thoroughly and carefully, the marketer can build up a very detailed and three-dimensional picture of the consumer. Building such profiles over very large groups of individuals can then allow the marketer to aggregate people with significant similarities in their profiles into named lifestyle segments. As you might expect, because lifestyles are so complex and the number of contributory variables so large, there is no single universally applicable typology of psychographic segments. Indeed, many different typologies have emerged over the years, emphasising different aspects of lifestyle, striving to provide a set of lifestyle segments that are either generally useful or designed for a specific commercial application.

In the USA, for example, advertising agencies have found the Values And Life Style (VALS-2) typology, based on Mitchell (1983), particularly useful. The typology is based on the individual's *resources*, mainly income and education, and *self-orientation*, i.e. attitude towards oneself, one's aspirations and the things one does to communicate and achieve them. The segments that emerge include, for example, *Achievers*, who fall within the category of 'status-oriented'. They have abundant resources and are career minded with a social life that revolves around work and family. They mind very much what other people think of them, and particularly crave the good opinion of those who they themselves admire. The implication is that Achievers have largely 'made it' in terms of material success, in contrast to *Strivers* (who are likely to be Achievers in the future) and *Strugglers* (who aspire to be Achievers, but may never make it). Both these segments are also status-oriented, but are less well endowed with resources and still have some way to go.

Schoenwald (2001) highlighted some of the dangers in taking psychographic segmentation so far that the relationship between segment characteristics and brand performance becomes lost. Although it may be useful for identifying broad trends, segment boundaries can change as the market changes and some individuals may not fit categories easily or neatly, for example being conservative on financial issues yet highly progressive when it comes to embracing high technology. Schoenwald reminds us that segmentation is a marketing tool for defining markets better and must, therefore, be actionable and not confusing.

eg

'I can't believe it's not meat!' The wide variety of Quorn products now available indicates the broader customer base being targeted.

Source: © Quorn http://www.quorn.co.uk

The 6 million vegetarians in the UK are members of an attractive segment defined in terms of the values that these consumers hold. Meat-free brand Quorn, with sales worth £95m per annum, has benefited not only from a demand for vegetarian meat substitutes, but also from demand for healthier food generally. The market as a whole was worth worth £626m in 2004, having increased by 38 per cent over five years.

Quorn's strapline 'It might just surprise you' reflects its repositioning as a mainstream healthy food brand rather than just appealing to vegetarians. The potential health dangers of red meat are increasingly being understood, so meat-free products are picking up new consumers who may not be fully vegetarian. It is these meat reducers and healthy eaters that have become the main target for meat-free foods. It has been estimated that 45 per cent of UK households are reducing their meat intake, so the potential market is very large indeed as long as producers can overcome any consumer prejudices about vegetarian food being boring or 'cranky'. It is true that bean burgers, soya sausages and nut cutlets represent over half the sales in the category, but snacks and deli-type products are growing fast, with 16 per cent of sales. Ready meals, accounting for around 25 per cent of sales, have declined, however, but that is expected to change as manufacturers develop new varieties and taste appeals (*Campaign*, 2005; *Marketing Week*, 2005).

Within the SEM, many organisations have been trying to produce lifestyle-based psychographic segment profiles that categorise the whole of Europe. One such study, carried out by Euro Panel and marketed in the UK by AGB Dialogue, was based on an exhaustive 150-page questionnaire administered across the EU, Switzerland and Scandinavia. The main research areas covered included demographic and economic factors, as well as attitudes, activities and feelings. Analysis of the questionnaire data allowed researchers to identify sixteen lifestyle segments based on two main axes, innovation/conservatism and idealism/materialism. The results also identified twenty or so key questions that were crucial to matching a respondent with an appropriate segment. These key questions were then put to a further 20,000 respondents, which then allowed the definition of sixteen segments, including for example Euro-Citizen, Euro-Gentry, Euro-Moralist, Euro-Vigilante, Euro-Romantic and Euro-Business.

Despite the extent and depth of research that has gone into defining typologies such as these, they are still of somewhat limited use. When it comes to applying this material in a commercial marketing context, the marketer still needs to understand the underlying national factors that affect the buying decisions for a particular product.

Nevertheless, there are compelling reasons for such methods of segmentation being worth considering and persevering with, despite their difficulties. Primarily, they can open the door to a better-tailored, more subtle offering to the customer on all aspects of the marketing mix. This in turn can create a strong emotional bond between customer and product, making it more difficult for competitors to steal customers. Euro-segmentation adds a further dimension, in that it has the potential to create much larger and more profitable segments, assuming that the logistics of distribution allow geographically dispersed members of the segment to be reached cost effectively, and may thus create pan-European marketing opportunities.

The main problem, however, as we have seen, is that psychographic segments are very difficult and expensive to define and measure. Relevant information is much less likely to exist already in the public domain. It is also very easy to get the implementation wrong. For example, the organisation that tries to portray lifestyle elements within advertisements is depending on the audience's ability to interpret the symbols used in the desired way and to reach the desired conclusions from them. There are no guarantees of this, especially if the message is a complex one (more of this in Chapter 9). Additionally, the user of Euro-segments has to be very clear about allowing for national and cultural differences when trying to communicate on lifestyle elements.

In summary, psychographic segmentation works well in conjunction with demographic variables to refine further the offering to the customer, increasing its relevance and defendability against competition. It is also valuable for products that lean towards psychological rather than functional benefits for the customer, for instance perfumes, cars, clothing retailers, etc. For such a product to succeed, the marketer needs to create an image that convinces consumers that the product can either enhance their current lifestyle or help them to achieve their aspirations.

■ Behaviour segmentation

All the categories of segmentation talked about so far are centred on the customer, leading to as detailed a profile of the individual as possible. Little mention has been made, however, of the individual's relationship with the product. This needs to be addressed, as it is quite possible that people with similar demographic and/or psychographic profiles may yet interact differently with the same product. Segmenting a market in these terms, therefore, is known as behaviour segmentation.

End use

What is the product to be used for? The answer to this question has great implications for the whole marketing approach. Think about soup, for instance. This is a very versatile product with a range of potential uses, and a wide variety of brands and product lines have been developed, each of which appeals to a different usage segment. A shopper may well buy two or three different brands of soup, simply because their needs change according to intended use, for example a dinner party or a snack meal. At this point, demographic and psychographic variables may become irrelevant (or at least secondary) if the practicalities of usage are so important to the customer. Table 4.3 defines some of the possible end uses of soup and gives examples of products available on the UK market to serve them.

Table 4.3 Usage segmentation in the soup market

Use	Brand examples
Dinner party starter	Baxter's soups; Covent Garden soups
Warming snack	Crosse & Blackwell's soups
Meal replacement	Heinz Wholesoups
Recipe ingredient	Campbell's Condensed soups
Easy office lunch	Batchelor's Cup-a-Soups

Benefits sought

This variable can have more of a psychological slant than end usage and can link in very closely with both demographic and psychographic segments. In the case of a car, for example, the benefits sought may range from the practical ('reliable'; 'economic to run'; 'able to accommodate mum, dad, four kids, a granny, a wet dog and the remains of a picnic') to the more psychographically oriented ('environmentally friendly'; 'fast and mean'; 'overt status symbol'). Similarly, the benefits sought from a chilled ready meal might be 'ease of preparation', 'time saving', 'access to dishes I could not make myself', 'a reassuring standby in case I get home late one evening', and for the low-calorie and low-fat versions, 'a tasty and interesting variation on my diet!' It is not difficult to see how defining some of these *benefit segments* can also indicate the kinds of demographic or lifestyle descriptors that apply to people wanting those benefits.

eg A new entrant in the chilled ready meals sector, Naked, is targeting those consumers who want healthy, tasty food without having to spend any significant time in preparation. The steamed meals and pan-fried dishes in exotic flavours within the Naked range are targeting professionals on the basis of the benefits being offered. Of course, the choice of brand name is purely incidental in that process! (*The Grocer*, 2005).

Usage rate

Not everyone who buys a particular product consumes it at the same rate. There will be heavy users, medium users and light users. Figure 4.1 shows the hypothetical categorisation of an organisation's customer base according to usage. In this case, 20 per cent of customers account for 60 per cent of the organisation's sales. This clearly raises questions for marketing strategies, for example should we put all our resources into defending our share of heavy users? Alternatives might be to make light users heavier; to target competitors' heavy users aggressively; or even to develop differentiated products for different usage rates (such as frequent-wash shampoo).

Again, this segmentation variable can best be used in conjunction with others to paint a much more three-dimensional picture of the target customer.

Figure 4.1 Consumer product usage categories

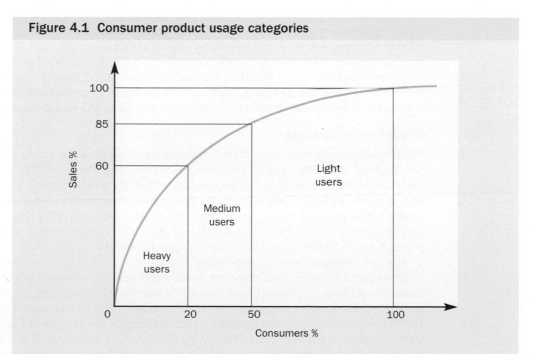

Loyalty

As with usage rate, loyalty could be a useful mechanism, not only for developing detail in the segment profile, but also for developing a better understanding of which segmentation variables are significant. For instance a carefully thought-out market research exercise might help an organisation to profile 'loyal to us', 'loyal to them' and 'switchers', and then discover what other factors seem to differentiate between each of these groups. More specifically, Wind (1982) identified six loyalty segments as follows:

1   Current loyal users who will continue to purchase the brand
2   Current customers who might switch brands or reduce consumption
3   Occasional users who might be persuaded to increase consumption with the right incentives
4   Occasional users who might decrease consumption because of competitors' offerings
5   Non-users who might buy the brand if it was modified
6   Non-users with strong negative attitudes that are unlikely to change.

What is certain is that brand loyalty can be a fragile thing, and is under increasing threat. This is partly as a result of the greater number of alternative brands available and incentives or promotions designed by competitors to undermine customer loyalty. The most serious threat in the UK, however, has come from supermarket own-brands, many of which look uncannily like the equivalent manufacturer brands but undercut them on price. Consumers thus believe that the own-brands are just as good, if not identical, and are thus prepared to switch to them and to be more price sensitive.

Assuming that loyalty does exist, even a simple combination of usage rate and loyalty begins to make a difference to the organisation's marketing strategy. If, for example, a large group of heavy users who are also brand switchers was identified, then there is much to be gained from investing resources in a tightly focused marketing mix designed to turn them into heavy users who are loyal to a particular company.

Attitude

Again, trespassing on the psychographic area, attitude looks at how the potential customer feels about the product (or the organisation). A set of customers who are already enthusiastic about a product, for example, require very different handling from a group who are downright hostile. A hostile group might need an opportunity to sample the product, along with an advertising campaign that addresses and answers the roots of their hostility. Attitude-based segments may be important in marketing charities or causes, or even in health education. Smokers who are hostile to the 'stop smoking' message will need different approaches from those who are amenable to the message and just need reassurance and practical support to put it into practice. Approaches aimed at the 'hostile' smoker have included fear ('look at these diseased lungs'), altruism ('what about your children?') and vanity (warning young women about the effect on their skin), but with little noticeable effect.

Buyer readiness stage

Buyer readiness can be a very valuable variable, particularly when one is thinking about the promotional mix. How close to purchasing is the potential customer? For example, at a very early stage the customer may not even be aware that the product exists, and therefore to get that customer moving closer to purchase, the organisation needs to generate *awareness* of the product. Then there is a need for information to stimulate *interest* in the product. The customer's ability to understand and interpret that information may lead to *desire* for the product, which in turn stimulates *action*: the purchase itself.

Figure 4.2 summarises this progression.

Behavioural segmentation, therefore, examines closely the relationship between the potential customer and the product, and there are a number of dimensions on which this can be done. Its main achievement is to bring the relationship between customer and product into sharper focus, thus providing greater understanding of the customer's specific needs and wants, leading to a better defined marketing mix. Another advantage of this kind of segmentation approach is that it provides opportunities for tailored marketing strategies to target brand switchers or to increase usage rates. All these benefits do justify the use of behavioural

Figure 4.2 The AIDA response hierarchy model

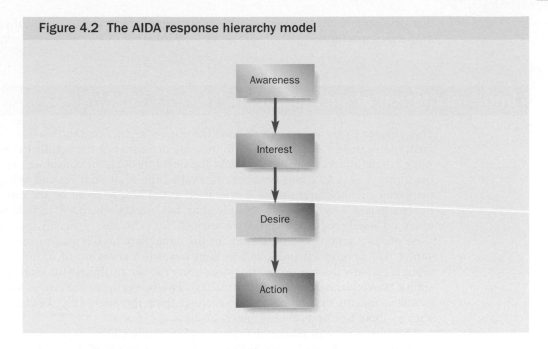

segmentation, as long as it does not lead to the organisation becoming product centred to the neglect of the customer's needs. The customer must still come first.

■ Multivariable segmentation

As has been hinted throughout the previous sections, it is unlikely that any one segmentation variable will be used absolutely on its own. It is more common for marketers to use a multivariable segmentation approach, defining a 'portfolio' of relevant segmentation variables, some of which will be prosaic and descriptive while others will tend towards the psychographic, depending on the product and market in question. The market for adult soft drinks includes age segmentation along with some usage considerations (for example as a substitute for wine as a meal accompaniment), some benefit segmentation (healthy, refreshing, relaxing), and lifestyle elements of health consciousness, sophisticated imagery and a desire for exotic ingredients. Similarly, the banking sector is moving from traditional segmentation based upon corporate and retail customers to approaches aimed at creating segments based upon combinations of customer attitudes towards bank services and expected benefits. Simply grouping customers according to demographic criteria failed to reflect their attitudes towards technology and their readiness to use it, which could be strategically important as internet banking develops further (Machauer and Morgner, 2001).

The emergence of geodemographics in recent years, as discussed at pp. 119 *et seq.* above, is an indicator of the way in which segmentation is moving, that is, towards multi-variable systems incorporating psychographics, demographics and geographics. These things are now possible and affordable, as Chapter 5 will show, because of increasingly sophisticated data collection mechanisms, developments in database creation and maintenance (*see* Chapter 11) and cheaper, more accessible computing facilities. A properly managed database allows the marketer to go even further and to incorporate behavioural variables as the purchaser develops a trading history with a supplier. Thus the marketers are creeping ever closer to the individual consumer. The UK supermarkets that have developed and launched store loyalty cards that are swiped through the checkout so that the customer can accumulate points towards discounts, for example, are collecting incredibly detailed information about each individual shopper's profile. It tells them when we shop, how often, which branches of the store we tend to use, how much we spend per visit, the range of goods we buy, and the choices we make between own brands and manufacturer brands. The supermarkets can use this information to help them define meaningful segments for their own customer base, to further develop and improve their overall marketing mix or to make individually tailored offers to specific customers.

Implementation of segmentation

This chapter so far has very freely used the phrase 'segmenting the market', but before segmentation can take place, there has to be some definition of the boundaries of that market. Any such definition really has to look at the world through the consumer's eyes, because the consumer makes decisions based on the evaluation of alternatives and substitutes. Thus a margarine manufacturer cannot restrict itself to thinking in terms of 'the margarine market', but has to take a wider view of 'the spreading-fats market' which will include butter and vegetable oil based products alongside margarine. This is because, generally speaking, all three of these product groups are contending for the same place on the nation's bread, and the consumer will develop attitudes and feelings towards a selection of brands across all three groups, perhaps through comparing price and product attributes (for example taste, spreadability, cooking versatility and health claims). This opens up a much wider competitive scene, as well as making the margarine manufacturer think more seriously about product positioning and about how and why consumers buy it.

This whole issue of market definition and its implications for segmentation comes back, yet again, to what should now be the familiar question of 'What business are we in?' It is a timely reminder that consumers basically buy solutions to problems, not products, and thus in defining market segments, the marketer should take into account any type of product that will provide a solution. Hence we are not in 'the margarine market', but in the 'lubricating bread' market, which brings us back full circle to the inclusion of butter and vegetable oil based spreads as direct competitors.

It is still not enough to have gone through the interesting exercise of segmenting a market, however it is defined. How is that information going to be used by the organisation to develop marketing strategies? One decision that must be made is how many segments within the market the organisation intends to target. We look first at targeting.

Targeting

There are three broad approaches available, summarised in Figure 4.3, and discussed in detail below.

Concentrated

The concentrated approach is the most focused approach of the three, and involves specialising in serving one specific segment. This can lead to very detailed knowledge of the target segment's needs and wants, with the added benefit that the organisation is seen as a specialist, giving it an advantage over its more mass-market competitors. This, however, carries a risk of complacency, leaving the organisation vulnerable to competitive entry into the segment.

In terms of management, concentration is attractive because costs are kept down, as there is only one marketing mix to manage, and there is still the potential for economies of scale. Strategically, the concentration of resources into one segment may lead to a stronger, more defendable position than that achievable by competitors which are spreading their effort more thinly. However, being a niche specialist may make it more difficult for an organisation to diversify into other segments, whether through lack of experience and knowledge, or through problems of acceptance arising from being identified with the original niche.

The benefits also need to be weighed against the other potential risks. First, all the organisation's eggs are in one basket, and if that segment fails, then there is no fallback position. The second risk is that if competitors see a rival establishing and clearly succeeding in a segment like this, then they may try to take some of it.

Figure 4.3 Segmentation targeting strategies

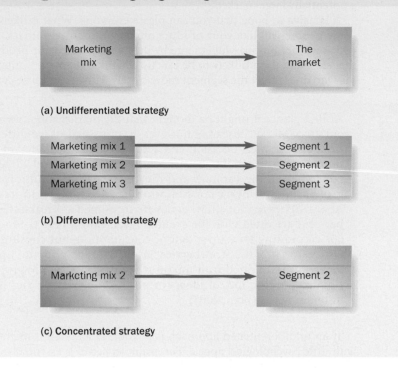

(a) Undifferentiated strategy

(b) Differentiated strategy

(c) Concentrated strategy

Differentiated

As Figure 4.3 implies, a differentiated strategy involves the development of a number of individual marketing mixes, each of which serves a different segment. For example, Ford manufactures a range of cars, covering a number of different segments, from the Focus at the bottom end of the price range, generally intended for the younger female driver, to the Scorpio in the higher price bracket, intended for the status-seeking executive.

As with the concentrated strategy, this approach does allow the organisation to tailor its offerings to suit the individual segments, thus maintaining satisfaction. It also overcomes one of the problems of concentration by spreading risk across the market, so that if one segment declines, the organisation still has revenue from others.

To be implemented properly, this approach requires a detailed overview of the market and how it is developing, perhaps leading to the early detection of new opportunities or emerging segments. This knowledge is valuable for an organisation with a healthy curiosity about its environment, but is acquired at a cost (in terms of both finance and managerial time). It also leads to increased costs in trying to manage the marketing mixes for a number of products, with possible diseconomies of scale.

Overall, a differentiated strategy dilutes the organisation's efforts through the thin spreading of resources. The organisation must, therefore, be very careful not to overreach itself in the number of segments it attempts to cover. Nevertheless, it can help an organisation to survive in highly competitive markets.

Undifferentiated

The undifferentiated approach is the least demanding of the three approaches, in that it assumes that the market is one great homogeneous unit, with no significant differences between individuals within that market. Thus a single marketing mix is required that serves the needs of the entire market. The emphasis is likely, therefore, to be on developing mass communication, mass distribution and as wide an appeal as possible.

An undifferentiated approach does have some apparent advantages. It involves relatively low costs, as there is only one marketing mix that does not require the depth of research, fine tuning and updating that a concentrated or differentiated strategy would entail. It could also lead to the possible maximisation of economies of scale, because of having a single product in a potentially large market.

It is naive to hope that you can please everyone. What is likely to happen in reality is that some people will like your product offering more than others, and thus a segment (not of your own definition) will emerge by default. Because your product has not been tailored to that segment, it is unlikely to be exactly what that segment wants, and therefore any competitor who does target the segment more closely will attract those customers.

eg At first glance it might be thought that the market for strawberries is largely undifferentiated. Market research, however, has revealed usage differences depending on the time of year, meal occasion and accompaniments. There are even different consumption patterns depending on the consumer's age. Around 40 per cent of strawberries are consumed in the summer and they feature in 619 million meals in the UK. Recent growth in strawberry consumption has been linked to its association with health. About 10 per cent of strawberries are consumed at breakfast, some with cereals, and 45 per cent are eaten with the evening meal. Consumers tend to be older, with the over-65s accounting for 28 per cent of consumption, but consumption among under-5s is also rising rapidly. Strawberries have a habit of popping up in fromage frais, in tub desserts and in dried fruit mixtures. All this data should give any marketer with a fertile imagination lots of ideas for promoting strawberries in different ways to meet different needs (Finn, 2005).

If an undifferentiated approach is possible at all, then it might best be suited for products with little psychological appeal. For example, petrol is essentially a very ordinary product that many of us purchase regularly but never even see (unless we are not very adept with a self-service pump). It makes the car go, regardless of whether it is a Rolls-Royce or a Lada and, traditionally, the only discriminating factor between brands has been price. Petrol retailers have now begun to create market segments, through the petrol itself (as with unleaded and petrols with extra additives), through the extended product (providing car washes, mini-supermarkets, etc.), and also through strong corporate images that create brands and engender loyalty. All of this is moving the petrol retailers away from undifferentiated strategies.

Quite apart from the advantages and disadvantages connected with each of the alternative approaches above, there are a number of factors influencing the choice of targeting strategy.

Marketing theory may well point to a particular strategy as being ideal, but if an organisation's resources cannot support and sustain that strategy, then an alternative must be found. A smaller organisation may, for example, need to adopt a concentrated strategy (perhaps based on a geographic segment in a consumer market, or on a specialist niche in a B2B market) to generate the growth required to allow a wider coverage of the market.

It is also important to make the choice of strategy in the context of the product itself. As has already been indicated, certain types of product lend themselves more readily to certain approaches, for example a product with many potential variations that involve a high level of psychological relationship with the customer (such as clothing or cosmetics) is better suited to a differentiated or concentrated approach. Other products with a more functional bias can be treated in a more undifferentiated way.

It must be reiterated, though, that undifferentiated approaches are becoming increasingly rare. Salt used to be held up to marketing students as the prime example of a commodity product sold in an undifferentiated way. Table 4.4 demonstrates how all that has changed.

Table 4.4 Differentiation in the salt market

· Table salt	· Iodised salt
· Cooking salt	· Low-sodium salt
· Sea salt	· Garlic salt
· Rock salt	· Celery salt
· Alpine rock salt	et cetera!

The product's lifecycle stage (*see* Chapter 6 for a full definition of this concept) might also affect the choice of strategy. For example, an innovative new product, of which neither the industry nor the consumer has past experience, may first be marketed with an undifferentiated strategy in order to gain practical knowledge of the market's behaviour and reactions. It is very difficult to undertake meaningful market research in advance of launching such a new product, because the market may have problems conceptualising the product or putting it into context. It will be in the growth and maturity stages of the lifecycle that differentiated strategies will emerge as competitors enter the market and organisations learn from experience.

That last comment is a reminder that strategic decisions cannot be taken in isolation from the activities of the competition. If competitors are clearly implementing differentiated strategies, then it is dangerous for you to adopt a more dilute, undifferentiated approach. It may make more sense to identify the segments within which the competition is strong and then to assess whether it would be possible to attack them head-on in those segments or to find a different niche and make that your own. Thus competition is affecting not only the choice of approach, but the actual choice of segment(s) to target.

corporate social responsibility in action

'As close to paradise as can be found'

Turtle Island represents for some the perfect holiday destination. The remote Fijian island in the Yasawa chain was purchased by Harvard graduate Richard Evanson in 1972 as a place to get away from it all, but also as the basis for a business so that his paradise could be shared. Development was needed before business was possible. A circular road was sympathetically built around the island, guest paths were established, Honduras mahogany trees were planted (some 300,000 trees over 26 years), to supplement the local species, and to encourage ecological diversity, stop soil erosion, create wind breaks and add to natural beauty. A three-acre organic vegetable garden was planted, extensive composting and recycling facilities were developed, and solar panel water heating installed to reflect a concern for ecology and the development of sustainable tourism.

The mission and values of the owner are to ensure that the marketing strategies fit with the culture and heritage to create sustainable tourism. Too many of the 'wrong' kind of tourists can soon degrade the local culture and environment. Turtle Island is at the opposite end of the spectrum from Benidorm or Blackpool. The capacity is just fourteen beachfront cottages on a private 500-acre estate and there are no plans to change that. Guests wanting to lie on the beach drinking all day, or sleeping all day and clubbing all night, are certainly not welcome. Turtle Island is designed to appeal to English-speaking couples who can communicate and enjoy each other's company and humour. It's first-name terms as soon as you arrive and a key part of the experience is the interaction with staff and other guests.

The island resort is positioned as the nearest thing to paradise, and clearly to the targeted segment it is just that, as occupancy is high and many bookings cannot be fulfilled for the required dates. The climate, the lush vegetation, the activity programme ranging from snorkelling to mountain biking, the all-inclusive pricing policy, and the opportunity to 'get away from it all' appear highly attractive. The price structure is designed to keep the resort exclusive. Excluding airfares (you need a small seaplane to get to the island) the charge is over $2000 per couple per night and the minimum permitted booking is six nights to provide plenty of opportunity to unwind. Around 60 per cent of its guests are from the United States and 30 per cent from Australia and New Zealand. There

Targeting the desire for the perfect holiday on a desert island but with all the facilities and service that the consumer needs to have a relaxing, carefree holiday, the Turtle Island resort more than satisfies the customers willing to pay for the privilege.

Source: © Turtle Island, Fiji
http://www.turtlefiji.com

is a 36 per cent rate of return visits which, considering its remote location, is exceptionally high.

What is important about Turtle Island is that the environmental responsibility and commitment demonstrated by the owner has been good for business and good for the island and its neighbouring community of over 6000 inhabitants. The concern with ecology, the deliberate attempt to restrict the number of tourists, the use of local materials (guests stay in traditional wood bures), the provision of medical facilities to the locals and a concern for monitoring, controlling and minimising the unfortunate impact of tourism, such as sewage, reef damage and social pollution, have given rise to international acclaim. Developed from an overgrazed and abused island with most of its trees cut down, the Turtle Island resort has won international recognition including a BA Environmental award.

The package of experiences and the ecological orientation have proved to have a strong appeal to a specific market segment and the owner deliberately sought to reflect that when designing the tourist package. Built on a stance that the owner describes as 'destination stewardship', the values of Turtle Island aim to balance and respect the needs of the land, the resources, the people, the community, heritage and culture, while at the same time providing a unique and friendly environment beyond standard hotel star-ratings.

The island has not been without controversy, however. The *Lonely Planet 1997* guide suggested that the island was distinctly unfriendly to gays given its exclusive nature and priority to social mixing between the guests. This was strongly denied, countering that creating the ideal social mix is challenging. The comments in subsequent editions of Lonely Planet were modified, but it goes to show that near perfection on one dimension of CSR can still leave a company open to accusations, however unfounded, on another. Bookings do not appear to have been affected, however, and the careful segmentation and positioning strategy continues to bring success.

Sources: Berno (2004) Chesshyre (2000); Evanson (1999); Turtle Island (2003); http://www.turtlefiji.com.

Benefits of segmentation

The previous sections of this chapter should at least have served to show that market segmentation is a complex and dangerous activity, in the sense that the process of choosing variables, their measurement and their implementation leaves plenty of scope for poor management and disappointment. Nevertheless, there are few, if any, markets in which segmentation has no role to play, and it is important to remember the potential benefits to be gained, whether looking at the customer, the marketing mix or the competition.

The customer

The obvious gain to customers is that they can find products that seem to fit more closely with what they want. These needs and wants, remember, are not only related to product function, but also to psychological fulfilment. Customers may feel that a particular supplier is more sympathetic towards them, or is speaking more directly to them, and therefore they will be more responsive and eventually more loyal to that supplier. The organisation that fails to segment deeply enough on significant criteria will lose custom to competitors that do.

The marketing mix

This is a timely reminder that the marketing mix should itself be a product of understanding the customer. Market segmentation helps the organisation to target its marketing mix more closely on the potential customer, and thus to meet the customer's needs and wants more exactly. Segmentation helps to define shopping habits (in terms of place, frequency and volume), price sensitivity, required product benefits and features, as well as laying the foundations for advertising and promotional decisions. The customer is at the core of all decisions relating to the 4Ps, and those decisions will be both easier to make and more consistent with each other if a clear and detailed definition of the target segments exists.

In the same vein, segmentation can also help the organisation to allocate its resources more efficiently. If a segment is well defined, then the organisation will have sufficient understanding to develop very precise marketing objectives and an accompanying strategy to achieve them, with a minimum of wastage. The organisation is doing neither more nor less than it needs to do in order to satisfy the customer's needs and wants.

This level of understanding of segments that exist in the market also forms a very sound foundation for strategic decisions. The organisation can prioritise across segments in line with its resources, objectives and desired position within the market.

■ The competition

Finally, the use of segmentation will help the organisation to achieve a better understanding of itself and the environment within which it exists. By looking outwards, to the customer, the organisation has to ask itself some very difficult questions about its capacity to serve that customer better than the competition. Also, by analysing the competitors' offerings in the context of the customer, the organisation should begin to appreciate the competition's real strengths and weaknesses, as well as identifying gaps in the market.

Dangers of segmentation

The benefits of segmentation need to be balanced against the dangers inherent in it. Some of these, such as the risks of poor definition and implementation of psychographic segmentation, have already been mentioned.

Jenkins and McDonald (1997) raise more fundamental concerns with market segmentation processes that are not grounded in the capabilities of the organisation. To them, there needs to be more focus on how organisations should segment their markets rather than a focus on how to segment using the range of variables mentioned earlier in this chapter. To decide on the 'should' means having an understanding of the organisation, its culture, its operating processes and structure which all influence the view of the market and how it could be segmented (Piercy and Morgan, 1993).

Other dangers are connected with the essence of segmentation: breaking markets down into ever smaller segments. Where should it stop? Catering for the differing needs of a large number of segments can lead to fragmentation of the market, with additional problems arising from the loss of economies of scale (through shorter production runs or loss of bulk purchasing discounts on raw materials, for instance), as mentioned at p. 129 above. Detail needs to be balanced against viability.

Within the market as a whole, if there are a number of organisations in direct competition for a number of segments, then the potential proliferation of brands may simply serve to confuse the customer. Imagine five competitors each trying to compete in five market segments. That gives the customer 25 brands to sort out. Even if customers can find their way through the maze of brands, the administration and marketing difficulties involved in getting those brands on to the supermarket shelves can be very costly.

Criteria for successful segmentation

Cutting through the detail of how to segment, and regardless of the complexities of segmentation in different types of market, are four absolute requirements for any successful segmentation exercise. Unless these four conditions prevail, the exercise will either look good on paper but be impossible to implement, or fail to deliver any marked strategic advantage.

■ Distinctiveness

Any segment defined has to be *distinctive*, that is, significantly different from any other segment. The basis of that difference depends on the type of product or the circumstances prevailing in the market at the time. It may be rooted in any of the segmentation variables discussed above, whether geographic, demographic or psychographic. Note too the use of the word *significant*. The choice of segmentation variables has to be relevant to the product in question.

Without a significant difference, segment boundaries become too blurred, and there is a risk that an organisation's offerings will not be sufficiently well tailored to attract the required customers.

Tangibility

It must be remembered that distinctiveness can be taken too far. Too much detail in segmentation, without sound commercial reasoning behind it, leads to fragmentation of effort and inefficiency. A defined segment must, therefore, be of a sufficient size to make its pursuit worthwhile. Again, the notion of size here is somewhat vague. For fmcg goods, viable *size* may entail many thousands of customers purchasing many tens of thousands of units, but in a B2B market, it may entail a handful of customers purchasing a handful of units.

Proving that a segment actually exists is also important. Analysis of a market may indicate that there is a gap that existing products do not appear to fill, whether defined in terms of the product itself or the customer profile. The next stage is to ask why that gap is there. Is it because no organisation has yet got round to filling it, or because the segment in that gap is too small to be commercially viable? Does that segment even exist, or are you segmenting in too much detail and creating opportunities on paper that will not work in practice?

Accessibility

As well as existing, a defined segment has to be *accessible.* The first aspect of this is connected with distribution. An organisation has to be able to find the means of delivering its goods and services to the customer, but this may not be so easy, for example, for a small organisation targeting a geographically spread segment with a low-priced infrequently purchased product. Issues of access may then become an extension of the segment profile, perhaps limiting the segment to those customers within a defined catchment area, or those who are prepared to order direct through particular media. Whatever the solution to problems of access, it does mean that the potential size of the segment has to be reassessed.

The second aspect of access is communication. Certain customers may be very difficult to make contact with, and if the promotional message cannot be communicated, then the chances of capturing those customers are much slimmer. Again, the segment profile may have to be extended to cover the media most likely to access those customers, and again, this will lead to a smaller segment.

Defendability

In talking about targeting strategies at pp. 128 *et seq.* above, one of the recurrent themes was that of the competition. Even with a concentrated strategy, targeting only one segment, there is a risk of competitors poaching customers. In defining and choosing segments, therefore, it is important to consider whether the organisation can develop a sufficiently strong differential advantage to defend its presence in that segment against competitive incursions.

B2B markets

Most of the above discussion has centred on consumer markets. With specific reference to B2B markets, Hlavacek and Ames (1986) propose a similar set of criteria for good segmentation practice. They suggest, for example, that each segment should be characterised by a common set of customer requirements, and that customer requirements and characteristics should be measurable. Segments should have identifiable competition, but be small enough to allow the supplier to reduce the competitive threat, or to build a defendable position against competition. In strategic terms, Hlavacek and Ames also propose that the members of a segment should have some logistical characteristic in common, for example that they are served by the same kind of distribution channel, or the same kind of sales effort. Finally, the critical success factors for each segment should be defined, and the supplier should ensure that it has the skills, assets and capabilities to meet the segment's needs, and to sustain that in the future.

Chapter summary

This chapter has focused on the complexities and methods involved in dividing markets into relevant, manageable and targetable segments in order to allow better-tailored offerings to be developed.

■ In B2B markets, segmentation techniques are divided into macro and micro variables or bases. Macro variables include both organisational characteristics, such as size, location and purchasing patterns, and product or service applications, defining the ways in which the product or service is used by the buyer. Micro segmentation variables lead to the definition, in some cases, of segments of one customer, and focus on the buyer's management philosophy, decision-making structures, purchasing policies and strategies, as well as needs and wants.

■ In consumer markets, five main categories of segmentation are defined: geographic, demographic, geodemographic, psychographic and behaviour based. Between them, they cover a full range of characteristics, whether descriptive, measurable, tangible or intangible, relating to the buyer, the buyer's lifestyle and the buyer's relationship with the product. In practice, a multivariable approach to segmentation is likely to be implemented, defining a portfolio of relevant characteristics from all categories to suit the market under consideration.

■ The implications of segmentation are wide-reaching. It forms the basis for strategic thinking, in terms of the choice of segment(s) to target in order to achieve internal and competitive objectives. The possibilities range from a niche strategy, specialising in only one segment, to a differentiated strategy, targeting two or more segments with different marketing mixes. The undifferentiated strategy, hoping to cover the whole market with only one marketing mix, is becoming increasingly less appropriate as consumers become more demanding, and although it does appear to ease the managerial burden, it is very vulnerable to focused competition.

■ Segmentation offers a number of benefits to both the consumer and the organisation. Consumers get an offering that is better tailored to their specific needs, as well as the satisfaction of feeling that the market is offering them a wider range of products to choose from. The organisation is more likely to engender customer loyalty because of the tailored offering, as well as the benefits of more efficient resource allocation and improved knowledge of the market. The organisation can also use its segmentation as a basis for building a strong competitive edge, by understanding its customers on a deeper psychological level and reflecting that in its marketing mix(es). This forms bonds between organisation/product and customer that are very difficult for competition to break. There are, however, dangers in segmentation, if it is not done well. Poor definition of segments, inappropriate choice of key variables or poor analysis and implementation of the outcomes of a segmentation exercise can all be disastrous. There is also the danger that if competing marketers become too enthusiastic in trying to 'outsegment' each other, the market will fragment to an unviable extent and consumers will become confused by the variety of choice open to them.

■ On balance, segmentation is a good and necessary activity in any market, whether it is a mass fmcg market of international proportions, or a select B2B market involving two or three well-known customers. In either case, any segment defined has to be distinctive (i.e. features at least one characteristic pulling it away from the rest that can be used to create a focused marketing mix), tangible (i.e. commercially viable), accessible (i.e. both the product and the promotional mix can reach it) and finally, defendable (i.e. against competition).

Questions for review and discussion

4.1 How might the market for personal computers, sold to B2B markets, be segmented?

4.2 Find examples of products that depend strongly on *demographic segmentation*, making sure that you find at least one example for each of the main demographic variables.

4.3 What is *psychographic segmentation* and why is it so difficult and so risky to do?

4.4 In what major way does *behavioural segmentation* differ from the other methods? Outline the variables that can be used in behavioural segmentation.

4.5 For each *targeting strategy*, find examples of organisations that use it. Discuss why you think they have chosen this strategy and how they implement it.

4.6 How can *market segmentation* influence decisions about the marketing mix?

case study 4

The pink pound

It is very difficult to estimate the size of the gay market in the UK. Although gay culture has increasingly become part of the mainstream, with many more openly gay celebrities and gay themes and characters featuring regularly in television dramas and comedies, Mintel (2000a, 2000b) has found that the gay market is largely a hidden population. Estimates of the size of the gay population vary between 3 per cent and 15 per cent of the total population but in Mintel's view it is likely to be towards the lower end of the scale overall with a higher concentration in urban areas. Estimates of its spending power also vary between £6bn and £8bn per annum in the UK and $464bn in the US.

There is some consensus on the characteristics of the gay market, however. Gay consumers are perceived to have a higher than average income, and almost 60 per cent of gay men are either single or not cohabiting. Those who are cohabiting are likely to be in dual-income households. In terms of spending patterns, therefore, the lack of dependants and responsibilities gives gay consumers more opportunities for lifestyle spending with a strong focus on leisure and socialising. *The Gay Times* has found that 80 per cent of its readership comes from the ABC1 socioeconomic groups, compared with 43 per cent of the general population.

There is plenty of opportunity for reaching the gay market. Mintel's (2000b) survey found that 77 per cent had internet access at home and/or at work which is much higher than the national average of 26 per cent. Research has also indicated that they spend up to ten times longer online than the average internet user, are more likely to buy the latest gadgets and are particularly appreciative of those organisations that reach out to communicate with them. The internet is important in that it allows gay people to build a stronger sense of community and it gives marketers a chance to locate and target the gay market efficiently and discreetly. The average household income of the gay internet user is £42,500. There are many ISPs and portals set up specifically for online gays (see, for example, http://uk.gay.com, http://www.rainbownetwork.com or http://www.pinklinks.co.uk). These sites attract mainstream advertisers, such as Tesco Direct, Marks and Spencer Financial, Virgin, British Airways, First Direct and IBM as well as companies specifically targeting the gay community.

There are also print media. In the UK, Chronos Publishing produces four national gay publications: *Boyz* (a free weekly magazine aimed at the younger end of the gay market), *The Pink Paper* (weekly newspaper sold via mainstream newsagents), *Fluid Magazine* (monthly style and listings magazine), and *Homosex* (free monthly glossy magazine focusing on sex and relationships). The other major media owner is the Millivres-Prowler Group which owns *The Gay Times* as well as a number of gay shops called Prowler. *The Gay Times* is a monthly, glossy publication which is one of Europe's best-selling gay magazines. Newsagent WH Smith classifies *The Gay Times* as a Tier One magazine, i.e. it must be stocked in every branch. Although the circulation figures for gay publications are not as high as those of mainstream media – *The Gay Times*, for example, has a circulation of around 70,000 – they do deliver a high quality affluent audience.

Many mainstream companies have still not realised the potential of the gay market. Market research has found that 86 per cent of companies have not communicated specifically with gay audiences. Many companies say that they target all groups, not just niche markets, and besides that, they can reach the same audience through mainstream media. In their view, many gays' purchasing decisions are made using the same criteria as those of heterosexual consumers. Companies could, however, be missing out. A phenomenal 92 per cent of gay consumers surveyed said that they were more likely to favour companies that acknowledge and support gay people, and 88 per cent said that it is important to them that a company is gay-friendly.

There are some product and service sectors in which gay consumers are explicitly targeted. The development of 'gay villages', particularly in London, Brighton and Manchester, has in turn led to many overtly gay pubs, bars, restaurants, clubs and shops opening close to each other. This creates a focal point for gay communities and indeed, gay pubs and clubs are important social venues. Mintel (2000b) found that 90 per cent of gay respondents were pub visitors (compared with 69 per cent of the general population) and 81 per cent had visited a club (compared with less than 30 per cent of the general population). Interestingly, club visiting does not decline with age among the gay community as dramatically as it does among the general population.

According to Mintel (2000b), the five most important factors which contribute towards enjoyment of a gay venue were cited as:

- Type of music (77 per cent)
- Not intense or intimidating (75 per cent)
- Have been before and liked it (68 per cent)
- Spacious with seating areas (62 per cent)
- Cheaper drinks and special offers (56 per cent).

The majority of gay bars and pubs are run by independents, although some mainstream breweries have committed themselves to the gay market. Bass, for example, runs 28 gay pubs across the UK while Scottish & Newcastle runs a number of gay pubs, mainly in London (six outlets) but with two in Manchester, purely due to their location on Canal Street at the heart of the 'gay village'. Some operators focus purely on the gay sector, such as the Manto Group (centred on Manchester) and Kudos Group (centred on London).

The holiday market too lends itself to gay targeting by both mainstream and specialised companies. VisitScotland targeted gay travellers, recognising the £72m that the pink pound brings to Scottish hotels every year. It hosted a number of visits by US tour operators that specialised in the gay market and launched a promotional campaign in magazines with high numbers of gay readers. It can be a struggle, however, when the industry sometimes attracts negative publicity such as that generated by the Highland B&B owner who turned away gay guests, describing them as 'deviants'.

Not all organisations actively target the pink pound but increasingly they are finding it difficult to discriminate on the grounds of sexual orientation. Sandals offers a number of all-inclusive adult-only and couples-only resorts in the Caribbean. However, there was considerable criticism when posters highlighted Sandals' resorts as a destination for 'romantic, mixed sex couples'. London Transport barred Sandals' advertisements from its trains after numerous complaints. Perhaps, in an open and non-discriminatory society, the pink pound as a concept may eventually become redundant and irrelevant as being gay becomes just another relatively minor consumer characteristic.

According to Mintel (2000a), respondents in its survey took an average of 2.07 holidays each per year, and 72 per cent of them had taken at least one holiday lasting a week or longer within the previous year. The *Gay Times* found that 41 per cent of its readership took two or more holidays per year. The beach/resort holiday destination is almost as popular with the gay community as with anyone else but gay holidaymakers are more likely to take city-based holidays (23 per cent of Mintel's respondents) than the general population (9 per cent). Mintel (2000a) points out that cities are more likely to have some form of gay infrastructure, in the form of bars and clubs, that would add value to a holiday.

Surprisingly, only 4 per cent of Mintel's respondents had been on a gay-themed holiday and only 3 per cent had booked their holiday using a gay travel agent or tour operator. Around 11 per cent had actually booked holidays over the internet, which is much higher than among the general population in which less than 2 per cent of holidays are booked on the internet. Via the gay websites mentioned earlier, it is easy to find gay-oriented travel agencies: http://www.throb.co.uk, for example, offers holidays to popular gay or gay-friendly resorts in Spain and offers incentives to encourage booking over the internet.

In summary, Mintel (2000a) says that gay holidaymakers want a more diverse array of gay travel products, targeting them with 'quality gay-friendly holidays, rather than gay-themed holidays'.

Sources: Fry (1998, 2000); Jamieson (2004); Lillington (2003); Mintel (2000a, 2000b); Muir (2003).

Questions

1 To what extent does the gay segment conform to the criteria for successful segmentation?

2 What segmentation bases are relevant to the gay pub/club and holiday markets?

3 What are the risks and rewards for a mainstream company targeting the gay segment?

References for chapter 4

Abratt, R. (1993), 'Market Segmentation Practices of Industrial Marketers', *Industrial Marketing Management*, 22, pp. 79–84.

Baker, L. (2004), 'Size Does Matter', *The Guardian*, 6 August, p. 6.

Bale, J. (2001), 'Seats Built for Those that Travel Light', *The Times*, 15 February.

Berno, T. (2004), *2004 World Legacy Awards: On-site Evaluation of Turtle Island, Yasawas, Fiji*, accessed via http:www.turtlefiji.com.

Broadhead, S. (1995), 'European Cup Winners', *Sunday Express*, 7 May, p. 31.

Campaign (2005), 'Quorn Awards Farm £8m Strategic Ad Brief', *Campaign*, 14 January, p. 8.

Chesshyre, T. (2000), 'Gay Can Be Green in Fiji', *The Times*, 19 February.

Douglas, S.P. and Craig, C.S. (1983), *International Marketing Research*, Prentice-Hall.

Evanson, R. (1999), 'A Global Icon in Sustainable Tourism', paper presented at the *2nd Annual Samoan Tourism Convention*, 24–25 February 1999.

Finn, C. (2005), 'Trends in the Consumption of Strawberries in the Home', *The Grocer*, 19 March, p. 55.

Fry, A. (1998), 'Reaching the Pink Pound', *Marketing*, 4 September, pp. 23–6.

Fry, A. (2000), 'Profits in the Pink', *Marketing*, 23 November, pp. 41–2.

Garrahan, M. (2004), 'Why Executives Will Always Be on the Move', *Financial Times*, 15 November, p. 1.

The Grocer (2005), 'Naked Gets its Kit on for the Chillers', *The Grocer*, 22 January, p. 64.

Hlavacek, J.D. and Ames, B.C. (1986), 'Segmenting Industrial and High Tech Markets', *Journal of Business Strategy*, 7 (2), pp. 39–50.

Jamieson, A. (2004), 'Death, Gambling and the Pink Pound: Is this Tourism's Future?', *The Scotsman*, 25 August, p. 19.

Jenkins, M. and McDonald, M. (1997), 'Market Segmentation: Organizational Archetypes and Research Agendas', *European Journal of Marketing*, 31 (1), pp. 17–32.

Johnson, K. (2005), Now Boarding: All Business-Class Flights', *Wall Street Journal*, 14 January, p. B1.

Lillington, K. (2003), 'Dream Ticket', *The Guardian*, 16 October, p. 25.

Machauer, A. and Morgner, S. (2001), 'Segmentation of Bank Customers by Expected Benefits and Attitudes', *International Journal of Bank Marketing*, 19 (1), pp. 6–18.

Marketing Week (2004a), 'Can Beattie Bring Subtlety to Gossard?', *Marketing Week*, 22 July, p. 25.

Marketing Week (2004b), 'Playtex Reveals Wonderbra Range Designed for Risqué Tops', *Marketing Week*, 5 August, p. 10.

Marketing Week (2005), 'Meat-free Food: the Pleasure Without the Flesh', *Marketing Week*, 26 May, p. 38.

Mazzoli, R. (2004), 'Les Jeunes, Leurs Tribus et Leurs Marques', *Marketing Magazine*, December, pp. 58–9.

McGill, A. (2004), Luxury Air Service Ready for Take-off', *The Belfast Newsletter*, 26 January, p. 5.

Mintel (2000a), 'The Gay Holiday Market, 8/11/00', accessed via **http://sinatra2/mintel.com**, October 2001.

Mintel (2000b), 'The Gay Entertainment Market, 12/12/00', accessed via **http://sinatra2/mintel.com**, October, 2001.

Mitchell, A. (1983), *The Nine American Lifestyles: Who Are We and Where Are We Going?*, Macmillan.

Moriarty, R. and Reibstein, D. (1986), 'Benefit Segmentation in Industrial Markets', *Journal of Business Research*, 14 (6), pp. 463–86.

Muir, H. (2003), 'Tube Bans "Anti-gay" Holiday Firm Adverts', *The Guardian*, 5 June, p. 13.

Piercy, N. and Morgan, N. (1993), 'Strategic and Operational Market Segmentation: a Managerial Analysis', *Journal of Strategic Marketing*, 1, pp. 123–40.

Plummer, J.T. (1974), 'The Concept and Application of Lifestyle Segmentation', *Journal of Marketing*, 38 (January), pp. 33–7.

Sarsfield, K. (2004), 'PrimeFlight Suspends its Belfast Operations', *Flight International*, 21 September.

Schoenwald, M. (2001), 'Psychographic Segmentation: Used or Abused', *Brandweek*, 22 January, pp. 34–8.

Sleight, P. (1997), *Targeting Customers: How to Use Geodemographic and Lifestyle Data in Your Business*, 2nd edn, NTC Publications.

Smith, W.R. (1957), 'Product Differentiation and Market Segmentation as Alternative Marketing Strategies', *Journal of Marketing*, 21 (July).

Smorszczewski, C. (2001), 'Corporate Banking', *Euromoney: The 2001 Guide to Poland*, May, pp. 4–5.

Stuttaford, T. (2001), 'The Heart Bears the Ultimate Burden', *The Times*, 15 February.

Turtle Island (2003), 'The Value Proposition of a Commitment to Environmental and Social Sustainability in Tourism', paper presented at the Small Luxury Hotels Annual Conference, Barbados, 27 May, accessed via **http://www.turtlefiji.com**.

Wedel, M. and Kamakura, W. (1999), *Market Segmentation: Conceptual and Methodological Foundations*, Dordrecht: Kluwer Academic Publishers.

Wind, Y. (1978), 'Issues and Advances in Segmentation Research', *Journal of Marketing Research*, 15 (3), pp. 317–37.

Wind, Y. (1982), *Product Policy and Concepts*, Methods and Strategy, Addison-Wesley.

Wind, Y. and Cardozo, R. (1974), 'Industrial Marketing Segmentation', *Industrial Marketing Management*, 3 (March), pp. 153–66.

chapter 5

marketing information and research

Updated by Lorna Young

learning objectives

This chapter will help you to:

1 recognise the importance of information to an organisation and the role information plays in effective marketing decision-making;

2 understand the role of a marketing information system and a decision support system, and develop an awareness of the various types of information available;

3 become familiar with the various steps involved in the marketing research process;

4 outline the sources of secondary and primary data, understand their role and the issues involved in their collection and analysis; and

5 appreciate some of the ethical concerns surrounding marketing research.

Introduction

The nature and role of market research in Europe have seen significant changes in recent years, as organisations increasingly look to do business in a wider range of EU and global markets. Global expenditure on market research is over US$19bn per year. The year-on-year increase in the amount spent on market research in territories such as Eastern Europe and South America is in double figures, as companies strive to understand new markets and audiences for their products and services. In established regions they have to devise ever more competitive strategies to succeed with a highly marketing-literate population, hence in the US, the largest single research market in the world, annual expenditure has increased at around 5 per cent. The UK, another of the most developed markets, tops the per capita expenditure charts, spending approximately £20 per head of population on market research annually. Whether organisations are concerned with breaking into developing markets, or maintaining or expanding their business within more established markets, the need to have effective information on those markets is essential to inform decisions on the most appropriate market entry and competitive strategies. To support all this, the organisation also needs a properly designed and managed information system to enable timely and appropriate information to be available for the marketing decision-maker (**http://www.esomar.com**).

Every aspect of marketing considered in this book, including the definition of markets and market segments, the formulation of an integrated strategy based on the 4Ps and planning and control mechanisms, requires the collection and analysis of information. The better the planning, data collection, information management and analysis, the more reliable and useful the outputs become, and thus marketers are able to make decisions that are more likely to satisfy the needs and wants of selected market segments. The organisation that is prepared to contemplate making a significant change to its marketing effort, without first assessing likely market reaction, is running a very high risk of failure.

In general, gathering information on the actual or potential marketplace not only allows the organisation to monitor trends and issues concerning its current customers, but also helps it to identify and profile potential customers and new markets, and to keep track of its competition, their strategies, tactics and future plans. In this context, market research and information handling offer the organisation a foundation from which it can adjust to the changing environment in which it operates.

eg Since first appearing in 1962, Spider-Man has featured in comic books, newspaper strips, television series, computer games and even as a theme park ride. In 2002, Columbia Pictures gave us Spider-Man the movie, which broke box office records by taking £77.6 million over its first weekend in the US. This meant that at its launch in 2004, Spider-Man 2 had a great deal to live up to, and not simply because of the anticipation generated by its predecessor. It had cost significantly more to make than the first movie ($200m vs $139m). It is also unusual for film sequels to match or better their predecessors, and the release date for the film meant that in its first few weeks it would be vying for cinema audiences against the third Harry Potter movie, Shrek 2, Fahrenheit 9/11, I Robot, The Bourne Supremacy and Catwoman. It was not only immediate competition from these films that was of concern to Columbia. In the two years since the release of Spider-Man 1 special effects had become more sophisticated and the computer-generated imagery in, for example The Lord of the Rings, Harry Potter, and Star Wars movies, had engendered increasingly higher expectations amongst cinemagoers.

To ensure that all marketing activity promoting the new film was motivating, relevant, and capable of maximising interest in the movie, the Columbia Tri-Star marketing group commissioned research into perceptions and expectations of the Spider-Man brand, as represented in the first film and in the context of the current film market. In

Tobey Maguire stars as Peter Parker/Spider-Man on the set of Sam Raimi's movie Spider-Man 2.

Source: © Melissa Moseley/Sony Pictures/Bureau L.A. Collections/Corbis advance of any promotional materials being developed, focus groups were conducted in seven countries among children and adults across a spectrum of 'Spider-Man enthusiasm', over three continents. The findings directly informed the marketing activity planned around the launch. In particular, the understanding that comic hero 'sequels' were often felt to have weak, self-contained plots led Columbia to adopt 'The story continues' line for all Spider-Man 2 communications, allying it with the more positively received 'saga' genre (Lord of the Rings, Harry Potter). In addition, an average of 850 audience members in each of the seven originally researched countries completed rating and recommendation questionnaires after watching the film on its first Saturday night, and the findings were used both to fine-tune sustained marketing activity and to persuade cinema chains to devote more screens and time to the movie. The film grossed $784 million at the box office worldwide and to ensure that marketing activity optimises consumer interest in Spider-Man 3 (due for release in summer 2007) a repeat of this research exercise is planned. Although other film marketers have yet to realise it, Columbia clearly recognises that when investing hundreds of millions of dollars in producing a film, there is value in market research 'to deliver integrated customer and market insights which inspire profitable business decisions' (John Markham, Director of Products and Business Insights, Nokia, as quoted by http://www.research-live.com). (Palmer and Kaminow, 2005; http://www.bbc.co.uk/news; http://www.research-live.com.)

This chapter first considers the role of marketing research and discusses the structure of the marketing information system (MIS) as a means of collecting, analysing and disseminating timely, accurate and relevant data and information throughout the organisation. It then looks at the marketing research planning framework. The stages in designing and implementing a marketing research project are considered, from defining the problem to writing a brief and then executing the project and disseminating the findings. The chapter also looks in detail at sourcing and collecting secondary (or desk) research, from existing or published sources, and primary (or field) research derived from scratch through surveys, observation or experimentation for a specific purpose. The important aspects of designing samples and data collection instruments are explored in some depth, since however well managed the rest of the research process is, asking the wrong questions in the wrong way to the wrong people is a recipe for poor quality marketing information.

Finally, because marketing research is potentially such a complex process, with so much riding on its findings, and because organisations often delegate it to agencies, it is important that it is carried out professionally and ethically. There is, therefore, a section on ethical issues involved in marketing research at pp. 172 et seq.

Throughout this chapter, the terms *client* and *researchers* have been used. Client means the organisation that has commissioned the marketing research, whether from an external agency or from an in-house department. Researchers means the individual or the team responsible for actually undertaking the research task, regardless of whether they are internal or external to the client organisation.

Marketing research: definition and role

Marketing research is at the heart of marketing decision-making and it is important to understand what it involves and its place within the organisation. This section thus discusses the meaning of marketing research and the role that it plays in helping managers to understand new or changing markets, competition, customers' and potential customers' needs and wants.

■ Defining marketing research

Marketing research is a critical input into marketing decisions and can be defined as follows:

Marketing research is the function which links the consumer, customer, and public to the marketer through information – information used to identify and define marketing opportunities and problems; generate, refine, and evaluate marketing actions; monitor marketing performance; and improve understanding of marketing as a process. Marketing research specifies the information required to address those issues; designs the method for collecting information; manages and implements the data collection process; analyses the results; and communicates the findings and their implications.

(AMA definition as quoted by McDaniel and Gates, 1996)

Marketing research links the organisation with the environment in which it is operating and involves specifying the problem, gathering data, then analysing and interpreting those data to facilitate the decision-making process. Marketing research is an essential link between the outside world and the marketer through the information used to identify and define marketing opportunities and problems, generate, refine and evaluate marketing actions, monitor marketing performance and improve understanding of marketing as a process. Marketing research thus specifies the information required to address these issues and designs the methods for collecting the necessary data. It implements the research plan and then analyses and interprets the collected data. After that, the findings and their implications can be communicated.

■ The role of marketing research

The role of marketing research in consumer markets has become well established across the EU. It is particularly important for manufacturers, because of the way in which retailers and other intermediaries act as a buffer between manufacturers and their end consumers. If the manufacturer is not to become isolated from market trends and changing preferences, it is important that an accurate, reliable flow of information reaches the marketing decision-maker. It might be very limiting if only feedback from the trade were used in making new product and marketing mix decisions.

Another factor facing the consumer goods marketer is the size of the customer base. With such a potentially large number of users and potential users, the onus is on the organisation to make sure that it generates a backward flow of communication from those customers. The potential size of consumer markets also opens up the prospect of adapting products and the general marketing offering to suit different target groups. Decisions on product range, packaging, pricing and promotion will all arise from a well-understood profile of the different types of need in the market. Think back to Chapter 4, where the links between market segments and marketing mixes were discussed in more detail. Marketing research is essential for ensuring that segments exist and that they are viable, and for establishing what they want and how to reach them. As markets become increasingly European and global in their scope, marketing research plays an even more crucial role in helping the organisation to Europeanise or globalise its marketing effort, and to decide when to standardise and when to vary its approaches as new markets are opened up.

marketing in action

Understanding you

From the moment you began thinking about continuing into higher education, the market researchers were interested in you. There are some 55,000 undergraduate courses available to applicants in the UK each year, and a great deal of competition for students amongst the universities and colleges which run them. Later in the process rival banks will compete for the deposit of your student loan cheque, and mobile phone companies, fashion, alcohol and cosmetics brands will all seek their share of it.

UCAS (Universities and Colleges Admissions Service) is the central organisation that processes applications for full-time undergraduate courses at universities and colleges in the UK. Dealing with, and holding the details of vast numbers of prospective students gives

UCAS enormous potential for intelligence gathering on this highly targeted audience which is of such interest to both educational establishments and commercial companies.

In 2004 UCAS launched the Ucascard, a loyalty card available to potential students using its applications service. The plastic card offers its holders a range of discounts through a voucher booklet or downloadable form. In its first year, 17 brands that felt there was a good 'fit' between their product or service and the student audience participated in the scheme, including Top Shop, Xbox,

Dell and the AA. With more than 115,000 student applicants registering for the card, these brands were afforded the opportunity for direct marketing dialogue with a captive and highly defined target audience.

At the end of Ucascard's first year, UCAS, in conjunction with Pursuit Media, undertook an online survey of cardholders – not difficult when 80 per cent of applicants opted-in to receive e-mail from UCAS and third parties. The objective of the survey was to identify which brands and services were considered most important by these young people, and their

preferred methods of receiving marketing communications. According to UCAS, 'the results of the survey helped us in our development of the next card'. Specifically, for the academic year 2005/06, the number of brand participants was reduced to 15: the AA, Dell and XBox left the scheme, but Top Shop continued, and was joined by among others HSBC, Orange, PC World, BSM and Vue Cinemas, all of whom benefit from the research findings on how to optimise their opportunities to communicate with you.

Sources: Marketing Week (2005); http://www.ucas.co.uk.

Students are an attractive target market for many branded goods and services.

Source: Image copyright Ben Harris/http://www.hallornothing.com

In B2B markets, the role of marketing research is still very similar to that in consumer markets, in that it helps the organisation to understand the marketing environment better and to make better-informed decisions about marketing strategies. Where the two types of market may differ is in the actual design and implementation of marketing research, because of some of the underlying factors peculiar to B2B markets, such as the smaller number of customers and the closer buyer–seller relationships, as introduced in Chapter 3. Despite any differences, the role of marketing research is still to provide an essential insight into opportunities, markets and customers.

The need for marketing research sometimes arises because the organisation needs specific details about a target market, which is a well-defined, straightforward descriptive research task. Sometimes, though, the research need arises from a much broader question, such as why a new product is not achieving expected market share. The organisation may have a theory about the nature of the problem, but it is up to marketing research to establish whether any assumptions are correct and to check out other possibilities. In practice, most marketing researchers spend a fair proportion of their time on informal projects, undertaken in reaction to specific requests for marketing information. Often these projects lack the scientific rigour associated with the more formal definition of market research. However, problems of a more innovative and complex nature have to be solved through major, formal pieces of market research, simply because of the risks involved in going ahead without the fullest possible insights.

Types of research

So far, the discussion of marketing research has been very general and has not distinguished between different types of research. There are, however, three main types of research, each suitable as an approach to different kinds of problem.

Exploratory research is often undertaken in order to collect preliminary data to help clarify or identify a problem, rather than for generating problem solutions. Before preparing a major proposal, some exploratory work may be undertaken to establish the critical areas to be highlighted in the main body of the research.

eg A major credit card company, looking to grow its market share in Eastern Europe, recognised from examining secondary data on economic and social trends that its products and the way they were promoted in the mature Western European market might not suit this new territory. It commissioned exploratory qualitative research in key countries across Eastern Europe to help it to understand attitudes to personal finance within the potential customer base before committing to a large-scale quantitative survey to inform product development. The results of the study pointed up not only the anticipated differences in consumer sophistication between the West and East, but also significant differences in the beliefs and outlook of residents of neighbouring countries. In particular, attitudes to being in debt and using credit were heavily influenced by the heritage and teachings of the Catholic Church in Poland, yet did not feature in feedback from the neighbouring Czech Republic. Once the presumption that there would be a degree of homogeneity in Eastern Europe had been dispelled, the company could then go on to design a quantitative questionnaire with sensitivity to local idiosyncrasies within this new geographic target market (with thanks to Fiona Jack, Green Light Research International).

Whether primary or secondary sources of data are used, the purpose is to make an initial assessment of the nature of a marketing problem, so that more detailed research work can be planned appropriately.

The second type of research, descriptive research, aims to provide the marketer with a better understanding of a particular issue or problem. This can range from quite specific briefs, for example profiling the consumers of a particular brand, assessing the actual purchase and repurchase behaviour associated with that brand and the reasons behind the behaviour exhibited. Most research in this category tends to be of a large-scale survey type, designed to provide a means of better understanding of marketing problems through the presentation of both quantitative and qualitative data.

Finally, causal or predictive research is undertaken to test a cause-and-effect relationship so that reasonably accurate predictions about the probable outcome of particular actions can be made. The difficulty with this kind of research for the marketing manager is that to be confident that more of x does cause more of y, all the other variables that influence y must be held constant. The real-world laboratory is rarely so obliging, with competitors, retailers and other intermediaries, and the marketing environment generally, all acting independently, doing things that will change the background conditions. Thus researchers trying to establish, for instance, whether or not a promotional 10 per cent price reduction would increase sales volume by 15 per cent during a specified period are faced with the problem of ensuring that all the other variables that might influence sales volume are held constant during the research. Random sampling may help in this process, so that the 10 per cent offer would only be made in a random selection of stores, with the other stores offering normal terms. Any difference in the performance of the product in the two groups of stores is likely to have been caused by the special promotion, since both the 'normal' and the 'promotional' product have been subjected to identical environmental factors, impacting on all the stores, during the same period.

The origins of research data

There are two main types of data, which are generated by fundamentally different research approaches.

Qualitative research

Qualitative research involves the collection of data that are open to interpretation, for example people's opinions, where there is no intention of establishing statistical validity. This type of research is especially useful for investigating motivation, attitudes, beliefs and intentions, rather than utilising probability-based samples. It is often based on very small-scale samples and, as a result, cannot be generalised in numerical terms. Although the results are often subjective, tentative and impressionistic, they can reflect the complexity that underlies consumer decision-making, capturing the richness and depth of how and why consumers act in the way they do.

Quantitative techniques, despite their statistical rigour, are rarely able to capture the full complexity and the wealth of interrelationships associated with marketing activity. The real value in qualitative research, therefore, lies in helping marketers to understand not what people say, but what they mean (or think they mean), and a range of techniques have been developed to assist in that task such as:

- survey research/questionnaires
- focus groups
- in-depth interviews
- observational techniques
- experimentation.

All of these are discussed further at pp. 155 *et seq.*

Quantitative research

Quantitative research involves the collection of information that is quantifiable and is not open to the same level of interpretation as qualitative research. It includes data such as sales figures, market share, market size, consumer product returns or complaints, and demographic information (see pp. 117 *et seq.*) and can be collected through primary research, such as questionnaire-based surveys and interviews, and through secondary sources, including published data.

Quantitative research usually involves larger-scale surveys or research that enable a factual base to be developed with sufficient strength to allow statistically rigorous analysis. Most of us have been on the receiving end of quantitative research at some time or another, having been collared by an interviewer armed with a clipboard interviewing respondents in the street. The success of quantitative research depends in part on establishing a representative sample that is large enough to allow researchers to be confident that the results can be generalised to apply to the wider population. It is then possible to specify that 'Forty-five per cent of the market think that . . . whereas 29 per cent believe . . .'. The research can be undertaken through telephone interviews, face-to-face interviews, or mail questionnaires (see pp. 155 *et seq.*), and can also utilise secondary data sources (see pp. 154 *et seq.*).

The internet is now starting to revolutionise quantitative research. The early emphasis was on gaining cooperation online and structuring questions, but now the techniques used are becoming more sophisticated, interactive, usable over time and more directly linked to systems to integrate all data sources, whether online or offline (James, 2001).

■ Continuous research

A large number of research projects are developed specifically to better understand and to overcome marketing problems as they are identified. At pp. 150 *et seq.* we trace the development of such projects from inception through to final evaluation. Some research, however, is conducted on a continuous basis. Continuous research is available on an ongoing basis for a subscription or agreement to purchase the updated findings. Usually offered by market research agencies, syndicated research provides much useful data on an ongoing basis. In the UK, retail purchases by consumers are tracked by ACNielsen, while Target Group Index (TGI), produced by BMRB, plots the fortunes of some 5000 brands. Similar services are available in all the main European markets. The quality of such research is very high, but the important advantage is shared cost, since ACNielsen data, for example, are essential to any large multiple retailer or brand manufacturer and they will all buy the data. The price for each organisation is still far, far less than the cost of doing or commissioning the research individually. The big disadvantage, of course, is that competitors also have access to exactly the same information.

There are a number of different approaches to generating continuous data.

Consumer panels

Market research companies recruit large numbers of households that are prepared to provide information on their actual buying and consumption patterns on a regular basis. The panel may be constituted to provide as wide a coverage of the population as possible, or it may be defined to home in on a particular segment. The make-up of a consumer panel can be quite specific. The Pre- and Post-Natal Survey (PNS), operated in the UK, runs a regular survey of 700 pregnant women and 600 mothers with babies up to six months old. For manufacturers of baby foods, nappies, toiletries and infant medicines, such inside information can be invaluable. Taylor Nelson Sofres Superpanel is the UK's leading continuous consumer panel and provides purchasing information on all main grocery markets. The panel was launched in 1991 and now consists of 15,000 households which are demographically and regionally balanced to offer a representative picture of the various sub-markets. Data are collected twice weekly through electronic terminals in the home, with purchases being recorded via home-scanning technology (**http://www.tnsofres.com**).

Data can be extracted from consumer panels in two main ways: home audits and omnibus surveys.

Home audits. A home audit means monitoring and tracking the purchasing and consumption patterns of individual households. ACNielsen Homescan has 126,000 households globally in 18 countries linked to in-home bar scanners that record grocery purchases as well as collect answers to survey questions (**http://www.acnielsen.com**). Information is simply downloaded to the research company on a regular basis using a modem. This method is increasingly replacing the old-style consumer diary, which recorded the same kind of information but using pen and paper technology!

Television viewership panels are very similar, in that they involve the recruitment of households and the installation of in-home monitoring equipment. This time, the objective is to use the equipment to enable minute-by-minute recording of audience viewing by channel. From these data, organisations such as AGB and RSMB are able to provide detailed ratings for programmes and viewing patterns during commercial breaks, a critical factor in the sale of advertising time.

Omnibus surveys. An omnibus survey, as the term suggests, enables an organisation to participate in an existing research programme whenever it is felt appropriate. When an organisation wants to take part, it can add a few extra questions to the next round of questionnaires sent to the large number of respondents who are regularly contacted. The big advantage is cost, although normally the number of questions that can be asked on behalf of a specific organisation is very small. The speed with which answers are received is also an important factor.

There are three types of omnibus survey: those carried out face-to-face during an interviewer visit to the home, telephone surveys and finally internet interviews. Face-to-face omnibuses tend to offer a larger sample size, often around 2000 adults, and allow support material to be used. They are also better for exploring more complex or sensitive issues (for example, health- or finance-related questioning) than the other two methods. Telephone omnibuses offer a faster turnaround time (about four to five days quicker than a face-to-face survey) but the sample sizes tend to be smaller and the scope of questioning is more limited. Internet omnibuses are new and are now spreading after their introduction in the United States. They are all based on self-completion of questionnaires and the sample must be carefully controlled to avoid unwanted respondents. It is, however, a very quick way of accessing the views of the internet population.

Taylor Nelson Sofres Consumer Omnibus has a number of options:

- *Capibus* is the UK's largest weekly omnibus offering a sample of 2000 adults, interviewed face-to-face with full results within ten days. Questions can be targeted and considerable information on the individual and household is collected.
- *PhoneBus* is run twice-weekly providing data from 2000 UK adults. It offers a four-day turnaround so if the questions are submitted by 10 a.m. on Tuesday, responses in full tables are available by Friday lunchtime. Most of the fieldwork is undertaken by CATI and random digit dialling is used to make the sample more representative by including ex-directory telephone users.
- *Ncompass* is Taylor Nelson Sofres' international omnibus, compiled through data collected by offices in over 80 countries. Results can be available within two weeks and if the Speedline is used, that can be reduced to just six days in the main European markets from a sample of 1000 adults per country.
- *Autobus* focuses on motoring samples with over 1000 motorists contacted each week of the year. Such specialist omnibus services are especially useful for the fast gathering of information on specific sectors.

Other companies such as Access Omnibus Surveys and RSGB Omnibus also offer regular omnibus surveys in a similar manner, allowing considerable choice in selecting the most appropriate survey for the target audience.

The internet is now starting to have a bigger impact on consumer panel research. ACNielsen, for example, has a 9000-strong panel of internet users in the UK and 90,000 worldwide and this is growing at a rapid rate as part of audience measurement research (Gray, 2000b). Every time a page is visited, specialised software installed in participants' computers records the information for ACNielsen. Some caution must, however, be exercised in the use of internet research. MORI, after using e-mail in an IT survey panel, dropped it because of falling response rates and reverted to telephone interviews. Although the online panel was a lower cost to clients, this had to be related to its effectiveness in actually generating data (http://www.researchlive.com).

Retail audits

The retail audit concept is perhaps the easiest to implement, as it relies on trained auditors visiting selected retail stores and undertaking regular stock checks. Increasingly, the use of barcode scanning is providing even more up-to-date information on what is sold where and when. Changes in stock, both on the shelf and in the warehouse, indicate an accurate figure for actual sales to consumers by pack size. This information is especially useful for assessing brand shares, response to sales promotions and the amount of stock being held within the retail trade. Along with information on price levels, the brand manager has much useful information with which to make revised marketing mix decisions.

Marketing information systems

In order to serve the information needs of the organisation and to support decision-making, marketers need to focus not only on collecting data and information, but also on how to handle and manage issues of storage, access and dissemination (McLuhan, 2001b). There is little point in having a highly complex information system that cannot readily deliver what managers want, when they want it and how they want it. Any system must be responsive to the needs of the users.

A marketing information system (MIS) has been defined as:

an organised set of procedures and methods by which pertinent, timely and accurate information is continually gathered, sorted, analysed, evaluated, stored and distributed for use by marketing decision makers.

(Zikmund and d'Amico, 1993, p. 108)

Nowadays, most of these systems are data-based and use high-powered computers. System requirements need to coordinate data collection and decision support, as shown in Figure 5.1. The MIS should be tailored to the specific requirements of the organisation. These will be influenced by the size of the organisation and the resources available as well as the specific needs of decision makers. While these needs are likely to be broadly similar between organisations, they will not be exactly the same and therefore the design of the systems and their sophistication will vary. What is important is that the information is managed in a way that facilitates the decision-making process, rather than just being a collection of data gathering dust.

It can be seen from Figure 5.1 that an MIS provides a comprehensive framework for managing information. Along with generating huge amounts of data about their day-to-day activities (sales, customer details, incoming and outgoing orders, transactions, service requirements, etc.), organisations are usually in various stages of gathering other data about

Figure 5.1 The marketing information system

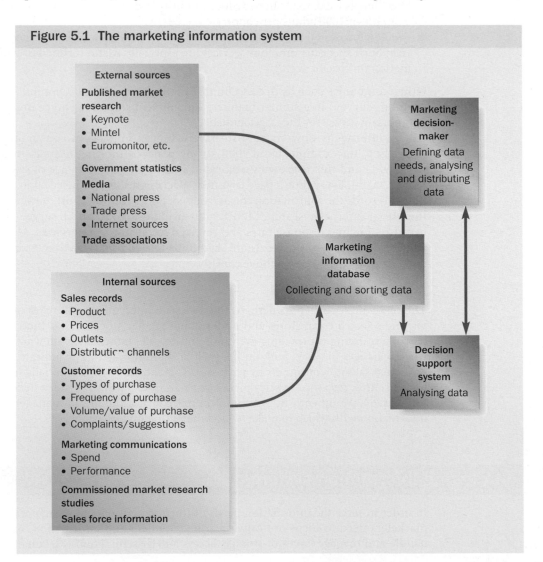

eg | The supermarket chain Somerfield utilised Ipsos's 'Customizer' framework to optimise use of their 4 million-strong Saver Card customer database. Ipsos first segmented the database according to customer transactions, then interviewed 2000 shoppers in 32 different Somerfield stores. By combining the transactional data with this further research data, then generalising it across the whole database, Ipsos could identify for Somerfield not only which groups of customers bought which products, but also why, and how to influence them. The resultant MIS allows Somerfield to target and tailor communications and offers to the most receptive customers (Alderson, 2005).

competitors, new product tests, improved service requirements and changing regulations, for example. Timeliness of information, whether it be for short- or long-term decision-making, is also of importance, as the provision of immediate feedback or projected trend details to decision-makers can provide a competitive advantage in the marketplace.

The other requirement of information is that it should be appropriate to the needs of those using it. Organisations have to manage the information they have, identify what information they need, and present it in the form that the various decision-makers require. Not all information that the organisation has is necessarily appropriate for all marketing decision-makers. It is therefore important to identify the various needs of those decision-makers and to ensure they are supplied with only the information that meets their needs.

Sources of marketing information

As indicated at the outset of this chapter and in Figure 5.1, there are two main sources of information for an MIS system, internal and external.

External sources

External sources are either *ad hoc* studies using secondary and primary research, or continuous data provided by the various syndicated and omnibus studies mentioned earlier. Information comes from sources external to the organisation, such as customers, suppliers, channels of distribution, strategic alliance partners, independent third parties, commercial agencies, industry associations, CSO, Eurostat, etc., and external sources like the internet. The challenge for the marketing manager is to integrate these findings into the organisation to effect change.

Internal sources

Information also comes from internal sources within the organisation. These include the internal record keeping system (production, accounting, sales records, purchase details, etc.), marketing research, sales representatives' field reports, call details, customer enquiries and complaints, product returns, etc. All of this information, again, must be managed appropriately and distributed in a timely fashion if it is going to be used effectively to assist decision-making.

eg | The development of Electronic Point of Sale (EPOS) technology has revolutionised the flow of information within retail operations, providing a base for fast and reliable information on emerging trends. Either by using a laser barcode scanner or by keying in a six-figure code, retailers can be right up to date in what is moving, where and what the immediate impact will be on stock levels. Retail managers can monitor movement on different product lines on a daily basis and adjust stock, orders and even in-store promotions, based on information either from individual stores or across all the branches. Tesco, with its Clubcard loyalty scheme, can track and record the purchasing and shopping habits of millions of individual customers, and tailor its marketing offerings, both locally and nationally, based on solid, internally generated information.

Clegg (2001) emphasised the importance not just of collecting externally generated marketing data but also of ensuring that there is effective communication within the organisation so that customer contact personnel in particular can contribute fully to building market research knowledge. If the marketing database is seen as being owned by the research department rather than being a knowledge reservoir for the whole organisation, it may not be so well informed of the experiences of customer-facing staff.

Organisations thus get everyday information, often as a matter of course, from a variety of sources that can influence their decision-making, but *intelligence* means developing a perspective on the information that provides a competitive edge, perhaps in new product opportunities or the opening up of a new market segment.

The main difficulty is information overload (Smith and Fletcher, 1999) where there is too much information and not enough intelligence. One study suggested that 49 per cent of managers surveyed cannot cope with the information they receive and another that organisations use as little as 20 per cent of their knowledge (Von Krogh *et al.*, 2000), meaning that a lot of perhaps useful intelligence is locked away or not evident to the decision-maker. Collecting marketing information should not, therefore, be an end in itself but should be part of a valuable and usable knowledge management source that can be accessed upon demand in a meaningful and digestible form.

Sometimes environmental scanning can provide useful insights. By deliberately looking at the various influences on product markets, an organisation may spot early warning signs before the competitors are aware of them. This will help in the forward planning process and will be especially useful as an input to strategic development decisions.

Decision support systems

The availability and use of a range of computer-based decision support systems (DSS) are changing the way information is used and presented to decision-makers, and the way in which they interpret it (Duan and Burrell, 1997). While an MIS organises and presents information, the DSS actually aids decision-making by allowing the marketer to manipulate information and explore 'what if . . .' type questions. A DSS usually comprises a software package designed for a personal computer, including statistical analysis tools, spreadsheets, databases and other programs that assist in gathering, analysing and interpreting information to facilitate marketing decision-making. By having the DSS connected to the MIS, marketers further enhance their ability to use the information available. Effectively, this brings the MIS to the desktop, and even to the personal laptop, with the appropriate connections, servers and modems. This can encourage wide use of information, although there may be some problems about restricting access to more sensitive areas and ensuring that the complexity can be handled from a systems perspective.

A DSS was developed, for example, to help decide the launch price of a new pharmaceutical product. The system enabled various marketing, sales force and pricing actions to be assessed to find the best price to charge. The system simulated market conditions as closely as possible to assess the impact of price on sales, share and profits over time (Rao, 2000).

The MIS or DSS will never replace decision-makers, only help them. Marketing decisions still need the imagination and flair that can interpret 'hard' information and turn it into implementable tactics and strategies that will maintain competitive edge.

The marketing research process

When an organisation has decided to undertake a research project, it is important to make sure that it is planned and executed systematically and logically, so that the 'right' objectives are defined and achieved as quickly, efficiently and cost effectively as possible. A general model of the marketing research process is presented here, which can be applied to a wide range of real situations with minor adaptations. Figure 5.2 shows the broad stages, and although it may suggest a logic and neatness that is rarely found in practice, it does at the very

Figure 5.2 The market research process

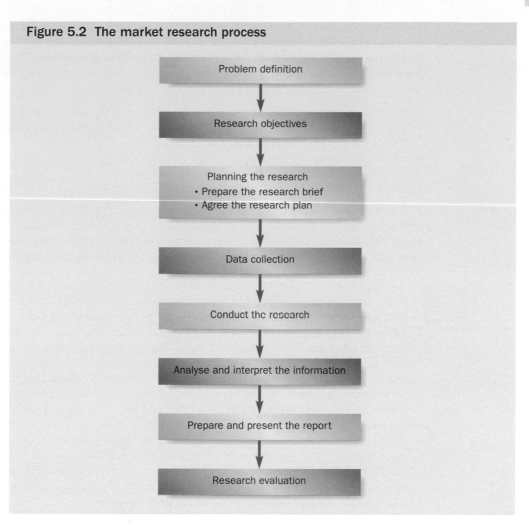

least offer a framework that can be tailored to meet different clients, situations and resources. Each stage in the process will now be discussed in turn.

■ Problem definition

Problem definition is the first and one of the most important stages in the research process, because it defines exactly what the project is about and as such influences how the subsequent stages are conducted, and ultimately the success of the project itself. The organisation sponsoring the research, whether it intends to use in-house researchers or an agency, needs to define precisely what the problem is and how that translates into research objectives. This may also lead to the identification of other concerns or problems that need to be included in the project. For example, if the fundamental problem has been defined as 'People are not buying our product', the organisation may feel that it should not only explore people's attitudes to the product itself, but also look at how they rate the product on other aspects of the marketing mix in comparison with the competition.

Once the broad nature of the problem has been established, the next stage involves more precise definition of objectives.

■ Research objectives

The tight specification of research objectives is important to ensure that the project is developed along the right lines. Usually, primary objectives need to be distinguished from secondary objectives. The primary objective for an electrical components manufacturer seeking to enter the French market, for example, might be to establish the market potential for the products specified and to indicate appropriate market entry strategies. The secondary objectives tend to be more specific and comprehensive. For the components manufacturer they might include:

- defining market trends and competitive structure over the past five years
- profiling the existing main suppliers in terms of strengths and weaknesses (products, prices, distribution, branding, service, etc.)
- identifying the main buyers of electrical components
- identifying the main buying criteria when purchasing
- surveying potential trade and end users for willingness to switch supply source.

The list above is not exhaustive, but the main point is that objectives clearly drive the whole research process, and should provide the necessary foundations for whatever management decisions will have to be taken at the end. In all cases, the research objectives need to be clearly and concisely stated in writing to ensure that the research brief can be adequately prepared.

eg A sportswear brand, originally well known for one core sport, had over time developed ranges for other sports and, in the process, also developed a number of different logos. Research was commissioned with the objective of discovering which single logo could best represent the brand across all sports. Specific outputs required from the research were guidance on the most appropriate and recognisable logo for the brand to adopt, and its optimum positioning on the clothing of sponsored elite athletes in each sport. A worldwide sample of 10,000 sports fans, recruited for their interest in the relevant sports, was questioned on brand awareness and brand image and asked both to nominate their preferred logo from a selection of five shown and to give reasons for their choice. The research company then analysed the most commonly used camera angles from a library of video and press coverage of major sporting events to identify areas of clothing with the highest frequency of exposure. The client gained clear and substantiated recommendations on logo design and siting to achieve maximum exposure on sports apparel (http://www.sportsmarketingsurveys.com).

To be successful at this stage, the project team needs good communication and a solid understanding of the issues involved. This is where exploratory research may be useful, in eliminating some of the possibilities or filling some basic gaps in knowledge and understanding. This could involve some preliminary discussions with distributors, experts or customers. The information collected, including any secondary data, can then be used to prepare the research brief for the formal commissioning of work.

■ Planning the research

The planning stage falls into two main parts: first, the preparation of the research brief, and second, agreeing the research plan. This applies equally whether the research is conducted in-house or not.

Prepare the research brief

The research brief originates from the client. Its quality and precision can vary widely. In some cases, the client has a vague idea of what the problem is, but is not sure what the underlying causes or dynamics are. They thus rely heavily on researchers to specify the problem and then decide on the best research design, effectively asking them to undertake the first two stages of the research process. In many ways, the development of this kind of brief is rather like consultancy and may be part of that kind of overall process.

The main points of the research brief (adapted from Hague, 1992) will be:

- a definition of the problem, including its history
- a description of the product to be researched

- a description of the market to be researched
- specific research objectives
- time and financial budget
- reporting requirements.

This brief may be the subject of modification and negotiation during the meetings.

Agree the research plan

On the basis of the brief, a research plan needs to be agreed before the project begins. Not only is this important for cost and timing considerations, but it also ensures that the data generated will enable management decisions to be resolved without the need for further analysis. There is nothing worse than completing a major research project only to find that the results are at best of only partial use to managers!

The details of the research plan will vary according to the project, but ideally it should contain:

- background information for the research
- research objectives (based on decisions that need to be made and the criteria to be used)
- research methods (secondary and/or primary)
- type of analysis to be employed
- degree of client involvement
- data ownership
- details of subcontractors (if any)
- level and timing of ongoing reporting
- format of final report
- timing and cost of research.

An organisation with a major research project may well ask a number of research agencies to tender for the business. Each agency will obviously propose different research plans. These need to be evaluated alongside the organisation's more usual buying criteria. The final decision by the clients should be based on confidence that the chosen agency can best meet its information needs through the research plan proposed, but within any constraints imposed.

■ Data collection

The first requirement in preparing the research plan is to identify clearly what additional data are needed and then to establish how they are to be collected. This may involve collecting both primary and secondary data, or just primary data.

Secondary research

Sometimes also referred to as *desk research*, secondary research consists of data and information that already exist and can be accessed by an organisation. Thus, for example, it would include published government statistics and published market research reports.

Clearly, if secondary research is available that answers the question or solves the problem, then that is the quickest and most efficient way of gathering the necessary data. In many cases, however, secondary data may not be directly applicable, or may only give half the picture.

The pursuit of secondary data should be exhaustive, as secondary data are usually far more cost-effective and quicker to collect than primary data. However, because secondary data were collected for another purpose they are not always in a form that is useful or appropriate, and thus they often have to be re-analysed to convert them into a form that can be used for a particular project. We will look in detail at secondary research below.

Primary research

Sometimes also called *field* research, primary research is undertaken or commissioned by an organisation for a specific purpose. The required information does not already exist in any available form and so the research has to be undertaken from scratch.

The advantage of primary research is that it is exactly tailored to the problem in hand, but it can be expensive and time consuming to undertake. We will look in detail at methods of primary research on pp. 155 *et seq*.

Once the researchers have recognised that information is needed that is not currently available, they must decide from what source they can most effectively get that information. It is well worth checking secondary data sources first to see what has already been done. Even if secondary data are available, or can be converted, they may still not be sufficient to meet all the researchers' needs, and thus a primary research study may still have to be developed to fill the gaps or further explore the issues. This means that a market research project will often incorporate both primary and secondary research, each complementing the other.

Secondary research

Secondary data can be either internal or external to the organisation. The former is considered to be part of the normal MIS (marketing information system), as outlined on pp. 147 *et seq.* The advantage of secondary research is that it can be much cheaper and quicker to access, and may provide information that the organisation would not otherwise have the time, resources or inclination to gather. External secondary data offer valuable information to researchers but, of course, the major drawback with secondary data is that the information has been collected for purposes other than this particular research project, and may not be in a suitable or usable form. The organisation also needs to be careful that secondary data are current and that they are appropriate and applicable to the problem in hand.

Secondary data can play a variety of roles in the research process. Its main role is probably in providing background information on industries and markets, in terms of trends, dynamics and structure. Some of this information may be useful in its own right in informing management decision-making, although it is more likely to provide pointers for further primary research. It can also provide useful information that may assist in sample selection for surveys by indicating the main competitor and customer groups.

■ Sources of secondary data

It would be impossible to list all potential sources of data, as the number of sources is vast and much will depend on the type of research project in question. A discussion with your friendly local business librarian will soon reveal how extensive such a list can be!

Secondary data vary widely in terms of relevance and quality. Boyd *et al.* (1977) suggest four criteria for evaluating secondary data sources:

1 Pertinency of the data
2 Who collects the data and why
3 Method of collecting data
4 Evidence of careful work.

Although secondary sources of data are widely used, as they tend to be low cost and usually easily obtainable once a source has been identified, the criteria above do suggest some potential problem areas. Often the data fail to get down to the micro level necessary to support management decisions. The focus is often at industry level rather than the sector or segment of particular interest, perhaps within a defined geographical area. Some data may have been collected to promote the well-being of the industry, rather than to provide wholly accurate figures, and sometimes they are not always accurate because of their source, their age or the way they were collected. However, for most surveys the sorting, sifting and analysis of secondary data are useful for purposes ranging from developing sample frames (see pp. 162 *et seq.*) to providing comprehensive insights into market size, structure and trends.

■ Online databases

Up until the 1990s most secondary data was print-based. Directories, both specialist and general, were essential tools for the market researcher. Although most directories are still in hard copy, most have been supplemented by CD-ROMs and by direct internet access via websites such as yell.com. They tend to appeal to different audiences. The key to the internet is offering an effective search engine so that the drudgery can be taken out of searching for and sourcing information. In internet versions, it is the relevance of the data to the task that is making them ever more attractive (Wilson, 2001).

Other market research databases are also going online. Euromonitor, through its Market Research Monitor, offers an online database available on subscription to cover 1300 consumer market and retail briefings. It covers consumer market analysis from 52 countries, and market profiles from four major industrialised countries: the UK, France, Germany and the US (Marshall, 2000; **http://www.euromonitor.com**). It pays, therefore, to explore thoroughly what is currently available before going out and generating more information at a far higher cost.

Primary research

Once the decision to use primary research has been made, researchers have to define what data need to be collected and how. This section looks specifically at 'how'. First, there is an overview of primary research methods.

Whatever method is chosen as most appropriate to the client's information needs, researchers then have to think about defining a sample of individuals or organisations from the total population of interest (defined as a market segment or an industry, for instance). This topic is covered in some depth on pp. 162 *et seq.* Finally, of particular interest to those conducting surveys, pp. 165 *et seq.* look specifically at questionnaires.

■ Research methods

The three most commonly used methods for collecting primary data are interviews and surveys, observation and experiments.

Interviews and surveys

Interviews and surveys involve the collection of data directly from individuals. This may be by direct face-to-face personal interview, either individually or in a group, by telephone or by a mail questionnaire. Each of these techniques, considered in turn below, has its own set of advantages and disadvantages, which are summarised in Table 5.1.

Personal interviews. A personal interview is a face-to-face meeting between an interviewer and a respondent. It may take place in the home, the office, the street, a shopping mall or at any prearranged venue. In one extreme case, a holiday company decided to interview respondents who were at leisure on the beach. One can imagine the varied responses!

There are three broad types of personal interview:

■ *The in-depth, largely unstructured interview*: Taking almost a conversational form, this is very useful for exploring attitudinal and motivational issues. It could last for one or two hours and can range fairly freely over a number of relevant issues. There is often considerable scope for the interviewer to explore some topics in more depth if additional unforeseen themes emerge in the interview, and thus high-level interviewing skills are needed, along with a sound knowledge of the product-market concept being examined. However, the time taken to complete an interview, and the cost of each interview, make large-scale surveys of this nature prohibitively expensive. In B2B markets, they are often used on a small-scale basis to fill gaps left by other approaches such as mail or telephone surveys.

■ *The structured interview*: This allows the interviewer far less flexibility to explore responses further and results in a more programmed, almost superficial interview. Little use is made of open-ended questions and the questionnaire is carefully designed for ease and speed of recording information and progress through the interview. The use of a standardised questionnaire means that the responses from a large number of individuals can be handled with considerable ease, as there is no need for further interpretation and analysis. The

Table 5.1 Comparative performance of interview and survey techniques

	Personal interviews	Group interviews	Telephone survey	Mail survey
Cost per response	High	Fairly high	Low	Very low
Speed of data collection	Fast	Fast	Very fast	Slow
Quantity of data collectable	Large	Large	Moderate	Moderate
Ability to reach dispersed population	Low	Low	High	High
Likely response rate	High	Very high	Fairly high	Low
Potential for interviewer bias	High	Very high	Fairly high	None
Ability to probe	High	High	Fairly high	None
Ability to use visual aids	High	High	None	Fairly high
Flexibility of questioning	High	Very high	Fairly high	None
Ability to ask complex questions	High	High	Fairly high	Low
Ability to get truth on sensitive questions	Fairly low	Fairly high	Fairly high	High
Respondent anonymity	Possible	Fairly possible	None	None
Likely respondent cooperation	Good	Very good	Good	Poor
Potential for respondent misunderstanding	Low	Low	Fairly low	High

limitations stem mainly from the need to design and pilot the questionnaire very carefully to ensure that it meets the specification expected of it. We look more closely at some of these questionnaire issues at pp. 165 *et seq.*

■ *The semi-structured interview*: This is a hybrid of the other two methods and is based around a programmed script, but the inclusion of some open-ended questions gives the interviewer scope to pursue certain issues more flexibly.

Group interviews or focus groups. Group interviews are used to produce qualitative data that are not capable of generalisation to the wider population, but do provide useful insights into underlying attitudes and behaviours relevant to the marketer. A group interview normally involves between six and eight respondents considered to be representative of the target group being examined. The role of the interviewer is to introduce topics, encourage and clarify responses and generally guide proceedings in a manner that is effective without being intrusive (Witthaus, 1999).

In this kind of group situation, individuals can express their views either in response to directed questions or, preferably, in response to general discussion on the themes that have been introduced. Often, the interaction and dialogue between respondents are more revealing of opinions. So that participants will relax enough to open out like this, it is often helpful to select the group concerned to include people of a similar status. For example, a manufacturer of an innovative protective gum shield for sports persons organised different group interviews for sports players (users) and dentists (specifiers). Further subdivision could have been possible by type of sport, or to distinguish the casual player from the professional.

A small group interview.

Source: Leapfrog Research & Planning Ltd http://www.leapfrogresearch.co.uk

Group interviews are especially useful where budgets are limited or if the research topic is not yet fully understood. If secondary data have clearly indicated in quantitative terms that there is a gap in the market, group interviews may be useful in providing some initial insights into why that gap exists, whether customers are willing to see it filled and with what. This could then provide the basis for more detailed and structured investigation. There are of course dangers in generalisation, but if between four and six different discussion groups have been held, some patterns may begin to emerge. For the smaller business with limited funds, group interviews may provide a useful alternative to more costly field techniques.

Telephone interviews. Telephone interviews are primarily used as a means of reaching a large number of respondents relatively quickly and directly. It is far more difficult to ignore a telephone call than a mail survey, although the amount and complexity of information that can be gathered are often limited. In the absence of any visual prompts and with a maximum attention span of probably no more than 10 minutes, the design of the questionnaire needs to be given great care and piloting is essential to ensure that the information required is obtainable.

The range of applications is wide but the telephone is especially useful for usage and purchase surveys where market size, trends and competitive share are to be assessed. Other applications include assessing advertising and promotional impact, customer satisfaction studies and establishing a response to a very specific phenomenon, such as the launch of a new export assistance scheme. Kwik Fit Exhausts telephones its recent customers to establish the degree of satisfaction with their recent purchase.

The interviewing process itself is highly demanding, but the use of software packages can enable the interviewer to record the findings more effectively and formally and to steer through the questionnaire, using loops and routing through, depending on the nature of the response. With the demand for such surveys, a number of agencies specialise in telephone research techniques.

eg Specialist business-to-business research agency B2B International (**http://www.b2binternational.com**) describes the main benefits of Computer Aided Telephone Interviewing (CATI) to its clients as accuracy and speed. As the questionnaire and routing appear automatically on the screen in front of interviewers, they are left free to concentrate on the interview itself and on recording responses accurately rather than concerning themselves with instructions on paper. The nature of the computer-aided approach means that feedback on results can be given in real time, and interviews are generally completed more quickly than with paper equivalents. The approach copes less well with open-ended response questions, however, and although it is time saving in execution, it can be time consuming to set up (after all, it requires the writing of computer software). With the increase in global and multi-territory research projects, most telephone interviewing teams within a research agency will have a quota of multi-lingual interviewers, and many agencies, like Survey Solutions (**http://www.surveysolutions.co.uk**), have built up partnerships with associate telephone interviewing specialists around the globe to provide clients with native-speaking telephone interviewers in most regions of the world.

Mail questionnaires. This popular form of research involves sending a questionnaire through the post to the respondent for self-completion and return to the researchers. Questionnaires can, of course, also be handed out at the point of sale, or included in product packaging, for buyers to fill in at their own convenience and then post back to the researchers. Hotels and airlines assess their service provision through this special kind of mail survey, and many electrical goods manufacturers use them to investigate purchasing decisions.

While the mail survey has the advantage of wide coverage, the lack of control over response poses a major problem. Researchers cannot control who responds and when and the level of non-response can create difficulties. Response rates can drop to less than 10 per cent in some surveys, although the more pertinent the research topic to the respondent, and the more 'user friendly' the questionnaire, the higher the response rate. The variable cost of a 1000-questionnaire postal survey is between £600 and £800. That excludes the cost of buying a mailing list or investment in specialised mail handling equipment. It is not the cost of the mailing that counts, however, but the cost per response gained when response rates can vary between 5 per cent and 50 per cent (**http://www.b2binternational.com**). Offering a special incentive can also work (Brennan *et al.*, 1991). In a survey of Irish hotel and guest house owners, the offer of free tickets to a local entertainment facility proved an attractive incentive. Other larger-scale consumer surveys promise to enter all respondents into a draw for a substantial prize.

Mail surveys are especially prevalent in B2B markets, where target respondents can be more easily identified from contacts or mailing lists. The process of mailing can also be readily implemented and controlled using the organisation's normal administrative and mailing infrastructure already set up for response logging, address label generation, folding and franking, etc. One way of trying to improve response rates for B2B mail surveys is to warn or notify the desired respondent in advance that the survey is on its way. Haggett and Mitchell (1994), reviewing the literature on pre-notification, found that overall it increases response rates by around 6 per cent and on average reduces by one the number of days taken to respond. The telephone shows the best results, increasing responses by 16 per cent, while postcards manage only a 2.5 per cent improvement. There is, however, no evidence to suggest that the quality of the response is also improved.

There is no one best method to select from the group discussed above. Much will depend on the nature of the research brief, especially in the light of the resources available and the quality and quantity of information required for decision-making. The other factor that has become of significant concern is the cost of the research survey. Face-to-face interviews, especially if conducted on an in-depth basis, tend to be the most costly and time consuming, thus making this form of survey less attractive. Other survey techniques, such as group interviews, telephone surveys and mail questionnaires, all provide alternative, cheaper ways of gathering data. Each of them, however, also has its own set of limitations. Ultimately, the decision on choice of technique has to put aside absolute cost considerations and think in terms of finding the most cost-effective way of collecting those vital data.

Internet research

The growth in the use of the internet is having a big impact on the market research industry. E-consultancy (2005) estimates that online market research will be worth £160m by the end of 2005. Business opportunities have been created by the significant increase in the number of dotcoms, 'clicks-and-mortar' companies, ISPs and online advertisers, all of them using market research to guide decision-making. Online research is, however, now also being increasingly used in preference to other research methods. It is estimated that around 10 per cent of market research in the UK is carried out using the internet, rising to up to 25 per cent for bespoke studies. With around 80 per cent of the population now using the internet, it is easier to achieve representative samples, and the cost-effectiveness and speed of turnaround have encouraged smaller companies that have never before had the budget to undertake market research to invest in this approach (*New Media Age*, 2004).

Internet usage rates will determine the speed and scope of internet market research. In the UK, the figure is 45 per cent compared to 60 per cent in the US, so obtaining a representative sample of the population is still highly problematic. It's fine if you want to research internet users, but for more targeted or representative samples it has severe limitations. A range of techniques is being employed, however, including online focus groups, questionnaires, pop-up surveys and extended e-mail groups. Table 5.2 highlights the advantages and disadvantages of online research, but as internet usage expands, technology improves and research industry experience and techniques grow, many of the disadvantages should be overcome.

Table 5.2 Advantages and disadvantages of internet research

	Type of online research	
	Quantitative	Qualitative
Benefits	Inexpensive compared with traditional research methodologies	Slightly faster and cheaper than traditional focus groups
	Fast turnaround	Avoids dominance by 'loud' personalities
	Automated data collection	
	Can show graphics, sometimes video	More client control
	No interviewer bias in data	Can show concepts or websites
	Data quality (logic checks and in-depth open-ended answers)	Easier to recruit respondents
		Can be coordinated internationally and allows for mixed nationalities
	Seamless international coordination	
Limitations	'Respondent universe'	Lose non-verbal elements of traditional focus groups
	Sampling issues: narrow target audience; difficult to identify; understanding the sample	Less useful for emotive issues
		Online moderation requires new skills
	Often self-completion-based, therefore potentially self-selecting	Some respondents can be hampered by slow typing speeds
	Technical problems	Technical problems
		Sampling issues: narrow target audience can be tricky to identify; can be difficult to understand the sample

Source: Alex Johnston, Technology and Communications Director for New Media Research International, as reported by Gray (2000b) 'How to use existing channels to target customers', *Admap*, December.

The big attractions are the significantly reduced data collection costs and the speed of setting up and implementing research activities. As with any research technique, however, it is important to ensure that what comes back is reliable and useful. There is always a risk that 'cheap' will mean devaluing the quality of the research. Nevertheless, the visual anonymity provided by cyber groups carried out on the internet can lead to an improvement in participation rates and the quality of findings from specific groups. It is easier, for example, to access the thoughts and feelings of obese consumers when there is no requirement for them to meet and be 'on show' to strangers (Pollitt, 2005).

The market research company Future Foundation has used the internet for qualitative research, including week-long e-mail groups, online moderated groups with panels, and offline groups (Cornish, 2001; **http://www.futurefoundation.net**). Others are making full use of the power of the internet to present media such as sounds, images and video clips or to use complex question routings that are incompatible with the printed page or interview (Bolden *et al.*, 2000).

The law on data collection over the internet is tightening. The UK's Data Protection Act prohibits the collection of data without consent, or for purposes not disclosed at the time. This means that the consumer must be made aware of any recording of websites browsed or online purchases in advance, allowing them to opt out if they want (Anstead, 2000). This also applies to online research. In order to undertake a survey prior permission has to be obtained from respondents before a potentially unwanted e-mail is sent. It is not enough that a customer's name is on a list: it is essential that people agree in advance to their e-mail addresses being used for that purpose. Obtaining e-mail addresses and ensuring that the consumer is happy to be sent information is one thing, but persuading people to e-mail back to verify their identity and signify their willingness to participate – a process known as closed-loop verification – is another (Billings, 2001). This is bad news from the researcher's point of view, because if a significant proportion of potential respondents opts out, it will reduce the representativeness of online research.

Observational research

This method involves, as its name implies, the observation by trained observers of particular individuals or groups, whether they are staff, consumers, potential consumers, members of the general public, children or whoever. The intention is to understand some aspect of their behaviour that will provide an insight into the problem that has been identified by the marketing research plan. For example, trials are often conducted with new products in which consumers are asked to use a particular product and are observed while they do so, thus giving information about design, utility, durability and other aspects, such as ease of use by different age groups, and whether people naturally use it in the intended way. This provides an opportunity to test the product and observe how it is used first hand.

eg A typical large UK supermarket will stock around 30,000 different products within about 20,000 square feet filled with signs, promotional banners, price tickets, gondola displays and, on an average to busy day, 200–300 shoppers to get in each other's way. Retailers and brand owners alike have realised that asking consumers to evaluate mocked-up store layouts or proposed point-of-sale concepts in the remote setup of a focus group may have no bearing on how the layout or promotion will work within a real store environment. This has led to a growth in accompanied shopping, where shoppers are accompanied on their normal trip by a researcher who can observe and ask questions about the customer's reaction to stimulus *in situ*, determining what is an effective influence on behaviour and why. As the use of the internet as a shopping medium has increased, accompanied browsing (a researcher sitting alongside an internet shopper and asking questions based on behaviour they see shoppers displaying whilst online) has been introduced as a parallel method of evaluating the effectiveness of online marketing communications. Similarly, as penetration of ambient media such as plasma screens carrying details of forthcoming promotions, events and advertising has grown in pubs and clubs, accompanied evenings-out have developed as a way of researchers assessing the efficacy of such communications among the target audience after a few pints. Nice work if you can get it! (Donald, 2005; Landy and Gale, 2003; Poynter and Quigley, 2001).

Another form of observational research that deliberately seeks feedback on employee performance is *mystery shopping*. This allows a researcher to go through the same experience as a normal customer, whether in a store, restaurant, plane or showroom. As far as the employees are concerned, they are just dealing with another customer and they are not aware that they are being closely observed. The 'shopper' is trained to ask certain questions and to measure performance on such things as service time, customer handling and question answering. The more objective the measures, the more valuable they are to marketing managers in ensuring that certain benchmark standards are being achieved. Mystery shopping is widely used by the larger retailers and service organisations to train staff and help the organisation to understand the customer–service provider interface (Bromage, 2000).

The potential problems that can be experienced with interviews are also likely with observation where human observers are used. That is, the training and supervision of observers are of great importance and, since it is more subjective, the likelihood of misinterpretation is higher. On the other hand, mechanical observation tools may be used to overcome bias problems, such as supermarket scanners monitoring the purchases of particular consumers or groups of consumers, and the ACNielsen people meters, used to monitor the viewing and listening habits of television watchers and radio listeners.

marketing in action

24/7 in São Paulo

'Although almost all consumer goods companies are active in countries such as Brazil, China and India, few take advantage of their full potential. Many concentrate on the minority of the population that can afford expensive western-style goods, leaving local competitors to target the overwhelming majority of consumers with modest means.'
(Sneader et al., 2005)

Not so Procter & Gamble and Sadia! P&G markets household cleaning and personal hygiene products in Brazil, and Sadia is one of Brazil's largest food manufacturers. They joined forces to better understand, meet the needs of, and ultimately profit from the country's 33 million low-income families. They commissioned Data Popular to have researchers spend seven days, 24 hours a day, in 25

low-income households, observing and shadowing the housewife as she went about her daily life. The objective was to build up a solid knowledge of this little-studied consumer group, observing both their articulated and non-articulated needs. Why do you think asking simple, direct questions in this instance would not have been an adequate substitute?

The security of the researchers and the representativeness of the sample and its behaviour in this unusual situation were obvious considerations. Sixty typical low-income households were initially screened for health, safety and basic hygiene. The resultant 38 households were then visited for six hours by a researcher who identified any tension within the family related to the presence of an observer, and gained a description of the housewife's preferred researcher in terms of age, gender, religion, ethnic background,

smoking habits, etc. From this, the final sample of 25 was determined. In order that there was comparability between the data collected in each household, in addition to what was spontaneously noted, the observers all collected information in a 'guided notebook' featuring 200 items that were to be observed and written about. After the study was completed, the housewives were invited to focus groups with other participants, whom they had not previously met, to discuss the experience. The consistent finding that family life had changed within the first 48 hours of having the researcher on the premises, but had returned to normal by day 3, justified the need for the researchers to be there 24/7, if they were to observe reality rather than a performance put on for their benefit.

Sources: Mariano et al. (2003); Sneader et al. (2005).

Other devices can be used to observe or monitor closely the physiological responses of individuals, such as their pupil dilation (using a tachistoscope) when watching advertisements, to indicate degree of interest. A galvanometer, which measures minute changes in perspiration, can also help to gauge a subject's interest in advertisements.

eg   Research agency Everyday Lives specialises in capturing observations of people doing everyday things on video – with the observed person's permission of course! With so many crowded, mature markets, it is often only by spotting an unconscious consumer need (one that they couldn't tell you about in response to a direct question) or anticipating needs that new products and brands can gain competitive advantage. Everyday Lives has videoed consumers for various client projects doing things like brushing their teeth, shopping in supermarket aisles, preparing food, eating meals and playing games on their mobile phones. The video footage is watched and analysed with a view to pinpointing new opportunities for product development or improved consumer communication. If new ideas arise from this analysis, the video footage is sometimes used as stimulus in further research with consumers to ask them if the new idea would change or improve their experience in a particular product category. Check out Everyday Lives' website http://www.edlglobal.net and see what they've been watching us do lately.

In some ways, observation is a more reliable predictor of behaviour than verbal assertions or intentions. Where interaction is not needed with the respondent, or where the respondent may be unable to recall the minutiae of their own behaviour, direct observation may be a valuable additional tool in the researcher's armoury. It is particularly informative when people are not aware that they are being observed and are thus acting totally naturally, rather than changing their behaviour or framing responses to suit what they think researchers want to see or hear.

Experimentation

The third method through which primary data can be collected is by conducting an experiment. This may involve the use of a laboratory (or other artificial environment), or the experiment may be set in its real-world situation, for example test marketing a product. In the experimental situation, researchers manipulate the independent variable(s), for example price, promotions or product position on a store shelf, and monitor the impact on the dependent variable, for example sales, to try to determine if any change in the dependent variable occurs. The important aspect of an experiment is to hold most of the independent variables constant (as well as other potentially confounding factors) while manipulating one independent variable and monitoring its impact on the dependent variable. This is usually possible in a laboratory, where control of the environment is within the power of researchers, but far less possible in a real-world situation where a myriad of external complications can occur that can confuse the results.

For example, a manufacturer may want to find out whether new packaging will increase sales of an existing product, before going to the expense of changing over to the new packaging. The manufacturer could conduct an experiment in a laboratory, perhaps by setting up a mock supermarket aisle, inviting consumers in and then observing whether their eyes were drawn to the new packaging, whether they picked it up, how long they looked at it and whether they eventually chose it in preference to the competition. The problem with this, however, is that it is still a very artificial situation, with no guarantees that it can replicate what would have happened in real life. Alternatively, therefore, the manufacturer could set up a field experiment, trialling the new packaging in real stores in one or more geographic regions and/or specific market segments and then monitoring the results.

Not all experimental research designs need to be highly structured, formal or set up for statistical validation purposes. For example, side-by-side experiments where shop A offers a different range or mix from shop B, which in all other respects is identical to shop A, can still reveal interesting insights into marketing problems, even though the rigour of more formal experimental designs is not present.

■ Sampling

Particularly in mass consumer markets, time and cost constraints mean that it is impractical to include every single target customer in whatever data gathering method has been chosen.

It is not necessary even to begin to try to do this, because a carefully chosen representative sample of the whole population (usually a target market) will be enough to give the researchers confidence that they are getting a true picture that can be generalised. In most cases, researchers are able to draw conclusions about the whole population (i.e. the group or target market) based on the study of a sample.

Figure 5.3, based on Tull and Hawkins (1990), shows the main stages in the sampling process. Each will be considered briefly in turn:

Figure 5.3 Stages in the sampling process

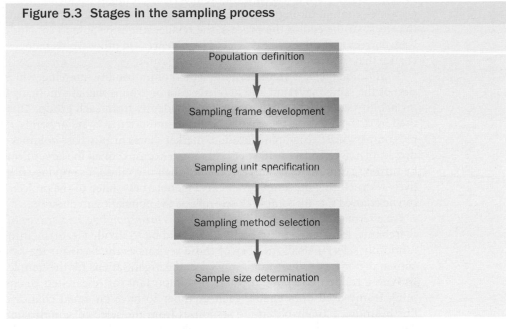

Source: Adapted from Tull and Hawkins (1990).

Population definition

The population to be surveyed will derive from the overall research objectives. Often this will be based on a target market or segment, but even then further definition based on markets, products or behaviours is unlikely to be necessary to create a tightly defined population.

Sampling frame

The sampling frame is the means of access to the population to be surveyed. It is basically a list from which individual names can be drawn. Registers of electors or lists of organisations compiled from directories such as *Kompass* and *Dun and Bradstreet* are examples of possible sampling frames. Internal customer records may also provide a sampling frame, although researchers need to be very sure that such records give a complete picture, and that there is no doubt that this is the required population for the study, rather than just a cheap, quick and easy way of generating an extensive list of names.

Sampling unit

The sampling unit is the actual individual from whom researchers want a response. In consumer markets, the sampling unit is usually the name attached to the address in the sampling frame. In B2B markets, however, this stage can be complex because, as we saw in Chapter 3, organisations have a number of individuals concerned with decision-making. It is very important to identify the right individual, as the responses of the purchasing manager in this case may be different from those of the managing director.

Sampling method selection

The next step in the process is to select the sample method, which is the means by which individual sample units and elements are selected from the larger sampling frame. The main and early decision is whether to use probability or non-probability sampling methods.

Probability sampling. Random, or *probability sampling*, where each member of the population has an equal or known chance of being selected for the sample, offers specified levels of confidence about the limits of accuracy of the results. So if a retailer wanted to do a survey to establish satisfaction levels with checkout services, it might decide to interview every thirtieth customer coming through the checkouts during research sessions held at different times of the week. At the end of the process, the retailer might be able to conclude that the findings were correct to the 95 per cent level of confidence – in other words there was only a one in 20 chance that the sample was biased or unrepresentative.

Stratified sampling is an important method of probability sampling, which involves the division of the sampling frame into defined strata or groups that are mutually exclusive. Random probability samples are then drawn independently from each group. This method is widely used in B2B markets, as they naturally divide into discrete layers or bands, reflecting for example company size, geographic location, market shares or purchase volumes. Researchers could decide, therefore, to take a 100 per cent sample (census) of all the larger firms (defined perhaps by turnover or number of employees) and then use random sampling with the rest. By effectively restructuring the sample frame in a manner best suited to the project, greater confidence can be enjoyed that the sample closely reflects the population in question.

An alternative form of stratified sampling is *area sampling*. In a survey of German builders' merchants, for example, the first stage would be to divide Germany into regions and then randomly select a small number of those regions as the basis for the sample. Within each chosen region, researchers randomly select the organisations for the sample.

With a random sampling method, it is important for researchers to ensure that the sampling frame used does enable each member to have an equal chance of being selected. Furthermore, actually obtaining responses from the selected sample can be quite difficult. What if the thirtieth customer through the checkout doesn't want to stop? What if there's nobody at home when the interviewer calls round or phones? What if the sampling frame is out of date and the selected consumer has moved house or died? Any of these circumstances violates the ideal of the random sample.

Non-random sampling. *Non-random samples* are much easier to identify than random samples because they are not based on the same strict selection requirements and allow researchers a little more flexibility. The results from these samples are not representative of the population being studied and may lack the statistical rigour generated by random sampling, but they are still often of considerable use to researchers. Two main non-random sampling methods may be used:

1 *Judgemental sampling.* This method is widely used in B2B market research. Sample units are selected deliberately by researchers, because they are felt to represent better sources of the required information. Given the concentrated nature of many industries, if a contracting company for pipework cleaning wanted to enter a new geographical market, for example, it would probably make sense to survey the larger users if that was the target segment of interest, rather than draw at random from all users, large and small. Of course, no inference could be drawn about the wider population from such a sample method.

2 *Quota sampling.* Quota samples are formed when researchers decide that a certain proportion of the total sample should be made up of respondents conforming to certain characteristics. It may be decided, for example, that for a particular study, the sample should consist of 400 non-working women aged between 25 and 35, 250 full-time working and 350 part-time working women in the same age group. This breakdown may reflect the actual structure of the market under consideration. Each interviewer is then told how many completed questionnaires to bring back within each quota category. The choice of respondents is not random, since the interviewer is actively looking for people who fulfil

the quota definitions and, once the quota is full, will reject any further respondents in that category. The advantage of quota sampling is that it is quicker and cheaper to do than a full random sample would be, as no sample frame has to be devised and researchers do not have to worry whether the sampling frame is up to date or not. Furthermore, interviewers are not committed to following up specific respondents. Under a quota sample, if a particular respondent does not want to cooperate, then that's fine – the interviewer will look for another one.

Sample size

A final yet very important consideration in the sampling process is sample size. There is no point in spending more time and money pursuing any bigger sample than you have to. With random sampling based on statistical analysis, researchers can have confidence within prescribed limits that the sample elements are representative of the population being studied.

As one would expect, the higher the levels of confidence required, the greater the size of the sample needed. In Europe, surveys of consumer buying habits are often of around 2000 units, which would typically yield a 95 per cent confidence level that the sample reflects the characteristics of the population. In B2B markets, sample sizes of between 300 and 1000 can be used to produce high levels of confidence. This would be especially true when suppliers operate within limited geographical areas (such as plumbers, or van hire firms), the value of sales is usually small (motor factors), and the buying organisations are also small (http://www.b2b international.com).

■ Questionnaire design

The questionnaire is a commonly used research instrument for gathering and recording information from interviews, whether face-to-face, mail or telephone surveys. Researchers soon learn that the best-planned surveys soon fall apart if the questionnaire is poorly designed and fails to gather the data originally anticipated. To minimise the risk of disappointment, however, there are several dimensions to consider in questionnaire design.

Objectives

The aim of a questionnaire is closely linked with the overall purpose of the research. It is tailormade to meet the information requirements of the study and therefore lies at the heart of the research process. If the questionnaire is to fulfil its role properly as a means of data collection, then there are several areas that need to be analysed, as outlined in Table 5.3.

Some thought also needs to be given to ensuring that the questionnaire will retain the interest of the respondent, so that full completion takes place. It is easy with self-administered questionnaires for the respondent to give up if the questionnaire becomes tedious, seems to be poorly explained, or is too long or complex.

It is thus important to make sure that the questionnaire takes as little time as possible to complete. Research in the US found that 20 per cent of consumers thought that questionnaires in general, including 30-minute telephone surveys, were too long (McDaniel *et al.*, 1985). According to Gander (1998), the 30-minute survey is still common, making the interviewer's job much more difficult.

Types of questions

There are two main types of question that can be asked in a questionnaire: open-ended questions and closed questions. The category of open-ended questions has many significant style variations within it, but they all allow considerable scope for the respondent to express views on the selected theme (and in some cases, on other themes!). Closed questions force the respondent to choose one or more responses from a number of possible replies provided in the questionnaire.

Open-ended questions. Questions such as 'In the buying of garden furniture, what factors do you find important?' or 'What do you think of the trend towards out-of-town shopping centres?' are open ended because they do not give a range of potential answers for the

Table 5.3 The objectives of a questionnaire	
Objective	**Suggestions**
To suit the nature of the target population	Pitch the questions in a way they can understand; ask questions they can be expected to be able to answer given their knowledge and experience.
To suit the research methods	For example, a telephone survey cannot use the kind of visual aids that a face-to-face interview can; a postal survey is less likely to get responses if it is lengthy or if it is probing feelings and/or attitudes.
To suit the research objectives	It must be designed appropriately to gather the right information for answering the research questions – no more, no less.
To collect the right kind of data	The quality and completeness of responses are important for a successful survey. There must also be the right depth of data, whether it is factual or probing attitudes, beliefs, opinions, motivations or feelings.
To aid data analysis	Ensure that it is as easy as possible to take the raw data from the questionnaires and input them accurately into any analytical framework/software package being used.
To minimise error and bias	Ensure that the questionnaire is 'tight' enough to allow it to be administered by any interviewer, to any respondent, at any time, in any location with consistency. Also ensure that questions cannot be misinterpreted or misunderstood.
To encourage accurate and full responses	Avoid leading or judgemental questions; ensure clarity in the way questions are asked; ensure that respondents feel at ease rather than threatened or intimidated by the questions.

respondent to choose from. In both cases, interviewers could be faced with as many different answers as there are respondents. Using such questions can, therefore, be rewarding, because of the rich insights given in a relatively unrestrained manner. The difficulties, however, emerge in recording and analysing the responses, given their potential length and wide variations. Nevertheless, it has been argued that using open-ended questions can help to build the goodwill of the respondent through allowing an unrestricted response (Chisnall, 1986).

Closed questions. Closed questions fall into two broad groups, dichotomous and multiple-choice questions. *Dichotomous questions* allow only two choices, such as 'yes or no' or 'good or bad'. These questions are easy to ask and easy to answer. With careful pre-coding, it is also relatively easy to analyse responses and to use them for cross-tabulation with another variable, for example to find out whether those who say that they do use a product pay more attention to product-specific advertising than those who say that they do not use it.

Multiple-choice questions are a more sophisticated form of closed question, because they can present a list of possible answers for the respondent to choose from. This could be, for example, a list of alternative factors that might influence a purchasing decision (price, quality, availability, etc.), or it could reflect alternative levels of strength of feeling, degree of importance or other shades of variation in response to the variable under consideration.

These questions need to be designed carefully, to incorporate and group as wide a range of answers as possible, since restraining the amount of choice available creates a potential source of bias. The alternative responses need to reflect the likely range, without overlap or duplication, since this too may create bias. By offering an 'other, please specify' category, these questions provide some opportunity to collect responses that were not originally conceived (but that should have been identified in the pilot stage) or responses that do not fit neatly into the imposed structure. However, the advantage of multiple-choice questions is that again they are relatively straightforward to analyse, if pre-coding has been used.

Multiple choices can also be used to overcome some respondent sensitivities. If asked 'How old are you?' or 'What do you earn?' as open questions, many people may refuse to answer because the questions are too specific and personal. Phrasing the question as 'To which of these age groups do you belong: 17 or under, 18–24, 25–34, 35–44, 45 or over?' allows respondents to feel that they have not given quite so much away. The bands need to be defined to reflect the likely scope of responses from the target respondents, and to be easy for them to relate to. Professionals, for example, will be more likely to relate to bands based on annual salary than manual workers, who are more likely to know what their weekly wage is.

Rating scales are a form of multiple-choice question, widely used in attitude measurement, motivational research and in situations where a number of complex, interacting factors are likely to influence a situation. There are a number of scaling methods, including the following:

1 *Likert summated ratings.* A large number of statements, relevant to the research study, are built up from preliminary research and piloting. These statements are then given to respondents who are asked to respond on a five- or seven-point scale, for example 'strongly agree', 'agree', 'neither agree nor disagree', 'disagree' and 'strongly disagree'. The responses are scored from 5 (strongly agree) down to 1 (strongly disagree). The average score across all respondents can then be used to establish the general strength of attitude towards the variable under consideration. An examination of the pattern of individual responses may also reveal issues of interest to the marketer.

2 *Semantic differential scales.* These scales were developed to measure differences in the meaning of words or concepts. This method involves a bipolar five- or seven-point rating scale, with each extreme defined by carefully selected adjectives representing opposite extremes of feeling. A study of retail store atmosphere might offer a series of scales including 'warm – cold', 'friendly – unfriendly', or 'fashionable – unfashionable', for example. Once the scales have been defined, the product (or whatever) is rated on each of them to reveal a profile of the respondent's opinion. Such scales can also be used for measuring corporate image or advertising image and for comparing different brands. In the latter case, if two products are plotted at the same time on the same scales, significant differences may emerge, and help the marketer to understand better the relative positioning of products in consumers' minds.

Examples of both types of rating scale can be found in Figure 5.4.

The wording of questions. The success or failure of a questionnaire lies as much in the detail as in the grand scheme and design. This includes the detailed wording of questions so that the respondent fully understands what is required and accurate responses are encouraged. The next few paragraphs raise a number of pertinent issues.

It is always important to ensure that the *meaning of words and phrases* is fully understood by the respondent. Particular effort should be made to avoid the use of jargon and technical language that may be unfamiliar to the respondent.

Ambiguity can lead to misunderstandings and thus poor or inaccurate responses. A question such as 'Do you buy this product frequently, sometimes, seldom or never?' seems to be clear and unambiguous, but think about it for a minute. What does 'frequently' mean? To one respondent it might mean weekly, to another it might mean monthly. Researchers should therefore be as specific as possible.

A further source of ambiguity or confusion occurs when the respondent is asked to cope with too many concepts at once. Two questions should therefore never be *piggy backed*, i.e. asked in one question, such as: 'How important is price to you, and how do you think we could improve on value for money?'

Leading questions may tempt the respondent to favour a particular answer. This is not, of course, the essence of good research. Thus asking 'Are you, or are you not, in favour of capital punishment?' is more balanced than 'Are you in favour of capital punishment?', which is edging the respondent towards 'Yes' as an answer.

Figure 5.4 Examples of rating scales

Likert scale

	Strongly agree	Agree	Neither agree nor disagree	Disagree	Strongly disagree
Morrisons prices are generally lower than those of other supermarkets					
Morrisons offers the widest range of groceries					
Morrisons staff are always friendly and helpful					
I never have to queue too long at the checkout					
Supermarket own-brands are just as good as manufacturers' brands					
Low prices are important to me in choosing a supermarket					
Supermarkets should provide more personal services					

Semantic differential scale

	1	2	3	4	5	6	7	
Modern								Old-fashioned
Friendly								Unfriendly
Attractive								Unattractive
Spacious								Crowded
High-quality goods								Low-quality goods
Wide choice of goods								Limited choice of goods
Convenient opening hours								Inconvenient opening hours
Tidy								Untidy
Short queues								Long queues
Low prices								High prices

Questions that are *too closed* are a kind of leading question that may also frustrate researchers. 'Is price an important factor in your purchase?' begs the answer 'Yes', but even if it was a balanced question, the responses tell very little. It does not indicate how important price is to the respondent or what other factors influence the purchase. An open-ended or multiple-choice question might tell much more.

Researchers need to be sympathetic to people's *sensitivity*. Some areas are highly personal, so building up slowly may be important and 'soft' rather than 'hard' words should be used, for example 'financial difficulties' rather than 'debt'. Of course, the more sensitive the information, the more likely the respondent is to refuse to answer, lie or even terminate the interview.

Coding and rules. It is more important to obtain accurate and pertinent information than to design a questionnaire that embraces everything but rarely gets completed. Hague (1992) proposes an *ideal length* for three different types of questionnaire:

- Telephone interviews: 5 to 30 minutes
- Visit interviews: 30 minutes to two hours
- Self-completion: four sides of A4, 20–30 questions.

A street interview would need to be very much shorter than 30 minutes to retain interest and prevent irritation.

The *layout* of the questionnaire is especially important for self-administered questionnaires. A cramped page looks unappealing, as well as making it difficult to respond. Where an interviewer is in control of the questionnaire, the layout should assist the recording and coding of responses and ease of flow through the interview to maintain momentum. Most questionnaires are now designed with *data coding* and ease of analysis in mind. This means that all responses to closed questions and multiple choices need to be categorised before the questionnaire is released, and that the layout must also be user friendly for whoever has to transfer the data from the completed questionnaire into a database.

The *order of the questions* is important for respondents, as the more confusing the flow and the more jumping around they have to do, the less likely they are to see it through to completion.

Support materials and explanation can be very important. For a mail survey a covering letter can be reassuring and persuasive while, at an interview, the interviewer needs to gain the respondent's attention and interest in participation. Visual aids, such as packaging or stills from advertising, can also get respondents more involved, as well as prompting their memories.

Piloting

Whatever care has been taken in the design of the questionnaire, problems usually emerge as soon as the questionnaire is tried on innocent respondents. Piloting a questionnaire on a small-scale sample can help to iron out any 'bugs', so that it can be refined before the full survey goes ahead. Initially, a fresh eye from colleagues can eliminate the worst howlers, but for most projects, it is best to set aside time for a full field pilot. This would mean testing the questionnaire on a small sub-sample (who will usually not then participate in the main survey) to check its meaning, layout and structure and, furthermore, to check whether it yields the required data and whether it can be analysed in the intended manner.

■ Conduct the research

Once the research plan has been developed and the methods of collection and proposed analysis identified, it is necessary to go about conducting the research itself. This stage will vary according to the type of research. The demands of a consumer survey involving perhaps thousands of respondents over a wide geographic area are very different from those of a select number of interviews in depth.

Particularly in primary research, it is this part of the process that often presents the biggest problem, because the collection of the data should not be left to poorly trained or badly briefed field researchers. In recent years, however, considerable progress has been made in professionalising research interviewers, moving away from the rather clichéd image of housewives earning extra cash. Training is now widespread and more male interviewers have been recruited both to enable access to previously no-go areas, such as high-crime housing estates and to handle situations where gender may matter during the interview (Gray, 2000a).

eg Recruiting market research interviewers is not an easy job. Staff have to be prepared to work afternoons and evenings to make sure that they get representative samples of all kinds of workers. They also have to be well organised and good at managing themselves and their time, especially if they are working out in the field rather than in a telephone interview call centre, for example. All researchers need a strong sense of responsibility and have to be prepared to take an ethical approach to what they do. Field researchers have to be tough, to cope with less cooperative interviewees or to deal with the stranger kinds of people one meets when spending a lot of time hanging around city streets with a clipboard.

Provided that interviewers read the questions exactly as they are written (an absolute rule in all market research codes of conduct), there is little difference between one interviewer and another on closed questions. There is, however, a huge difference when prompting and probing for open-ended questions. An interviewer who writes down ver-batim exactly what the respondent says, encouraging them to clarify and add anything else continually, until the response 'nothing else' is achieved, will improve the quality and richness of data generated. Interviewers who are conscious of taking up too much of the respondent's time, paraphrase their responses and probe less fully will miss opportuni-ties to generate richness in the data (Schafer, 2003).

Research companies thus take a great deal of care in recruiting and training researchers. Some companies undertake lengthy initial telephone screening, partly to give applicants a better idea of what the job entails and partly to help develop a profile of the candidate. Many companies then insist on a face-to-face interview to check a candi-date's appearance (especially for field researchers), their interaction skills and their ability to deal with situations. This is important because staff are effectively representing the research company and its clients and they have to be able to develop a rapport with interviewees quickly, reassure them and hold their attention, often through a fairly long and detailed survey.

Research company Gallup maintains that only 1 out of 16 candidates makes it through its selection procedures, a clear indication that the company sees the quality of its staff as an important asset. Those recruiting interviewers for telephone research call centres are less concerned about the appearance of their staff but more concerned about their telephone voice and ability to establish rapport without the face-to-face contact. Some companies even recruit people with certain regional accents to help this process (Gander, 1998).

There are a number of areas, in any kind of face-to-face research, where careful attention to detail can pay dividends. The greater the need for the interviewer to depart from a carefully prepared script and *modus operandi*, the greater the skill involved and the higher the cost of the interview. This is particularly emphasised in the implementation role of the interviewer who conducts a group discussion or an in-depth interview. The dangers of interview bias are always present where the interviewer records what they think has been said or meant, not what has actually been said in response to a question. This sort of bias can be particularly pronounced where open-ended questions are being used. There are some situations where conducting field research is especially challenging, such as when particular targets or subjects need to be covered. The extremely affluent or poor, ethnic minorities, youth and corporate executives are often harder to reach than many target groups in the UK (Gray, 2000a). Community intermediaries are often used, for example, to reach target groups such as older Asian women and the Jamaican community and persuade them to participate in research.

New technology is making a big impact in the implementation of field research by assist-ing in the questioning and recording process. Computer aided telephone interviewing (CATI) and computer aided personal interviewing (CAPI) have revolutionised data collection tech-niques and are now widely used. CAPI means that each interviewer is provided with a laptop computer which has the questionnaire displayed on screen. The interviewer can then read out text from the screen and key in the responses. The pre-programmed questionnaire will auto-matically route the interviewer to different parts of the questionnaire as appropriate (e.g. those who have/have not purchased in the previous three months) and will prompt the inter-viewer to clarify any illogical answers. It helps quality control by creating greater consistency in interviewer questioning and the recording of answers and furthermore allows the inter-viewer to concentrate on building a rapport with the respondent to help prevent fatigue and loss of interest in more complex questionnaires. CATI provides similar technology for tele-phone interviewing and again allows for greater consistency in interviewing and the recording of information.

■ Analyse and interpret the information

While the quality of the research data is essential, it is the analysis of the data, i.e. turning raw data into useful information, that provides the most value to the organisation. It is on the basis of the reports prepared from the data analysis that significant managerial decisions are likely to be made. The use of sophisticated computer hardware and software packages provides a powerful means of processing large quantities of data relatively easily. CAPI, CATI, scanners that can read completed questionnaires, complex statistical analysis and data manipulation have improved the speed, accuracy and depth of the analysis itself. However, it is still the human element, the researcher's expertise in identifying a trend or relationship or some other nugget hidden within the results, that provides the key component for decision-makers and transforms the data and techniques used into valuable information.

eg Speed of analysis is often just as important as the depth of analysis in some situations. Some clients want information within days of starting a campaign rather than waiting until three weeks after it has finished. With time-sensitive products, such as video/DVD and CD releases, the sales data from the first few days are a good indicator of the success of the campaign. If adjustments have to be made to the campaign, they often have to happen in the first week (McLuhan, 2001a).

Some care needs to be exercised in the interpretation of quantitative data. Outputs of calculations should never overrule sound common sense in assessing the significance and relevance of the data generated. There is sometimes the danger of analysis paralysis, where the use of highly sophisticated techniques almost becomes an end in itself, rather than simply a means of identifying new relationships and providing significant new insights for management. While the old saying that trends, differences or relationships are only meaningful if they are obvious to even the untrained statistical eye may be going too far, it does highlight the danger of misinterpreting cause and effect and the differences between groups of consumers, arising from over-reliance on finely balanced statistics pursued by researchers.

Not all data are quantitative, of course. Qualitative data arising from in-depth interviews or group discussions pose a different kind of challenge to researchers. Whereas quantitative data have to prove their reliability when compared with the wider population, qualitative data can never be claimed to be representative of what a wider sample of respondents might indicate. The main task of qualitative data, therefore, is to present attitudes, feelings and motivations in some depth, whether or not they are representative of the wider population.

To handle qualitative data analysis, great care must be taken in the recording of information. Video or taped interviews are thus helpful in enabling classification and categorisation of the main points to be checked and explored in depth. Similarly, issue or content analysis enables particular themes to be explored across a range of interviews. For example, if researchers wanted to identify the barriers to exporting in small firms, they might define such themes as market entry, market knowledge, finance or using agents as indicative of the main barriers to be assessed. The data analysis might be supported by a range of quotations from the interviews. Because of the richness and complexity of this kind of data, skilled psychologists are often used to explore and explain much of what is said and, indeed, not said.

So although the risks of bias are great in qualitative analysis, both in data selection and analysis, and although the results can, in untrained hands, be rather subjective and conjectural, the advantage arises from the fresh insights and perspectives that more rigorous statistical techniques would simply not generate.

■ Prepare and present the report

The information provided by researchers must be in a form that is useful to decision-makers. Too often, research reports are written in highly technical language or research jargon that, to a layperson, is confusing or meaningless. Marketers who want to use these reports to make decisions need them to be easily understandable. A report that is too complex is all but useless. That is why the formal presentation of the report, whether written or verbal (which allows the client to ask questions and seek clarification of points made), should be given as much thought, care and attention as any previous stage in the research process. It also allows the results to be personalised for the receiving organisation which can improve the perceived credibility of the findings and thus increase willingness to take action (Schmalensee, 2001).

Although a verbal presentation can play an important part in sharing understanding, it is the report itself that has the power to influence thinking significantly. Arguments can be carefully presented, with data used appropriately in their support, and the detail surrounding the main findings can be displayed to increase the client's confidence that the research was well executed to plan. There are no standard report formats, as much will depend on the nature of the research task undertaken.

■ Research evaluation

Research projects rarely go completely to plan. Although greater care in conducting pilot studies and exploratory research will make it more likely that the actual outcomes will match those planned, problems may still emerge that will require careful consideration in weighing up the value of the project. Thoughtful analysis of the planning, conduct and outcomes of the project will also teach valuable lessons for the future to both clients and researchers.

This stage can involve a review of all aspects of the research plan described above. Any deviations need to be understood, both in terms of the current results and for designing future research. With regard to the research project undertaken, the most important point is whether the research actually provided a sufficient quality and quantity of information to assist management decision-making. Sometimes, the research objectives may have been ambiguous or poorly framed in the context of the marketing problem being addressed. Ultimately, it is the marketing manager who must take responsibility for ensuring that the objectives and research plan were compatible and reflected the requirements, although researchers can help in this task.

Ethics in marketing research

The ethical concerns surrounding market research have been the subject of an ongoing debate in the industry for a long time. Because much consumer research involves specific groups of consumers, including children and other groups that might be considered vulnerable, it is essential that the researchers' credibility is maintained and that the highest standards of professional practice are demonstrated, and so the industry has established a set of professional ethical guidelines. These guidelines include such matters as protecting the confidentiality of respondents or clients, not distorting or misrepresenting research findings (for example, two major newspapers could both claim to be the market leader by using readership figures gathered over different time spans and failing to mention the time period), using tricks to gain information from respondents, conducting an experiment and not telling those being studied, and using research as a guise for selling and sales lead building.

The European Society for Opinion and Marketing Research (ESOMAR), a leading marketing research association, is actively trying to encourage members to stamp out the practice of 'sugging' (selling under the guise of market research) through an agreed code of practice.

corporate social responsibility   in action

Finding out what kids are up to

When market researchers have to investigate children's behaviour and motivation as consumers, they have to proceed with extreme caution. It is very easy to step over both the legal line and industry codes designed to protect children and young people from predatory practices. Nevertheless, marketers cannot afford to ignore the needs of a segment estimated to be worth £300bn. Children have never before had more disposable income for discretionary purchases, had more influence over household purchases, or been in a better position to persuade guilty, busy parents that a particular purchase will make up for lack of time spent together. Little wonder, then, that they are a consumer group marketers are keen to understand. In recent years, some brand owners have come under fire for using their understanding of children in an irresponsible and exploitative way.

With topics such as growing levels of child obesity and commercialisation of schools continually in the headlines, and fingers pointing firmly at major advertisers, we have recently seen Coca-Cola pledging to target children no longer, McDonald's promoting healthier lifestyles and carrot sticks, and Ribena switching its primary target audience from children to the 18–30 age group. But the need for marketers in certain product categories to understand how to influence children and their parents in favour of their brands remains imperative, albeit complicated by the new requirement to balance effective promotion with 'responsibility'.

Marketers rely on the market research industry to help them understand what makes today's kids tick. The Market Research Society has a firm Code of Conduct which must be applied when any researcher is dealing with children in a research situation. The objective is 'to protect the rights of children (under 16s) and young people (16 and 17 year olds) physically, mentally, ethically and emotionally and to ensure that they are not exploited.' The rules apply mainly to practicalities: ensuring that parental consent is given; ensuring that children are aware that they can refuse to answer questions or can opt out; and making sure that another adult is present or nearby. The Code also requires researchers to ensure that the content is appropriate, i.e. that

nothing is discussed that is inappropriate to the age group; that nothing happens that is likely to cause tension between child and parents or peer group; and that there is nothing that is likely to upset or worry a child. There is a strong focus here on the design of the research and the process of data collection, but there are also some concerns about whether children are being adequately and ethically protected and not exploited through the way in which some research findings are used.

Quite apart from their spending power, today's children have been described as 'the first generation born with a mouse in their hand and a computer screen as their window on the world' (Lindstrom and Seybold, 2004) and research methods have had to adapt to this. The online website http://www.yorg.com conducts research during school ICT lessons, with 21,000 children aged between 6 and 16 years old completing their surveys with full teacher approval during the course of a school year. The website says, 'We don't bore them with books of multiple choice answers that are worse than homework. Our research programme involves them completely by using technology they love and understand. These kids respond live, on screen and with their peers. They interact with our software online so that the data gets to you fast, making your planning work in kid's time, not past times. You experience the

honesty of today's kids as they have fun learning about themselves. Enrol your brand and learn fast what kids are really saying when the adults get out of their way.' (http://www.yorg.com). It has also become increasingly popular for research agencies to give children the hardware to compile video or audio diaries of their daily lives with the resultant footage being discussed within a research session, and some agencies report improved results when encouraging children and young people to run their own focus groups with an adult moderator there only for minor guidance.

As research methods develop to delve deeper into children's commercial motivation and behaviour, some practitioners have become concerned about the 'ethics involved in teasing out desires of children and their parents for marketers' (Clegg, 2005) and the need for the market research industry to face up to its share of social responsibility. The Market Research Society's current position is that the marketing and advertising industries have guidelines they follow on marketing to children, and as long as the market research industry reflects those, it is not up to researchers to lead on the issue. But it is a debate that is likely to continue.

Sources: Choueke (2005); Clegg (2005); Lindstrom and Seybold (2004); Wolfman (2005); http://www.mrs.org.uk; http://www.yorg.co.uk.

BMRA, the British Market Research Association, is a trade association representing the interests of market research companies and helping to regulate them. It requires its members to subscribe to a code of conduct and insists that its larger members are accredited by the Market Research Quality Standards Association (BMRA, 1998). Of course, not all providers of market research are committed to compliance and not all bad practice can be eliminated, but considerable progress is being made.

Chapter summary

■ Marketing managers find it impossible to make decisions effectively without a constant flow of information on every aspect of marketing. Everything, from defining target markets to developing marketing mixes to making long-term strategic plans, has to be supported with appropriate information.

■ The organisation needs to coordinate its information, collected from a variety of sources, into an MIS. A formal MIS brings everything together under one umbrella and provides timely and comprehensive information to aid managers in decision-making. DSS build on the MIS, also to help decision-making. The DSS uses a variety of computer tools and packages to allow a manager to manipulate information, to explore possible outcomes of courses of action and to experiment in a risk-free environment. There are three different types of market research, exploratory, descriptive and causal, each one serving different purposes. Depending on the nature of the problem under investigation, any of the three types of market research may use qualitative or quantitative data. Rather than individually pursuing a series of marketing research studies, an organisation can participate in continuous research, undertaken by a market research agency on an ongoing basis and usually syndicated.

■ There is a general framework for the conduct of a marketing research project that can be applied to almost any kind of market or situation. It consists of eight stages: problem definition, research objectives, planning the research, data collection, research implementation, data analysis, reporting findings and research evaluation.

■ *Secondary research* provides a means of sourcing marketing information that already exists in some form, whether internal or external to the organisation. Gaps in secondary data can be filled through *primary research*. The main methods of primary research are interviews and surveys, observation and experiments. *Sampling* is a crucial area for successful market research. There is no need to survey an entire population in order to find answers to questions. As long as a representative sample is drawn, answers can be generalised to apply to the whole population. *Questionnaires* are often used as a means of collecting data from the sample selected, and they must reflect the purpose of the research, collect the appropriate data accurately and efficiently, and facilitate the analysis of data.

■ Ethical issues in market research are very important. Researchers have to comply with codes of practice to protect vulnerable groups in society from exploitation. They also have to ensure that respondents recruited for market research studies are fully aware of what they are committing themselves to and that they are not misled at any stage in the research process.

Questions for review and discussion

5.1 Why is *market research* an essential tool for the marketing manager?

5.2 What kinds of marketing problems might be addressed through:
   (a) *exploratory*;
   (b) *descriptive*; and
   (c) *causal* research projects?

5.3 Define the stages of the *market research process* and outline what each one involves.

5.4 Discuss the role and content of an *MIS* and how it might relate to a *DSS*.

5.5 Evaluate the appropriateness of each of the different *interview- and survey-based primary research methods* for:
   (a) investigating the buying criteria used by B2B purchasers;
   (b) defining the attitudes of a target market towards a brand of breakfast cereal;

   (c) profiling purchasers of small electrical goods; and
   (d) measuring levels of post-purchase satisfaction among customers.
   Clearly define any assumptions you make about each of the situations.

5.6 Design a questionnaire. It should contain about 20 questions and you should use as many of the different types of question as possible. Pay particular attention to the concerns discussed at pp. 153–7 of the chapter. The objective is to investigate respondents' attitudes to music CDs and their purchasing habits. Pilot your questionnaire on 12–15 people (but preferably not people on the same course as you), analyse the results and then make any adjustments. Within your seminar group, be prepared to discuss the rationale behind your questionnaire, the outcome of the pilot and any data analysis problems.

case study 5

SMA: Finding the right formula

It can be difficult to achieve brand distinction and relevance when you have a full range of product, place, price and promotion choices that you can make. Imagine how much more difficult it can be when there are restrictions placed on how you present your product and communicate its benefits. Particularly when the target audience is generally eager for, and receptive to, information about your product category. This is the position that those who are responsible for marketing formula milk for babies find themselves in.

It is an extraordinary market for a number of reasons. At the heart of it is the fact that current government health policy is that breastfeeding should be promoted and encouraged, and thus formula milk manufacturers are not permitted to engage in consumer advertising or promotion in mass media to pregnant women or new mums, nor is the depiction of babies allowed on their packaging. Furthermore, formula milk manufacturers may provide information to mums only through direct request, or via support material they issue to healthcare professionals (midwives and health visitors). This means that marketing communication opportunities are limited and thus it is a product category that people give no thought to until they are on the point of using it – because of the 'breast is best' policy and the resulting high levels of intention to breastfeed, even during pregnancy formula milk is rarely considered. Nevertheless, despite high intentions to breastfeed, for a number of reasons, 31 per cent of the 690,000 women having babies in the UK each year bottle-feed from birth and 54 per cent introduce bottle feeding within the first year of their child's life. As milk represents a baby's only form of sustenance for the first four months and a key form of sustenance for the rest of the first year of life, the decision about which brand to choose is a highly emotive one for the mother, and yet one to which she may have given little previous thought, and about which she is likely to have little information. Once in the market, bottle-feeding mums will tend to remain brand loyal because of the risk of upsetting their child's digestive system through chopping and changing. That's good news for the manufacturers, but they also have to take account of the fact that purchasers are only in the market for an average of 12 months before moving their child onto cow's milk, so the target audience is always changing.

Given these peculiar market characteristics, SMA Nutrition, a leading formula milk manufacturer in the UK since 1956, was keen to:

In order to improve the marketing strategies for its formula milk, SMA invested in research into the purchasing and usage habits of young mothers.
Source: SMA Nutrition http://www.wyeth.com

■ ensure that it was providing the right products, formats and communications for the complex needs of mothers
■ enhance the support it gives via healthcare professionals
■ develop a customer relationship management (CRM) programme.

This required an overview of the entire market, and an approach to segmenting all the different consumer types within it. SMA commissioned Leapfrog, a research agency it had worked in partnership with for a decade, to design and undertake a large-scale research project. It was completed in two phases.

The first phase consisted of qualitative research. A total of 38 pairs of friends were involved in qualitative discussions in their own homes, in eight different locations across Britain and Ireland. The sample recruited represented a spread of pregnant women and mums of babies from newborn to 12 months old; covered all brand and milk type usage; involved first-time and subsequent mums, and in contrast to more mainstream research projects, included very low income mums, under-age mums and those using specific milk products for special dietary needs. This phase generated a wealth of data on mothers, the things that influenced them and their decision process when selecting formula, and suggested strong hypotheses for market segmentation, all of which had to be validated and quantified.

The second phase involved quantitative research. Because a large sample size was required, capable of allowing pregnant women, first-time, and subsequent mums to be analysed as separate groups, and because there was a need to cover a wide geographic area, including isolated rural areas and areas of high deprivation, telephone interviewing was selected rather than personal interviewing. As the questionnaires covered full details of feeding behaviour, influences on every single feeding decision and attitudinal questions, the interviews took an average of 25 minutes, and were sometimes interrupted and reconvened as a result of baby demands, but compliance of interviewees was extremely high.

The result was the identification of eight discrete consumer segments, including for example 'modern capable Mum' and 'lonesome Mum'. For each of the eight segments the research was able to establish:

- size
- demographics
- key values
- behaviour in relation to feeding practices, information-seeking, etc.
- brand usage propensity
- key influences
- likelihood to influence others
- most appropriate communication style to address them
- key influential messages in making brand selection.

A further stage involving CACI's Acorn profiling identified each segment down to postcode level, i.e. could show which types of mother were most likely to live in which UK postcodes.

Source: Adapted with kind permission from a case study presented at the MRS Conference 2005 by Fidelma Hughes (SMA Nutrition) and Julie Hindmarch (Leapfrog Research and Planning).

Questions

1 Sometimes clients feel the need for a 'fresh look' at their market, and employ a new research agency. What do you think the benefits to SMA were in using Leapfrog, its long-term research partner, for this specific project?

2 Why do you think the qualitative phase was conducted in friendship pairs rather than individual interviews or larger focus groups, and why in the respondents' own homes?

3 Twenty-five minutes is a long telephone interview, and would usually exceed a respondent's tolerance level. What factors do you think contributed to the respondents' willingness to participate in this lengthy questionnaire?

4 If you were the marketing director of SMA, what uses could you put the research findings to, bearing in mind the constraints in this sector?

References for chapter 5

Alderson, T. (2005), 'Target Practice', *Research*, June.

Anstead, M. (2000), 'Taking a Tough Line on Privacy', *Marketing*, 13 April, p. 31.

Billings, C. (2001), 'Researchers Try Electronic Route', *Marketing*, 29 March, pp. 27–8.

BMRA (1998), 'BMRA – What Does BMRA Stand For?', advertisement in *Marketing Week*, 25 June, p. 50.

Bolden, R., Moscarola, J. and Baulac, Y. (2000), 'Interactive Research: How Internet Technology Could Revolutionise the Survey and Analysis Process', paper presented at *The Honeymoon is Over! Survey Research on the Internet* Conference, Imperial College, London, September 2000.

Boyd, H.W. *et al.* (1977), *Marketing Research*, 4th edn, Irwin.

Brennan, M. *et al.* (1991), 'The Effects of Monetary Incentives on the Response Rate and Cost Effectiveness of a Mail Survey', *Journal of the Market Research Society*, 33 (3), pp. 229–41.

Bromage, N. (2000), 'Mystery Shopping', *Management Accounting*, April, p. 30.

Chisnall, P.M. (1986), *Marketing Research*, 3rd edn, McGraw-Hill.

Choueke, M. (2005), 'Growing Up and Out', *Marketing Week*, 4 August, p. 27.

Clegg, A. (2001), 'Talk Among Yourselves', *Marketing Week*, 6 December, pp. 41–2.

Clegg, A. (2005), 'Out of the Mouths of Babes', *Marketing Week*, 23 June, p. 43.

Cornish, C. (2001), 'Experiences of Qualitative Research on the Internet', in Westlake, A., Sykes, W., Manners, T. and Rigg, M. (eds), *The Challenge of the Internet*, proceedings of the second ASC International Conference on Survey Research Methods.

Donald, H. (2005), 'Find Out What's in Store', *Marketing Week*, 24 February, pp. 41–2.

Duan, Y. and Burrell, P. (1997), 'Some Issues in Developing Expert Marketing Systems', *Journal of Business and Industrial Marketing*, 12 (2), pp. 149–62.

E-consultancy (2005), Internet Statistics Compendium, March, accessed via **http://www.e-consultancy.com/publications**.

Gander, P. (1998), 'Just the Job', *Marketing Week*, 25 June, pp. 51–4.

Gray, R. (2000a), 'How Research Has Narrowed Targets', *Marketing*, 10 February, pp. 31–2.

Gray, R. (2000b), 'The Relentless Rise of Online Research', *Marketing*, 18 May, p. 41.

Haggett, S. and Mitchell, V.W. (1994), 'Effect of Industrial Prenotification on Response Rate, Speed, Quality, Bias and Cost', *Industrial Marketing Management*, 23 (2), pp. 101–10.

Hague, P. (1992), *The Industrial Market Research Handbook*, 3rd edn, Kogan Page.

James, D. (2001), 'Quantitative Research', *Marketing News*, 1 January, p. 13.

Landy, L. and Gale, S. (2003), 'Measuring Ambient Media in Pubs and Clubs', paper presented at the ESOMAR Conference, June.

Lindstrom, M. and Seybold, P. (2004), *BRANDchild: Remarkable Insights into the Minds of Today's Global Kids and their Relationship with Brands*, Kogan Page Business Books.

Mariano, F., Susskind, R., Torres, H., Gotelli Varoli, A., Maciel, D. and Cunha, R. (2003), 'Living 24/7: A Week with Consumers in Search of the Objective Truth', paper presented at the ESOMAR *Congress 2003 – Management, Accountability and Research.*

Marketing Week (2005), 'UCAS Relaunches Student Loyalty Card with 15 Brands', *Marketing Week*, 3 March, p. 9.

Marshall, J. (2000), 'Monitoring Market Research Online', *Information World Review*, October, p. 31.

McDaniel, C. and Gates, R. (1996), *Contemporary Marketing Research*, 3rd edn, West.

McDaniel, S. *et al.* (1985), 'The Threats to Marketing Research: an Empirical Reappraisal', *Journal of Marketing Research*, 22 (February), pp. 74–80.

McLuhan, R. (2001a), 'How to Aid Clients Using Technology', *Marketing*, 30 August, p. 48.

McLuhan, R. (2001b), 'How Data Can Help Target Customers', *Marketing*, 27 September, p. 25.

New Media Age (2004), 'Online Increasingly Popular for Research', *New Media Age*, 13 August.

Palmer, S and Kaminow, D. (2005), 'Kerpow! Kerching! Understanding and Positioning the Spiderman Brand', paper presented at the Market Research Society Conference.

Pollitt, H. (2005), 'Obesity Through the Eyes of the Obese', *State of the Nation*, Association of Qualitative Researchers, May.

Poynter, R. and Quigley, P. (2001), 'Qualitative Research and the Internet', paper presented at the ESOMAR Conference, October.

Rao, S. (2000), 'A Marketing Decision Support System for Pricing New Pharmaceutical Products', *Marketing Research*, 12 (4), pp. 22–9.

Schafer, M. (2003) 'An Informal Guide to Probing', November, accessed via **http://www.research-live.com**.

Schmalensee, D. (2001), 'Rules of Thumb for B2B Research', *Marketing Research*, 13 (3), pp. 28–33.

Smith, D. and Fletcher, J. (1999), 'Fitting Market and Competitive Intelligence into the Knowledge Management Jigsaw', *Marketing and Research Today*, 28 (3), pp. 128–37.

Sneader, K., Sibony, O. and Haden, P. (2005), 'New Directions for Consumer Goods', *Market Leader*, Spring, pp. 32–7.

Tull, D.S. and Hawkins, D.T. (1990), *Marketing Research: Measurement and Method*, Macmillan.

Von Krogh, G., Ichijo, K. and Nonaka, I. (2000), *Enabling Knowledge Creation: How to Unlock the Mystery of Tacit Knowledge and Release the Power of Innovation*, New York: OUP.

Wilson, R. (2001), 'Search Engines', *Marketing Week*, 5 July, pp. 53–4.

Witthaus, M. (1999), 'Group Therapy', *Marketing Week*, 28 January, pp. 43–7.

Wolfman, A. (2005), 'Kids Research Meets Reality TV', *Young Consumers*, 6 (2).

Zikmund, W.G. and d'Amico, M. (1993), *Marketing*, West.

chapter 6

product

learning objectives

This chapter will help you to:

1 define and classify products and the key terms associated with them;

2 understand the nature, benefits and implementation of product and brand development;

3 understand the product lifecycle concept, its influence on marketing strategies and its limitations;

4 appreciate the importance of product positioning and how it both affects and is affected by marketing strategies;

5 define the role and responsibilities of the product or brand manager; and

6 outline the issues surrounding pan-European branding.

Introduction

The product is at the heart of the marketing exchange. Remember that customers buy products to solve problems or to enhance their lives and thus the marketer has to ensure that the product can fully satisfy the customer, not just in functional terms, but also in psychological terms. The product is important, therefore, because it is the ultimate test of whether the organisation has understood its customer's needs.

The example below raises a number of interesting questions about what makes a product and the importance of brand image and customer perceptions of it. To start the process of thinking about these issues, therefore, this chapter examines some fundamental concepts. The definition of product and ways of classifying products lead to some basic definitions of product ranges. Then, the underlying concepts, such as branding, packaging, design and quality, that give the product its character and essential appeal to the buyer will be examined along with issues relating to brand management.

An important concept linked with product and brand management is that of the product lifecycle. This traces the life story of the product, helping managers to understand the pressures and opportunities affecting products as they mature. To create and sustain long-lived brands, the product range needs to be managed in sympathy with changes in the customer and competitive environment through the concept of product positioning and repositioning. This may involve changes in marketing strategies, including promotion, packaging, design or even in the target market profile. Every product has to be assessed and managed according to how the consumer perceives it in relation to the competition. This chapter then turns to the practical problems of managing these processes, presenting a brief overview of product management structures. Finally, the issues surrounding the development and management of pan-European brands will be considered.

eg Perhaps the best known product and brand name in the world is Coca-Cola. First trade-marked in 1887, everything about the product such as the bottle shape, the colours and packaging design, and the logo design that has been developed from the word Coca-Cola, is instantly recognisable, distinctive and familiar to almost everyone globally. As one of its advertising campaigns of the 1990s put it, 'If you don't know what it is, Welcome to Planet Earth' (Pavitt, 2001). An earlier campaign called 'Hilltop' featured a diverse world society wanting to teach the world to sing and to buy the world a Coke. To the company the brand is everything, as it represents enduring values of authenticity, optimism and confidence.

In blind tasting, Coca-Cola may not score significantly better than its rivals in terms of taste and quality, but the strength of the brand name and the brand image have certainly helped it to maintain its market dominance. Some critics, however, are not so sure whether Coke's strength is sustainable. FMCG markets are generally mature, and brands less powerful than they were ten and twenty years ago. It's Google and eBay that now 'teach the world to sing' and many newer brands such as Innocent that are innovating and creating new niches. Although the brand name of Coke is still strong, the trend towards healthier drinks and concerns about sugar content and artificial sweeteners could actually work against the brand and result in gradual decline (Bainbridge and Green, 2004; *Brand Strategy*, 2004).

Anatomy of a product

A formal definition of product may be that:

a product is a physical good, service, idea, person or place that is capable of offering tangible and intangible attributes that individuals or organisations regard as so necessary, worthwhile or satisfying that they are prepared to exchange money, patronage or some other unit of value in order to acquire it.

A product is, therefore, a powerful and varied thing. The definition includes tangible products (tins of baked beans, aircraft engines), intangible products (services such as hairdressing or management consultancy) and ideas (public health messages, for instance). It even includes trade in people. For example, the creation and hard selling of pop groups and idols are less about music than about the promotion of a personality to which the target audience can relate. Does a Madonna fan buy her latest album for its intrinsic musical qualities or because of the Madonna name on the label? Places are also saleable products. Holiday resorts and capital cities, for example, have long exploited their natural geographic or cultural advantages, building service industries that in some cases become essential to the local economy.

Whatever the product is, whether tangible, intangible or Madonna, it can always be broken down into bundles of benefits that mean different things to different buyers. Figure 6.1 shows the basic anatomy of a product as a series of four concentric rings representing the core product, the tangible product, the augmented product and finally the potential product.

The *core product* represents the heart of the product, the main reason for its existence and purchase. The core benefit of any product may be functional or psychological and its definition must provide something for the marketer to work on to develop a differential advantage. Any make of car will get the purchaser from A to B, but add on to that the required benefits of spaciousness, or fuel economy or status enhancement, and a definition of a core product to which a market segment will relate begins to emerge. The core benefit of a holiday could be to lie in the sun doing absolutely nothing, being pampered for two weeks, at one end of the spectrum or, at the other end, to escape from the world by seeking adventure and danger in unknown terrain. Although it might be argued that a Club 18–30 holiday could satisfy both those core benefit requirements, generally speaking very different packages will emerge to meet those needs.

Figure 6.1 The anatomy of a product

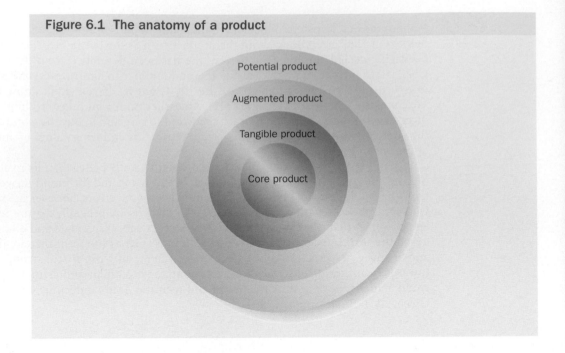

Potential product

Augmented product

Tangible product

Core product

The definition of the core benefit is important because it influences the next layer, the *tangible product*. The tangible product is essentially the means by which the marketer puts flesh on the core product, making it a real product that clearly represents and communicates the offer of the core benefit. The tools used to create the product include design specification, product features, quality level, branding and packaging. A car that embodies the core benefit of 'fast and mean status symbol', for example, is likely to have a larger engine, sexy design, leather upholstery, lots of electric gadgets, built-in CD player, definitely be available in black or red metallic paint (among other choices) and certainly carry a marque such as BMW rather than Lada.

eg Sometimes, product designers have to have a radical rethink of the way in which the core benefit of a product is delivered, perhaps because of a changing marketing environment. Air travel, for example, is under pressure from rising fuel costs, a shortage of slots at major airports, the adverse health effects of cramped seating, and increasingly vocal criticism of its performance on both environmental and noise pollution. And yet more and more people want to fly, to more places, more often. To respond to this environment, a collaborative three-year project called The Silent Aircraft Initiative has been launched involving Cambridge University, Massachusetts Institute of Technology, Rolls-Royce, Boeing and other aerospace companies, airlines and airports to rethink and redesign passenger aircraft.

After two years' work, the 40-strong team of researchers has proposed a 'flying wing' with its engines embedded in the aircraft's body and air intakes on top of the fuselage. It is claimed that this arrangement would mean that the noise would be partly absorbed by the aircraft body and partly bounced upwards, so that it wouldn't be heard beyond an airport perimeter. Initially, the team is looking at a 250-seat aircraft with a range of 4000 miles, but there is no reason why it could not be enlarged to take 800 passengers. The interior arrangement will also differ from more traditional aircraft: there will be few window seats, and thus more flexibility to create private cabins and give passengers more room to move about. One project team member said that it would be more like a ferry deck than an aircraft interior.

This design does answer a lot of the problems facing the industry. As well as reducing noise pollution, it is more fuel efficient, it provides a better environment for passengers, and if does end up as an 800-seater, then it will be able to deliver more passengers per landing slot. Don't, however, put your travel plans on hold while you wait for the new aircraft to enter commercial service; that's not likely to happen until 2025 (Cookson, 2005; Hawkes, 2005).

The *augmented product* represents add-on extras that do not themselves form an intrinsic element of the product, but may be used by producers or retailers to increase the product's benefits or attractiveness. A computer manufacturer may offer installation, user training and after-sales service, for instance, to enhance the attractiveness of the product package. None of this affects the actual computer system itself, but will affect the satisfaction and benefits that the buyer gets from the exchange. Retailers also offer augmented products. An electrical retailer selling national and widely available brands such as Hoover, Zanussi, Indesit or Hotpoint needs to make its own mark on each transaction so that the buyer will want to shop there again in the future. Augmenting the product through extra guarantees, cheap financing, delivery and breakdown insurance is more likely to provide memorable, competitively defendable and relatively inexpensive mechanisms for creating a relationship with the consumer than is price competition.

Finally, the *potential product* layer acknowledges the dynamic and strategic nature of the product. The first three layers have described the product as it is now, but the marketer also needs to think about what the product could be and should be in the future. The potential product can be defined in terms of its possible evolution, for example new ways of differentiating itself from the competition.

Product classification

To bring order to a wide and complex area of marketing, it is useful to be able to define groups of products that either have similar characteristics or generate similar buying behaviour within a market.

Product-based classification

A product-based classification groups together products that have similar characteristics, although they may serve very different purposes and markets. There are three main categories: durable products, non-durable products and service products.

- *Durable products*: Durable products last for many uses and over a long period before having to be replaced. Products such as domestic electrical goods, cars and capital machinery fall into this group. A durable is likely to be an infrequently purchased, relatively expensive good. It may require selective distribution through specialist channels and a communications approach that is primarily centred on information and function rather than psychological benefits.
- *Non-durable products*: Non-durable products can only be used once or a few times before they have to be replaced. Food and other fmcg goods fall into this category, as do office consumables such as stationery and computer printer cartridges. A non-durable is likely to be a frequently purchased, relatively low-priced item requiring mass distribution through as wide a variety of outlets as possible and mass communication centred on psychological benefits.
- *Service products*: Services represent intangible products comprising activities, benefits or satisfactions that are not embodied in physical products. Items such as financial services, holidays, travel and personal services create problems for marketers, because of their intangibility and inherent perishability (see Chapter 13). Service providers have to find ways of either bringing the service to the consumer or persuading the consumer to come to the service delivery point. Communication has to develop both functional and psychological benefit themes as well as reassuring the potential customer of the quality and consistency of the service offered.

Although these classifications are ostensibly based on product characteristics, it has proved to be impossible to talk about them without some reference to buyer behaviour, so perhaps it is time to make this dimension more explicit and instead to think about user-based classifications of products.

■ User-based classifications: consumer goods and services

The contents of this section are very closely linked with the content of pp. 76 *et seq.*, where differences in buyer behaviour were based on whether the purchase was a routine response situation, a limited problem solving situation or an extended problem solving situation. If we begin with these behavioural categories, it is possible to identify parallel groups of goods and services that fit into those situations, giving a very powerful combination of buyer and product characteristics for outlining the basic shape of the marketing mix.

Convenience goods

Convenience goods correspond to the routine response buying situation. They are relatively inexpensive, frequent purchases. The buyer puts little effort into the purchasing decision and convenience often takes priority over brand loyalty. If the desired brand of breakfast cereal is inexplicably unavailable within the store that the shopper is visiting, they will probably buy an alternative brand or do without rather than take the trouble to go to another shop.

Shopping goods

Linked with limited problem solving behaviour, shopping goods represent something more of a risk and an adventure to consumers, who are thus more willing to shop around and plan their purchases and even to enjoy the shopping process. Comparison through advertisements and visits to retail outlets may be supplemented by information from easily accessible sources, such as consumer organisations' published reports, word of mouth from family and friends and brochures, as well as advice from sales assistants in the retail setting. A moderately rational assessment of the alternative products based on function, features, service promises and guarantees will lead to a decision. Within the shopping goods classification, there may be brand and/or store loyalty involved, or no loyalty at all. There may also be a pre-existing short list of preferred brands within which the detailed comparison and final choice will be made.

If you want a toaster that oozes class, then treat yourself to the Classic Vario toaster by Dualit. It's built to last a lifetime.

Source: © Dualit 01293 652500 http://www.dualit.com

Forget the £20 version of a toaster. If you want a Dualit toaster, they start at over £100 and can go up to over £200. Each one is hand-built and they are made in limited quantities, despite increasing demand. The toaster does not pop up; it stops cooking when the timer tells it to and then keeps the toast warm until you throw a lever to get it out. It is designed to last, with cast aluminium ends, stainless steel bodywork and patented heating elements that can produce two, three, four or six variations. Although old-fashioned production methods are used, including a whole toaster being made by one worker from beginning to end and their identification number stamped on the base plate, it offers superior performance for those who are fussy about their toast. You would have to shop around to find one, however. You have little chance of finding one in the High Street electrical stores, but you might strike lucky in selected stores such as John Lewis. Dualit prides itself in offering a 'shopping good' (Carlyle, 2004; Pearman, 2001; http://www.dualit.co.uk).

Speciality goods

Speciality goods equate with the consumer's extensive problem-solving situation. The high-risk, expensive, very infrequently purchased products in this category evoke the most rational consumer response that a manufacturer could hope to find. It is not entirely rational, however. The psychological and emotive pull of a brand name like Porsche could still override objective assessment of information, leading to a biased, but happy, decision for the consumer. If you allow the inclusion in this category of products like designer perfumes, those that cost several hundred pounds for 50 ml and would be a once (or never) in a lifetime purchase for most consumers, then rationality goes right out of the window and the purchase is made entirely on the basis of the dream and the imagery woven around the product.

The products in this category need very specialist retailing that will provide a high level of augmented product services, both before and after the sale. Limiting distribution to a small number of exclusive and well-monitored outlets not only protects the product from abuse (for example inappropriate display or sales advice), but also helps to enhance the product's special image and the status of the buyer.

Unsought goods

Within the unsought goods category, there are two types of situation. The first is the sudden emergency, such as the burst water pipe or the flat tyre. The organisation's job here is to ensure that the consumer either thinks of its name first or that it is the most accessible provider of the solution to the problem.

The second unsought situation arises with the kinds of products that people would not normally buy without aggressive hard-selling techniques, such as timeshare properties and some home improvements.

■ User-based classifications: B2B goods and services

This type of classification of B2B goods and services is linked closely with the discussion at pp. 99 *et seq.*, where the spectrum of buying situations from routine re-buy to new task purchasing was discussed. The novelty of the purchase influences the time, effort and human resources put into the purchasing decision. If that is then combined with the role and importance of the purchase within the production environment, it is possible to develop a classification system that is both widely applicable and indicative of particular marketing approaches.

Capital goods

Capital equipment consists of all the buildings and fixed equipment that have to be in place for production to happen. Such items tend to be infrequently purchased and, given that they are expected to support production over a long lifetime and that they can represent a substantial investment, they are usually regarded as a high-risk decision in the new task category. They thus tend to use extensive decision-making, involving a wide range of personnel from all levels of the organisation and perhaps independent external consultants as well. This category might also include government-funded capital projects such as the building of motorways, bridges, housing and public buildings like hospitals and theatres.

Accessory goods

Accessory goods are items that give peripheral support to the production process without direct involvement. Included in this group, therefore, will be items such as hand tools, fork-lift trucks, storage bins and any other portable or light equipment. Office equipment is also included here, such as PCs, desks, chairs and filing cabinets.

Generally speaking, these items are not quite as expensive or as infrequently purchased as the capital goods. The risk factor is also lower. This suggests that the length of and the degree of involvement in the purchasing process will be scaled down accordingly into something closer to the modified re-buy situation.

Raw materials

Raw materials arrive more or less in their natural state, having been processed only sufficiently to ensure their safe and economical transport to the factory. Thus iron ore is delivered to Corus; fish arrives at the Findus fish-finger factory; beans and tomatoes are delivered to Heinz; and fleeces arrive at the textile mill. The raw materials then go on to further processing within the purchaser's own production line. The challenge for the supplier of raw materials is how to distinguish its product from the competition's, given that there may be few specification differences between them. Often, the differentiating factors in the purchaser's mind relate to non-product features, such as service, handling convenience, trust and terms of payment, for example.

Semi-finished goods

Unlike raw materials, semi-finished goods have already been subject to a significant level of processing before arriving at the purchaser's factory. They still, however, need further processing before incorporation into the ultimate product. A clothing manufacturer, therefore, will purchase cloth (i.e. the product of spinning, weaving and dyeing processes), which still needs to be cut and sewn to create the ultimate product.

Components and parts

Components and parts are finished goods in their own right, which simply have to be incorporated into the assembly of the final product with no further processing. Car manufacturers, for example, buy in headlamp units, alarm systems and microchips as complete components or parts and then fit them to the cars on the assembly line.

If the components are buyer-specified, then the sales representative's main responsibility is to make sure that the right people are talking to each other to clarify the detail of the buyer's precise requirements. Even when the product has been agreed, there is still a need to maintain the relationship. In contrast, supplier-specified products demand clear appreciation of customer needs, carefully designed and priced products and effective selling and promotion to exploit the opportunities identified by market research.

Supplies and services

Finally, there are several categories of minor consumable items (as distinct from the accessory goods discussed above) and services that facilitate production and the smooth running of the organisation without any direct input. Operating supplies are frequently purchased consumable items that do not end up in the finished product. In the office, this group mainly includes stationery items such as pens, paper and envelopes, as well as computer consumables such as printer toner or ink cartridges and floppy disks. Maintenance and repair services ensure that all the capital and accessory goods continue to operate smoothly and efficiently. This category can also include minor consumable items, such as cleaning materials, which assist in providing this service. Business services may well be a major category of purchases for an organisation, involving a great deal of expenditure and decision-making effort, since they involve the purchase of services like management consultancy, accounting and legal advice and advertising agency expertise. This takes the discussion back to new task purchasing and its associated problems of involvement and risk.

Understanding the product range

Most organisations offer a variety of different products and perhaps a number of variations of each individual product, designed to meet the needs of different market segments. Car companies clearly do this, producing different models of car to suit different price expectations, different power and performance requirements and different usage conditions, from the long-distance sales representative to the family wanting a car largely for short journeys in a busy suburban area.

To understand any product fully, it is essential to appreciate its position in the wider family of the organisation's products. The marketing literature uses a number of terms when talking about the product family that are easy to confuse because of their similarity. Here are some definitions that sort out the confusion and offer some insight into the complexity of the product family.

■ Product mix

The product mix is the total sum of all the products and variants offered by an organisation. A small company serving a specialist need may have a very small, tightly focused product mix. Van Dyck Belgian Chocolates, for example, offers boxed chocolates, chocolate bars, liqueur chocolates, fruit-flavoured chocolate, nut chocolates, etc. A large multinational supplier of fmcg products, such as Nestlé, has a very large and varied product mix, from confectionery to coffee to canned goods.

■ Product line

To impose some order on to the product mix, it can be divided into a number of product lines. A product line is a group of products that are closely related to each other. This relationship may be production-oriented, in that the products have similar production requirements or problems. Alternatively, the relationship may be market-oriented, in that the products fulfil similar needs, or are sold to the same customer group or have similar product management requirements.

■ Product item

A product line consists of a number of product items. These are the individual products or brands, each with its own features, benefits, price, etc. In the fmcg area, therefore, if Heinz had a product line called table sauces, the product items within it might be tomato ketchup, salad cream, mayonnaise, reduced calorie mayonnaise, etc.

■ Product line length

The total number of items within the product line is the product line length. Bosch, for example, might have a product line of DIY power tools, as shown in Figure 6.2. Its equivalent industrial range of power tools would probably be even longer.

■ Product line depth

The number of different variants of each item within a product line defines its *depth*. A deep product line has many item variants. A deep line may be indicative of a differentiated market coverage strategy where a number of different segments are being served with tailored prod-

Figure 6.2 Bosch DIY power tools product line

	LINE LENGTH	Catalogue Number	Power (Watts)	Speed (rpm)	LINE DEPTH
	• Cordless screwdriver				
	• Cordless drill				
	• Impact drill ←	PSB 500 RE	500	0–3000	
	• Planes	PSB 550 RA	550	0–3000	
	• Sanders	PSB 700 RE	700	3000	
	• Jigsaws	PSB 750–2 RE	750	1000/3000	
	• Grinders	PSB 1000 RPE	1010	2700	
	• Heat guns	PSB 1000 RCA	1010	0–2700	

ucts. If we look again at the Bosch example in Figure 6.2, we can break impact drills down into a number of variants, giving a depth of six, each of which has different performance and application capabilities, as well as fitting into different price segments ranging from under £50 to over £120.

Similarly, in an fmcg market, the Lynx brand (known as Axe outside the UK) produced by Lever Fabergé offers great product line depth in male toiletries. Under the Lynx umbrella, aftershave, shaving gel, shower gel, body spray, deodorant (in stick, roll-on and spray forms), shampoo and conditioner are offered in a variety of fragrances with suitably exotic and macho names such as Voodoo, Gravity, Africa, Phoenix, Apollo and Atlantis. This depth does not aim to cover different market segments, but does offer sufficient variation and choice to keep the target segment interested and loyal. The line includes all the basic male toiletry products so that the customer does not need to purchase anything from outside the line, and the variety of fragrances, with a new one introduced every year to keep the line fresh and interesting, allows the customer to experiment and have a change from time to time!

The Lynx range encourages brand loyalty by varying the fragrances and by using eye-catching advertising that targets male fantasies.

Source: Image courtesy of The Advertising Archives

■ Product mix width

The *width* of the product mix is defined by the number of product lines offered. Depending on how broadly or narrowly defined the product lines are, a wide mix might indicate an organisation with a diverse interest in a number of different markets, such as Nestlé.

Branding

Branding is an important element of the tangible product and, particularly in consumer markets, is a means of linking items within a product line or emphasising the individuality of product items. This points to the most important function of branding: the creation and communication of a three-dimensional character for a product that is not easily copied or damaged by competitors' efforts. The prosaic definition of brand, accepted by most marketers, is that it consists of any name, design, style, words or symbols, singly or in any combination that distinguish one product from another in the eyes of the customer. Brands are used by people to establish their status far more than religion or political party. We are often judged by the brands we select, the football teams we support, the television programmes we watch, the clothes we buy, the car marque we drive, where we eat and even what we eat. It is, therefore, perhaps of no great surprise that brands are often not about physical attributes but a set of values, a philosophy that can be matched with the consumer's own values and philosophy. Orange represents a bright future, Nike is about achievement ('just do it') and Avantis about life.

■ The meaning of branding

The definition of brand provided above offered a variety of mechanisms through which branding could be developed, the most obvious of which are the name and the logo. As with the product mix jargon discussed in the previous section, you are likely to meet a number of terms in the course of your reading and it is important to differentiate between them.

Brand name

A brand name is any word or illustration that clearly distinguishes one seller's goods from another. It can take the form of words, such as Weetabix and Ferrero Rocher, or initials, such as AA. Numbers can be used to create an effective brand name, such as 7-Up. Brand names can also be enhanced by the use of an associated logo, such as the one used by Apple computers, to reinforce the name, or through the particular style in which the name is presented. The classic example of this is the Coca-Cola brand name, where the visual impact of the written name is so strong that the onlooker recognises the design rather than reads the words. Thus Coca-Cola is instantly identifiable whether the name is written in English, Russian, Chinese or Arabic because it always somehow *looks* the same.

Trade name

The trade name is the legal name of an organisation, which may or may not relate directly to the branding of its products.

Some companies prefer to let the brands speak for themselves and do not give any prominence to the product's parentage. Washing powder brands produced by either Unilever or Procter & Gamble do not prominently display the company name, although it is shown on the back or side of the pack. Few consumers would realise that Persil, Surf and Radion come from the same stable.

Trade mark

A trade mark is a brand name, symbol or logo, which is registered and protected for the owner's sole use. To bring the UK into line with EU legislation, the Trades Marks Act, 1994 allowed organisations to register smells, sounds, product shapes and packaging, as well as brand names and logos (Olsen, 2000). This means that the Coca-Cola bottle, the Toblerone bar and Heinz's tomato ketchup bottle are as protectable as their respective brand names. Advertising slogans, jingles and even movements or gestures associated with a brand can also be registered as trade marks. The Act prevents competitors from legally using any of these things in a way that may confuse or mislead buyers, and also makes the registration process and action over infringement much easier.

eg China has long been a country generating serious trademark infringements that worry Western manufacturers. Since its entry to the WTO, however, China has taken considerable steps to clamp down and to protect intellectual property. The State Administration for Industry and Commerce (SAIC) plays the leading role among government organisations in registering and administering trademarks nationwide, and also guides local administrations of industry and commerce in their pursuit of trademark and counterfeiting cases. Three cases demonstrate the challenge it faces. A dress manufacturer in Shanghai produced and sold 15,000 garments marked with the labels 'Nike' and 'Adidas' for a total of Rmb177,368. It was prosecuted, fined Rmb180,000, and had the goods confiscated. A company based in Wuxi used the trademark 'Hongda' to market its motorcycle parts. Honda objected to this and forced the company to cease its activity and pay a large fine. Finally, a manufacturer of aluminium and plastic boards in Ningbo sold goods bearing the '3M' mark. These goods again were confiscated. Overall in 2003, SAIC handled 26,488 cases specifically involving trademark infringement and counterfeiting (*China Law and Practice*, 2004).

Brand mark

The brand mark is specifically the element of the visual brand identity that does not consist of words, but of design and symbols. This would include things like McDonald's golden arches, Apple's computer symbol, or Audi's interlocking circles. These things are also protectable, as discussed under trade marks above.

■ The benefits of branding

Branding carries benefits for all parties involved in the exchange process and in theory at least makes it easier to buy or sell products. This section, summarised in Figure 6.3, looks at the benefits of branding from different perspectives, beginning with that of the buyer.

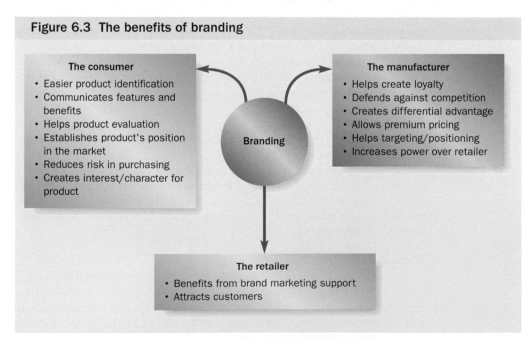

Figure 6.3 The benefits of branding

The consumer
- Easier product identification
- Communicates features and benefits
- Helps product evaluation
- Establishes product's position in the market
- Reduces risk in purchasing
- Creates interest/character for product

Branding

The manufacturer
- Helps create loyalty
- Defends against competition
- Creates differential advantage
- Allows premium pricing
- Helps targeting/positioning
- Increases power over retailer

The retailer
- Benefits from brand marketing support
- Attracts customers

Consumer perspective

Branding is of particular value to the buyer in a complex and crowded marketplace. In a supermarket, for example, brand names and visual images make it easier to locate and identify required products. Strong branding can speak volumes about the function and character of the product and help consumers to judge whether it is their sort of product, delivering the functional and psychological benefits sought. This is especially true for a new, untried product. The branding can at least help the evaluation of product suitability, and if there is an element of corporate branding it can also offer reassurance about the product's quality pedigree.

This all aids in the shopping process and reduces some of its risks, but it goes further. Giving a product what amounts to a three-dimensional personality makes it easier for consumers to form attitudes and feelings about the product. It gets them sufficiently interested to want to be bothered to do that. This has the double effect of creating brand loyalty (the product as a trusted friend) and of creating something special in the consumer's mind that the competition would find difficult to touch.

This has thus led to brands being regarded as 'packaged meanings' that shoppers can identify with and that organisations are happy to engender. Being able to humanise products with characteristics such as being honest, friendly, trustworthy, fun or *avant garde* all helps to build stronger customer relationships and makes the product attributes almost secondary.

Manufacturer perspective

The manufacturer benefits, of course, from the relationship of the buyer with branding. The ease of identification of the product at the point of sale, the connotations of quality and familiarity and the creation of a three-dimensional product personality all help the manufacturer. The manufacturer's key interest is in the building of defendable brand loyalty to the point where the trust, liking and preference for the brand overcome any lingering price sensitivity, thus allowing a reasonable measure of premium pricing and the prevention of brand switching.

Some of the best known brands that have emerged over the past 50 years have become almost synonymous with the product sector: Kellogg's for cereal, Hoover for vacuum cleaners, Nike for sports shoes and Sony Walkman for the personal stereo market. Achieving such a 'generic brand' position creates considerable strength for the manufacturer in shaping marketing strategy, but it is no guarantee of continued success – ask Levi's or Marks & Spencer.

Other more subtle advantages of branding for the manufacturer are linked with segmentation and competitive positioning strategies. Different brands can be used by one organisation to target different segments. Because the different brands have clearly defined individual characteristics, the consumer does not necessarily link them and thus does not become confused about what the organisation stands for. Even where there is a strong corporate element to the branding, as with Ford cars, the individual models within the range are clearly seen as separate products, serving different market needs, with price differences justified in terms of design and technical specification. Consumers view this wide range of brands positively, as a way of offering as tailored a choice as possible within the confines of a mass market.

Strong branding is also important for providing competitive advantage, not just in terms of generating consumer loyalty, but also as a means of competing head-on, competing generally across the whole market in an almost undifferentiated way or finding a niche in which to dominate. Brand imagery can help to define the extent of competition or exaggerate the differentiating features that pull it away from the competition.

Retailer perspective

The retailer benefits from branding to a certain extent. Branded products are well supported by advertising and other marketing activities, and so the retailer has some assurance that they will sell. Branded products do draw customers into the store, but the disadvantage is that if a brand is unavailable in one store, then the shopper is likely to patronise another instead. The retailer may prefer the shopper to be less brand loyal and more store loyal! Supermarkets have always recognised the value and necessity of manufacturer-branded goods, but they have also looked for ways of reducing the power that this gives the brand owner. This issue will be looked at in detail later in this chapter.

■ Brand valuation

It is clear from the previous section that successful brands are an asset to the brand owner. Successful brands can be long lasting and create a competitive advantage that others find difficult to challenge, as seen in the example of Cadbury's Dairy Milk. Interbrand claims that on average, brands account for more than one-third of shareholder value and in some cases as much as 70 per cent (Lindemann, 2004).

A brand asset has been defined as:

A name and/or symbol used to uniquely identify the goods and services of a seller from those of its competitors, with a view to obtaining wealth in excess of that obtainable without a brand.

(Tollington, 1998)

To have a meaningful brand asset requires identification and quantification. Brand valuation emerged through the 1990s as an important measure for brand owners assessing the effectiveness of their brand marketing strategies, their long-term advertising and even the overall worth of the company. Brands represent a financial value to a company reflected through the goodwill component of a balance sheet. The physical assets of a company often now only represent a small part of the value of that company: it is reputation that is worth paying for, as it can bring you loyal customers and committed staff. When Ford bought Jaguar it was estimated that the physical assets were just 16 per cent of the value of the company, and when Vodafone bought Orange, physical assets were just 10 per cent of the value (Bunting, 2001). This reflects the real value of strong brand names.

The value of brands to many companies has now become so important that it has been argued that the chief executive should ultimately be the brand manager and that all staff need to realise that they are in the front line of brand delivery. Such an approach is clearly demonstrated by Richard Branson at Virgin, where the strength of the Virgin brand name has successfully carried it into many sectors.

The recognition of brands as assets is likely to become more emphasised in future as finance directors and accountants increasingly use brand-valuation techniques in balance sheets. However, because of issues of the subjectivity and reliability of valuation measurement, the accounting profession still treats brand valuation with some caution (*Brand Strategy*, 2003).

Lest this discussion should seem too enthusiastic about branding, we now turn to some of the disadvantages. Echoing one of the risks of segmentation (discussed in Chapter 4, p. 133), there is the danger of proliferation if brands are created to serve every possible market niche. Retailers are under pressure to stock increasing numbers of lines within a product area, which means in turn that either less shelf space is devoted to each brand or retailers refuse to stock some brands. Both options are unpleasant for the manufacturer. The consumer may also begin to see too much choice and, at some point, there is a risk that the differences between brands become imperceptible to the consumer and confusion sets in.

■ Types of brands

The discussion so far has centred on the brands created and marketed by manufacturers and sold through retail outlets. An area of growing importance, however, is the brand created by a wholesaler or retailer for that organisation's sole use. This development has taken place partly because of conflicts and power struggles between manufacturers and retailers, and partly because the retailers also need to generate store loyalty in a highly competitive retail sector.

This section, therefore, distinguishes between the brands emanating from different types of organisation.

Manufacturer brands

Most manufacturers, particularly in the fmcg sector, are at arm's length from the end buyer and consumer of their product. The retail sector is in between and can make the difference between a product's success and failure through the way the product is displayed or made available to the public. The manufacturer can attempt to impose some control over this through trade promotions, but the manufacturer's best weapon is direct communication with the end buyer. Planting brand names and recognition of brand imagery in the consumer's mind through advertising or sales promotion gives the manufacturer a fighting chance of recognition and selection at the point of sale. Furthermore, the creation of a strong brand that has hard-core loyalty can tip the balance of power back in favour of the manufacturer, because any retailer not stocking that brand runs the risk of losing custom to its competitors.

Retailer and wholesaler brands

The growth of own-label brands (i.e. those bearing the retailer's name) or own-brands has become a major factor in retailing. Why do it? One possible problem a retailer has is that if a consumer is buying a recognised manufacturer's brand, then the source of that purchase is less relevant. A can of Heinz baked beans represents the same values whether it is purchased from a corner shop or from Harrods. Retailers can differentiate from each other on the basis of price or service, but they are looking for more than that. The existence of a range of exclusive retailer brands that the consumer comes to value creates a physical reason for visiting that retailer and no other. These brands also serve the purpose of giving the consumer 'the retailer in a tin', where the product in the kitchen cupboard is a constant reminder of the retailer and embodies the retailer's values in a more tangible form, reinforcing loyalty and positive attitudes.

Other reasons include the fact that the retailer can earn a better margin on an own-brand and still sell it more cheaply than a manufacturer's brand. This is because the retailer's own-brand is sold on the back of the retailer's normal marketing activity and not with the massive advertising, promotion and selling costs that each manufacturer's brand has to bear.

The use of own-brand varies across different retailers. Some retailers, such as Kwik Save, use their own label to create a no-nonsense, no-frills, value-for-money, generic range. Others, such as Marks & Spencer, Sainsbury's and the Albert Heijn chain in the Netherlands, have created own-brands that are actually perceived as superior in quality to the manufacturer's offerings.

Given that own-label products seem to put so much power into the hands of the retailers, why do manufacturers cooperate in their production? For a manufacturer of second string brands (i.e. not the biggest names in the market), it might be a good way of developing closer links with a retailer and earning some sort of protection for the manufacturer's brands. In return for the supply, at attractive prices, of own-brand products, the retailer might undertake to display the manufacturer's brands more favourably, or promise not to delist them, for example. The extra volume provides some predictability for the manufacturer and it also could help to achieve economies of scale of benefit to both parties. The danger, of course, is that of the manufacturer becoming too dependent on the retailer's own-brand business.

Product management and strategy

This chapter has already hinted at a number of important dimensions to be considered in developing and maintaining a branding strategy. Each one will now be treated separately.

■ Creating the brand

New product development

New product development (NPD) is important to organisations for many reasons, including the need to create and maintain competitive advantage through innovation and better serving the customer's changing needs and wants. Whether a product is a totally new innovation, an update of a familiar product or an imitation of a competitor's product, it needs careful planning and development to ensure that it meets customers' needs and wants, that it has a significant competitive advantage and that it is accepted within the marketplace. NPD can be a long and expensive process, with no guarantees that the resulting product will succeed, and therefore to minimise the risks, it needs careful and skilful management to ensure that the best ideas are successfully developed into commercially viable, potentially profitable products with a future.

Product design, quality and guarantees

Design. Design is an integral part of the product itself, affecting not only its overall aesthetic qualities but also its ergonomic properties (i.e. the ease and comfort with which it can be used) and even its components and materials. All of this together can enhance the product's visual appeal, its ability to fulfil its function and its reliability and life span.

eg

The PC has struggled to achieve big design leaps forward. PCs may have become more powerful, smaller and faster, but still the basic designs remain the same and the colour choice is usually limited. In an age in which the computer is an essential part of any home, there has been little progress on PCs designed for particular jobs, for particular rooms, and particular people. There are some attempts to present the PC as an entertainment centre or photographic centre, but generally the efforts have not been convincing. Five ideas suggested for change are:

- *Think smaller:* small enough to fit in a pocket but powerful enough to run high-end software, all making the laptop redundant. MS Systems have incorporated a processor into key-sized circuitry, but there is still the issue of plugging into keyboards and monitors.
- *Show it bigger:* flat-screen monitors have taken over from cathode ray tubes, but they tend to go up to only about 17- or 19-inch screen sizes. Microsoft is experimenting with a 44-inch high resolution curve-round screen so that multiple programs can be viewed at once or the ultimate gaming experience can be realised.
- *Entertain:* the PC should become the command centre for home entertainment. Using high definition video, quality sound processing and wi-fi, a wide range of entertainment applications can be managed from one central point.
- *Make it fit in:* new designs can reduce cable sprawl and save space. IDEO has built an entertainment PC with the computer hidden in the black screen display.
- *Aesthetics:* Apple has led the way in this area with use of colour and interesting designs.

It remains to be seen how quickly PC manufacturers will start to think outside the 'box' when it comes to the next generation of designs (Park, 2004).

Design is increasingly being recognised as being more than just the shape and colour of new products. It also involves the process by which new products and service are produced to meet customer needs and bring creative ideas to reality. Research by the UK Design Council, however, has indicated that smaller companies are often far less design-oriented than larger ones and in some companies, design still plays only a small role in the marketing and product development process. Governments have, however, recognised the importance of design in helping industry to gain a sustainable competitive edge in global markets. Bodies such as the UK's Design Council, the Netherlands Design Institute and the French Agence pour la Promotion de la Création Industrielle promote and support good design practice. The EU also encourages design with initiatives such as the biannual European Community Design Prize aimed at small and medium-sized businesses.

Quality. Unlike design, quality is a very well-understood concept among managers. Many organisations now recognise the importance of quality and have adopted the philosophy of total quality management (TQM), which means that all employees take responsibility for building quality into whatever they do. TQM affects all aspects of the organisation's work, from materials handling to the production process, from the product itself to the administrative procedures that provide customer service. Marketers, of course, have a vested interest in all these manifestations of quality, because creating and holding on to customers means not only providing the quality of product that they want (and providing it consistently), but also supporting the product with quality administrative, technical and after-sales service.

'Let's off-road!'

That memorable catchphrase from the BBC's *Fast Show*, 'Let's Off-Road', is the target of Greenpeace and other environmentalists along with road-safety campaigners, who want large off-road Sports Utility Vehicles (SUVs) off the road for good. Contemptuously labelled 'Chelsea Tractors', their high fuel consumption, the road space they occupy, and the risks to pedestrians in the event of a collision have all come in for severe criticism. Consumption rates can vary between 12 and 20 miles to the gallon, depending upon whether it has a diesel or petrol engine. There is also a view that the sheer size and height of these vehicles makes drivers more aggressive and gives them a false sense of security.

Despite the criticism, the SUV is a growth sector of the car industry with sales up 12.8 per cent during 2004 and by 40 per cent over five years. The leading SUV brands from Jeep, Toyota, Land Rover, Range Rover, Mitsubishi, Suzuki and Nissan have enjoyed good profitability over that period. Generally SUVs are most attractive to 35- to 54-year-olds but there are variations, with Suzuki having a younger profile and Nissan and Toyota appealing to older drivers.

Only a small percentage of the nation lives in remote rural areas where off-road vehicles may be needed, but SUV brands present a powerful image of a versatile, family-oriented yet stylish car to urban dwellers. Although the vehicles may suggest wealth, the average income of buyers is very much middle income, but the family size, excluding the Suzuki, tends to be four or more people. It is too early to establish whether the top of the range Volvo XC90, BMW X5 or Porsche Cayenne will change that profile. Perhaps the biggest attraction is the style value, with 55 per cent looking to trade up to maintain the status element. Research has indicated that 20 per cent buy SUVs for style alone (*Marketing Week*, 2005). Only 12 per cent actually take them off-road (*Marketing Week*, 2004)!

The advertising and image building for SUVs is, however, very direct and very aspirational with a strong macho tone. One manufacturer uses phrases such as 'dominate the highways', 'take the town by storm' and 'conquer the streets', leaving the reader in no doubt about the brand proposition. Most of the locations for photography are rural or coastal and never feature the school run. Honda took a more balanced approach when advertising its CR-V with the strapline 'Is that the wild calling, or just the local garden centre? Sometimes it's difficult to tell.' This reflects the reality: SUVs are made for one thing but used for another and marketers have a lot to answer for in that. The wider functional benefits of safety, design and space are often lost in the messaging and this has become a major PR problem for the manufacturers (*Professional Engineering*, 2004).

Despite their popularity with their drivers, SUVs are very unpopular with the general public and this may feed through into legislation. Interestingly, SUVs have failed to penetrate the business market due to their high fuel consumption and thus high tax liability. This is not likely to change, as two-thirds of the population want special taxes slapped on SUVs and over half want them banned from city centres (*Marketing Week*, 2004). There is just not much opportunity to off-road in Oxford Street. The Mayor of London described urban 4×4 drivers as 'complete idiots' and would like higher congestion charges to drive them away. He made no reference, however, to the increased number of buses on British roads, sometimes running almost empty, following bus deregulation, and the fact that these vehicles can do far more damage. Sweden and France are also considering higher taxation for SUVs. In France 14 out of 18 cars on the environmentally harmful list are SUVs.

The road safety lobby argues that a child is 17 times more likely to be killed or seriously injured if hit by an SUV rather than a saloon car. With road safety becoming higher on the EU political agenda, it is likely that there will be more regulation on design and a requirement for manufacturers to give more information on the dangers of SUVs, moves inspired by groups arguing that SUVs are anti-social. Special taxes are also a real possibility, either direct taxation at the point of purchase or indirect taxation through congestion charging rates. Any regulation or legislation will be opposed, however, on the basis that it is not the role of government to tell people what cars they can drive.

Where will the debate end? Some groups are taking matters into their own hands. Thirty-five Greenpeace activists invaded the Range Rover plant in the West Midlands, chained themselves to the production line and prevented production until they were arrested. The industry has argued that legislation is not necessary, because it is punitive on a group of consumers exercising free purchasing choice, but also because SUVs may become the GTIs of tomorrow. The industry goes through fashion cycles – ten years ago the GTI badge was the pinnacle of driving chic, today it's the SUV, and in ten years' time ... who knows? What is needed, however, is a more careful presentation of SUV benefits and an image that is not concerned with status and driving others off the road!

Sources: Mackintosh (2005); *Marketing Week* (2004; 2005); *Professional Engineering* (2004).

In judging the quality of the product itself, a number of dimensions may be considered.

Performance. Performance is about what the product can actually *do*. Thus with the Bosch impact drills mentioned earlier (see Figure 6.2), a customer might perceive the more expensive model with a variable speed of 3000 rpm as being of 'better quality' than a more basic lower-powered drill. The customer might have more difficulty judging between competing products, however. Black & Decker, for example, produces a range of impact drills that are very similar to the Bosch ones, with minor variations in specification and price levels. If both the Bosch model and the equivalent Black & Decker model offer the same functions, features, benefits and pricing levels, the customer might have problems differentiating between them in terms of performance and will have to judge on other characteristics.

Durability. Some products are expected to have a longer life span than others and some customers are prepared to pay more for what they perceive to be a better-quality, more *durable* product. Thus the quality level built into the product needs to be suited to its expected life and projected usage. Thus a child's digital watch fitted into a plastic strap featuring a licensed character such as Barbie or Batman, retailing at around £5, is not expected to have the same durability or quality level as a Swiss Tissot retailing at £125. Disposable products in particular, such as razors, biros and cigarette lighters, need to be manufactured to a quality level that is high enough to allow them to perform the required function for the required number of uses or for the required time span, yet low enough to keep the price down to a level where the customer accepts the concept of frequent replacement.

Reliability and maintenance. Many customers are concerned about the probability of a product breaking down or otherwise failing, and about the ease and economy of repairs. As with durability, some customers will pay a price premium for what are perceived to be more *reliable* products or for the peace of mind offered by comprehensive after-sales support. These days most makes of car, for example, are pretty reliable if they are properly maintained and so car buyers may differentiate on the basis of the cost and ease of servicing and the cost and availability of spare parts.

Design and style. As mentioned earlier, the visual and ergonomic appeal of a product may influence perceptions of its quality. The sleek, stylish, aerodynamic lines of the Lamborghini contrast sharply with the functional boxiness of the Lada. Packaging design can also enhance quality perceptions.

Corporate name and reputation. If, after all that, customers are still uncertain about the relative quality offerings of the alternative products under consideration, they may fall back on their *perceptions of the organisation*. Some may feel that Black & Decker is a well established, familiar name, and if they have had other Black & Decker products that have served well in the past, then that might swing the quality decision in Black & Decker's favour. Others may decide in favour of Bosch because of its associations with high-quality German engineering.

Marketers recognise that quality in the marketplace is a matter of perception rather than technical specification. This is particularly true in consumer markets, where the potential customer may not have the expertise to judge quality objectively and will use all sorts of cues, such as price, packaging or comparison with competitors, to form an opinion about quality level.

Guarantees. One way in which an organisation can emphasise its commitment to quality and its confidence in its own products and procedures is through the *guarantees* it offers. Although customers are protected under national and EU laws against misleading product claims and goods that are not fit for their intended purpose, many organisations choose to extend their responsibility beyond the legal minimum. Some will offer extended warranties. Others are less ambitious and simply offer 'no questions asked' refunds or replacements if the customer is unhappy with a product for any reason at all. Such schemes not only reflect the organisation's confidence in its product and its commitment to customer service, but also reduce the risk to the customer in trying the product.

eg The Haberman Anywayup® Cup is a prized possession to stop a toddler dripping juice all over you or, worse still, your neighbour's carpet. It used innovation in design, with a slit valve to control the flow of liquid, and yet still matched the alternatives for style. Designed by a mother who had suffered from more traditional cups, the non-spill cup was named as a Design Council Millennium Product; it won the Gold Medal at the Salon International des Inventions in Geneva; and it has won other awards, such as the 'Female Inventor of the Year' for the company's owner. Its superior design has led to sales of over £10m in over 70 countries since its launch in 1995 (Bridge, 2003; **http://mandyhaberman.com**).

The award-winning Haberman Anywayup® Cup comes in three different models, for children and adults who need cups that hold drinks without them spilling.

Source: © Mandy Haberman http://www.mandyhaberman.com

It may also be possible for the organisation to use its guarantees to create a differential advantage over its competitors. The danger is, however, that promises can be copied and once similar guarantees have become widespread within a particular market or industry, they start to be seen as a normal part of the product package and their impact may be lost as customers look for other differentiating factors.

Naming, packaging and labelling the brand

Selecting a brand name. A brand name must be memorable, easy to pronounce and meaningful (whether in real or emotional terms). As manufacturers look increasingly towards wider European and international markets, there is a much greater need to check that a proposed name does not lead to unintended ridicule in a foreign language. Neither the French breakfast cereal Plopsies (chocolate-flavoured puffed rice) nor the gloriously evocative Slovakian pasta brand Kuk & Fuk are serious contenders for launch into an English-speaking market. From a linguistic point of view, care must be taken to avoid certain combinations of letters that are difficult to pronounce in some languages.

Language problems apart, the ability of a brand name to communicate something about the product's character or functional benefits could be important. Blackett (1985) suggests that approaches to this can vary, falling within a spectrum ranging from freestanding names, through associative names, to names that are baldly descriptive. This spectrum is shown with examples of actual brand names in Figure 6.4. Names that are totally freestanding are completely abstract and bear no relation to the product or its character. Kodak is a classic example of such a name.

Figure 6.4 The brand name spectrum

← Descriptive	Associative	Freestanding →
Bitter Lemon	Walkman	Kodak
Dairy Milk Chocolate	Natrel	Esso
Shredded Wheat	Burger King	Pantene
Liquorice All Sorts	Bold	Mars Bar
	Sensodyne	

Associative names suggest some characteristic, image or benefit of the product, but often in an indirect way. Pledge (furniture polish), Elvive (shampoo) and Impulse (body spray) are all names that make some kind of statement about the product's positioning through the consumer's understanding of the word(s) used in the name. The extremely prosaic end of the spectrum is represented by descriptive names. Names such as Chocolate Orange, Shredded Wheat and Cling Film certainly tell you about what the product is, but they are neither imaginative nor easy to protect. Bitter Lemon, for example, began as a brand name and was so apt that it soon became a generic title for any old bottle of lemon-flavoured mixer. Somewhere between associative and descriptive names come a group with names that are descriptive, but with a distinctive twist. Ex-Lax (laxative), Lucozade (fizzy glucose drink) and Bacofoil (aluminium cooking foil) are names that manage to describe without losing the individuality of the brand.

In summary, there are four 'rules' for good brand naming. As far as possible, they need to be:

1 *distinctive*, standing out from the competition while being appealing to the target market and appropriate to the character of the product;
2 *supportive* of the product's positioning with respect to its competitors (pp. 211 *et seq.* will discuss positioning in further detail), while remaining consistent with the organisation's overall branding policy;
3 *acceptable*, recognisable, pronounceable and memorisable, in other words user-friendly to the consumer; and finally,
4 *available*, registerable, protectable (i.e. yours and only yours).

With respect to this last point, it is important to ensure that the suggested brand name is not infringing the rights of existing brands. This is particularly difficult with international brands.

Packaging. Packaging is an important part of the product that not only serves a functional purpose, but also acts as a means of communicating product information and brand character (Harrington, 2005). The packaging is often the consumer's first point of contact with the actual product and so it is essential to make it attractive and appropriate for both the product's and the customer's needs.

eg McVitie's (http://www.unitedbiscuits.co.uk) has managed to differentiate its Jaffa Cakes (http://www.jaffacakes.co.uk) brand from supermarket 'look-alike' own brands by producing innovative packaging for mini-Jaffa Cakes. The pack consists of six individually sealed plastic segments, joined by perforations, which can be easily separated. The pack is bright orange, with the texture of orange peel to emphasise the nature of the product. Each segment provides a portion of Jaffa Cakes and can be packed into a lunch box or just used as a convenient snack. Meanwhile, the other five segments remain sealed and therefore stay fresh until required.

Packaging is any container or wrapping in which the product is offered for sale and can consist of a variety of materials such as glass, paper, metal or plastic, depending on what is to be contained. The choice of materials and the design of the packaging may have to take account of the texture, appearance and viscosity of the product, as well as its perishability.

Dangerous products such as medicines or corrosive household cleaners need special attention. Other design issues might include the role of the packaging in keeping the product ready for use, the means of dispensing the product and the graphic design, presenting the brand imagery and the statutory and desired on-pack information.

Naturally, there is a cost involved in all of this. Although it can cost £100,000 to create a packaging design for an fmcg product, it seems a very reasonable sum compared with the £3 million or more that will be spent on the advertising to launch that same product. McKenzie (1997) found that the packaging design was becoming a vital element in developing a brand proposition to the consumer both in advertising and point-of-sale promotion. This could be the case both for a new product launch and for relaunching existing products that might be starting to look tired.

With the rise of the self-service ethos in consumer markets, packaging has indeed grown in importance. It has to communicate product information to help the consumer make a choice, to communicate brand image and positioning and, mostly, to attract attention at the point of sale and invite the consumer to explore the product further (Pieters and Warlops, 1999). Thus packaging is an important part of the overall product offering and has a number of marketing and technical dimensions, some of which are discussed below.

Functions of packaging. First among the functions of packaging are the practicalities. Packaging must be *functional*: it must protect the product in storage, in shipment and often in use. Other packaging functions centre on convenience for the consumer, in terms of both ease of access and ease of use. In the convenience food sector, ease of use has come with the development of packaging that can be placed straight inside a microwave oven and thus serves as a cooking utensil. This underlines the necessity for packaging materials, design and technology to develop in parallel with markets and emerging market needs. Consumer pressure for fewer preservatives and additives in food products has also encouraged the development of packaging that better preserves pack content. Products also need to be protected from tampering, and many jars or packages now have at least a visually prominent seal on the outer pack with the verbal warning that the product should not be used if the seal is damaged.

In addition to offering functional information about product identity and use, packaging also serves a *promotional* purpose. It needs to grab and hold the consumer's attention and involve them with the product. It has been suggested that packaging may be the biggest medium of communication for three reasons (Peters, 1994):

■ its extensive reach to nearly all purchasers of the category;
■ its presence at the crucial moment when the purchase decision is made; and
■ the high level of involvement of users who will actively scan packaging for information.

This involvement of the user makes the packaging an essential element in branding, both in the communication of brand values and as an essential part of the brand identity (Connolly and Davidson, 1996).

Packaging can also be used, for example, as a means of distributing coupons, for advertising other related products, announcing new products, presenting on-pack offers or distributing samples and gifts. A special can was developed for Lucozade Sport, for example, that allowed 'instant win' vouchers to be sealed into the packaging, separate from the liquid. There is more on all of this in Chapter 11.

eg The added psychological value of the packaging is an absolutely essential part of some products. Perfumes, for example, rely heavily on their packaging to endorse the qualities of luxury, expense, exclusivity, mystery and self-indulgence that they try to represent. Champagne, a perfume by Yves St Laurent, comes in a crimson-lined gold box, which opens out like a kind of casket to reveal an elegant bottle representing a champagne cork, complete with gold wire. It is estimated that the packaging for such a product actually costs about three times as much as the content of the bottle itself. Closer to the mass market, Easter eggs are also an example of the packaging outshining the content. Novelty carton shapes, bright graphics, ribbons and bows are central to the purchasing decision and dull any natural inclination to compare the price with the actual chocolate content.

Packaging in the marketing mix. Packaging plays an important part in the marketing mix. This chapter has already outlined its functional importance, its communication possibilities and its crucial role as a first point of physical contact between the buyer and the product. Effective and thoughtful packaging is recognised as a means of increasing sales.

Even the choice of the range of pack sizes to offer the market can reinforce the objectives of the marketing mix. Trial-size packs, clearly labelled as such, help with new product launch (see also Chapter 11) by encouraging low-risk product trial. Small-sized packs of an established product may reinforce a commitment to a market segment comprising single-person households or infrequent users. Larger packs target family usage, heavy users generally or the cost-conscious segment who see the large pack as better value for money. The increase in out-of-town shopping by car means that consumers are far better able than ever before to buy large, bulky items. This trend has developed further into the demand for multiple packs. Pack sizes may also be closely linked with end-use segmentation (see p. 124). Ice-cream can be packaged as either an individual treat, a family block or a party-sized tub. The consumer selects the appropriate size depending on the end use, but the choice must be there or else the consumer will turn to another brand.

In developing a new product or planning a product relaunch, an organisation thus needs to think carefully about all aspects of packaging and its integration into the overall marketing mix of the product. Although only a small number of brands can be supported by heavy national advertising, for the rest, packaging represents the investment priority for communicating the brand message (Underwood *et al.*, 2001). The technical and design considerations, along with the likely trade and consumer reactions, need to be assessed. Consumers in particular can become very attached to packaging. It can be as recognisable and as cherished as a friend's face and consumers may not, therefore, take kindly to plastic surgery! Sudden packaging changes may lead to a suspicion that other things about the product have also changed for the worse. All of this goes to show that, as with any aspect of marketing, packaging design and concepts need careful research and testing, using where possible one of the growing number of professional consultancies in the field.

Labelling. Labelling is a particular area within the packaging field that represents the outermost layer of the product. Labels have a strong functional dimension, in that they include warnings and instructions, as well as information required by law or best industry practice. Labels state, at the very least, the weight or volume of the product (often including a stylised letter 'e', which means that the variation in weight or volume between packs is within certain tolerances laid down by the EU), a barcode and the name and contact address of the producer. Consumer demand has also led to the inclusion of far more product information, such as ingredients, nutritional information and the environmental friendliness of the product.

The prominence and detail of health and safety instructions are also becoming increasingly important, as organisations seek to protect themselves against prosecution or civil liability should the product be misused. These instructions range from general warnings to keep a product out of the reach of children, to prohibitions on inhaling solvent-based products, through to detailed instructions about the use of protective clothing.

■ Developing the brand

An organisation that uses branding effectively is in a powerful position with the retail trade in gaining shelf space and cooperation. It can also be in a better position to engender consumer loyalty, whether to an individual product or to a range (which would allow product switching within the variety offered in the range, without the loss of overall sales). All of this helps to make branding a very active and strategically important area in marketing. The following sections thus look at some of the more strategic issues arising from the need to make the most of the effort and expense that have gone into a product's initial development.

Product range brand policy

For most fmcg organisations, the decision on whether to brand the product range or not is an easy one. Branding is essential for most products in these markets. Difficulty arises with some homogeneous products because in theory the customer does not perceive sufficient difference between competing products to make branding feasible. As suggested on pp. 129 *et seq.* in the discussion on undifferentiated products, however, there are fewer and fewer truly homogeneous products to be found. Petrol brands, for example, have now been created that differentiate on the basis of service factors and the use of sales promotions as an integral part of the offering.

Once the decision to brand has been made, there are still a number of choices, one of which is the degree of independence that the brand is to be given in terms of its relationship with both other brands and the originating organisation.

Generic brands represent one extreme, where a single brand image covers a wide range of different products. This is mainly found in supermarkets, where a range of very low-priced, basic staple products are packaged with the minimum of frills and often the minimum permissible information on the packaging, such as Tesco's Value Lines. This is still a form of branding, in the sense that it is creating a distinctive character for a set of products.

At the opposite extreme, individual products are given entirely separate individual brand identities. There is thus no obvious relationship between different products produced by the same organisation. This is known as *discreet branding*. It is a useful policy to adopt if the intention is to compete in a number of different segments because it reduces the risk of one product's positioning affecting the consumer's perception of another product. It also means that if one product gets into trouble, perhaps through a product-tampering scare or through production problems causing variable quality, the other products are better insulated against the bad reputation rubbing off onto them too. The big disadvantage of the discreet approach to branding, however, is that each brand has to be set up from scratch, with all the expense and marketing problems associated with it. The new brand cannot benefit from the established reputation of any other brand.

One way of allowing brands to support each other is by using a monolithic approach to branding, which uses a family name (usually linked with the corporate name) with a single brand identity for the whole product range.

eg Heinz (**http://www.heinz.com**) is a prime example of the monolithic approach. The Heinz brand is well respected and very strong, but individual Heinz products have little identity of their own. Brand names are descriptive and always include the word Heinz to link them, such as Heinz Cream of Tomato Soup, Heinz Baked Beans, Heinz Low Calorie Mayonnaise, etc. Even the label design of each product shows that it clearly belongs to the Heinz family, further drawing the products together. Such family unity creates a strong overall image and allows new products easy entry into the existing product lines (although it might take consumers a while to notice a new flavour of soup in among the rest). It is also possible to achieve economies of scale in communication, if desired, and distribution, through treating the family as a unit rather than as a number of independent products. The danger is, however, that if one product fails or gains a bad reputation, the rest may suffer with it.

A compromise between monolithic and discreet branding is an approach that allows individual brand images, but uses a corporate or family name as a prominent umbrella to endorse the product. Some organisations, such as Ford and Kellogg's, use a *fixed endorsed* approach. Here, there is a rigid relationship between the company name and the brand, with a high degree of consistency between the presentation of different brands (but not as extreme as the Heinz approach). A *flexible endorsed* approach, such as that practised by Cadbury's, gives the brand more latitude to express its individuality. The company name may be more or less prominent, depending on how much independence the organisation wants the brand to have. These products seem to enjoy the best of both worlds. The family name gives the products and any new products a measure of credibility, yet the individuality of the products allows variety, imagination and creativity without being too stifled by the 'house style'. Marketing costs are, however, going to be higher because of the need to develop and launch individual identities for products and then to communicate both the family image and the individual brand images.

Product range and brand extension

A kind of flexible endorsement that does not involve the corporate name is where a brand name is developed to cover a limited number of products within a product line. Consumers may be more favourably inclined towards brands that are associated with known and trusted products (DelVecchio, 2000).

The confectionery sector has been especially active in building brand extension strategies. There are three advantages: it builds awareness and thus the scope for impulse buying, it supports the launch of new products as the consumer is already basically familiar with the core brand, and finally it can maximise revenue. MARS, for example, pioneered extending chocolate brands into ice-creams. Strategically, this was an interesting move: in summer if chocolate sales drop there is always the opportunity to improve ice-cream sales. It is now possible to find MARS, Galaxy, Snickers, Bounty and Twix products in the ice-cream cabinet. MARS also extended into individually wrapped cakes featuring Galaxy and Milky Way through a partnership with United Biscuits. Extension has also taken place into the biscuit market with biscuits topped with Twix, MARS and Bounty, aimed at indulgence in the home (Adwan, 2003).

When it's hot and you want something sweet, sticky and firm, a MARS® ice cream should hit the spot. ® MARS is a registered trademark of Masterfoods.

Source: © Masterfoods 2006 http://www.mars.co.uk

Extending the brand range. This example raises the issue of *brand extension*. Such a policy is cost efficient in that it saves the cost of developing totally new images and promoting and building them up from nothing: for example, easyJet is actively extending its brand name into 'easyEverything'. The launch of cyber cafés was the first such move using a formula similar to the one that made easyJet so successful. The cafés offer low-cost internet access to the public with easyJet's trademark no-frills service. It has been argued, however, that the introduction of additional products to the brand family can dilute the strength of the brand (John *et al.*, 1998). As the number of products affiliated to a brand name increases, the original brand beliefs may become less focused and start to be fuzzier in consumers' minds. To some extent, Virgin has suffered from this. Extending the brand name from a successful airline to the more problematic rail service could damage the core brand reputation.

Brand extension happens not only 'horizontally' as in the Mars case. Brands can be extended upwards, downwards or in both directions. An upwards extension might involve introducing a higher-priced, higher-quality, more exclusive product, while a downwards extension might require a basic, no-frills product at a rock-bottom, mass-market price.

In thinking about such an extension, the marketer needs to be sure that the gaps thus filled are worth filling. Will sufficient customers emerge to take up the new product? Will the trade accept it? Is it a significant profit opportunity? Will it simply cannibalise existing products? This last issue is particularly important; there is no point in extending a product range downwards if the main effect is to pull customers away from an existing mid-range product.

An upwards extension could create a product with higher margins (see Chapter 7) as well as enhancing the organisation's image. It also helps to build a kind of staircase for the customer to climb. As the customer becomes more affluent or as their needs and wants become more sophisticated, they can trade up to the next product in the range and still maintain their loyalty to one organisation.

eg Pringle, a Scottish knitwear firm best known for its sweaters and golf sponsorship, tried to extend upwards into luxury goods, such as high-quality luggage and accessories. At the same time, it was also expanding sideways into non-knitwear clothing and its own retail outlets. This combination of upwards and sideways expansion did not work well. The Pringle brand name was appearing on too many items that were too far removed from its core image. This diluted the impact and exclusivity of the name and meant that customers did not perceive the luxury goods as being suitably classy or elite.

A downwards extension can be used to attack competitors operating at the volume end of the market. It can build a larger base of sales if a lower-priced product broadens the number of potential customers. Then, by introducing people to the bottom of the range product and forming some kind of relationship with them, it may be possible to get them to trade up, thus assisting sales of the mid-range product. This would be the ideal situation, but do remember the risks of cannibalisation if the bottom of the range product acts as a magnet to existing mid-range customers. There can be a risk of undermining brand equity by extensions at the bottom of the range. This can cause an overall loss of equity to the whole range that is greater than the incremental sales of the new products (Reibstein *et al.*, 1998).

Filling the product range. The option of filling the product range involves a very close examination of the current range, then creating new products to fill in any gaps between existing products. One way of filling out the range could be to increase the number of variants available. The product remains the same, but it has a range of different presentations. Thus a food product might be available in single-serving packs, family-sized packs or catering-sized freezer packs. Tomato ketchup is available in squeezy bottles as well as in glass ones.

eg Volkswagen may have extended its product umbrella too far (Mitchell, 2004). Not so long ago, there was a range of distinctive products and sub-brands appealing to different market segments. It was clear to car users what 'The Beetle', 'The Golf' and 'The Passat' stood for and the segments they were targeting. As the VW empire expanded through acquisition, however, it became more difficult with Audi, Seat, Skoda, Bentley, Bugatti and Phaeton all now included in the VW stable. It was decided that rather than retaining independent brands, the VW umbrella should be applied. One group included Skoda, VW, Bentley, Bugatti and Phaeton under the theme 'class beating standards' with the price range extending from the VW Lupo starting at just over £7000 to the top-of-the-range Bentley at around £180,000. The other group covered Audi and Seat with the shared competencies of 'sportiness, technology and design'. Without logic or consistency, brand structures can become difficult to maintain. Consumers then become confused about what is being offered and the values each brand represents (Mitchell, 2004).

Filling the range can be a useful strategy for keeping the competition out, by offering the consumer some novelty and a more detailed range of products closer to their needs, and to add incrementally to profits at relatively low risk. The danger, however, is the risk of adding to costs, but with no overall increase in sales. This is the risk of cannibalisation, of fragmenting existing market share across too many similar products. There is the added irony that the consumer might well be indifferent to these variants, being perfectly satisfied with the original range.

Deleting products. The final stages of a product's life are often the hardest for management to contemplate. The decision to eliminate a poor seller that may be generating low or even negative profits is a tough one to make. The economic rationale for being ruthless is clear. A product making poor returns absorbs management time and can quickly drain resources if it is being kept alive by aggressive selling and promotion. There is, however, often a reluctance to take action. There are various reasons for this, some of which are purely personal or political. Managers often form emotional attachments to the products they have looked after: 'I introduced this product, I backed it and built my career on it.' If the offending product was launched more recently, then its deletion might be seen as an admission of failure on the part of its managers. They would, therefore, prefer to try just once more to turn the product round and to retain their reputations intact.

Other reasons for being reluctant to delete a product are based on a desire to offer as wide a range as possible, regardless of the additional costs incurred. While there is still some demand (however small) for a particular product, the organisation feels obliged to continue to provide it, as a service to its customers. Suddenly deleting that product might result in negative feelings for some customers. Car owners in particular become attached to certain models and react badly when a manufacturer decides to withdraw them from the available range.

All of this means that there is a need for a regular systematic review to identify the more marginal products, to assess their current contribution and to decide how they fit with future plans. If new life can be injected into a product, then all well and good, but if not, then the axe will have to fall and the product be phased out or dropped immediately.

eg Colman's French Mustard is no more. This was not strictly a commercial decision, as it was based on a ruling from the European Union. When the parent company, Unilever, bought a competitor, Amora Maille, in 2000, the EU ruled that Unilever had too high a market share and so Colman's French Mustard was deleted to reduce the alleged monopoly position. From now on, it will have to be mustard from Dijon or Bordeaux rather than Norwich. Unilever chose, however, not to sell the brand, contrary to the EU view, as it could have been a threat in the hands of a strong competitor. Instead, Unilever discontinued it to focus on better developing the Amora Maille brand name (Bridgett, 2001).

The product lifecycle

The product lifecycle (**PLC**) concept reflects the theory that products, like people, live a life. They are born, they grow up, they mature and, eventually, they die. During its life, a product goes through many different experiences, achieving varying levels of success in the market. This naturally means that the product's marketing support needs also vary, depending on what is necessary both to secure the present and to work towards the future. Figure 6.5 shows the theoretical progress of a PLC, indicating the pattern of sales and profits earned. The diagram may be applied either to an individual product or brand (for example Kellogg's Cornflakes) or to a product class (breakfast cereals).

Figure 6.5 indicates that there are four main stages – introduction, growth, maturity and decline – and these are now discussed in turn along with their implications for marketing strategy.

■ Stage 1: introduction

At the very start of the product's life as it enters the market, sales will begin to build slowly and profit may be small (even negative). A slow build-up of sales reflects the lead time required for marketing efforts to take effect and for people to hear about the product and try

Figure 6.5 The product lifecycle

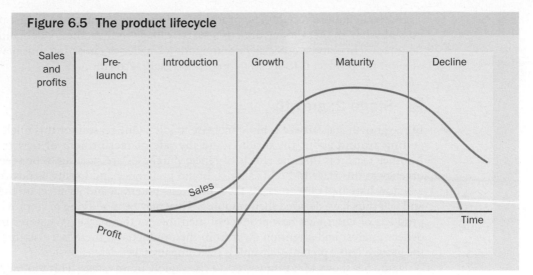

it. Low profits are partly an effect of the low initial sales and partly a reflection of the possible need to recoup development and launch costs.

The marketer's main priority at this stage is to generate widespread awareness of the product among the target segment and to stimulate trial. If the product is truly innovative, there may be no competitors yet and so there is the added problem of building primary demand (i.e. demand for the class of product rather than simply demand for a specific brand) as a background to the actual brand choice.

There is also a need to gain distribution. With new fmcg lines, the retail trade may be hard to convince unless the product has a real USP (unique selling point), because of the pressure on shelf space and the proliferation of available brands. In parallel with that, there is still the task of generating awareness among consumers and moving them through towards a purchase. The decision on the product's price, whether to price high or low or whether to offer an introductory trial price, could be an important element in achieving that first purchase.

eg

Love it or hate it, Microsoft is the world's biggest software company and can pack a punch when it enters a market. Despite the dominance of the Sony PlayStation, Microsoft entered the video games console market with Xbox. Similarly, it entered the online music download market to rival Apple's iTuncs (see pp. 11–12). At the heart of Microsoft's business, however, rests the Windows operating system, and that is proving more problematic for new product development. With two decades of history since the launch of Windows 1.0 in 1985, it has become more and more difficult for Microsoft to innovate significantly due to the demands of a large and established network of customers.

Longhorn represents the next generation of Microsoft operating system, to be launched in 2006, five years after Windows XP. Although the shape of the new system is not yet known, it has become difficult to make sweeping changes to tried and tested programs as, in the pursuit of backward compatibility, any new code could clash with the program's older elements that users have purchased previously. This was one of the reasons why the innovative WinFS that enables the user to find documents and pictures more easily is unlikely to be included in the early packages.

A further complication rests with the changing user base for Windows. Originally, the customer base was dominated by personal users with businesses mainly using mainframes. Now, of course, many business users have adopted Windows and Office Application suites (about 30 per cent of Microsoft revenue) making them more resistant to change because of switching costs and they are more concerned with functionality and reliability than cutting-edge developments. It remains to be seen therefore whether the introduction of Longhorn will fulfil the hopes of driving an upgrade cycle, which in turn will generate higher sales (Gapper, 2004; Waters, 2005).

Given the failure rate of new products and the importance of giving a product the best possible start in life, the introduction stage is likely to make heavy demands on marketing resources. This can be especially draining for a smaller organisation, but nevertheless is necessary if the product is to survive into the next stage: growth.

■ Stage 2: growth

In the growth stage, there is rapid increase in sales. One reason for this might be that word is getting around about the product and the rate of recruitment of new triers accelerates. Another reason is that the effects of repeat purchases are starting to be seen. There is some urgency at this stage to build as much brand preference and loyalty as possible. Competitors will now have had time to assess the product, its potential and its effect on the overall market, and will thus have decided their response. They may be modifying or improving their existing products or entering a new product of their own to the market. Whatever they do, they will deflect interest and attention away from the product and there is a risk that this will flatten the growth curve prematurely unless the company takes defensive steps.

Figure 6.5 shows that profits start to rise rapidly in this stage. This too might be affected by competitive pressure, if other organisations choose to compete on price, forcing margins down. Again, repeat purchases that build brand loyalty are the best defence in these circumstances.

Even though the product might seem to be still very young and only just starting to deliver its potential, towards the close of the growth stage might be a good time to think about product modifications or improvements, either to reinforce existing segments or to open up new ones. This is about keeping one step ahead of the competition. If the initial novelty of your product has worn off, buyers might be vulnerable to competitors' new products. This might also threaten the security of your distribution channels, as heavy competition for shelf space squeezes out weaker products perceived as heading nowhere. This all reinforces, yet again, the need for constant attention to brand building and the generation of consumer loyalty, as well as the necessity for the cultivation of good relationships with distributors.

eg   The 'active health drinks' market for functional or 'active' yoghurt drinks grew by nearly 75 per cent in 2004, to £185m. In market development terms, that is very rapid growth indeed. In the UK over that period the average UK household consumed 7.6 kg of active health drinks. The market is dominated by Danone's Actimel, which has gained a market share of over 50 per cent. To help maintain and further improve its strong leadership position, over £9.4m has been invested in advertising, and new flavours have been added to the range to keep ahead of rivals such as Benecol and Müller Vitality. Danone knows that rivals will be keen to gain a stronger share in such a fast-growing market, so this investment in the brand is essential (*The Grocer*, 2005).

Another good reason for considering modifying the product is that by now you have real experience of producing and marketing it. The more innovative the product (whether innovative for your organisation or innovative within the market), the more likely it is that experience will have highlighted unforeseen strengths and weaknesses in the product and its marketing. This is the time to learn from that experience and fine-tune the whole offering or extend the product range to attract new segments.

At some point, the growth period comes to an end as the product begins to reach its peak and enters the next stage: maturity.

■ Stage 3: maturity

During the maturity stage, the product achieves as much as it is going to. The accelerated growth levels off, as everyone who is likely to be interested in the product should have tried it by now and a stable set of loyal repeat buyers should have emerged. The mobile phone market, for example, had achieved 70 per cent penetration in the UK by the end of 2001 and sales levelled off to

A drop of scotch, anyone?

It is at once the most civilised and barbaric of drinks. Treat it with respect and it will repay you with incomparable kindness; abuse its beneficence and it will send you reeling into the gutter.
(Murray, 2004)

Scotch whisky in the UK is in the mature stage of the lifecycle and is showing signs of going into decline. To make matters worse, it is seen as a mature drink for mature people, more cruelly described as fitting the 'pipe and slippers' generation. The whisky market in the UK was worth £2.9bn in 2004, but its core market remains men aged over 45. Although the population is ageing, so any decline may be gradual, the industry's challenge is to appeal to younger drinkers who will join the pipe and slippers brigade in ten or twenty years' time!

Whisky products are grouped into blended (at least three years old) and malts, which are typically ten years old. Blended is dominant, accounting for over 75 per cent of the market, but this sector has also seen heavy discounting by the supermarkets to maintain sales. Nevertheless, despite this discounting, sales of blended whiskies have declined. The premium malt segment is, however, growing by around 10 per cent per year as consumers trade up in the search for better quality. It is one thing to offer your friends a cheap blended whisky, and another to offer a distinctive malt.

Although the perception of whisky producers is of the small independent distiller located in the Highlands nurturing its special brand, the reality is that, at the time of writing, 75 per cent of all the Scottish distillers are owned by just three global players: Diageo, Allied Domecq and Pernod Ricard. Diageo owns Bells, the UK market leader, Johnnie Walker and classic malts such as Dalwhinnie, Oban and Talisker. Allied controls Teachers, Laphroaig and Canadian

Club. Finally Pernod generates 40 per cent of its sales from whisky brands such as Chivas Regal, Aberlour and The Glenlivet. One of the last remaining independent distillers in Scotland was recently sold to French company Moët Hennessy, along with Glenmorangie, Glen Moray and Ardbeg whiskies. So the industry is highly concentrated in terms of manufacturers, but with many brands: estimates suggest that there are over 2000 whiskies from around the world and those owned by the two main players enjoy considerable marketing muscle.

Despite the UK market being in late maturity, whisky is a global product and Scotch whisky has a strong reputation around the world (being sold in over 200 markets). Most of the UK manufacturers have extensive export sales and new markets are being opened up, for example in Portugal, Spain and Greece. Pernod's Chivas Regal and The Glenlivet grew by 12 per cent and 9 per cent respectively in 2004 due to global sales. Sales in China have been particularly strong with 170 per cent growth in 2003 for all Scotch whisky to a Chinese market worth £9.7m. Overall, global sales for Scotch whisky grew by 2 per cent to £982m in 2003. Strong

performances were also recorded from Brazil (up 44 per cent), India (15 per cent) and Russia. There are new challengers, however. Japanese distillers are becoming stronger and Yoichi single malt beat Scottish and American competition to win the *Whisky Magazine* 'best of best' competition in 2001. Although it may take another ten years, Japanese whisky could do what New World wines did to the European wine industry.

Although exporting has helped to offset the impact of the maturity of the home market, attempts are being made to attract younger drinkers (not teenagers!). The Famous Grouse has repositioned through more modern bottle design featuring black and gold to give it a premium look. The supporting advertising campaign featured the grouse icon to promote the brand's youthful position and promoted serving suggestions, such as a Game Bird recipe that included elderflower cordial and apple schnapps to suggest a more modern drink. It remains to be seen whether such strategies can breathe new life into the domestic whisky market.

Sources: Black (2005); Bowker (2005); Lyons (2004); Murray (2004); Solley (2004); http://www.scotchwhiskey.net.

THE FAMOUS GROUSE MALT. MAKE AN ENTRANCE.

The Famous Grouse uses its grouse icon to create amusing and eye-catching advertising to appeal to drinkers younger than its traditional core market.

Source: © The Famous Grouse

upgrading and replacement rather than converting those harder-to-win customers. This is not a cause for complacency, however. There are few new customers available and even the laggards have purchased by now. This means that there is a high degree of customer understanding of the product and possibly of the market. They know what they want, and if your product starts to look dated or becomes unexciting compared with newer offerings from the competition, then they might well switch brands. Certainly, the smaller or more poorly positioned brands are going to be squeezed out. In these circumstances, the best hope is to consolidate the hard-core loyal buyers, encouraging heavier consumption from them. It may also be possible to convert some brand switchers into loyal customers through the use of sales promotions and advertising.

At this stage, there is likely to be heavy price competition and increased marketing expenditure from all competitors in order to retain brand loyalty. Much of this expenditure will be focused on marketing communication, but some may be channelled into minor product improvements to refresh the brand. Distribution channels may also need careful handling at this stage. Unless the product remains a steady seller, the retailer may be looking to delist it to make room on the shelves for younger products.

The sales curve has reached a plateau, as the market is saturated and largely stable. Any short-term gains will be offset by similar losses and profits may start to decline because of price competition pressure. It is thus very important to try, at least, to retain existing buyers. Sooner or later, however, the stability of the maturity phase will break, either through competitive pressure (they are better at poaching your customers than you are at poaching theirs) or through new developments in the market that make your product increasingly inappropriate, pushing the product into the decline stage.

■ Stage 4: decline

Once a product goes into decline for market-based reasons, it is almost impossible to stop it. The rate of decline can be controlled to some extent, but inevitably sales and profits will fall regardless of marketing effort.

Decline can often be environment-related rather than a result of poor management decisions. Technological developments or changes in consumer tastes, for example, can lead to the demise of the best-managed product. New technologies are increasingly becoming a powerful force that can destroy an established market in a few years. Polaroid built a market around instant photos, but digital cameras offer the same facility with a lot more flexibility. Cravens *et al.* (2000) highlighted the danger of becoming obsessed with improving and extending products in the mature or decline stages and not recognising more fundamental changes to the market. A similar pattern could be experienced in the future as MP3 and MP4 formats with download facilities render conventional CD formats obsolete.

eg The nappy market still has not bottomed out. The market is contracting through no fault of the brand manufacturers, as the birth rate has been declining over recent years. The disposable nappy market has slipped from maturity into decline, falling by over 19 per cent between 1999 and 2003 (Mintel, 2004). The two main players in this market are Procter & Gamble with its Pampers range, and Kimberly-Clark with Huggies. While Pampers' market share stayed pretty steady between 1999 and 2000, hovering around the 61–62 per cent level, Huggies improved its share (at the expense of retailer own-label products) from 26 per cent to 30 per cent. This might look like good news for both companies, but it must be remembered that these are shares of a declining market. Pampers actually saw its sales fall over this period from £260m to £210m, and Huggies' sales fell from £111m to £103m. This happened despite heavy expenditure on brand building with a wide range of marketing communications initiatives (Mintel, 2004).

Faced with a product in decline, the marketer has a difficult decision of whether to try slowing down the decline with some marketing expenditure, or to milk the product by withdrawing support and making as much profit out of it as possible as it heads towards a natural death. In the latter case, the withdrawing of marketing support aimed at distributors in particular is quite likely to speed up the delisting process.

■ Facets of the PLC

The PLC is more of a guide to what could happen rather than a prescription of what will happen. At its best, it does provide some useful indications at each stage of some of the marketing problems and issues that could arise. It is, after all, a form of collective wisdom based on the history of many brands. But before applying the concept in practice, it is necessary to dig deeper and think about a number of issues before the PLC becomes a really useful tool.

Length

It is very difficult to predict how long it will take a product to move through its life. The length of the PLC varies not only from market to market, but also from brand to brand within a market. Some board games, for example, such as Monopoly, Scrabble and more recently Trivial Pursuit, are well-established, long-term sellers, whereas other games, particularly those linked with television shows (remember Countdown, Blockbusters and Neighbours board games?), have much shorter spans.

The problem is that the length of the PLC is affected by so many things. It is not only the pace of change in the external environment, but also the organisation's handling of the product throughout its life. The organisation's willingness and ability to communicate effectively and efficiently with both the trade and the consumer, its policy of supporting the product in the critical early period and its approach to defending and refreshing its products will all affect how the PLC develops.

Self-fulfilling prophecy

Linked with the previous point, there is a real danger that the PLC can become a self-fulfilling prophecy (Wood, 1990). A marketing manager might, for example, imagine that a product is about to move from growth into maturity. Theory may suggest appropriate marketing strategies for this transition and, if these are implemented, the product will start to behave as though it is mature, whether it was really ready for it or not.

Shape

The shape of the PLC offered in Figure 6.5 is necessarily a generalisation. Products that get into marketing problems at any PLC stage will certainly not follow this pattern. Products that spend relatively longer in one stage than another will also have distorted PLC curves. A product that has a long and stable maturity, for instance, will show a long flat plateau in maturity rather than Figure 6.5's gentle hillock. Different market circumstances could also distort this hypothetical curve. Five different scenarios, the innovative product, the imitative product, the fashion product, the product failure and the revitalisation, each with its own PLC shape, are shown in Figure 6.6.

Innovative product. The innovative product is breaking totally new ground and cannot really utilise consumers' previous experience as a short cut to acceptance. People feel that they have managed perfectly well without this product in the past, so why do they need it now? Having to educate the market from scratch is neither easy nor cheap. Sony, in introducing the Walkman, had to undertake this task and, of course, it not only laid the foundations for its own product, but also broke the ground for 'me too' subsequent imitative entrants.

Imitative product. Imitative products, such as new confectionery brands or the first non-Sony personal stereo, do not require as much spadework as the innovative product. They take advantage of the established market and the buyer's existing knowledge and past experience, and thus will move into the growth stage very quickly. The main considerations for the imitative marketer are establishing clear, differentiated positioning of the product against existing brands, encouraging trial and making repeat purchase as easy as possible.

Fashion product. Fashion products have a naturally short PLC. Fads are an extreme form of fashion product, accentuating the rapid sales increase followed by the rapid decline. The timing of entry into the market is critical and those who succeed in making a quick

Figure 6.6 PLC variations on a theme

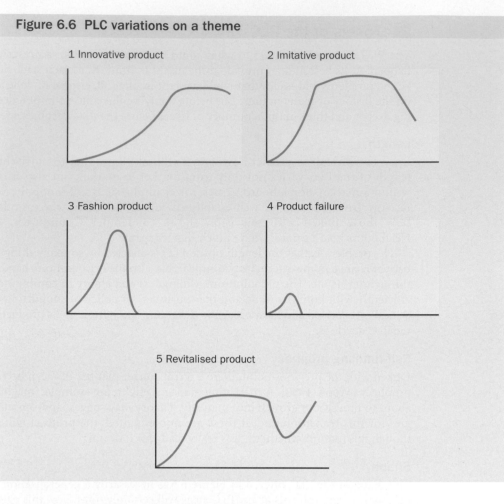

return in these markets are those who spot the trend early. There is little opportunity for late entrants. It is interesting to note that some fads retain a hard core of enthusiasts, for example skateboarding.

Product failure. Some products never even achieve a growth stage: they fail. This may be because the product itself is badly thought through or because it never gained awareness or distribution. New food products from small manufacturers without the resources to create strong brands may fail because they simply cannot gain mass distribution from retailers unwilling to take risks with unknown producers or brands.

Revitalisation product. The revitalisation phase of the PLC shows that marketing effort can indeed influence the course of a lifecycle. By updating a product, either through design or through a fresh marketing approach, new life can be injected to regenerate customer and retailer interest and loyalty. Tango, for example, was a standard, uninteresting fizzy orange drink until some surreal, controversial and imaginative advertising repositioned it as a trendy teenage drink. Hiam (1990) argued that many products can be revitalised and that 'maturity simply reflects saturation of a specific target market with a specific product form'. Changing the form of product and expanding the target market could help new growth creation. Generally it is argued that 'it is a myth that products have a predetermined life span'.

Product level, class, form and brand

As said at the beginning of this section, the PLC can operate on a number of different levels. It is important to distinguish between the PLCs of total industries (such as the motor industry), product classes (such as petrol-driven private vehicles), product forms (such as hatchback cars) and individual brands (such as the Fiat Uno).

Industries and product classes tend to have the longest PLCs, because they are an aggregate of the efforts of many organisations and many individual products over time. An industry, such as the motor industry, can be in an overall state of fairly steady maturity for many years even as individual product forms and brands come and go. In the motor industry, for example, the hatchback is probably a mature product form, while the people carrier is still in its growth stage. Although a number of hatchback 'brands' have come and gone, the number of people carrier 'brands' is still growing. At the same time, the earliest entrants in the European market are starting to reach maturity.

Despite these weaknesses, the PLC is a well-used concept. Product marketing strategies should, however, take into account other considerations as well as the PLC, as the next section shows.

Market evolution

The marketing manager needs to understand how markets develop over time, in order better to plan and manage products, their lifecycles and their marketing strategies.

■ The diffusion of innovation

The product lifecycle is clearly driven by changes in consumer behaviour as the new product becomes established. The rate at which the growth stage develops is linked in particular to the speed with which customers can be led through from awareness of the product to trial and eventual adoption of the product, in other words how fast the AIDA model (see Figure 4.2 on p. 127) works. The problem is, however, that not all customers move through it with equal speed and eagerness and some will adopt innovation more quickly than others. This has led to the concept of the diffusion of innovation (Rogers, 1962), which looks at the rate at which innovation spreads across a market as a whole. Effectively, it allows the grouping or classification of customers depending on their speed of adoption into one of five adopter categories, as shown in Figure 6.7.

Innovators

Innovators are important in the early stages of a product's lifecycle to help get the product off the ground and start the process of gaining acceptance. They form only a small group, but

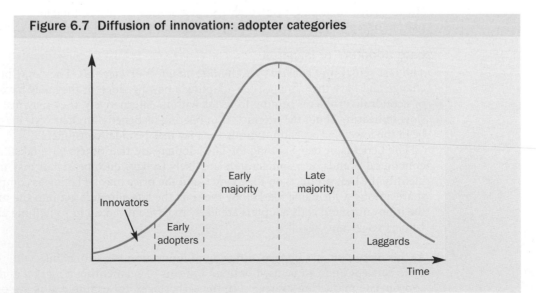

Figure 6.7 Diffusion of innovation: adopter categories

they buy early and are prepared to take a risk. In consumer markets, innovators tend to be younger, better educated, more affluent and confident. In B2B markets, innovators are likely to be profitable and, again, willing to take risks in return for the potential benefits to be gained from being first.

Early adopters

Early adopters enter the market early, but are content to let the innovators take the real pioneering risks with a new product. They do, however, soon follow the lead of the innovators and are always alert to new developments in markets of interest to them. Once the early adopters begin to enter the market, the growth stage of a PLC can then develop.

Both innovators and early adopters tend to be opinion leaders and thus it is important for the promoter of a new product to target them and win them over. The mass market, however, looks particularly to the early adopters for a lead, as they are more of a mainstream group than the innovators. The early adopters are thus critical for making a product generally acceptable and for spreading word-of-mouth recommendations about the product's value and benefits.

Early majority

With the *early majority* the mass market starts to build up, as more and more people enter it. The early majority are more risk averse than previous groups and want some reassurance that the product is tried and tested before they will commit themselves to it. This group may be relatively well educated, with above-average incomes, but that may depend on the nature of the product concerned. Digital cameras, for example, have entered this stage, but many consumers may be holding back until the price comes down. When a product does reach the early majority, social pressure may begin to build: 'You really must get yourself an ice-cream maker – you can't possibly manage without one.' This begins to move the product towards the late majority.

Late majority

The *late majority* customers are perhaps less interested or bothered about the product category, or are content to wait until they see how the market develops. They are a little behind the early majority and want more reassurance about the product's benefits and worth. It could be argued that DVD players have entered this stage. The late majority may have more choice of alternative products in the market, as competition builds, and will certainly have the benefit of the accumulated knowledge and experience of the previous groups. Once the late majority has been converted, the product is likely to be reaching its mature stage, a steady plateau of repeat purchases, with very few new customers left to enter the market.

Late adopters or laggards

The last remaining converts are the *late adopters* or *laggards*. They may be very averse to change and have therefore resisted adopting a new product, or they may have had attitudinal or economic problems coming to terms with it. Alternatively, they may just have been very slow in hearing about the product or in relating its benefits to their own lifestyles. They may be in the lower socioeconomic groups or they may be older consumers.

The benefits of being among the late adopters are that others have taken all the risks, the ephemeral brands or manufacturers are likely to have disappeared, it may thus be easier to identify the best products on the market, and the price may be falling as competitors fight for share among a shrinking market. By the time the late adopters get into the market, however, the innovators and early adopters are likely to have moved on to something else and thus the whole cycle begins again!

As this discussion has implied, diffusion of innovation has strong links with the product life-cycle concept and can be used both as a means of segmenting a market and for suggesting appropriate marketing strategies. In the early stages, for example, it is important to understand the needs and motivations of the innovators and early adopters and then to attract attention and generate trial among these groups. Other than knowing that they have innovative tendencies, however, it can be difficult to profile the groups using more concrete demographic or psychographic variables. In that case, it is important for the marketer to think in product terms. Perhaps hi-fi innovators and early adopters may be reached through specialist magazines that review new products, for example.

Positioning and repositioning products

A crucial decision, which could affect the length of a product's life and its resilience in a market over time, concerns the product's positioning. Product positioning means thinking about a product in the context of the competitive space it occupies in its market, defined in terms of attributes that matter to the target market. The important criterion is how close to the ideal on each of those attributes, compared with competing products, your product is judged to be by the target market. Harrods, for example, is positioned as a high-quality, exclusive department store. In order to reinforce this positioning with its target market, Harrods (**http://www.harrods.com**) makes sure that its product ranges, its staff expertise, its displays and overall store ambience are of equally high quality.

It is the target customer's definition of important attributes and their perception of how your product compares on them that matter. Marketing managers have to stand back from their own feelings and must ensure that the attributes selected are those that are critical to the customer, not those that marketing managers would like to be critical. The range of attributes judged to be important will vary according to the particular market segments under consideration.

The concept of product positioning is clearly focused on a customer-based perspective, but it still has serious implications for product design and development. The decision about positioning is made during the product's development and will be reflected in a whole range of the product's characteristics, including brand image, packaging and quality, as well as in the pricing and communication elements of the marketing mix.

Defining and selecting an appropriate position for a product involves three stages.

Stage 1. Detailed market research needs to be carried out during the first stage in order to establish what attributes are important to any given market segment and their order of preference. This background research will centre on a class of products rather than on individual brands within the class. Thus a particular segment, for example, might regard softness, absorbency and a high number of sheets on the roll as the three most important attributes of toilet tissue, in that order of preference.

Stage 2. Having identified the important attributes, in the second stage further research now shortlists the existing products that offer those attributes. Brands such as Kleenex Velvet and Andrex might be seen as fulfilling the needs of the toilet tissue segment mentioned above.

Stage 3. In the third stage, it is necessary to find out:

(a) what the target market considers to be the ideal level for each of the defined attributes; and
(b) how they rate each brand's attributes in relation to the ideal and to each other.

The conclusions from this hypothetical research may be, for instance, that while Andrex has more sheets per roll than Kleenex (thus apparently achieving a better rating for Andrex on an important attribute), in relation to the ideal Andrex is perceived to have too many (too bulky for the roll holder), whereas Kleenex might be perceived to have too few (runs out too quickly). Both products could thus improve their offering.

Once the positioning process has been completed for all the relevant attributes, it is useful to be able to visualise the complete picture graphically, by creating a perceptual map of the market. Figure 6.8 shows such a hypothetical map of the toilet tissue market, using price and softness as two dimensions that might represent important attributes. This shows that Brand A is serving the bottom end of the market in Segment 1, offering a cheap, purely functional product, whereas Brand B is aimed at the discerning customer in Segment 2 who is prepared to pay a little more for a gentler experience. Brand C seems to be closer to Segment 1 than Segment 2,

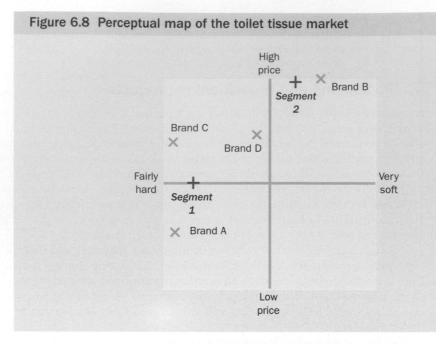

Figure 6.8 Perceptual map of the toilet tissue market

but is overpriced compared with Brand A for a similar quality of product. Brand D is floating between the two segments, with nothing to offer that is particularly appealing to either.

In some cases, of course, two dimensions are insufficient to represent the complexities of target market opinion. Although this creates a far more difficult mapping task, any number of further dimensions can be included using multidimensional scaling techniques (Green and Carmone, 1970).

Perceptual mapping helps to provide insights into appropriate competitive actions. For instance, a fundamental decision could be whether to try to meet the competition head-on or to differentiate your product away from them. The map can show just how far away from the competition your product is perceived to be and where its weaknesses lie, leading to an understanding of the marketing tasks involved in improving the product offering. If the intention is to differentiate, the map can indicate whether your product is sufficiently different in terms of attributes that matter and whether market niches exist that your product could be adapted to fill.

All of this implies that assessing and defining meaningful product positioning is an important early step in marketing management. This process can bring to light opportunities, it can highlight potential dangers of cannibalising one's own products and it can help to define competitive pressures, strengths and weaknesses. It is also a step in making the decision to modify a current product range by repositioning selected products.

Repositioning and modifying products

Positioning might have to be adjusted for many reasons as both the product and its market mature. Developing technology, evolving competition, changing customer needs and wants all mean that products have to be constantly appraised and reviewed. Nevertheless, a major product repositioning exercise can be very costly and risky (alienating or confusing existing buyers and failing to attract new ones, for instance). This means that the marketing manager needs to be sure that the changes will be perceptible and relevant to the target market, that the market is willing to accept change and that the repositioning will produce measurable benefits.

Repositioning has a number of serious implications. It might involve redefining or enlarging segments and it may well involve redesigning an entire marketing strategy. Such a fundamental revamp of a product is most likely to take place in the maturity stage of the PLC, when the product is beginning to fade a little.

There are three main areas for repositioning and product improvement.

Quality. As discussed at pp. 193 *et seq.*, quality has a number of dimensions. With physical products, quality can be defined in terms of reliability, durability and dependability, which are generally applicable across most products. There are, however, product-specific quality dimensions that the target market could use as indicators of a quality product, such as speed, taste, colour, materials, ingredients and even price and packaging.

eg Jimmy Choo Ltd, the luxury shoe group with a turnover of about £40m, is very protective of its up-market position. The last thing it wants to do is advertise, as that suggests that the brand is available to anyone, even with prices starting at £300. There are some tensions, however, between a natural desire to build upon the luxury brand associations and protection of its market position. It was a difficult decision to take out an Oxford Street concession in Selfridges, as that suggests availability, but by keeping prices high, Jimmy Choo expects to keep the aspiration level also high, as its products would be unaffordable for most consumers. Jimmy Choo has also been looking at brand extensions, building upon its quality reputation. While the name could be extended to handbags and upmarket sunglasses and cosmetics, Jimmy Choo branded socks and toilet covers are definitely not going to appear in the shops (Grande, 2003; Saigol, 2004).

Raising the quality of a physical product could be achieved perhaps through better components or refined manufacturing. For a service product, it could mean major refurbishment for the premises or developing the way in which the experience is packaged. Whatever the product or the means employed, raising the quality offers the prospect of charging higher prices and increasing profit margins. It might, however, lead to increased competition from other organisations greedy for a share of that prosperity. The other point to consider carefully is whether the target market will either recognise or value the newly raised quality.

Design. Thinking in an aesthetic rather than an engineering context, design affects the impact of the product on the senses. This concept can be difficult to handle, as it covers areas such as the appearance, texture, taste, smell, feel or sound of the product, all of which involve the customer in some very subjective assessments. These areas do, however, provide many combinations of variables that could offer the opportunity for change. If the objective is to reposition a product, just changing its visual appearance or its packaging (probably with 'new improved . . .' splashed across it) could give customers sufficient cues and justification for revising their opinions of it.

It must be stressed that any design changes are a waste of time and resources unless they matter to the market, can be communicated to that market and are implemented to achieve defined objectives.

Performance. Like design, performance relies on the customer's initial, rather impressionistic assessment. A more concrete appreciation of performance may only come after product use. The kind of factors under consideration here include convenience, safety, ease of handling, efficiency, effectiveness and adaptability to different situations. A car's performance, for instance, can be measured in terms of its acceleration, braking ability or fuel economy, depending on what is important to the buyer. Improving the fuel economy at the expense of acceleration might change the character of the car, making it less appealing to a 'boy racer' type of segment, but positioning it more firmly and more positively in the 'heavy urban usage' segment. Even the fuel itself has been repositioned in terms of its performance-enhancing capabilities, with some brands promising to be more engine friendly or to improve engine performance.

What's the core benefit of a washing machine?

One useful way of reviewing product design and performance specifications is to gather information from service engineers and/or the distributors and retailers who are in the front line of dealing with customer complaints and product breakdowns. Sometimes, this can yield surprising insights into customer behaviour and their relationships with products. Washing machine manufacturer Haier's service engineers, for example, found that a lot of washing machines in rural areas of China were breaking down because they were being used for washing vegetables as well as clothes, and the peel was blocking the pipes. Many companies would have responded by putting a big warning and disclaimer in the product manual tactfully but firmly pointing out that this machine is designed only for washing clothes and refusing to accept responsibility for breakdowns caused by carrots. Haier, however, being a customer-centred organisation, responded much more pragmatically by redesigning its washing machines so that they could be used for vegetables, and giving customers helpful tips on how to use the machine safely for

this purpose. Having once opened its corporate mind to the weird and wonderful things that washing machines can be used for, Haier also designed a washing machine that could be used to make goat's cheese (adding a whole new dimension to the concept of customer churn). Now that's what we call a differential advantage!

Another of Haier's product lines is compact refrigerators. As with the washing machines, you might assume that you know exactly what the main features and benefits of such a product are: it has to keep food cold and it has to fit into a limited space, perhaps in a small apartment or a small kitchen. In the US, Haier found that a lot of its refrigerators were being used by students in halls of residence and that quite often, students were putting a board across the top of two fridges, and calling it a table. So the product designers made a fridge with fold-out flaps on top so it could be made into a table when needed. Haier now has nearly 50 per cent share of the US compact refrigerator market.

Zhang Ruimin, CEO of Haier, emphasises the importance of the link between market orientation, product design and competitive advantage:

Consumers in the United States are used to popular brands like

GE and Whirlpool, so they'll wonder why they should choose a brand they've never heard of. But large companies are established and slow moving, and we see an opportunity to compete against them in their home markets by being more customer focused than they are. To win over those consumers we have two approaches: speed and differentiation – speed, of course, to satisfy the consumers' needs as quickly as possible, differentiation to introduce brand-new products or products with features to meet different needs.
(as quoted by Wu, 2003)

The two product examples in this vignette demonstrate how Haier's customer orientation and willingness to question its preconceptions about what its products are for have led directly to design and performance enhancements. They also help to explain why this Chinese company is not only the market leader in its own domestic market but is one of the top five global appliance makers with a turnover in 2003 of $9.7bn generated by sales in over 160 countries.

Sources: Ruelas-Gossi and Sull (2004); Wu (2003).

Quality, design and performance are often inextricably interlinked. Proposed changes under one heading have implications for the others. Improving a car's fuel economy may involve better-quality components under the bonnet as well as a more aerodynamic body design.

It does not really matter whether a proposed change is classified as relating to quality, design or performance, or all three. What does matter is that as part of the product management process, all the relevant options are assessed to make sure that the product continues to achieve its maximum potential, either within its existing segment(s) or through repositioning into a new one. Quality, design and performance all provide possibilities for the major or minor changes that will ensure this.

Product management and organisation

There is a range of management structures for marketing, depending on the tasks required and the environmental opportunities and threats. Products are extremely important as revenue earners and so they need careful management. Product-centred management structures can help to ensure that they do get the care they deserve. A product or brand manager handles part of a range or even an individual brand if it is very critical. Product managers operate across all functional areas, especially marketing, but also liaise with R&D, production and logistics to ensure the best opportunities and treatment for their product(s). Their job is to manage the product throughout its lifecycle, from launch, through any modifications, to its eventual demise. It can often be a total commitment and may include commissioning research, liaising with distribution and even handling sales with major account negotiations. The product manager will also be involved in planning advertising approaches, media selection and packaging.

In terms of planning, controlling and monitoring product performance, the product manager is likely to have to produce an annual product plan, specifying actions, resources and strategies for the coming trading period. This helps the manager to justify the investment of resources in the product and also allows early recognition of problems with the product and proposed corrective action.

This kind of product management structure is used in larger fmcg organisations in particular, where there is significant emphasis on new product development and major mass-market brands. It may also be applicable in some B2B markets, but as Davis (1984) suggests, the structure and complexity of some B2B markets mean that other options may also have to be considered. If, for example, the same product or component is sold to a range of different end users, then it may be better to divide management responsibility by end user (or segment) rather than by product. A car component, for example, may be sold to car manufacturers, servicing and repair workshops or specialist retailers. Each of these customer groups needs different handling and the component manufacturer may prefer to have specialist marketing managers for each one. A different approach is to divide marketing management responsibility on a geographic basis, particularly where international marketing is the norm. The logic is the same as for the end-user focus: each territory has a unique profile and very different demands and handling needs, requiring a specialist manager. Both of these alternatives, allocating responsibility by end user or geographic area, take account of the day-to-day marketing needs of the organisation's products but potentially leave an unfilled gap for a 'product champion'. The last thing the organisation wants is for managers to develop the attitude that they only sell the product and that its wider strategic development is 'somebody else's problem'.

European product strategy

Creating a brand that can be established across Europe, a Eurobrand, is neither easy nor cheap, as the motor industry has found in striving to create a 'world car' that can suit all tastes internationally. Lynch (1994) is uncompromisingly blunt in defining the criteria essential for Eurobrand building:

1 *Resources*: Lynch estimates that a marketing communications budget of no less than $60 million is needed for three years to establish the brand, unless, of course, a much longer-term phased introduction is planned.
2 *Quality*: The need for consistent quality in both the product itself and the production, logistical and administrative procedures that support it should not be underestimated. Operating on a pan-European basis is more difficult than operating within a national market.
3 *Timing*: According to Lynch, it will take at least five years to establish a Eurobrand and short-term returns on investment should not be expected.

These three criteria alone put Eurobranding out of the reach of most organisations. There are also practical considerations, for example culture and language. These can affect everything from the brand name (remember Plopsies and Kuk & Fuk, not to mention other gems from non-English speaking markets, such as Fanny, Spunk, Bum and Crap?) to the imagery associated with the brand, to the advertising. The marketer has to decide whether to use an identical approach in all corners of the European market, or whether to make adaptations, perhaps to the advertising or the packaging, for particular local or cultural conditions. English is the main second language for most continental Europeans which means that packaging could become more multilingual with English alongside a number of different language versions, but most markets are a very long way from using just one common language.

eg Since joining the EU, a number of Polish companies have been active in building a presence in the large EU markets, such as Germany. The main method has been acquisition, to build upon any brand reputation that has been already established, thus avoiding difficult brand renaming and introduction decisions. Unimil, a Krakow-based condom manufacturer, acquired Germany's Condomi to gain 20 per cent of the European market with an established brand name. It also gained access to an established distribution system which it intended to exploit with new designs and marketing methods (Cienski, 2005).

Halliburton and Hunerberg (1987) found that strategic variables such as positioning and product range transferred more readily across borders than pricing, which needs to reflect local conditions. Advertising and distribution tended to vary between standardised and differentiated approaches. It is, however, difficult to generalise. Nescafé, while giving the impression of being a standardised international brand, actually varies in blend, flavour and product description to suit local taste (Rijkens, 1992). This highlights the difference between the concept and the brand in terms of standardisation. For Nescafé, there is often considerable conformity across Europe on packaging, labelling and basic communications mix strategies, whereas specific message design and pricing are subject to more local control.

All of this assumes that there is a pan-European market for the product, demanding volumes that justify the investment. Despite the potential problems, however, there are many pan-European brands (some of which are also global brands). The car manufacturers successfully sell the same model across Europe, while Procter & Gamble, Johnson & Johnson, Colgate Palmolive, Heinz and Nestlé all maintain pan-European fmcg brands. Although many of those brands have been around for many years, it is still possible to launch a new brand on a pan-European basis. Gillette's Natrel deodorant was launched with heavy marketing support across the EU, using not only identical product and brand imagery in all countries, but also identical packaging and advertising. All of this not only increases production and administrative efficiency, and provides a sales force better tailored to the market's needs, but also allows the organisation to use its European size to compete effectively against national competitors in each country.

Chapter summary

- Product is defined as covering a wide variety of goods, services and ideas that can be the subject of a marketing exchange. The product itself is layered, consisting of the core product, the tangible product and, finally, the augmented product. Using the tangible and augmented product, manufacturers, service providers and retailers can create differential advantage. Products can be classified according to either their own characteristics (durable, non-durable or service) or buyer-oriented characteristics. In consumer markets, these are linked with the frequency of purchase and the length and depth of the information search. In B2B markets, they are more likely to relate to the final use of the product. An organisation's product mix, made up of individual product items, can be divided into product lines. These are groups of items that have some common link, either operational or marketing-based. Product mix width is established by the number of product lines, while product line depth is defined according to the number of individual items within a line.

- Branding is an important way of creating differentiated tangible products. It helps the manufacturer to establish loyalty through the three-dimensional character imposed on the product, as well as deflecting consumer attention away from price. Branding is carried out not only by manufacturers, but also by retailers who want to create a more tangible character for themselves, as well as wanting consumers consciously to prefer to shop at their outlets. Relevant issues concerning brand owners include the creation and design of products and their brand identities as expressed through the core and tangible product via elements such as naming, quality, packaging and labelling. The strategic management of product and brand ranges is also important.

■ The product lifecycle (PLC) concept is the foundation for the idea that products move through stages in their lives and that they may, therefore, have different marketing needs over time. The PLC suggests four stages: introduction, growth, maturity and decline. Inevitably, the PLC is a very general concept, perhaps too general to be of real use, and there are many practical problems in using it. For an organisation, product management is important not only for making sure that existing products live profitable and efficient lives, and that they are deleted at the most appropriate time, but also to enable it to plan for the future and the flow of new products, taking advantage of new technologies and other opportunities. This implies the need for a balanced portfolio of products: some still in development, some in the early stages of their lives, some more mature and some heading for decline.

■ One way of ensuring that products get the most out of their lifecycles is to think about how they are positioned. This means defining what attributes or benefits are important to the market, then researching how your product, its competitors and a hypothetical ideal product are rated against those criteria, then analysing each brand's position in relation to the others and to the ideal. Perceptual mapping, using two or more dimensions, can help to visualise the state of the market. All of this can stimulate debate as to whether a product needs to be further differentiated from its competitors or brought closer to the market segment's ideal. Over a product's lifecycle, repositioning may become necessary in response to the changing marketing and competitive environment.

■ In fmcg companies in particular, product or brand managers may be given the responsibility of looking after a particular product or group of products. Although a similar product management structure may be found in B2B markets, alternative options may be considered. Management responsibility may be divided by end user or on a geographic basis, again because the needs of different regions may differ. In either case, the organisation can develop managers with depth of expertise relating to a specific group of end users or a particular geographic market.

■ The creation of the SEM opened up opportunities for pan-European branding. For many smaller organisations, however, this is not a serious issue and they do not have the resources or the real desire to move beyond their own national boundaries. Organisations interested in pan-European branding need abundant resources, to be sure that they can deliver consistent quality in all aspects of the operations and marketing and that they are prepared to support the brand through a long lead time before the product begins to make a return on its investment.

Questions for review and discussion

6.1 Choose three different brands of shampoo that you think incorporate different core products.
(a) Define the core product for each brand.
(b) How does the tangible product for each brand reflect the core product?

6.2 What is a speciality product and how might its marketing mix and the kind of buying behaviour associated with it differ from those found with other products?

6.3 Develop a weighted set of five or six criteria for 'good' labelling. Collect a number of competing brands of the same product and rate each of them against your criteria. Which brand comes out best? As a result of this exercise, would you adjust your weightings or change the criteria included?

6.4 Discuss the relationship between product adopter categories and the stages of the PLC. What are the implications for the marketer?

6.5 Choose a consumer product area (be very specific – for example, choose shampoo rather than haircare products) and list as many brands available within it as you can.
(a) What stage in the PLC has each brand reached?
(b) Does any one organisation own several of the brands and, if so, how are those brands distributed across the different PLC stages?

6.6 Define product positioning and summarise the reasons why it is important.

case study 6

Small, but perfectly formed

The original Mini became an icon for the sixties generation, a triumph of its time for innovative style and mechanical engineering. Its owners included The Beatles, Mick Jagger, Peter Sellers and Twiggy and it played a star role with Michael Caine in the movie *The Italian Job*. As an aside, it also won the Monte Carlo rally three times. At its launch in 1959, however, its creators had no such pretensions or ambitions for the car. It was simply a response to the possibility of petrol rationing. Its fuel economy and a competitive price tag of £497 set it aside from the rest, and it became almost a generic name for small cars.

Although The Beatles' music and Mick Jagger all survived well beyond the swinging '60s, by 1972 fashions had changed and the Mini brand was in decline. It increasingly became a small-volume, niche car with a cult following re-living earlier times. An influx of competitive small cars, a shift in consumer preference for more space and comfort, and changing design appreciation meant that the Mini became stuck with being a likeable, but dated brand. Although the Mini was kept in production, the then owner BL (British Leyland) was looking for a replacement. Its efforts were not an unqualified success, however. The Mini Metro launched in the 1980s, again an economical, low-priced brand, was again soon left behind by later entrants in terms of quality, design and performance. To succeed in the small car segment requires production efficiency and volume sales along with some distinguishing features. The Metro did not survive the Mini and is best remembered as the car people learned to drive in after the British School of Motoring adopted the brand for its fleet in the 1980s.

In the 1990s, the Mini passed into BMW's hands and plans were laid for a new Mini. The brand name was considered so strong and evocative that it was capable of a renaissance. The challenge was to create a car that was readily identified with the old Mini and handled like a Mini, yet had 21st-century quality and comforts. It was described as a baby BMW at £10,300 for the entry-level Mini One and £11,600 for the sporty Mini Cooper. The new Mini retained its sense of fun, in both its looks and its heart. The Cooper S version had a 1.6-litre engine offering 130 bhp for those seeking the on-road experience of the original. BMW avoided making the same mistake as VW, however. When VW launched the new Beetle in 1999 it was priced at £15,000, well beyond the target market's price limit, especially for a two-car household. BMW had originally planned to launch the Mini at £14,000, but changed it to the more competitive £10,000, just a little higher than some of the popular alternatives.

The new version of the classic Mini Traveller, launched at the Tokyo Motor Show, reflects the Japanese appreciation of all things British. The car will feature new, experimental access and storage systems, including a cargo box which can be attached to the side window. When open this will create a table for serving tea and scones.

Source: © BMW AG http://www.mini.co.uk

At the UK launch, it already had 6000 advance orders, 2500 in Britain alone, and prospective buyers soon had to join a six-month waiting list. Registrations in the first eight weeks were claimed to be double those of the Ford Puma in 1997 and more than ten times the number of new VW Beetles sold over the equivalent two-month launch period in 1999. To meet demand, a rolling launch was planned with the rest of Europe two months behind the UK launch, and the USA and Japan were targeted for 2002. Even at its launch, however, some critics had doubts about its likely success. Some believed that the small car market was already crowded and as a 'fashion vehicle' the Mini's shelf life in the showroom could be short, without regular freshening up. Often, car models are given a facelift every three years, not the seven years planned by BMW for the Mini. There was also a question as to whether BMW would make money out of the Mini. The problem with small cars with small price tags is small profits, if they make any profit at all. Nevertheless, BMW does tend to take a long-term view on its investments, which is probably a good thing as the Mini required a new production line, cost one-third more to develop than had been budgeted, and was late to market.

So how successful has the Mini been? By 2004, £208m had been invested in the new Mini; it was on sale in 73 markets across the world; and the factory had turned out its 500,000th car two years ahead of schedule. Although there had been no major overhaul of the brand, the introduction of the Mini Cooper and the Mini Convertible, for example, had helped to maintain the market's enthusiasm for it. The car's image was probably helped too by its starring role in the Austin Powers movies and photos in the media of celebrities such as Madonna and Elijah Wood driving Minis. Demand was outstripping supply. The critics were right about one thing, however. O'Connell (2004) reports that 'BMW had concluded that a combination of the car's ambitious specification and a deliberate decision to offer low basic prices had restricted its profitability'. In 2008, therefore, when the successor to the current Mini is likely to go into production, its specification will be more basic, and components will be sourced more cheaply.

The Mini also proved to be a big hit in the US, which is perhaps surprising in a market that is perceived as preferring big 'gas-guzzlers' and SUVs. Original forecasts suggested that about 20,000 vehicles per year could be sold in the US. In fact, 20,000 were sold within days of the launch in March 2002! In 2003, Mini sold about 36,010 Cooper and Cooper S models alone, and in just the first six months of 2005, nearly 22,000 Minis were delivered to US customers, which is not bad for a range that starts at around $17,000. According to White (2004), the Mini helped to popularise the 'premium small car' niche in the US, which is now starting to attract competitors as well as consumers. Subaru, Mazda, Toyota and Honda are all reported to be planning to launch more stylish small cars to compete against the Mini in the US. It will be very interesting to see how the Mini's sales hold up against such serious competition.

Sources: Barrett (2001); Chittenden (2001); Edwards (2001); Golding (2001); Griffiths (2004); Lister (2001); Moyes (2003); O'Connell (2004); White (2004); http://www.bmwgroup.com.

Questions

1 What is the core product that the Mini offers compared with the mainstream BMW range? Why do you think BMW was prepared to invest so much to have the Mini in its range?

2 How could the Mini's core product be translated into tangible, augmented and potential products as represented in Figure 6.1? To what extent might the planned changes to specifications and components in 2008 affect the brand image of the Mini?

3 What are the advantages and disadvantages of using an existing brand name for this new product launch?

4 Why do you think the Mini has been so successful in the US?

References for chapter 6

Adwan, L. (2003), 'The Role of Confectionery Brand Extensions', *Euromonitor Archive*, 17 March, accessed via http://www.euromonitor.com.

Bainbridge, J. and Green, L. (2004), 'The Coca-Cola Challenge', *Campaign*, 22 October, pp. 28–9.

Barrett, L. (2001), 'The Baby Beamer', *Marketing Week*, 21 June, pp. 24–5.

Black, E. (2005), 'Scotch Under Threat from Japan's New Generation', *The Scotsman*, 23 April, p. 8.

Blackett, T. (1985), 'Brand Name Research – Getting it Right', *Marketing and Research Today*, May, pp. 89–93.

Bowker, J (2005), 'Pernod Can Toast Success of Whiskies', *The Scotsman*, 4 February, p. 51.

Brand Strategy (2003), 'No Magic Formula for Valuation', *Brand Strategy*, August, p. 3.

Brand Strategy (2004), 'Brand MOT: Coca-Cola', *Brand Strategy*, 6 December, p. 10.

Bridge, R. (2003), 'Seal of Success for Inventor', *Sunday Times*, 18 May, p. 15.

Bridgett, D. (2001), 'Now Europe Forces Colman's to Cut the French Mustard', *Mail on Sunday*, 15 April, p. 41.

Bunting, M. (2001), 'The New Gods', *The Guardian*, 8 July, p. 2.4.

Carlyle, R. (2004), 'Dualit Toaster', *Daily Telegraph*, 4 December, p. 3.

China Law and Practice (2004), 'Foreign Trademark Protection in China: Case Studies from 2003', *China Law and Practice*, July, p. 1.

Chittenden, M. (2001), 'Mini Comes Back as a Trendy Teuton', *Sunday Times*, 8 July, p. 8.

Cienski, J. (2005), 'Poles Vault into Europe's Big League', *Financial Times*, 5 January, p. 11.

Connolly, A. and Davidson, L. (1996), 'How Does Design Affect Decisions at the Point of Sale?', *Journal of Brand Management*, 4 (2), pp. 100–7.

Cookson, C. (2005), 'Silent Aircraft is More than a Flight of Fancy', *Financial Times*, 10 September, p. 4.

Cravens, D., Piercy, N. and Prentice, A. (2000), 'Developing Market-driven Product Strategies', *Journal of Product and Brand Management*, 9 (6), pp. 369–88.

Davis, E.J. (1984), 'Managing Marketing', in N.A. Hart (ed.), *The Marketing of Industrial Products*, McGraw-Hill.

DelVecchio, D. (2000), 'Moving Beyond Fit: The Role of Brand Portfolio Characteristics in Consumer Evaluations of Brand Reliability', *Journal of Product and Brand Management*, 9 (7), pp. 457–71.

Edwards, O. (2001), 'The Big Hydrogen Gamble', *Eurobusiness*, September, pp. 36–40.

Gapper, J. (2004), 'Microsoft is Starting to Feel its Age', *Financial Times*, 2 September, p. 17.

Golding, R. (2001), 'The Mini is Back but What's the Return?', *The Independent*, 2 May, p. 4.

Grande, C. (2003), 'Stepping Out, but Oh So Discreetly', *Financial Times*, 29 July, p. 8.

Green, P.E. and Carmone, F.J. (1970), *Multidimensional Scaling and Related Techniques in Marketing Analysis*, Allyn and Bacon.

Griffiths, J. (2004), 'BMW Struggling to Get Max out of Mini', *Financial Times*, 26 August, p. 4.

The Grocer (2005), 'Focus on Active Health Drinks', supplement to *The Grocer*, May, p. 4.

Halliburton, C. and Hunerberg, R. (1987), 'The Globalisation Dispute in Marketing', *European Management Journal*, 4 (Winter), pp. 243–9.

Harrington, S. (2005), 'Innovation in Packaging', *The Grocer*, 5 February, pp. 38–40.

Hawkes, N. (2005), 'Aircraft of Future Promised Passengers the Space of a Ferry and a Quiet Life for Those Down Below', *The Times*, 10 September, p. 30.

Hiam, A. (1990), 'Exposing Four Myths of Strategic Planning', *Journal of Business Strategy*, September/October, pp. 23–8.

John, D., Loken, B. and Joiner, C. (1998), 'The Negative Impact of Extensions: Can Flagship Products be Diluted?', *Journal of Marketing*, 62 (1), pp. 19–32.

Lindemann, J. (2004), 'Brand Valuation', in *The Economist* (ed.), *Brands and Branding*, Economist Books.

Lister, S. (2001), 'Sixties Throwback is Instant 21st-century Hit', *The Times*, 12 July, p. 11.

Lynch, R. (1994), *European Business Strategies: The European and Global Strategies of Europe's Top Companies*, Kogan Page.

Lyons, W. (2004), 'Chinese Sales of Scotch Whisky Soar 170%', *The Scotsman*, 27 October, p. 47.

Mackintosh, J. (2005), 'Production of Off-road Cars Halted by Protest', *Financial Times*, 17 May, p. 3.

Marketing Week (2004), 'Driving SUVs Off the Road', *Marketing Week*, 9 September, p. 24.

Marketing Week (2005), 'Plenty of Off-roaders on the Street', *Marketing Week*, 3 February, p. 34.

McKenzie, S. (1997), 'Package Deal', *Marketing Week*, 11 September, pp. 67–9.

Mintel (2004), 'Nappies and Baby Wipes', *UK Market Intelligence*, April, accessed via **http://www.mintel.com**.

Mitchell, A. (2004), 'Lessons in Successfully Using a Master Brand', *Marketing Week*, 27 May, p. 28.

Moyes, S. (2003), 'How Austin Powered a Mini Craze', *Daily Mirror*, 9 January, p. 31.

Murray, I. (2004), 'Will the Whisky Maltopops Marketers Get Hammered?', *Marketing Week*, 29 July, p. 74.

O'Connell, D. (2004), 'Cheaper Mini Heads for Cowley', *Sunday Times*, 30 May, p. 3.

Olsen, J. (2000), 'Disharmony in Europe Puts Brand Owners at Risk', *Managing Intellectual Property*, December/January, pp. 52–63.

Park, A. (2004), 'PCs Have Barely Changed Styles Since their Birth', *Business Week*, 21 June, p. 86.

Pavitt, J. (2001), 'Branded: A Brief History of Brands 1: Coca-Cola', *The Guardian*, 9 July, p. 2.4.

Pearman, H. (2001), 'Dualit Toaster', *Sunday Times*, 4 November, p. 6.

Peters, M. (1994), 'Good Packaging Gets Through to the Fickle Buyer', *Marketing*, 20 January, p. 10.

Pieters, R. and Warlops, L. (1999), 'Visual Attention During Brand Choice: The Impact of Time Pressure and Task Motivation', *International Journal of Research in Marketing*, 16, pp. 1–16.

Professional Engineering (2004), 'Bulky, Thirsty Image "May Harm SUV Sales"', *Professional Engineering*, 8 September, p. 5.

Reibstein, D.J. *et al.* (1998), 'Mastering Marketing. Part Four: Brand Strategy', *Financial Times Supplement*, pp. 7–8.

Rijkens, R. (1992), *European Advertising Strategies: The Profiles and Policies of Multinational Companies Operating in Europe*, Cassell.

Rogers, E.M. (1962), *Diffusion of Innovation*, The Free Press.

Ruelas-Gossi, A. and Sull, D. (2004), 'The Art of Innovating on a Shoestring', *Financial Times*, 24 September, p. 3.

Saigol, L. (2004), 'For Sale Sign on Jimmy Choo', *Financial Times*, 1 November, p. 22.

Solley, S. (2004), 'Famous Grouse Bids for Younger Market', *Marketing*, 18 August, p. 5.

Tollington, T. (1998), 'Brands: The Asset Definition and Recognition Test', *Journal of Product and Brand Management*, 7 (3), pp. 180–92.

Underwood, R., Klein, N. and Burke, R. (2001), 'Packaging Communication: Attentional Effects of Product Imagery', *Journal of Product and Brand Management*, 10 (7), pp. 403–22.

Waters, R. (2005), 'Gates to Reveal Office Target', *Financial Times*, 19 May, p. 19.

White, J. (2004), 'Challenges Rise for BMW's Mini in US Market', *Wall Street Journal*, 24 March, p. 1.

Wood, L. (1990), 'The End of the Product Life Cycle? Education Says Goodbye to an Old Friend', *Journal of Marketing Management*, 6 (2), pp. 145–55.

Wu, Y. (2003), 'China's Refrigerator Magnate', *McKinsey Quarterly*, 3, pp. 340–2.

price

Introduction

At first glance, price might seem to be the least complicated and perhaps the least interesting element of the marketing mix, not having the tangibility of the product, the glamour of advertising or the atmosphere of retailing. It does, however, play a very important role in the lives of both marketers and customers, and deserves as much strategic consideration as any other marketing tool. Price not only directly generates the revenues that allow organisations to create and retain customers at a profit (in accordance with one of the definitions of marketing in Chapter 1), but can also be used as a communicator, as a bargaining tool and as a competitive weapon. The customer can use price as a means of comparing products, judging relative value for money or judging product quality.

Ultimately, the customer is being asked to accept the product offering and (usually) to hand money over in exchange for it. If the product has been carefully thought out with the customer's needs in mind, if the distribution channels chosen are convenient and appropriate to that customer, if the promotional mix has been sufficiently seductive, then there is a good chance that the customer will be willing to hand over some amount of money for the pleasure of owning that product. But even then, the price that is placed on the product is crucial: set too high a price, and the customer will reject the offering and all the good work done with the rest of the marketing mix is wasted; too low, and the customer is suspicious ('too good to be true'). What constitutes 'a high price' or 'a low price' depends on the buyer, and has to be put into the context of their perceptions of themselves, of the entire marketing package and of the competitors' offerings. Pricing has a spurious certainty about it because it involves numbers, but do not be misled by this; it is as emotive and as open to misinterpretation as any other marketing activity.

It is thus important for the marketer to understand the meaning of price from the customer's point of view, and to price products in accordance with the 'value' that the customer places on the benefits offered.

This chapter expands on these initial concepts of price. It will look further at what price is, and what it means to marketers and customers in various contexts. It will also examine more closely the role of price in the marketing mix, and how it interacts with other marketing activities. This sets the scene for a focus on some of the internal factors and external pressures that influence pricing thinking within an organisation. The final section of the chapter then draws all this together to give an overview of the managerial process that leads to decisions on pricing strategies and price setting.

eg The hotel accommodation sector has grown a lot in recent years, as Europeans have become far more mobile, taking more business and leisure trips. Much of the growth has been driven by the development of budget chains (see pp. 226–7) and the UK's bed and breakfast establishments have had to respond to remain competitive. The traditional image has not been good. Cheap, yes, but often downmarket and sometimes shabby.

Things have, however, changed as a new generation of 'luxury' B&B owners have entered the market. Their aspiration is to offer standards similar to those of a small hotel, with a friendly, easy-going environment making it a 'home from home'. Alternatives have crept onto the breakfast menu, including quality kippers and full organic fry-ups. A lot more attention has been paid to the quality of the rooms, décor, fabric and colour scheme so that guests feel that they are in a comfortable and relaxing environment. Prices have also risen to cover the additional services and help pay for the investment, with some charging almost as much as local hotels, in excess of £40–£50 per night. If they price too cheaply, experience has taught them that the number of enquiries can actually drop as the target customers expect to pay more for something special. This also reflects a new segment of B&B customers: those wanting a quality short break and international guests, especially Americans, who are sensitive to levels of service and standards.

One problem still remains for the luxury B&B owners, that is how to promote to a wider audience. The higher prices charged must in part be ploughed back into promotional expenditure to keep the enquiries and bookings coming in. Often the investment must be in niche publications and websites such as Wolsey Lodges, Alistair Sawday's Special Places to Stay, or Unique Home Stays. For some B&Bs, these can generate as much as 60 per cent of their enquiries. So, for this sector the pricing decision is critical, as from that comes the opportunity to provide better service and higher standards, as well as generating new business. If, however, you opt for the alternative at £20 per person per night, you can experience the price–value trade-off first hand (Glasgow, 2004).

The role and perception of price

Price is the value that is placed on something. What is someone prepared to give in order to gain something else? Usually, price is measured in money, as a convenient medium of exchange that allows prices to be set quite precisely. This is not necessarily always the case, however. Goods and services may be bartered ('I will help you with the marketing plan for your car repair business if you service my car for me'), or there may be circumstances where monetary exchange is not appropriate, for example at election time when politicians make promises in return for your vote. Any such transactions, even if they do not directly involve money, are exchange processes and thus can use marketing principles (go back to Chapter 1 for the discussion of marketing as an exchange process). Price is any common currency of value to both buyer and seller.

Even money-based pricing comes under many names, depending on the circumstances of its use: solicitors charge fees; landlords charge rent; bankers charge interest; railways charge fares; hotels charge a room rate; consultants charge retainers; agents charge commission; insurance companies charge premiums; and over bridges or through tunnels, tolls may be charged. Whatever the label, it is still a price for a good or a service, and the same principles apply.

Price does not necessarily mean the same things to different people, just because it is usually expressed as a number. You have to look beyond the price, at what it represents to both the buyer and the seller if you want to grasp its significance in any transaction. Buyer and seller may well have different perspectives on what price means. We now turn to that of the buyer.

■ The customer's perspective

From the buyer's perspective, price represents the value they attach to whatever is being exchanged. Up to the point of purchase, the marketer has been making promises to the potential buyer about what this product is and what it can do for that customer. The customer is going to weigh up those promises against the price and decide whether it is worth paying (Zeithaml, 1988).

In assessing price, the customer is looking specifically at the expected benefits of the product, as shown in Figure 7.1.

Functional

Functional benefits relate to the design of the product and its ability to fulfil its desired function. For example, a washing machine's price might be judged on whether or not it can handle different washing temperatures, operate economically and dry as well as wash.

Quality

The customer may expect price to reflect the quality level of the product (Erickson and Johansson, 1985). Thus a customer may be prepared to pay more for leather upholstery in a car, or for solid wood furniture rather than veneer, or for hand-made Belgian chocolates rather than mass produced. Quality perceptions may be to do with the materials or components used in the product, as in these examples, or with the labour involved in making it. Quality may also, however, be a less tangible judgement made on the basis of corporate image. BMW, Heinz and Cadbury's are perceived as quality companies, and therefore they are perceived as producing quality products. The consumer can thus accept that those organisations might charge higher prices.

Operational

In B2B markets, price may be judged in relation to the product's ability to influence the production process. For example, a new piece of machinery might be assessed on its ability to increase productivity, make the production line more efficient or reduce the labour content of the finished goods. Even in a consumer market, operational issues might be considered.

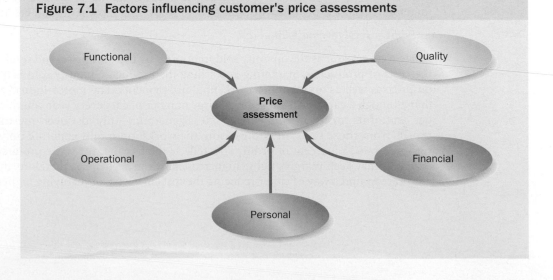

Figure 7.1 Factors influencing customer's price assessments

For instance, the purchase of a microwave oven increases the operational efficiency of the kitchen, both making it easier to cater for the staggered mealtimes resulting from the modern family's fragmented lifestyle, and giving the chief cook more time to pursue other interests.

Financial

Particularly in B2B markets, many purchases are seen as investments, and therefore the expected return on that investment is important in judging whether the price is worthwhile or not. New machinery, for example, is expected to pay for itself over time in terms of increased efficiency, output, labour saving, etc. Note that this judgement is made not only in terms of production outputs, but also in terms of long-term cost savings, efficiency gains and productivity improvements.

Personal

Personal benefit is a difficult category for the marketer to gauge, as it attempts to measure price against intangible, individual, psychological benefits such as status, comfort, self-image (Chapter 3 reminded you about these benefits), etc. Some high-involvement products, such as perfumes, use high pricing deliberately as a means of amplifying the upmarket, with sophisticated, exclusive images portrayed in their packaging, distribution and advertising strategies, thus increasing the status enhancement and 'feel good' factor of the purchase.

Remember too that B2B markets are not immune from the effects of personal factors. Purchasing can be influenced by the individual motivations of people involved (as discussed at pp. 106 *et seq.*), and even by a desire to enhance a corporate self-image.

The problem is, of course, that different buyers put different values on different benefits. This endorses the need for market segmentation (see Chapter 4), which can begin to sort out groupings of like-minded customers so that appropriately tailored marketing mixes (including price) can be developed.

So far, it has been assumed that price perception and judgements of value are constant in the mind of the potential buyer. They are, however, variable according to circumstances. For example, a householder thinking of replacing water pipes would probably be very price sensitive and get quotes from a number of plumbers before making a decision. A burst pipe in the winter, however, would have that same householder paying almost any price to get a plumber round immediately. In any such distress purchase, the value placed on immediate problem solution justifies paying a premium price.

Another factor influencing price perception is scarcity. Where supply is severely limited and demand is high, prices can take on a life of their own and begin to spiral.

■ The seller's perspective

Price is a distinctive element of the marketing mix for the *seller*, because it is the only one that generates revenue. All the other elements represent outgoing costs. Price is also important, therefore, because it provides the basis of both recovering those costs and creating profit:

Profit = Total revenue − Total cost

where total revenue is the quantity sold multiplied by the unit price, and total cost represents the costs of producing, marketing and selling the product. Quantity sold is itself dependent on price as well as on the other marketing mix elements. The motor industry has suggested that although a car dealership selling a large number of cars every year could well generate 80 per cent of its turnover from car sales, it is generating only just over one third of its total profits from those sales. In comparison, the workshop might generate only 5 per cent of turnover, but 25 per cent of profit. This reflects the fact that for some products, competitive pressures may keep margins tight. To increase profit in such areas, therefore, the organisation may have to find a way of either reducing the costs involved, or justifying higher prices.

eg Camera manufacturers produce wide ranges of products, priced differently to cater for different segments' needs. Even when focusing on the relatively new technology of digital cameras, manufacturers recognise that at the bottom end of the market is the customer who sees a camera as a means to an end. This customer wants to capture the moment and may not be concerned with the number of pixels, connectivity, or the media card options. They just want to point and shoot, and let the camera do the rest. Many products at this end of the market cost less than £100.

The serious amateur, on the other hand, might be interested in the process of taking the picture and will, therefore, take far greater interest in the technical specifications and the quality and flexibility of any output. Aspects such as zoom capability, backlighting and flash modes could all be important and as a result prices can range from £300 to over £1000, as customers are prepared to trade features and benefits for price. This sector is being revolutionised with the introduction of digital SLRs below £1000. By giving the flexibility for lens change and the feel of a traditional SLR, the attraction to the serious amateur is far greater. Finally, the professional photographer might be prepared to go straight to the top of the range to maximise the quality of output. Specifications will thus often be closely studied and add-on items considered. To get the right package, the professional photographer could well be prepared to pay several thousand pounds. The lower end of the professional sector of the digital market is, however, now becoming increasingly attractive as a trade-up for the serious amateur.

The seller, however, must always take care to think about price from the perspective of the customer. In pure economic terms, it would be assumed that reducing a price would lead to higher sales because more people could then afford and want the product. As the introduction to this chapter suggested, however, a low price may be interpreted as making a negative statement about the product's quality, and a sudden reduction in price of an established product may be taken to mean that the product's quality has been compromised in some way. Even petrol, the stereotypical homogeneous product, has been a victim of this.

Similarly, a high price may not always be a bad thing for a seller. If buyers equate price with quality (and in the absence of information or knowledge of the market, it may be the only indicator they pick up), then a higher price might actually attract customers. Part of the psychological benefit of the purchase for the customer might well be derived from its expense, for example in purchasing gifts where one feels obliged to spend a certain amount on the

The customer is paying for both the brand and the quality that promises success when buying the Olympus E-500 – a top of the range digital SLR camera.

Source: Olympus UK Ltd http://www.olympus.co.uk

recipient either to fulfil social expectations or to signal affection. The higher the price, the more exclusive the market segment able to afford the product or service. Many more rail travellers, for example, choose to travel second class than in the higher-priced first-class accommodation.

The seller also needs to remember that sometimes the cost to the customer of purchasing a product can be much greater than its price. These broader considerations might have an inhibiting effect on purchase. When consumers were buying DVD players for the first time, for example, they did not only look at the ticket price of the machine, but also weighed up the costs of replacing favourite video cassettes with discs. A business buying a new computer system has to consider the costs of transferring records, staff training and the initial decrease in productivity as they learn to find their way around the new system and the costs of instal-lation (and of removing the old equipment). The whole marketing strategy for a product has to recognise the real cost to the customer of accepting the offering and work to overcome such objections, whether through pricing, a better-tailored product offering or effective com-munication and persuasion.

Whatever type of market an organisation is in, whatever market segments it seeks to serve, it must always be aware that price can never stand apart from the other elements of the mar-keting mix. It interacts with those elements and must, therefore, give out signals consistent with those given by the product itself, place and promotion. Price is often quoted as a reason for not purchasing a product, but this reflects a tendency to use price as a scapegoat for other failings in the marketing mix. Price is a highly visible factor and at the point of purchase it hits the buyer where it hurts – in the pocket. As has been said before in this chapter, if the rest of the marketing mix has worked well up to the point of sale, then the price should not be too great an issue, because the buyer will have been convinced that the benefits supplied are com-mensurate with the price asked. Price is seen here as a natural, integrated element in harmony with the rest of the offering. It could be argued that a buyer who is wavering and uses price as the ultimate determinant of whether to purchase is either shopping in the wrong market seg-ment or being ill-served by sloppy marketing.

marketing **in action**

A cheap and cheerful bed for the night

Since the late 1980s, the UK hotel market has been revolutionised by the growth of the budget sector, characterised by Travel Inn, Ibis, and Express by Holiday Inn. Between 1999 and 2005, the number of budget hotel rooms in the UK grew from 39,000 to 65,000, and the forecast for 2010 is 100,000. Even at that figure, however, the budget hotels' share of all hotel rooms would be just 10 per cent in the UK, compared with 15 per cent in France and 18 per cent in the United States. The number of budget hotel sites in the UK is around 1000 and there are new additions each year. It is not just the business traveller who has fuelled the expansion, as the leisure market has also been buoyant.

Whitbread has the biggest share of the UK budget hotel market.

Having acquired the Premier Lodge chain in 2004, it has 40 per cent share. Travelodge has 15,000 rooms spread across 265 hotels and plans to add 2500 rooms a year to double its size by 2011. Premier Travel Inn now has 449 hotels with over 28,000 beds and it intends to expand that to 35,000 by 2008.

The original budget hotels tended to be fairly basic but operated to a consistent standard, often operated by chains to a flat-rate pricing structure. There were often no service frills, no restaurants within the hotel itself and minimal extra facilities in the rooms, such as telephones and mini-bars. Instead, hotels in this sector offered an alternative to higher-priced hotels with wider services and bed and breakfast/guest houses that were of variable standard. To the weary traveller, the possibility of booking in advance via a centralised

reservation system and getting a guaranteed level of service, and the convenience of arriving and departing to the guest's schedule, rather than fitting into the landlady's schedule, offered an attractive advantage. Prices were set to fall below the typical full-service hotel but above the typical bed and breakfast. Furthermore, customers paid per room, not per person, so a family could stay for the same price as an individual, subject to maximum room occupancy, of course.

More recent developments have tended to add back some of the service. Six-foot-wide beds, secure parking, 24-hour reception, and an adjacent, on-site bar and restaurant are now standard features. The Sleep Inn at Cambridge, for example, offers internet access, direct-dial telephones, clothes presses, hairdryers and even a TV with a PlayStation in the rooms, but still costs only £50.40 for a room

To complement easyJet's flights and car hire services, you can now also use easyHotel for good value accommodation.

Source: © easyHotel http://www.easyhotel.com

for two. Express by Holiday Inn offers free breakfast to guests at the adjacent restaurant and, although each bedroom has a work area, dataport and telephone, guests can still book a meeting room, which also has fax and photocopying facilities. At the other end of the scale, super-economy brand Formule 1 offers rooms for £19.95 without en-suite bathrooms.

Price structures have also changed. Rather than pricing by season or individual location, tiered pricing now tends to operate according to the general location and day of the week. Thus prices

may vary depending on whether a hotel is in a city centre or not, with London as the most expensive. Express by Holiday Inn usually operates different prices for weekdays and weekends. In short, the early emphasis on price competition is being replaced with a value for money approach when service levels and delivery are of a consistent standard. Travel Lodge is experimenting with a business model that sets prices according to anticipated demand, thus following the example of the low-cost airlines, rather than using a formal tiered structure. Rooms could,

therefore, vary from just over £20 to over £50, the emphasis being on filling capacity and generating whatever marginal income can be achieved when most of the costs are fixed. Occupancy rates are typically high, above 70 per cent per annum, which is better than for most other hotel sectors (*Business Europe*, 2004). This more flexible approach to pricing is helped by a greater use of the internet for room bookings, although this still accounts for only around 25 per cent of all bookings, a lower percentage than typically found in the budget airline sector.

Developing a strong, consistent brand is an important part of the business formula in achieving high occupancy rates. As competition increases, however, there may be pressure to develop more facilities rather than to cut prices. Interestingly, in many of the US budget chains extras such as continental breakfast and swimming pools are regularly used to differentiate, often with only a small price premium. The low-cost budget hotel sector is, therefore, now starting to break down even further, as different service/facility options are being offered at different price levels, although the ease of reservation, convenience and brand consistency all tend to be similar.

Sources: *Business Europe* (2004); *Marketing Week* (2003, 2005); Singh (2001); Stevenson (2005); Upton (2001).

External influences on the pricing decision

The previous sections of this chapter have shown that there is more to pricing than meets the eye. It is not a precise science because of the complexities of the marketing environment and the human perceptions of the parties involved in the marketing exchange. There will always be some uncertainty over the effect of a pricing decision, whether on distribution channels, competitors or the customer. Nevertheless, to reduce that uncertainty, it is important to analyse the range of issues affecting pricing decisions. Some of these are internal to the selling organisation, and are thus perhaps more predictable, but others arise from external pressures, and are therefore more difficult to define precisely. There is also some variation in the extent to which the organisation can control or influence these issues. Figure 7.2 summarises the main areas of *external influence*, while this section of the chapter defines them and gives an overview of their impact on the pricing decision, in preparation for the more detailed scrutiny of price setting and strategies towards the end of the chapter.

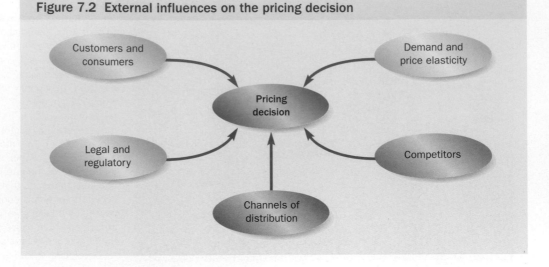

Figure 7.2 External influences on the pricing decision

Customers and consumers

As pp. 223 *et seq.* showed, pricing cannot be considered without taking into account the feelings and sensitivities of the *end buyer*. Different market segments react to price levels and price changes differently depending on the nature of the product, its desirability and the level of product loyalty established.

> **eg** The discerning coffee drinker who likes the taste of Nescafé and always buys that brand may not notice when the price rises, but even if they do spot the price rise, they might still continue to purchase Nescafé because they value the brand's benefits so highly. A segment that perceives coffee as a commodity and does not mind what it tastes like as long as it is hot and wet might be more inclined to be price sensitive. They might have been buying the same brand on a regular basis, but if its price rises then they certainly will notice and switch to something cheaper.

The marketer has to be careful to set prices within an area bounded at the bottom end by costs and at the top end by what the market will tolerate. The bigger that area, the more discretion the marketer has in setting price. The organisation can increase its pricing discretion either by reducing costs (thereby lowering the bottom boundary) or by raising the consumers' threshold (by better-targeted communication or by improving the product offering).

The consumers' upper threshold is difficult to define as it is linked closely with perceptions of the product and its competitive standing. A product perceived as better than the competition will have a higher upper threshold than one perceived as poor value. In the latter case, the upper limit on price may be very close to cost. Similarly, a product with strong brand loyalty attached to it can push its upper limit higher because the product's desirability blunts any price sensitivity, enabling a price premium to be achieved. By basing a price on the perceived value of the offer, a close match can be found with what the customer is prepared to pay (Nimer, 1975; Thompson and Coe, 1997).

Demand and price elasticity

Customers' attitudes towards price and their responsiveness to it are reflected to some extent in economic theories of *demand*. Marketers' pricing objectives and the estimation of demand are thus very closely linked (Montgomery, 1988). As pricing objectives change, for example if there is a decision to move upmarket into a premium-priced segment, the nature and size of potential demand will also change. Similarly, it is important for the marketer to be able to estimate demand for new product. The definition of demand is flexible here; it may mean demand across an entire product market, or demand within a specific market segment, or be organisation specific.

Demand determinants

For most products, it seems logical that if the price goes up, then demand falls and, conversely, if the price falls, then demand rises. This is the basic premise behind the standard demand curve shown in Figure 7.3, which shows the number of units sold (Q1) at a given price (P1). As price increases from P1 to P2, demand is expected to fall from Q1 to Q2. This classic demand curve may relate either to a market or to an individual product. As an example, if the dollar is weak against other currencies, Americans generally find foreign holidays more expensive and thus do not travel. Similarly, the Asian financial crisis reduced the number of Japanese tourists.

The shape of the demand curve, however, will be influenced by a range of factors other than price. Changing consumer tastes and needs, for example, might make a product more or less desirable regardless of the price. The economic ability to pay is still there, but the willingness to buy is not. Fluctuations in real disposable income could similarly affect demand, particularly for what could be considered luxury items. In a recession, for instance, consumers may cut back on demand for foreign holidays or new cars. In this case, the willingness exists, but the means to pay do not. The availability and pricing of close substitute products will also change the responsiveness of demand. For example, the introduction of the CD player into the mass market had a disastrous effect on demand for record players.

All of these factors are demand determinants that the marketer must understand in order to inject meaning into the demand curve. As Diamantopoulos and Mathews (1995) emphasise, however, demand curves are very subjective in nature. They depend very much on managerial judgements of the likely impact of price changes on demand, since most organisations do not have the kind of sophisticated information systems that would allow a more objective calculation. In reality, then, it is a *perceived* demand curve that drives managerial decisions rather than a 'real' one.

eg One of the side effects of the tsunami disaster in the Indian Ocean was the impact on the world's fish supply chain. The damage to the fishing fleet, shore logistics facilities and infrastructure meant a shortage of supply, and a knock-on effect on prices was predicted in markets across the world. A number of species including tuna are extensively fished off Sri Lanka and the Maldives, and shrimp are brought ashore in Thailand. Prices were expected to rise for these species if the supply situation was not restored quickly, as sustained demand chases more limited supplies (*The Grocer*, 2005a).

Figure 7.3 The classic demand curve

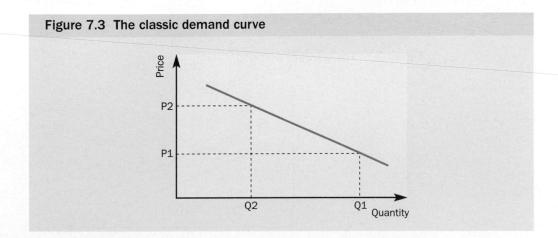

Not all products conform to the classic demand curve shown in Figure 7.3. Some products with a deep psychological relationship with the consumer, perhaps with a high status dimension, can show a reverse price–demand curve where the higher the price is the higher the demand. As Figure 7.4 shows, as the price goes down from P1 to P2 and demand falls from Q1 to Q2, the product loses its mystique and demand falls. There is, however, still an upper threshold beyond which the good becomes too expensive for even a status-conscious market. Then as the price rises higher, beyond P3, a more normal relationship holds true in which higher price leads to lower demand. This creates a boomerang-shaped demand curve. Knowing at what point the curve begins to turn back on itself could be useful for a marketer wishing to skim the market. Price too high and you could have turned the corner, becoming too exclusive.

Another dimension of the demand curve is that marketers can themselves seek to influence its shape. Figure 7.5 shows how the demand curve can be shifted upwards through marketing efforts. If the marketer can offer better value to the customer or change the customer's perceptions of the product, then a higher quantity will be demanded without any reduction in the price. It is valuable for the marketer to be able to find ways of using non-price-based mechanisms of responding to a competitor's price cut or seeking to improve demand, to avoid the kind of mutually damaging price wars that erode margins and profits. This may create a new demand curve, parallel to the old one, so that demand can be increased from Q1 to Q2 while retaining the price at P1.

Price elasticity of demand

It is also important for the marketer to have some understanding of the sensitivity of demand to price changes. This is shown by the steepness of the demand curve. A very steep demand curve shows a great deal of price sensitivity, in that a small change in price, all other things remaining equal, leads to a big change in demand. For some essential products, such as electricity, the demand curve is much more shallow; changes in price do not lead to big changes

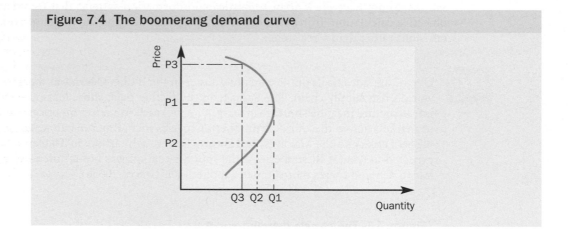

Figure 7.4 The boomerang demand curve

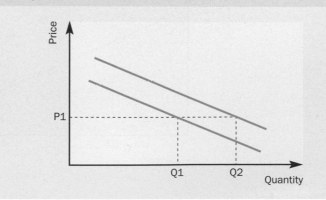

Figure 7.5 The parallel demand curve

eg

Fine fragrances, especially those with designer names, might fall into this category of demand curve. The fragrance houses have been careful to price them sufficiently highly to position them well away from ordinary toiletries. This means that fine fragrances appeal not only to a well-to-do segment who can easily afford this sort of product on a regular basis, but also to those who aspire to be part of this elite and are prepared to splash out what seems to them to be a large sum of money occasionally to bring themselves closer to a world of luxury and sophistication. In either case, the high price is part of the appeal and the excitement of the product. The higher the price, the bigger the thrill. If the price became too high, however, the aspiring segment would probably fall away and live out their fantasies with something more affordable. They might find £30 to £80 acceptable, but £70 to £120 might be perceived as too extravagant. Even the elite segment might have its upper threshold. If the price of designer-label fine fragrances becomes too high, then they might as well buy the designer's clothes instead if they want to flaunt their wealth and status!

in demand. In this case, demand is said to be inelastic because it does not stretch a lot if pulled either way by price. The term price elasticity of demand thus refers to the ratio of percentage change in quantity over percentage change in price:

$$\text{Price elasticity} = \frac{\text{\% change in quantity demanded}}{\text{\% change in price}}$$

Thus the higher the price elasticity of demand, the more sensitive the market. Goods like electricity have a price elasticity much closer to zero than do goods like convenience foods. For most goods, as the quantity demanded usually falls if the price rises, price elasticity is often negative, but by convention the minus sign is usually ignored.

It is important for the marketer to understand price elasticity and its causes, whether for an organisation's brand or within the market as a whole, as a basis for marketing mix decisions. There are a number of factors that will influence the price sensitivity (i.e. the price elasticity of demand) of customers. According to economic theory, the emergence of more, or closer, substitutes for a product will increase its price elasticity as buyers have the option of switching to the substitute as the price of the original product rises. From a marketing perspective, however, it does not seem quite so simple. The emergence of vegetable-based spreadable fats, for example, has offered consumers an alternative to butter and thus something with which to compare the price of butter. Further than that, however, it has completely changed the character of butter's demand curve from that of a necessity (a fairly flat straight line) to that of a luxury (more of a boomerang shape). Those who now choose to buy butter because of its superior taste or because of the status it bestows on the contents of the buyer's fridge will be no more price sensitive now than they ever were and, indeed, may even be less so.

As well as looking at the influence of substitutes on the shape and steepness of demand curves, it is also interesting to consider the relative importance of the purchase to the buyer. A purchase involving a relatively large cash outlay compared with the buyer's income will make that buyer more price sensitive. As discussed in Chapter 3, the more risky and infrequent the purchase, the more rational the buyer becomes, and more important the value for money aspects of the offering become. A rise in the price of cars, for example, might deter a potential buyer from replacing an old car.

■ Channels of distribution

An organisation's approach to pricing has also to take into account the needs and expectations of the other members of the *distribution chain*. Each of them will have a desired level of profit margin and a requirement to cover the costs associated with handling and reselling the product, such as transport, warehousing, insurance and retail display, for example. Even with a service product, such as insurance or a holiday, distributing through agents who claim commission on sales to cover premises, staffing, administration and profit has an impact on the price of the service.

All of this tends to erode the manufacturer's pricing discretion, because effectively it adds to the producer's costs and takes the total much nearer to the consumer's upper limit. How much erosion there is will depend on the balance of power between manufacturer and intermediaries.

■ Competitors

The point has been made several times during the course of this chapter that pricing decisions have to be made in a *competitive* context. The level and intensity of competition and the pricing decisions that other organisations make in the market will influence any producer's own pricing. It is not just about relative positioning ('If the budget version is £10 and the premium quality version is £70, then if we want to signal a mid-range product we have to charge £45'). It also concerns strategic decisions about the extent to which the organisation wishes to use price as an aggressive competitive weapon. Price and non-price competition will be discussed later in this chapter.

The influence of competition on price will depend on the nature of the product and the number and size of competitors within the market.

Monopoly

Few monopoly situations, where there is only one supplier serving the whole market, exist. Traditionally, monopolies have been large state-owned enterprises providing public services such as utilities, telecommunications and mail, or operating economically crucial industries such as steel and coal. Legislation protected the monopoly from competition. In theory, monopolists have no competitive framework for pricing and can, therefore, set whatever prices they like as the customer has no choice but to source from them. In practice, however, governments and independent watchdog bodies have imposed regulations and pressurised monopolists into keeping prices within socially acceptable limits. Even if that was not enough, the growth of international competition and the availability of alternatives also have an impact. The price and availability of fuel, oil, gas or nuclear power, for instance, all affect the price and demand for coal.

Oligopoly

The UK's deregulated telecommunications market is an oligopoly, where a small number of powerful providers dominate the market between them. Each player in the market is very conscious of the rest and makes no move without due consideration of the likely competitive response. Pricing is a particularly sensitive issue in such markets and, where oligopolists choose to price very closely with each other, accusations of collusion are bound to arise. Sudden changes in price by one organisation might be construed as a threat by the rest, but prior and public notification of price rises can be used to defuse suspicion.

These developments are not surprising, as a price war between oligopolists is something that all parties involved would prefer to avoid. Since oligopolists are likely to be fairly evenly matched, it is difficult for any one of them to be sure that it can win. While the war goes on, the consumer may be happy, but the oligopolists are simply eroding their profit margins to dangerously thin levels, not gaining any competitive ground, and causing themselves much stress about the eventual outcome.

Monopolistic competition

Most markets fall into the category of monopolistic competition where there are many competitors, but each has a product differentiated from the rest. Price is not necessarily a key factor in these markets, as product features and benefits serve to differentiate a product and diffuse the competitive effect. The emphasis in these markets is on branding or adding value so that the customer is prepared to accept a different price from its competitors. Miele, a German manufacturer of kitchen and laundry appliances, for example, has developed a reputation for selling very high-quality goods at a price premium. It can thus price its products substantially higher than those of its competitors, because Miele's customers believe that they are getting good value for money in terms of quality, durability and service.

Perfect competition

As with its direct opposite, the monopoly, perfect competition is hard to find. It implies that there are very many sellers in the market with products that are indistinguishable from each other in the eyes of the buyer. There is, therefore, little flexibility on price, because no one seller has either enough power to lead the rest or the ability to differentiate the product sufficiently to justify a different price. If one seller increases the price, either the rest will follow suit or customers will change suppliers, bringing the aberrant supplier back into line. One supplier's reduction in price will attract custom until such time as other suppliers follow suit.

To avoid this kind of powerless stalemate, most markets have evolved into offering differentiated products, even with the most uninteresting commodities (see the example at p. 130 on salt, for instance). Nor does the equality of suppliers last for long in most markets. One or two more astute or powerful suppliers usually emerge to lead the market into monopolistic competition.

■ Legal and regulatory framework

European marketers increasingly need to understand the national and European *legal and regulatory framework* when setting and adjusting prices. Aspects of this were discussed at pp. 58 *et seq.* Some organisations, such as public utilities, tend to have their pricing policies carefully scrutinised by the government to make sure that they are in the public interest, especially where a near-monopoly is operating. Even after privatisation, such organisations are not entirely free to price as they wish. As mentioned in Chapter 2, for example, the privatised water, gas, telephone and electricity companies in the UK are answerable to quasi non-governmental organisations (QUANGOs), watchdog bodies set up by the government. Even the National Lottery has its pricing, distribution of funds and profits overseen by a QUANGO, Oflot.

In the UK, resale price maintenance, that is, the power of manufacturers to determine what the retail price of their products should be, was abolished in the early 1960s. Although it was retained in a few selected product areas, over the years it has been gradually dropped. The latest area in which resale price maintenance has been abolished is vitamins, minerals and dietary supplements. The idea behind this price maintenance was to protect small, neighbourhood pharmacies by ensuring that the bigger High Street chains had no price advantage over them. Some bigger retailers resented this, however. The supermarket chain ASDA cut up to 20 per cent off the prices of brands in those categories, forcing the manufacturers to take ASDA to court to uphold their right to dictate the price. The case went against ASDA, which then had to increase prices again and await the outcome of an OFT review of the situation. In the meantime, all the major supermarkets pointedly and heavily discounted their own-label vitamins, minerals and supplements, as they were perfectly entitled to do. The price maintenance on this category of products was finally abolished in 2001.

Internal influences on the pricing decision

Pricing is, of course, also influenced by various *internal factors*. Pricing needs to reflect both corporate and marketing objectives, for example, as well as being consistent with the rest of the marketing mix. It is also important to remember, however, that pricing may also be related to costs, if the organisation is looking to generate an acceptable margin of profit. Figure 7.6 summarises the internal influences on price, and the rest of this section discusses each of them in further detail.

■ Organisational objectives

The area of *organisational objectives* is an internal influence, linked with corporate strategy. Marketing plans and objectives have to be set not only best to satisfy the customer's needs

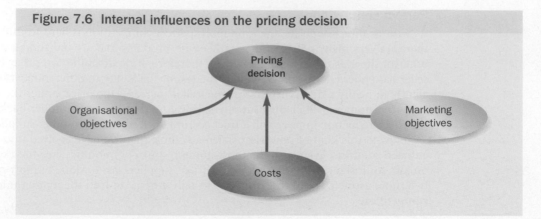

Figure 7.6 Internal influences on the pricing decision

and wants, but also to reflect the aspirations of the organisation. These two aims should not be incompatible! Organisational objectives such as target volume sales, target value sales, target growth in various market segments and target profit figures can all be made more or less attainable through the deployment of the marketing mix and particularly through price.

Corporate strategy is not concerned simply with quantifiable target setting. It is also concerned with the organisation's relative position in the market compared with the competition. Pricing may be used to help either to signal a desire for leadership (whether in terms of lowest cost or price, or superior quality) or to establish a clearly differentiated niche, which can then be emphasised and consolidated through the other elements of the marketing mix. In launching the *Midnight Sun* brand of butter onto the UK market, the Finnish company Valio used high-quality silver packaging as well as pricing the product to match the market leader, Lurpak, to communicate an upmarket image to the customer.

At the other end of the pricing spectrum, discount supermarket chains, such as Netto, Aldi, Lidl and Kwik Save, are trying to achieve objectives relating to price leadership in the market. Obviously, low pricing within their stores is their primary tool, but this can only be achieved through cost reduction (hence the minimalist retail environment and low levels of customer service) and accepting lower profit margins (1 per cent, compared with the industry average of between 5 per cent and 8 per cent). Achieving all of this is also dependent on attracting many more customers through the doors to generate the higher volume of sales needed to make a reasonable profit. The higher volumes also give the discount retailer scope for negotiating more favourable terms with the manufacturers for bulk buying.

Organisational objectives can change over time as the organisation and its markets evolve. A new business, or a new entrant into a market, faces initial problems of survival. There is a need to generate orders to use excess capacity and to establish a foothold in the market. Relatively low pricing (at the sacrifice of profit margins rather than quality) is just one possible way of doing that. Once established, the organisation can begin to think in terms of target profits and building a competitive position, which may involve a revised approach to pricing. Using price as part of an integrated marketing mix, the organisation can aim to achieve market leadership in terms of whatever criteria are important. Once leadership is achieved, objectives have to be redefined to maintain and defend that leadership, thus keeping competition at arm's length.

Corporate objectives can also have both short- and long-term dimensions to them. In the short term, for example, a small business on the verge of collapse might use low price as a survival tactic to keep it afloat, even if its longer-term ambitions include quality leadership at a higher price.

■ Marketing objectives

As the previous subsection has implied, marketing and organisational objectives are very closely interrelated and influence each other to a great extent. The distinction, though, is that while organisational objectives relate primarily to the operation, the well-being and the personality of the organisation as a whole, *marketing objectives* are more closely focused on specific target markets and the position desired within them.

Marketing objectives are achieved through the use of the whole marketing mix, not just the price element, emphasising again the need for an integrated and harmonious marketing mix. An organisation may have a portfolio of products serving different segments, each of which requires a different approach to pricing. Such a differentiated strategy can be seen in telecommunications, with British Telecommunications developing a range of tariffs for both domestic and business users to suit different needs and priorities.

eg The manufacturer of KEF Audio (UK) Ltd (**http://www.kef.com**) has a range of 40 products in its range (hi-fi stereo pairs and home theatre multi-speaker systems), plus sixteen custom installation loudspeakers (for building into room walls and use outside). Prices start at £99.99 per pair for the entry level Cresta 10 hi-fi pair, rising to £8999.99 for the flagship Reference 207 hi-fi pair. As long as the market recognises the functional and quality differences between the models in such a range, the wide spread of prices need not cause confusion or conflict as to what the organisation stands for.

In that sense, it is no different from a car manufacturer making a cheap and cheerful £8000 run-about model at one end of the range and a sleek, executive £40,000 status machine at the other. The key is to use the other elements of the marketing mix to support the price or to provide a rationale for it. The concept of the product portfolio and the management issues surrounding it are fully covered in Chapter 12.

Another product concept that might influence the pricing of a particular product over a period of time is the product lifecycle (see pp. 202 *et seq.*). In the introductory stage, a lower price might be necessary as part of a marketing strategy to encourage trial. Advertising this as 'an introductory trial price' would be one way of preventing 'low price = low quality' judgements. As the product becomes established through the growth and early maturity stages, and gains loyal buyers, the organisation may feel confident enough to raise the price. As indicated

The top end of the KEF Loudspeaker range – KEF 207 speakers.

Source: KEF Audio (UK) http://www.kef.com

earlier, this has to be done with due reference to the competitive situation and the desired positioning for both product and organisation. In late maturity and decline, it is possible that price reductions could be used to squeeze the last breath out of the dying product.

■ Costs

From a marketing perspective, price is primarily related to what the customer will be prepared to pay for a particular product offering. The actual *cost* of providing that offering cannot, however, be completely ignored. Marketing is about creating and holding a customer at a profit, and if an organisation cannot produce the product for less than it can sell it for, then its presence in that market is questionable.

The cost of producing the product, therefore, represents a floor below which the product cannot be sold profitably. However, defining cost may not be so straightforward. In a hotel, for example, the majority of its costs are fixed in the short term (staffing, facilities provision, maintenance, etc.) and are incurred regardless of the room occupancy. The variable costs associated with an actual guest (such as laundry and consumables) are relatively low. In setting the price of a room, therefore, the organisation has to reflect both the estimated variable costs and an element of contribution towards fixed costs and profit based on predicted levels of business, so that in the long run all costs are met and an acceptable level of profit is made.

In the short term, however, it may not be possible to adhere strictly to a cost-recovery formula. The price has to stand in a competitive and unpredictable environment, and may have to be flexible enough to be used as a competitive weapon or as a promotional tool to maintain volume of sales. Thus a hotel may be prepared to let a room at a discount of anything up to 40 per cent of the normal rate at a quiet time of the year when the supply of hotel rooms far exceeds the demand. This is acceptable as long as the price covers the variable costs of letting that room and makes some contribution towards fixed costs and profit. Similarly, at busy times when rooms are hard to find, hotels can afford to stand by their published rates.

Another important dimension of cost is the concept of joint or shared costs that are divided between a number of products produced by one organisation. Central provision of, for example, R&D facilities, maintenance, quality assurance and administrative costs has to be paid for through revenue generated and therefore has to be reflected in prices. Often the rules for allocating these costs across product lines are arbitrary, and not necessarily closely linked with predicted sales and the market's price sensitivity.

It is therefore clear that costs do play an important role in price setting. They will be further discussed in the following section.

The process of price setting

This section examines the stages that organisations go through to establish the price range and to set the final prices for their products. A certain amount of managerial skill is required to assess how both consumers and competitors will respond to a particular pricing decision in the context of a particular marketing mix. The pricing decision is simple only for an organisation that consciously follows the rest of the market rather than tries to lead it.

Figure 7.7 gives an overview of the managerial process involved in price setting. The first stage, setting price objectives, ensures that the corporate and marketing objectives of the organisation are taken into consideration in the pricing decision. Stage 2, estimating demand, assesses likely market potential and consumer reaction to different price levels, and was covered at pp. 228 *et seq*. Within this structure, marketing managers can then begin to define pricing policy in stage 3. This is the guiding philosophical framework within which pricing strategies and decisions are determined.

eg Despite some of the claims made about the impact of the EU in lowering price levels, car manufacturers are feeling the impact of EU-driven legislation on their costs. It is claimed that there are 282 separate pieces of legislation that could add between €4000 and €6000 per vehicle. The main thrust of the legislation is to make cars cleaner and safer. Some examples include bonnets equipped with airbags to minimise the consequences of low-impact collisions, and a device that will stop a car if the owner has not paid tax or insurance and that will also record mileage and toll charges and even monitor speeding. The question is whether the European consumer will feel the need for these benefits and whether they are prepared to pay more for them. And will non-EU car manufacturers lead or follow these changes? All these factors have to be taken into account when setting price levels (Boles, 2005).

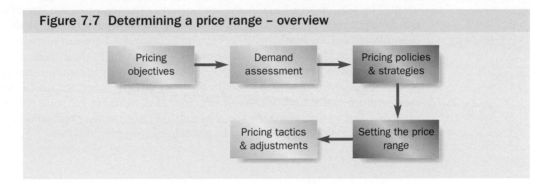

Figure 7.7 Determining a price range – overview

Pricing strategies deal with the long-term issues of positioning within the market and the achievement of corporate and marketing objectives. Establishing cost–volume–profit relationships at stage 4 checks that the estimated sales of the product can generate acceptable levels of income at any given price in order to cover costs and make an adequate profit. Implicit in all of this is the fact that pricing has to take place in a competitive environment, and thus the marketing manager must assess how competitors will react to various possible prices, and the extent to which the proposed price reflects the desired competitive positioning of the organisation and its products.

These first four stages culminate in stage 5, pricing tactics and final adjustments that focus on the practical application of pricing in the marketing mix and in the context of the market segments to be served.

Although Figure 7.7 presents a neat, logical flow, in reality the pricing decision is likely to involve many reiterations and merging of stages. Some stages may be omitted, others may be extended to take into account special conditions within a market. There may also be conflict, for example between corporate level pressure to maximise profit and competitive assessment that indicates a market that is already well served at the higher-priced end. Such conflicts need to be resolved to avoid the risks of inconsistent pricing within a poorly defined marketing mix. It is also difficult to generalise about the price-setting process, not only because it operates uniquely in every organisation, but also because it will vary greatly between different types of product and market depending on the dynamics and maturity of the specific situation.

Pricing objectives

Any planned approach needs to be founded on what has to be achieved, and that applies as much to pricing as to anything else. Its role in the marketing mix as well as its role as the generator of revenue and profit has to be defined. In that sense, price is a delicate balance between serving the customer's needs and wants and serving the need of the organisation to recoup its costs of manufacturing and marketing and to make a profit.

Price objectives, therefore, should be closely linked with organisational and marketing objectives (Baumol, 1965). Some of these may be financially based, whereas others may be related to volume of sales. If in the short term, for example, finance detects a cash flow problem, marketers may be pressurised into dropping prices to convert products into cash quickly. In the longer term, the corporate strategists may see the organisation's only means of survival to be the defeat of a major competitor, and price may be a key weapon in that. This also underlines the fact that objectives need not be absolutely fixed; they can vary in the short or long term to meet changing needs and pressures.

eg BOGOFF (buy one get one for free) offers made by retailers can be a real pain for a manufacturer trying to preserve a brand's premium market position. Lynx, Anchor, Covent Garden Soups, Johnson & Johnson, Birds Eye and Goodfella's Pizza have all been affected (Bashford, 2004). Then there are 3 for 2 offers, 50 per cent extra free and other forms of indirect discounting which have the potential to cheapen a brand's image. The supermarkets are interested in retaining competitiveness and price promotions do move stock. The side effect of low prices and offers is that competitors are often forced to match them, thus making consumers more, not less, price sensitive. It also encourages brand switching so that consumers share their loyalty between a selection of brands rather than sticking with just one choice. Of course, from the retailer's perpsective, it could reinforce the price–value store perception and thus encourage store loyalty. Nevertheless, the fear is that price promotions initially designed for the short term to create volume sales have a habit of sticking, as consumers get used to paying a lower price and that in turn shifts the focus away from brand quality to brand price. That may not be in the long-term interests of brand owners (Garner, 2004).

As with objectives in any area of management, pricing objectives must be clearly defined, detailed, time specific and never inconsistent with each other (Diamantopoulos and Mathews, 1995). Clearly, these ideals are easier to achieve in an organisation dealing with a small number of large transactions or a few products. The complexity increases, however, for an organisation dealing in a number of markets, with a large number of customers, or with a number of products. Many Japanese companies tend to take a longer-term view of pricing and consider the profit not from individual product lines alone, but from the whole portfolio of products (Howard and Herbig, 1996). By taking a long-term view, price is considered in the context of the value of the relationship over the longer term, rather than as a short-term opportunity to increase profits. Rather than letting costs dictate prices, the tendency among Japanese companies is to set the price on long-term market considerations and then to work backwards to get costs into line.

Financial objectives

Financial objectives can have both short- and long-term dimensions. For instance, the necessity to generate sufficient cash flow to fund the day-to-day operation of the organisation is a short-term objective, whereas the need to generate funds to allow reinvestment in research and development is a longer-term goal. Long-term objectives ultimately provide the means of satisfying shareholder expectations and generating the means of investing in sound foundations for the future.

Sales and marketing objectives

Clearly, sales and marketing objectives are important influencers of the pricing decision. Target market share, relative position within the market and target volume sales can all be affected through pricing choices.

Market share and positioning. An organisation's marketing objectives may relate to either maintaining or increasing market share. The implications of this for pricing need to be carefully considered. Maintenance of market share in a highly competitive market may mean that prices cannot be increased for the next trading period, or even that they have to be reduced to face competitors who undercut. Increasing market share may mean aggressively low pricing to attract switchers from competing products. Alternatively, high prices might help to establish a high-quality position that appeals to more discerning customers.

Volume sales. Seeking volume sales may well be related to market share objectives, but arises more from an operational focus on capacity. In different kinds of production activity, pricing may be used as a means of maintaining the operational smooth running of the organisation. With continuous production, involving the mass production of identical products, there is the ability to pile up stocks of the finished product until it is sold. At some point, however, the stockpiles may become unacceptably large, leading to pressure to sell at a discount to clear them. In a recession, for instance, many car manufacturers face this problem if they keep their production lines running at more or less normal capacity in the hope that the market will pick up soon.

Status quo. Linked closely with maintaining market share, the objective of preserving the *status quo* implies an organisation that is happy for things to continue as they are and does not want the market's boat to be rocked. Even a market leader may be happy simply to retain share rather than seek even more, and may prefer not to challenge a smaller, lower-priced competitor for fear of damaging its own position in the process.

One of the problems of using pricing as a means of gaining share is indeed the risk of a price war. One organisation reduces its prices and then all the others start a downward spiral of undercutting. The ultimate outcome of this is that margins become increasingly small, the weakest organisations fall by the wayside, relative market shares are unlikely to change, and nobody wins other than the consumer. This is a very expensive way of maintaining the *status quo*. Even a smaller supplier may elect to maintain the *status quo* by matching rather than challenging competitors' prices. According to Perks (1993), to win a price war, an organisation should only target weaker competitors, fight from a position of strength and extend the war over a long period to wear down the competition.

An organisation may, of course, choose to match prices in some product areas, but not in others. Even the upmarket UK supermarkets, for example, are seen to compete aggressively on price on a select number of basic product lines, yet quietly make up for this by charging price premiums on others.

Price matching rather than undercutting may well maintain the *status quo*, but it also opens the door for non-price competition, where the focus is on the other elements of the marketing mix. An organisation that can demonstrate that it offers a better product (by whatever criteria matter to the target market) can neutralise, to some extent, the market's sensitivity to price. This is difficult to do, but it does mean that it is easier to build and retain loyalty, thus defending against competitive erosion of both market share and margins. The more price sensitive the customers, the less loyal they are.

Survival

In difficult economic circumstances, survival can become the only motivating objective for an organisation. Long-term strategic objectives have no currency if you are likely to be out of business tomorrow. Imagine a small company that has found that its market does not have the potential it originally predicted. Price is a very obvious and flexible marketing mix element to change in order to keep goods flowing out and cash flowing in. Even a larger firm, such as a shipbuilder, may be prepared to suffer short-term losses to keep the operation intact, even though this cannot be sustained indefinitely without reducing the size of the operation in some way.

Demand assessment

It is important for marketers to assess the likely levels of demand for a product at any given price. Again, it must be stressed that this is not a mechanical mathematical exercise: it requires a sound and detailed understanding of both customers' and competitors' attitudes and sensitivities towards pricing as well as paying due respect to the organisation's own pricing objectives. It would be too simplistic, for example, to say that if we cut our price by 10 per cent then volume sales would rise by 15 per cent. Such a price cut might trigger a price war with an aggressive competitor, which in turn might lead to either unacceptable erosion of profit margins or loss of sales and/or market share to the competitor. Even if a price war is avoided, the price cut might serve to cheapen the product's positioning in the customer's perceptions and weaken its brand image to its long-term detriment.

eg Research by the Henley Centre suggested that different groups of consumers value time differently. 'Cash rich' but 'time poor' customers might be prepared to pay more for their products and services if they can access the service more quickly and conveniently than if they waste time queuing. This has led to some supermarkets considering the introduction of a fast-moving checkout line in which customers pay more for the benefit of moving through the line more quickly. One problem is avoiding offence to the majority of customers who want good service but are not prepared to pay a premium. There could also be problems if the majority of customers elect to take the fast lane. Research has suggested that one in four full-time workers would be interested in using such a system.

Demand assessment clearly has an important role to play in helping to justify the feasibility of certain decisions. Think about the supermarket senior managers considering whether to go ahead with the fast-track checkout idea described in the above example. Whether customers would like the idea or be offended by it is obviously one important consideration, but there are also practical issues linked with its cost-effectiveness. One in four full-time workers might well be 'interested' in the service, but how many of them would actually use it in practice? How long would the fast-track queues have to be (or indeed how short would the mainstream queues have to be!) or how long would the perceived waiting time have to be before customers decide that the fast-track service is not worth the price premium charged? The higher the price premium, the higher the customer's expectations of service quality and speed. All of this will affect decisions on how many fast-track checkouts will be needed, and at what times during the week, which in turn will affect the costs and thus the profitability of providing the service. Thus the seemingly simple question of how demand for the service will vary with the price premium charged turns into a complex equation involving many variables, some of which are more tangible and measurable than others!

Overall, then, demand assessment involves a great deal of managerial skill in defining and exploring 'what if' scenarios and has to be reviewed in the light of other elements of the price-setting process.

■ Pricing policies and strategies

Pricing policies and strategies guide and inform the pricing decision, providing a framework within which decisions can be made with consistency and with the approval of the organisation as a whole. Policies and strategies help to specify the role of pricing and its use in the context of the marketing mix (Nagle, 1987). Such frameworks are especially important in larger organisations where pricing decisions may be delegated with some discretion to line managers or sales representatives. They need sufficient rules to maintain a consistent corporate image in front of the market without being unduly restricted.

There are many situations in which a sales representative, for instance, may need policy guidance. Imagine a sales representative visiting a customer who tells him that a competitor is offering a similar product more cheaply. Company policy will help the representative to decide whether or not to get involved in undercutting or whether to sell the product benefits harder.

Other situations where policy and strategy guidelines may be of use include responding to a competitive price threat in a mass market, setting prices for new or relaunched products, modifying price in accordance with prevailing environmental conditions, using price with other marketing mix elements and, finally, using price across the product range to achieve overall revenue and profit targets. Some of these situations are discussed in more detail below. In any situation, guidelines can provide the basis for more detailed pricing strategies designed to achieve price objectives. These guidelines should be founded on sound pricing research that encompasses competitors' strategies and customers' views of value, as well as internal costs (Monroe and Cox, 2001).

eg You pay for what you get with olive oil … or do you? A preference for flavoured oils will cost you twice the price of a standard oil, and then 'infused oils' can cost a further 25–50 per cent on top of that. Flavoured oils, offering a touch of garlic, for example, can be used as a salad dressing, while spiced oils are useful for cooking, and for that benefit there is less price sensitivity. Consumers understand what they are getting and are prepared to pay a premium price for it. Infused oils are generally made from fresh raw materials with cold-pressed olive oil, and heat is added to provide a more natural tasting oil. For many consumers, the word 'infusion' creates a positive upmarket feel, linking with something organic and natural. The additional costs associated with the production of these value-added oils bear little relationship to the price premiums charged (*The Grocer*, 2005b).

New product pricing strategies

In addition to all the other pressures and risks inherent in new product development, as discussed in Chapter 6, it is important to get the launch price right as it can be difficult to change it later. It can be easy and tempting to set a low price to attract customers to a new launch, but this can establish attitudes and perceptions of the quality and positioning of the brand that would be difficult to overturn. A subsequent price rise might be viewed with some hostility by the customer. The safest route to low price entry with an option of raising it later is to make the price a promotional issue. Clearly signalling the low price as an introductory offer, a short term trial price both attracts attention and encourages trial of the new product, and when the price does rise to its 'normal' level, there is no confusion or suspicion in the customer's mind.

Another aspect of the high or low price setting decision is the likely impact on the competition. A high price might encourage them to enter the market too, as they see potentially high profit margins. The organisation launching the new product may not, however, have too much choice. Internal pressure to recoup development costs quickly may force a high price, or alternatively a price-sensitive market might simply reject a high price and force prices lower.

According to Monroe and Della Bitta (1978), much depends on how innovative the new product is. A new brand in a crowded market can be precise with its price positioning as there are many competitors to compare with, and both the price setter and the consumer can 'read' the price signals clearly. A completely unknown product, such as the very first domestic video recorder, has no such frame of reference. The price setter can work on three things. First, the prices of other domestic electrical goods might give clues as to the sort of prices consumers expect to pay. This is a tenuous link because this new product is so obviously different it may not be comparable, especially in the mind of an opinion-leading consumer. Second, market research may have been carried out to discover how enthusiastic consumers are about the new idea, and hypothetically what they would pay to possess it. Again, this may be misleading because the consumers have no experience of this product and may not themselves be able to foresee in theory how they would respond in practice. Third, the price setter can work on internal factors such as costs, breakeven analysis and return on investment. This serves as a starting point, and experience and emerging competition will allow a more realistic price structure to evolve. It is a dangerous route, however. If that cost-based price turns out to be inappropriate, rescuing the product could be almost impossible, particularly if astute competitors are learning from your mistakes and launching realistically priced products themselves.

With all this in mind, the high or low entry price decision boils down to two alternative strategies, skimming or penetration, first proposed by Dean (1950).

Price skimming. In order to skim, prices are set high to attract the least price-sensitive market segments. Such pricing might appeal, for instance, to opinion leaders who want to be seen to be first with any new product regardless of the price, or to those who seek status and see high price as the mark of an exclusive product.

Skimming has a number of advantages. It allows the organisation to establish a quality brand image that could serve as a stepping stone to future development of lower-priced, more mass-market versions. If the product in question is a difficult one to produce, then pricing to keep the market small and exclusive can also give breathing space to gain learning experience on lower volumes while still marketing the product in a real market. The risk here, of course, is that high price raises high expectations, and if that learning experience does not go well, then the market will think that the product quality is too poor or inconsistent to justify the price, a bad reputation will stick and the future of the product becomes questionable. Finally, it is easier to reduce price than to raise it. If an initial high price does not generate the required response, it can be slowly lowered until an appropriate level is found.

eg   The early entrants to the digital SLR market were priced at over £1000 and some of the semi-professional cameras cost in excess of £5000. This put them both out of reach for the mainstream camera user, so a large number of alternative 'point and shoot' cameras flooded the market with price tags well below the cheapest digital SLR. In 2003, the mould was broken when Canon launched the EOS 300D with 6.3 megapixels selling below the £1000 barrier. Canon sold 1.2 million units. As sales volumes increased, the opportunity for economies of scale and price reductions grew. A series of alternative models from competitors also followed, again below the £1000 price point. Technology has since continued to improve, with most models and now digital SLRs offering most of the features and controls found on traditional film-based SLRs. Thus the serious amateur photographer can take exactly the picture wanted, but all for less than £1000. Some models offer genuinely innovative features, such as the image stabilisation anti-shake capability available on the Konica Minolta 7D. Prices have fallen as competition has heated up, and a new user segment has been opened up as serious photographers switch, and the 'point and shoot' experts decide to rise to the challenge of the digital SLR (Taylor, 2005).

Penetration pricing. In an attempt to gain as big a market share as possible in the shortest possible time, an organisation may price aggressively below existing competition, deliberately paring its margins for the sake of volume. This is *penetration pricing*. It may be a necessary strategy if cost structures are such that a very large volume of sales is required to break even or to achieve economies of scale in production or marketing terms. It is a risky strategy because it could establish a poor-quality brand image and also, if it does not work, it would be very difficult to raise the price.

It is, nevertheless, a legitimate strategy to seek to deny the competition volume share within the market. Penetration pricing of a new product, particularly in a market where product differentiation is difficult, reduces the attractiveness of market entry to competitors unless they can be sure that they can produce and market much more efficiently and on a tighter cost base. Penetration pricing is also useful in elastic demand situations where price is a critical factor for the buyer.

As emphasised above, the choice of launch price should take into account future plans for the pricing and positioning of the product. Some products can enter a market with a skimming price and retain it, particularly luxury goods that are well differentiated from each other and have an element of uniqueness about them. The Swiss company Bueche Girod, for example, advertised a 9 carat gold and diamond ladies' watch for £1675 with a matching necklace for a further £2975. In markets where a new product has a high level of technological innovation and customers have no benchmark against which to compare prices, the introductory price may skim, but this will give way to something more competitive as rival products enter the market, economies of scale are achieved and costs reduce with the learning curve. In contrast, penetration pricing at launch sets an aggressive, value-for-money stance that the manufacturer would find hard to break away from, regardless of what the competition does. This product will always have to be priced competitively.

Product mix pricing strategies

A product that is part of a product range cannot be priced in isolation from the rest of the range. The range has to be viewed as an entity, and different products serve different purposes that come together to benefit the whole. In seeking to serve the needs of a number of market segments and build a strong competitive defence across the market, one product may be allowed to earn a relatively low return while another is skimming.

Within an individual product line (see pp. 185 *et seq.* for the distinction between range and line), such as SLR cameras, each product within the line offers additional features and their pricing needs to be spaced out accordingly. Customers see the set of products within the line and relate the price steps with additional features, benefits or quality. This may also encourage consumers to trade up to a more expensive model in the line as they begin to indulge in a type of marginal analysis: 'For an extra £20 I can have a zoom facility as well. Seems like a better deal . . .'. The process may not be so rational. As discussed at p. 225, price may be used as an indicator of quality in the absence of other knowledge or indicators. Thus a buyer may find a model within the product line at (or slightly beyond) the preconceived spending limit and feel that the best possible quality purchase has been made, regardless of whether the product benefits and features are useful or appropriate.

Rather than presenting a predetermined collection of standard products with standard prices, some organisations prefer to offer a basic-priced product to which the consumer can then add extras, each of which adds to the overall price. The beauty of this is that the basic price seems very reasonable and affordable, and thus the consumer can easily get to the stage of wanting the product. Once that stage is reached, the odd few pounds here and there for extra features seem insignificant, even though the final total price may be somewhat higher than the consumer would have been comfortable with in the first place. At least the customer is getting a personally tailored purchase.

eg Holiday packages prominently feature low prices on their brochures to attract attention and make themselves seem eminently affordable. Two weeks in the sun for only £99 per person soon increases to something closer to £300 when airport transfers and taxes are added, along with the supplements for a local departure, insurance, better-quality accommodation with a sea view, full board and an August rather than May holiday. Buying a car is also a minefield of extras. Delivery charges, taxes, registration plates, metallic paint, sunroof, alarm system and central locking are among the items that may not necessarily be quoted in the advertised price.

The problem with any such approach is knowing what to leave out and what to include in the basic price. A basic price that does not include non-optional items such as tax is likely to lead to an unimpressed customer. There is also the danger that a competitor who comes in with an all-inclusive price may be seen as attractive by customers who feel that they have been deceived by overpriced extras that are actually essentials.

Managing price changes

Prices are rarely static for long periods. Competitive pressures may force prices down, either temporarily or permanently, or new market opportunities might increase the price premium on a product. The pressure of cost inflation means that the marketing manager has to decide whether to pass these cost increases on to customers through prices charged, and when. However, changing prices can have a serious effect on profit margins and on market stability. If the changes are too significant, whether on transatlantic air fares or the price of vegetables in the local market, it is almost inevitable that competitors will respond in some way. Price changes not only cause ripples through the market, but also have an impact on sales volume. Normally, it is likely that a price cut will increase volume, and it is sometimes a very fine calculation to predict whether the profit margin earned on the extra volume gained more than compensates for the lost margin caused by the price cut. At various times, an organisation might be faced with the prospect of initiating price changes, or of responding to competitors' price changes.

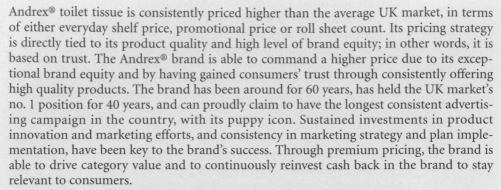

Andrex® toilet tissue is consistently priced higher than the average UK market, in terms of either everyday shelf price, promotional price or roll sheet count. Its pricing strategy is directly tied to its product quality and high level of brand equity; in other words, it is based on trust. The Andrex® brand is able to command a higher price due to its exceptional brand equity and by having gained consumers' trust through consistently offering high quality products. The brand has been around for 60 years, has held the UK market's no. 1 position for 40 years, and can proudly claim to have the longest consistent advertising campaign in the country, with its puppy icon. Sustained investments in product innovation and marketing efforts, and consistency in marketing strategy and plan implementation, have been key to the brand's success. Through premium pricing, the brand is able to drive category value and to continuously reinvest cash back in the brand to stay relevant to consumers.

Conditions in the marketplace during 2001, combined with product innovation capabilities, led Andrex® to reduce the number of sheets on a roll, proportionally reduce its pack price in line with sheet reduction, and improve product performance. By holding its price per sheet, Andrex® delivered a better product at proportionally the same price per sheet, hence maintaining its historical premium-priced and equity positioning. This launch, alongside a campaign of 'Andrex® at a price you'll love', helped to defend and grow market share into 2002, whilst maintaining brand health and brand equity (*Marketing Week*, 2001).

® Andrex and the Andrex Puppy are registered trademarks of Kimberly-Clark Ltd.

The cute puppy in this ad emphasises the soft yet strong qualities which Andrex highlights for its toilet tissue.

Source: Kimberly-Clark Ltd
http://www.andrexpuppy.co.uk

■ Setting the price range

Once the strategic direction of the pricing decision has been specified, a price range needs to be set within which the final detail of price can be established. A pricing method is needed that can generate purposeful and sound prices throughout the year. The method and its rigidity will obviously vary depending on whether the organisation is setting one-off prices for a few products or many prices for a large product range or is in a fast-moving retailing environment.

There are three main pricing methods, which take into account some of the key pricing issues already discussed. They are cost-based, demand-based and competition-based. The organisation may adopt one main method of operation or use a flexible combination depending on circumstance. Each method will be discussed in turn, once the general principles of cost–volume–profit relationships have been established.

The cost–volume–profit relationship

The demand patterns discussed at pp. 228 *et seq.*, although established and understood in their own right, also need to be understood in the context of their relationship with costs, volume of production and profit. The marketer needs to understand how the organisation's costs behave under different conditions, internally and externally generated, in order to appreciate fully the implications of marketing decisions on the operation of the organisation. The marketer should understand the different types of costs and their contribution to the pricing decision. The four most important cost concepts are fixed costs, variable costs, marginal cost and total cost. These are now defined.

Fixed costs. Fixed costs are those that do not vary with output in the short term. This category thus includes management salaries, insurance, rent, buildings and machine maintenance, etc. Once output passes a certain threshold, however, extra production facilities might have to be brought on stream and so fixed costs will then show a step-like increase.

Variable costs. Variable costs are those that vary according to the quantity produced. These costs are incurred through raw materials, components and direct labour used for assembly or manufacture. Variable costs can be expressed as a total or on a per unit basis.

Marginal cost. The change that occurs to total cost if one more unit is added to the production total is the marginal cost.

Total cost. Total cost is all the cost incurred by an organisation in manufacturing, marketing, administering and delivering the product to the customer. Total cost thus adds the fixed costs and the variable costs together.

Costs may not be the only factor involved in setting prices, but they are an important one. No organisation would wish to operate for very long at a level where its selling price was not completely recovering its costs and making some contribution towards profit.

Breakeven analysis. Breakeven analysis offers a simple, convenient approach to examining the cost–volume–profit relationship. It is a technique that shows the relationship between total revenue and total cost in order to determine the profitability of different levels of output. The breakeven point is the point at which total revenue and total cost are equal (i.e. no profit is made, nor are any losses incurred). Producing beyond this point generates increasing levels of profit.

Knowing how many units at any given price would have to be made and sold in order to break even is important, especially in new product and small business situations where an organisation has limited resources to fall back on if losses are incurred. Combining the breakeven analysis with known market and competitive conditions may make an organisation realise that it cannot compete unless it either reduces costs or develops a marketing strategy to increase volume sales.

Cost-based methods

The emphasis in *cost-based* pricing methods is on the organisation's production and marketing costs. Analysis of these costs leads to an attempt to set a price that generates a sufficient profit. The obvious disadvantage is the lack of focus on the external situation. An organisation implementing such a method would need to be very sure of the market's response. It is, however, a simple method to use, drawing the sort of direct parallels between cost and price that make accountants very happy. There are some variations in cost-based pricing.

Mark-up. Especially in the retail sector, where it can be difficult to estimate demand patterns for each product line, percentage mark-up is used as a means of price setting. This means that the retailer starts with the price paid to the supplier for the goods and then adds a percentage to reach the retail price to the customer. In fmcg high-volume markets this can be as low as 8 per cent, whereas in low-volume fashion clothing markets it can be 200 per cent or more. Mark-ups may be standard across all retailers in a particular sector, although the smaller business may have to accept a lower mark-up to compete with the retail prices of bigger operators who can negotiate better cost prices from suppliers. A retailer such as Costco that deliberately violates the mark-up traditions of its sector can be seen as initiating an all-out price war.

corporate social responsibility   in action

What price factory gate pricing?

When a market is highly competitive on price, it is natural that companies will seek to operate as cost-effectively and as cost-efficiently as possible in order to improve their profit margins or to give them scope to cut prices. For the big retailers in the UK grocery market, cost management is not just an internal issue, but extends to suppliers and those companies that service the supply chain, such as hauliers and logistics providers. The retailers are concerned to minimise the total cost of getting goods from production lines to your local supermarket shelf. An initiative that is increasingly being adopted by the major retailers is factory gate pricing (FGP).

According to Potter *et al.* (2003), FGP is:

> ... the use of an ex-works price for a product and the organisation and optimisation of transport by the purchaser to the point of delivery.

This means that the price quoted by the supplier does not include any transport costs of the finished goods; with FGP these costs are taken over and controlled by the customer which in this case is the retailer. While FGP has been successfully used in other sectors, such as car manufacture and the fashion trade, it is a relatively new phenomenon in the very fast-moving, highly complex world of grocery goods. Traditionally, suppliers took responsibility for the cost of getting goods to the retailer's distribution centre (primary distribution) and then the retailer was responsible for getting them from the distribution centre to the individual stores (secondary distribution). Under FGP, the retailer now takes over at the factory gate (in some cases, the 'factory gate' may be the supplier's

distribution centre). The retailer can then take a holistic view of both its primary and secondary distribution with respect to a large number of suppliers and manage the entire system strategically.

FGP in the UK has been initiated and driven by the biggest grocery retailers, such as Tesco and ASDA, and when it works well, there are undoubtedly a number of benefits:

- Hauliers who do a lot of FGP work for a retailer can achieve better economies of scale than they would through working for a number of suppliers independently.
- Manufacturers (especially smaller ones) can concentrate on managing their product development and production rather than worrying about managing logistics and transport costs, etc. They can benefit from the retailer's experience of complex logistics systems.
- FGP allows more consolidated loads, i.e. one lorry picking up small consignments from a number of suppliers on a specific route. ASDA's view is that '... delivering together rather than separately makes more sense in terms of costs and takes a lot of the hassle out of dealing with a big retailer' (as quoted by Pendrous, 2004).
- By taking an overview of the whole system, the retailer can cut the time which goods spend in transit, improve stock availability, and yet operate with lower stock levels in the system as well as being more responsive to fluctuations in demand.
- FGP reduces 'transport miles' because of consolidated loads and back-hauling (i.e. ensuring that lorries are always travelling as full as possible and are travelling empty as seldom as possible). This efficiency means fewer lorries on the road, which

not only reduces operating costs but also addresses environmental concerns about the number of lorries on the roads. ASDA claims to have taken €22 million out of its transport costs in 2003 through FGP, and expected to cut 20 million road miles in 2004 (Davies, 2004).
- The process of negotiating and implementing FGP can be a catalyst to better communication and trust between retailers and suppliers.
- FGP can also be a catalyst to encourage suppliers to analyse their cost base in more serious detail.

Some critics have, however, expressed concern about the implications of FGP:

- FGP requires suppliers to be quite open and transparent about their costs and thus to share what might be viewed as commercially sensitive internal information to the retailer.
- FGP could actually increase a manufacturer's cost of delivering to other non-FGP retailers because there is less volume going through the supplier's own delivery system.
- The larger retailers have long felt that they have been subsidising deliveries from manufacturers to smaller retailers because manufacturers have set their supply prices on the basis of their total costs rather than apportioning costs to specific retail customers on the basis of the 'real' cost of delivering to them. FGP strips all that out, which will increase prices charged to smaller retailers, making them even less competitive.
- These smaller non-FGP retailers might also suffer if hauliers reduce their service levels because they are losing revenue

due to volume lost to FGP business.

- FGP puts an even greater level of control and power into the large retailers' hands. Smaller suppliers might find it difficult to negotiate a 'good' FGP deal with a large retailer in the first place, which might make them more financially vulnerable. It could also make a supplier more dependent on a retailer if it is locked into that retailer's logistics system and makes the threat of de-listing even more devastating.
- There are some claims of 'enforced participation', i.e.

suppliers being told that they must accept FGP if they want to do business with a particular retailer. It is certainly in the retailer's interests to achieve the greatest economies of scale by having as many of its suppliers as possible within its FGP system.

- There are also claims that retailers are not necessarily passing on all the savings up the supply chain. It might be argued that if the retailer is using the savings to reduce retail prices to the end customer then suppliers will indirectly benefit through higher sales

volumes, but if the savings are going straight into the retailer's profit margins …

FGP is here to stay: the retailers will make sure of that. The issue, though, is whether it will be implemented and operated fairly in an industry in which there are frequent allegations about retailers abusing their power over their suppliers, and in which smaller retailers and suppliers already feel vulnerable.

Sources: Davies (2004); Jack (2004); Pendrous (2004); Potter *et al.* (2003); Wyman (2004); **http://www.scottishfoodanddrink.com**; **http://www.igd.com**.

Although this is basically a cost-based pricing method, it does not operate in isolation from external events. Retailers will be wary of implementing a mark-up that leads to a retail price way out of line with the competition, or that violates the consumer's expectations.

Cost-plus pricing. Cost-plus pricing involves adding a fixed percentage to production or construction costs. It is mainly used on large projects or for custom-built items where it is difficult to estimate costs in advance. The percentage will be agreed between buyer and seller in advance, and then just before, or after, the project's completion, buyer and seller agree the admissible costs and calculate the final price. It sounds straightforward enough, but in large, complex construction projects, it is not so easy to pin down precise costs. Problems arise where the seller is inflating prices, and it can take some time for buyer and seller to negotiate a final settlement.

An industry operating on this kind of pricing method, using a standard percentage, is oriented less towards price competition, and more towards achieving competitiveness through cost efficiency.

Experience curve pricing. Over time, and as an organisation produces more units, its experience and learning lead to more efficiency. This can also apply in service situations (Chambers and Johnston, 2000). Cost savings of 10–30 per cent per unit can be achieved each time the organisation doubles its experience.

Some organisations use this learning curve, essentially predicting how costs are going to change over time, as part of the price-planning process. Such planning means not only that the organisation is under pressure to build the volume in order to gain the experience benefits, but also that if it can gain a high market share early on in the product's life, it can achieve a strong competitive position because it gains the cost savings from learning sooner (Schmenner, 1990). It can thus withstand price competition.

Although the savings are made mainly in production, there is still a close link with the volume share and price-dominating strategies discussed earlier. Scanners and WAP phones are examples of products that are reducing their relative prices, partly because of the experience curve effect.

The problem with cost-based methods is that they are too internally focused. The price determined has to survive in a marketplace where customers and competitors have their own views of what pricing should be. An organisation's price may thus make perfect sense in cost terms and generate a respectable profit contribution, but be perceived as far too high or far too low by customers in comparison with the features and benefits offered. The price may also be way out of line compared with a competitor with a different kind of cost base.

Demand-based pricing

Demand-based pricing looks outwards from the production line and focuses on customers and their responsiveness to different price levels. Even this approach may not be enough on its own, but when it is linked with an appreciation of competition-based pricing, it provides a powerful market-oriented perspective that cost-based methods just do not provide.

At its simplest, demand-based pricing indicates that when demand is strong, the price goes up, and when it is weak, the price goes down. This can be seen in some service industries, for example, where demand fluctuates depending on time. Package holidays taken during school holidays at Christmas, Easter or in the summer when demand is high are more expensive than those taken at other times of the year when it is more difficult for families to get away. Similarly, holidays taken when weather conditions at the destination are less predictable or less pleasant are cheaper because there is less demand. Even within the course of a single day, travel prices can vary according to demand. Tickets on shuttle flights between Heathrow and UK regional airports vary in price depending on when the peak times for business travellers occur.

marketing **in action**

Flying just above the breakeven line

The budget airline model is the same: single fleets of planes for better buying power and lower servicing costs, fast turnarounds, use of cheap, sometimes even remote airports, no-frills, everything on board costs extra, and in return, the traveller gets offered very low fares that rise as the flight fills up. Prices are flexible depending upon demand. Book early and prices can be very low, book when demand is expected to be high (around Christmas, for example) and they can be very high. Weekends will cost more than weekdays on any leisure routes. The purpose is to fill all seats and generate marginal income rather than no income at all to contribute towards overheads. One of your authors tried to change the return flight with a low-cost airline and was quoted nearly £150 on a ticket originally priced at £30!

Low-cost airlines were launched in Europe after the domestic airline market was deregulated in 1997. Ryanair and easyJet were the pioneers, and the business model was unashamedly based on that used by South West Airlines and ValuJet (now AirTran) in the US. Interestingly, these two US airlines are starting to move upmarket, whereas the evidence from Europe is that the same or an even more downmarket position will be pursued. Ryanair has introduced

fixed seats (i.e. the seating configuration within the cabin cannot be changed) as they cost less to maintain, and consideration is even being given to eliminating all baggage other than carry-on bags.

In Europe, the market is still in transition as new entrants launch themselves, quickly run into trouble and then disappear, just as in the US where 32 out of 34 budget airlines did not survive very long. The main reason reflects low fares, low margins and then failure to fill the plane. Some of the doomed budget airlines offered crazy prices even compared with easyJet and Ryanair in a desperate bid to build capacity and a customer base. The expansion of the EU to create an even bigger deregulated aviation market has fuelled a further round of route expansion. Whereas in the early period of European budget airline development competition was with the main network carriers such as British Airways, now it is competition with other budget airlines that causes the biggest headaches, as often it is only route and price that are the distinguishing features. Ryanair and easyJet also, however, emphasise service reliability and performance, in sharp contrast to a smaller airline that has real problems offering its service if one of its two planes has a technical difficulty!

The growth in the budget sector is probably far from over. Ryanair ordered 100 Boeing 737s and

By keeping its fleet up to date and constantly opening new routes, easyJet maintains its market position. Shown here is the Boeing 737-700.

Source: © easyJet airline company http://www.easyjet.co.uk

easyJet 107 Airbus A319s, all to be delivered by 2008. This would provide an additional capacity of 250,000 passengers per plane per year on top of the 44 million people carried by budget airlines in 2003–04. That means passenger numbers would have to double to ensure the planes earn their keep. Achieving this growth will not prove easy, as the current pattern is dominated by British/Irish operators and other nations have a different propensity to travel for leisure. Finding slots at the main airports might also prove a problem, as often, as at Charles de Gaulle airport, despite paying the same landing fees as the main carriers, budget operators are allocated gates well away from the main terminals. Gaining greater access to airports in France and Germany will be essential if low-cost carriers are to expand.

One of the 50 or so low-cost carriers in Europe is Aeris in France. Originally a charter operator, it decided to try low-cost flights from Paris to the south of France. Although Ryanair and easyJet flew to some of the destinations, such as Perpignan, Aeris regarded Air France as its main competitor. Air France offered four daily round trips to Paris and Aeris offered three, but the price difference was as high as €200. Despite the price differential, however, Aeris managed to fill only 60 per cent of its seats on average, and flights ceased in 2003. Air France's dominance and state support has made it tough for smaller airlines in France. Three airlines other than Aeris – Air Liberté, Air Littoral and AOM – also filed for bankruptcy in 2003 alone. Until that grip is broken it is likely to be difficult for French-based budget airlines to succeed.

Sources: Arnold (2003); *The Economist* (2004); Rowling (2003).

There is an underlying assumption that an organisation operating such a flexible pricing policy has a good understanding of the nature and elasticity of demand in its market, as already outlined at pp. 228 *et seq.*

One form of demand-based pricing is psychological pricing. This is very much a customer-based pricing method, relying as it does on the consumer's emotive responses, subjective assessments and feelings towards specific purchases. Clearly, this is particularly applicable to products with a higher involvement focus, i.e. those that appeal more to psychological than to practical motives for purchase. Thus, for example, high prices for prestige goods help to reinforce the psychological sense of self-indulgence and pampering that is such an important part of the buying experience. At the other end of the scale, lots of big splashy '10% off' or 'buy one get one free' offers scattered around a retail store on key items helps to create and reinforce a value-for-money image and the sense of getting a bargain.

Competition-based pricing

This chapter has frequently warned of the danger of setting prices without knowing what is happening in the market, particularly with respect to one's competitors. According to Lambin (1993), there are two aspects of competition that influence an organisation's pricing. The first is the *structure of the market*. Generally speaking, the greater the number of competitors, i.e. the closer to perfect competition the market comes, the less autonomy the organisation has in price setting. The second competitive factor is the product's *perceived value* in the market. In other words, the more differentiated an organisation's product is from the competition, the more autonomy the organisation has in pricing it, because buyers come to value its unique benefits.

eg The $55bn global toy industry has become very cut-throat with considerable price competition that is in the process of restructuring distribution channels. In the EU, speciality toy shops accounted for 38.6 per cent of traditional toy and game sales in 2003, down 4 percentage points from 1998. It is this sector that is feeling the squeeze, while supermarkets and hypermarkets increased their share by 4 points to 25 per cent. This pattern has been repeated in the US where Wal-Mart and Target have made big inroads into the sector using their buying power to force prices downward and being more selective about which products they decide to stock. Some of the pricing approaches employed are considered predatory, as the big retailers get toys in early and cut prices deep. The greater the concentration of buying power in the retail sector, the more powerful pricing forces will become.

One of the specialist retailers that could come under threat is the category killer Toys 'Я' Us with its 1500 stores. In the US, it has a 15 per cent market share, but this is under severe threat and one of the company's options could be to retrench back to the US to concentrate on competing with Wal-Mart head-on. Some toy manufacturers are delighted to supply the large superstores as the space devoted to toys is large and high volumes are shifted. This is important to manufacturers in a market which is contracting as 8–12 year-olds look for high-technology toys and games. Research has indicated that top of an 8–11-year-old's wish list is a mobile phone, a DVD player and a gift voucher (Foster, 2004; Hodgson, 2004).

Most markets are becoming increasingly competitive, and a focus on competitive strategy in business planning emphasises the importance of understanding the role of price as a means of competing. An organisation that decides to become a cost leader in its market and to take a price-oriented approach to maintaining its position needs an especially efficient intelligence system to monitor its competitors. Levy (1994) looked at organisations that offer price guarantees in B2B markets. Any supplier promising to match the lowest price offered by any of its rivals needs to know as much as possible about those rivals and their cost and pricing structures in order to assess the likely cost of such a promise.

In consumer markets, market research can certainly help to provide intelligence, whether this means shopping audits to monitor the comparative retail prices of goods, or consumer surveys or focus groups to monitor price perceptions and evolving sensitivity relative to the rest of the marketing mix. Data gathering and analysis can be more difficult in B2B markets, because of the flexibility of pricing and the degree of customisation of marketing packages to an individual customer's needs in these markets. There is a heavy reliance on sales representatives' reports, information gained through informal networks within the industry and qualitative assessment of all those data.

Competitive analysis can focus on a number of levels, at one end of the spectrum involving a general overview of the market, and at the other end focusing on individual product lines or items. Whatever the market, whatever the focus of competitive analysis, the same decision has to be made: whether to price at the same level as the competition, or above or below them.

An organisation that has decided to be a price follower must, by definition, look to the market for guidance. The decision to position at the same level as the competition, or above or below them, requires information about what is happening in the market. This is pricing based on the 'going rate' for the product. Conventional pricing behaviour in the market is used as a reference point for comparing what is offered, and the price is varied from that. Each supplier to the market is thus acting as a marker for the others, taking into account relative positioning and relative offering. Effectively, pricing is based on collective wisdom, and certainly for the smaller business it is easier to do what everyone else does rather than pay for market research to prove what the price ought to be, and run the risk of getting it wrong. In a seaside resort, for example, a small bed and breakfast hotel is unlikely to price itself differently from the one next door, unless it can justify doing so by offering significantly better services. Within an accepted price range, however, any one organisation's move may not be seen as either significant or threatening by the rest.

The dangers of excessive price competition, in terms of both the cost to the competitors and the risk to a product's reputation, thus attracting the 'wrong' kind of customer, have already been indicated. But if neither the organisation nor the product has a particularly high reputation, or if the product has few differentiating features, then price competition may be the only avenue open unless there is a commitment to working on the product and the marketing mix as a whole.

■ Pricing tactics and adjustments

Pricing tactics and adjustments are concerned with the last steps towards arriving at the final price. There is no such thing as a fixed price; price can be varied to reflect specific customer needs, the market position within the channel of distribution or the economic aspects of the deal.

Particularly in B2B markets, *price structures* give guidelines to the sales representative to help in negotiating a final price with the customer. The concern is not only to avoid overcharging or inconsistent charging, but to set up a framework for pricing discretion that is linked with the significance of the customer or the purchase situation.

A variation on price structures, *special adjustments* to list or quoted prices can be made either for short-term promotional purposes or as part of a regular deal to reward a trade customer for services rendered.

At one extreme, price structure may involve a take it or leave it, single price policy such as IKEA operates. It offers no trade discount for organisational purchasers, seeing itself largely as a consumer-oriented retailer. Compare this with some industrial distributorships, which offer different levels of discount to different customers. Most try to find a middle ground, between consistent pricing and flexibility for certain key customers.

Discounts consist of reductions from the normal or list price as a reward for bulk purchases or the range of distribution services offered. The level and frequency of discounts will vary according to individual circumstances. Blois (1994) points out that most organisations offer discounts from list prices and that these discounts form an important part of pricing strategies. There are examples of both types of discount in consumer and B2B markets. The promotional technique of 'buy two and get the third free' is effectively a bulk discount and is found on many products in many supermarkets. Similarly, a promotion that requires a consumer to collect tokens then send them off for a cash rebate is a form of cumulative discount. In B2B markets, a retailer may be offered a twelfth case of a product free if eleven are initially purchased (quantity discount), or a rebate on the number of cases of a product sold by the end of the trading period (cumulative discount).

Allowances are similar to discounts, but usually require the buyer to perform some additional service. Trade-in, for example, makes a transaction more complicated because it involves the exchange of a good as well as money for whatever is being purchased. It is a common practice in the car market, where consumers trade in their old cars as part exchange for a new one. The qualitative judgement of the value of the trade-in disguises the discount offered, and it is further complicated by the attitudes of the respective parties. A car that is an unreliable liability to the owner may have potential to a dealer with a particular customer in mind or a good eye for scrap. The owner thinks they are getting a good deal on the old car, while the dealer thinks they can actually recoup the trade-in value and make a bit more besides.

Finally, geographic adjustments are those made, especially in B2B markets, to reflect the costs of transport and insurance involved in getting the goods from buyer to seller. In consumer markets, they can be seen in the case of mail-order goods, which carry an extra charge for postage and packing. Zoned pricing relates price to the geographic distance between buyer and seller. A DIY warehouse, for example, might add a £5 delivery charge to any destination within five miles, £7.50 for up to ten miles, £10 for up to fifteen miles and so on, reflecting the extra time and petrol involved in delivering to more distant locations. Operating a single zone means that the delivery price is the same regardless of distance, as is the case with the domestic postal service, which charges on the weight of letters rather than the destination. The international mail service does, however, operate on a multiple-zone basis, dividing the world up into areas and pricing to reflect different transport costs.

Chapter summary

■ Pricing is a broad area, defined as covering anything of value that is given in exchange for something else. 'Price' is a blanket term to cover a variety of labels and is a key element in the marketing exchange. Price is usually measured in money, but can also involve the bartering of goods and services.

■ Price serves a number of purposes. It is a measure against which buyers can assess the product's promised features and benefits and then decide whether the functional, operational, financial or personal advantages of purchase are worthwhile or not. The seller faces the difficult job of setting the price in the context of the buyers' price perceptions and sensitivities. In a price-sensitive market, finding exactly the right price is essential if customers are to be attracted and retained. The seller also needs to remember that price may involve the buyer in more than the handing over of a sum of money. Associated costs of installation, training and disposal of old equipment, for example, are taken into account in assessing the price of a B2B purchase.

- The external influences influencing the pricing decision include customers, channels of distribution, competition and legal and regulatory constraints.

- Corporate and marketing objectives set the internal agenda in terms of what pricing is expected to achieve, both for the organisation as a whole and for the specific product. The organisation's costs relating to the development, manufacture and marketing of the product will also affect price.

- The process of price setting involves a great deal of research and managerial skill. The five stages of the process are setting pricing objectives; estimating demand; setting pricing policies and strategies; determining the price range; and finally, defining any pricing tactics and adjustments that may be necessary.

Questions for review and discussion

7.1 Define *price elasticity*. Why is this an important concept for the marketer?

7.2 To what extent and why do you think that *costs* should influence pricing?

7.3 Define the various stages involved in *setting prices*.

7.4 Find an example of a *price-sensitive* consumer market. Why do you think this market is price sensitive and is there anything that the

manufacturers or retailers could do to make it less so?

7.5 Choose a consumer product and explain the role that pricing plays in its marketing mix and *market positioning*.

7.6 To what extent and why do you think that a marketing manager's pricing decision should be influenced by the competition's pricing?

case study 7

An away win for the OFT

Love it or hate it, Manchester United is big business. It is a worldwide brand name that generates a loyalty and affinity that enables the soccer club, like many others, to develop merchandise, media products and alliances with service providers on a scale not thought possible in the era before the English Premier League was established. Merchandising sales have been helped as soccer has repositioned itself from a working-class game, sometimes dominated by violent youth, to a family entertainment dominated by middle and higher earners. For many clubs, what happens on the pitch or terrace is just a small part of a powerful marketing organisation.

Manchester United can be considered a typical 'passion brand', characterised by a sometimes fanatical following and a strong sense of belonging that is far removed from the discerning and rational consumer. Its following spreads far wider than its Old Trafford ground

and many supporters have never seen a live game. Even passion brands are not immune from criticism, however, and there is a risk of over-commercialisation, which can undermine the special relationship between the club and the consumer.

A major source of revenue is the sale of replica kit. The market for replica shirts alone is worth over £210m per annum. Between 1993 and 2001, Manchester United introduced about twenty new kits, and at around £40 per shirt, that represented a major investment for its keenest fans. One really dedicated fan even paid £4600 for a second-hand Manchester United shirt, although admittedly it was the one worn by Ole Gunnar Solskjaer when he scored the injury-time winner against Bayern Munich in the 1999 Champion's League Final in Barcelona. The incentive for clubs to change kits is clear and does not necessarily relate to fashion or sponsorship: the absence of a new Manchester United strip in the 1997–98 season meant a drop in merchandise sales of 16 per cent from the previous year's level.

Fans had long been grumbling about the high prices of replica kit and allegations of price-fixing had been rife. In 1999, the Football Association, the Premier League and the Scottish Football Association thus agreed to try to stop price-fixing for replica football kits, for instance by stopping practices such as shops being threatened with not receiving supplies if they slash prices. Prices had been expected to drop by up to one-third – but it didn't happen. Table 7.1 shows 2001 and 2005 prices for an adult replica shirt.

Table 7.1 Replica football shirt prices: 2001 vs 2005 (selected clubs: adult men's shirt)

Club	2001 price	2005 price
Arsenal	£39.99	£45.00
Chelsea	£39.99	£44.99*
Derby County[†]	£39.99	£44.99
Leeds United[†]	£39.99	£35.00
Manchester United	£48.00	£44.99*
Newcastle United	£40.00	£40.00
West Ham United	£39.99	£44.99

* VAT added at 17.5 per cent where price has been quoted excluding VAT on the website.
[†] Club not in English Premier League in 2005–06 season (all clubs cited were in the English Premier League in 2001).
Sources: online club shops and **http://www.kitbag.com**, accessed 2 October 2005.

According to Arkell (2001), the biggest winners are the manufacturers rather than the football clubs. If a shirt costs £40, about £20 goes to the manufacturer (yet it allegedly costs only about £7 to make one), about £13 goes to the retailer and £7 on tax, leaving a minimal amount for the club. The clubs gain from selling licences to the manufacturers in the first place and from royalties on each kit sold. The clubs also obviously earn more by cutting out the middleman and selling kit via their own retail stores and mail-order operations.

Nevertheless, as a result of years of criticism from fans that top clubs had been financially exploiting them, a charter, incorporated into the Premiership rules, came into force in the 2000–01 season covering a range of issues such as ticket prices, complaints handling and replica kit. In terms of replica kit, the charter states that they will have a minimum lifespan of two years and carry a sticker on them stating the launch date. Premiership clubs could, therefore, be fined for changing their kits too regularly or for failing to conduct research among fans on the design and number of new strips. The charter does not, however, deal with the issue of pricing replica kit.

In addition, the Competition Act came into force in 2000 which allows fines of up to 10 per cent of turnover to be imposed on companies proved to have been involved in price-fixing. In September 2001, OFT officials raided the British offices of sportswear retailers and manufacturers, including JJB Sports, Nike and Umbro, as part of a probe into price-fixing of replica sports kits. While all this was happening, sales of replica football kits were falling, partly because of changing fashions (hardly a consideration for the die-hard fans, surely) and partly because of parents rebelling against the cost. A Mintel survey showed that 43 per cent of respondents with families felt that football clothing was too expensive. It is interesting to note that Manchester United found that replica kit sales through its own outlets were holding up well, but sales through other retailers were declining.

Meanwhile, the OFT enquiry took two years. In August 2003, it was announced that price fixing had gone on, especially during key periods such as the launch of new kits and England's qualifying for Euro 2000. Fines totalling £18.6m were imposed on ten companies, including a variety of sportswear manufacturers and retailers, as well as on Manchester United and the Football Association. The biggest fines were handed out to JJB Sports, the UK's largest sportswear retailer (£8.37m), Umbro, the licensed manufacturer of replica shirts (£6.64m), and Manchester United (£1.65m). The Football Association was also fined £158,000 for participating in the illegal agreements (Black, 2003; Butler, 2004). Just over a year later, in October 2004, appeals against the decisions had been heard, but the decisions were largely upheld. A further appeal in May 2005 resulted in reductions in some of the fines, with JJB Sports' fine reduced to £6.4m, for example (Bowers, 2005).

The OFT was confident that its ruling would bring prices down in the marketplace. Draw your own conclusions from the 2005 prices quoted in Table 7.1 about what has happened to prices in club shops. It must be said, however, that JJB Sports' online shop was selling Arsenal shirts for £37, Chelsea for £25, Manchester United for £33 and Newcastle United for £25 (kit for the other clubs featured in our table was not available on this website), so the bargains are out there at last, if you search for them.

As Fresco (2001) points out, many clubs are trying to protect their revenue by diversifying their range of merchandise. Now that we've told you about them, can you continue to live without a three-pack of Chelsea women's thongs for £7.65 (excluding VAT, and out of stock in all sizes at the time of writing!), Shep Woolley's

'Pompey' Til I Die' CD for £4.00 from Portsmouth, or Sunderland's £5.99 DVD of the 1973 Cup Final? Leeds United has good reason to want to forget the 1973 Cup Final, but does offer twelve issues of the *Leeds Leeds Leeds* magazine for £39.

Sources: Arkell (2001); Black (2003); Bowers (2005); Butler (2004); Chaudhary (2000); Farrell (1998); Fresco (2001); Mintel (2000); Mitchell (1998); Narain (2001); Porter (2004).

Questions

1 Why is merchandise so important to a Premier League soccer club? Why do clubs go into retailing and mail-order when their core business is football?

2 What do you think are the internal factors influencing a club like Manchester United's pricing decision for replica kit?

3 What kind of factors are consumers taking into account when assessing the retail price of replica kit? Do you think they are sensitive to price or to the number of new kits that come out?

4 Why do you think the 2005 kit prices listed in Table 7.1 are still so similar from club to club? Undertake an informal survey of the current price of a Manchester United shirt on e-tail sites and in local retail stores. Analyse and discuss your findings.

References for chapter 7

Arkell, H. (2001), 'Raid on Replica Soccer Kit Companies as "Price-Fixing" is Probed', *Evening Standard*, 6 September, p. 18.

Arnold, M. (2003), 'Aeris Files for Bankruptcy', *Financial Times*, 23 September, p. 1.

Bashford, S. (2004), 'Price Promotion: The Brand Killer', *Marketing*, 30 June, p. 42.

Baumol, W.J. (1965), *Economic Theory and Operations Analysis*, Prentice Hall.

Black, D. (2003), 'Man United Fined over Football Kit Price-fixing Cartel', *The Guardian*, 2 August, p. 7.

Blois, K. (1994), 'Discounts in Business Marketing Management', *Industrial Marketing Management*, 23 (2), pp. 93–100.

Boles, T. (2005), 'EU Laws Will Drive Car Prices Up by €6,000', *Sunday Business*, 17 April, p. C3.

Bowers, S. (2005), 'JJB Fights On Despite Cut in Replica Fine', *The Guardian*, 20 May, p. 20.

Business Europe (2004), 'Web Bookings Fuel Budget Hotel Growth', *Business Europe*, 23 November, accessed via http://www.businesseurope.com.

Butler, S. (2004), 'Retailer Fights Price-fix Finding', *The Times*, 2 October, p. 58.

Chambers, S. and Johnston, R. (2000), 'Experience Curves in Services: Macro and Micro Level Approaches', *International Journal of Operations and Production Management*, 20 (7), pp. 842–59.

Chaudhary, V. (2000), 'Greedy Clubs are Called to Account: Premier Fans Promised New Deal over Ticket Prices and Replica Kits', *The Guardian*, 17 August, p. 1.32.

Davies, C. (2004), 'Cutting-edge Logistics: Factory Gate Pricing', *Supply Chain Europe*, July/August, pp. 15–17.

Dean, J. (1950), 'Pricing Policies for New Products', *Harvard Business Review*, 28 (November), pp. 45–53.

Diamantopoulos, A. and Mathews, B. (1995), *Making Pricing Decisions: A Study of Managerial Practice*, Chapman & Hall.

The Economist (2004), 'Turbulent Skies', *The Economist*, 10 July, p. 68.

Erickson, G.M. and Johansson, J.K. (1985), 'The Role of Price in Multi-attribute Product Evaluations', *Journal of Consumer Research*, 12, pp. 195–9.

Farrell, S. (1998), 'Clubs Accused of Fixing Replica Soccer Kit Prices', *The Times*, 24 February, p. 6.

Foster, L. (2004), 'Cut-throat Pricing is Driving Speciality Toy Shops Out of Business and Squeezing Manufacturers', *Financial Times*, 17 September, p. 17.

Fresco, A. (2001), 'Football Club Profits Hit as Fans Rip Off Replica Shirts', *The Times*, 3 April, p. 9.

Garner, E. (2004), 'A Promo Too Far', *Brand Strategy*, April, p. 35.

Glasgow, F. (2004), 'Ditch the Doilies, Darling', *Financial Times*, 11 December, p. 15.

The Grocer (2005a), 'Tsunami Hits Fishing', *The Grocer*, 8 January, p. 54.

The Grocer (2005b), 'Oils Buoyed by Natural Infusiasm', *The Grocer*, 23 July, p. 44.

Hodgson, J. (2004), 'Bidders Circle European Stores of Toys R Us', *Sunday Business*, 7 November, p. C1.

Howard, C. and Herbig, P. (1996), 'Japanese Pricing Policies', *Journal of Consumer Marketing*, 13 (4), pp. 5–17.

Jack, S. (2004), 'FGP Grows its Supporters', *Motor Transport*, 4 January, p. 16.

Lambin, J.J. (1993), *Strategic Marketing: A European Approach*, McGraw-Hill.

Levy, D.T. (1994), 'Guaranteed Pricing in Industrial Purchases: Making Use of Markets in Contractual Relations', *Industrial Marketing Management*, 23 (4), pp. 307–13.

Marketing Week (2001), 'Andrex Ads to Focus on Price Cuts', *Marketing Week*, 9 August, p. 7.

Marketing Week (2003), 'Frills-seeking Antics of the Budget Hotels', *Marketing Week*, 25 September, p. 19.

Marketing Week (2005), 'Budget Hotels Battle to Get Brits into Bed', *Marketing Week*, 17 March, p. 25.

Mintel (2000), 'The Football Business', 8 November, accessed via http://www.mintel.com.

Mitchell, A. (1998), 'Sky's the Limit for New Breed of Passion Brands', *Marketing Week*, 17 September, pp. 44–5.

Monroe, K. and Cox, J. (2001), 'Pricing Practices that Endanger Profits', *Marketing Management*, September/October, pp. 42–6.

Monroe, K. and Della Bitta, A. (1978), 'Models for Pricing Decisions', *Journal of Marketing Research*, 15 (August), pp. 413–28.

Montgomery, S.L. (1988), *Profitable Pricing Strategies*, McGraw-Hill.

Nagle, T.T. (1987), *The Strategy and Tactics of Pricing*, Prentice Hall.

Narain, J. (2001), 'United are Beaten at Home by Tesco Bonanza for Families as Supermarket Sells Replica Kit at Half Price', *Daily Mail*, 30 April, p. 23.

Nimer, D. (1975), 'Pricing the Profitable Sale Has a Lot to Do with Perception', *Sales Management*, 114 (19), pp. 13–14.

Pendrous, R. (2004), 'Asda Presses Ahead with Factory Gate Pricing', *Food Manufacture*, October, p. 21.

Perks, R. (1993), 'How to Win a Price War', *Investor's Chronicle*, 22 October, pp. 14–15.

Porter, A. (2004), 'English Teams Top Euro Ticket Price League', *Sunday Times*, 15 August, p. 11.

Potter, A., Lalwani, C., Disney, S. and Velho, H. (2003), 'Modelling the Impact of Factory Gate Pricing on Transport and Logistics', *proceedings of 8th International Symposium of Logistics*, Seville, 6–8 July, pp. 625–31.

Rowling, M. (2003), 'French Airlines Struggle to Go Low-cost', *BBC News*, 18 September, accessed via http://www.bbc.co.uk.

Schmenner, R. (1990), *Production/Operations Management*, New York: Macmillan.

Singh, S. (2001), 'The Move to Cheaper Sleeping', *Marketing Week*, 14 June, pp. 38–9.

Stevenson, R. (2005), 'Budget Hotel Boom Creates 4,500 Jobs', *The Independent*, 15 March, p. 38.

Taylor, P. (2005), 'A Snapshot of the SLR Market', *Financial Times*, 6 May, p. 16.

Thompson, K. and Coe, B. (1997), 'Gaining Sustainable Competitive Advantage Through Strategic Pricing: Selecting a Perceived Value Price', *Pricing Strategy and Practice*, 5 (2), pp. 70–9.

Upton, G. (2001), 'Budget Hotels, But They Have All the Frills', *Evening Standard*, 19 February, p. 72.

Wyman, V. (2004), 'He Who Pays the Piper …', *Food Manufacture*, January, pp. 35–6.

Zeithaml, V.A. (1988), 'Consumer Perceptions of Price, Quality and Value', *Journal of Marketing*, 52 (July), pp. 2–22.

chapter 8

place

learning objectives

This chapter will help you to:

1 define what a channel of distribution is and understand the forms it can take in both consumer and B2B markets;

2 discuss the rationale for using intermediaries and their contribution to efficient and effective marketing efforts;

3 differentiate between types of intermediary and their roles; and

4 appreciate the factors influencing channel design, structure and strategy and the effect of conflict and cooperation within channels.

Introduction

Shopaholics of the world unite! Retailing is one of the highest-profile areas of marketing and, like advertising, has had a tremendous impact on society, culture and lifestyles. To some, shopping is an essential social and leisure activity, while to others, it is a chore. It offers some a chance to dream and, for most of us, an opportunity at some time or other to indulge ourselves. We often take for granted the availability of wide ranges of goods and know that if we search hard enough, we will find just what we are looking for. Some people, indeed, find that half the fun is in the searching rather than the ultimate purchase.

Although to us as consumers retailing means fun, excitement and the opportunity to splash out vast quantities of cash (thanks to plastic cards!), it is a very serious business for the managers and organisations that make it happen. It is often the last stage in the channel of distribution before consumption, the final link in fulfilling the responsibility of a marketing-oriented supply chain to get the product to the customer in the right place at the right time. The retail store is thus at the end of an extremely efficient and sophisticated distribution system designed to move goods down the distribution channel from manufacturer to consumer. A retailer can be just one of the intermediaries whose role is to facilitate that movement of goods and to offer them at a time and place (and at a price) that is convenient and attractive to the end consumer.

In considering how and why goods get to consumers, the chapter begins with a definition of channels of distribution, highlighting the roles played by different types of intermediaries, and looks at the relative merits of using intermediaries compared with direct selling. Attention then turns to the strategic decision-making necessary to design and implement a channel strategy. Although channels of distribution are important economic structures, they are also social systems involving individuals and organisations. This chapter, therefore, also considers issues associated with the general conduct of the relationship.

eg Perhaps one of the killer questions is 'if this retailer did not currently exist, would you invent it?' Some have argued that if that question was asked about WHSmith, the answer might not be positive. Sales have been static and profit margins squeezed by increased competition. The problem is that WHSmith has yet to redefine its core merchandise proposition in a retail environment that has changed dramatically from the days when it dominated the high street for books, cards, music and stationery supplies. New competitors such as Staples for stationery and Borders for books have been slicker and more aggressive, while supermarkets such as Tesco have been nibbling at the other end, offering wide ranges of magazines and cards, and unbeatable deals on a small number of the very best sellers in CDs/DVDs and books. WHSmith is no longer regarded as the automatic specialist destination store for anything in particular.

As part of a recovery plan, the focus is on merchandising. Products are to be presented more attractively, shelf heights have increased to obtain more turnover per square foot, and availability is to be improved through better supply chain management. Stockouts were frequent and, despite having 545 stores, the top-selling lines were available in just 92 of them (Ryle, 2004)! That is being corrected, but it's about more than this. The essence of the shopping experience at WHSmith is having to be re-examined to position it against the new rivals. For the kind of standard merchandise that WHSmith sells, retail differentiation is difficult to achieve, especially when it is so widely and cheaply available elsewhere. It could be that WHSmith cannot survive in its current high street form (Barnes, 2005a; *Marketing Week*, 2004b).

Channel structures

A marketing channel can be defined as the structure linking a group of individuals or organisations through which a product or service is made available to the consumer or industrial user. The degree of formality in the relationships between the channel members can vary significantly, from the highly organised arrangements in the distribution of fmcg products through supermarkets, to the more speculative and transient position of roadside sellers of fruit and vegetables.

eg When Carrefour decided to expand into China, it found that a number of factors influencing its retail and distribution strategy differed from those it experienced in its domestic market, France. Although the Chinese market is huge, with potentially 1.3 billion consumers, it is widely dispersed and the distances between major population centres can be vast. Given the poor transportation infrastructure, the notion of national buying and local distribution is not as feasible in China as it is in France. For some goods, Carrefour has had to select three different suppliers to provide the same product to its 61 hypermarkets spread across 15 Chinese cities. Even then, lorries are often delayed due to road congestion, and at times some lorries have been 'lost' altogether. While a typical store in France might receive eight to ten lorries per day from a regional distribution centre, a Chinese branch might receive up to 300 deliveries per day direct from suppliers (although some deliveries are made by bicycle!).

Carrefour also found wide differences in income levels, local customs, food tastes, local bureaucracy and consumer demands between Chinese regions. In the larger cities such as Shanghai and Beijing, consumer tastes are adapting and becoming much more sensitive to Western food retail formats, which is not surprising, given that there are 25 hypermarkets in Shanghai alone. In some of the 34 provinces, however, the experience is much more limited. There is still a preference, for example, for fresh produce bought from street markets, and since many households do not have freezers, it is rare to find demand for a wide range of frozen food. Unlike in France, the product assortment offered tends to vary by region and according to local circumstances. Despite these differences, Carrefour plans to expand further in China and sees the potential for 500 retail outlets ultimately (Hollinger, 2005).

This is on the back of a wave of growth; the number of modern trade outlets increased by over 40 per cent in 2003 alone (Longo, 2004). Although a typical store in China generates about 60 per cent of the turnover of a similarly sized store in France, the average spend is four times lower. The density of population within a store's catchment area, however, provides considerable compensation (Goldman, 2001; Hunt, 2001).

The route selected to move a product to market through different intermediaries is known as the *channel structure*. The chosen route varies according to whether the organisation is dealing with consumer or B2B goods. Even within these broad sectors, different products might require different distribution channels.

■ Consumer goods

The four most common channel structures in consumer markets are shown in Figure 8.1. As can be seen, each alternative involves a different number of intermediaries, and each is appropriate to different kinds of markets or selling situations. Each will now be discussed in turn.

Figure 8.1 Channel structures for consumer goods

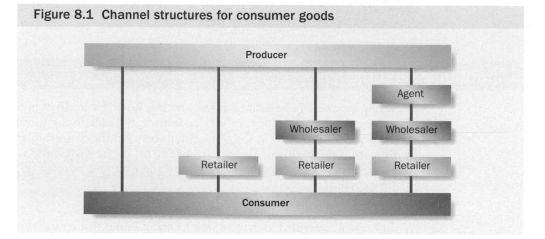

Producer–consumer (direct supply). In the producer–consumer direct supply channel, the manufacturer and consumer deal directly with each other. There are many variants on this theme. It could be a factory shop or a pick-your-own fruit farm. Door-to-door selling, such as that practised by double-glazing companies, and party plan selling, such as Tupperware and Ann Summers parties, are all attempts by producers to eliminate intermediaries.

Producer–retailer–consumer (short channel). The producer–retailer–consumer route is the most popular with the larger retailers, since they can buy in large quantities, obtaining special prices and often with tailormade stock-handling and delivery arrangements. This route is typically used by large supermarket chains and is most appropriate for large manufacturers and large retailers who deal in such huge quantities that a direct relationship is efficient.

In the car trade, a local dealer usually deals directly with the manufacturer, because, unlike fmcg products, there is a need for significant support in the supply infrastructure and expertise in the sales and service process. This is an example of the grey area between retailing and distributorships.

Producer–wholesaler–retailer–consumer (long channel). The advantage of adding a wholesaler level can be significant where small manufacturers and/or small retailers are involved. A small manufacturing organisation does not necessarily have the skills or resources to reach a wide range of retail customers and, similarly, the small corner shop does not have the resources to source relatively small quantities direct from many manufactures. The wholesaler can provide a focal point for both sides, by buying in bulk from manufacturers, then splitting that bulk into manageable quantities for small retailers; by bringing a wider assortment of goods together for the retailer under one roof; by providing access to a wider range of retail customers for the small manufacturer; and by similarly providing access to a wider range of manufacturers' goods for the small retailer. Effectively, the wholesaler is marketing on behalf of the manufacturer.

eg
The independent grocery sector is serviced by a number of wholesalers and cash-and-carry providers. Booker is the biggest wholesaler in the UK with 173 cash-and-carry depots, and it has 100,000 retail and 300,000 catering customers. Deliveries are made from the cash and carries to retail customers, but the plan is to concentrate on developing between six and ten local delivery centres across the UK to improve availability and service. To service the catering trade specifically, 100 Booker branches offer the Booker Express delivery service (Hamson, 2005b).

Sugro UK, a Nantwich-based wholesale group that is part of a German-based parent company, is an amalgam of 79 wholesalers and cash-and-carry operators specialising mainly in confectionery, snacks and soft drinks. It services 41,000 outlets including CTN (confectionery, tobacco, news) stores, convenience stores, petrol forecourt stores and pubs. To provide the service, it has 350 field and telesales personnel and 450 delivery vehicles to negotiate and support sales. The whole international group handles 250,000 different products. The advantages for small independent retailers sourcing from the group are mainly linked with the group's centralised bulk buying from major manufacturers, the availability of Sugro own-brands on some lines, as well as an efficient and comprehensive stocking and delivery service. To be competitive itself, Sugro aims to provide a 'point of difference' for the retailer so that a win–win situation is created (**http://www.sugro.co.uk**).

The wholesaler can also act on behalf of relatively large manufacturers trying to sell large volumes of frequently reordered products to a wide retail network. Daily national newspapers, for example, are delivered from the presses to the wholesalers, which can then break bulk and assemble tailormade orders involving many different titles for their own retail customers. This is far more efficient than each newspaper producer trying to deal direct with each small corner shop newsagent.

Producer–agent–wholesaler–retailer–consumer. This is the longest and most indirect channel. It might be used, for example, where a manufacturer is trying to enter a relatively unknown export market. The agent will be chosen because of local knowledge, contacts and expertise in selling into that country, and will earn commission on sales made. The problem is, however, that the manufacturer is totally dependent on the agent and has to trust the quality of the agent's knowledge, commitment and selling ability. Nevertheless, this method is widely used by smaller organisations trying to develop in remote markets, where their ability to establish a strong presence is constrained by lack of time, resources or knowledge.

■ B2B goods

As highlighted in Chapter 3, B2B products often involve close technical and commercial dialogue between buyer and seller, during which the product and its attributes are matched to the customer's specific requirements. The type and frequency of purchase, the quantity purchased and the importance of the product to the buyer all affect the type of channel structure commonly found in B2B markets. Office stationery, for example, is not a crucial purchase from the point of view of keeping production lines going and, as a routine repurchase, it is more likely to be distributed through specialist distributors or retailers such as Staples or Rymans. In contrast, crucial components that have to be integrated into a production line are likely to be delivered direct from supplier to buyer to specific deadlines. The variety of B2B distribution channels can be seen in Figure 8.2. Each type will now be discussed in turn.

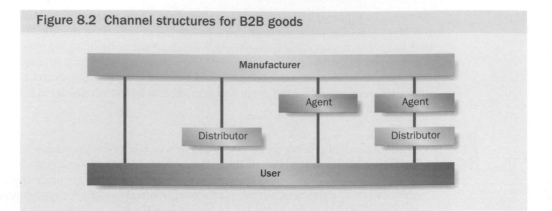

Figure 8.2 Channel structures for B2B goods

Manufacturer–user. The direct channel is most appropriate where the goods being sold have a high unit cost and perhaps a high technical content. There is likely to be a small number of buyers who are perhaps confined to clearly defined geographical areas. To operate such a channel, the manufacturer must be prepared to build and manage a sales and distribution force that can negotiate sales, provide service and administer customer needs.

eg AB Konstruktions-Bakelit, one of Sweden's largest manufacturers of industrial plastic components, deals directly with customers such as Volvo, Saab and Alfa Laval. This is because of the need for considerable dialogue during the design and development stage to ensure a close fit between the customer's specification and components that are made to order. There would be a very high risk of misunderstanding if a third party were introduced.

Sales branches tend to be situated away from the manufacturer's head office in areas where demand is particularly high. They are a conveniently situated focal point for the area's sales force, providing them with products and support services so that they in turn can better meet their customers' needs more quickly. Sales branches may also sell products themselves directly to small retailers or wholesalers.

Sales offices do not carry stock, so, although they might take orders from local customers, they are only acting as agents and will pass the order on to head office. Again, they provide a locally convenient focus in busy areas.

Manufacturer–distributor–user. Less direct channels tend to be adopted as the number of customers grows, the size of customers reduces, and the number of intermediary functions also increases. Building materials, for example, are often sold to builders' merchants, who then sell to the building trade based on lower order quantities, and consequently with a greater range of stock availability but greater proximity to local need. The philosophy is similar to that of the short channel of distribution discussed in the consumer context on p. 258.

eg This less direct type of structure can also apply to software products. Moser GmbH is one of the leading software houses in Germany and specialises in selling to trade and handicraft organisations. Although it had over 10,000 software installations in Germany and the Netherlands, it decided to seek expansion elsewhere in Europe. This was done by selling through other software and system houses which already had the sales and technical appreciation to generate sales for Moser.

Manufacturer–agent–user. Sometimes an agent is introduced to act on behalf of a group of manufacturers in dealing with users in situations where it would not be economically viable to create a direct selling effort, but where there is a need for selling expertise to generate and complete transactions.

eg Teijo Pesukoneet from Nakkila in Finland specialises in technically advanced cleaning machines for metal components in enclosed cabinets. Although it has its own sales offices in Sweden and Norway, it operates through agents in other main European markets such as the UK and Germany. Agents are trained to handle technical queries and sales enquiries but relay orders to Finland for direct delivery.

Generally speaking, agents do not take title to goods, but may buy and sell, usually on a commission basis, on behalf of manufacturers and retailers. They facilitate an exchange process rather than participating fully in it. They tend to specialise in particular markets or product lines and are used because of their knowledge, or their superior purchasing or selling skills, or their well-established contacts within the market. The distinction between an agent and a broker is a fine one. Agents tend to be retained on a long-term basis to act on behalf of a client, and thus build up working rapport. A broker tends to be used on a one-off, temporary basis to fulfill a specific need or deal.

The main problem with agents is the amount of commission that has to be paid, as this can push selling costs up. This cost has to be looked at in context and with a sense of proportion. That commission is buying sales performance, market knowledge and a degree of flexibility that would take a lot of time and money to build for yourself, even if you wanted to do it. The alternative to using agents, therefore, may not be so effective or cost efficient.

marketing in action

South African oranges

The next time you tuck into a South African orange, stop to think of the many stages in the distribution channel through which the product has moved, from the South African orange growers to the local supermarket. Each year South Africa exports some 50 million cartons of oranges, with western Europe consuming over 50 per cent of them. The industry is made up of 200 private farmers and 1200 growers in cooperatives. Many growers and cooperatives pool their output for marketing and distribution purposes under the Capespan International selling operation (50 per cent owned by Fyffes). Capespan is a giant in the global fruit market. It operates worldwide through a network of subsidiaries, joint ventures and alliance partners, with international assets that include interests in shipping, port handling and cold storage, warehousing, distribution and marketing. The challenge for Capespan has been to align its distribution strategy with increased

international competition, greater customer sophistication and the demands of ever-powerful supermarket chains. Product freshness, variety, quality and supply must all meet customer demand and the product must move smoothly through the supply chain from grower to buyer.

The oranges move from the growers to the fruit-handling facilities run by Capespan near the major ports such as Durban, Cape Town and Port Elizabeth. Capespan purchases the oranges and then adds handling and transportation costs and a profit margin. The services provided include some initial de-greening, environmental control, labelling and packing, all before shipment. It also arranges shipment, increasingly in large bulk bins for ease of handling, from the ports. At this stage, data is collected on the fruit, size, type, quality grade, treatment and origin.

Another service that Capespan undertakes is to move the oranges to cold storage before they depart for Europe. Most of these processes are provided by

Capespan subsidiaries: Fresh Produce Terminals provides cold storage and warehousing facilities, Cape Reefers provides shipping coordination, and CSS Logistics provides the clearing and forwarding documentation.

European ports such as Flushing, Sheerness and Tilbury have been selected as destinations. A partnership approach between Capespan and the port authorities has resulted in a specialist infrastructure for handling and storing palletised or binned oranges. In order to ensure that the right oranges arrive at the right EU port, data is sent to Capespan planners in Europe, who then decide which fruit should be unloaded at which port to meet local demand. On arrival, Capespan re-inspects the produce. Where necessary, the cartons are labelled and quality control checks undertaken to ensure that the fruit is consistent with specific buyers' expectations. This all helps to preserve the reputation of the Capespan brand name, Outspan. There are plans to add more valuable services such as pre-packing, size grading and fruit preparation for fresh fruit salad. After processing, the oranges are ready either to enter the UK domestic distribution chain or to go for further storage. Because an electronic data system has been used, fruit that has ripened during transit is ready to leave port quickly in 'table-fresh' condition.

Shipment can be to external pre-packers contracted by the supermarkets or straight to the wholesale and supermarket distribution systems at regional or central warehouse collection points. These shipments fulfil orders placed either direct by the supermarkets or through selling agents dealing with Capespan in the UK. Some oranges go into the fruit and vegetable distribution chain and end up being sold in markets and through wholesalers dealing with specialist fruit and vegetable stores.

Capespan relies heavily on timely information produced at every step of the supply chain to manage the procurement, distribution, marketing and sales processes. Customised information

systems and pallet tracking systems such as Paltrack are used for pallet tracking and stock control. Using data provided by the order and shipments, a decision support infrastructure ensures that information is generated to support Capespan's key decisions, such as destination priorities, and that information is also provided in the most useful form to suppliers. Capespan also uses web technology throughout the supply chain, such as its extranet (**http://www.ourgrowers.co.za**) which links Capespan with its growers/suppliers, allowing access to critical market information in real time from marketplaces around the world. Other internet sites provide an encyclopaedia of information to customers and support grower/customer interaction.

The success of Capespan has, therefore, been driven by the provision of specialist technical skills to add value in the distribution chain. This includes:

- Ensuring consistent quality and leading brand packaging
- Enabling economies of scale to be achieved in logistics

shipping, and packing materials
- Creating access to worldwide markets for growers who would otherwise have difficulty establishing and managing an international distribution chain
- Providing customer-specific packaging services at source, for example punnets and boxes
- Installing an effective IT system, internet and intranet for the benefit of channel members, with web-based stock trading and product flow information that would be cost-prohibitive for an individual grower
- Globally coordinated marketing.

The value added by Capespan is clear, as independent, sometimes small growers would not have the resources or expertise to undertake all these tasks, and the wholesalers in the buying markets would not have the local knowledge of the African fruit growing industry. That knowledge and expertise is what Capespan's customers are willing to pay for.

Sources: Shapley (1998);
http://www.capespan.com;
http://www.networking.ibm.com;
http://www.oracle.com.

Manufacturer–agent–distributor–user. A model comprising manufacturer–agent–distributor–user links is particularly useful in fast-moving export markets. The sales agent coordinates sales in a specified market, while the distributors provide inventory and fast restocking facilities close to the point of customer need. The comments on the longest channel of distribution in the consumer context (see pp. 258–9) are also applicable here.

Increasingly, using multiple channels of distribution is becoming the rule rather than the exception (Frazier, 1999). Where there is choice, the retailer could have a virtual, web-based store as well as physical retail outlets. In global markets stronger branded manufacturers could adopt different methods to reach customers, depending upon local distribution structures. Using multiple channels enables more market segments to be reached and can increase penetration levels, but this must be weighed against lower levels of support from trade members who find themselves facing high degrees of intra-channel competition.

The type of structure adopted in a particular sector, whether industrial or consumer, will ultimately depend on the product and market characteristics that produce differing cost and servicing profiles. These issues will be further explored in the context of the main justification for using marketing intermediaries, described next.

Rationale for using intermediaries

Every transaction between a buyer and a seller costs money. There are delivery costs, order picking and packing costs, marketing costs, and almost certainly administrative costs associated with processing an order and receiving or making payment. The role of the intermediary is to increase the efficiency and reduce the costs of individual transactions. This can be clearly seen in Figure 8.3.

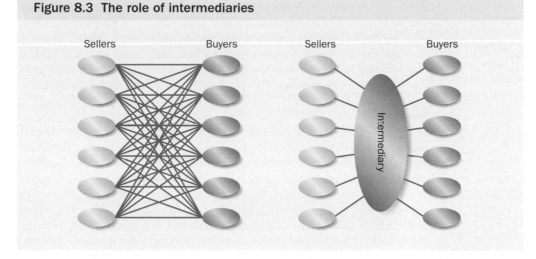

Figure 8.3 The role of intermediaries

If six manufacturers wished to deal with six buyers, a total of 36 links would be necessary. All of these transaction links cost time and money to service, and require a certain level of administrative and marketing expertise. If volumes and profit margins are sufficient, then this may be a viable proposition. However, in many situations this would add considerably to the cost of the product. By using an intermediary, the number of links falls to just twelve, and each buyer and each seller needs to maintain and service only one link. If this makes sense when considering only six potential buyers, just imagine how much more sensible it is with fmcg goods where there are millions of potential buyers! On economic grounds alone, the rationale for intermediaries in creating transaction efficiency is demonstrated.

However, there are other reasons for using intermediaries, because they add value for the manufacturer and customer alike. These value-added services fall into three main groups (Webster, 1979), as shown in Figure 8.4.

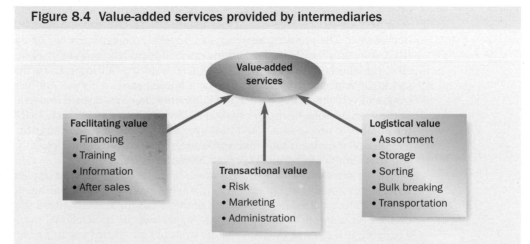

Figure 8.4 Value-added services provided by intermediaries

■ Transactional value

The role of intermediaries in assisting transaction efficiency has already been highlighted. To perform this role adequately, the intermediary, as an interconnected but separate entity, must decide on its own strategic position in the marketplace, and therefore assemble products that it believes its own desired customers need and then market them effectively. The selection is extremely important, and requires careful purchasing in terms of type, quantity and cost to fit the intermediary's own product strategy.

Risk

The *risks* move to the intermediary, who takes *title* to the goods and, as legal owner, is responsible for their resale. Of course, it is in the manufacturer's interest to see the product moving through the distribution system in order to achieve sales and profit objectives. However, the risk of being lumbered with obsolete, damaged or slow-moving stock rests with the intermediary, not the manufacturer. This is a valuable service to that manufacturer.

Marketing

With the transfer of title and risk, the need to *market effectively* increases. Intermediaries may recruit and train their own sales forces to resell the products that they have assembled. This is another valuable service to the manufacturer, as it means that the product may have a greater chance of being brought to the attention of the prospective customer, especially in B2B markets. In consumer markets, retailers are an important interface between the manufacturer and the consumer. Retailers take responsibility for the pricing, display and control of the products offered, the processing of cash and/or credit transactions, and, if necessary, delivery to the customer. If retailers fail to ensure that adequate stocks of products are available to buy, or if they provide inadequate customer service or an unappealing retail environment, then sales could be lost.

In most retail situations, the consumer enters a carefully planned and controlled environment designed to create a retail environment that helps to establish and reinforce the ambience and image desired. In some, this may be a low-cost minimalist approach that reinforces a no-frills, value for money philosophy, with simple picking from racks and pallets or drums. In others, music, decor and display are all subtly developed and designed around themes to create a more upmarket, higher-quality shopping experience.

The retail environment can also include a range of additional services. Convenient parking is a critical issue where customers are buying in bulk, or want fast takeaway services (the 'drive-thru' fast food operator has found the logical solution to this one!). Additional services in the form of credit, delivery, returns and purchasing assistance can help to differentiate a retailer.

eg   IKEA, despite having had a €13.5bn turnover and over 400 million customers visiting its 201 stores in 30 countries, has been criticised over the level of customer service and advice it offers. It has achieved high degrees of consistency worldwide in its operations, with self-assembly, self-service, high-design merchandise that is affordable, especially for the first-time homeowner. The problem, however, can be seen (and experienced) by anyone visiting an IKEA store on a busy Saturday. Parking can be difficult, the availability of instore advice variable, the checkout queues long, and there is an overall impression that the retailer is seemingly reluctant to make the shopper's burden easier. This was not helped by the disastrous and very public fiasco when the Edmonton store was opened in north London. As part of the opening, sofas normally priced at £325 were offered at £49 each. IKEA underestimated the number of people who would turn up, and thus the store was swamped, and had to close after just 30 minutes. It took nine ambulances to take people suffering from heat exhaustion and crush injuries to hospital! (Barnes, 2005b; Scheraga, 2005).

The service solutions are straightforward, but have not yet been implemented. Opening more stores would help, but primarily it is about staffing levels, so hiring more in-store staff, installing more checkouts, and finding promotional methods to spread shopper visits more evenly over the week could all help. Making the website transactional would also help a lot. Currently, it is claimed by IKEA that its strategies are 'geared towards generating customers into stores where they can actually sit on and touch products' (as quoted by Stewart-Allen, 2001). IKEA is, however, piloting an online ordering system as well as an e-mail customer enquiry line. Other retailers have provided an adequate shopping experience online and few people nowadays want to spend a whole or half day battling for a parking space, searching for trolleys and queueing at checkouts. IKEA's challenge is to improve customer service satisfaction to match the high levels of merchandise satisfaction it achieves.

IKEA shows its products in room settings so that customers can match their lifestyle aspirations to what is on offer.

Source: © IKEA

■ Logistical value

Assortment

A critical role for the intermediary is the assembly of an *assortment of products* from different sources that is compatible with the needs of the intermediary's own customers. This assortment can operate at product or brand level. A drinks wholesaler, for example, may offer a full range of merchandise from beer to cognac, but within each category considerable brand choice may also be offered. The benefit to the customer is the wide choice available from one source, supported perhaps by a competitive and comprehensive pre- and post-sales service. However, for other intermediaries the choice may be more limited. If one manufacturer occupies a dominant position, the choice of competing brands may be severely restricted to just complementary products. In many car dealerships, for example, only one manufacturer's new cars can be sold, although there might be more flexibility over second-hand cars.

Assortment strategy is a critical variable in a retailer's marketing strategy. The key is to build an assortment to reflect the needs of the target market.

Within a particular product area or market, variety is ensured, as retailers seek to differentiate their offerings from those of their competitors, although increasingly this is becoming more difficult. In any assortment strategy there are risks in misjudging changes in customer fads or tastes. This is particularly noticeable in high fashion areas where even the sale rails do not move assortments that have been left behind.

Wholesalers can play a major role in providing the wide assortment of goods required. While some retailers deal directly with manufacturers, others, particularly smaller stores, may prefer the convenience and accessibility of the wholesaler, especially where fast, responsive supply is assured. In the book trade, for example, it is difficult for a retailer to offer anything like the total number of titles available. Instead, the retailer acts as an order conduit, so that either the wholesaler or the publisher can service individual orders that have been consolidated into economic shipment sizes. The wholesaler can maintain a much wider range of products than is possible in all but the largest retail groups, and can provide efficient support activities for rapid stock replenishment.

Storage, sorting and bulk breaking

A further dimension of logistical value is the *accumulation and storing of products* at locations that are appropriate and convenient to the customer. The small manufacturer can make one large delivery of output to the wholesaler's warehouse, where it can be stored until a retailer wants it, and broken down into smaller lots as necessary. The hassles of transporting small quantities to many different locations, finding storage space and insuring the goods are taken away from the manufacturer.

eg A walk around a market in a developing country reveals row upon row of sellers with small tables offering piles of undifferentiated home-grown carrots or turnips and little

Appealing to the customer as a convenience product, Florette sells pre-packed salad leaves which come from a variety of suppliers.

Source: Image courtesy of The Advertising Archives

else, a far cry from town centre markets in the UK or France. By using intermediaries, farmers or market gardeners do not need to find their own markets. A fruit and vegetable wholesaler can accumulate small quantities of different products from specialist growers, sort them, and then make larger deliveries of assorted goods to the next point in the chain, thus gaining economies in transport costs.

Soléco is France's largest producer of pre-packed salads and fresh stir-fry and snack vegetables. Trading under the Florette and Manon brands, nearly 60 per cent of its €293m turnover in 2004 was generated in the French market, in which it is the leader, with well over 40 per cent share of the pre-packed salad market. In the UK, however, it takes second place, with only 15 per cent market share. This is because of the strength of retailer own-brand pre-packed salads which account for 82 per cent of the market (Mintel, 2005).

To make its European-wide business a success, Soléco had to invest in high levels of quality control, strict temperature control and specialist preparation machinery. It also needs regular supply. Not only has it contracted with 450 French growers, but about 15 per cent of its supply needs comes from Italy, Spain and Portugal. All crops are allocated batch numbers as part of an ISO 9001 system. Through such transparency, Soléco can assure the trade that the 'use by' date will never exceed seven days after processing, fewer on more fragile items such as lettuce. Soléco knows the field of origin, the variety, the date of harvesting, and the date and place of packaging to ensure that even when distribution lines are extended, freshness of the produce can be guaranteed. All of this enables the consumer to enjoy top quality, fresh produce (**http://www.florette-corporare.com; http://www.soleco.co.uk**).

Sorting is a very basic step in the logistical process, and means grouping many diverse products into more uniform, homogeneous groups. These groups may be based on product class and further subdivided by such factors as size, shape, weight and colour. This process may also add value by *grading*, which means inspecting, testing or judging products so that they can be placed into more homogeneous quality grades. These standards may be based on intermediary or industry predetermined standards. Large supermarket chains, for example, are particularly demanding about the standardisation of the fruit and vegetables that they retail. If you look at a carton of apples in a supermarket, you will see that they are all of a standard size, colour and quality. Mother Nature hasn't quite worked out how to ensure such uniformity, so the producers and wholesalers have to put effort into sorting out and grading the top quality produce for the High Street. The second-class produce ends up in less choosy retail outlets, while the most irregular specimens end up in soup, fruit juices and ready meals.

A further important role for the intermediary, as already implied, is bulk breaking, the division of large units into the smaller, more manageable quantities required by the next step in the chain. Whereas a builder's merchant may purchase sand by the lorry load, the small builder may purchase by the bagged pallet load, and the individual consumer by the individual bag. The value of bulk breaking is clear to the DIY enthusiast, who certainly would not wish to purchase by the pallet load. There is, of course, a price to pay for this convenience, and the consumer would expect to pay a higher price per bag purchased individually than the builder would pay per bag purchased by the pallet load.

Transportation

A final role is in actually *transporting the product* to the next point in the chain. Lorry loads may be made up of deliveries to several customers in the same area, thus maximising the payload, and with careful siting of warehouse facilities, minimising the distances the products have to travel. Again, this is more efficient than having each manufacturer sending out delivery vans to every customer throughout the country.

The provision of storage and transportation has become increasingly important with the widening distance, in terms of both geography and the length of distribution channels, between producer and consumer. Purchasing patterns increasingly include products sourced from wherever the best deal can be offered, whether local or international. As production becomes more concentrated into a relatively small number of larger operations, the need to move products over large distances increases. The distance can be even greater in the food-stuffs area, with the demand for exotic and fresh foods from elsewhere in Europe and well beyond. The availability of Chilean grapes in UK supermarkets in winter, for example, is the end point of a long series of distribution decisions including a number of intermediaries.

Retailers and wholesalers, by allowing larger shipments to be made and then breaking bulk, play an important role in establishing economies of scale in channels of physical distribution. Some wholesalers are themselves heavily involved in performing physical distribution roles such as inventory planning, packing, transportation and order processing in line with customer service objectives. This assists the manufacturer as well as the retailer. Often the wholesaler will incur costs in inward-bound transportation, maintain a safety stock buffer and absorb associated inventory and materials handling expenses, all of which represent savings for the manufacturer.

■ Facilitating value

Financing

The intermediary also offers a range of other value-added services either to the manufacturer or to the customer. Not only do intermediaries share the risks, as outlined above, they also provide a valuable *financing* benefit. The manufacturer has to manage only a small number of accounts (for example with two or three wholesalers rather than with 200 or more individual retailers) and can keep tighter control over credit periods, thus improving cash flow. As part of the service to the consumer, retailers may offer credit or other financial services such as credit card acceptance, easy payment terms and insurance. Manufacturers selling direct would not necessarily be interested in such financial services.

Information, training and after-sales service

Both retailers and wholesalers are part of the forward information flow that advises customers and persuades them to buy. Although in the supermarket environment the role of personal advice is minimal, many retailers, especially those in product lines such as clothing, hobbies, electrical goods and cars, are expected to assist the consumer directly in making a purchase decision and to advise on subsequent use. These are the kinds of goods that require limited or extended decision-making behaviour, as discussed at pp. 73–4 earlier. Manufacturers might well invest in training wholesale or retail staff in how to sell the benefits of their product ranges and provide after-sales service support.

Wholesalers are also important sources of advice for some retailers and users. The more specialised a wholesaler, the greater the opportunity for developing an in-depth market understanding, tracking new or declining products, analysing competitive actions, defining promotions needed and advising on best buys. This role may be especially valuable to the smaller retailer who has less direct access to quality information on broader trends in a specific market. Similarly, an industrial distributor may be expected to advise customers on applications and to assist in low-level technical problem solving.

Market *information* and *feedback* are precious commodities, as we saw in Chapter 5. The intermediary is much closer to the marketplace, and therefore alert to changes in consumer needs and competitive conditions. Passing on this information up the channel of distribution can enable manufacturers to modify their marketing strategies for the benefit of all parties. While there is no replacement for systematic, organised market research, information derived from sales contacts and meetings with intermediaries provides specific, often relevant intelligence. For the small manufacturer, with very limited market research resources, this can be particularly invaluable.

All the above functions need to be performed at some point within the marketing channel. The key decision concerns which member undertakes what role. This decision may be reached by *negotiation*, where the power in the channel is reasonably balanced, or by *imposition*, when either manufacturer or retailer dominates. Whatever the outcome, the compensation system in terms of margins needs to be designed to reflect the added value role performed.

Types of intermediary

As we have already seen, many marketing channels involve the physical movement of goods and the transfer of legal title to the goods to various types of intermediary. This section summarises the key characteristics of each of those types.

■ Distributors and dealers

Distributors and dealers are intermediaries who add value through special services associated with stocking or selling inventory, credit and after-sales service. Although these intermediaries are often used in B2B markets, they can also be found in direct dealing with consumers, for example computer or motor dealers. The term usually signifies a more structured and closer tie between the manufacturer and intermediary in order that the product may be delivered efficiently and with the appropriate level of expertise. Clearly, some retail outlets are also closely associated with dealerships and the distinction between them may be somewhat blurred.

■ Agents and brokers

Agents and brokers are intermediaries who have the legal authority to act on behalf of the manufacturer, although they do not take legal title to the goods or indeed handle the product directly in any way. They do, however, make the product more accessible to the customer and in some cases provide appropriate add-on benefits. Their prime function is to bring buyer and seller together. Universities often use agents to recruit students in overseas markets.

■ Wholesalers

Wholesalers do not normally deal with the end consumer but with other intermediaries, usually retailers. However, in some situations sales are made directly to the end user, especially in B2B markets, with no further resale taking place. An organisation may purchase its catering or cleaning supplies from a local cash and carry business that serves the retail trade. A wholesaler does take legal title to the goods as well as taking physical possession of them.

■ Franchisees

A franchisee holds a contract to supply and market a product or service to the design or blueprint of the franchisor (the owner or originator of the product or service). The franchise agreement covers not only the precise specification of the product or service, but also the selling and marketing aspects of the business. The uniformity of different branches of McDonald's is an indication of the level of detail covered by a franchise agreement. There are many products and services currently offered through franchise arrangements, especially in the retail and home services sector.

■ Retailers

Retailers sell direct to the consumer and may either purchase direct from the manufacturer or deal with a wholesaler, depending on purchasing power and volume. Retailers can be classified on a number of criteria, not all of which are immediately obvious to the average shopper. These are discussed in this section which will also help to shed further light on what retailers actually do and why they are important to both manufacturer and consumer.

Form of ownership

Retailing was for many years the realm of the small-independent business. Some grew by adding more branches and some grew by acquisition, but it is only since the 1950s that the retail structure of the high street has evolved significantly, favouring the larger organisation. Nevertheless, there are still several predominant forms of ownership to be found.

Independent. Still the most common form of ownership in terms of number of retail outlets is independent, with over 62 per cent of UK outlets falling into this category. In sales volume terms, however, this group accounts for less than 30 per cent. Marked variances exist between retail categories, with a significant role for the small independent in the drinks sector and in CTN (confectionery, tobacco and news) retailing. Similar patterns exist across Europe, especially in France, Spain and the Benelux countries, which have above-average densities of small retailers. Typically, the independent retail outlet is managed by a sole trader or a family business. For the consumer, the main benefits are the personalised attention and flexibility that can be offered. These operations can be highly individualistic in terms of the variety and quality of merchandise stocked, ranging from very upmarket to bargain basement.

Although it may not be possible for the small independent to compete on price and breadth of range offered, the key is to complement the big multiples rather than to try to compete head-on. Howe (1992) is clear about forces that work against the small retailer, such as changing population patterns, the drift towards out-of-town shopping, supply and resource problems, and the sheer scale and professionalism of the large multiple chains. To combat this, the small retailer thus needs to look for niches, specialised merchandise, flexible opening hours and special services and to make more effective use of suppliers. This boils down to sound management and marketing thinking.

eg Small village grocery shops are becoming an endangered species. Estimates have suggested that 300 close every year and that around one-third of all villages now have no local store. Turnover varies widely. Some smaller stores are hard pushed to generate £2,000 per week, but more favoured locations can easily double that. The Rural Shops Alliance estimates that there are only about 12,000 rural shops left; the rest have become victims of increased consumer mobility and the attraction of the supermarkets, some of which actually run weekly free bus services to their stores. The key to survival is diversification. Having the local Post Office franchise can be a big help, as it attracts people into the store, but it is also about offering fax and photocopying facilities, internet access, lottery access, cash points, video hire, flexible opening hours and fresh local produce. Although shopping for convenience items or those forgotten on the main shopping trip provides basic turnover for the village store, what is really needed to increase the value and loyalty of customers is a change in the retailer's attitude and the creation of a service-oriented multi-activity centre appealing to the cross-section of the community that could create a captive audience (Gregory, 2001a, 2001b).

Corporate chain. A corporate chain has multiple outlets under common ownership. The operation of the chain will reflect corporate strategy, and many will centralise decisions where economies of scale can be gained. The most obvious activity to be centralised is purchasing, so that volume discounts and greater power over suppliers can be gained. There are, of course, other benefits to be derived from a regional, national or even international presence in terms of image and brand building. Typical examples include Next and M&S. Some chains do allow a degree of discretion at a local level to reflect different operating environments, in terms of opening hours, merchandise or services provided, but the main strength comes from unity rather than diversity.

Contractual system. The linking of members of distribution channels through formal agreements rather than ownership (i.e. a contractual system) is discussed later in this chapter. For retail or wholesale sponsored cooperatives or franchises, the main benefit is the ability to draw from collective strength, whether in management, marketing or operational procedures. In some cases, the collective strength, as with franchises, can provide a valuable tool for promoting customer awareness and familiarity, leading in turn to retail loyalty. The trade-off for the franchisee is some loss of discretion, both operationally and strategically, but this may be countered by the benefits of unity. Franchising might also pass on the retailing risk to the franchisee. When Benetton's performance was poor in the US market, 300 stores closed, with all the losses borne by the franchisees rather than by Benetton (Davidson, 1993).

If the independent retailer wants to avoid the risks of franchising, yet wants to benefit from collective power, then affiliation to either a buying group or a voluntary chain might be the answer. Buying groups are usually found in food retailing and their purpose is to centralise the purchasing function and to achieve economies of scale on behalf of their members.

Level of service

The range and quality of services offered vary considerably from retailer to retailer. Some, such as department stores, offer gift-wrapping services, and some DIY stores offer home delivery, but in others most of the obligation for picking, assessing and taking the product home rests with the customer. The following three types of service level highlight the main options.

Full service. Stores such as Harrods provide the full range of customer services. This includes close personal attention on the shopfloor, a full range of account and delivery services, and a clear objective to treat each customer as a valued individual. Such high levels of service are reflected in the premium pricing policy adopted.

Limited service. The number of customers handled and the competitive prices that need to be charged prevent the implementation of the full range of services, but the services that are offered make purchasing easier. Credit, no-quibble returns, telephone orders and home delivery may be offered. This is a question of deciding what the target market 'must have' rather than what it 'would like', or defining what is essential for competitive edge. A retailer, such as Next, that claims to sell quality clothing at competitive prices cannot offer too many extra services because that would increase the retailer's costs. They do, however, have to offer a limited range of services in order to remain competitive with similar retailers.

Self-service. In self-service stores, the customer performs many of the in-store functions, including picking goods, queueing at the checkout, paying by cash or perhaps credit card, and then struggling to the car park with a loaded trolley. Some food and discount stores operate in this mode, but the trend is towards offering more service to ease bottleneck points that are particularly frustrating to the customer. This could include the provision of more staff at the delicatessen counter, more checkouts to guarantee short queues, and assistance with packing.

Merchandise lines

Retailers can be distinguished by the merchandise they carry, assessed in terms of the breadth and depth of range.

Breadth of range. The breadth of range represents the variety of different product lines stocked. A department store (see pp. 273 *et seq.* for a fuller discussion) will carry a wide variety of product lines, perhaps including electrical goods, household goods, designer clothing, hairdressing and even holidays.

eg A catalogue retail showroom (see p. 278), such as Argos, is not expected to display its whole range of stock 'live' and is thus able to provide much greater breadth and depth of range than its department store rivals. It is limited only by its logistical systems and ability to update and replenish its in-store warehouses quickly. Argos has 600 stores, including 33 Index stores acquired from Littlewoods. The Extra catalogue offers an additional 3000 products on top of Argos's mainstream 17,000 product range. Despite the breadth of range it offers, it was felt that Argos was not capitalising on the increased demand for home-based PCs, so the new line was introduced at most of its stores. Also, as a means of reducing the complexity of the Argos offering for customers, a number of more focused catalogues have been introduced. One of these is Argos Additions, a clothing and home catalogue including brands such as Reebok, Levi's and Gossard. In addition, online shopping and ordering has been introduced that can involve secure payment, home delivery or showroom collection. The main problem for Argos is its image.

Although refurbishment is taking place, some of its stores look tired and a little down-market; many people buy well-known brands from them, but few admit to it, although its shopping catalogue has massive penetration and sales have consistently grown. Argos has remained true to its strengths, providing convenience, availability and choice at low prices. Internet sales, although accounting for only 7 per cent of total revenue, are growing rapidly. Argos's experience with the catalogue approach to retailing, when the product cannot be seen before purchase, the catalogue's penetration into 70 per cent of UK homes, and the established in-store technology along with an established home delivery operation all mean that it is well placed to build further on its initial success with internet selling (Jardine, 2001; Kleinman, 2001; *Marketing*, 2004; *Marketing Week*, 2005; Quilter, 2005).

Depth of range. The depth of range defines the amount of choice or assortment within a product line, on whatever dimensions are relevant to that kind of product. A music store stocking DVDs, CDs, tapes, minidiscs and vinyl records could be said to have depth in its range. Similarly, a clothing store that stocks cashmere jumpers might be said to have a shallow range if the jumpers are available only in one style, or a deep range if they are available in five different styles. Introducing further assortment criteria, such as size range and colour, creates a very complex definition of depth. A speciality or niche retailer, such as Tie Rack, would be expected to provide depth in its product lines on a number of assortment criteria.

eg Hennes and Mauritz (H&M) is Sweden's fifth largest company and operates around 1121 stores in 22 countries. It is still expanding in the UK, USA, Germany and Austria. It owns over a dozen own-labels covering men's, women's and children's clothing, casual and classic wear, and underwear and outerwear. These labels are targeted at specific segments in the 14–45 age range, for example Clothes is very trend conscious, Hennes is classic fashion, and Mama is the maternity range. The assortment is, however, varied by region to suit local demographics and tastes. The formula has been a great success: since 2000, sales have increased by 70 per cent, compared with almost no growth for M&S, and H&M now looks set to topple M&S as Europe's biggest clothing retailer (Lyons, 2004). Its key to success is flexible supply lines, strong ranges and ability to identify the coming trend, hitting it quickly and then moving on. It shares many of the characteristics that have made IKEA successful: keen prices, good design, and sourcing from low-cost countries. Quality may not be at the forefront, but is adequate for the life expectancy of a fashion item.

Although it is a speciality retailer, concentrating on fashion, it provides a broad but shallow range, compared with other fashion retailers which specialise in just women's wear or jeans (narrow and deep). H&M is happy to offer low prices, reasonable quality and a wide range of fashionable clothing. To keep customers interested in its stores and to broaden the width of range further, new products designed by in-house staff such as those from the Karl Lagerfeld women's collection are introduced every day and no product is kept in the stores for longer than one month. That means some stores receive between two and four deliveries each day, and slower-moving items soon hit the markdown racks. It also means an extensive logistics operation involving regional warehouses, with half supplied from within Europe and the rest from Asia. Most other fashion retailers tend to change ranges only two to four times a year (*Financial Times*, 2004; Lyons, 2004; Scardino, 2001; Teather, 2001).

Operating methods

The area of operating methods has seen significant change, with the recent growth of alternatives to the traditional approach. Traditional store retailing, which itself includes a wide number of types of retailer, still predominates. These various types are considered in the next section. Non-store retailing, however, where the customer does not physically travel to visit the retailer, has become increasingly popular. This is partly because of changing customer attitudes, partly because of the drive upmarket made by the mail-order companies in particular, and partly because of technological advances in logistics. The whole area of non-store shopping will be further discussed at pp. 278 *et seq*.

Store types

A walk down any high street or a drive around the outskirts of any large town reveals a wide range of approaches to selling us things. There are retailers of all shapes and sizes, enticing us in with what they hope are clearly differentiated marketing mixes. The following discussion groups retailers according to the type of retail operation that they run. Each type will be defined, and the role it plays within the retail sector will be discussed.

Department stores. Department stores usually occupy a prominent prime position within a town centre or a large out-of-town shopping mall. Most towns have one, and some centres, such as London's Oxford Street, support several. Department stores are large and are organised into discrete departments consisting of related product lines, such as sports, ladies' fashions, toys, electrical goods, etc.

eg Royal Vendex KBB is the main non-food retail company in the Netherlands, with a portfolio of department stores and speciality stores. The company operates 12 well-known retail formats, including department stores, variety stores and speciality stores, across more than 1700 outlets in seven countries, and generates total net sales of €4.1bn. Its department stores have three formats, Vroom & Dreesman, Hema and Bijenkorf, each acting as separate business units, with different positioning strategies and customer profiles. The stores have own-label women's, babies' and children's clothing, personal care products, spectacles, shoes, home and interior decoration products, consumer and household electronics including computers, books, in-store catering services, external restaurants, bakery, internet shopping services and photo service. Although the combined sales of these stores is €990m, operating margins are between 4 and 6 per cent, reflecting the competitive markets in which department stores operate (**http://www.vendexkbb.com**).

To support the concept of providing everything that the customer could possibly want, department stores extend themselves into services as well as physical products, operating hairdressing and beauty parlours, restaurants and travel agencies. In some stores, individual departments are treated as business units in their own right. Taking that concept a little further, it is not surprising that concessions or 'stores within a store' have become common. With these, a manufacturer or another retail name purchases space within a department store, paying either a fixed rental per square metre or a percentage commission on turnover, to set up and operate a distinct trading area of its own. Jaeger, a classic fashion manufacturer and retailer, operates a number of its own stores throughout the UK, but also generates over one-third of its turnover from concessions within department stores such as House of Fraser.

eg Behavioural aspects of sex shopping were considered in Chapter 3. Tabooboo wanted to reach the two-thirds of women who would not visit a sex shop or buy a toy online and so it took out a concession in Selfridges. Amid a range of contemporary womenswear can thus be found a large range of multi-coloured vibrators, lubes and whips. Associating sex toys with branded clothing labels gives legitimacy to something that a few years ago was regarded as much more seedy and taboo. The idea is to generate impulse purchases and, after all, the products can easily be hidden in the generic yellow Selfridges carrier bag. It remains to be seen whether the two-thirds of uninitiated women actually take the plunge (Godson, 2004).

Variety stores. Variety stores are smaller than department stores, and they stock a more limited number of ranges in greater depth. Stores such as BhS and Marks & Spencer in the UK, and Monoprix in France, provide a great deal of choice within that limited definition, covering ladies' wear, menswear, children's clothing, sportswear, lingerie, etc. Most, however, carry additional ranges. BhS, for example, offers housewares and lighting, while Marks & Spencer offers shoes, greeting cards, plants, and extensive and successful food halls within its stores.

Like department stores, the major variety stores such as Monoprix in France and Kaufhalle in Germany operate as national chains, maintaining a consistent image across the country, and some also operate internationally. Whatever the geographical coverage of the variety store chain, given the size of the stores, they need volume traffic (i.e. lots of customers), and thus to develop a mass-market appeal they need to offer quality merchandise at no more than mid-range price points. Variety stores tend to offer limited additional services, with a tendency towards self-service, and centralised cashier points. In that sense, they are something between a department store and a supermarket.

Supermarkets. Over the last few years, the supermarket has been accused of being the main culprit in changing the face of the high street. The first generation of supermarkets, some 30 years ago, were relatively small, town-centre operations. As they expanded and cut their costs through self-service, bulk buying and heavy merchandising, they began to replace the small, traditional independent grocer. They expanded on to out-of-town sites, with easy free parking, and took the customers with them, thus (allegedly) threatening the health of the high street.

The wheel then turned full circle. As planning regulations in the UK tightened, making it more difficult to develop new out-of-town superstores, retailers began looking at town centre sites again. They developed new formats, such as Tesco Metro and Sainsbury's Local, for small stores carrying ready meals, basic staple grocery goods such as bread and milk, and lunchtime snacks aimed at shoppers and office workers.

The dominance of supermarkets is hardly surprising, because their size and operating structures mean that their labour costs can be 10–20 per cent lower than those of independent grocers, and their buying advantage 15 per cent better. This means that they can offer a significant price advantage. Additionally, they have made efficiency gains and increased their cost effectiveness through their commitment to developing and implementing new technology in the areas of EPOS, shelf allocation models, forecasting and physical distribution management systems. The effective management of retail logistics has, therefore, become a major source of sustainable competitive advantage (Paché, 1998). Most supermarkets, however, work on high turnover and low operating margins.

Hypermarkets. The hypermarket is a natural extension of the supermarket. While the average supermarket covers up to 2500 m^2, a superstore is between 2500 and 5000 m^2 and a hypermarket is anything over 5000 m^2 in size (URPI, 1988). A hypermarket provides even more choice and depth of range, but usually centres mainly around groceries. Examples of hypermarket operators are Intermarché and Carrefour in France, Tengelmann in Germany and ASDA in the UK. Because of their size, hypermarkets tend to occupy new sites on out-of-town retail parks. They need easy access and a large amount of space for parking, not only because of the volume of customers they have to attract, but also because their size means that customers will often buy a great deal at a time and will therefore need to be able to bring the car close to the store.

Obtaining planning permission is becoming increasingly difficult for new hypermarket locations anywhere in Europe. Nevertheless, a small number of developments are still taking place as part of new out-of-town shopping centres, with hypermarkets such as Auchan playing a central role. The new 'hypermarket for better living' in Val d'Europe, Marne-la-Vallée (Paris region, France), is a further example of continued development. The extended range of services include a beauty salon, a nursery, computers for use by customers, the possibility of watching DVD trailers and listening to the CDs on offer, and an optician. The Irish planning authorities have looked at the effects of hypermarket and superstore developments in other EU countries and concluded that they damage town centres, leading to the closure of small shops, and cause traffic congestion. As a result of this, the Irish government introduced new planning guidelines designed to place further restrictions on the development of superstores and hypermarkets.

The impact on the environment and town planning is, therefore, a far more important consideration than in the past in granting planning permission. Arrangements for the recycling of packaging, store architecture which blends in with surroundings, access arrangements, and the impact on retail diversity are now to the fore. In the UK the rules also remain stringent. Although primary shopping area extension is still possible with out-of-town development, the rules indicate that suitable sites in town centres or on the edge of centres must be fully considered first. Even if that hurdle is jumped successfully, opposition from environmentalists and anti-supermarket bodies is likely to be intense (Hamson, 2005a). The situation across the rest of Europe is little different from in the UK and Ireland. Spanish law favours small local stores with a surface area of below 300 m^2, and in Poland before planning permission is granted, the impact of the hypermarket on the employment structure in an area has to be specified (Auchan, 2001). In France, the birthplace of European hypermarkets, planning regulations have become more stringent in recent years for any developments over 1000 m^2. This has slowed down the domestic expansion of hypermarkets and encouraged the likes of Auchan and Carrefour to expand internationally.

Out-of-town speciality stores. An out-of-town speciality store tends to specialise in one broad product group, for example furniture, carpets, DIY or electrical. It tends to operate on an out-of-town site, which is cheaper than a town-centre site and also offers good parking and general accessibility. It concentrates on discounted prices and promotional lines, thus emphasising price and value for money. A product sold in an out-of-town speciality store is likely to be cheaper than the same item sold through a town centre speciality or department store.

The store itself can be single storey, with no windows. Some care is taken, however, over the attractiveness of the in-store displays and the layout. Depending on the kind of product area involved, the store may be self-service, or it may need to provide knowledgeable staff to help customers with choice and ordering processes. Recent years have seen efforts to improve the ambience of such stores and even greater care over their design.

Toys 'Я' Us in particular has become known as a *category killer* because it offers so much choice and such low prices that other retailers cannot compete. Its large out-of-town sites mean that it is efficient in terms of its operating costs, and its global bulk buying means that it can source extremely cheaply. Shoppers wanting to buy a particular toy know that Toys 'Я' Us will probably have it in stock, and shoppers who are unsure about what they want have a wonderful browsing opportunity. Additionally, the out-of-town sites are easily accessible and make trans-

Toys 'Я' Us locates its stores on out-of-town sites with plenty of parking to make it easy for anyone to shop for a wide variety of toys.

Source: © Ferruccio/Alamy

porting bulky items much easier. The small, independent toy retailer, in contrast, cannot match buying power, cost control, accessibility or choice and is likely to be driven out of business.

eg Pets at Home is the category killer for the UK's 7.5 million cats, 6.1 million dogs, 1.1 million hamsters and 750,000 budgies. It is the market leader in the £2.3bn pet supplies market which is growing at 4 per cent per year (Hall, 2004). The formula is based on large, 10,000 ft^2 edge-of-town sites with good parking, well-trained staff, and store events to attract attention. Grooming parlours and vets' surgeries have generated more traffic. Although the main emphasis is on supplies, small pets such as fish, budgies and hamsters are sold too. When an area cannot support a superstore, smaller high street stores are opened (there are around 200 in the UK) to increase overall market penetration. Margins are further expanded by own-brand products and by sourcing products from the Far East. The specialised nature of the stores has meant that the supermarkets can compete on only a few lines, such as pet foods, while at the other end of the scale, the traditional small pet shop cannot offer the variety or achieve the bulk buying or economies of scale to compete on price.

Town centre speciality stores. Like out-of-town speciality stores, town centre speciality stores concentrate on a narrow product group as a means of building a differentiated offering. They are smaller than the out-of-town speciality stores, averaging about 250 m^2. Within this sector, however, there are retailers such as florists, lingerie retailers, bakeries and confectioners that operate in much smaller premises. Well-known names such as H&M (see p. 272), Superdrug, Thorntons, Next and HMV all fit into this category.

Other examples of products sold through town centre speciality stores are footwear, toys, books and clothing (although often segmented by sex, age, lifestyle or even size). Most are comparison products, for which the fact of being displayed alongside similar items can be an advantage, as the customer wants to be able to examine and deliberate over a wider choice of alternatives before making a purchase decision. Given their central locations, and the need to build consumer traffic with competitive merchandise, the sector has seen the growth of multiple chains, serving clearly defined target market segments with clearly defined product mixes, such as most of the high street fashion stores. To reinforce the concept of specialisation and differentiation, some, especially the clothing multiples, have developed their own-label brands.

eg A visit to Thorntons is strictly about self-indulgence or buying gifts. Its slogan, 'Chocolate Heaven since 1911', captures the core values of the brand. It now has 380 company-owned stores and around 200 franchised confectionery shops throughout the UK and also sells by catalogue and online. The format is always the same, only the range stocked expands or contracts depending on the size and profile of each shop. Thorntons aims to be the finest sweetshop in town. Although the locations vary from shopping malls to airports and railway stations, the retail formula normally specifies the products to promote by season, the required selling area, the type of window displays, and the serving arrangements. Thorntons found, however, that concentrating on the high street restricted sales opportunities and did not capitalise on the brand strengths. The decision was made to close some of the stores and to sell Thorntons branded products through retailers such as Tesco, Sainsbury's, WHSmith and Woolworths, and this now contributes almost 15 per cent of Thorntons sales (McArthur, 2005; O'Grady, 2001; http://www.thorntons.co.uk).

Town centre speciality stores usually offer a mixture of browsing and self-service, but with personnel available to help if required. The creation of a retail atmosphere or ambience appropriate to the target market is very important, including for instance the use of window display and store layout. This allows the town centre speciality store to feed off consumer traffic generated by larger stores, since passing shoppers are attracted in on impulse by what they see in the window or through the door. The multiples can use uniform formulae to replicate success over a wide area, but because of their buying power and expertise, they have taken a great deal of business away from small independents.

Convenience stores. Despite the decline of the small, independent grocer in the UK, there is still a niche that can be filled by convenience stores. Operating mainly in the groceries, drink and CTN sectors, they open long hours, not just 9 a.m. until 6 p.m. The typical CTN is still the small, independent corner shop that serves a local community with basic groceries, newspapers, confectionery and cigarettes, but the range has expanded to include books, stationery, video hire, and greetings cards.

They fill a gap left by the supermarkets, which are fine for the weekly or monthly shopping trip, if the consumer can be bothered to drive out to one. The convenience stores, however, satisfy needs that arise in the meantime. If the consumer has run out of something, forgotten to get something at the supermarket, wants freshness, or finds six unexpected guests on the doorstep who want feeding, the local convenience store is invaluable. If the emergency happens outside normal shopping times, then the advantages of a local, late-night shop become obvious. Such benefits, however, do tend to come at a price premium. To try to become more price competitive, some 'open-all-hours' convenience stores operate as voluntary chains, such as Spar, Londis, Today's and Mace, in which the retailers retain their independence but benefit from bulk purchasing and centralised marketing activities. The priority for many CTNs is to keep trying new services and lines that might sell in the local community. A large number now have off-licences, fax facilities, and the provision of other outsourced services, including dry cleaning and shoe repairs. The National Lottery ticket terminals have provided a boost to income, while even sales of travel cards and phone cards have generated new streams of revenue.

Two more recent developments in convenience retailing are forecourt shops at petrol stations and computerised kiosks. Many petrol retailers, such as Jet and Shell, have developed their non-petrol retailing areas into attractive mini-supermarkets that pull in custom in their own right. In some cases, they are even attracting customers who go in to buy milk or bread and end up purchasing petrol as an afterthought. Sales through forecourts in 2004 were worth around £3.8bn, nearly a 16 per cent share of the convenience market, showing what an important revenue earner forecourt retailing has become (IGD, 2005). The next stage of development could be more cash dispensers installed at forecourt sites, and eventually internet access. Forecourts could also become pick-up locations for home shopping orders. Offering a diversified portfolio of services can be a critical factor in the survival of some rural petrol stations and fuel sales are expected to drop below 20 per cent of sales, on average, over the next few years.

eg The launch of Tesco Metro was a wake-up call for small urban independent convenience stores. It forced many to think very carefully about the catchment area they were serving and what customers really want from a convenience store. Some independents moved quickly to join symbol groups such as Spar and Costcutter to gain the benefits of increased buying power and marketing and merchandising expertise. Independent membership of symbol groups increased by 64 per cent in 2003–04, whereas the number of unaffiliated independent stores fell by 14 per cent. Tesco has only around 5 per cent of the convenience sector but with its enormous buying power there is plenty of scope to offset costs and maintain margins, and yet compete strongly on price. It is true to say that many consumers expect to pay more in a convenience store, and that they are willing to pay a premium for the convenience provided. But there are limits. According to the IGD, most consumers are content to pay a premium of around 5–10 per cent, and yet prices in many independents are more than 15 per cent higher than in the supermarkets. Tesco Express and Sainsbury's Local typically charge only 5 per cent more than in their superstores, thus presenting a tough challenge to their competitors. Interestingly, and adding to the independents' problems, many consumers perceive that the prices they are paying in convenience stores are higher than they actually are, which is a problem for independents seeking to retain business in areas where consumers have a choice of where to shop (Gregory, 2004; Harrington, 2004).

Discount clubs. Discount clubs are rather like cash and carries for the general public, where they can buy in bulk at extremely competitive prices. Discount clubs do, however, have membership requirements, related to occupation and income.

eg   Costco is a form of discount club for both traders and individual members, operating from 16 UK locations, 65 in Canada and 338 in the United States and four other countries. The format is large warehouses selling high-quality, nationally branded and selected private-label merchandise at low prices to businesses purchasing for commercial use or resale, and also to individuals who are members of selected employment groups. Products are packaged, displayed and sold in bulk quantities in a no-frills, warehouse atmosphere on the original shipping pallets. The warehouses are self-service and the member's purchases are packed into empty product boxes. By stripping out the service and merchandising, the prices can be kept low. Costco has no advertising or investor relations department and comparatively few staff. Overheads must also be kept as low as possible to ensure profitability (Birchall, 2005a, 2005b; *The Grocer*, 2001; http://www. costco.co.uk).

The discount clubs achieve their low prices and competitive edge through minimal service and the negotiation of keen bulk deals with the major manufacturers, beyond anything offered to the established supermarkets. Added to this, they pare their margins to the bone, relying on volume turnover, and they purchase speculatively. For instance, they may purchase a one-off consignment of a manufacturer's surplus stock at a very low price, or they may buy stock cheaply from a bankrupt company. While this allows them to offer incredible bargains, they cannot guarantee consistency of supply, thus they may have a heap of televisions one week but once these have been sold, that is it, there are no more. The following week the same space in the store may be occupied by hi-fis. At least such a policy keeps customers coming back to see what new bargains there are.

Markets. Most towns have markets, as a last link with an ancient form of retailing. There are now different types of market, not only those selling different kinds of products but street markets, held on certain days only; permanent markets occupying dedicated sites under cover or in the open; and Sunday markets for more specialised products.

Catalogue showrooms. A fairly recent development, catalogue showrooms try to combine the benefits of a high street presence with the best in logistics technology and physical distribution management. The central focus of the showroom is the catalogue, and many copies are displayed around the store as well as being available for the customer to take home for browsing. Some items are on live display, but this is by no means the whole product range. The consumer selects from the catalogue, then goes to a checkout where an assistant inputs the order into the central computer. If the item is immediately available, the cashier takes payment. The consumer then joins a queue at a collection point, while the purchased product is brought round from the warehouse behind the scenes, usually very quickly.

A prime example of this type of operation is Argos, which carries a very wide range of household, electrical and leisure goods. It offers relatively competitive prices through bulk purchasing, and savings on operating costs, damage and pilfering (because of the limited displays).

Non-store retailing

A growing amount of selling to individual consumers is now taking place outside the traditional retailing structures. Non-store selling may involve personal selling (to be dealt with in Chapter 10), selling to the consumer at home through television, internet or telephone links or, most impersonally, selling through vending machines.

In-home selling. The longest-established means of selling to the consumer at home is through door-to-door selling, where the representative calls at the house either trying to sell from a suitcase (brushes, for example), or trying to do some preliminary selling to pave the way for a more concerted effort later (with higher-cost items such as double glazing, burglar alarms and other home improvements). Cold calling (i.e. turning up unexpectedly and unannounced) is not a particularly efficient use of the representative's time, nor is it likely to evoke a positive response from the customer.

A more acceptable method of in-home selling that has really taken off is the party plan. Here, the organisation recruits ordinary consumers to act as agents and do the selling for them in a relaxed, sociable atmosphere. The agent, or a willing friend, will host a party at a house and provide light refreshments. Guests are invited to attend and during the course of the evening, when everyone is relaxed, the agent will demonstrate the goods and take orders.

Since the pioneering days of the Tupperware party, many other products have used the same sort of technique. Ann Summers, for instance, is an organisation that sells erotic lingerie and sex aids and toys through parties. The majority of the customers are women who would otherwise never dream of going into 'that kind of shop', let alone buying 'that kind of merchandise'. A party is an ideal way of selling those products to that particular target market, because the atmosphere is relaxed, the customer is among friends, and purchases can be made without embarrassment amidst lots of giggling. One of the best features of party selling is the ability to show and demonstrate the product. This kind of hands-on, interactive approach is a powerful way of involving the potential customer and thus getting them interested and in a mood to buy.

The main problem with party selling, however, is that it can be difficult to recruit agents, and their quality and selling abilities will be variable. Supporting and motivating a pyramid of agents and paying their commission can make selling costs very high.

Mail order and teleshopping. Mail order has a long history and traditionally consists of a printed catalogue from which customers select goods that are then delivered to the home, either through the postal service or via couriers. This form of selling has, however, developed and diversified over the years. Offers are now made through magazine or newspaper advertisements, as well as through the traditional catalogue, and database marketing now means that specially tailored offers can be made to individual customers. Orders no longer have to be mailed in by the customer, but can be telephoned, with payment being made immediately by credit card. The strength of mail order varies across Europe, but it is generally stronger in northern Europe than in the south. It is strong in Germany through companies such as Otto Versand, Quelle and Nekermann.

marketing **in action**

Home delivery or 'drive thru' grocery shopping?

Not every shopper enjoys the 'fun' of shopping, especially when it involves a trip to the supermarket. It is this group, those who cannot or prefer not to visit the supermarket but who must buy, that has been the target of several attempts to develop home ordering and home delivery grocery services. The latest estimates, however, suggest that home shopping still accounts for only around 1 per cent of UK grocery sales (Bainbridge and Gladding, 2005).

The reasons why home shopping should be popular are clear: increasingly busy lives with extended working hours; the increasing number of people at work, especially women; the feeling that people have better things to do with their free time such as 'real' leisure pursuits; and growing acceptance of home delivery in a range of sectors such as books, pizza, flowers, etc. All of this, combined with the increasing use of the internet, sets the scene for significant growth in home grocery shopping. The trouble is that the supermarket chains that have experimented with online grocery shopping have reported variable results. Somerfield and Budgens closed down their home delivery operations in 2000 due to poor take-up. In contrast, Tesco and Sainsbury's are often quoted as the two most successful operators.

The 'Sainsbury's To You' online service claims to cover around 75 per cent of the country and to receive 35,000 orders per week. Although this is still a small percentage compared with checkout sales, it does provide a valuable service to some customers. In 2004 it launched a '1 hour delivery promise', reflecting confidence in its ability to process and expedite orders very quickly. Its main rival Tesco offered only a two-hour promise. Sainsbury's also went further in offering a £10 discount off the customer's next order if delivery fell outside the one-hour time slot. Supported by a marketing campaign, hopes were high that the 10 per cent sales increase observed in trials could be replicated on the full roll-out (*Marketing Week*, 2004a). Unfortunately within two months the scheme had to be withdrawn, not for operational reasons, but because customers were taking advantage of a loophole in the Sainsbury website that allowed codes on vouchers to be used again and again. For a while, a chatroom used for discount code trading became one of the most popular on the internet as customers repeatedly cashed in on the £10 vouchers (Johnstone, 2004). It is now uncertain how Sainsbury's will develop its home delivery service, as there have been some criticisms of poor availability and unsuitable substitutions being made since it moved to store-based distribution. Tesco thus remains dominant (Hegarty, 2005).

Tesco.com has persevered with home shopping for nearly 10 years and is now seeing some results. Although the level of profit earned from the venture is unknown, it is claimed that there are over 750,000 registered customers, that it covers 96 per cent of Tesco's 270 stores and that it receives 120,000 orders a week (*Marketing Week*, 2004a). Tesco claims that it has opened up new market segments and attracted business away from Waitrose in the south and Sainsbury's in the north of the UK. Customers do not just order groceries; CDs, DVDs and wine are also popular. Perhaps what is more important is that while the typical shopper at Tesco spends under £25 per visit, the online shopper spends over £80 (presumably on the basis that if you are going to pay a £5 delivery fee, you might as well make it worthwhile). Waitrose has now also joined the market through a joint venture with Ocado, although it operates only in selected regions to combat Tesco. Nevertheless, Waitrose does have a reputation for good delivery and service (Bainbridge and Gladding, 2005). Ocado has massive sheds carrying stock in breadth and depth so that it can reduce the number of substituted items for Waitrose. Meanwhile, ASDA has doubled the number of products that it offers on the web to 20,000 (Tesco offers 40,000) and soon expects to be able to reach 60 per cent of UK households.

Verdict Research estimates that sales will continue to grow, reaching £2bn in 2005, nearly 2 per cent of grocery turnover. The number of shoppers buying through this method is around 2 million, and as broadband becomes more popular, numbers are likely to grow further. Others, such as Dresdner Kleinwort Benson, forecast that by 2008 around 10 per cent of UK food sales will be generated this way. This supports Tesco's belief that online shopping could be the biggest revolution in supermarket shopping since self-service was introduced. Independent research is less encouraging, however. An Institute of Grocery and Distribution survey has suggested that most consumers have little interest in buying groceries over the internet: they prefer to choose food in-store, don't like paying online and enjoy the spontaneity and exploration of shopping. The level of understanding is also low, as they think that the product range will be limited with shorter shelf-life and that they will lose out by having fewer price promotions. The challenge is still to ensure fast delivery and no substitutes so that online shoppers can be completely satisfied.

Sources: Bainbridge and Gladding (2005); Dickinson (2005); Hegarty (2005); Johnstone (2004); *Marketing Week* (2004a); Parry and Cogswell (2005); Ryle (2001).

Teleshopping represents a much wider range of activities. It includes shopping by telephone in response to television advertisements, whether on cable, satellite or terrestrial channels. Some cable and satellite operators run home-shopping channels, such as QVC, where the primary objective is to sell goods to viewers. Teleshopping also covers interactive shopping by computer, using mechanisms such as the French Minitel system or the internet. The internet in particular offers interesting opportunities to a variety of sellers, including established retailers. Many, such as Toys 'Я' Us and Blackwell's Bookshop, have set up 'virtual' stores on internet sites, so that a potential customer can browse through the merchandise, select items, pay by credit card and then wait for the goods to be delivered.

Vending. Vending machines account for a very small percentage of retail sales, less than 1 per cent. They are mainly based in workplaces and public locations, for example offices, factories, staffrooms, bus and rail stations, etc. They are best used for small, standard, low-priced, repeat purchase products, such as hot and cold drinks, cans of drink, chocolate and snacks, bank cash dispensers and postage stamps. They have the advantage of allowing customers to purchase at highly convenient locations, at any time of the day or night. Vending machines can also help to deliver the product in prime condition for consumption, for example the refrigerated machines that deliver a can of ice-cold Coke. A human retailer cannot always maintain those conditions.

Channel strategy

With the various added-value roles implicit in the marketing channel, decisions need to be taken about the allocation and performance of these roles, the basis of remuneration within the system, and the effectiveness of alternative configurations in enabling market penetration to be achieved competitively and efficiently. This is channel strategy.

■ Channel structures

The basic forms of channel design were outlined in Figures 8.1 and 8.3. These are known as conventional channels, in which the various channel activities are agreed by negotiation and compromise, recognising that both sides need each other. The particular structure adopted should reflect the market and product characteristics, taking into consideration such factors as market coverage, value, quantity sold, margin available, etc. (Sharma and Dominguez, 1992).

Where a manufacturer needs to reach distinct target markets, a dual or multiple distribution approach may be adopted, which means that each target market may be reached by two or more different routes. For example, IBM will sell direct to large users and organisations, but will go through the retail trade to reach the consumer segment. This pattern works well, provided that discreteness is maintained and as long as the arrangement reflects the various buyers' differing pre- and post-purchase servicing needs. However, problems can emerge if the same product is sold to the same target market through different channels. A book publisher, for example, may create some friction with the book trade if it actively encourages direct ordering and other subscription services at lower prices than the retail trade can manage. This potential for conflict may well increase as direct marketing and home shopping gain in popularity.

Competition in channels

Not all competition in channels comes from traditionally expected direct sources, as we see from Figure 8.5. Sometimes, internal channel competition can reduce the efficiency of the whole channel system. Each of the four types of competition identified by Palamountain (1955) is considered in turn below.

Horizontal competition. Horizontal competition, as can be seen in Figure 8.5, is competition between intermediaries of the same type. This type of competition, for example between supermarkets, is readily visible. Each one develops marketing and product range strategies to gain competitive advantage over the others.

Intertype competition. Intertype competition refers to competition at the same level in the channel but between different types of outlet. Thus, for example, the battle between the department stores, the High Street electrical retailers and large out-of-town warehouse operations to sell hi-fi equipment to the same customer base is a form of intertype competition. The manufacturer that has a choice may need to develop different approaches to handle each retailer type. Of course, there are dangers if a manufacturer is seen to give unwarranted preference to one type over another, given the intense rivalries that can develop. This may start to lead to dysfunctional channel behaviour.

Vertical competition. Vertical competition can soon become a serious threat to the integrity and effectiveness of a channel. Here, the competition is between different levels in the channel, such as wholesaler and retailer, or even retailer and manufacturer. This type of

Figure 8.5 Competition in channels

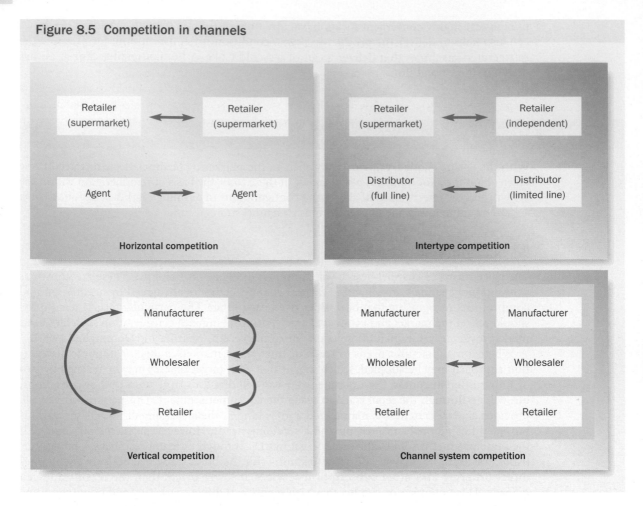

competition can soon lead to internal rivalry, where the focus shifts from cooperative market penetration, focused outwards, to mutual cannibalism, focused inwards.

Channel system competition. The last form of channel competition is where a particular channel is in competition with different, parallel channels. The focus for the operator, therefore, is on ensuring that its system is more efficient and competitive than the others. The emphasis is on total channel efficiency, which may, however, involve some suboptimisation in the interests of a more effective chain.

eg The car manufacturers operate through competing channel systems, especially where there are exclusive arrangements with dealers. Ford, therefore, wants to make sure that its channel system is functioning better than Renault's or Honda's to create extra value for existing and potential customers. This has implications for all aspects of marketing, including promotion, distribution, customer service, technical support and product development.

Vertical marketing systems

To minimise the risks of internal competition within the channel and the risks of conflict, channel members, who wish to cooperate and gain the maximum possible benefits from channel membership, may form closely knit vertical marketing systems (VMS). These systems can become highly organised and dominated, to a point where the independence of some of the members disappears into a vertically integrated channel, with one member owning all or some of the other levels. There are three types of VMS.

Corporate vertical marketing systems. A corporate VMS exists where an organisation owns and operates other levels in the channel. This may be at any level, and the dominant organisation may be manufacturer, wholesaler or retailer. *Forward integration* means that the manufacturer owns and operates at the retail or wholesale level. A number of oil companies, for example, own their own petrol stations, while Firestone, the tyre manufacturer, owns its own tyre retailers. *Backward integration* occurs when the retailer owns and operates at a wholesale or manufacturing level. Retailers such as Zara operate in backwardly integrated markets.

Contractual vertical marketing systems. The most prevalent form of VMS is the contractual VMS. Members of the channel retain their independence, but negotiate contractual agreements that specify their rights, duties and obligations, covering issues such as stock levels and pricing policies, for example. This prevents unnecessary internal conflict and suboptimal behaviour. Three types of contractual system are commonly found.

> The corporate VMS has the advantage of creating a channel that is tailormade for the owner's product and marketing objectives. Furthermore, those objectives are shared throughout the channel. The owner also has ultimate control over the activities of the channel and its members. TUI, the German tour operator, operates a VMS so that it can tailor its holiday packages to client needs and ensure that these objectives are shared throughout the channel, as it has the ultimate control of its members' activities. The VMS includes travel agents selling the packages, airlines taking customers to holiday destinations, and the hotels looking after them, all packaged by owned, branded tour operators. In these situations, care must be taken to allay public fears that such close arrangements could restrict customer choice and result in biased advice from travel agents supporting one tour operator at the expense of others.

A retail cooperative exists where groups of retailers agree to work together and to combine and increase their purchasing power by supporting their own wholesaling operation. This sort of agreement helps the small independent retailers who are members of the cooperative with greater range, access to promotion and more competitive pricing.

A wholesaler voluntary chain is one where a wholesaler promotes a contractual relationship with independent retailers, whereby the latter agree to coordinated purchasing, inventory and merchandising programmes. The coordination enables some of the benefits of bulk buying and group promotion to be realised by smaller operators. Mace and the Independent Grocers' Alliance are UK examples.

Franchising is fast becoming a major model of contractual arrangement across Europe. Franchising is an ongoing contractual relationship between a franchisor who owns the product concept and a franchisee who is allowed to operate a business, within an agreed territory, in line with the methods, procedures and overall blueprint provided by the franchisor. Managerial support, training, merchandising and access to finance are effectively exchanged for conformity and a specified fee and/or royalties on sales.

Administered vertical marketing systems. Coordination and control are achieved in an administered VMS through the power of one of the channel members. It is, in reality, a conventional channel within which a dominant force has emerged. Therefore, although each member is autonomous, there is a willingness to agree to interorganisational management by one of its members. Contracts may or may not be used to govern the parameters of behaviour.

> Marks & Spencer uses an administered VMS to forge very close links with its suppliers, and to dominate decisions about what is supplied, how it is manufactured, quality levels and pricing. Suppliers accept this dominance because they regard M&S as a prestigious and trustworthy customer, and respect its experience of the market. Similarly, Ahold, the Dutch retailer, offers leadership within its distribution channels in terms of product development, manufacturing and purchasing.

The emergence of these integrated forms of channel system is increasingly questioning the traditional approach to channel management. They also provide a context within which behavioural aspects of channel relationships can be examined.

■ Market coverage

One way of thinking about which types of channel are appropriate is to start at the end and work backwards. The sort of questions to ask relate not only to the identity of the end customer, but also to their expectations, demand patterns, frequency of ordering, degree of comparison shopping, degree of convenience and the associated services required. All of these elements influence the added value created by place, and the density and type of intermediaries to be used, whether at wholesaler or distributor or retail level. Market coverage, therefore, is about reaching the end customer as cost effectively and as efficiently as possible, while maximising customer satisfaction. To achieve this, three alternative models of distribution intensity can be adopted, as shown in Table 8.1, each of which reflects different product and customer requirements from place (Stern *et al.*, 1996). They are discussed below, in turn.

Table 8.1 Alternative distribution intensities: general characteristics

	Intensive	Selective	Exclusive
Total number of outlets covered	Maximum	Possibly many	Relatively few
Number of outlets per region	As many as possible	A small number	One or very few
Distribution focus	Maximum availability	Some specialist retailer knowledge	Close retailer/ consumer relationship
Type of consumer product	Convenience	Shopping	Speciality
Number of potential purchasers	High	Medium	Low
Purchase frequency	Often	Occasionally	Seldom
Level of planned purchasing by consumers	Low	Medium	High
Typical price	Low	Medium	High

Intensive distribution

Intensive distribution occurs where the product or service is placed in as many outlets as possible, and no interested intermediary is barred from stocking the product. Typical products include bread, newspapers and confectionery, but more generally, most convenience goods (see p. 182) fall into this category. The advantage to the consumer is that convenience and availability may be just around the corner, and they can invest a minimum of time and effort in the purchasing process. Using this kind of market coverage also assumes that availability is more important than the type of store selling the product, hence the growth of non-petrol products on sale in garages.

Intensive distribution usually involves a long chain of distribution (manufacturer–wholesaler–retailer–consumer). It is an efficient means of getting the product as widely available as possible, but total distribution costs may be high, especially where small retailers are concerned and unit orders are low.

Selective distribution

As the term suggests, a more selective approach is designed to use a small number of carefully chosen outlets within a defined geographic area. These are often found with shopping products (again, see p. 182) where the consumer may be more willing to search for the most appropriate product and then to undertake a detailed comparison of alternatives. Unlike intensively distributed goods, which can virtually be put on a shop shelf to sell themselves, selectively distributed products might need a little more help from the intermediary, perhaps because they have a higher technical content that needs to be demonstrated, for instance. Manufacturers may also need to invest more in the distribution infrastructure, point-of-sale materials and after-sales service. It may thus pay to select a smaller number of intermediaries, where support such as training and joint promotions can be offered and controlled.

eg The major fine fragrance manufacturers have long adopted a selective distribution strategy. Their rationale for this is that they are selling a luxury, upmarket product that needs to have an appropriate level of personal selling support and the right kind of retail ambience to reinforce and enhance the product's expensive image. In the early 1990s, they repeatedly refused to supply discount chemist chains such as Superdrug in the UK, who wanted to undercut the prices charged by upmarket department stores and other existing fragrance retailers. Pressure from Superdrug and other discount retailers which obtained unofficial but perfectly legal supplies from third parties has thus led to a relaxation of the manufacturers' attitudes and thus to the wider availability of fragrances with a significant focus on price competition from all but the most upmarket retailers.

Exclusive distribution

Exclusive distribution is the opposite of intensive distribution, and means that only one outlet covers a relatively large geographic area. This type of distribution may reflect very large infrastructure investments, a scattered low density of demand or infrequently purchased products. In B2B markets, the impact on the customer may not be particularly significant if a sales force and customer service network are in place. However, in consumer markets there may be some inconvenience to the customer, who may have to travel some distance to source the product and may effectively have no choice about who to purchase from.

eg Bang & Olufsen (B&O) has adopted a strategy of working closely with small retailers on a global scale. It has 400 B&O branded stores across the world operated by independent businesses. By adopting a branded store format, it is better able to control how these exclusive dealers display and demonstrate B&O audio-visual equipment. Keeping this level of exclusivity and control is essential, because if stock levels are not maintained and if demos are not available then multi-brand hi-fi retailers are prone to 'switch selling', i.e. selling the customer an alternative brand which they *do* have in stock and which *does* have demos available.

B&O's dealers have to be highly motivated and dedicated to B&O. Getting customers to experience a demo is a critical part of the selling process, so the purpose of most of the marketing effort is to encourage potential customers to make an enquiry and become willing to visit a dealer. Similarly, the current web strategy is to drive customers to dealers, not to encourage direct sales, although for the longer term B&O is keeping its options open. The B&O website supports this effort, so that customers can book a local demo through the main company website. Using the Synkron web platform B&O has also been able to give each dealer a higher quality micro-site designed by B&O. Our local store, for example, is based in Oxford and its micro-site not only gives the expected information about store location and contact details and generic information about the ranges it stocks, but also shows a photograph of the store and gives profiles of its owner and his staff which gives it a much more friendly, intimate, small business feel. In further acknowledgement of the importance of the link between the consumer and the retailer, now that we have established that Oxford is our local store, every time we log onto the B&O main website, a hyperlink direct to the Oxford store micro-site features on the homepage (*New Media Age*, 2004; **http://www.bang-olufsen.com**).

Such an exclusive approach may even fit in with the product's own exclusivity. It would also be appropriate where high degrees of cooperation in inventory management, service standards and selling effort are required between manufacturer and intermediary (Frazier and Lassar, 1996).

■ Influences on channel strategy

There are several alternative channel design decisions facing the manufacturer who has a choice, but there are also several factors that may constrain these choices. These factors are outlined below, and are shown in Figure 8.6. While it may be desirable to adopt an optimal design in terms of marketing effectiveness and efficiency, rarely do organisations have the luxury of a clean sheet of paper. More often, they inherit the consequences of previous decisions, and the risks of changing design midstream need to be carefully considered before any planned improvement.

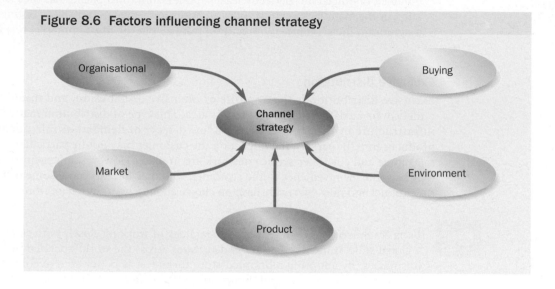

Figure 8.6   Factors influencing channel strategy

Organisational objectives, capabilities and resources

The channel strategy selected needs to fit in with the organisation's objectives, capabilities and resources. If the objective is to generate mass appeal and rapid market penetration, then an intensive distribution approach would be necessary. This would have to be supported, however, with an equally intense investment in other marketing activities such as promotion. If the focus was on repositioning upmarket into a more exclusive niche, then a selective or even an exclusive distribution approach would be called for.

Objectives may change over time as environmental circumstances evolve. For example, demands for an improved delivery service or increased geographic coverage may require new distributors, more distributors or incorporating better service levels in the service structure of existing distributors.

Market size, dispersion and remoteness

No channel strategy decision can ignore the impact of the market. If a manufacturer wishes to penetrate a market some distance from its base, it may lack the contacts, market knowledge or distribution infrastructure to deal directly. There may be little choice but to deal with intermediaries. Similarly, a small organisation might lack the resources necessary for building sales contacts and maintaining customer service, especially if resources are limited and there is a need to develop sales volume quickly.

When demand is more highly concentrated, or where there are a few, readily identifiable customers, it may be possible to build a direct operation, keep full control and eliminate intermediaries. Efficiency may be obtained in negotiation, delivery and support services. By way of contrast, a large, dispersed market, such as that for magazines, may require a well-structured, efficient chain of intermediaries.

Buying complexity and behaviour

Understanding customer needs and buying criteria goes to the heart of effective marketing and has a major influence on channel selection (Butaney and Wortzel, 1988). Questions such as who buys, where they buy and how frequently they buy all indicate the kind of intermediary best suited to reach target customers. Matching the intermediary with customer needs, buyer expectations and product position is a challenging task. The move to out-of-town shopping, with its advantages of easy parking, convenience and large assortments under one roof, has meant a refocusing of effort by some manufacturers to ensure that they are well represented. Similarly, if a product occupies a specialist position, there is little point in dealing with a wholesaler that is primarily concerned with mass distribution.

eg Following on from the B&O example on p. 285, its competitor Linn Hi-Fi believes that the retailer must take the complexity out of the hi-fi buying decision for the consumer. The retailer has to be able to demonstrate, help design the best system, provide specialist listening facilities and be prepared to install a system. Some are even allowing home trials. But when the customer is potentially spending thousands on a sound system or home cinema set-up, everything has to be right.

Product characteristics

Products that are complex to purchase, install or operate, products that are of high unit value and products that are customer specific tend to be distributed directly to the customer or through highly specialised intermediaries. This reflects the need for close dialogue during the pre- and post-sale situations that may be lost if additional parties are involved. By way of contrast, fairly standard, routinely purchased, low-unit-value products tend to be distributed intensively through intermediaries.

eg McQuillan Engineering Industries (MEI) is a supplier of a wide assortment of components for aircraft interiors, such as overhead bins, galleys, sink units and even nuts and bolts. However, although considerable stocks are held, everything is manufactured to customer designs and specifications, and when demanded they can be assembled on site. Customers include Boeing, Saab and Airbus. With a specialism in batch or prototype production, the distribution and sales method is direct because of the complexity of individual customer orders. This contrasts with replacement parts for domestic electrical equipment, which are standardised by model and are widely stocked either in manufacturers' warehouses or through intermediaries such as repairers.

Other product factors may also have an impact. Highly perishable products need short distribution channels to maintain product quality or to assist in rapid turnover. Items that are non-standard or difficult to handle or items that have the potential to create transport problems may be less attractive to intermediaries (Rosenbloom, 1987).

Changing environment

The changing business environment, discussed in Chapter 2, creates new problems and opportunities for channel design. Three issues demonstrate the effect.

Technology. Technology offers the potential for closer integration between the manufacturer and the intermediary. Online systems may enable direct access to stock availability, electronic ordering and automated dispatch with the minimum of negotiation, if any. Electronic point-of-sale (EPOS) data can facilitate very rapid responses within the distribution system. Smaller organisations still relying on older technology such as the telephone and manual checking may soon become marginalised.

Working patterns. The growth in the number of women working has had a profound effect on some distribution channels, making some channels more difficult to operate, such as door-to-door selling during the daytime, while home shopping and convenience shopping outside usual trading hours have become much more widely accepted.

European Union regulations. Generally speaking, manufacturers have the right to decide which intermediaries should or should not distribute their products. Both national and European regulatory bodies start to become interested, however, where exclusion of certain intermediaries might be seen as a deliberate attempt to distort competition or to achieve price fixing. See, for example, Case Study 7 (at p. 252) and also the legal debate over Levi Strauss's refusal to supply supermarket chains with jeans. The debate hinged on whether the refusal to supply was based on a legitimate concern over trademark protection and the quality of the retail premises and staff, or whether it was simply an attempt to prevent retail prices falling.

Selecting a channel member

The final phase of the channel design strategy is the selection of specific intermediaries. The selection decision tends to become more critical as the intensity of distribution itself becomes more selective or exclusive. In mass-distribution decisions, such as those concerning products like confectionery, any willing outlet will be considered. However, where a selective distribution approach is adopted, great care must be taken over the final selection of intermediary, as a poor decision may lead to strategic failure. For example, the selection of a wholesaler to allow entry into a new European market may be critical to the degree and speed of penetration achieved.

eg Klemm is part of the Bauer group and specialises in a range of German-built hydraulic rigs and drilling accessories for construction sites. Its channel approach is often to appoint sole distributors in target countries. Thus in the UK, Skelair handles all sales, while in the Netherlands, Dutch Drilling Consultants v.o.f. has exclusive rights. Klemm seeks to develop a close and effective relationship with its distributors. Although individual domestic markets may be relatively small, the selling task is complex in defining machines for applications, and good after-sales service is also crucial. This demands close technical support and a level of trust and confidence between manufacturer and distributor (**http://www.klemm-bt.com**).

In situations where organisations need to select intermediaries on a fairly frequent basis, it would be useful to select on the basis of predetermined criteria. Table 8.2 highlights a range of issues that should be examined as part of an appraisal process.

Table 8.2 Selection criteria for intermediaries

Strategic	Operational
• Expansion plans	• Local market knowledge
• Resource building	• Adequate premises/equipment
• Management quality/competence	• Stockholding policy
• Market coverage	• Customer convenience
• Partnership willingness	• Product knowledge
• Loyalty/cooperation	• Realistic credit/payment terms
	• Sales force capability
	• Efficient customer service

The relative importance of the various criteria will vary from sector to sector and indeed over time. Inevitably, there is still a need for management judgement and a trading off of pros and cons, as the 'ideal' distributor that is both willing and able to proceed will rarely be found. Remember too that intermediaries have the choice of whether or not they will sell the products offered. This luxury of choice is not restricted just to supermarkets and large multiple retailers. Travel agents can stock only a limited number of holidays, and are very careful about offering new packages from smaller tour operators. In some industrial distribution channels, the intermediary can decide whether or not to stock ancillary products around the main products that it sells on a dealership basis.

Skelair International provides expertise to develop sales in the UK for Klemm Bohrtechnik, a renowned ground engineering specialist.

Source: Klemm Bohrtechnik/Skelair International Ltd

Conflict and cooperation

Most of this chapter so far has concentrated largely on economic issues involved in channel decisions. However, all channel decisions are ultimately made between people in organisations. There is, therefore, always the potential for disagreement over the many decisions such as expected roles, allocation of effort, reward structures, product and marketing strategies that ensure the system operates effectively. A channel is an interorganisational social system comprising members who are tied together by a belief that by working together (for the time being at least), they can improve the individual benefits gained. A climate of cooperation is perhaps the most desirable within a channel system. It does not just happen, but needs to be worked on and cultivated.

Good communication, in terms of amount, direction, medium and content, is also essential for closer cooperation in a channel (Mohr and Nevin, 1990). In a study of computer dealers, Mohr *et al.* (1999) found that effective communication led to greater satisfaction, stronger commitment and better coordination. The development of electronic sharing of data and intelligence is strengthening many channel relationships as technology helps all members to make better decisions in times of market uncertainty as well as reducing selling and coordination costs (Huber, 1990).

corporate social responsibility   in action

Keeping tabs on tablets

When we talk about counterfeit goods, we probably think about fake designer clothing and accessories or pirated DVDs. We don't think of it as anything that does much harm – perhaps some lost tax revenue to a few governments, lost profits to a few fat-cat organisations that won't miss it, and a little wounded pride for the consumers who were daft enough to think that they were buying the real thing at a knock-down price. It can be a far more serious issue than this, however. It has been estimated that 10 per cent of drugs sold worldwide are counterfeit, and that in the developing world, the figure is over 25 per cent. In Nigeria, it is more like 60 per cent. This is a huge issue for the pharmaceutical industry and its supply chain – at best, counterfeit drugs may supply a reduced or ineffective dosage, but at worst, they may kill the patient. The whole question of the security of the pharmaceutical supply chain has to be addressed if patients are to have confidence that the drugs they collect from the local pharmacy are actually those that left legitimate manufacturing plants. It's a very complex question, in a $400bn global industry in which drugs companies often outsource manufacture to suppliers in a number of different low-cost countries, and then distribute those goods worldwide via a number of intermediaries. It is fair to say that some of these countries perhaps take a less than rigorous view of patent and intellectual property protection.

Some counterfeiting is extremely difficult to control, such as the fake pills manufactured from brick dust, paint, floor wax and water and then sold via dodgy 'no questions asked' websites, although the police and other regulatory bodies worldwide are cooperating to locate and close down the illegal factories that produce these drugs. Similarly, companies such as Pfizer are using the full force of the law to pursue website owners that are selling fake or illegitimate supplies of

drugs such as Viagra. Some counterfeit drugs do get into more traditional distribution channels – it takes only one unscrupulous link in what can be a complex and geographically widespread chain of intermediaries. Some products can change hands many times through the perfectly legal process of parallel trading in which drugs can be bought more cheaply in other EU countries and then imported into the UK, for example. By this time, their origins may have become somewhat obscure. Further scope for problems arises from the regulation that requires these imported medicines to be opened so that an English language patient information leaflet can be inserted. So much for tamper-proof packaging. Around 20 per cent of medicines dispensed in the UK have been repackaged and there have been calls in the industry for the regulations to be changed to allow over-boxing (i.e. leaving the original packaging unopened and inserting it with its required leaflet into a new box).

In the interests of protecting all the legitimate members of the supply chain, measures are being developed to try to ensure drug safety at the point of dispensing it. For example, a pilot scheme ran from autumn 2004 into early 2005 in 44 pharmacies in the UK using RFID (radio frequency identification) tags to help identify counterfeit medicines that had got into the supply chain. Six drug manufacturers also participated and 20,000 products were given an RFID tag or barcode. When the

product is scanned at the point of sale, its details are relayed to a secure database to check that everything matches up with the manufacturer's original record on that specific item. If a product is not recognised, it is rejected. This is a big improvement on more traditional printed bar codes as they identify only a 'type' of product, whereas RFID can differentiate each individual package. This means not only that counterfeit medicines can be identified, but also that drugs that have expired or that belong to a batch that has been recalled can be picked up easily. Of course, this confirms only that the packaging is 'real', but what if the contents have been switched at some point in the supply chain? There is a lot of investment going into the development of non-toxic, durable and impossible-to-fake technologies for the overt and covert marking of individual tablets.

With governments and regulatory bodies taking a keen interest in this issue, it is vital that the pharmaceutical manufacturers and other members of this supply chain work together to protect the integrity of the products they deal with and their journey through the marketplace. This is not only about safeguarding the investment that has been made in building brand and corporate images, but also about safeguarding the health and welfare of consumers and their trust in the supply chain.

Sources: *FDA Consumer* (2005); Humble (2005); Jackson (2005); Lantin (2004); Muddyman (2005); *Packaging Magazine* (2005).

Some view conflict and cooperation as being at opposite ends of a continuum, while others view them as distinct concepts. Whatever the view, strong cooperation can lead to a feeling of satisfaction and partnership, one of give and take. Cooperation may lead to strong personal and organisational ties that are difficult for outsiders to break. However, not all cooperation need be voluntary. A weaker channel member may think it best to cooperate and comply with the wishes of a more powerful member, rather than risk retribution.

Conflict is a natural part of any social system. Conflict may exist where, for example, one channel member feels that another member is not dealing fairly with it, or that the system is not working sufficiently in its favour. There are numerous possible causes of conflict, some arising from poor understanding, others from a fundamental difference of opinion that goes to the heart of the relationship.

Conflict needs to be spotted early and dealt with before it becomes too overt. This can be helped by regular meetings, frequent communication and ensuring that all parties emerge satisfied from negotiations. It is critical that each channel member should fully understand their role and what is expected of them, and that this is agreed in advance. If conflict does become overt, communication, formation of channel committees, a fast arbitration service and top management commitment to resolution are all essential to prevent an irrevocable breakdown of the channel.

eg Nisa-Today is the largest independent buying group in Europe for retail and wholesale companies. Its commercial objective is to negotiate the lowest cost-price of products and provide the most efficient supply chain for its member companies. Using its collective buying power it negotiates on behalf of its affiliated independent retailers to obtain more competitive terms than they could get individually. In doing that, however, Nisa-Today ran into trouble with its suppliers when it demanded that they should make cost reductions. A 20p per case reduction was asked for on all chilled and frozen products, and suppliers complained that this was presented as non-negotiable. Nisa-Today said that the cuts were requested to help offset increased investment in IT and the supply chain (*The Grocer*, 2005).

Chapter summary

■ The channel of distribution is the means through which products are moved from the manufacturer to the end consumer. The structure of channels can vary considerably depending on the type of market, the needs of the end customer and the type of product. Consumer goods might be supplied direct, but in mass markets for convenience goods this might not be feasible and longer channels might be used. B2B markets are far more likely to involve direct supply from manufacturer to B2B buyer. Some B2B purchases, however, particularly routine repurchases of non-critical items such as office stationery, might be distributed in ways that are similar to those used in consumer markets, with various intermediaries involved.

■ Intermediaries play an important role in increasing efficiency and reducing costs, reduce the manufacturer's risk, gather, store, sort and transport a wide range of goods, and ease cash flow for manufacturers and for customers. These functions are not all necessarily performed by the same member of the distribution channel and the decision as to who does what may be made by consensus or by the use of power in the channel. Distributors, agents and wholesalers tend to act as intermediaries in B2B markets or as an interface between manufacturers and retailers. Retailers tend to serve the needs of individual consumers and can be classified according to a number of criteria: form of ownership (independents, corporate chains or contractual systems), level of service (full or limited), merchandise lines (breadth and depth) and operating methods (type of store, whether department store, supermarket, variety store or other). Non-store retailing, closely linked with direct marketing, has also become increasingly popular and widespread. It includes in-home selling, parties, mail-order operations, teleshopping and vending machines.

■ Channel design will be influenced by a number of factors, including organisational objectives, capabilities and resources. Market size might also constrain the choice of channel, as might the buying complexity associated with the product and the buying behaviour of the target market. The changing environment can also influence the choice of channel. Selecting specific intermediaries to join a channel can be difficult but this choice can be a critical success factor since, for example, the speed of entry and the degree of penetration into a new market can depend on the right choice of intermediary. Sometimes, however, the intermediary has the power to reject a manufacturer or a specific product. Vertical marketing systems (VMS) have evolved to create a channel that is more efficient and effective for all parties, ideally working towards the common good in a long-term relationship. Clearly, voluntary cooperation is the best way of achieving an effective and efficient channel. However, conflict might arise and, if it is not dealt with promptly and sensitively, might lead, sooner or later, to the dissolution of that channel.

■ Manufacturers are not restricted to using only one channel. There are three broad levels of intensity of distribution, each implying a different set of channels and different types of intermediary: intensive distribution, selective distribution and exclusive distribution.

Questions for review and discussion

8.1 What are the different types of *intermediary* that might be found in a distribution channel?

8.2 What are the five factors influencing *channel strategy*?

8.3 To what extent and why do you think that the creation of a VMS can improve the performance of a channel and its members?

8.4 What kind of market coverage strategy might be appropriate for the following, and why:
(a) a bar of chocolate;
(b) a toothbrush;
(c) a home computer;
(d) a marketing textbook.

8.5 Using Table 8.2 on p. 288 as a starting point, develop lists of criteria that a manufacturer might use in defining:
(a) 'good' retailers; and
(b) 'good' wholesalers
to recruit for consumer market channels.

8.6 In what ways and to what extent do you think that *non-store retailing* poses a threat to conventional retailers?

case study 8

The fresh appeal of the farmers' market

Farmers' markets are springing up in towns and cities all over the place! You only have to read the lifestyle pages of the quality newspapers to see how the cookery editors are raving over the quality and range of produce these markets supply, and how a farmers' market in the neighbourhood can increase the value of your house. So what are farmers' markets and why have they suddenly become so trendy?

According to the National Farmers' Retail & Markets Association (FARMA),

> *A farmers' market is one in which farmers, growers or producers from a defined local area are present in person to sell their own produce, direct to the public. All products sold should have been grown, reared, caught, brewed, pickled, baked, smoked or processed by the stallholder.* (**http://www.farmersmarkets.net**)

'Local area' is defined by FARMA as being within 50 miles or within the county boundary. The precise criteria vary from market to market, however. Most impose a 30-mile boundary, while London Farmers' Markets allow a 100-mile radius around the M25.

The idea came from the USA, and the first farmers' markets in the UK were held in 1997/98, in Bath and London. They spread quickly: by 2000 there were 240 such markets, and by 2005 more than 500 across the whole country, providing over 10,000 market days between them. The biggest is in Winchester, with 100 stalls and an estimated 10,000 visitors on a Sunday. Most farmers' markets attract between 1000 and 2000 shoppers. Farmers' markets' turnover in 2004 was estimated to be around £300m, one-third of which was generated from organic produce. FARMA sees these markets as a valuable way of encouraging two-way interaction and dialogue between food producers and consumers, and furthermore,

> *Farmers' markets are for all kinds of food producers and offer a low-cost entry point for many farmers who have not 'sold direct' before. Farmers' markets are the embodiment of the availability of home grown foods. They are the British farming industry's most high-profile shop-window.* (**http://www.farmersmarkets.net**)

This is also echoed by La Trobe (2001) who sees farmers' markets as a means of small-scale producers cutting out intermediaries and thus being able to plough back more of the revenue directly into rural economies. La Trobe also suggests that the kind of small-scale producers who sell at farmers' markets are more likely to operate in an environmentally friendly way and are less likely to use intensive or otherwise questionable forms of animal rearing. In the current climate of consumer concern, the opportunity that a farmers' market offers for dialogue between producer and consumer 'improves accountability and helps customers to overcome any concerns they may have regarding the ethical issues of farming animals, as well as the quality, traceability and safety of the food they are buying' (La Trobe, 2001).

While it all sounds very idyllic, a survey of a number of farmers' markets undertaken by ACNielsen in the summer of 2005 did note that not many of the stalls complied exactly with the code. The stalls did not just stock their own produce or even local produce, but offered quite a lot of imported fruit and vegetables too. This may be because the title 'farmers' market' is not protected and 'unofficial' farmers' markets can do what they like (Palmer, 2005).

Many stalls also combined produce with specialist 'healthfood' or lifestyle products, although a lot less organic or free-range produce was available than expected. It is interesting too that many stalls offered a mixture of basic produce and premium items. In terms of product range and pricing, as might be expected of markets that bring together a wide variety of autonomous small producers, wide variations were observed from market to market and from region to region. Some items were significantly cheaper than could be found in supermarkets, some were significantly more expensive. Table 8.3 shows comparative prices for a selection of produce that is typically found in a farmers' market.

Another study, commissioned by the London Development Agency, similarly found that the price differences between farmers' markets and supermarkets are variable, but relatively small. The conclusion was that farmers' markets are overall more price competitive than consumers perceive them to be (Woolf, 2005).

Pricing is not necessarily the main criterion for shopping at a farmers' market, however. The typical farmers' market shopper tends to be female, in the ABC1 socioeconomic groups, either retired or with a young family, and is willing to pay a premium for perceived value in terms of freshness, quality and local produc-tion. Healthy eating may be important to her, exacer-bated by media coverage of the unhealthiness of processed foods and various food scares. In this light, farmers, especially organic farmers, may well be regarded as more trustworthy suppliers of food than supermarkets. This shopper may also be somewhat disillusioned with the uniformity and predictability of the supermarket shopping experience and perhaps gets a 'buzz' from the busy, sociable atmosphere of a market and the opportunity to discover new or different things there. She may well have an ethical conscience, and might have been disturbed by what she has heard in various media about the sourcing policies of the gro-cery multiples. If that is the case, then the opportunity to question producers and buy directly from them at a farmers' market will be very appealing.

ACNielsen thus summarises the main motivations for buying from farmers' markets as linked with percep-tions of their being green, local, and healthy, as shown in Figure 8.7.

And what of the impact of a farmers' market on the more established retailers in a local area? Palmer (2005) looked at the impact of Barnes farmers' market in London. Some local retailers feel that market stalls have an unfair advantage because they do not have the retail overheads that the shops have to bear, such as Council Tax and rent. Furthermore, they feel that market products are marketed and perceived as somehow 'better' than what is in the local shops. As one butcher put it, 'All our beef comes from the Orkney Islands, and we do a lot of organic pork. I think they consider their stuff is better because it's got mud on it but in the end you're just paying

Table 8.3 Examples of produce prices: supermarket vs farmers' market

Produce	Quantity	National grocery multiples (w/c 16 May 2005)	Farmers' markets – North	Farmers' markets – Central	Farmers' markets – South
Carrots	Kilo	£0.69	£0.68	£0.79	£0.80
New potatoes	Kilo	£1.19	£0.88	£1.02	£0.96
Cherry tomatoes	Kilo	£2.72	£0.95	£1.88	£2.64
Local apples	Kilo	£1.48	£1.41	£1.17	£1.52
Plums	Kilo	£2.96	£2.41	£2.19	£2.30
Eggs (extra large)	6	£0.98	£0.70	£0.86	£0.82
Pork chops	Kilo	£4.48	£5.44	£4.86	£5.55
Pork sausage	Kilo	£3.79	£4.17	£4.05	£3.52
Back bacon	Kilo	£5.60	£4.98	£5.10	£9.90
Chicken fillets	Kilo	£6.50	£4.67	£5.85	£6.75
Mature cheddar	Kilo	£4.68	£4.17	£7.15	£8.96
Fresh salmon fillet	Kilo	£6.29	£6.23	£8.61	N/A

Source: ACNielsen.

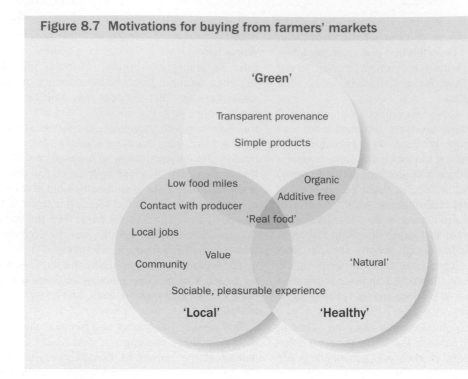

Figure 8.7 Motivations for buying from farmers' markets

Source: ACNielsen.

for the mud' (as quoted by Palmer, 2005). Others feel that the markets draw more shoppers into the area and that local shopkeepers actually benefit from this increased traffic. Nevertheless, La Trobe (2001) makes the point that if farmers' markets are going to displace super-markets or other retailers in people's routine shopping habits, then they need to be held regularly, perhaps weekly or twice a month. There also needs to be a wide range of stalls, between them offering a varied selection of foods.

As the number of markets and stalls expands, regu-lation also becomes a bigger problem. Organisers of 'official' markets run under the FARMA code do check the credentials of potential stallholders before they are accepted, run random checks of produce that is on sale in the market, and follow up consumer com-plaints against stallholders. Nevertheless, especially in 'unofficial' farmers' markets, Trading Standards Officers are starting to pick up cases of stallholders passing off 'ordinary' produce as organic, falsely claim-ing accreditation by reputable monitoring bodies such as The Soil Association, or selling produce that they themselves have not produced (Doward and Wander, 2005). Clearly, to unscrupulous operators, the profits to be made from the premium prices that can be charged on the basis of consumers' perceptions of the superior quality and benefits of farmers' market foods make the risk worthwhile.

Sources: Doward and Wander (2005); La Trobe (2001); Palmer (2005); Woolf (2005); and with grateful thanks to Geraldine Jennings, ACNielsen.

Questions

1 What factors and trends have driven the growth of farmers' markets so far?

2 What is the difference, from the consumer's point of view, between the experience of buying a kilo of apples at a farmers' market and buying exactly the same produce from a supermarket?

3 One of the biggest supermarket chains in the UK has expressed an interest in the farmers' market phenomenon. Write a brief report outlining and justifying what you see as the major threats currently posed to a supermarket chain by farmers' markets and make recommendations for countering or minimising those threats.

4 What factors and trends are likely to further encourage or limit the growth potential for farmers' markets in the future?

References for chapter 8

Auchan (2001), 'Hypermarkets Won't Be Built Without Prior Employment Forecast', *Polish News Bulletin*, 14 December, accessed via **http://www.auchan.com**.

Bainbridge, J. and Gladding, N. (2005), 'Net Gains', *Marketing*, 25 May, pp. 38–9.

Barnes, R. (2005a), 'Can Non-specialists Survive?', *Marketing*, 26 January, p. 13.

Barnes, R. (2005b), 'Appealing to the Masses', *Marketing*, 2 March, p. 26.

Birchall, J. (2005a), Costco Sets Out Plan for Expansion', *Financial Times*, 27 May, p. 27.

Birchall, J. (2005b), 'Pile High, Sell Cheap and Pay Well', *Financial Times*, 11 July, p. 12.

Butaney, G. and Wortzel, L. (1988), 'Distribution Power Versus Manufacturer Power: The Customer Role', *Journal of Marketing*, 52 (January), pp. 52–63.

Davidson, H. (1993), 'Bubbling Benetton Beats Recession', *Sunday Times*, 4 April, pp. 3–11.

Dickinson, H. (2005), 'Online Grocers Must Keep Delivering', *Marketing*, 17 August, p. 10.

Doward, J. and Wander, A. (2005), 'If You Buy "Organic Produce", Can You Trust What You Get?', *The Observer*, 21 August, p. 8.

FDA Consumer (2005), 'Update on Counterfeit Drugs', *FDA Consumer*, September/October pp. 6–7.

Financial Times (2004), 'Hennes & Mauritz', *Financial Times*, 16 December, p. 24.

Frazier, G. (1999), 'Organizing and Managing Channels of Distribution', *Journal of the Academy of Marketing Science*, 27 (2), pp. 226–40.

Frazier, G. and Lassar, W. (1996), 'Determinants of Distribution Intensity', *Journal of Marketing*, 60 (October), pp. 39–51.

Godson, S. (2004), 'Let's Go Sex Shopping', *The Times*, 13 March, p. 6.

Goldman, A. (2001), 'The Transfer of Retail Formats into Developing Economies: The Example of China', *Journal of Retailing*, 77 (2), pp. 221–42.

Gregory, H. (2001a), 'Country Ways', *The Grocer*, 31 March, pp. 36–8.

Gregory, H. (2001b), 'What it Takes', *The Grocer*, 24 November, pp. 26–8.

Gregory, H. (2004), 'The Price of Convenience', *Marketing*, 22 September, pp. 32–4.

The Grocer (2001), 'Costco Total is Now 13', *The Grocer*, 1 September, p. 8.

The Grocer (2005), 'Suppliers Refuse Nisa-Today Demands for Price Cuts', *The Grocer*, 2 April, p. 8.

Hall, W. (2004), 'How Superstore Chain Became a UK "Category Killer"', *Financial Times*, 8 June, p. 13.

Hamson, L. (2005a), 'Out of Town Restriction Stays Says Government', *The Grocer*, 26 March, p. 8.

Hamson, L. (2005b), 'Hans Kristians Hands Are On', *The Grocer*, 2 April, pp. 30–1.

Harrington, S. (2004), 'They Stock Everything Except Humble Pie', *Financial Times*, 22 June, p. 6.

Hegarty, R. (2005), 'Sainsbury Stumbling Online', *The Grocer*, 2 April, p. 8.

Hollinger, P. (2005), 'Hypermarket Hell: a Price War Forces Carrefour to Defend the Home Front', *Financial Times*, 25 January, p. 15.

Howe, W. (1992), *Retailing Management*, Macmillan.

Huber, G. (1990), 'A Theory of the Effects of Advanced Information Technologies on Organizational Design, Intelligence, and Decision Making', *Academy of Management Review*, 15 (1), pp. 47–72.

Humble, C. (2005), 'Inside the Fake Viagra Factory', *Sunday Telegraph*, 21 August, p. 011.

Hunt, J. (2001), 'Orient Express', *The Grocer*, 12 May, pp. 36–7.

IGD (2005), *Convenience Retailing Market Overview*, 4 May, accessed via **http://www.igd.org.uk**.

Jackson, A. (2005), 'Maintaining the Safety of EU Drugs', *Pharmaceutical Technology Europe*, April, p. 74.

Jardine, A. (2001), 'Argos Diversifies to Update Image', *Marketing*, 5 August, p. 4.

Johnstone, H. (2004), 'Shoppers Cash in on Store's Website Error', *Daily Telegraph*, 4 November, p. 9.

Kleinman, M. (2001), 'Can Argos Hold on to a Position of Strength?', *Marketing*, 27 September, p. 13.

Lantin, B. (2004), 'The Danger of Drugs on the Net', *Daily Telegraph*, 22 November, p. 18.

La Trobe, H. (2001), 'Farmers' Markets: Local Rural Produce', *International Journal of Consumer Studies*, 25 (3), pp. 181–92.

Longo, D. (2004), 'In China, Local and Multinational Retailers Share Similar Problems', *Progressive Grocer*, 1 December, pp. 8–9.

Lyons, W. (2004), 'H&M's Fast Lane Fashions Leave M&S Behind Times', *The Scotsman*, 18 November, p. 8.

Marketing (2004), 'Argos', *Marketing*, 6 October, p. 87.

Marketing Week (2004a), 'Sainsbury's in 1hr Pledge on Deliveries', *Marketing Week*, 9 September, p. 7.

Marketing Week (2004b), 'Days Numbered for Retail Giants?', *Marketing Week*, 14 October, p. 5.

Marketing Week (2005), 'Will a Change of Agency Help Put Argos Back on Track?', *Marketing Week*, 25 August, p. 7.

McArthur, A. (2005), 'Thorntons Wraps Up a Tasty Year Despite Drop in Sales', *Evening News*, 19 July, p. 2.

Mintel (2005), 'Pre-packed and Dressed Salads', *Mintel Market Intelligence*, August, accessed via http://www.mintel.com.

Mohr, J. and Nevin, J. (1990), 'Communication Strategies in Marketing Channels: a Theoretical Perspective', *Journal of Marketing*, 54 (October), pp. 36–51.

Mohr, J., Fisher, R. and Nevin, J. (1999), 'Communicating for Better Channel Relationships', *Marketing Management*, 8 (2), pp. 38–45.

Muddyman, G. (2005), 'What You Can Learn from a Pharmaceutical Supply Chain', *World Trade*, September, pp. 54–7.

New Media Age (2004), 'Strategic Play – Bang & Olufsen: Can Online be a Sound Choice?', *New Media Age*, 24 June, p. 18.

O'Grady, S. (2001), 'Sweet Smell May Be Thornton's Success', *The Independent*, 8 December, p. 5.

Paché, G. (1998), 'Logistics Outsourcing in Grocery Distribution: a European Perspective', *Logistics Information Management*, 11 (5), pp. 301–8.

Packaging Magazine (2005), 'Taking on Counterfeiters', *Packaging Magazine*, 16 June, p. 25.

Palamountain, J. (1955), *The Politics of Distribution*, Harvard University Press.

Palmer, M. (2005), 'Farmers' Markets – a Rural Idyll in the City', *Evening Standard*, 4 November, p. 51.

Parry, C. and Cogswell, J. (2005), 'To the Checkout Without Going Out', *Marketing Week*, 6 January, pp. 26–7.

Quilter, J. (2005), 'Argos', *Marketing*, 22 June, p. 22.

Rosenbloom, B. (1987), *Marketing Channels: A Management View*, Dryden.

Ryle, S. (2001), '@business: Delivering the Goods Brings Net Success', *The Observer*, 12 August, p. 6.

Ryle, S. (2004), 'Mammon: Sticking Her Neck Out', *The Observer*, 25 April, p. 16.

Scardino, E. (2001), 'H&M: Can it Adapt to America's Landscape?', *DSN Retailing Today*, 17 September, pp. A10–A11.

Scheraga, D. (2005), 'Balancing Act at IKEA', *Chain Store Age*, June, pp. 45–6.

Shapley, D. (1998), 'The Cape Crusaders', *The Grocer*, 20 June, pp. 59–63.

Sharma, A. and Dominguez, L. (1992), 'Channel Evolution: a Framework for Analysis', *Journal of the Academy of Marketing Science*, 20 (Winter), pp. 1–16.

Stern, L., El-Ansary, A. and Coughlan, A. (1996), *Marketing Channels* (5th edn), Prentice Hall.

Stewart-Allen, A. (2001), 'Ikea Service Worst in its Own Backyard', *Marketing News*, 23 April, p. 11.

Teather, D. (2001), 'H&M Plans to Open 50 Fashion Stores', *The Guardian*, 22 June, p. 1.23.

URPI (1988), *List of UK Hypermarkets and Superstores*, Unit for Retail Planning Information.

Webster, F. (1979), *Industrial Marketing Strategy*, John Wiley & Sons.

Woolf, M. (2005), 'Produce Better Value at Farmers' Markets than Superstores', *The Independent on Sunday*, 6 November, p. 31.

chapter 9

promotion: integrated marketing communication

learning objectives

This chapter will help you to:

1 understand the importance of planned, integrated communication in a marketing context;

2 appreciate the variety and scope of marketing communication objectives;

3 explain the use of promotional tools in the communication process;

4 identify the factors and constraints influencing the mix of communications tools that an organisation uses; and

5 define the main methods by which communications budgets are set.

Introduction

The promotional mix is the direct way in which an organisation attempts to communicate with various target audiences. It consists of five main elements, as shown in Figure 9.1. Advertising represents non-personal, mass communication; personal selling is at the other extreme, covering face-to-face, personally tailored messages. Sales promotion involves tactical, short-term incentives that encourage a target audience to behave in a certain way. Public relations is about creating and maintaining good-quality relationships with many interested

Figure 9.1 The elements of the promotional mix

groups (for example the media, shareholders and trade unions), not just with customers. Finally, direct marketing involves creating one-to-one relationships with individual customers, often in mass markets, and might involve mailings, telephone selling or electronic media. Some might classify direct marketing activities as forms of advertising, sales promotion or even personal selling, but this text treats direct marketing as a separate element of the promotional mix while acknowledging that it 'borrows' from the other elements.

Ideally, the marketer would like to invest extensively in every element of the mix. In a world of finite resources, however, choices have to be made about which activities are going to work together most cost-effectively with the maximum synergy to achieve the communications objectives of the organisation within a defined budget. Budgets obviously vary widely between different organisations, and depending on the type of product involved and the communications task in hand.

This chapter, along with the two that follow it, will aim to explain why such choices are made.

eg   Ocado, the online grocery provider for supermarket Waitrose, uses different elements of the promotional mix to communicate different messages to target consumers depending on their relationship history with the brand. Radio advertisements and posters are used to communicate Ocado's competitive advantages (for example free delivery on orders over £75, one-hour delivery slots, and groceries carried to your kitchen) to encourage trial. The distinctive Ocado delivery vans are a mobile advertisement in themselves, and when a new delivery area is added the vans drive around with the objective of raising awareness of the service's availability, and they are supported by direct mail in the catchment area. Having placed orders, customers will receive regular magazines containing information and offers, and free, often seasonal gifts with their shopping. This promotes loyalty and encourages word-of-mouth recommendation. Once customers are shopping regularly with the service, they receive weekly e-mail reminders to do their shopping, and may be sent electronic vouchers or offers to encourage continued use of the service. When in 2005 Ocado was crowned as the best online grocer by both *Which?* and *Good Housekeeping* magazines, it gained the perfect PR platform to reassure existing customers of having made a good choice, and to encourage prospective customers to give the service a try (Armitt, 2005).

In vans decorated with enormous fruits and vegetables, Ocado's home delivery service makes itself an advertisement on wheels.

Source: Reproduced with permission of Ocado Limited

This chapter provides a general strategic overview by focusing on th communications planning process. Pickton and Broderick (2001, p. marketing communication as

> *... a process which involves the management and organisation of all agents planning, implementation and control of all marketing communications con messages and promotional tools focused at selected target audiences in such a the greatest economy, efficiency, effectiveness, enhancement and coherence of m communications effort in achieving predetermined product and corporate marke ng communications objectives.*

This definition emphasises the need to plan and manage the integrated marketing communications function carefully and strategically within the market context and using the full range of communications tools effectively and efficiently. This chapter, therefore, looks at some of the influences that shape an appropriate blend within the promotional mix, allowing the marketer to allocate communication resources most effectively.

The main focus of the chapter is on developing a planning framework within which managerial decisions on communication activity can be made. Each stage in the planning flow is discussed in turn, with particular emphasis being given to relevant issues and the kind of integrated promotional mix that might subsequently be appropriate. It is becoming increasingly important for organisations to design and implement effective integrated marketing communications strategies as they expand their interests beyond their known domestic markets.

Communications planning model

Figure 9.2, adapted from Rothschild's (1987) communications decision sequence framework, includes all the main elements of marketing communications decision-making. Given the complexity of communication and the immense possibilities for getting some element of it wrong, a thorough and systematic planning process is crucial for minimising the risks. No organisation can afford either the financial or the reputational damage caused by poorly planned or implemented communications campaigns.

Each element and its implications for the balancing of the promotional mix will now be defined and analysed in turn. The first element is the situation analysis, which has been split into three subsections: the target market, the product and the environment. Bear in mind,

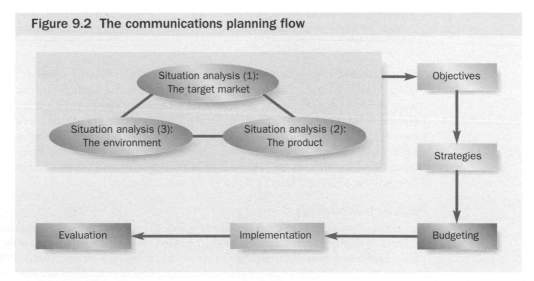

Figure 9.2 The communications planning flow

Source: Michael L. Rothschild, *Marketing Communications: From Fundamentals to Strategies*. Copyright © 1987 D.C. Heath and Company. By permission of Houghton Mifflin Company.

however, that in reality it is difficult to 'pigeon hole' things quite so neatly as this might imply, and there will, therefore, be a lot of cross-referencing.

■ Situation analysis (1): the target market

B2B or consumer market

The *target market* decision most likely to have an impact on the balancing of the overall promotional mix is whether the market is a consumer market or a B2B market. Recalling the comparison made in Chapter 3 between consumer and B2B markets, Table 9.1 summarises the impact of the main distinguishing features on the choice of promotional mix. The picture that emerges from this is that B2B markets are very much more dependent on the personal selling element, with advertising and sales promotion playing a strong supporting role.

Table 9.1 B2B vs consumer marketing communications: characteristics and implications

B2B	Consumer
Fewer, often identifiable customers	Usually mass, aggregated markets
• *Personal and personalised communication feasible*	• *Mass communication, e.g. television advertising, most efficient and cost effective*
Complex products, often tailored to individual customer specification	Standardised products with little scope for negotiation and customisation
• *Need for lengthy buyer–seller dialogue via personal selling*	• *Impersonal channels of communication convey standard message*
High-value, high-risk, infrequent purchases	Low-value, low-risk, frequent purchases
• *Need for much information through literature and personal representation, with emphasis on product performance and financial criteria*	• *Less technical emphasis; status and other intangible benefits often stressed; incentives needed to build or break buying habits*
Rational decision-making process over time, with a buying centre taking responsibility	Short time scale, often impulse purchasing by an individual or family buying unit
• *Need to understand who plays what role and try to influence whole buying centre*	• *Need to understand who plays what role and to try to influence family*

The converse is generally true in consumer markets. A large number of customers each making relatively low value, frequent purchases can be most efficiently contacted using mass media. Advertising, therefore, comes to the fore, with sales promotion a close second, while personal selling is almost redundant. Figure 9.3 shows this polarisation of B2B and consumer promotional mixes. This does, of course, represent sweeping generalisations about the nature of these markets, which need to be qualified. The product itself, for instance, will influence the shape of the mix, as will the nature of competitive and other environmental pressures. These will be addressed later (pp. 306 *et seq.* and 309 *et seq.*).

Push or pull strategy

Remember, however, that even consumer goods marketers are likely to have to consider B2B markets in dealing with channels of distribution. Figure 9.4 offers two strategies, push and pull, which emphasise different lines of communication (Oliver and Farris, 1989). With a push strategy, the manufacturer chooses to concentrate communications activity on the member of the distribution channel immediately below. This means that the wholesaler, in this example, has a warehouse full of product and thus an incentive to use communication to make a special

Figure 9.3 B2B vs consumer promotional mix

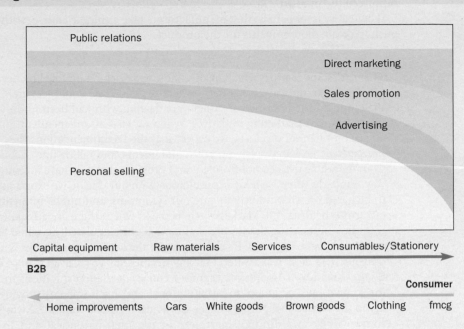

Figure 9.4 Push–pull strategy

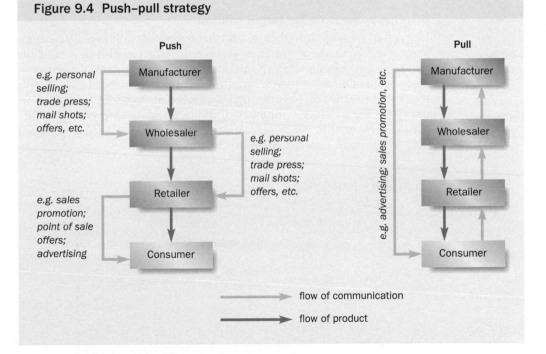

effort to sell it quickly on to the retailer, who in turn promotes it to the end consumer. The product is thereby pushed down the distribution channel, with communication flowing from member to member in parallel with the product. There is little or no communication between manufacturer and consumer in this case.

In contrast, the pull strategy requires the manufacturer to create demand for the product through direct communication with the consumer. The retailers will perceive this demand and, in the interests of serving their customers' needs, will demand the product from their wholesaler, who will demand it from the manufacturer. This bottom-up approach pulls the product down the distribution channel, with communication flowing in the opposite direction from the product!

The reality is, of course, that manufacturers take a middle course, with some pull and some push to create more impetus for the product.

eg

There are some markets which involve intermediaries – a middle link between the manufacturer and the consumer/end-user – where the end-user would feel highly uncomfortable if they thought the intermediary they were dealing with had been unduly influenced by the manufacturer's marketing initiatives. When we visit an Independent Financial Advisor for advice on financial products, we expect that the recommendations they make to us will be *independent*, i.e. based solely on our requirements, and taking into account what is on offer from the whole market, not from a brand provider that may have incentivised them in some way. Similarly, when we have a consultation with our doctor, we expect any drugs prescribed to be based on what is likely to cure our symptoms, and not be influenced by a Christmas gift from the drug rep. Markets such as these, where there are ethical considerations surrounding influencing the supply chain, are highly regulated. So while you may see a drug company's name on your GP's coffee mug, or the logo of a pension provider on the calendar on your IFA's desk, rest assured that any freebie they've received cannot cost more than £5. By the same token, brands may sponsor conferences and exhibitions in these markets, but the content must be judged to be educational, and any hospitality provided must be secondary to the educational purpose of the gathering. So if you want to be wined and dined, or do some wining and dining, steer clear of the pharmaceutical and investment markets (**http://www.abpi.org.uk; http://www.mhra.gov.uk; http://www.unbiased.co.uk**).

Buyer readiness of the target market

In terms of message formulation, a further tempering influence on communication with consumers will be the buyer readiness stage of the target market. It is most unlikely that a target market is going to undergo an instant conversion from total ignorance of a product's existence to queuing up at the checkout to buy it. Particularly in consumer markets, it is more likely that people will pass through a number of stages *en route* from initial awareness to desire for the product. A number of models have been proposed – for example Strong's (1925) AIDA model, which put various labels on these stages, as shown in Figure 9.5 – but broadly speaking, they all amount to the same sequence.

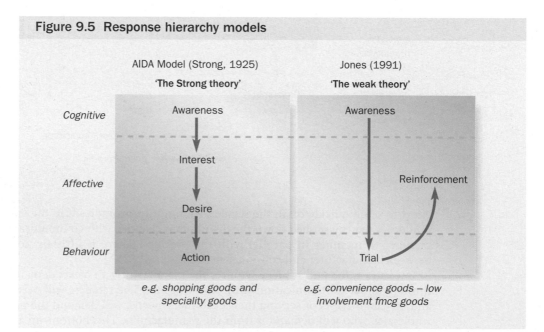

Figure 9.5 Response hierarchy models

Cognitive. The cognitive stage involves sowing the seeds of a thought, i.e. catching the target market's attention and generating straightforward awareness of the product: 'Yes, I know this product exists.' As part of the launch of the Mini, for example, BMW used media advertising, PR, and hospitality events to get the updated brand known and understood as being something different and special.

eg Once a car is more than three years old, and its warranty has expired, many owners believe it is no longer worth returning to the manufacturer's dealership to have the vehicle serviced. As long as the owners remain on the dealer's database, however, they can be mailed, encouraged and incentivised to return. But what about those car owners who have moved, or those buying cars second-hand? Honda wanted to target these people, but first had to find out who they were, and assess their circumstances in order to maximise the potential to convert them to dealer servicing. Teams of street marketers were sent out to scour the local areas surrounding Honda dealerships, for example in car parks, looking for Honda models, over three years old, with registration plates not on the dealer's database. Every vehicle matching this description had a pack placed under the windscreen wiper. The alarm that car owners finding these packs might have initially experienced (the pack strongly resembled a parking ticket in a clear plastic wrapper) was ill-founded, as the packs contained a high-quality chamois and a freepost data-gathering mini-questionnaire. Completion was incentivised with the chance to win one of three new Honda cars.

The best-performing dealerships experienced a 32 per cent response rate, and the data collected allowed them to target and tailor mailings, having already laid the foundations of a relationship via the windscreen pack (**http://www.mad.co.uk**).

Affective. The affective stage involves creating or changing an attitude, i.e. giving the consumer sufficient information (whether factual or image-based) to pass judgement on the product and to develop positive feelings towards it: 'I understand what this product can do for me, and I like the idea of it.'

Behaviour. The behaviour stage involves precipitating action, i.e. where the strength of the positive attitudes generated in the affective stage leads the consumer to desire the product and to do something about acquiring it: 'I want this product and I'm going to go and buy it.' Many press advertisements incorporating a mail order facility are operating at this level.

marketing in action

Video Arts: the home of memorably entertaining training (and trashing!)

Video Arts, a company specialising in the production and marketing of training videos, was established in 1972. Its founders were a small group of television professionals, including John Cleese, who pioneered the use of humour in training. It was their belief, which has since been proved with a string of major training awards, that if people are entertained while being educated, there is a better chance of their remembering what they've learnt. As well as using humour, the organisation has always insisted on the highest standards of production quality. Household names such as Ricky Gervais, Martin Clunes, Robert Lindsay, Dawn French, Paul Merton and Hugh Laurie have appeared in Video Arts programmes, covering subjects such as Interviewing Skills, Managing People, Communication, Management Skills, Creativity, Customer Service, Selling Skills and Finance.

Video Arts products would typically be bought and used by specialist training agencies or consultancies, and the Human Resource Management departments of large companies. There are currently over 200 Video Arts titles used by more than 100,000 organisations across 50 countries worldwide. The most recent title to be added to the Video Arts catalogue is 'Jamie's School Dinners – A Recipe for Managing and Living with Change'. This two-part package uses the chef Jamie Oliver's efforts to change the attitude and behaviour of those responsible for the provision and preparation of school meals to bring the whole area of change management to life. This would be of interest to any organisation whose management and staff are having to deal with change in the workplace.

Obviously, Video Arts itself has experienced change during the three decades since its launch. Now, in addition to videos, some of its training packages are available online or on CD-ROM, and as in domestic life, the DVD format is superseding video. Knowing that many customers had tattered and dusty collections of its training videos, Video Arts was keen to encourage them to clear out their old hoard, and upgrade to new and updated programmes on DVD. It approached agency Partners Andrews Aldridge with the brief to persuade the customer base to have a clearout and reorder. Knowing that the target audience would feel that it was never the right

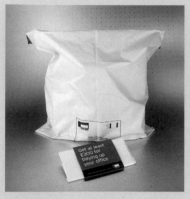

The art of recycling put to work for Video Arts.

Source: © Video Arts/Partners Andrews Aldridge

time for a purge, either because it was such a chore or because it seemed wasteful to throw out resources, Partners Andrews Aldridge devised a major incentive: £300 discount from the usual DVD price (typically in the region of £1200) coupled with an engaging method of returning old videos.

Customers were sent a Video Arts bin-bag with the call-to-action 'Get at least £300 for tidying-up your office'. This provided a catalyst and encouragement to clear out old training videos, and return them in the addressed bin-bag. Apart from being an impactful piece of mail, this initiative reflected the personality of Video Arts for which fun and humour have always been key attributes. The results were impressive. During the two-month period of the promotion, 35 per cent of Video Arts' total revenue came from DVD sales, representing a 15 per cent increase on the previous period. In effect, Video Arts saw an £18 return on every £1 spent on this campaign. And the agency was rewarded with a win in the Best Business to Business category of the 2005 *Precision Marketing Response Awards*.

Sources: http://www.videoarts.com and with thanks to Partners Andrews Aldridge.

The speed with which a target market passes through these stages depends on the kind of product, the target market involved and the marketing strategies adopted by the organisation. Nevertheless, each stage becomes increasingly more difficult to implement, since more is being asked of the consumer. Generating awareness, the first stage, is relatively easy as it involves little risk or commitment from the consumer, and may even operate unconsciously. The second stage needs some effort from consumers if it is to be successful, because they are being asked to assimilate information, process it and form an opinion. The third and final stage requires the most involvement – actually getting up and doing something, which is likely to involve paying out money!

The Strong (1925) theory of communication proposed these stages as forming a logical flow of events driven by marketing communication. Advertising, for example, creates the initial awareness, stimulates the interest and then the desire for the product, and only then does trial take place. In other words, the attitude and opinion are formed before the consumer ever gets near the product. There is, however, another school of thought that maintains that it does not always happen like that. The weak theory of communication (Jones, 1991) accepts that marketing communication can generate the awareness, but then the consumer might well try the product without having formed any particular attitude or opinion of it. Only then, after the purchase and product trial, does the marketing communication begin to contribute to attitude and opinion working alongside consumer experience of the product. This would make sense for low-involvement products, the frequently purchased boring goods about which it is difficult to get emotional, such as washing powder.

Whatever the route through the response hierarchy, the unique characteristics of each stage imply that differing promotional mixes may be called for to maximise the creative benefits and cost-effectiveness of the different promotional tools. Figure 9.6 suggests that advertising is most appropriate at the earliest stage, given its capacity to reach large numbers of people relatively cheaply and quickly with a simple message. Sales promotions can also bring a product name to the fore and help in the affective stage: using a sample that has been

eg A consumer might see a television advertisement for a new kitchen roll with improved absorbency, then forget about it until they are faced with it on the supermarket shelf during their next shopping trip. At that point they might think 'I saw an ad for that – I'll give it a go' and buy a pack. Having tried it, if they've found that it performs well, they might pay more attention to the content of subsequent advertisements for that product as a way of legitimising and reinforcing their positive opinion.

delivered to the door certainly generates awareness and aids judgement and recognition of a product. Adding a coupon to the sample's packaging is also an incentive to move into the behaviour stage, that of buying a full-sized package.

Notice that in Figure 9.6 the role of advertising diminishes as the behaviour stage moves closer and personal selling comes to the fore. Advertising can only reiterate and reinforce what consumers already know about the product, and if this wasn't enough to stimulate action the last time they saw or heard it, it may not be so this time either. At this point, potential buyers may just need a last bit of persuasion to tip them over the edge into buying, and that last kick may be best delivered by a sales representative who can reiterate the product benefits, tailoring communication to suit the particular customer's needs and doubts in a two-way dialogue. With many fmcg products sold in supermarkets, however, this is not a feasible option, and the manufacturer relies on the packaging and, to some extent, the sales promotions to do the selling at the point of sale without human intervention. Many fmcg products, therefore, strive for distinctively coloured packaging that stands out on the supermarket shelf, commanding attention. This issue will be readdressed in the following subsection.

In reality, individuals within the target market may pass through the stages at different times or may take longer to pass from one stage to the next. This means that it may be necessary to develop an integrated promotional mix recognising that the various elements are appealing to sub-segments at different readiness stages, with imagery and content tailored accordingly. The implementation of the various elements may be almost simultaneous, with some fine-tuning of the campaign over the longer term.

Knowledge of the target market is an important foundation stone for all of the communication decisions that you are going to make. The more you know about the people you want to talk to, the more likely you are to create successful communication. This means not only

Figure 9.6 Buyer readiness stages and the promotional mix

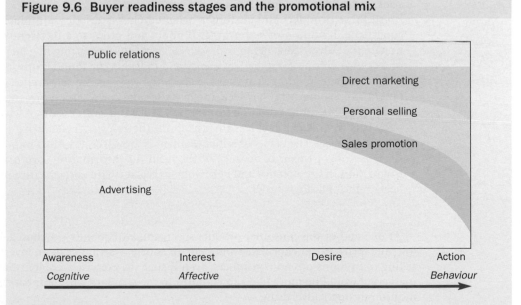

having a clear demographic profile of the target market, but also having as much detail as possible about their attitudes, beliefs and aspirations, and about their shopping, viewing and reading habits. In addition it is important to understand their relationship with your product and their perceptions of it. This will be explained in relation to communication objectives at pp. 311 *et seq.*

This is a good time for you to look back at Chapter 4 and revise some of the methods of segmenting markets, whether consumer or B2B, since the criteria by which the target market is defined (including product-oriented criteria) may well have a strong influence not only on the broad issue of balancing the promotional mix, but also on the finer detail of media choice and creative content.

■ Situation analysis (2): the product

Inextricably linked with consideration of the target market is consideration of the *product* involved. This section will look again at the area of B2B and consumer products in the light of the influence of other product characteristics, and then explore the specific influence of the product lifecycle on the promotional mix.

B2B and consumer products

It is simplistic in the extreme to define a product either as a B2B purchase, personal selling being the best way to sell it, or as a consumer product, which must be advertised. Other product characteristics or the buying habits associated with the product may make such a distinction meaningless.

eg An illustration of this 'grey area' is the sale of double glazing to domestic householders. Strictly speaking, this is a consumer market, in that the product is being purchased by individuals or families for private consumption. There are, however, a number of features suggesting that this particular product has more in common with typical B2B purchases than with other consumer goods. It is an expensive, infrequent purchase with a high level of technical personalisation required to match the product exactly with the customer's needs. It involves a fairly rational decision-making process that takes place over time, and there is a high demand for product information and negotiation before commitment to purchase is made. To the buyer, it is a high-risk purchase that may well involve several members of the family (effectively acting as a buying centre) and will almost certainly involve a great deal of persuasion, reassurance and dialogue from a sales representative.

All these product- and customer-oriented characteristics completely override the superficial definition of a consumer product and point to a different kind of promotional mix. Advertising, along with website content, plays a role in generating awareness of a double glazing company's existence and in laying the foundations for corporate and product image building. They also prepare the way for the sales representative, since a potential customer who has seen an advertisement for a sales representative's company or has read the information on its website will have an impression of what kind of company this is, and will feel less uneasy about the sales representative's credibility and trustworthiness. The personal selling element is, however, the most important and effective element of this mix because of the need for information, product tailoring and negotiation in the affective and behaviour stages. It is also cost-effective in relation to the likely value of a single order.

At one end of the consumer product spectrum, a frequently purchased, low-involvement, low-unit-price bar of chocolate would not, of course, warrant such an investment in personal selling to millions of end consumers, even if such an exercise were logistically possible. The marketing would be more likely to conform to the standard mix, emphasising mass communication through advertising.

Another example chosen to illustrate the grey area between consumer and B2B markets is that of day-to-day consumable office supplies, such as pencils, pens and paperclips, for small businesses. This has more in common with the chocolate bar than the double glazing, although technically it is a B2B product, in that it is used to support the production of goods for resale. Compared with most B2B purchases, it is a routine re-buy, a low-priced, low-risk, low-involvement purchase, probably delegated to an individual who goes out to the nearest stationer's or office supplies retailer at lunchtime with the contents of the petty cash tin. It is simply not cost-effective to use personal selling of such a range of products to that buyer who belongs to a large and ill-defined target market (there are thousands of small businesses, in every kind of activity and market, and geographically widespread) and who makes such small-value purchases. At best, personal selling should be targeted at the stationer's or the office supplies retailer.

The two examples above serve as a warning that some B2B products behave more like consumer products and vice versa.

The product lifecycle stage

One further product characteristic that may affect the approach to communication is the *product lifecycle stage* reached (see pp. 202 *et seq.*). Since the overall marketing objectives tend to change as the product moves through each stage, it is likely that the specific communications objectives will also change. Different tasks need to be fulfilled and thus the balance of the promotional mix will alter.

Introduction. With the launch of a new consumer product, it is likely that there will be high initial expenditure on the promotional mix. Advertising will ensure that the product name and benefits become known and spread quickly among the target market, while sales promotions, perhaps based on coupons and sampling, help to generate trial of the product. Sales promotions will also be used in conjunction with intense personal selling effort to gain retailer acceptance of the product.

Growth. Communications activity is likely to be a little less intense as the product begins to find its own impetus and both retailers and consumers make repeat purchases. There might also be less emphasis on awareness generation and information giving, and more on long-term image and loyalty building. As competitors launch similar products, it is important to ensure that differential advantage is maintained, and that customers know exactly why they should continue to buy the original product rather than switching over to a competitor. This could mean a shift towards advertising as a prime means of image creation that works over a longer period.

Baileys Irish Cream Liqueur has always had a strong franchise amongst female at-home drinkers. Diageo, the brand owner, is continually seeking ways in which to recruit new, younger drinkers to the brand. There have been product initiatives to meet this objective, such as the launch of the single-shot minis format, but one of its most successful investments was in sponsoring the Channel 4 programme *Sex and the City*. Baileys was aiming to shake off lingering associations with sweetness and an old-fashioned, conservative kind of femininity and create a new, sassier image. Carat, Diageo's media agency, identified the core target audience for this image change message as 'Self Assured Realists' characterised by confidence, contentment with their standard of living and upmarket media choices. The fit between *Sex and the City*'s programme values, and sensuous, sassy characters could not have been better. A husky female voice-over posed questions full of sexual innuendo while Baileys was suggestively poured over ice at the beginning and end of the programme. The sponsorship 'grey area' got around the problems that Baileys would have had in featuring such content in straightforward advertising. Ofcom, the industry watchdog, forbids any association between alcohol and sexual success, prowess or attractiveness in advertisements. A welcome by-product of the sponsorship initiative was the independent development of Baileys-based 'Sex and the City cocktails' by trendy pubs and clubs, adding to the impetus of making younger women reappraise the brand (Elms and Svendsen, 2005; Singh, 2004; Wilkinson, 2004).

Baileys' smooth use of sponsorship targeting the same audience as Sex and the City

Source: Image courtesy of The Advertising Archives

Maturity. The maturity stage is likely to be a defensive or holding operation, since competitors with younger products may be threatening to take custom away from the product. Most people know about the product; most people (apart from a few laggards) who are likely to try it have already done so. Thus the role of communication is reminding (about the brand image and values) and reassurance (about having chosen the right product), probably through mass advertising. In B2B markets, this stage is likely to be about further developing and consolidating relationships with customers in preparation for newer products in your portfolio.

Decline. Marketing communication is not going to rescue a product that is clearly on its way out; it can only stave off the inevitable for a while. The majority of consumers and, for that matter, distributors will have already moved on to other products, leaving only a few laggards. A certain level of reminder advertising and sales promotion might keep them in the market for this product for a while, but eventually even they will drift off. There is little point in diverting resources that could be better used on the next new product.

eg Walkers is the UK's number one grocery brand, accounting for over 37 per cent of sales in the lucrative crisp market, and spending an estimated £17m per year on consumer advertising. However, with the recent publicity surrounding the nutritional shortcomings of some children's preferred foodstuffs (the salt and fat content in crisps, the salt and sugar in breakfast cereals, for instance), and the growing public concern about child obesity, things are getting tougher for the nation's favourite snacks. In the year to October 2004, sales of bagged snacks were down 1.7 per cent and sales of Walkers' core range down 1.9 per cent. As brand leader, Walkers had to protect its core franchise, and look at new product development areas to fuel growth. The saturated fat content of the core product was reduced, and technicians are working on reducing the salt content by between 5 and 11 per cent. During 2004, a promotion based on giving away free Walkers branded walk-o-meters (pedometers) to encourage active lifestyles and tie in with the brand name, was carried by the core product. These initiatives tackled negative associations with the category head-on. A further promotion giving away 9000 iPod minis ran in autumn 2005. The pre-promotion publicity on the Walkers website describing the opportunity to 'win a iPod mini every 5 minutes during September' was designed to renew interest in the core range. At the same time Walkers developed and heavily advertised the Potato Heads range, low in fat, with no artificial flavouring, colouring or preservatives, which was further extended with Potato Heads Naked, a low-salt variant. This ensures there is a Walkers product to meet the needs of those who are falling out of the core category (Harwood, 2005; Parry, 2005).

The above analysis assumes that a product takes an unexceptional course through the classical stages of the lifecycle. Many consumer goods, however, are revamped at some time during the maturity stage to extend their lifecycle. In such a case, there is every reason to rethink the communications package and treat the process more like a new product launch. There is much to communicate both to the trade and to the consumer about the 'new improved' brand, the increased value for money, the enhanced performance, more stylish looks or whatever aspects are being emphasised. In a sense, this stage is even more difficult than the new product launch, as the marketer has to tread a fine line between overturning old preconceptions about the product, convincing the market that there is something new to consider and confusing and alienating existing users who might think that the familiar, comforting brand values have been thrown out.

The lifecycle concept, as discussed at pp. 207 *et seq.*, does have its problems, and in the context of marketing communication, its unthinking, rigid application as a primary basis for communications planning is dangerous. If a product is assumed to be mature or declining, then the application of a communications package appropriate to that stage may well hasten its demise. There are other, more relevant factors, both internal and external, which should have a far greater bearing on the planning process. Some of the external factors will now be discussed.

■ Situation analysis (3): the environment

Again, some revision of an earlier chapter might stand you in good stead here. Chapter 2 analysed the marketing environment in some detail. This section will, therefore, only look at ways in which environmental elements specifically affect communications.

Social and *cultural* aspects of the environment will mostly have an impact on the message element of communication. What is said about the product and the scenario within which it is depicted in advertisements will reflect what is socially acceptable and culturally familiar to the target market. There must be something that they can recognise, identify with and/or wish to aspire to, if they are going to remember the message, and particularly if they are expected to act on it. This reinforces what was said at pp. 300 *et seq.* about the necessity of knowing the target market well.

Organisations are particularly keen to spot changes and shifts in social mores and then to capitalise on them, often creating a bandwagon effect. The 'green' issue is a good example of this. Many companies perceived that there was pressure on them to produce environmentally friendlier products, but rather than lose time in developing really new alternatives (and risk lagging behind their competitors), a few simply created new advertising messages and emphasised green-oriented product claims on their packaging to create the desired image. However, questionable approaches have been widely publicised, such as labelling washing-up liquid 'phosphate free' when that kind of product never contains phosphate anyway, and emphasising that packaging can be recycled when the recycling facilities do not exist, leading to confusion and suspicion in the consumer's mind about all green claims.

eg

On 9 January 2005, 1759 passengers boarded the luxury P&O liner *Aurora* for a 103-day round-the-world cruise. It was billed as the 'voyage of a lifetime', and certainly cost many of the passengers a lifetime's savings. But the vessel immediately experienced engine trouble, and for the first few days only sailed around the Isle of Wight. Frustrated at the lack of information on progress, and severely disappointed, 300 passengers abandoned the cruise. *Aurora* finally embarked on the planned route on 19 January, but after only 110 miles, and just off the coast of Devon, the trip was cancelled due to propulsion problems, and the ship and passengers returned to Southampton. During the 10 days while the would-be cruisers were literally and metaphorically 'at sea', the *Aurora* story was headline news in all broadcast and print media. The editorial focus was on the 'limbo' passengers left in, and the stark contrast between the reality of the experience and what the *Aurora's* customers had expected. It didn't take long for details of the ship's ominous history to be played out whenever the 'latest update' article appeared – the champagne bottle had failed to smash during her naming ceremony, she had broken down in the Bay of Biscay on her maiden voyage, 600 passengers and crew had been laid low in 2003 with the highly contagious Norovirus vomiting bug. Mitchell (2005) described the lack of positive action and PR during the 10-day hiatus as leaving P&O looking 'unprofessional, uncaring and unimaginative'. Had P&O pulled out the stops in giving those on board a great time, and heavily publicising it (damage limitation), it might not have found itself having to divert some of its £11.5m annual budget on a promotional rehabilitation of *Aurora* when she came back into service (*Daily Mail*, 2005; *Marketing Week*, 2005; Mitchell, 2005).

A more general criticism of advertisers' influence in the social and cultural area is about their alleged use and reinforcement of stereotypes. The advertisers argue that they simply reflect society as it is, and that it is not their business to change it – they *respond* to the customer's changing attitudes and lifestyle. Should there, however, be concern that if people see stereotypes being constantly presented through advertising as the norm, and even as states to be aspired to, then maybe the impetus to question their validity and to break them will be less urgent? This is a complex 'chicken and egg' debate that you may want to pursue for yourself outside these pages. There are no easy answers.

To be fair to the advertisers, the whole area of stereotypes does perhaps present one of the great insoluble dilemmas of mass communication. In moving away from one stereotype, it is too easy to replace it with another. Because the advertiser is trying to appeal to a relatively large number of individuals (even in a niche market), it is impossible to create an image that reflects every member of the target market in detail. What emerges, therefore, is a superficial sketch of the essential characteristics of that group and its aspirations, i.e. a stereotype! Thus the stereotypical housewife who lives in the kitchen and is fulfilled through the quality of her cooking has been usurped at the opposite extreme by the equally unrealistic power-dressing, independent dragon of the boardroom with only the slightest whiff of Chanel and femininity. It seems that the advertisers cannot win.

eg

Stereotypes can provide a rich seam of humour in advertising. In recent years there has been a rise in the number of campaigns depicting hopeless men, unable to complete the simplest task without the help of a smart, capable woman. The trend began as a kind of amusing corrective to the portrayal of women in advertising as simpleton housewives, but our neighbours across the pond have had enough! Men in the US have launched a campaign against sexual stereotyping. The Society for the Prevention of Misandry (opposite of misogyny) in the Media identifies man-bashing advertisements, then encourages boycotting of the advertised product. Reebok's execution that uses the 'This is a Man's World' song while showing a clumsy oaf falling over the equipment in a gym full of fit women, and needing to be rescued by one of them, has put it on the blacklist. One hugely popular campaign that achieves both the 'ahhhh' factor and humour through role-reversal stereotyping is for the Vauxhall Zafira. We hear Harry, George and

Amir, fellow dwellers in a suburban cul-de-sac, discuss the minor trials and tribulations of transporting their families around in their Zafiras, referring to everyday hiccups of their charges forgetting to go to the toilet and being overtired. Harry, George and Amir are, however, only 8 years old, and the subjects under discussion are their parents (Murray, 2005; **http://www.vauxhall.co.uk**).

No communications plan can be shaped without some reference to what *competitors* are doing or are likely to do, given the necessity of emphasising the differential advantage and positioning of the product in relation to theirs. This could affect every stage of the planning, from the definition of objectives, through the creative strategy, to the setting of budgets. These themes will be taken up under the appropriate headings later in this chapter, and will also feature in the chapters on the individual tools of the promotional mix.

Another important factor to take into account is the *legal/regulatory* environment, as discussed in Chapter 2. Some products are restricted as to where and when they can be advertised. In the UK, for instance, cigarette advertising is not permitted on television. Restrictions may also exist about what can or must be said or shown in relation to the product. Toy advertising cannot imply a social disadvantage through not owning a product, and must also indicate the price of the toy. More generally, advertising aimed at children cannot encourage them to pester their parents to purchase (not that they normally need encouragement). Some regulations are enshrined in law, while others are imposed and applied through monitoring watchdog bodies such as the Advertising Standards Authority. Professional bodies, such as the UK's Institute of Sales Promotion or the Direct Marketing Association, often develop codes of practice to which their members undertake to adhere. As yet, no unified codes have been developed that apply across Europe.

■ Objectives

Now that the background is in place and there exists a detailed profile of the customer, the product and the environment, it is possible to define detailed objectives for the communications campaign.

Table 9.2, based on the work of DeLozier (1975), summarises and categorises possible communications objectives. The first group relates to awareness, information and attitude generation, while the second group is about affecting behaviour. The final group consists of corporate objectives, a timely reminder that marketing communications planning is not only about achieving the goals of brand managers or marketing managers, but also about the contribution of marketing activity to the wider strategic good of the organisation.

corporate social responsibility   in action

Don't drink and advertise!

Responsible advertising, particularly in relation to the promotion of food and alcohol, was the dominant issue for the UK advertising industry throughout 2004–05. The advertising of alcohol has always been subject to stringent guidelines, but in line with the Government's declared strategy to reduce the harm caused by alcohol, new rules have been introduced. With the specific objectives of protecting under-18s, preventing binge drinking and curbing anti-social behaviour as a result of drinking, Ofcom, the media super-regulator, handed an amended set of restrictions to the ASA (Advertising Standards Authority) to enforce in November 2004.

Under the new guidelines no alcohol advertisement should be likely to appeal to those under 18 years of age by reflecting or being associated with youth culture. There should be no link between alcohol and sexual activity or success, nor any implication that alcohol can enhance attractiveness. Specifically on television, alcohol advertising must not show, imply or refer to 'daring', 'toughness', 'aggression' or 'unruly', 'irresponsible' or 'anti-social behaviour' or in any way glamorise yob culture. That puts paid to the WKD campaign, then! Another campaign to bite the dust in the wake of these new rules is the Bacardi Party advertisements which fall foul of the requirement that no alcohol advertisement should suggest that drinking is 'essential to the success of a social occasion'. Prior to the new rules, alcohol advertisers were prohibited from using celebrity endorsement or depicting success. So what options are left open to them?

In-pub promotions, which are currently unregulated, are soon to be subject to a code of practice prohibiting initiatives which encourage speed drinking or excessive consumption. Already some brands have come up with lateral solutions to meet their communication requirements. Absolut Vodka created an 'Absolut Love' room in Hotel Pelirocco, dubbed 'Brighton's sauciest stopover'. The Absolut room, one of 19 individually designed bedrooms in this trendy establishment, is exotic, romantic and designed both to reflect the brand and to embrace the wilder side of the Brighton scene. Tennents lager sponsored an installation at Glasgow's famous King Tut's music venue featuring a huge wallpaper graphic of thousands of lyrics from bands that have played there. The Italian bottled beer brand Peroni created a live advert in Sloane Street, London, using a shop window display of a giant bottle of Peroni, a fridge full of product and a handsome Italian gentleman posing as a security guard. This attracted much attention from passing shoppers, and the media. So it really is a case of watch this space.

Sources: Brough (2005); Butcher (2005); Porter (2004).

What Table 9.2 does not do is to distinguish between short-, medium- and long-term objectives. Obviously, the short-term activities are the most pressing and are going to demand more detailed planning, but there still needs to be an appreciation of what happens next. The nature and character of medium- and longer-term objectives will inevitably be shaped by short-term activity (and its degree of success), but it is also true that short-term activity can only be fully justified when it is put into the context of the wider picture.

Finally, Table 9.2 also stresses the importance of precision, practicality and measurability in setting objectives. Vague, open objectives such as 'to increase awareness of the product' are insufficient. Who do you want to become aware of the product: the retail trade, the general public, or a specific target segment? How much awareness are you aiming to generate within the defined group and within what time scale? A more useful objective might therefore be 'to generate 75 per cent awareness of the product within three months among A, B and C1 home-owners aged between 25 and 40 with incomes in excess of £25,000 per annum who are interested in opera and the environment'.

Until such precise definitions of objectives have been made, the rest of the planning process cannot really go ahead – how can decisions be made if you don't really know what it

Table 9.2 Possible communications objectives

Area	Objective
Cognitive	Clarify customer needs Increase brand awareness Increase product knowledge
Affective	Improve brand image Improve company image Increase brand preference
Behaviour	Stimulate search behaviour Increase trial purchases Increase repurchase rate Increase word-of-mouth recommendation
Corporate	Improved financial position Increase flexibility of corporate image Increase cooperation from the trade Enhance reputation with key publics Build up management ego

Source: DeLozier (1975). Copyright © 1975 The Estate of the late Professor M. Wayne DeLozier.

is you are aiming for? Precise objectives also provide the foundation for monitoring, feedback and assessment of the success of the communications mix. There is at least something against which to measure actual performance.

■ Strategies

Having defined objectives, it is now necessary to devise strategies for achieving them. The analysis done so far may already have established the broad balance of the promotional mix, but there is still the task of developing the fine detail of what the actual message is to be, how best to frame it and what medium or media can be used to communicate it most efficiently and effectively.

Designing the message content, structure and format poses questions for managing any element of the promotional mix. Message content is about what the sender wants to say,

The Advertising Standards Authority (ASA) received 375 complaints about Velvet Toilet Tissue's 'Love Your Bum' campaign. The advertisements featured a range of bare bottoms, encouraging people to treat their rears to a 'feel-good experience'. Despite some members of the public being unimpressed, the ASA decided there was no justification for a formal investigation, as there was little to cause offence. When the advertising agency Saatchi and Saatchi produced billboards for Club 18–30 holidays carrying slogans such as 'Beaver España' and 'The Summer of 69' and featuring graphic close-up crotch shots of young men in boxer shorts to exemplify 'package holidays', 492 disgruntled witnesses complained to the ASA. Despite Saatchi's claim that the advertisements reflected the true essence of such holidays, the ASA ruled that the posters should be withdrawn (Burrell, 2005).

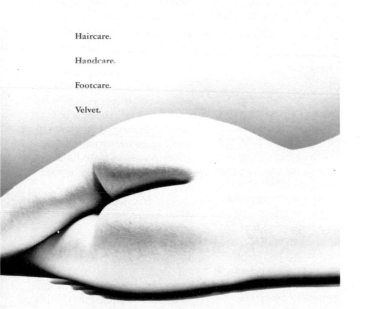

By carefully avoiding the use of the word 'bum', this Velvet ad stayed within acceptable boundaries.

Source: Image courtesy of The Advertising Archives

while message structure is about how to say it in terms of propositions and arguments. The message format depends on the choice of media used for transmitting or transferring the message. This will determine whether sight, sound, colour or other stimuli can be used effectively. These are important themes, which will be further addressed in the context of each element of the promotional mix in the following five chapters. A money-off sales promotion, for example, is certainly appropriate for stimulating short-term sales of a product, but will it cheapen the product's quality image in the eyes of the target market? Is the target market likely to respond to a cash saving, or would they be more appreciative of a charity tie-in where a donation is made to a specific charity for every unit sold? The latter suggestion has the added benefit of enhancing corporate as well as brand image, and is also less easy for the competition to copy.

With advertising in particular, the organisation might use a character or a celebrity to communicate a message on its behalf to give it source credibility. The audience will see the spokesperson as the source of the message and thus might pay more attention to it or interpret it as having more credibility (Hirschman, 1987).

marketing in action

'Til death (or disgrace) do us part: the pros and cons of celebrity endorsement

A recent Millward Brown tracking study estimated that one in five advertisements in the UK features the face, voice or testimony of a celebrity. Rines (2004) believes that celebrity endorsement can be a cost-effective way to achieve image transfer and enhance brand attributes, but cautions that as in any relationship, things can turn sour. If the celebrity on your brand's payroll starts making the wrong kind of headlines, the objective to ally the celebrity's image and values with your brand backfires. Coca-Cola signed up Manchester United and England striker Wayne Rooney for £1m until the end of the 2006 World Cup. Ongoing tabloid revelations about his antics on and off the pitch, and media speculation as to whether he is a suitable 'role model', have continually embarrassed the brand. Revelations about his England team-mate David Beckham's private life do not seem to have affected the various brands that pay him an estimated £50m a year for endorsement in the same way. This appears to be because of the distinction between 'celebrity' and 'role model'.

A celebrity could be anyone from a Big Brother contestant to a much-photographed aristocrat, famous for being famous, and having some lifestyle attribute a particular target audience might aspire to. Role models are more likely to embody positive and admirable values that are made public consistently through their behaviour. Nelson Mandela was chosen to launch the 'Make Poverty History' campaign because he was the ideal role model – everything we know about his behaviour throughout his life underlines his belief and commitment to the cause, and nothing we know contradicts it. Gary Lineker was chosen as the face of Walkers' crisps over 10 years ago because in his long, top-flight footballing career he had never so much as received a yellow card – a good role model. Although the endorsement deals may have started rolling in for David Beckham after the strength of character he showed in rehabilitating himself as the hard-working family man after his crucial sending-off in the World Cup match against Argentina in 1998, his deals with brands like Police sunglasses, Brylcreem, Gillette and Vodafone are more about celebrity glamour and lifestyle.

Although many column inches are devoted to undeserving brand ambassadors in the media, there are some brands that hit the jackpot with their celebrity spokespeople. B&Q signed up yachtswoman Ellen MacArthur when she was a virtual unknown, claiming there was a good fit between her can-do attitude and B&Q's brand values. And she did it, very publicly, in true 'role model' style by completing her solo round-the-world voyage, and B&Q reaped the knock-on rewards. When Sainsbury's signed up Jamie Oliver it knew it was getting a cheeky Cockney chappie who knew about food. Since his high-profile initiatives to give disadvantaged teenagers the opportunity to train as chefs, and improve school meals, Sainsbury's now finds itself with a national hero and food quality ambassador at its disposal. 'Laaaverly' as the man himself might say.

As in life, some celebrity/brand relationships end in divorce. In the same way that careful spouses with a lot to lose insist on a pre-nuptial agreement, advertisers can take out 'Death and Disgrace' insurance. This allows them to recoup some of the costs of pulling or recasting advertisements should their famous face die or do something else regrettable!

Sources: Johnson (2005); Rines (2004); Saunders (2005).

Whether the spokesperson, or presenter of the message, is a well-known celebrity or an invented character, it is important to link their characteristics with the communication objectives. The marketing manager might also have to decide whether or not to use personal or impersonal media. Table 9.3 compares the marketing advantages and disadvantages of a range of media, from informal word-of-mouth contact such as friends recommending products to each other through to a formal professional face-to-face pitch from a sales representative.

Table 9.3 Comparison of personal and impersonal media for communications

| | Personal → | | → Impersonal | |
	Word of mouth	Sales representative	Personalised mail shot	Mass media advertising
Accuracy and consistency of delivery	Questionable	Good	Excellent	Excellent
Likely completeness of message	Questionable	Good	Excellent	Excellent
Controllability of content	None	Good	Excellent	Excellent
Ability to convey complexity	Questionable	Excellent	Good	Relatively poor
Flexibility and tailoring of message	Good	Excellent	Good	None
Ability to target	None	Excellent	Good	Relatively poor
Reach	Patchy	Relatively poor	Excellent	Excellent
Feedback collection	None	Excellent – immediate	Possible – depends on response mechanism	Difficult – costly and time consuming

Whichever element of the communications mix is being used, the important consideration is to match the message and media with both the target audience and the defined objectives. These issues are covered in further detail for each element of the mix in the following chapters.

Budgeting

Controlled communication is rarely free. The marketer has to develop campaigns within (often) tight budgets, or fight for a larger share of available resources. It is important, therefore, to develop a budgeting method that produces a realistic figure for the marketer to work with in order to achieve objectives. Even in the same sector, the spend on advertising can vary considerably. In the chicken and burger fast food sector, for example, in 2003, McDonald's spent around £84m on advertising, while its biggest-spending rivals, KFC and Burger King, spent around £29m and £20m respectively (Mintel, 2004). Similarly, in laundry products, in the first 10 months of 2004, Lever Fabergé spent £20m advertising Persil, while Procter & Gamble (P&G) spent only £10m advertising the Ariel brand (Mintel, 2005).

There are six main methods of budget setting, some of which are better suited to predictable, static markets rather than dynamic, fast-changing situations.

Judgemental budget setting

The first group of methods of determining budgets are called judgemental budget setting because they all involve some degree of guesswork.

Arbitrary budgets. Arbitrary budgets are based on what has always been spent in the past or, for a new product, on what is usually spent on that kind of thing.

Affordable method. The affordable budget, closely linked to the arbitrary budget, is one which, as its name implies, imposes a limit based either on what is left over after other more important expenses have been met or on what the company accountant feels to be the maximum allowable. Hooley and Lynch (1985) suggest that this method is used in product-led rather than in marketing-led organisations because it is not actually linked with what is to be achieved in the marketplace.

Percentage of past sales method. The percentage of past sales method is at least better, in that it acknowledges some link between communication and sales, even though the link is illogical. The chief assumptions here are that sales precede communication, and that future activities should be entirely dependent on past performance. Taken to its extreme, it is easy to imagine a situation in which a product has a bad year, therefore its communication budget is cut, causing it to perform even more poorly, continuing in a downward spiral until it dies completely. The judgemental element here is deciding what percentage to apply. There are industry norms for various markets; for example in the pharmaceutical industry, 10 to 20 per cent is a typical advertising/sales ratio, but this drops to less than 1 per cent in clothing and footwear. For industrial equipment the advertising/sales ratio is often lower than 1 per cent although the sales force cost/sales ratio is often considerably higher in such industries. However, this is only part of the picture. The industrial equipment manufacturer might well invest much more in its sales force. Such percentages might simply be the cumulative habits of many organisations and thus might be questionable when considered in the context of the organisation's own position and ambitions within the market.

Percentage of future sales method. None of the budgeting methods so far considered takes any account of the future needs of the product itself. However, the percentage of future sales method is an improvement, in that communication and sales are in the right order, but again there is the question of what percentage to apply. There is also an underlying assumption about there being a direct relationship between next year's expenditure and next year's sales.

Data-based budget setting

None of the methods examined so far has taken account of communications objectives – a reminder/reinforcement operation is much cheaper than a major attitude change exercise – or indeed of the quality or cost-effectiveness of the communication activities undertaken. There is a grave risk that the money allocated will be insufficient to achieve any real progress, in which case it will have been wasted. This then paves the way for the second group of techniques, called data-based budget setting methods, which eliminate the worst of the judgemental aspects of budgeting.

Competitive parity. The competitive parity method involves discovering what the competition is spending and then matching or exceeding it. It has some logic, in that if you are shouting as loudly as someone else, then you have a better chance of being heard than if you are whispering. In marketing, however, it is not necessarily the volume of noise so much as the quality of noise that determines whether the message gets across and is acted on.

If it is to have any credibility at all, then the competitive parity method must take into account competitors' own communications objectives, how they compare with yours and how efficiently and effectively they are spending their money. For all you know, the competitors have set their budgets by looking at how much you spent last year, which takes you all back into a stalemate similar to that of the arbitrary budget method.

Objective and task budgeting. The final method of budgeting, arguably the best, is objective and task budgeting. This is naturally the most difficult to implement successfully. It does, however, solve many of the dilemmas posed so far and makes most commercial sense. It requires the organisation to work backwards. First define the communications objectives, then work out exactly what has to be done to achieve them. This can be costed to provide a budget that is directly linked to the product's needs and is neither more nor less than that required. A new product, for example, will need substantial investment in integrated marketing communication in order to gain acceptance within distribution channels, and then to generate awareness and trial among consumers. A mature product, in contrast, might need only 'maintenance' support, which will clearly cost much less. The only danger with objective and task budgeting, however, is that ambition overtakes common sense, leading to a budget that simply will not be accepted.

The art of making this technique work lies in refining the objectives and the ensuing budget in the light of what the organisation can bear. It may mean taking a little longer than you would like to establish the product, or finding cheaper, more creative ways of achieving objectives, but at least the problems to be faced will be known in advance and can be strategically managed.

Mitchell (1993), as reported by Fill (2002), suggested that 40 per cent of companies use the objective and task method, while 27 per cent use a percentage of future sales, 8 per cent use a percentage of past sales, and 19 per cent use their own methods. Overall, across the whole promotional mix, organisations are likely to use some kind of composite method that includes elements of judgemental and data-based techniques (Fill, 2002).

Positioning the budgeting element so late in the planning flow does imply that the objective and task method is the preferred one. To reiterate, there is no point in throwing more money at the communication problem than is strictly necessary or justifiable in terms of future aims, and equally, spending too little to make an impact is just as wasteful.

eg Over the August Bank Holiday weekend in 2003, the UK directory enquiries number 192, run by BT for the previous 47 years, was switched off. Following decisions to deregulate the service, it was replaced by 30 new players, all keen to challenge BT, all with six-digit numbers beginning with 118. With a launch marketing budget of £22.5m, and absolute determination to succeed, The Number UK Ltd planned a multimedia campaign. Since directory enquiries was a low-interest area, and one that was about to be saturated, the first decision was to start early – eight months before the switch-on date, and as it turned out, five months before any of the competition. The imperative to stand out and stamp the brand on the UK householder's memory led to £2m of the budget being invested in the acquisition of the number 118 118. The duplication in the number provided creative inspiration; all communications material was based on two shaggy-haired, moustachioed runners, each wearing the number 118 on their vests. The twins featured in high-profile national television and print advertising, and were the subject of a spoof fan site called MysteryRunners.com, which spawned viral initiatives. There were also live stunts with lookalike runners appearing on local high streets. 118 118 achieved 44 per cent market share of the UK directory enquiries market as soon as 192 was switched off, and maintained that level throughout the following year (http://www.dandad.org.uk/inspiration).

The 118 118 campaign has developed over time without losing its ability to make its message memorable through humour.

Source: *Image courtesy of The Advertising Archives*

Implementation and evaluation

The aim of planning is *not* to create an impressive, aesthetically pleasing document that promptly gets locked in a filing cabinet for a year. It is too easy for the planning process to become an isolated activity, undertaken as an end in itself with too little thought about the realities of the world and the practical problems of making things happen as you want them to. Throughout the planning stages, there must be due consideration given to 'what if . . .' scenarios and due respect given to what is practicable and manageable. That is not to say that an organisation should be timid in what it aims to achieve, but rather that risks should be well calculated.

Planning also helps to establish priorities, allocate responsibilities and ensure a fully integrated, consistent approach, maximising the benefits gained from all elements of the communications mix. In reality, budgets are never big enough to do everything, and something has to be sacrificed. Inevitably, different activities will be championed by different managers and these tensions have to be resolved within the planning framework. For example, many organisations are reappraising the cost-effectiveness of personal selling in the light of developments in the field of direct marketing.

An equally important activity is collecting feedback. You have been communicating with a purpose and you need to know at least whether that purpose is being fulfilled. Monitoring during the campaign helps to assess early on whether or not the objectives are being met as expected. If it is really necessary, corrective action can thus be taken before too much time and money is wasted or, even worse, before too much damage is done to the product's image.

It is not enough, however, to say that the promotional mix was designed to generate sales and we have sold this much product, and therefore it was a success. The analysis needs to be deeper than this – after all, a great deal of time and money has been invested in this communication programme. What aspects of the promotional mix worked best and most cost-effectively? Was there sufficient synergy between them? Do we have the right balance within each element of the mix, for example choice of advertising media? Are consumers' attitudes and beliefs about our product the ones we expected and wanted them to develop? Have we generated the required long-term loyalty to the product?

It is only through persistent and painstaking research effort that these sorts of question are going to be answered. Such answers not only help to analyse how perceptive past planning efforts were, but also provide the basis for future planning activity. They begin to shape the nature and objectives of the continued communication task ahead and, through helping managers to learn from successes and mistakes, lead to a more efficient use of skills and resources. The following chapters will discuss some of the techniques and problems of collecting feedback on specific elements of the promotional mix, and Chapter 5 is also relevant in a more general sense.

Communications planning model: review

Rothschild's (1987) model of the communications planning process (see Figure 9.2) is an invaluable framework, as it includes all the main issues to be considered in balancing the promotional mix. In reality, however, the process cannot be as clear cut or neatly divided as the model suggests. Planning has to be an iterative and dynamic process, producing plans that are sufficiently flexible and open to allow adaptation in the light of emerging experience, opportunities and threats.

It is also easy, when presented with a flow-chart type of model like this one, to make assumptions about cause and effect. There is a great deal of logic and sense in the sequencing of decisions indicated by this model – definition of target market defines objectives; objectives determine strategies; strategies determine budgets and so on – but in reality there have to be feedback loops between the later and earlier elements of the model. Budgets, for instance, are likely to become a limiting factor that may cause revision of strategies and/or objectives and/or target market detail. Objective and task is the preferred approach to budget setting, but it still has to be operated within the framework of the resources that the organisation can reasonably and justifiably be expected to marshal, as discussed earlier.

The concluding messages are, therefore, that the planning process:

1 is very important for achieving commercial objectives effectively and efficiently;
2 should not be viewed as a series of discrete steps in a rigid sequence;
3 should not be an end in itself, but should be regarded as only a beginning;
4 should produce plans that are open to review and revision as appropriate;
5 should be undertaken in the light of what is reasonably achievable and practicable for the organisation; and
6 should be assessed with the benefit of hindsight and feedback so that next year it will work even better.

Chapter 12 looks at marketing planning more generally, and will further discuss the techniques and problems of implementing plans within the organisational culture.

Chapter summary

■ An integrated approach to marketing communication planning is vital, given the importance of effective communication to the success of products and given the level of investment often required for integrated marketing communication activity. The main stages in the planning flow include analysing the situation, defining objectives, defining strategies, setting budgets, and implementation and evaluation.

■ Communications objectives must be precise, practical and measurable. They can be cognitive (e.g. creating awareness and disseminating knowledge), affective (e.g. creating and manipulating brand images), behavioural (e.g. stimulating the consumer to purchase action) or corporate (e.g. building and enhancing corporate image).

■ Different promotional tools are effective for different types of objective. While advertising might be more appropriate for cognitive objectives, personal selling and sales promotions could be better for behavioural objectives, for example. Direct marketing can be very useful in creating and enhancing longer-term relationships with customers.

■ Communications budgets can be set in a number of ways. Judgemental methods involve a degree of guesswork, for example being set arbitrarily or on the basis of what can be afforded. They can also be set on the basis of expected future sales, or made dependent on historical sales figures. Data-based methods are more closely related to what is actually happening in the marketplace and include competitive parity and the objective and task method.

Questions for review and discussion

9.1   What are the five main elements of the *promotional mix*?

9.2   What are the stages in the *marketing communications planning flow*?

9.3   What are the three broad stages of *buyer readiness*, and how might the balance of the promotional mix vary between them?

9.4   What are the main categories of *marketing communication objectives*?

9.5   What are the main advantages and disadvantages of *objective and task* budget setting compared with the other methods?

9.6   How and why might the balance of the promotional mix differ between:
(a) the sale of a car to a private individual; and
(b) the sale of a fleet of cars to an organisation for its sales representatives?

case study 9

Flying in from Rio

In the same way that Scotland has a national spirit in whisky, and Russia in vodka, Brazil has cachaca (pronounced coshasa). The spirit, made from sugar cane, has been produced in Brazil for over 500 years, and the Brazilian population drink their way through 1.3 billion litres of it every year. But whereas Russia exports 50 per cent of the vodka it produces, less than 1 per cent of the cachaca produced in Brazil each year leaves the country. As with many national spirits, there is a variation in quality from the 'rough stuff' to the brands for aficionados. Brazil's premium quality cachaca brand is Sagatiba (pronounced sagachiba). The brand owners decided it was time for the rest of the world to experience Sagatiba, and thus embarked on a £20m European launch campaign during 2005. The long-term objective was to make Sagatiba as well-known and popular as Bacardi, but starting from a zero awareness base, there was a long way to go.

The first stop was at advertising agency Saatchi and Saatchi, which was charged with developing press and poster advertising that could run in style magazines and on metropolitan billboards across Europe, in parallel with other brand awareness and image building

By referring to an iconic Brazilian image, Sagatiba ads encourage drinkers to try something exotic and different.

Source: Image courtesy of The Advertising Archives

initiatives that would 'spread the word'. Saatchi's produced an arresting campaign featuring a model who closely resembled the iconic 'Christ the Redeemer' statue that looks out across Rio de Janeiro. In each of four advertisements this young, stylised Brazilian was pictured in the midst of modern, hip, Brazilian life, adopting the same Christ-on-the-Cross pose, e.g. with arms wrapped around a pool cue in a bar, or with arms outstretched across the back of a taxi seat with the city in the background. Each execution carried the line 'Sagatiba – pure spirit of Brasil'. Creatives in the agency also worked on designs for strongly branded merchandise such as ash trays, bar seats and ice cube trays using the distinctive 'S' shape from the Sagatiba logo, with a view to their being placed in stylish bars in major cities. Viral initiatives such as a 'forward to your mates' e-mail quiz, which ended with directions on where to find a bar to sample Sagatiba, and a graffiti interpretation of the print campaign spray-painted on walls and buildings in fashionable parts of London's East End were also undertaken. The objection to this latter initiative by traditional graffiti artists, on the grounds that it was commercial interests hijacking their art form, only served to heighten interest in Sagatiba, and generate a curiosity amongst younger consumers who are often immune to conventional advertising.

When it was announced that Selfridges department store in London's Oxford Street was to hold a 'Brazilian Month', 1600 bottles of Sagatiba were shipped to the store where the brand owners created a Brazilian beach bar in one of the shop windows. Here, models served and drank Sagatiba, danced to Brazilian music, and invited shoppers to try the brand, which was then available in store for them to buy. In an attempt to drive listings in the right sorts of places, 12 of the top barmen from the UK's hippest venues were invited to a London bar where they were introduced to Sagatiba, and encouraged to experiment with the spirit. As an extension of this, Sagatiba sponsored the UK Bartender's Guild Cocktail Competition, where the challenge was to create a cocktail using a minimum of 35 ml of Sagatiba. Regional heats ran in major cities throughout the summer, and the winner bagged a luxury holiday in Brazil, and the right to represent the UK at the International Bar Association World Cocktail championships in Helsinki.

Sagatiba also ran a bar at The Taste of London event in Regent's Park where over four days gourmet food and drink from over 100 exhibitors was sampled and subsequently talked about, and written about in the press. Sagatiba's co-sponsors at the event included 40 of the capital's top restaurants serving signature dishes, the Wine and Spirit Educational Trust running a Wine and Spirit Academy, and Laurent Perrier champagne. Next steps include launching the brand in Rome, Amsterdam and other major European cities, following the print advertising campaign with cinema and television, and depending on the impact the brand manages to have in Europe, achieving global brand awareness and trial of the product.

Sources: BBC (2005); *Design News* (2005); Malvern (2005); http://www.ukbg.co.uk; http://www.tasteoflondon.co.uk.

Questions

1 Categorise the various communications activities mentioned in the case according to whether they represent push or pull tools.

2 Why do you think advertising alone was not considered sufficient for the brand launch?

3 What role do you think the specific venues and other brand names present there will have had on Sagatiba's brand image at the events it was associated with?

4 Why do you think viral or contagion mechanisms are often adopted by alcohol brands specifically?

References for chapter 9

Armitt, C. (2005), 'Food for Thought', *New Media Age*, 11 August, pp. 16–17.

BBC (2005), Inside Saatchi & Saatchi, broadcast on BBC2, 15 February.

Brough, C. (2005), 'Last Orders', *Brand Strategy*, July/August, pp. 32–3.

Burrell, I. (2005), 'No Such Thing as Bad Publicity – The 10 Most Controversial Billboards', *The Independent*, 27 July, pp. 12–13.

Butcher, J. (2005), 'New Alcohol Ad Rules Launch Today', 9 June, accessed via http://www.mad.co.uk.

Daily Mail (2005), 'Ill-fated Aurora Cruise Clocks up £30 Million Bill', *Daily Mail*, 15 February.

DeLozier, M. (1975), *The Marketing Communications Process*, McGraw-Hill.

Design News (2005), 'Wallpaper Express, Salone', *Design News*, April, accessed via http://www.wallpaper.com.

Elms, S. and Svendsen, J. (2005), 'The Mind, the Brain and the Media', *Admap*, April, pp. 28–31.

Fill, C. (2002), *Marketing Communications: Contexts, Strategies and Applications* (3rd edn), Financial Times Prentice Hall.

Harwood, S. (2005), 'Consumer Brands Give Web a Key Role', *New Media Age*, 4 (August), p. 10.

Hirschman, E. (1987), 'People as Products: Analysis of a Complex Marketing Exchange', *Journal of Marketing*, 51 (1), pp. 98–108.

Hooley, G. and Lynch, J. (1985), 'How UK Advertisers Set Budgets', *International Journal of Advertising*, 3, pp. 223–31.

Johnson, B. (2005), 'No More Heroes', *Marketing Week*, 12 May, pp. 26–9.

Jones, J. (1991), 'Over Promise and Under Delivery', *Marketing and Research Today*, 19 (November), pp. 195–203.

Malvern, J. (2005), 'Graffiti Artists Pour Scorn on Saatchi Street Art Campaign', *The Times*, 23 May, p. 26.

Marketing Week (2005), 'P&O Diverts Ad Spend to Boost Troubled Aurora', *Marketing Week*, 27 January, p. 11.

Mintel (2004), 'Chicken and Burger Bars', *Mintel Leisure Intelligence UK*, March, accessed via http://www.mintel.com.

Mintel (2005), 'Clothes Washing Detergents and Laundry Aids', *Mintel Market Intelligence UK*, January, accessed via http://www.mintel.com.

Mitchell, L. (1993), 'An Examination of Methods of Setting Advertising Budgets: Practice and Literature', *European Journal of Advertising*, 27 (5), pp. 5–21.

Mitchell, V. (2005), 'An Aurora of Bad PR Around P&O', *Marketing Week*, 27 January, p. 29.

Murray, I. (2005), 'Men Fight Back as Battle of the Sexes Hits Adland', *Marketing Week*, 10 February, p. 78.

Oliver, J. and Farris, P. (1989), 'Push and Pull: A One-Two Punch for Packaged Products', *Sloan Management Review*, 31 (Fall), pp. 53–61.

Parry, C. (2005), 'Snacks Under Attack', *Marketing Week*, 21 July, p. 31.

Pickton, D. and Broderick, A. (2001), *Integrated Marketing Communications*, Financial Times Prentice Hall.

Porter, N. (2004), 'Ofcom Unveils New Rules on Alcohol Ads', 1 November, accessed via http://www.mad.co.uk.

Rines, S. (2004), 'Wayne Wonder', 6 September, accessed via http://www.mad.co.uk.

Rothschild, M. (1987), *Marketing Communications: From Fundamentals to Strategies*, Heath.

Saunders, S. (2005), 'Rights and Wrongs', *Creative Review*, June, pp. 58–9.

Singh, S. (2004), 'Will TV be Teetotal if Ofcom Gets Its Way?', *Marketing Week*, 30 September, pp. 22–3.

Strong, E. (1925), *The Psychology of Selling*, McGraw-Hill.

Wilkinson, A. (2004), 'It's Hard Work to Fill a Prior Sponsor's Shoes', *Marketing Week*, 4 November, pp. 17–18.

chapter 10

promotion: advertising and personal selling

Introduction

This chapter discusses advertising, an indirect form of communiction, and personal selling, a very direct way of getting a marketing message across. It examines the role of advertising in the promotional mix and the important aspects of message design and media selection in the development of successful campaigns. The stages in developing an advertising campaign are then presented, along with the main management decisions at each stage. Sometimes these decisions are made in conjunction with the support of an external advertising agency, while in other organisations the campaign process is controlled almost exclusively in-house. The decision to use an agency and the importance of the client–agency relationship are thus also considered within the chapter.

eg Throughout a brand's life the market situation changes and evolves, so there is a need to reappraise brand objectives and strategy continually. Advertising has historically played a key role in positioning and repositioning brands to relevant consumers to help meet brand objectives. Pfizer Consumer Healthcare's mouthwash brand Listerine had been brand leader in the UK market since the 1970s. Between 1985 and 1995 the brand was synonymous with the animated dragon, Clifford, a halitosis sufferer who appeared in the advertisements, and after sloshing some Listerine around his mouth, always pulled the princess. During this decade, however, more brands and a proliferation of own-label products entered the sector; chewing gum and mints were being used increasingly as quick-fix breath fresheners, and oral care became more therapeutic with added-value toothpastes and brushes appearing on the market. Listerine's positioning as a breath freshener was less relevant and sales were declining. In order to arrest decline, advertising was used to reposition Listerine as a contributor to healthier teeth and gums through its germ- and plaque-reducing qualities. The creative vehicle for this message from 1997 onwards was a loveable rogue tooth fairy, constantly frustrated at the lack of adult teeth to collect because of Listerine use. Having arrested decline (as well as decay) through this campaign, the brand's new objective was to grow, and so a campaign was developed with the more dramatic underlying message that Listerine users didn't need to visit the dentist. The television advertisement featured vignettes of bored dentists, listlessly filling their time with absurd, trivial tasks while patients stayed away with their healthy teeth and gums. During the advertising periods in 2002 and 2003 there was a 40 per cent increase in base sales compared to the same periods in previous years (Fenn, 2004).

The role of advertising

■ Within the promotional mix

Advertising can be defined as any paid form of non-personal promotion transmitted through a mass medium. The sponsor should be clearly identified and the advertisement may relate to an organisation, a product or a service. The key difference, therefore, between advertising and other forms of promotion is that it is impersonal and communicates with large numbers of people through paid media channels. Although the term 'mass media' is often used, it has to be interpreted carefully. The proliferation of satellite and cable television channels, along with the increasing number of more tightly targeted special interest magazines and the use of the internet, means that on the one hand advertising audiences are generally smaller, but on the other the audiences are 'better quality'. This implies that they are far more likely to be interested in the subject matter of the advertising carried by their chosen medium.

Advertising normally conforms to one of two basic types: product-oriented or institutional (Berkowitz *et al.*, 1992), as shown in Figure 10.1. A product-oriented advertisement focuses, as the term suggests, on the product or service being offered, whether for profit or not. Its prime task is to support the product in achieving its marketing goals.

Product-oriented advertising can itself take one of three alternative forms: pioneering, competitive, or reminder and reinforcement advertising.

Figure 10.1 Types of advertising

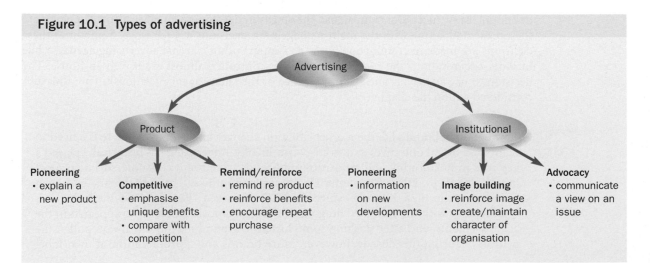

Pioneering advertising

Pioneering advertising is used in the early stages of the lifecycle when it is necessary to explain just what the product will do and the benefits it can offer. The more innovative, technically complex and expensive the product is, the more essential this explanation becomes. Depending on the product's newness, the prime emphasis might well be on stimulating basic generic demand rather than attempting to beat competition.

In these cases, the prime emphasis in the advertising is to provide enough information to allow potential buyers to see how this product might relate to them, and thus to stimulate enough interest to encourage further investigation and possibly trial.

Competitive advertising

Competitive advertising is concerned with emphasising the special features of the product or brand as a means of outselling the competition. Usually the seller seeks to communicate the unique benefits, real or imaginary, that distinguish the product and give it its competitive edge. Given that most markets are mature and often crowded, this type of advertising is very common and very important.

eg In Western Europe, the bottled mineral water market has become commoditised, making things particularly difficult for a premium-priced brand like Evian. In order to differentiate itself from the competition, and to justify the price tag, Evian ran a television and cinema advertisement in France, Belgium, Luxembourg and the UK throughout 2003. The advertisement featured a variety of healthy-looking, energetic adults singing the Queen hit 'We Will Rock You' in children's voices. The idea was to portray Evian as the 'spirit of youthfulness', keeping its consumers young in mind and body. Although not steeped in a product truth, and therefore something of a generic claim, the assonance of the endline 'Evian – Live Young', particularly when pronounced with a marked French accent, would make it difficult for another brand to encroach on the territory effectively (EuroRSCG, 2004).

A form of competitive advertising that has grown in significance in recent years is comparative advertising. This means making a direct comparison between one product and another, showing the advertiser's product in a much more favourable light, of course (Muehling *et al.*, 1990). Alternatively, the comparison may be more subtle, referring to 'other leading brands' and leaving it up to the target audience to decide which rival product is intended. Initially, it was thought unwise to use a direct comparison approach as it gave a free mention to competitors and was likely to bring about a 'knocking copy' reaction. However, advertisers have now realised that in a competitive world, even if they do make a comparison with a market leader with already high awareness levels, the effect need not be negative.

marketing **in action**

Laughing all the way to the ... building society?

Many Europeans who have visited the USA during an election campaign will comment on both the amount and nature of advertising for political candidates to which they are exposed. Comparative advertising has always played a part in American communications, and in Western Europe, where there has been little tradition of comparative advertising, audiences can find the harsh, 'knocking' copy of US commercials detailing a candidate's often highly personal unsuitability for office distasteful. Until recently, comparative advertising was outlawed in some EU countries, and in others there was an industry belief that it was better to promote your product on the basis of its strengths rather than the competition's weaknesses. Apart from anything else, it can seem counter-intuitive to spend precious advertising budgets talking about your competitors (albeit their faults) rather than talking-up your brand. The EC Directive on Comparative Advertising in the late 1990s, however, legitimised comparative advertising as being in the interests of competition and public information. Coming from cultures unused to knocking the competition to score brand points in

By poking fun at the negative perceptions of other building societies, Nationwide made viewers take more notice of the alternative approach it offers.

Source: © Nationwide Building Society

advertising, a number of European industry players went on record urging caution and proposing loose guidelines for the use of this approach (see Shannon, 1999; Gray, 2001; Mason, 2000; Staheli, 2000). One guideline related to humour and how its use could soften the blow of direct comparison for an audience unused to and uncomfortable with having their brand choices slagged off.

Nationwide Building Society and its advertising agency Leagas Delaney have used humour in comparative advertising to great effect. As it is the difference in its status – building society as opposed to bank – that is Nationwide's USP, it had little option but to draw comparisons. While a series of advertisements listing all the things that banks do wrong might sound dull and negative, the lightness of touch in the execution of the eight 60-second TV commercials makes them anything but. By writing the advertisements as comedy sketches, hiring Armando Iannucci, the award-winning comedy writer and director (Alan Partridge, Brass Eye) to direct them, and casting well-known comedy actor Mark Benton as the stereotypical Bank Manager, the agency was inviting the target audience to have a laugh at the exaggeratedly (but legitimate) customer-unfriendly antics of banks. In one, we witness the Bank Manager changing the subject, for example to riding penny farthings and lions, every time the customer tries to close their account. In another, a customer, irate at having been charged for taking money out of an autobank abroad, is told by the Bank Manager to view it 'like a tip – and at the end of the year we add all those tips up and it goes towards the bubbly at the shareholders' meeting'. In a third, a customer is informed they were not offered as competitive a rate on their mortgage as a friend because the bank teller didn't like their cardigan or nose as much. All of the commercials end with the line 'Nationwide, proud to be different'. The humour in the executions makes the comparative elements of the message more palatable to the audience.

Sources: Creative Review (2005); Gray (2001); Mason (2000); Shannon (1999); Staheli (2000); Wood (2003).

Reminder and reinforcement advertising

Reminder and reinforcement advertising tends to operate after purchase. It reminds customers that the product still exists and that it has certain positive properties and benefits. This increases the chances of repurchase and sometimes might even persuade consumers to buy larger quantities. The main emphasis is not on creating new knowledge or behaviour but on reinforcing previous purchasing behaviour, and reassuring consumers that they made the right choice in the first place.

eg Most football and rugby grounds rely heavily on the up-front revenue generated by season ticket holders. Eden Park, the home of rugby union in Auckland, New Zealand, is no exception. Yet between 1998 and 2003 the number of annual season ticket holders had dropped from 9476 to 6588. Many previous ticket holders were still attending games *ad hoc*, but obviously represented a less profitable and reliable income stream. Reasons for this drop seemed to be a combination of Sky coverage of key matches, disappointment that the venue had not hosted as many of the 2003 Rugby World Cup matches as anticipated, some flirtation with a newly successful local rugby league side, and a general 'taking for granted' having the prestigious venue on the doorstep (where at least one All Blacks test match is played each season). A multi-media print campaign was mounted to remind locals that the only way to guarantee a seat for the big matches was to hold a season ticket – or effectively have YOUR SEAT at the ground. The visual was of the seats in the stadium, whichever medium it appeared in. The result was 4519 new season ticket seats sold the following season (Big Communications, 2004).

This kind of advertising clearly relates to established products in the mature stage of the product lifecycle where the emphasis is on maintaining market share at a time of major competition.

Institutional advertising

In contrast, institutional advertising is not product specific. It aims to build a sound reputation and image for the whole organisation to achieve a wide range of objectives with different target audiences. These could include the community, financial stakeholders, government and customers, to name but a few.

Institutional advertising may be undertaken for many reasons, as shown in Figure 10.1, for example pioneering in the sense of presenting new developments within the organisation, image building, or advocacy in the sense of presenting the organisation's point of view on an issue. Some institutional advertising might be linked with presenting the organisation as a caring, responsible and progressive company. These advertisements are designed to inform or reinforce positive images with target audiences. Others may adopt an advocacy perspective, indicating the organisation's view on a particular issue for political, social responsibility or self-interest reasons.

■ Within the marketing mix

The above categorisation of product and institutional advertising broadly describes the direct uses of advertising. Within the marketing mix, advertising also plays a less direct but equally important role in supporting other areas of marketing activity. In B2B markets, advertising often directly supports the selling efforts of the sales team by generating leads, providing information on new developments to a wider audience more quickly, and creating a generally more receptive climate prior to the sales visit.

---

corporate social responsibility   in action

Brands stripping off for a good cause

Cause-related marketing (CRM), a promotional link-up between a brand and a cause or charity, can provide an interesting focus for an advertising campaign, as well as generating positive publicity. Two years after launching the Recycle for London initiative, the Greater London Authority launched a £1.5m advertising campaign to run for eight weeks throughout September, October and November 2005 in the capital. Posters which appeared on buses, at bus stops and in and around the London Underground network featured a total of 35 recyclable products from household brand names such as Gillette, Aquafresh, Heinz, Orangina, Red Bull, Ribena and Sure. In each of the creative executions the brands' packaging was adapted to communicate the campaign's strapline – 'London, Let's Recycle More'. The products and brands featured were chosen to represent the spectrum of packaging householders can recycle, including some items they may be surprised

Posters using recognisable shapes of containers that can be recycled have encouraged the public to think twice before throwing everything in the bin.

Source: © Recycle for London/Greater London Authority

to know they can recycle – aerosol cans as well as food cans, magazines and directories as well as newspapers.

The poster campaign coincided with and promoted the launch of a text service designed to make recycling easier. By texting the word 'recycle' and their postcode to 63131, Londoners could gain information on which materials could be recycled, where their nearest recycling facilities were, and collection dates in their area. Those visiting the website **http://www.recycleforlondon. com** had access to the same information.

Sources: *Marketing Week* (2005c); **http://www.recycleforlondon.com.**

Similarly, with sales promotion, a short-term incentive offer may be actively advertised to encourage increased traffic. For example, airlines offering 'two for one' deals or a free ticket competition frequently support their promotions with media advertising. Furniture stores also make frequent use of television and press advertising to inform the public of short-term promotional price cuts or low/no interest financing deals to stimulate interest in furnishing and to draw people into stores that they might not otherwise have thought of visiting at that particular time.

More strategically, advertising may be used to reposition a product for defensive or aggressive reasons in order to improve its competitive position. This may be achieved by demonstrating new uses for the product or to open up new segments, either geographically or benefit-based.

In other situations, advertising may support other marketing mix activities to spread demand or to reduce sales fluctuations. The problems of seasonality are well known in the services field, whether in relation to holidays, restaurants or cinemas. Combined with pricing, advertising may seek to spread or even out demand patterns, saving the service provider from having to accept periods of marked under-utilisation of capacity. The various cross-channel ferry companies, for example, advertise low-priced deals to France during the winter to boost passenger numbers.

Overall, advertising's role within an organisation depends on a range of contexts, environments and competitive challenges, and may even change within the same organisation over time. The detailed role of advertising will be specified in the marketing plan, which will clearly specify objectives, resources, activities and results expected. These issues will be revisited at pp. 340 *et seq.*, where the stages in developing an advertising campaign are considered.

Formulating the advertising message

The essence of communication, as outlined in the previous chapter, is to decide what to say, to whom, by what means and with what results. This section centres on the very demanding decision area of designing an appropriate message, with the emphasis on the message content, its tone and how it can then be presented for either print or broadcast communication.

Message

Before producing an advertisement, you need to know who the target audience is and to give careful consideration to what you want to say to them. This requires a sound understanding of the targets, their interests, needs, motivations, lifestyles, etc. In addition, there needs to be an honest appraisal of the product or service to determine the differential characteristics or benefits that are worth highlighting to achieve the desired results.

Clearly, marketing and promotional objectives are at the heart of message formulation. If the prime objective is to generate awareness, then the message must offer clear information to alert the audience to what is on offer. If the objective is to stimulate enquiries, then the focus would need to be on moving the customer through to action, making sure that the response mechanism is clear and easy to use. There also needs to be consistency between the product positioning (see pp. 211 *et seq.*) desired and the content and style of the advertisement.

The main aim in message design and execution is to prepare an informative and persuasive message in terms of words, symbols and illustrations that will not only attract attention but retain interest through its presentation so that the target audience responds as desired. Grabbing and holding attention may mean making someone watch an entire 30-second television advertisement, read a long, wordy print advertisement, or simply dwell long enough on a non-verbal graphic image to start thinking about what it means. Whatever the medium or the style of communication, it is therefore essential that the message is understandable and relevant to the audience.

You might reasonably assume that the objective of all recruitment campaigns would be to increase the number of applicants. Not so with the police force. With one in three eligible people claiming they would be prepared to consider a career in the force, and more people prepared to consider the police than any of the armed forces, numbers were not the issue for the Home Office. What it wanted advertising agency M&C Saatchi to deliver was a better quality of applicant: not the ranks of those eager for the fast car chases and forensic breakthroughs of television dramas, nor those who imagined an easy life of cruising around in squad cars and moving the odd motorist on, but people genuinely equipped to deal with the extraordinary situations modern police officers often find themselves in. By focusing on just such scenarios – separating a reluctant child from an abusive parent, interviewing a grieving mother after her infant's cot death, clearing a bar full of drunk football fans without incident – the advertising emphasised the realities of the job. By having famous and respected figures like Sir Bob Geldof, Lennox Lewis, Simon Weston and John Barnes describing these situations and concluding they couldn't do it, but posing the question to the audience 'Could You?', the advertisements were trying to isolate only those candidates truly up to the job. This campaign appeared on television, radio, in the cinema and press, and online banners linked potential applicants directly to the website **http://www.policecouldyou.co.uk** (Storey, 2001).

The juxtaposition of celebrities' comments and stark images of police work challenges potential recruits to think about whether they might be able to make a difference.

Source: Image courtesy of The Advertising Archives

Sometimes the message may be sent out through both broadcast and print media using the same theme. In other cases, a number of different messages may be communicated in different ways over the length of the campaign.

eg
Abbott (2005) argues that for effective integration between brand and consumer, 'the most basic customer facing situation – the sales environment' needs to be considered. More and more marketers are realising that POS (point of sale) communications can have an impact on the achievement of communications objectives, particularly when they reinforce advertising messages appearing in other media. With retail environments increasingly crowded with shelf-wobblers, banners, posters and displays, however, the issue of impact and standout has arisen. One area experiencing growth is floor media. Tesco Media charges £400 for an advertisement to appear on a floor panel for four weeks in each of Tesco's 400 stores, and reports that clients often use this media opportunity in conjunction with posters, petrol pump nozzles and trolley cards to emphasise a brand message throughout a customer's shopping trip (Benady, 2005).

Microsoft negotiated with Adrail to put dinosaur footprints down on a number of rail station concourses leading to stands where its software was being demonstrated, tying in with its mass media campaign portraying the computer-illiterate as dinosaurs. Similarly, BT has used floor media to direct travellers to its internet terminals within rail stations.

■ Creative appeals

After the marketing issues of message content have been considered, the creative task can proceed. It is here that agencies can play a particularly major role in the conceptualisation and design of messages that appeal effectively.

Rational appeals centre on some kind of logical argument persuading the consumer to think or act in a certain way. However, often it is not just a case of *what* is said, but also *how* it is said. The bald logic in itself may not be enough to grab and hold the consumers' attention sufficiently to make the message stick. How it is said can introduce an *emotional appeal* into the advertisement to reinforce the underlying logic of the message. The concern here is not just with facts but also with the customer's feelings and emotions towards what is on offer. It is often the emotional element that gives the advertisement an extra appeal.

eg
'Experts' are often used in advertisements based on rational appeals. An expert might typically be a white-coated scientist demonstrating or affirming the germ-killing power of a loo cleaner, or the outstanding ability of a washing powder to turn your murky grey undies brilliant white. Saab, the Swedish car manufacturer, has used its heritage and expertise in aircraft engine design to promote its cars in its advertising. Whether it is a TV commercial with a Saab model racing down the runway alongside a jet aeroplane, or a magazine advertisement carrying the headline 'Based on an original idea by the Wright brothers' (pioneers in flight), Saab persuades the consumer, rationally, that its expertise in aeronautics is translated into building better-performing cars.

Positive emotions can be very effective in creating memorable and persuasive messages, which do not necessarily need any solid rational basis in order to be effective. Humour and sex are particularly powerful tools for the advertiser, particularly in appealing to people's needs for escapism and fantasy.

It may be argued that television is better at creating emotional appeals, as it is more lifelike, with sight, sound and motion to aid the presentation, whereas print is better for more rational, factually based appeals.

Product-oriented appeals

Product-oriented appeals centre on product features or attributes and seek to emphasise their importance to the target audience. The appeals may be based on product specification (airbags or side impact protection bars in cars, for example), price (actual price level, payment terms or extras), service (availability) or any part of the offering that creates a potential competitive edge in the eyes of the target market.

With a product-oriented appeal, there are several options for specific message design strategy. These include, for example, showing the audience how the product provides the solution to a problem. The message could also centre on a 'slice of life', demonstrating how the product fits into a lifestyle that either approximates that of the target market or is one with which they can identify or to which they can aspire.

Getting closer to real life, news, facts and testimonials offer hard information about the product or proof through 'satisfied customers' that the product is all it is claimed to be. Magazine advertisements trying to sell goods that the target market might perceive to be more expensive, or goods that sound too good to be true, or goods that a customer would normally want to see or try before purchase, often use testimonials from satisfied customers. These might help to alleviate some of the doubt or risk and encourage the reader to respond to the advertisement.

> **eg**
>
> The UK population currently chomps its way through £93m worth of tortilla chips every year, which represents an increase of 40 per cent in the five years between 2000 and 2005. Doritos, the brand leader, is mainly responsible for this growth as a result of a consumer opportunity insight, and the use of a hugely successful slice-of-life advertising campaign to exploit it. A large-scale quantitative study in 2001 revealed that 'adult, in-home, evening snacking, when people relax in front on the TV or with friends' was an area worth targeting for Doritos. Larger Doritos bags for sharing and chips and dips packs were developed, and the £7m 'Friendchips' television advertising campaign was launched. The advertisements focused on a group of mates, male and female (not dissimilar to the group in the classic American sitcom *Friends*), sitting around chatting, with the product acting as a catalyst for their conversation. To date there have been more than 20 different commercials featuring the group's frivolous, risqué and witty banter around bags of Doritos and dips, always shown between 8 p.m. and 11 p.m. in advertising breaks for programmes popular with 18–35-year-old sociable types. The media slots are chosen to coincide with the times when members of the target audience are likely to be chilling with their partners or friends, and if they're not, then the advertisements might encourage them to think they should be (*Brand Republic*, 2005; FritoLay/AMV, 2003).

In magazines and trade publications, news and fact-based approaches can also take the form of advertorials. These are designed to fit in with the style, tone and presentation of the publication so that the reader tends to think of them as extensions to the magazine rather than advertisements. The overall objective is that the reader's attention should be able to flow naturally from the magazine's normal editorial content into and through the advertorial and out the other side, maintaining interest and retention. This is particularly effective where the advertorial is short.

> **eg**
>
> Print media advertorials are very popular. Research by magazine publisher Emap showed that advertorials work just as well as normal advertising in moving the reader through from awareness to interest, but are a lot better for getting information across and feeling as if they are part of the publication. Because of the association with the editorial style of the publication and the effectiveness of advertorials, media owners tend to charge more for the space, sometimes up to 20 per cent more than if exactly the same space in the same issue was used for ordinary advertising. Research has also shown that readers understand the difference between advertorial and editorial and do not feel 'conned' into

reading advertorial. In fact, readers trust advertorials more because of the implied link between them and the publication itself. As long as there is interestingly presented information and no hard sell, readers actually enjoy advertorials (*Marketing*, 1999).

In the spring of 2004, Wella, the haircare company, placed a full-colour advertorial in the *Daily Telegraph Magazine* as part of a six-month national drive to increase awareness of its Trend Vision 04 campaign. The Trend Vision campaign promoted three hairstyles that Wella had branded 'hottest of the year'. This was the first time that Wella had spent any advertising budget with the Telegraph group, but claimed that the environment was right as the *Daily Telegraph Magazine* was building a strong reputation for cutting-edge fashion and trend spotting under the well-known fashion editor Hilary Alexander (Davidson, 2004).

As print publications expand from the paper page to online, advertorials follow. In the summer of 2005, Sony Ericsson ran a special advertorial feature on Vogue.com whereby each member of the fashion team at *Vogue* took a photo of an item from their wardrobe using a Sony Ericsson phone, and posted it on the site with an explanation of why it was their most treasured piece of clothing. Sony Ericsson felt that this initiative complemented its reputation for stylish handset design (*New Media Age*, 2005).

Customer-oriented appeals

Customer-oriented appeals are focused on what the consumer personally gains through using this product. Such appeals encourage the consumer by association to think about the benefits that may be realisable through the rational or emotional content of the advertisement. Typically, they include the following.

Saving or making money. Bold 2-in-1, for example, could sell itself simply on the product-oriented appeal that it incorporates both a washing powder and a fabric conditioner in its formulation. In fact, its advertising takes the argument further into a customer-oriented appeal, demonstrating how this two-in-one product is cheaper than buying the two components separately, thus putting money back in the purchaser's pocket.

Fear avoidance. The use of fear avoidance appeals is a powerful one in message generation and has been extensively used in public, non-profit-making promotions, for example AIDS prevention, anti-drinking and driving, anti-smoking and other health-awareness programmes. Getting the right level of fear is a challenge: too high and it will be regarded as too threatening and thus be screened out, too low and it will not be considered compelling enough to act on.

Security enhancement. A wide range of insurance products aimed at the over-50s are advertised not only on the rational basis that they are a sensible financial investment, but also on the emotional basis that they provide peace of mind. This is a customer-oriented appeal in that it works on self-interest and a craving for security. Stairlifts are also sold on the basis of security enhancement, with the implication that they make going up and down stairs easier for the elderly. The advertisements also suggest that with a stairlift, the elderly will be able to retain their independence and remain in their own homes longer, a great concern to many older people.

Self-esteem and image. Sometimes, when it is difficult to differentiate between competing products on a functional basis, consumers may choose the one that they think will best improve their self-esteem or enhance their image among social or peer groups. Advertisers recognise this and can produce advertisements in which the product and its function play a very secondary role to the portrayal of these psychological and social benefits. Perfumes, cosmetics and toiletries clearly exploit this, but even an expensive technical product such as a car can focus on self-esteem and image.

eg

Mazda ran two online advertisements for its flagship model the RX-8 sports coupé. One, titled 'Revolution', showed a page from Sky Sports.com collapsing and the instruction 'bring down the old order'. Each advertisement featured the question 'Can you drive the revolution?' and encouraged a click-through to **www.drivetherevolution.com** where potential RX-8 drivers were encouraged to take a psychometric 'zoom zoom challenge' test to establish whether they really had the mettle to drive the RX-8. Those passing had the opportunity to drive one of the cars around a British racetrack. The whole macho racing challenge idea is designed to trade on the young male executive audience's self-esteem (**http://www.gluelondon.co.uk; http://drivetherevolution.com**).

Usage benefits – time, effort, accuracy, etc. An approach stressing usage benefits is very similar to a rational, product-oriented appeal, but shows how the consumer benefits from saving time, or gains the satisfaction of producing consistently good results through using this product. Such savings or satisfactions are often translated into emotional benefits such as spending more time with the family or winning other people's admiration. They even work in B2B advertising.

eg

Zanussi Electrolux launched its Jetsystem washing machine with magazine advertisements posing the question 'Everyone knows showers are more efficient than baths. So why do other machines work like baths?' It then went on to describe how Jetsystem effectively power-showers clothes clean, saving time, water and energy. The corporate line 'makes life a little easier' that appears on all Zanussi Electrolux advertisements indicates that whatever product is being advertised, there should always be a usage-benefit message to exemplify the corporate claim (*Homes and Gardens*, 2005).

Advertising media

Advertising media are called on to perform the task of delivering the message to the consumer. The advertiser needs, therefore, to select the medium or media most appropriate to the task in hand, given their relative effectiveness and the budget available. Most organisations either cannot afford expensive television advertising or find it inappropriate. Print media, such as local and national newspapers, special interest magazines and trade publications, have thus become the primary focus for most organisations' advertising efforts.

This section will look further at each advertising medium's relative merits, strengths and weaknesses, but first defines some of the terms commonly used in connection with advertising media.

Some definitions

Before we proceed to examine the advertising media, several basic terms need to be defined, based on Fill (2002).

Reach

Reach is the percentage of the target market that is exposed to the message at least once during the relevant period. If the advertisement is estimated to reach 65 per cent of the target market, then its reach would be classified as 65. Note that reach is not concerned with the entire population, but only with a clearly defined target audience. Reach can be measured by newspaper or magazine circulation figures, television viewing statistics or analysis of flows past advertising boarding sites, and is normally measured over a four-week period.

Ratings

Ratings, otherwise known as TVRs, measure the percentage of all households owning a television that are viewing at a particular time. Ratings are a prime determinant of the fees charged for the various advertising slots on television.

> **eg** As the amount charged for an advertising slot is based on the number of people likely to be watching, it is the breaks in the most popular soap operas, such as *Coronation Street*, that tend to be the most expensive. The most expensive slots in the world, however, occur during the annual broadcast of the American Superbowl. With more than 130 million US viewers tuning in to the event, and 800 million worldwide, a 30-second slot can cost upwards of $2m. Because of its extraordinary reach, and general newsworthiness, some advertisers, notably Apple and Chrysler, have used the event to showcase new advertising for new products (Yelkur *et al.*, 2004).

Frequency

Frequency is the average number of times that a member of the target audience will have been exposed to a media vehicle during the specified time period. Poster advertising space, for example, can be bought in packages that deliver specified reach and frequency objectives for a target audience.

Opportunity to see

Opportunity to see (OTS) describes how many times a member of the target audience will have an opportunity to see the advertisement. Thus, for example, a magazine might be said to offer 75 per cent coverage with an average OTS of 3. This means that within a given time period, the magazine will reach 75 per cent of the target market, each of whom will have three opportunities to see the advertisement. According to White (1988), it is generally accepted that an OTS of $2\frac{1}{2}$ to 3 is average for a television advertising campaign, whereas a press campaign needs 5 or more. As Fill (2002) points out, an OTS figure of 10 is probably a waste of money, as the extra OTSs are not likely to improve reach by very much and might even risk alienating the audience with overkill!

Ideally, advertisers set targets to be achieved on both reach and frequency. Sometimes, however, because of financial constraints, they have to compromise. They can either spend on achieving breadth of coverage, that is, have a high reach figure, or go for depth, that is, have a high level of frequency, but they cannot afford both. Whether reach or frequency is better depends entirely on what the advertisement's objectives are. Where awareness generation is the prime objective, then the focus may be on reach, getting a basic message to as many of the target market as possible at least once. If, however, the objective is to communicate complex information or to affect attitudes, then frequency may be more appropriate.

Of course, when measuring reach, the wider the range of media used, the greater the chances of overlap. If, for instance, a campaign uses both television and magazine advertising, some members of the target market will see neither, some will see only the television advertisement, some will see only the print advertisement, but some will see both. Although the overall reach is actually likely to be greater than if just one medium was used, the degree of overlap must enter into the calculation, since as a campaign develops the tendency is towards duplicated reach.

■ Broadcast media

Television

Television's impact can be high, as it not only intrudes into the consumer's home but also offers a combination of sound, colour, motion and entertainment that has a strong chance of grabbing attention and getting a message across. Television advertising presents a tremendous communication opportunity, enabling a seller to communicate to a broad range of potentially large audiences. This means that television has a relatively low cost per thousand (the cost of reaching a thousand viewers) and that it has a high reach, but to largely undifferentiated audiences. Some differentiation is possible, depending on the audience profile of the programmes broadcast, and thus an advertiser can select spots to reach specific audiences, for example during sports broadcasts, but the advertising is still far from being narrowly targeted.

The problem, therefore, with television is that its wide coverage means high wastage. The cost per thousand may be low, and the number of thousands reached may be very high, but the relevance and quality of those contacts must be questioned. Television advertising time can be very expensive, especially if the advertisement is networked nationally. Actual costs will vary according to such factors as the time of day, the predicted audience profile and size, the geographic area to be covered, the length of time and number of slots purchased and the timing of negotiation. All of this means that very large bills are soon incurred.

eg Any new product launch is likely to be an expensive undertaking, particularly if it is into a highly competitive and crowded market such as gaming. When Nintendo launched Gameboy Advance, a model designed to appeal to an older audience than the original Gameboy, it spent over €20m on television, press, radio and outdoor advertisements. It is not only the cost of the media in which advertisements are placed that marketers need to consider. There is also the cost involved with producing the executions. Guinness's 'surfer' advertisement cost more than £1m and took over a year to make. Although using a celebrity in an advertisement may be more straightforward than creating special effects like the Guinness white horse waves, it can still prove expensive (see p. 314).

Quite apart from the cost involved, television is a low-involvement medium. This means that although the senders control the message content and broadcasting, they cannot check the receiver's level of attention and understanding, because the receiver is a passive participant in what is essentially one-way communication. There is no guarantee that the receiver is following the message, learning from it and remembering it positively. Retention rates tend to be low, and therefore repetition is needed, which in turn means high costs.

The growth of internationally broadcast cable and satellite television channels is changing the shape of television advertising by creating pan-European segment interest groups. MTV, for example, has opened up communication with a huge youth market linked by a common music culture.

Radio

Radio has always provided an important means of broadcast communication for smaller companies operating within a restricted geographic area. It is now, however, beginning to emerge as a valuable national medium in the UK because of the growth in the number of local commercial radio stations and the creation of national commercial stations such as Classic FM, Virgin Radio and talkSPORT.

While still not as important as television and print, in general terms radio can play a valuable supportive role in extending reach and increasing frequency. Despite being restricted to sound only, radio still offers wide creative and imaginative advertising possibilities and, like television, can deliver to fairly specific target audiences. Narrow segments can be attractive for specialist products or services.

eg In 2005, Guardian Media Group relaunched jazzfm.com as a standalone online radio service with highly targeted advertising opportunities. 650,000 'jazz head' individuals are attracted to the online radio service each month, and are typically ABC1 30–45-year-olds. By offering standard banners, buttons, branded microsites and bespoke online advertising solutions for clients, jazzfm.com can provide high-end advertisers like British Airways, Microsoft and Mercedes with access to this niche but influential audience, at a fraction of the cost of traditional media (Jones, 2005).

Compared with television, radio normally offers a low cost per time slot. However, as a low involvement medium, it is often not closely attended to, being used just as background rather than for detailed listening. More attention might be paid, however, to the car radio during the morning and evening journey to and from work. Nevertheless, learning often takes place only slowly, again requiring a high level of repetition, carrying with it the danger of counter-productive audience irritation at hearing the same advertisements again and again. Radio is, therefore, a high frequency medium. Television for the same budget will provide more reach, but far less frequency. The choice between them depends on objectives, and brings us back to the earlier 'reach vs frequency' discussion. Large advertisers can, however, use the two media in conjunction with each other, with radio as a means of reminding listeners of the television advertisements and reinforcing that message.

■ Cinema

Cinema is not a major medium, but can be used to reach selected audiences, especially younger and male. In the UK, for example, nearly 80 per cent of cinema goers are in the 15–34 age group. The improvement in the quality of cinema facilities through the development and marketing of multiplexes has led to something of a resurgence in cinema audiences over the last 10 years or so.

Cinema goers are a captive audience, sitting there with the intention of being entertained. Thus the advertiser has an increased chance of gaining the audience's attention. The quality and impact of cinema advertising can be much greater than that of television, because of the size of the screen and the quality of the sound system. Cinema is often used as a secondary medium rather than as a main medium in an advertising campaign. It can also screen advertisements, rated consistently with the film's classification, that would not necessarily be allowed on television.

■ Print media

Magazines

The main advantage of a printed medium is that information can be presented and then examined selectively at the reader's leisure. A copy of a magazine tends to be passed around among a number of people and kept for quite a long time. Add to that the fact that magazines can be very closely targeted to a tightly defined audience, and the attraction of print media starts to become clear. Advertisers also have an enormous range of types and titles to choose from.

There exist an enormous number of special-interest magazines, each tailored to a specific segment. As well as broad segmentation, by sex (*Freundin* for women in Germany; *Playboy* for men anywhere), age (*Bliss* and *Mizz* for teenage girls; *The Oldie* for the over-50s in the UK) and geography (*The Dalesman* for Yorkshire and its expatriates), there are many narrower criteria applied. These usually relate to lifestyle, hobbies and leisure pursuits, and enable a specialist advertiser to achieve a very high reach within those segments.

Trade and technical journals are targeted at specific occupations, professions or industries. *Industrial Equipment News*, *The Farmer*, *Accountancy Age* and *Chemistry in Britain* each provide a very cost-effective means of communication with groups of people who have very little in common other than their jobs.

Whatever the type of publication, the key is its ability to reach the specific target audience. New technology has created this diversity of magazines to suit a very wide range of targets.

Magazines have other benefits. Some may have a long life, especially special-interest magazines that may be collected for many years, although the advertising may lose relevance. Normally, though, an edition usually lasts as long as the timing between issues. The regular publication and the stable readership can allow advertisers to build up a campaign with a series of sequential advertisements over time to reinforce the message. An advertiser may also choose to take the same slot – for example the back page, which is a prime spot – to build familiarity. The advertiser may even buy several pages in the same issue, to gain a short burst of intense frequency to reinforce a message, or to present a more complex, detailed informational campaign that a single- or double-page spread could not achieve.

eg Looking at the ever-elongating shelves in any newsagents, it might not come as a surprise to learn that consumer expenditure on magazines in the UK has grown in real terms every year since 2000. According to the Advertising Association, in 2005 more than £2bn was spent buying magazines. Although there is a tendency for commentators to describe the market as reaching saturation point, recent launches seem to suggest that reader appetite expands to accommodate new titles. Emap's *Grazia*, Condé Nast's *Easy Living* and IPC's *Pick Me Up*, all launched early in 2005, achieved very respectable circulation figures during their first six months according to the Audit Bureau of Circulation (ABC). And while the launch of the new men's titles *Nuts* and *Zoo* was predicted to cannibalise established publications like *FHM* and *Loaded*, they have actually increased overall market readership, without stealing from existing titles (**http://www.mad.co.uk**).

Magazines also have one potentially powerful advantage over broadcast media, which is that the mood of the reader is likely to be more receptive. People often save a magazine until they have time to look at it properly, and because they are inherently interested in the magazine's editorial content, they do pay attention and absorb what they read. This has a knock-on effect on the advertising content too. People also tend to keep magazines for reference purposes. Thus the advertising may not prompt immediate action, but if readers suddenly come back into the market, then they know where to look for suppliers.

■ Newspapers

The main role of newspapers for advertisers is to communicate quickly and flexibly to a large audience. National daily papers, national Sunday papers and local daily or weekly papers between them offer a wide range of advertising opportunities and audiences.

Classified advertisements are usually small, factual and often grouped under such headings as furniture, home and garden, lonely hearts, etc. This is the kind of advertising used by individuals selling their personal property, or by very small businesses (for example a one-woman home hairdressing service). Such advertisements are a major feature of local and regional newspapers. Display advertising has wider variations in size, shape and location within the newspaper, and uses a range of graphics, copy and photography. *Display advertisements* may be grouped under special features and pages: for instance, if a local newspaper runs a weddings feature it brings together advertisers providing the various goods and services that the bride-to-be would be interested in. Such groupings offer the individual advertisers a degree of synergy. Local newspapers are an important advertising medium, not only for small businesses, but for national chains of retailers supporting local stores and car manufacturers supporting local dealerships. In 2004, regional press had a 20 per cent share of total UK advertising revenue, second only to television's 26 per cent. National newspapers had a share of only 13 per cent (**http://www.newspapersoc.org.uk**).

The main problem with newspaper advertising is related to its cost-efficiency – if the advertiser wants to be more selective in targeting. Wastage rates can be high, as newspapers can appeal to very broad segments of the population. Furthermore, compared with magazines, newspapers have a much shorter lifespan and can have problems with the quality of reproduction possible. Although colour and photographic reproduction quality in newspapers is rapidly improving, it is still inferior to that offered by magazines, and can be inconsistent. The same advertisement, for instance, published in different newspapers or on different days can take on varying colour values and intensities, and be more or less grainy or focused.

■ Advertising hoardings, ambient and outdoor media

The last group of advertising media includes posters and hoardings, ambient media (such as advertising on bus tickets, toilet walls and store floors) as well as transport-oriented advertising media (advertising in and on buses, taxis and trains and in stations). It can be very cost-effective. According to Ray (2002), it can cost £30 to reach 1000 people through television but only £2.80 through outdoor media.

Advertising posters range from small home-made advertisements placed on a noticeboard to those for giant hoardings. This section concentrates on the latter group. Hoarding sites are normally sold by the fortnight. Being in a static location, they may easily be seen 10–20 times in a fortnight by people on their way to and from work or school, etc. In the UK, over one-third of poster sites are taken by car or drink advertisers. The reach may be small, but the frequency can be quite intense. They can, however, be affected by some unpredictable elements, out of the control of the advertiser. Bad weather means that people will spend less time out of doors, and are certainly not going to be positively receptive to outdoor advertising. Hoardings and posters are also vulnerable to the attentions of those who think they can improve on the existing message with some graffiti or fly posting.

Size is one of the greatest assets of the advertising hoarding, creating impact. Over 80 per cent of hoarding space in the UK is taken by 4-, 6- or 48-sheet sites (a 48-sheet hoarding measures 10 feet by 20 feet). Also, sites can be selected, if available, according to the match between traffic flows and target audience. However, in appealing to a mobile audience, the message needs to be simple and thus usually links with other elements of a wider campaign, either for generating initial awareness or on a reminder and reinforcement basis.

Finally, there are the *transport-oriented media*. These include advertisements in rail or bus stations, which capture and occupy the attention of waiting passengers who have nothing better to do for a while than read the advertisements. Similarly, advertising inside trains, taxis and buses has a captive audience for as long as the journey takes. Advertising on the outside of vehicles, perhaps even going so far as to repaint an entire bus with an advertisement, extends the reach of the advertisement to anyone who happens to be around the vehicle's route.

Using advertising agencies

It is not surprising, given the complexity and expense involved, that many organisations employ an agency to handle the development and implementation of advertising programmes. It is important, however, to select the right kind of agency, and in this section we will discuss criteria for selecting an agency and present a few thoughts on client–agency relationships.

Selecting an agency

Clearly, selecting an agency is very important since its work can potentially make or break a product. Different writers suggest different checklists against which to measure the appropriateness of any given agency. The following list has been compiled from the work of Fill (2002), Pickton and Broderick (2001), Smith and Taylor (2002), and White (1988), and is also shown in Figure 10.2.

Relative size of agency and client. As already mentioned, it might be useful to try to match the relative sizes of the client and the agency, certainly in terms of the proposed advertising spend. This is to ensure the right level of mutual respect, attention and importance. The client might also want to think ahead strategically, and choose an agency that will either grow with the client or be able to meet increased future needs. This might mean coping with a bigger account, coping with integrated communications, or coping with international advertising.

Location and accessibility. A smaller business with a limited geographic market might prefer to work with a small agency that has deep local knowledge and understanding. A larger business, wishing to keep a close eye on what the agency is doing and thus wanting frequent face-to-face meetings with the account team, might also find it more convenient to use an agency located nearby.

Type of help required. Clearly, a client wants an agency that can supply the kinds of services and expertise required. The client might want a full service agency, or just specialised help in media buying, for example. The client might also want an integrated service, covering a wide

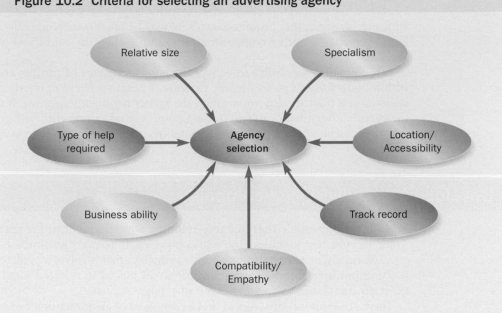

Figure 10.2 Criteria for selecting an advertising agency

range of communications techniques, not just advertising. Any prospective agency thus needs to be measured against its ability to deliver an appropriate package.

Specialism. Some agencies have a reputation for specialising in particular products or services, for example higher education advertising or financial services advertising. Some clients might find this attractive on the basis that they can be sure that the agency has detailed knowledge of the relevant marketing and competitive environments. Others, however, might find it off-putting. They might feel that the agency works for the client's competitors or that they are 'stale' from doing too much work in one field. Nevertheless, a degree of relevant experience in some related area might be a good indicator of an agency's ability to handle this new account.

Track record. Regardless of whether the agency specialises in particular types of advertising or not, a new client is going to be interested in its track record. How has the agency grown? Who is on its client list? How creative is its work? How effective is its work? Does it seem able to retain its clients, generate repeat business from them and build strong relationships?

Compatibility, empathy and personal chemistry. Compatibility and empathy are about corporate culture and outlook and about individual personalities. Clearly, a client wants an agency that is sympathetic to what the client is trying to achieve and can find the right way of talking to the target audience. A great deal of this depends on client–agency communication and the ability of the agency personnel who will be working on the account to get on well with the individuals from the client company with whom they will be liaising. It is quite legitimate, therefore, for the client to ask just who will be working on the account.

Business ability. Advertising is extremely expensive and so a client wants to be reassured that the agency can work within budget, cost-effectively, efficiently and within deadlines. This might, therefore, mean looking at their research and planning capabilities. Furthermore, a client should make sure that they understand the basis on which they will be charged by the agency and precisely what is and is not included.

■ The client–agency relationship

Whatever the type of agency used, a good relationship is essential. With sound briefing, mutual understanding, and an agreed system of remuneration, the agency becomes an extension of the organisation's own marketing team. Cooperation may depend on mutual importance. For instance, a large client working with a large agency is fine, but a small client dealing with a large agency may become lost. There may be other constraints affecting agency choice. If an agency deals with a competitor, for example, then the conflict of interest needs to be avoided.

It is clear that the ability to deliver the goods, in terms of timing, creative content and within budget, is crucial to success. Communication and developing deeper mutual understanding and trust are also important if the agency is going to diagnose, understand and solve the client's advertising problem. If these points are taken out of the advertising agency context, they can be seen to be the fundamental criteria for any good buyer–supplier relationship.

Developing an advertising campaign

It is almost impossible that one free-standing advertisement in the press or on television would be sufficient to achieve the results expected, in terms of the impact on the target audience. Normally, advertisers think about a campaign that involves a predetermined theme but is communicated through a series of messages placed in selected media chosen for their expected cumulative impact on the specified target audience.

There are a number of stages in the development of an advertising campaign. Although the emphasis will vary from situation to situation, each stage at least acknowledges a need for careful management assessment and decision-making. The stages are shown in Figure 10.3 and are discussed in turn below.

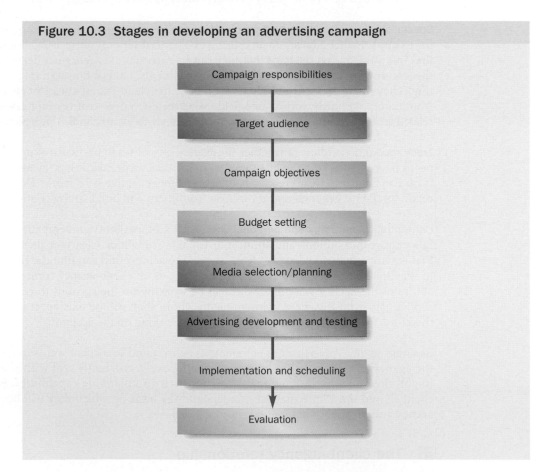

Figure 10.3 Stages in developing an advertising campaign

Campaign responsibilities

Target audience

Campaign objectives

Budget setting

Media selection/planning

Advertising development and testing

Implementation and scheduling

Evaluation

■ Deciding on campaign responsibilities

This is an important question of organisational structure and 'ownership' of the campaign. If management is devolved on a product basis, then overall responsibility may rest with the brand or product manager. This certainly helps to ensure that the campaign integrates with sales promotion, selling, production planning, etc., since the brand manager is very well versed in all aspects of the product's life. If, however, management is devolved on a functional basis, then the responsibility for an advertising campaign will lie with the advertising and promotion manager. This means that the campaign benefits from depth of advertising expertise, but lacks the involvement with the product that a brand manager would supply. Whatever the arrangement, it is essential to define who is ultimately responsible for what tasks and what elements of the budget.

■ Selecting the target audience

As discussed at pp. 300 *et seq.*, knowing who you are talking to is the foundation of good communication. Based on segmentation strategy, the target audience represents the group at whom the communication is aimed within the market. In some cases, the segment and the target audience may be one and the same. Sometimes, however, the target audience may be a subdivision of the segment. If, for instance, an organisation served a particular hobby segment, different approaches to advertising would be taken depending on whether they wanted to talk to serious, casual, high spenders, low spenders, general-interest or specific-interest subgroups. This underlines the need to understand the market and the range of target audiences within it.

A profile of the target audience increases the chances of successful promotion and communication. Any details, such as location, media viewing (or listening or reading) habits, geodemographics, attitudes and values, can be used to shape the propositions contained within the campaign or to direct the creative approach and media choice.

eg Global advertising is on the increase, and in some sectors the continent of Europe is treated as a single territory, with a single advertising approach. But as Europe comprises 44 different nations, using 60 different languages, there are some products that simply cannot be promoted in the same way across Europe. Nestlé, for example, has always had to run completely different advertisements for its instant coffee brand Nescafé in individual European countries because of the vastly different coffee heritage and culture in each (Polak, 2005).

Whatever the type of product, if the assessment of the target audience is incomplete or woolly, there may be problems in directing campaign efforts later.

■ Campaign objectives

Communication objectives were considered at pp. 311 *et seq.*, and provide a clear view of what the advertising should accomplish. These objectives need to be specific, measurable and time related. They must also indicate the level of change sought, defining a specific outcome from the advertising task. If there are no measurable objectives, how can achievements be recognised and success or failure judged?

Most advertising is focused on some stage of a response hierarchy model, such as those presented in Figure 9.5 (p. 302). These models highlight the stages in the process of consumer decision-making from initial exposure and awareness through to post-purchase review. Issues such as liking, awareness or knowledge, preference and conviction are important parts of that process, and advertising can aim to influence any one of them. These can thus be translated into advertising objectives with measurable targets for awareness generation, product trial and/or repurchase, attitude creation or shifts, or positioning or preferences in comparison with the competition.

These objectives should be driven by the agreed marketing strategy and plan. Note the difference between marketing and advertising objectives. Sales and market share targets are legitimate marketing objectives as they represent the outcomes of a range of marketing mix decisions. Advertising, however, is just one element contributing to that process, and is designed to achieve specific tasks, but not necessarily exclusively sales.

■ Campaign budgets

Developing a communication budget was considered at pp. 315 *et seq*. Look back to these pages to refresh your memory on the methods of budget setting. Remember that there is no one right or wrong sum to allocate to a campaign, and often a combination of the methods proposed earlier acts as a guide.

Often the setting of budgets is an iterative process, developing and being modified as the campaign takes shape. There is a direct link between budgets and objectives such that a modification in one area is almost certainly likely to have an impact in the other. Even if the underlying philosophy of the budget is the 'objective and task' approach, practicality still means that most budgets are constrained in some way by the cash available. This forces managers to plan carefully and to consider a range of options in order to be as cost-effective as possible in the achievement of the specified objectives.

The first job is to link marketing objectives with the tasks expected of advertising and promotion. Targets may be set, for example, in relation to awareness levels, trial and repeat purchases. Not all these targets would be achieved by advertising alone. Sales promotion, and of course product formulation, may play a big part in repeat purchase behaviour.

■ Media selection and planning

The various media options were considered individually at pp. 333 *et seq*. The large range of alternative media needs to be reduced down to manageable options and then scheduling (discussed at p. 343) planned to achieve the desired results. The resultant media plan must be detailed and specific. Actual media vehicles must be specified, as well as when, where, how much and how often. The important aim is to ensure a reasonable fit between the media vehicles considered and the target audience so that sufficient reach and frequency are achieved to allow the real objectives of the advertising a fighting chance of success. This is becoming more difficult as audience profiles and markets change (Mueller-Heumann, 1992). The plan has an important role to play in integrating the campaign effort into the rest of the marketing plan and in communicating requirements clearly to any support agencies.

eg The office equipment company Brother sponsored Channel 4's programme *Risking It All* as part of a £2m promotional campaign. The first series had attracted more than 3 million viewers, and during the 10-week run of the second series, Brother provided the idents at the beginning and end of the programme, and in the breaks. In addition, anyone visiting the Channel 4 website for details of the programme saw the Brother sponsorship badge. Brother's marketers believed that the programme, which follows the fortunes of people who have given up jobs to start their own business, was a perfect vehicle for their brand. The organisation claims to recognise the pressures faced by small businesses, particularly start-ups, and believes that its printers and all-in-one ranges are ideally suited to those specific needs. The sponsorship deal was signed with the objective of aligning Brother with the small new business market (*Marketing Week*, 2005b).

A number of considerations guide the selction of media. First, the media selected must ensure consistency with the overall *campaign objectives* in terms of awareness, reach, etc. The *target audience* is, however, critical to guiding the detailed media selection. As close a fit as possible is required between medium and audience. A consideration of the *competitive factors* includes examining what competitors have been doing, where they have been doing it, and with what outcomes. A decision may have to be made whether to use the same media as the competition or to innovate. The *geographic focus* might be relevant, depending on whether the target audience may be international, national or regional, and sometimes a selection of media or vehicles may have to be used to reach dispersed groups within the target audience. As discussed at p. 342, *budget constraints* mean that practicality and affordability usually enter into the planning at some stage. A proposal of 20 prime-time slots on television might well give the chief accountant apoplexy and have to be replaced with a more modest print campaign that makes its impact through stunning creativity. *Timing* too is an issue, as the plan needs to take into account any lead-in or build-up time, particularly if the product's sales have a strong element of seasonality. Perfumes and aftershaves, for example, look to Christmas as a strong selling period. Advertisers of these products use glossy magazine advertising all year round, but in the weeks up to Christmas, add intensive and expensive television campaigns (it's a good job we don't have smellyvision yet) to coincide with consumers' decision-making for gifts. Similarly, timing is important in launching a new product, to make sure that the right level of awareness, understanding and desire have been generated by the time the product is actually available.

As with any plan, it should provide the reader with a clear justification of the rationale behind the decisions, and should act as a guide as to how it integrates with other marketing activities.

◾ Advertising development and testing

At this stage, the advertisements themselves are designed and made, ready for broadcasting or printing. The creative issues involved have already been covered elsewhere within this chapter. As the advertisement evolves, pre-testing is often used to check that the content, message and impact are as expected. This is particularly important with television advertising, which is relatively expensive to produce and broadcast, and also would represent an extremely public embarrassment if it failed.

Tests are, therefore, built in at various stages of the advertisement's development. Initial concepts and storyboards can be discussed with a sample of members of the target audience to see if they can understand the message and relate to the scenario or images in the proposed advertisement. Slightly further on in the process, a rough video of the advertisement (not the full production – just enough to give a flavour of the finished piece) can also be tested. This allows final adjustments to be made before the finished advertisement is produced. Even then, further testing can reassure the agency and the client that the advertisement is absolutely ready for release. Print advertisements can similarly be tested at various stages of their development, using rough sketches, mock-ups and then the finished advertisement.

Pre-testing is a valuable exercise, but its outcomes should be approached with some caution. The testing conditions are rather artificial, by necessity, and audiences (assuming even that the testers can assemble a truly representative audience) who react in certain ways to seeing an advertisement in a theatre or church hall might respond very differently if they saw that same advertisement in their own homes under 'normal' viewing conditions.

◾ Implementation and scheduling

In the implementation phase, a number of professional experts may be needed to develop and deliver the advertising campaign. These will include graphic designers, photographers, commercial artists, copywriters, research specialists and, not least, media and production companies. The role of the advertising manager is to coordinate and select these professionals within a budget to achieve the planned objectives.

A key part of the implementation phase is the scheduling of the campaign. There are many different scheduling patterns (Sissors and Bumba, 1989). Sometimes, advertising takes place in *bursts*, as shown in Figure 10.4. This means short-term, intense advertising activity, such as that often found with new product launches. Most organisations do not have the resources

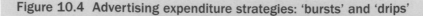

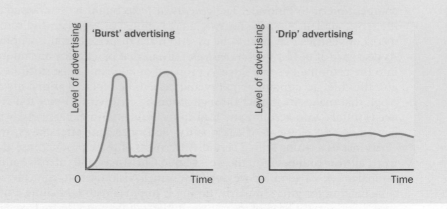

Figure 10.4 Advertising expenditure strategies: 'bursts' and 'drips'

(or the inclination) to keep up such intense advertising activity indefinitely, and thus the bursts are few and far between. The alternative is to spread the advertising budget out more evenly, by advertising in *drips*, also shown in Figure 10.4. The advertising activity is less intense, but more persistent. Reminder advertising for a frequently purchased mature product might take place in drips rather than bursts.

A number of factors will help to determine the overall schedule. *Marketing factors* might influence the speed of the impact required. An organisation launching a new product or responding to a competitor's comparative advertising might want to make a quick impact, for example. If *turnover of customers* is high, then there is a need to advertise more frequently to keep the message available for new entrants into the market. Similarly, *purchase frequency* and *volatility* could be relevant factors. If demand is *highly seasonal* or *perishable*, then the scheduling might provide for a short period of high-frequency advertising. The peak time for advertising perfumes and toys, for example, is in the run up to Christmas. Similarly, various chocolate products peak at Easter or Mother's Day, for example. Alternatively, there may be a link with brand loyalty. Higher loyalty may need less frequency, provided that the product is not under competitive attack. This is, however, a dangerous assumption.

If the danger of forgetting is high, then the advertiser is likely to need a more active campaign implemented at regular intervals. Different groups learn and forget at different rates. Therefore these *retention and attrition rates* of the target audience are yet another assessment that needs to be made. *Message factors* relate to the complexity of the message. A campaign for a new product may need more repetition than one for an established product, because of the newness of the message. More generally, simple messages or those that stand out from the crowd demand less repetition. Similarly, smaller advertisements or those placed in less noticeable spots within a print medium may need more frequency to make sure they are seen.

Media factors relate to the choice of media. The fewer media or advertising vehicles in the plan, the fewer OTSs are likely to be needed. This smaller limit may be important for a smaller business with a limited budget or for a major business seeking to dominate a particular medium by means of monopolising the best slots or positions. Such dominance increases the repetition to those in the target audience. The more congested the medium, the more OTSs there need to be, to cut through the background 'noise'.

None of this makes one media plan better than another. It depends on objectives and the particular market circumstances prevailing. If the product is new or seasonal, a more intensive effort may be appropriate. The scheduling plan may, of course, evolve over time. During the introduction stage of the product lifecycle an intensive burst of advertising will launch the product, and this may then be followed by a more spread-out campaign as the growth stage finishes. Creating awareness in the first place is expensive, but critical to a product's success.

■ Campaign evaluation

The evaluation is perhaps the most critical part of the whole campaign process. This stage exists not only to assess the effectiveness of the campaign mounted, but also to provide valuable learning for the future.

There are two stages in evaluation. *Interim evaluation* enables a campaign to be revised and adjusted before completion to improve its effectiveness. It enables a closer match to be achieved between advertising objectives and the emerging campaign results.

Alternatively or additionally, *exit evaluation* is undertaken at the end of the campaign. Post-testing can check whether the target audience has received, understood, interpreted and remembered the message as the advertiser wished, and whether they have acted upon it.

Personal selling: defintion, role and tasks

According to Fill (2002, p. 16), personal selling can be defined as:

> *An interpersonal communication tool which involves face to face activities undertaken by individuals, often representing an organisation, in order to inform, persuade or remind an individual or group to take appropriate action, as required by the sponsor's representative.*

As a basic definition, this does capture the essence of personal selling. *Interpersonal communication* implies a live, two-way, interactive dialogue between buyer and seller (which none of the other promotional mix elements can achieve); *an individual or group* implies a small, select audience (again, more targeted than with the other elements); *to inform, persuade or remind … to take appropriate action* implies a planned activity with a specific purpose.

Note that the definition does not imply that personal selling is only about making sales. It may well ultimately be about making a sale, but that is not its only function. It can contribute considerably to the organisation both before and, indeed, after a sale has been made. As a means of making sales, personal selling is about finding, informing, persuading and at times servicing customers through the personal, two-way communication that is its strength. It means helping customers to articulate their needs, tailoring persuasive selling messages to answer those needs, and then handling customers' responses or concerns in order to arrive at a mutually valued exchange. As a background to that, personal selling is also a crucial element in ensuring customers' post-purchase satisfaction, and in building profitable long-term buyer–seller relationships built on trust and understanding (Miller and Heinman, 1991).

eg Avon, the cosmetics company, employs over 160,000 sales representatives in the UK (3.5 million worldwide) supported by 450 area sales managers, as part of the largest direct sales operation in the world. The representatives play a key role in providing advice, demonstrating products, allowing sampling, closing sales and relationship building on their territories. In the UK over 10,000 orders are processed every day. Recently Avon became the first company to test direct selling in the Chinese market, although the rate of expansion in China is uncertain due to a reluctance to allow unregulated competition at the consumer's expense. For example, the 30 per cent cap on commission rates is much lower than elsewhere in the world, which will reduce the remuneration potential for the representatives and area management structure (McDonald, 2004; *Wall Street Journal*, 2005).

Chapter 9 has already offered some insights into where personal selling fits best into the promotional mix. We discussed how personal selling is more appropriate in B2B than consumer markets at p. 300, while pp. 306 *et seq.* looked at its advantages in promoting and selling high-cost, complex products. The discussion at p. 305 also notes that personal selling operates most effectively when customers are on the verge of making a final decision and committing themselves, but still need that last little bit of tailored persuasion.

■ Advantages of personal selling

Impact

If you do not like the look of a TV advertisement, you can turn it off, or ignore it. If a glance at a print advertisement fails to capture your further attention, you can turn the page. If an envelope on the doormat looks like a mailshot, you can put it in the bin unopened. If a sales representative appears on your doorstep or in your office, it is a little more difficult to switch off. A person has to be dealt with in some way, and since most of us subscribe to the common rules of politeness, we will at least listen to what the person wants before shepherding them out of the door. The sales representative, therefore, has a much greater chance of engaging your initial attention than an advertisement does.

It is also true, of course, that an advertisement has no means of knowing or caring that you have ignored it. Sales representatives, on the other hand, have the ability to respond to the situations in which they find themselves, and can take steps to prevent themselves from being shut off completely. This could be, for instance, by pressing for another appointment at a more convenient time, or by at least leaving sales literature for the potential customer to read and think about at their leisure. Overall, you are far more likely to remember a person you have met or spoken to (and to respond to what they said) than you are to remember an advertisement. In that respect, personal selling is very powerful indeed, particularly if it capitalises on the elements of precision and cultivation (see below) as well.

Precision

Precision represents one of the great advantages of personal selling over any of the other promotional mix elements, and explains why it is so effective at the customer's point of decision-making. There are two facets of precision that should be acknowledged: targeting precision and message precision.

Targeting precision arises from the fact that personal selling is not a mass medium. Advertising can be targeted within broad parameters, but even so, there will still be many wasted contacts (people who are not even in the target market; people who are not currently interested in the product; people who have recently purchased already; people who cannot currently afford to purchase, etc.). Advertising hits those contacts anyway with its full message, and each of those wasted contacts costs money. Personal selling can weed out the inappropriate contacts early on, and concentrate its efforts on those who offer a real prospect of making a sale.

Message precision arises from the interactive two-way dialogue that personal selling encourages. An advertisement cannot tell what impact it is having on you. It cannot discern whether you are paying attention to it, whether you understand it or whether you think it is relevant to you. Furthermore, once the advertisement has been presented to you, that is it. It is a fixed, inflexible message, and if you did not understand it, or if you felt that it did not tell you what you wanted to know, then you have no opportunity to do anything about it other than wait for another advertisement to come along that might clarify these things. Because personal selling involves live interaction, however, these problems should not occur. The sales representative can tell, for example, that your attention is wandering, and therefore can change track, exploring other avenues until something seems to capture you again. The representative can also make sure that you understand what you are being told and go over it again from a different angle if you are having difficulty with the first approach. Similarly, the representative can see if something has particularly caught your imagination and tailor the message to emphasise that feature or benefit. Thus, by listening and watching, the sales representative should be able to create a unique approach that exactly matches the mood and the needs of each prospective customer. This too is a very potent capability.

Cultivation

As Chapter 3 implied, the creation of long-term, mutually beneficial buyer–seller relationships is now recognised as extremely important to the health and profitability of organisations in many industries. The sales force has a crucial role to play in both creating and maintaining such relationships. Sales representatives are often the public face of an organisation, and their ability to carry the organisation's message professionally and confidently can affect judgement of that organisation and what it stands for. When Avon, the cosmetics company, decided to target the teenage beauty business, it realised that to build and maintain customer relationships it had to reconsider whether the direct sales force employed was suitable for the different customer group. The new range 'exclusively for teens' was launched globally in 2003, but instead of using an army of 'Avon ladies', the company recruited teenagers who are better placed to demonstrate and promote the products to that audience (Singh, 2001).

Selling cosmetics and toiletries to friends and neighbours in the comfort of your own home is the way in which Avon works very successfully.

Source: © Avon Cosmetics Ltd

Cost

All the advantages and benefits discussed above come at a very high cost, as personal selling is extremely labour intensive. In addition, costs of travel (and time spent travelling), accommodation and other expenses have to be accounted for. It can cost between £50,000 and £75,000 per year to keep a sales representative on the road and for the more demanding roles this can rise to over £100,000 (Newman, 2005). Generally, the salary paid is only around 50 per cent of the total cost of keeping a sales representative mobile and connected. The actual time spent selling to a customer can vary considerably, and estimates of 50 per cent of time spent on travelling, 20 per cent on administration, 20 per cent on call planning and 10 per cent on actual face-to-face contact are not uncommon (McDonald, 1984; Abberton Associates, 1997). Proudfoot Consulting found in an international study that just 7 per cent of sales activity was face to face with the customer (*Management Services*, 2002). When added to time spent in unproductive administration and travelling, and the effects of poor territory management, the result can be very high call costs, in excess of £250 per call if around 10–15 calls are made each week. Sales Directors in 25 per cent of cases did not know how much time the sales team spent actually spent on selling in their working week (**http://www.proudfootconsulting.com**). Some caution has to be exercised when interpreting these figures, however, as ultimately it is sales effectiveness that counts and relationship building and keeping in touch with customers both support the ongoing sales activity.

■ Tasks of personal selling

There is a tendency to think of the sales representative in a one-off selling situation. What the discussion in the previous sections has shown is that, in reality, the representative is likely to be handling a relationship with any specific customer over a long period of time. The representative will be looking to build up close personal ties because much depends on repeat sales. In some cases, the representative might even be involved in helping to negotiate and handle joint product development. All of this suggests a range of tasks beyond the straight selling situation.

Figure 10.5 summarises the range of typical tasks of the sales representative, each of which is defined below.

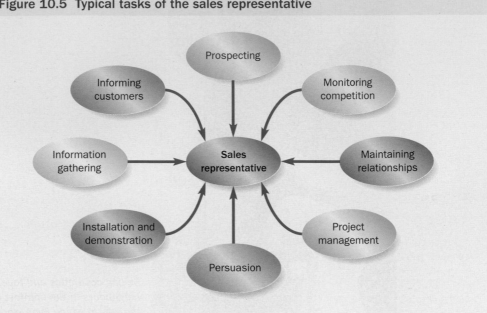

Figure 10.5 Typical tasks of the sales representative

Prospecting

Prospecting is finding new potential customers who have the willingness and ability to purchase. For Rentokil Tropical Plants, for example, the role of the sales representative is to contact a range of potential clients including offices, hotels, shopping centres and restaurants to design and recommend individual displays of tropical plants on a supply and maintenance basis. Prospecting is an important task, particularly for organisations entering a new market segment or for those offering a new product line with no established customer base.

Informing

Informing is giving prospective customers adequate, detailed and relevant information about products and services on offer. In B2B markets, once contact has been made with prospects, the sales representative needs to stimulate sufficient information exchange to ensure a technical and commercial match that is better than the competition.

Persuading

Persuading is helping the prospective customer to analyse the information provided, in the light of their needs, in order to come to the conclusion that the product being offered is the best solution to their problem. Sometimes, presenting the main product benefits is sufficient to convince the buyer of the wisdom of selecting that supplier. On other occasions, especially with purchases that are technically or commercially more complex, the persuasion might have to be very subtle and varied, according to the concerns of the different members of the buying team.

Installing and demonstrating

Particularly with technical, B2B purchases, the buyer may need considerable support and help to get the equipment installed and to train staff in its use. The sales representative may join a wider team of support personnel to ensure that all this takes place according to whatever was agreed and to the customer's satisfaction. The representative's continued presence acts as a link between pre- and post-purchase events, and implies that the representative has not stopped caring about the customer just because the sale has been made.

Coordinating within their own organisation

The role of the sales representative is not just about forward communication with the buyer. It is also concerned with 'representing' the customer's interests within the selling organisation. Whether concerned with financial, technical or logistical issues, the sales representative must coordinate and sometimes organise internal activities on a project basis to ensure that the customer's needs are met. At Duracell, the UK market leader in batteries, a national account manager is responsible for all aspects of the relationship with the large grocery chains. This includes external roles of display, distribution and promotional planning as well as internal coordination of logistics and product category management.

---

marketing | in action

The sales rep: an endangered species

A sales representative is an expensive asset for an organisation to maintain. Representatives need cars, computers, mobile phones, samples, presentation equipment and administrative support. They also run up bills for hotel accommodation and entertaining clients. When economic times are hard, therefore, many organisations cut their sales forces or rationalise them to save on costs. Other factors have also led to a reduction in the number of sales representatives. In consumer goods markets, for instance, there has been a reduction in the number of small independent retailers and a corresponding increase in the share of business taken by the big multiples. The bigger retailers tend to have computerised stock control systems with online ordering, so that there is no need for a representative to visit individual branches so often (if at all). HP Foods, for example, had between 70 and 100 sales representatives in the 1970s. By the millennium, the number had been slimmed down to twelve business development executives who each manage a portfolio of national and regional accounts. The largest proportion of HP's orders, however,

comes in via computers or the telephone.

There is, of course, still a role for the representative in consumer goods markets in visiting smaller retailers, both to take orders and to help with promotional events or point-of-sale displays. Many organisations, however, find it cheaper and more efficient to use contract sales staff from field marketing agencies for such tasks. Retailers and brand owners are realising that in their own fiercely competitive environments, they must be more aggressive when fighting their own corner. The struggle to generate sales volumes by ensuring that the right quantity of product is available when consumers want to buy is one numbers game that is far from dull for those involved (*Marketing Week*, 2004). When Mars launched Celebrations, for example, a field marketing agency was used rather than Mars' own sales force to work with cash-and-carry and other wholesalers to provide free samples, provide product information and negotiate special point-of-sale displays. The benefit of contract staff is that the organisation has to pay for them only when they want them, and can have as large or small a 'sales force' as a particular task or project requires. Contract sales staff tend

to work in small territories and thus have established close relationships with the retailers and other customers that they regularly visit.

Field marketing (FM) has grown in popularity over the last ten years as an effective substitute for client-owned sales forces where the emphasis is on the more routine tasks of order taking and in-store demonstrations. FM has been defined as 'the business of creating, directing and managing full-time merchandising, sales and training teams to influence change at the point of purchase' (Gary MacManus, Aspen Field Marketing, as quoted by Middleton, 2001). The main activities are sales (i.e. acting as a client's sales team or supplementing the activities of the client's sales team or meeting specific coverage or time requirements), merchandising, auditing and mystery shopping.

Douwe Egberts and Philips wanted to focus on in-store demonstration when they launched the Philips Senseo Coffee Pod System as they wanted to motivate consumers to sample and buy the coffee maker. They funded 1300 retail demonstration days over 27 weeks to promote sales. More than 11,500 coffee machines were sold during the period, roughly 56 per cent of all system sales over the trial period (*Marketing Week*, 2005a). By using field marketing, both companies were able to get their market established more quickly and to ensure that distribution targets were met.

Some organisations might worry, however, that because contract sales staff are not employed by them full time, there might be questions about their loyalty and motivation. Agencies are well aware of this and try to overcome it by setting up quality control systems to monitor the performance of their staff in the field, and ensuring that staff are fully and properly briefed at the start of an assignment. To try to engender 'loyalty' to the task in hand, the agency will also ensure that a member of staff is working for only one client in a particular product market at a time. Because of the amount of time contract staff spend in the field and because of the wide range of customers and product types they deal with, these agencies can amass a wealth of data about what is going on in the market that a company's own sales force would not have either the time or the resources to collect. Agencies can thus feed information back to clients, providing an additional benefit to their service.

As field marketing has grown in popularity, so its role has expanded from being just point-of-sale merchandising. The contract sellers' sales forces are becoming better trained, more IT literate and more skilled in providing useful market information back to the contracting company. There are two broad areas in which contract sales staff are currently used: in fmcg, dealing with retailers, and in door-to-door selling, covering a wide range of products and services including cable television, utilities and financial services. High pressure selling and mis-selling were exposed in the utilities sector, where untrained and unscrupulous sales people made a wide range of promises that could not be honoured to encourage consumers to change energy suppliers. Most reputable field marketing agencies seek to avoid such problems through careful recruitment, appropriate training and local control. For example, it has been suggested that the ratio of sales representatives to managers should be 10:1 in fmcg and 6:1 in door-to-door selling.

Thus, although the grocery trade still dominates the use of FM agencies, other sectors have now started to realise the benefits of more flexible sales force arrangements. The major credit card companies recruit new card holders through direct selling using agencies, and car manufacturers such as Honda, BMW and Volvo use FM to encourage sampling and test drives. Some smaller companies have found that using FM agencies can provide them with a dedicated sales team they could never previously have afforded. The next stage of development is likely to be closer integration of FM into pan-European promotional campaigns. According to field marketing agency CPM, however, few truly pan-European FM campaigns are being run, with companies such as Mars and Disney preferring to run separate country-by-country FM campaigns. Some larger companies are seeking to find one agency to handle all their different campaigns across Europe. Achieving pan-European campaigns is not easy, however, when standardised laws are not yet applicable across the EU (*Precision Marketing*, 2005b). So, the need to address local market situations and culture will for some time act as a brake on genuine pan-European FM campaigns.

It seems, therefore, that the sales representative might not be about to become extinct. What is certain is that organisations are rethinking how they manage and organise their sales forces and their selling processes. It is virtually impossible for any new product to achieve 100 per cent distribution in the multiple retailers, but levels of 85 to 95 per cent can be achieved and that means that field marketing can make a significant difference. Thus the role and the tasks of representatives will change, and how they are employed might change, but they will always be needed in some capacity.

Sources: Gofton (2002); *Marketing Week* (2004, 2005a); McLuhan (2001a, 2001b); Middleton (2001); Miles (1998); *Precision Marketing* (2005b); http://www.ukfm.co.uk.

Maintaining relationships

Once an initial sale has been made, it might be the start of an ongoing relationship. In many cases, a single sale is just one of a stream of transactions and thus cannot be considered in isolation from the total relationship. An important role for the sales representative is to manage the relationship rather than just the specifics of a particular sale. This means that in many organisations, more substantial and critical relationships have a 'relationship manager' to handle the various facets of the buyer–seller evolution (Turnbull and Cunningham, 1981). In some cases, the sales representative might have only one relationship to manage, but in others, the representative might have to manage a network based in a particular sector.

The prime responsibility of an account manager at Colgate-Palmolive is to maintain and develop business relationships with major multiple retailer accounts. These relationships in some cases go back over many years. In order to achieve this, the emphasis is on co-operation and customer development through working together in such areas as category management, logistics and merchandising. There is a need to ensure a close fit between retail requirements and Colgate-Palmolive's brand strategies. This means that the account manager must be able to analyse brand and category information in order to develop plans that will help sales of Colgate's personal and household care products. Any account manager who sought short-term sales gains at the expense of customer trust and goodwill would not benefit Colgate-Palmolive's long-term plans for the account.

Information and feedback gathering

The gathering of information and the provision of feedback emphasises the need for representatives to keep their eyes and ears open, and to indulge in two-way communication with the customers they deal with. 'Grapevine' gossip about what is happening in the industry might, for example, give valuable early warning about big planned purchases in the future, or about potential customers who are dissatisfied with their current supplier. Both of these situations would offer opportunities to the organisation that heard about them early enough to make strategic plans about how to capitalise on them. In terms of relationships with existing customers, sales representatives are more likely than anyone to hear about the things that the customer is unhappy about. This feedback role is even more important when developing business in export markets, where the base of accumulated knowledge might not be very strong. Personal contacts can help to add to that knowledge over time (Johanson and Vahlne, 1977).

Monitoring competitor action

The representative works out in the field, meeting customers and, in all probability, competitors. As well as picking up snippets about what competitors are planning and who they are doing business with, the representative can provide valuable information about how his or her organisation's products compare with those of the competition in the eyes of the purchasers. During the course of sales presentations, prospective customers can be subtly probed to find out what they think are the relative strengths and weaknesses of competing products, what they consider to be the important features and benefits in that kind of product, and how the available offerings score relative to each other (Lambert *et al.*, 1990).

The personal selling process

At the heart of the sales process is the sales representative's ability to build a relationship with the buyer that is sufficiently strong to achieve a deal that benefits both parties. In many situations the main decision relates to *supplier choice* rather than whether or not to buy. The sales representative's role is to highlight the attractions of the specification, support, service and commercial package on offer. Differences between products, markets, organisational philosophies and even individuals will all have a bearing on the style and effectiveness of the selling activity.

Although it has just been suggested that personal selling does not lend itself to a prescribed formula, it is possible to define a number of broad stages through which most selling episodes will pass (Russell *et al.*, 1977). Depending on the product, the market, the organisations and individuals involved, the length of time spent in any one of the stages will vary, as will the way in which each stage is implemented (Pedersen *et al.*, 1986). Nevertheless, the generalised analysis offered here provides a useful basis for beginning to understand what contributes to successful personal selling.

Figure 10.6 shows the flow of stages through a personal selling process.

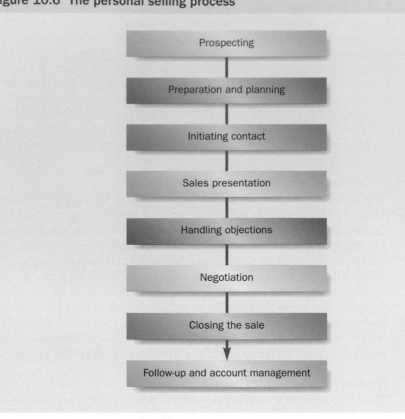

Figure 10.6 The personal selling process

Prospecting

Before sales representatives can get down to the real job of selling something, they need to have someone to sell to. In some organisations, perhaps those selling an industrial product with a specific application to a relatively small number of easily defined B2B customers, this will be a highly structured activity, involving sales representatives and support staff, and will lead to the representative going out on a call knowing that the prospect is potentially fruitful. In contrast, double glazing companies often employ canvassers to walk the streets knocking on doors to see if householders are likely prospects. This is not a particularly efficient use of the representatives' time, as most people will say that they are not interested, but in promoting an infrequently purchased, high-priced product, yet in a mass market, it is difficult to see what else in the way of prospecting they can do.

In a B2B rather than a consumer market, the sales representative needs a prospect bank, a pool of potential customers to be drawn on as appropriate. This bank could include potential customers who have made enquiries or responded to advertising, but not been followed up already. Second, there are those who have already been approached in an exploratory way, for example through telemarketing, and look promising enough to deserve further encouragement. Third, and most problematic, are the lists of names. These lists might be purchased from a list broker or be compiled from a trade directory or a list of organisations attending a particular trade exhibition. Sales representatives may have to develop their own prospect banks, either from word of mouth from contacts outside the organisation, or from the telemarketing support staff discussed above. They can also compile lists from directories, or from scanning the media for relevant company news that might open up an opportunity. As with the telemarketers above, this might lead to a session of preliminary cold calling (by phone or in person) to establish whether this person or organisation really is a viable prospect.

Preparation and planning

Identifying a qualified prospect is only the beginning of the process. Before the real selling begins, it is very important to obtain further information on the prospect in order to prepare the best and most relevant sales approach and to plan tactics.

In selling to a B2B customer, this may mean scanning a number of company reports, assessing the norms for that industry in relation to likely buying criteria and needs. Analysing the prospect's company report might promise indications of the strategic direction in which it is moving, as well as revealing its financial situation. It is also necessary to think about the kind of purchasing structures that the representative is going to have to work through, identifying the most likely influencers and decision-makers. In addition, it is also useful to find out as much as possible about the application of the product and the features and benefits required. This allows the representative to construct a sales presentation that will be relevant to the buyer and thus will have more chance of engaging their attention and being persuasive.

Sales representatives in B2B markets are fortunate that sufficient information exists about their buyers to allow them to prepare so well in advance. In consumer markets, it is more likely that representatives have to think on their feet, analysing customers while they are face to face with them.

Where it is possible, therefore, doing the homework is essential, and it often needs to be very thorough, especially in situations involving large, complex projects with stiff competition. Also, if the competition is already well entrenched in doing business with a prospect, it is even more important to find out as much as possible in advance, since getting that customer to switch supplier will probably be an uphill task unless you can find the right approach with the right people.

Initiating contact

Making the first contact with the prospect is a delicate operation. There are two ways of approaching this stage. First, the initial telephone call that qualifies the prospect may be used to solicit an appointment. Failure to achieve that means that the selling process cannot begin. The second approach is to use cold calling. This means turning up on the doorstep in the hope that someone will see you, as the double glazing sales representative does. This can be very wasteful in terms of time and travel. There is no guarantee that the representative will get access to the key people, who probably would not in any case be able to spare time without a prior appointment. Even if the representative does get access, it is unlikely that a properly tailored sales presentation will have been prepared if there has not been preliminary contact with the prospect. Cold callers are often seen as time-wasters, and do not do themselves or their organisations any favours in the eyes of the prospects.

eg Whether it is double glazing, paved drives, kitchens, insurance or fresh fish, the cold calling, door-to-door sales representative is often seen as an unwelcome, intrusive time-waster. Although the door can always be slammed, elderly people in particular often become flustered and are vulnerable to predatory or persistent callers. The OFT estimated that there were 16,000 bogus trading cases where vulnerable customers were pressurised into buying shoddy goods and services at an average price of £2000 (*Precision Marketing*, 2005a). The reputable sellers, however, obviously do not like having their image tainted by the activities of fly-by-night builders and con artists. The Direct Selling Association (DSA) has thus sought to encourage self-regulation in the UK through the introduction of a code of conduct. Sales staff from its 60 members must carry clear identification and make it clear that there is a 14-day cooling-off period to cancel products and services. Otherwise, it is a case of 'buyer beware' as disreputable companies tend not to subscribe to trade associations and exploit legal loopholes that bypass the Office of Fair Trading rights and leave the consumer vulnerable to overcharging and poor quality and service (Stewart, 2002).

Once an approach has been made and an appointment secured, the next stage is the initial call. This helps the representative to discover whether the initial assessment of the customer's likely need is borne out in practice. In these early meetings, it is important to build up rapport, mutual respect and trust between buyer and seller before the more serious business discussion gets under way. The time spent in establishing this relationship is well spent. It helps to build a solid foundation for the later stages of discussion.

■ The sales presentation

At last, the representative has enough insight and information to allow the preparation of the sales presentation itself that lies at the heart of the selling process. The ease of its preparation and its effectiveness in practice owe a great deal to the thoroughness and quality of the work done in the earlier stages. The objective of the sales presentation is to show how the product offering and the customer's needs match. The presentation must not be product-oriented, but be concerned with what the product can do for that particular customer. In other words, do not sell the features, sell the benefits.

There may be some practicalities to be handled as part of the presentation. The representative may have to demonstrate the product, for example. The product or sample used must look right, and will need to be explained, not in technical terms, necessarily, but in terms of how it offers particular benefits and solutions. A demonstration is a powerful element of a sales presentation, because it gets the prospect involved and encourages conversation and questions. It provides a focus that can dispel any lingering awkwardness between buyer and seller. Also, in getting their hands on the product itself, or a sample, the prospect is brought very close to the reality of the product and can begin to see for themselves what it can do for them.

eg When a 61-year-old man enquired about a £5000 spa bath at a Merlin Timber Products showroom, it allegedly led to his death. Although the prospective customer just wanted a brochure, the keen salesman invited him and his wife to witness a demonstration of the water turbulence created by high-powered air pumps, blowers and jets. Unfortunately, as the unsuspecting customer was invited to feel the therapeutic turbulence, the jets of air also sprayed him with a fine mist. Two days later he complained of 'flu-like symptoms and just 17 days later died of multiple organ failure from legionnaire's disease. Samples taken from the water confirmed that the bacteria were present three weeks after the incident. The Surrey Health Council, under whose environmental responsibility the showroom came, found that the ozoneator was not working properly and if it had been, the bacteria would have been killed. The Council also found that sales staff had not been properly trained about the health risks associated with demonstrating spa baths, so the accident that happened was, to some, entirely predictable. The coroner recorded a verdict of accidental death on the poor customer (Payne, 2002).

Handling objections

It is indeed a rare and skilful sales representative who can complete an entire sales presentation without the prospect coming out with words to the effect of 'that's all very well, but …'. At any stage in the selling process that involves the customer, objections can and probably will be made. These may arise for various reasons: lack of understanding, lack of interest, misinformation, a need for reassurance or genuine concern. The sales representative must be prepared to overcome objections where possible, as otherwise the sale is likely to be lost completely. If the customer is concerned enough to raise an objection, then the representative must have the courtesy to answer it in some way. Homespun wisdom among seasoned sales representatives argues that the real selling does not begin until the customer raises an objection.

Organisations that do not subscribe to the formula approach to selling often do train their sales staff to handle specific objections that commonly arise in their field in a set way. If a buyer says, for example, 'I think your product is not as good as product *x*', the sales representative should explore what is meant by the use of the word 'good'. This could cover a whole range of different areas in the competitive offering. The representative's response may therefore be designed to explore in more detail the underlying problem by asking 'In what way is it not as good?' Agreeing with the objection and countering it is often called the 'yes, but' technique. Where the objection is founded in fact, all the representative can legitimately do is agree with the substance of it, then find a compensating factor to outweigh it. Thus if the prospect argues that the product being sold is more expensive than the competition's, the representative can reply with 'Yes, I agree that value for money is important. Although our product is more expensive initially, you will find that the day-to-day running costs and the annual maintenance add up to a lot less ...'. Such a technique avoids creating excessive tension and argument, because the customer feels that their objection has been acknowledged and satisfactorily answered.

All in all, handling objections requires a very careful response from representatives. They must not see objections as a call for them to say just anything to clinch the sale, since doing so will only lead to legal or relationship problems later. The representative must assess the situation, the type of objection and the mood of the customer and then choose the most appropriate style of response, without overstepping any ethical boundaries in terms of content. It is critical that winning the argument used to overcome the objection does not lead to a lost sale. Objections may interrupt the flow of the sales process either temporarily or permanently, and unless they are overcome, the final stages of the selling process cannot be achieved.

Negotiation

Once the main body of the sales presentation is drawing to a close, with all the prospect's questions and objections answered for the time being, the selling process may move into a negotiation phase. Negotiation is a 'give and take' activity in which both parties try to shape a deal that satisfies both of them. Negotiation assumes a basic willingness to trade, but does not necessarily lead to a final deal. The danger for the sales representative, of course, is that a deadlocked or delayed negotiation phase may allow a competitor to enter the fray.

Despite the fact that deals are becoming more complex, sales staff are still expected to be able to negotiate. If they are going to be given the power to negotiate on behalf of the organisation, then they need clear guidelines on how far they are permitted to go in terms of concessions, and what the implications of those concessions would be. An extra month's credit, for example, could be quite expensive, particularly for an organisation with short-term cash flow problems, unless it is traded for another prized concession. This effectively means that the sales representative needs financial as well as behavioural training in order to handle complex and sometimes lengthy negotiations.

As a final point, it must be said that negotiation need not be a separate and discrete stage of the selling process. Negotiation may emerge implicitly during the process of handling objections, or may be an integral part of the next stage to be discussed, closing the sale.

Closing the sale

The closing stage of the personal selling process is concerned with reaching the point where the customer agrees to purchase. In most cases, it is the sales representative's responsibility to close the sale, to ask for the order. Where the representative is less sure of the prospect's state of mind, or where the prospect still seems to have doubts, the timing of the closure and the way in which it is done could affect whether a sale is made. Try to close the sale too soon, and the buyer might be frightened off; leave it too long, and the buyer might become irritated by the prolonged process and all the good work done earlier in the sales presentation will start to dissipate.

Watching the buyer's behaviour and listening to what they are saying might indicate that closure is near. The buyer's questions, for example, may become very trivial or the objections might dry up. The buyer might go quiet and start examining the product intently, waiting for the representative to make a move. The buyer's comments or questions might begin to relate to the post-purchase period, with a strong assumption that the deal has already been done.

A representative who thinks that the time to close is near, but is uncertain, might have to test the buyer's readiness to commit to a purchase. Also, if the prospect seems to be teetering on the edge of making a decision, then the representative might have to use a mechanism to give the buyer a gentle nudge in the direction of closure, for instance by offering the buyer a number of alternatives, each of which implies an agreement to purchase. The buyer's response gives an insight into how ready they are to commit themselves. Thus if the representative says 'Would you like delivery to each of your stores or to the central distribution point?', there are two ways in which the buyer might respond. One way would be to choose one of the alternatives offered, in which case the sale must be very close, since the buyer is willing to get down to such fine detail. The other response would be something like 'Wait a minute, before we get down to that, what about ...', showing that the buyer has not yet heard enough and may still have objections to be answered.

Follow-up and account management

The sales representative's responsibility does not end once a sale has been agreed. As implied earlier at pp. 349 *et seq.*, the sales representative, as the customer's key contact point with the selling organisation, needs to ensure that the product is delivered on time and in good condition, that any installation or training promises are fulfilled and that the customer is absolutely satisfied with the purchase and is getting the best out of it.

At a more general level, the relationship with the customer still needs to be cultivated and managed. Where the sale has resulted in an ongoing supply situation, this may mean ensuring continued satisfaction with quality and service levels. Even with infrequently purchased items, ongoing positive contact helps to ensure that when new business develops, that supplier will be well placed. In the case of the consumer buying a car, the sales representative will make sure in the early stages that the customer is happy with the car, and work to resolve any problems quickly and efficiently. In the longer term, direct responsibility usually passes from the representative to a customer care manager who will ensure that the buyer is regularly sent product information and things like invitations to new product launches in the showrooms.

In the B2B market, an important role for the sales representative is to manage the customer's account internally within the selling organisation, ensuring that appropriate support is available as needed. Thus the representative is continuing to liaise between the customer and the accounts department, engineering, R&D, service and anyone else with whom the customer needs to deal.

Sales management

The previous section concentrated on the mechanics of selling something to a prospective buyer. That is important, certainly, because if the selling process does not work well, then there will be no sales and no revenue. Equally important, however, is the management of the sales force. Whether in a multi-national organisation or a small company, the selling effort needs to be planned and managed, and sales management provides an essential link between the organisation's strategic marketing plans and the achievement of sales objectives by the representatives in the field.

■ Planning and strategy

The sales plan outlines the objectives for the selling effort and the details of how the plan should be implemented. This plan itself arises from, and must fit closely with, the marketing objectives set for products and market share, etc. These marketing objectives need to be translated into sales objectives, both for the sales force as a whole, and for individuals or groups within the sales force.

Setting sales objectives provides an essential yardstick against which to measure progress and to motivate and influence the selling effort. Normally, quantitative measures are used to specify exactly what is required. At the level of the total sales force, the targets will be in terms of sales value and/or volume. Setting objectives in sales and profit terms is often necessary either to avoid the dangers of chasing low profit sales or to lessen the temptation to reduce margins to generate more sales volume but less gross profit. Targets for individual sales representatives need not relate only to selling quantities of products. Performance targets might be agreed in terms of the number of sales calls, the number of new accounts recruited, the call frequency, call conversion rates (i.e. turning prospects into buyers) or selling expenses.

Assuming that the selling effort is to be managed internally, the sales manager also has to decide how the sales force will be organised: by geography (e.g. each sales representative is allocated a geographic region as their sales territory); by product (e.g. each sales representative is allocated a particular brand or family of product lines to sell); by customer type (e.g. each sales representative concentrates on a particular industry in which to sell); or by customer importance (e.g. the most important customers, perhaps in terms of sales, are identified and allocated their own sales representative or account team).

There is no one universally applicable and appropriate organisational structure. Sometimes a mixed structure may be best, combining geographic and major customer specialisation. Johnson & Johnson, for example, employs regionally based territory sales managers for its UK consumer products, but with specific responsibility for certain types of customer, such as independent pharmacies and wholesale cash and carries. This allows the organisation to benefit from the advantages of both types of allocation, while reducing the effect of their disadvantages. The chosen structure will be the right one as long as it reflects the objectives and marketing strategy of the firm.

A further decision has to be made on the ideal size of the sales force. A number of factors need to be considered, such as the calling frequency required for each customer, the number of calls possible each day, and the relative division of the representative's time between administration, selling and repeat calls (Cravens and LaForge, 1983). All these matters will have an impact on the ability of the sales force to achieve the expected sales results from the number of accounts served. For a smaller business, the issue may be further constrained by just how many representatives can be afforded!

Recruitment and selection

As with any recruitment exercise, it is important to begin by developing a profile of who the organisation is looking for. A detailed analysis of the selling tasks should lead to a list of the ideal skills and characteristics of the representative to be recruited. Table 10.1 lists the attributes of sales representatives typically appreciated by buyers.

A common dilemma is whether previous experience is an essential requirement. Some organisations prefer to take on recruits new to selling, then train them in their own methods rather than recruit experienced representatives who come with bad habits and other organisations' weaknesses. Others, especially smaller organisations, may deliberately seek

Table 10.1 Sales representative attributes typically appreciated by buyers

- Thoroughness and follow-up
- Knowledge of seller's products
- Representing the buyer's interests within the selling organisation
- Market knowledge
- Understanding the buyer's problems
- Knowledge of the buyer's product and markets
- Diplomacy and tact
- Good preparation before sales calls
- Regular sales calls
- Technical education

experienced staff, wishing to benefit from training programmes that they themselves could not afford to provide.

The actual selection process needs to be designed to draw out evidence of the ability of each candidate to perform the specified tasks, so that an informed choice can be made. The cost of a poor selection can be very high, not just in terms of recruitment costs and salary, but also, and perhaps more seriously, in terms of lost sales opportunities or damage to the organisation's reputation. In view of the importance of making the right choice, in addition to normal interview and reference procedures, a number of firms employ psychological tests to assess personality and some will not confirm the appointment until the successful completion of the initial training period.

■ Training

The recruitment process generally provides only the raw material. Although the new recruit might already have appropriate skills and a good attitudinal profile, training will help to sharpen both areas so that better performance within the sales philosophy of the employing organisation can be developed. Sales force training applies not just to new recruits, however. Both new and existing staff, even well-established staff, may need skills refinement and upgrading.

Training may be formal or informal. Some organisations invest in and develop their own high-quality training facilities and run a regular series of introductory and refresher courses in-house. This has the advantage of ensuring that the training is relevant to the organisation and its business, as well as signifying an ongoing commitment to staff development.

Other organisations adopt a more *ad hoc* approach, using outside specialists as required. This means that the organisation pays only for what it uses, but the approach carries two serious risks. The first problem is that the training may be too generalised and thus insufficiently tailored to the organisation's needs. The second problem is that it is too easy for the organisation to put off training or, even worse, to delete it altogether in times of financial stringency.

eg When Eli Lilly planned to launch Cialis, the male impotence drug, into the UK market, it decided to undertake extensive training of 250 out of 450 UK sales representatives. The role of the representatives is to contact health professionals about the drugs on offer and to seek their adoption for prescription. The sales force is organised around customer groups. Primary care representatives call on GPs, nurses and pharmacists, specialist representatives call on hospital doctors and consultants, while the NHS team calls on budget holders and policy makers. Planning the training was not easy as erectile dysfunction is a sensitive topic, especially when there is a 60:40 female–male split in the sales force. It had to fit the needs of the different field teams. The training delivery strategy included distance learning, home-based study, residential plenaries and small group syndicates to put into practice the information gained through discussion and role plays. Unless the sales manager considered that enough progress had been made, the representatives did not pass the course. The total cost was

Cialis solves a recurrent problem for some older men and brings a smile to their faces.

Source: © Image Source/Alamy http://www.alamy.com

£230,000 for 1200 training days. The product was successfully launched, staff turnover has dropped and contact rates have improved from 2.8 to 4.8 per day (Pollitt, 2004).

Finally, a third group uses informal or semi-formal 'sitting with Nelly', on-the-job coaching. This involves the trainee observing other representatives in the field, and then being observed themselves by experienced sales representatives and/or the sales manager. There is nothing quite like seeing the job being done, but with this approach the organisation needs to take great care to deal with a number of points. One concern is to ensure that such training is comprehensive, covering all aspects of the job. Another is to ensure that bad habits or questionable techniques are not passed on. The main problem with this kind of on-the-job training is that the training is not usually done by professional trainers. Therefore the quality can be variable, and there is no opportunity for fresh ideas to be introduced to the sales force.

■ Motivation and compensation

An organisation will not only want to motivate new recruits to join its sales force, but also have an interest in making sure that they are sufficiently well rewarded for their achievements that they will not easily be poached by the competition (Cron *et al.*, 1988). There are many ways in which the sales team can be motivated to achieve outstanding results and rewarded, but they are not all financially based. Opportunities for self-development through training, well-defined career progression routes, and a feeling of being valued as an individual within a team can all increase job satisfaction.

Nevertheless, pay still remains a vital ingredient in attracting and retaining a committed sales force. Three main methods of compensation exist: straight salary, straight commission

Table 10.2 Comparison of compensation plans

	Commission only	Salary only	Part salary/ part commission
Motivation for rep. to generate sales	High	Low	Medium
Motivation for rep. to build customer relationship	Low	High	Medium
Motivation for rep. to participate in training	Low	High	Medium
Cost-effectiveness for organisation	High	Potentially low	Medium
Predictability of cost to organisation	Low	High	Medium
Predictability of income for rep.	Low	High	Medium
Ease of administration for organisation	Low	High	Low
Organisation's control over rep.	Low	High	Medium
Organisation's flexibility to push sales of particular products	High	Low	High
Overall, best where ...	• Aggressive selling is needed • There are few non-selling tasks	• Training new reps • Difficult sales territories exist • Developing new territories • There are many non-selling tasks	• Organisation wants both incentive and control • Sales territories all have similar profiles

and a combination of salary and commission. Each method implies a number of advantages and disadvantages, listed in Table 10.2. The straight salary compensation plan is where a fixed amount is paid on a salary basis. The straight commission compensation plan means that earnings are directly related to the sales and profit generated. Finally, the most popular method is the combination plan, involving part salary and part commission. The selection of the most appropriate method will partly be determined by the nature of the selling tasks, and the degree of staff turnover that can be tolerated given the training and recruiting costs.

■ Performance evaluation

Given that many sales representatives work away from an office base, the monitoring and control of individual selling activity are vital functions in the sales management role. The sales representative's performance can be measured in both quantitative and qualitative terms. Quantitative assessments can be related to either input or output measures, usually with reference to targets and benchmarks (Good and Stone, 1991). Input measures assess activities such as the number of calls and account coverage. Output measures focus on the end rather than the means, and include measurement of sales volume, sales development, number of new accounts and specific product sales.

To create a rounded picture of the sales representative's performance, qualitative measures that tend to be informal and subjective are also used. These could include attitude, product knowledge, appearance and communication skills. Using them in conjunction with quantitative measures, the sales manager may be able to find explanations for any particularly good or bad performance underlying the quantitative evidence of the formal results achieved (Churchill *et al.*, 2000).

Either way, the assessment can form the basis of a deeper analysis to encourage a proactive rather than reactive approach to sales management. The analysis might indicate that action needs to be taken on call policy, training or motivation, or even that problems may lie not with the sales force, but with the product or its marketing strategies.

Chapter summary

■ Advertising is a non-personal form of communication with an identified sponsor, using any form of mass media. Advertising can help to create awareness, build image and attitudes and then reinforce those attitudes through reminders. It is an invaluable support for other elements of the promotional mix, for example by creating awareness and positive attitudes towards an organisation in preparation for a sales team, or by communicating sales promotions. Advertising also has strategic uses within the wider marketing mix. It can contribute to product positioning, thus supporting a premium price, or it could help to even out seasonal fluctuations in demand.

■ The advertising message is extremely important. It has to be informative, persuasive and attention grabbing. It has to be appropriate for the target audience and thus speak to them in terms to which they can relate. There are several types of creative appeal that advertisers can use: rational, emotional and product-centred. Once the message and its appeal have been decided, the advertisement has to be prepared for print or broadcasting. In either case, the advertisement has to be relevant to the target audience, making a sufficient impact to get the desired message across and to get the audience to act on it.

■ The advertiser has a wide choice of media. Television has a wide reach across the whole population, but it can be difficult to target a specific market segment precisely. Radio can deliver fairly specific target audiences, and is an attractive medium for smaller companies operating in a defined geographic area covered by a local radio station. Cinema is a relatively minor medium delivering captive, well-profiled audiences. It can make a big impact on the audience because of the quality of the sound and the size of the screen. Print media broadly consist of magazines and newspapers. Magazines tend to have well-defined readerships who are receptive to the content of advertisements relevant to the magazine's theme. Newspapers, on the other hand, have a very short life span and are often skimmed rather than read properly. A reader is unlikely to read through the same copy more than once. Outdoor media includes advertising hoardings, posters, ambient and transport-related media. They can provide easily digested messages that attract the attention of bored passengers or passers-by. They can generate high frequency as people tend to pass the same sites regularly, but can be spoiled by the weather and the ambience of their location.

■ Advertising agencies are often used to provide expertise. Choosing an agency is an important task, and an organisation needs to think carefully about the relevant criteria for choice. Once the client has signed up an agency, it is then important to continue to communicate and to build a strong mutual understanding, with both sides contributing according to expectations.

■ Managing advertising within an organisation involves a number of stages. First, campaign responsibilities need to be decided so that the process and the budget are kept under proper control. Once the target market and their broad communication needs have been defined, specific campaign objectives can be developed. Next, the budget can be set in the light of the desired objectives. Media choices, based on the habits of the target audience, the requirements of the planned message and the desired reach and frequency, can then be made. Meanwhile, the advertisements themselves are developed. Testing can be built in at various stages of this development to ensure that the right message is getting across in the right kind of way with the right kind of effect. Once the advertising has been fully developed, it can be implemented. Both during and after the campaign, managers will assess the advertising's effectiveness, using aided or unaided recall, enquiry tests or sales tests, depending on the original objectives.

■ Although personal selling can be an expensive and labour-intensive marketing communication activity, it has a number of advantages over other forms of communication. It makes an *impact*, because it involves face-to-face contact and is less likely to be ignored; it can deliver a *precise and tailored* message to a target customer who has already been checked out to ensure that they fit the right profile; and it helps in the *cultivation* of long-term buyer–seller relationships.

■ The personal selling process can be a long and complicated marketing activity to implement. The process starts with the identification of prospective customers, and then the representative has to do as much background work on the prospect as possible in order to prepare an initial approach and a relevant sales presentation. Initial contact breaks the ice between buyer and seller, allowing an appointment to be made for the real selling to begin. The sales presentation will give the representative the opportunity to present the product in the best possible light, using a variety of samples and audio-visual aids, while allowing the customer to ask questions and to raise any objections they may have. Negotiating the fine details of the deal may lead naturally to closing the sale, and then all that remains is for the representative to ensure the customer's post-purchase satisfaction and work towards building a long-term relationship leading to repeat business and further purchases.

■ Sales management is an important area of marketing, and involves a number of issues. *Sales planning and strategy* means making decisions about sales objectives, both for the organisation as a whole and for individual sales representatives or teams. *Recruitment* and *training* are also both important aspects of sales management. Apart from benefiting from training programmes, sales representatives have to be properly *motivated and compensated* for their efforts. A natural part of all this is *performance evaluation*. Sales managers need to ensure that representatives are achieving their targets and, if not, why not.

Questions for review and discussion

10.1 In what ways can advertising support the other elements of the promotional mix?

10.2 Find examples of advertising that uses:
(a) a rational appeal; and
(b) a fear appeal.
Why do you think the advertisers have chosen these approaches?

10.3 Find a current advertising campaign that uses both television and print media. Why do you think both media are being used? To what extent is each medium contributing something different to the overall message?

10.4 Develop a checklist of criteria against which a prospective client could assess advertising agencies. Which criterion would you say is the most important, and why?

10.5 What are the stages in the *personal selling process*?

10.6 Find 20 job advertisements for sales representatives and summarise the range of characteristics and skills sought. Which are the most commonly required and to what extent do you think that they are essential for a successful sales representative?

case study 10

Getting real about getting behind the wheel

The Government, or more specifically the Department of Transport, Local Government and the Regions (DTLR), has run anti-drink/drive campaigns in the UK for nearly 40 years. Over the last 10 years the annual budget for these advertisements has averaged around £2m. Despite this continuous investment, nearly 600 road users die in drink/drive collisions each year, and a further 18,000 are injured, several hundred seriously. According to statistics collected by the RAC Foundation, drinking and driving accounts for one in six road deaths, drivers under the age of 25 are much more likely to be involved in drink/drive crashes, and men are three times more likely to fail a breath test than women.

Over the years, a number of different advertising approaches have been adopted to try to change drink/driving behaviour, and with obvious budgetary constraints, target audiences and media deployment have had to be prioritised. There have been advertisements that have shown the horrific damage that drink/drivers have wrought on other people's lives – an approach that is still used in Ireland with their 'Could you live with the SHAME?' campaign. While this 'take responsibility' message was shown to affect some, research indicated that those most resistant to amending their drink/drive behaviour were more likely to be influenced by selfish motives. This led to executions which concentrated on the personal consequences of drink/driving, both practical, such as losing your licence and job, being fined or imprisoned, having a criminal record and higher insurance premiums, and physical, such as being rendered a human 'vegetable' like Dave in the 1995 'Come on Dave, just one more' campaign.

For budgetary reasons, campaigns were historically concentrated around the Christmas period, when it was considered that drivers would be more likely to take risks with drinking and driving. Following the Christmas 2001 campaign, which featured real-life footage of the emergency services attending devastating drink/drive crash scenes with incongruous upbeat Christmas songs and carols playing in the background, an article appeared in the *Daily Telegraph* newspaper titled 'Don't drink and drive, and don't preach' (Williams, 2001). The copy went on to say 'As regular as Morecambe and Wise repeats, but considerably less entertaining, government anti-drink/drive campaigns have been a sad feature of Christmas television programming for 25 years'. While not reflecting a universal view, the points made in the article about the preaching tone, and the Christmas-centric focus when evidence suggests that drink/drive accidents occur year-round, had some validity. Although not able to finance a year-round campaign, by developing a more integrated approach to all road safety campaigns (speeding, seatbelts and drinking) by running the line

1998 drink/drive campaign

THINK on all of them, the DTLR endeavoured to make thinking about safer driving a year-round issue.

In 2005, a summer campaign was mounted in recognition that longer days, warmer weather and an increasing number of *al fresco* drinking venues and occasions were contributory factors to drink/driving. After focusing on Christmas for such a long time, the DTLR was keen to point out that just as many drink/drive casualties occur in the summer as at Christmas. The target audience was young males, and the multimedia campaign tackled the realities of this audience's attitude, and its influence on their behaviour, head on. 'Getting caught' was a bigger worry to them than any damage they might do when drinking and driving; they believed they knew 'their limit', and could have several drinks without being affected; they thought it was only when you were blind drunk that you were really at risk.

During June, July and August 2005 the commercial 'Crash' was shown on television, specifically on Thursdays, Fridays, Saturdays and Sundays. The same advertisement ran in cinemas to coincide with the summer blockbuster movies. The radio commercial 'Your Round' was broadcast on national stations from June until September in slots from Friday to Sunday, and posters and leaflets were placed during the same period. Although taking different angles on the theme, the same

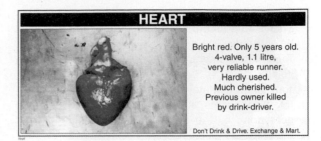

Gradually campaigns to encourage people not to mix drinking and driving have become more hard hitting, showing the reality of the death and destruction it causes.

Source: Image courtesy of the Advertising Archives

underlying messages were present in all of the advertising activity – the decision to drink and drive is made in the *pub*, not on the *road*, and it takes less than you think to become a drink/driver. The scenarios depicted were less immediately dramatic than in previous advertisements, essentially focusing on the mundane reality of a trip to the pub, but it was hoped that in dramatising that in-pub moment when the decision to have a drink, or another drink, was made, there would be more self-identification on the part of the young male audience, who had not recognised themselves as the potential crash victims of previous, more gory executions.

The 30-second commercial that was screened on television and in the cinema showed three guys meeting up after work for a quiet drink. One of the guys gets in a second round, and the 'hero' of the advertisement tries to decline because he's driving, but quickly gives in ('After all, it's only two'). For the duration of this exchange an attractive blonde at the bar and our seated 'hero' have been giving each other the eye, something that his mates have been unable to resist commenting on. She makes to come towards their table at the exact moment he decides to have a second drink, then she is flung across the room, landing in a heap as the result of being hit by an 'invisible' car. At the same time we see the group of mates whiplashed forward and backward at their table as if involved in a head-on crash. This dramatised the catastrophic consequences of drink/driving – a crash, carnage – in the hitherto quiet and calm environment of the pub, where the decision to have another was so lightly made.

The 'Your Round' radio advertisement, focuses on a similar scenario. It opens with Tom and a mate having a quiet drink after work, and throughout there is the low hum of pub noise in the background:

Tom's Mate: Another drink Tom?
Tom: I can't, mate, I'm off to meet Rach.
Tom's Mate: And?
Tom: I've already had one, and I'm driving, aren't I?
Tom's Mate: Come on mate. It's your round, one more can't hurt.

2001 drink/drive campaign

Source: © Crown Copyright. Reproduced with permission of the Home Office

(Mate's thoughts, audible) One more might hurt, but I don't want him to leave until he buys me that drink he owes me.

Tom: Alright, alright, one more, but then I'm definitely going.

Tom's Mate: Whatever you say, Tom, you're the man. (Mate's thoughts, audible) He won't be the man if he gets done by the police, but it's his licence, not mine. It's his problem.

Both: Cheers!

Voice-over: Remember who's driving. Remember whose licence it is. Think. Don't drink and drive.

The posters and leaflets also featured two mates drinking pints in a bar, with their bodies calibrated at different levels in blue. The message here was 'You can't calculate your alcohol limit. So don't try', and was supported with facts such as how an individual's weight, sex, age, metabolism, stress levels, amount of food eaten, and type and amount of alcohol consumed, all contribute to the effect alcohol has on different people at different times.

So there has been a move away from depicting the extraordinary road crash dramas, to dramatising the mundane reality of drink/driving, which like the puppy in the RSPCA advertisement is a fact of everyday life, not just for Christmas!

Sources: Williams (2001); **http://www.thinkroadsafety.gov.uk/campaigns**; **http://www.racfoundation.org**; **http://rospa.com/roadsafety**.

Questions

1 It is unusual for actual days of the week to be specified on a media plan. Why do you think specific days were nominated for the television and radio advertisements to air in this case?

2 List the individual elements in the advertising executions described that can be directly linked to insights into the target audience's attitude.

3 This campaign made use of television, cinema, radio, posters and leaflets. What function do you think each individual medium performed within the campaign? What would have been lost if all monies had been spent in a single medium?

4 Think of another advertising campaign that is seeking to influence and change entrenched attitudes. In what ways is it similar to or different from this campaign?

References for chapter 10

Abberton Associates (1997), *Balancing the Selling Equation: Revisited*, accessed via **http://www.cpm-int.com**.

Abbott, G. (2005), 'Promises, Promises, … Take to PoP Instead', *Marketing Week*, 15 September, p. 30.

Benady, D. (2005), 'Marketing to Look Down On', *Marketing Week*, 14 July, pp. 39–40.

Berkowitz, E.N. *et al.* (1992), *Marketing*, Irwin.

Big Communications (2004), 'Rugby Seats', *The Communication Agencies Association of New Zealand Paper*.

Brand Republic (2005), 'Superbrand Case Studies: Doritos', *Brand Republic*, 8 August.

Churchill, G., Ford, N., Walker, O., Johnston, M. and Tanner, J. (2000), *Sales Force Management*, 6th edn, Irwin.

Cravens, D. and LaForge, R. (1983), 'Salesforce Deployment Analysis', *Industrial Marketing Management*, July, pp. 179–92.

Creative Review (2005), 'The Serious Business of Comedy', *Creative Review*, January, p. 16.

Cron, W. *et al.* (1988), 'The Influence of Career Stages on Components of Salesperson Motivation', *Journal of Marketing*, 52 (July), pp. 179–92.

Davidson, D. (2004), 'Wella's Hair Raising Campaign', 23 February.

EuroRSCG (2004), 'Evian: We Will Rock You', *Euro-Effie Awards Paper*.

Fenn, N. (2004), 'Listerine: How Advertising Gave People an Imperative to Pick Up a Bottle', *IPA Advertising Effectiveness Paper*, sourced via **http://www.warc.com**.

Fill, C. (2002), *Marketing Communications: Contexts, Strategies and Applications*, 3rd edn, Financial Times Prentice Hall.

FritoLay/AMV (2003), 'Friendchips', *Euro-Effies Award Paper*.

Gofton, K. (2002), 'Field Marketing Grows Up', *Campaign*, 25 January, p. 22.

Good, D. and Stone, R. (1991), 'How Sales Quotas are Developed', *Industrial Marketing Management*, 20 (1), pp. 51–6.

Gray, R. (2001), 'Fighting Talk', *Marketing*, 20 September, pp. 26–7.

Homes and Gardens (2005), advertisement featured in *Homes and Gardens*, October, p. 98.

Johanson, J. and Vahlne, J. (1977), 'The Internationalisation Process of the Firm: A Model of Knowledge Development and Increasing Foreign Market Commitment', *Journal of International Business Studies*, 8 (1), pp. 23–32.

Jones, G. (2005), 'GMG Transposes Jazz FM into Standalone Online Radio Station', *New Media Age*, 2 June, p. 5.

Lambert, D. *et al.* (1990), 'Industrial Salespeople as a Source of Market Information', *Industrial Marketing Management*, 19, pp. 141–5.

Management Services (2002), 'Sales People Spend Just Seven Percent of their Time – Selling', *Management Services*, August, p. 7.

Marketing (1999), 'Reading Between the Lines', *Marketing*, 21 January, pp. 21–2.

Marketing Week (2004), 'Forces on the Ground', *Marketing Week*, 18 November, p. 37.

Marketing Week (2005a), 'Wake Up to an Early Start', *Marketing Week*, 4 August, p. 37.

Marketing Week (2005b), 'Brother Signs £2m Sponsor Deal with C4 Business Show', *Marketing Week*, 8 September, p. 18.

Marketing Week (2005c), 'Brands Sign Up to London Recycle Push', *Marketing Week*, 15 September, p. 9.

Mason, J. (2000), 'Judge Throws Out BA Attack on Ryanair', *Financial Times*, 6 December, p. 4.

McDonald, J. (2004), 'A Ding Dong Battle to Keep Ahead of the Pack', *Daily Telegraph*, 2 December, p. 6.

McDonald, M. (1984), *Marketing Plans*, Butterworth-Heinemann.

McLuhan, R. (2001a), 'Food Remains Top for Field Activities', *Marketing*, 30 August, p. 37.

McLuhan, R. (2001b), 'UK Agencies Focus on European Arena', *Marketing*, 30 August, p. 42.

Middleton, T. (2001), 'Field Questions', *Marketing Week*, 22 November, pp. 51–3.

Miles, L. (1998), 'Discipline on the Doorstep', *Marketing*, 19 November, pp. 37–40.

Miller, R. and Heinman, S. (1991), *Successful Large Account Management*, Holt.

Muehling, D. *et al.* (1990), 'The Impact of Comparative Advertising on Levels of Message Involvement', *Journal of Advertising*, 19 (4), pp. 41–50.

Mueller-Heumann, G. (1992), 'Markets and Technology Shifts in the 1990s: Market Fragmentation and Mass Customisation', *Journal of Marketing Management*, 8 (4), pp. 303–14.

Newman, A. (2005), 'Death of the Salesman?', *Insurance Brokers' Monthly and Insurance Adviser*, July, pp. 4–5.

New Media Age (2005) 'Vogue.com in Deal with Sony Ericsson', *New Media Age*, 14 July, p. 3.

Payne, S. (2002), 'Shopper at Garden Centre Died after Testing Spa Bath', *Daily Telegraph*, 15 February, p. 8.

Pedersen, C. *et al.* (1986), *Selling: Principles and Methods*, Irwin.

Pickton, D. and Broderick, A. (2001), *Integrated Marketing Communications*, Financial Times Prentice Hall.

Polak, E. (2005), 'Going Global: How Local Origin Affects Brand Strategy', *Admap*, May.

Pollitt, D. (2004), 'Eli Lilly Gets the Right Prescription for Training Cialis Sales Representatives', *Human Resource Management International Digest*, 12 (5), p. 11.

Precision Marketing (2005a), 'Doorstep Firms Seal OFT Approval', *Precision Marketing*, 4 March, p. 2.

Precision Marketing (2005b), 'Playing the Field', *Precision Marketing*, 25 March, p. 15.

Ray, A. (2002), 'Using Outdoor to Target the Young', *Marketing*, 31 January, p. 25.

Russell, F. *et al.* (1977), *Textbook of Salesmanship*, 10th edn, McGraw-Hill.

Shannon, J. (1999), 'Comparative Ads Call for Prudence', *Marketing Week*, 6 May, p. 32.

Singh, S. (2001), 'Avon Plans Global Teen Assault', *Marketing Week*, 16 August, p. 5.

Sissors, J. and Bumba, L. (1989), *Advertising Media Planning*, 3rd edn, NTC Business Books.

Smith, P. and Taylor, J. (2002), *Marketing Communications: An Integrated Approach*, 3rd edn, Kogan Page.

Staheli, P. (2000), 'We're the Best but We're Not Allowed to Tell You', *Evening Standard*, 26 April, p. 59.

Stewart, C. (2002), 'Cold Comfort for Those Cold Callers', *The Times*, 26 January, p. 8.

Storey, R. (2001), 'COI – Police, When Respect is Due', *Account Planning Group Creative Planning Awards Paper*.

Turnbull, P. and Cunningham, M. (1981), *International Marketing and Purchasing: A Survey Among Marketing and Purchasing Executives in Five European Countries*, Macmillan.

Wall Street Journal (2005), 'China, in Boon to Firms Like Amway, to Ease Ban on Direct Sales', *Wall Street Journal*, 18 August, p. A9.

White, R. (1988), *Advertising: What It Is and How To Do It*, McGraw-Hill.

Williams, A. (2001), 'Don't Drink and Drive, and Don't Preach', *Daily Telegraph Motoring Section*, 12 December.

Wood, J. (2003), 'Does Negative and Comparative Advertising Work?', *Admap*, January, pp. 37–8.

Yelkur, R., Tomkovick, C. and Traczyk, P. (2004), 'Super Bowl Advertising Effectiveness', *Journal of Advertising Research*, 44 (1), pp. 143–59.

chapter 11

promotion: other tools of marketing communication

learning objectives

This chapter will help you to:

1 define sales promotion and appreciate its role in the communications mix through the objectives it can achieve and the methods it uses in targeting consumers, retailers and B2B customers;

2 understand what direct marketing is and appreciate its role in the communications mix through the objectives it can achieve and the various methods it employs;

3 appreciate the importance of creating and maintaining a database of customers and understand the importance of using the database as a direct marketing tool;

4 appreciate the contribution that trade shows and exhibitions can make to achieving B2B marketing objectives;

5 define PR and understand its role in supporting the organisation's activities, and outline the techniques of PR and their appropriateness for different kinds of public;

6 understand the role of sponsorship in the marketing communications mix and the benefits and problems of different types of sponsorship; and

7 understand the nature of cause-related marketing and the benefits it offers to all parties involved.

Introduction

This chapter discusses a wide range of marketing communications tools. First, we shall explore sales promotion. Traditionally the poor cousin of advertising, sales promotion actually covers a fascinating range of short-term tactical tools that can play a vital complementary role in long-term promotional strategy. Its aim is to add extra value to the product or service, over and above the normal product offering, thus creating an extra inducement to buy or try it. Although individual sales promotions are usually regarded as short-term tactical measures, sales promotion generally, as an element of the promotional mix, is increasingly being recognised as a valid strategic tool, working alongside and supporting other promotional elements.

This chapter will define more clearly what sales promotion is, the techniques it employs and what strategic role it can play within the promotional mix.

Sales promotion takes many different forms but can impact significantly on our lives. The Scots are up in arms about the threat to one of the most popular sales promotions, the 'Happy Hour'. All sorts of deals are offered by pubs to attract customers into the bar early with the aim of keeping them late. 'Two for one' drinks and other price-cutting sales promotion deals are under threat as the Scottish Parliament seeks to curb under-age and binge drinking. The new bill, if passed, will ban promotions which 'encourage or seek to encourage a person to buy or consume a larger measure of alcohol than the person had otherwise intended to buy or consume' (*Marketing Week*, 2005j).

Sports retailer JJB may not face the same restrictions, but it does similarly use sales promotion to encourage store traffic. Printed game cards were inserted into a football magazine that gave readers a unique number. They then had to visit a JJB store and enter their number into a keypad to see whether they had won a prize. For the lucky ones, it was redeemable through the JJB website (Gander, 2005).

The next area considered is direct marketing. Direct marketing is more than just 'junk mail'. It encompasses a wide range of commonly used techniques, not only direct mail but also telemarketing, direct response mechanisms, mail order and internet marketing. The chapter will look at each of those areas, although internet and new media issues will be covered in more detail later in Chapter 14.

Trade shows and exhibitions are also briefly considered, as a useful part of the B2B communications mix in particular. We examine their role and value to organisations, not least their ability to generate qualified sales leads and to reinforce the organisation's presence and image in the marketplace as a basis for future direct marketing campaigns.

Public relations (PR) is the area of marketing communications that specifically deals with the quality and nature of the relationship between an organisation and its publics, such as its financial backers, its employees and trades unions, its suppliers, the legal and regulatory bodies to which it is accountable, interested pressure groups, the media, and many other groups or 'publics' which have the ability to affect the way in which the organisation does business. Its prime concern is to generate a sound, effective and understandable flow of communication between the organisation and these groups so that shared understanding is possible. While publicity or press relations can make a significant contribution, PR utilises a much wider range of activities, which this chapter will cover.

The final sections of this chapter consider sponsorship and cause-related marketing (CRM). Sponsorship of sport, television programmes and the arts will be discussed in terms of the benefits gained by both parties. CRM is loosely related to sponsorship, in that part of its remit is looking at how corporate donors or sponsors can help charities or other non-profit organisations. It also covers PR and sales promotion activities that link companies with non-profit organisations and examines the benefits gained by all those involved.

It is not just commercial organisations that have embraced direct marketing in their promotional strategies. A number of cause-related organisations have also adopted direct marketing into their fund-raising strategies due to its contact effectiveness and relatively low cost compared with media advertising. Diabetes UK aims to improve the lives of people suffering from diabetes, some 1.8 million in the UK alone. It has 180,000 members and the target is 250,000 by 2007. The promotional strategy included some press advertising and direct mail aimed at potential givers along with point of contact material in pharmacies and health centres. Healthcare professionals were also targeted with messages concerning the needs of diabetes sufferers (*Precision Marketing*, 2005b).

Orbis is an international sight-saving charity and needs to raise funds to support its work in the developing world. Around 85 per cent of its funds come from individual donations. Its saving sight programmes include the DC-10 Flying Eye Hospital, a fully equipped, state-of-the-art eye surgery hospital and teaching facility that can travel to locations that need support. It decided to send direct mail to 110,000 households to raise its profile and to attract donors. The target was women aged over 55 and the mail shot featured the Flying Hospital. To reach the audience it also planned inserts in a range of religious and medical magazines whose readership profile matched the target group (*Precision Marketing*, 2005a).

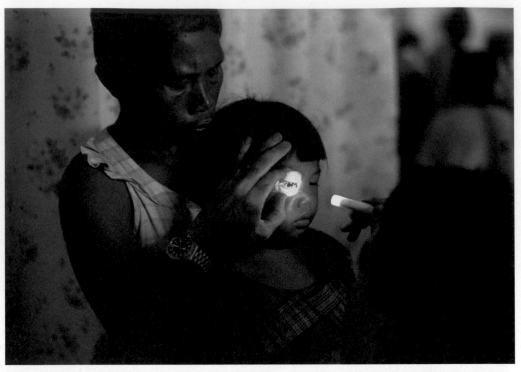

Helping people to be able to see the light again is the main aim of the charity ORBIS.

Source: ORBIS http://www.orbis.org.uk Photograph © Matt Shonfeld

Sales promotion

■ Definition and role

According to the Institute of Sales Promotion, sales promotion is:

> ... a range of tactical marketing techniques designed within a strategic marketing framework to add value to a product or service in order to achieve specific sales and marketing objectives.

The word 'tactical' implies a short, sharp burst of activity that is expected to be effective as soon as it is implemented. The fact that this activity is *designed within a strategic marketing framework* means, however, that it is not a panic measure, not just something to wheel out when you do not know what else to do. On the contrary, sales promotion should be planned into an integrated communications mix, to make the most of its ability to complement other areas such as advertising and its unique capacity to achieve certain objectives, mostly tactical but sometimes strategic (Davies, 1992).

The key element of this definition, however, is that the sales promotion should *add value to a product or service*. This is something over and above the normal product offering that might make buyers stop and think about whether to change their usual buying behaviour, or revise their buying criteria. This takes the form of something tangible that is of value to the buyer, whether it is extra product free, money, a gift or the opportunity to win a prize, that under normal circumstances they would not get.

Perhaps the main problem with the definition is that the area of sales promotion has almost developed beyond it. The idea of the short-term tactical shock to the market is very well established and understood, and will be seen to be at the heart of many of the specific techniques outlined in this chapter. With the development of relationship marketing, that is, the necessity for building long-term buyer–seller relationships, marketers have been looking for ways of developing the scope of traditional sales promotion to encourage long-term customer loyalty and repeat purchasing behaviour. Loyalty schemes, such as frequent flyer pro-grammes, are sales promotions in the sense that they offer added value over and above the normal product offering, but they are certainly not short-term tactical measures – quite the opposite. Wilmshurst (1993) clearly states that creatively designed sales promotions can be just as effective as advertising in affecting consumers' attitudes to brands. This means, per-haps, that the definition of sales promotion needs to be revised to account for those strategic, franchise-building promotional techniques:

> *... a range of marketing techniques designed within a strategic marketing framework to add extra value to a product or service over and above the 'normal' offering in order to achieve specific sales and marketing objectives. This extra value may be of a short-term tactical nature or it may be part of a longer-term franchise-building programme.*

Sales promotion objectives

Overview

Sales promotion objectives all fall into three broad categories: communication, incentive and invitation.

Sales promotion has a capacity to communicate with the buyer in ways that advertising would find hard to emulate. Advertising can tell people that a product is 'new, improved', or that it offers certain features and benefits, but this is conceptual information, which people may not fully understand or accept. Sales promotion can, for instance, put product samples into people's hands so that they can judge for themselves whether the claims are true. Learning by one's own experience is so much more powerful and convincing than taking the advertiser's word for it.

The incentive is usually the central pillar of a sales promotion campaign. The potential buyer has to be given encouragement to behave in certain ways, through an agreed bargain between seller and buyer: if you do this, then I will *reward* you with that.

eg
It may be easy to set up incentive schemes but it is much harder to remove them. Those collecting Eurotunnel loyalty points had a shock when it was decided to scrap the Points Plus Offers and Property Owners Club schemes at short notice, giving savers very little time to redeem any remaining points. Eurotunnel claimed that the withdrawal was part of a pricing overhaul to make crossings cheaper for a larger group than the 130,000 scheme participants. Some regular customers were, however, furious with the withdrawal: the canny ones estimated that it meant the loss of a free crossing for every six paid for and that the overall lower fares would not compensate for this. The risk Eurotunnel ran in withdrawing the incentive scheme was that it would encourage people to switch to low cost airlines or the cheaper ferry option (Chesshyre and Bryan-Brown, 2004).

Through its incentives, the promoted product is saying 'Buy ME, and buy me NOW'. The promotion is, therefore, an invitation to consider this product, to think about your buying decision, and to do it quickly. The ephemeral nature of most sales promotions reinforces the urgency of taking up the invitation immediately. It prevents the buyer from putting off trial of the product, because the 'extra something' will not be around for long. For the consumer, in particular, the point of sale represents the crucial decision-making time. A product that is jumping up and down, shouting 'Hey, look at me!' through its sales promotion is offering the clearest possible invitation to do business.

The rest of this section will focus further on the objectives that sales promotion can achieve within the context of the relationship within which they are used.

Manufacturer–intermediary (trade promotion)

The intermediary provides a vital service for the manufacturer in displaying goods to their best advantage and making them easily available to the consumer. In a competitive market, however, a manufacturer might wish to use sales promotion techniques to encourage the intermediary to take a particular interest in particular products for various purposes. Intermediaries might expect or insist on sales promotions before they will cooperate with what the manufacturer wants.

As shown in Figure 11.1, and discussed below, trade promotions revolve around gaining more product penetration, more display and more intermediary promotional effort. As Fill (2002) points out, however, this might cause conflict between the manufacturer and the intermediary, since the intermediary's prime objective is to increase store traffic. The level of incentive might thus have to be extremely attractive!

Figure 11.1 Manufacturer–intermediary sales promotion objectives

Increase stock levels. The more stock of a particular product that an intermediary holds, the more committed they will be to put effort into selling it quickly. Furthermore, intermediaries have limited stockholding space, so the more space that your product takes up, the less room there is for the competition. Money-based or extra-product-based incentives might encourage intermediaries to increase their orders, although the effect might be short-lived and in the longer term might even reduce orders as intermediaries work through the extra stock they acquired during the promotion.

Gain more and better shelf space. There is intense competition between manufacturers to secure shelf space within retail outlets. Demand for shelf space far outstrips supply. Intermediaries are, therefore, willing to accept incentives to help them to allocate this scarce resource to particular products or manufacturers. Again, this may link with money- or product-based trade promotions, but could also be part of a joint promotion agreement or a point-of-sale promotion, for instance. The quality of the shelf space acquired is also important. If a product is to capture the consumer's attention, then it needs to be prominent. This means that it must be displayed either at the customer's eye level or at the end of the aisles in a supermarket where the customer is turning the corner and all the trolley traffic jams occur. There is keen competition for these highly desirable display sites, also called *golden zones*, and again, intermediary-oriented sales promotion may help a manufacturer to make its case more strongly.

New product launch. The launch period is a delicate time in any new product's life, and if the distribution aspects of the marketing strategy are weak, then it could be fatal. A new product needs to be accepted by the appropriate intermediaries so that it is available for all those consumers eager to try it. To the trade, however, a new product is a potential risk. What if it doesn't sell? Trade promotions (particularly with a push strategy – see pp. 300 *et seq.*) can reduce some of that risk. Money-based promotions reduce the potential financial losses of a product failure, while 'sale or return' promotions remove the fear of being left with unsaleable stock. Sales force support, meanwhile, can reassure the intermediary that staff are ready, willing and able to sell the product and fully understand its features and benefits. This is particularly appropriate with more complex, infrequently purchased items, such as electrical goods.

Even out fluctuating sales. Some products, such as lawnmowers, ice-cream and holidays, suffer from seasonality. While the design of the product offering or the pricing policies adopted can help to overcome these problems, sales promotion can also play a part. If manufacturers are able to encourage intermediaries to take on more stock or to push the product harder during the 'quieter' periods, sales can be spread a little more evenly throughout the year. This process can also be enhanced by a related consumer-oriented promotion, so that the manufacturer is gaining extra synergy through simultaneous push and pull activity.

Counter the competition. It has already been indicated that a manufacturer is competing with every other manufacturer for an intermediary's attention. Sales promotions, therefore, make very useful tactical weapons to spoil or dilute the effects of a competitor's actions. If, for instance, you are aware that the competition is about to launch a new product, you might use a trade sales promotion to load up a key intermediary with your related products, so that at best they will be reluctant to take on the competition's goods, or at worst, they will drive a much harder bargain with the competitor.

Retailer–consumer (retailer promotions)

In the same way that manufacturers compete among themselves for the intermediary's attention, retailers compete for the consumer's patronage. Store-specific sales promotions, whether jointly prepared with a manufacturer or originating solely from the retailer, can help differentiate one store from another, and entice the public in. Retailers also try to use sales promotions in a longer-term strategic way to create store loyalty, for example through card schemes that allow the shopper to collect points over time that can be redeemed for gifts or money-off vouchers. Retailers use sales promotion for many reasons and these are summarised in Figure 11.2.

Increase store traffic. A prime objective for a retailer is to get the public in through the shop door. Any kind of retailer-specific sales promotion has a chance of doing that. Money-off coupons delivered from door to door or printed in the local newspaper, for example, might bring in people who do not usually shop in a particular store. Such promotions might also encourage retail substitution, giving shoppers an incentive to patronise one retailer rather than another. An electrical retailer might advertise a one-day sale with a few carefully chosen items offered on promotion at rock-bottom prices. This bait brings potential customers to the store, and even if the real bargains have gone early, they will still look at other goods.

Increase frequency and amount of purchases. Even if a customer already shops at one retailer's outlets, the retailer would prefer them to shop there more often and to spend more.

Short-term promotions are often used by retailers to increase store traffic. Supermarkets, for instance, often use price-based offers to draw shoppers into their stores. By advertising rock-bottom bargains on a selected number of big-name brands in the local press and through door-to-door leafleting within a store's catchment area, shoppers are tempted to pay a visit. The range of offers changes week by week, thus keeping the shopper's interest fresh. The hope is that the shopper will keep returning every week and that once in the store, they will buy far more than just a limited range of discounted brands.

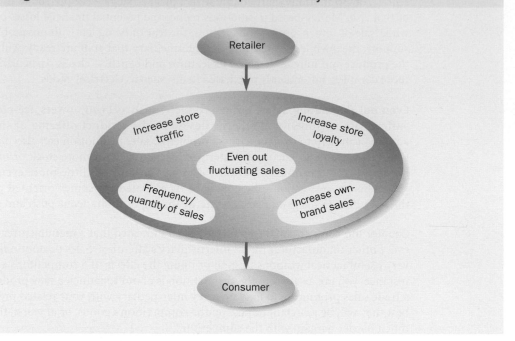

Figure 11.2 Retailer–consumer sales promotion objectives

Increase store loyalty. Supermarkets in particular use sales promotion as a means of generating store loyalty. The kinds of activities outlined in relation to increasing the frequency and amount of purchases help towards this, as does a rolling programme of couponing and money-off offers. The problem with this type of promotion, however, is that it risks creating a 'deal-prone' promiscuous customer who will switch to whichever retailer is currently offering the best package of short-term promotions. To counteract this, some retailers have introduced loyalty schemes using swipe cards.

eg   In the UK, Tesco was the first with its Clubcard, and Sainsbury's followed with its Reward card (which later became Nectar). Shoppers have an incentive to shop regularly at a particular retailer in order to accumulate points. Using the customer database, coupons and money-off vouchers can be regularly issued and delivered to the customer's own home, thus creating a stronger, more personal retailer–customer link.

Increase own-brand sales. Retailers are increasingly investing in their own-brand ranges. These are, therefore, legitimate subjects for a whole range of consumer-oriented promotions. These promotions do not have to be overtly price or product based.

eg   In-store free recipe cards can help to promote the store's fresh foods or own-label products by giving the shopper meal ideas and encouraging them to buy the ingredients. This can be linked with other promotions so that, for instance, one of the own-label ingredients could feature a price reduction to encourage purchase further. The magazines sent out with loyalty card statements and vouchers can also promote own-label goods, again through recipes, through editorial copy explaining how products can be used and their benefits, or through the more obvious mechanism of extra money-off vouchers.

Even out busy periods. In the same way that manufacturers face seasonal demand for some products, retailers have to cope with fluctuations between the very busy periods of the week or year, and the very quiet times. Offering sales promotions that apply only on certain days or within certain trading hours might divert some customers away from the busier periods.

eg A one-day sale on a Wednesday or Thursday can be a good way for a retailer to divert shoppers away from the busier weekend, especially if it is well advertised in the local area. One DIY retailer also instituted Wednesday afternoon discounts for senior citizens, presumably because that is an easily defined group who can change their shopping day because they are not likely to be working. Supermarkets in particular find the wide variation in the number of people shopping each day very difficult from the point of view of both making sure that there is adequate staff cover available and keeping the shelves full for shoppers. They are thus considering price-based promotion to reward those who shop at quieter times and penalise those who are 'cash rich, time poor'.

Manufacturer–consumer (manufacturer promotion)

While it is obviously important for manufacturers to have the distribution channels working in their favour, there is still much work to be done with the consumer to help ensure continued product success. After all, if consumer demand for a product is buoyant, that in itself acts as an incentive to the retail trade to stock it, effectively acting as a pull strategy. There are many reasons for manufacturers to use sales promotions to woo the consumer, and some of these are outlined below and summarised in Figure 11.3.

Encourage trial. The rationale in encouraging trial is similar to that discussed earlier in relation to the intermediary and new product launches. New products face the problem of being

Figure 11.3 Manufacturer–consumer sales promotion objectives

unknown, and therefore consumers may need incentives to encourage trial of the product. Samples help consumers to judge a product for themselves, while coupons, money off and gifts reduce the financial penalty of a 'wrong' purchase. Sales promotions thus play an important role in the early stages of a product's life.

Expand usage. Expanding usage involves using sales promotion to encourage people to find different ways of using more of the product so that, of course, they purchase more.

> **eg** Mayonnaise brand Hellmann's offered consumers a free recipe book when they purchased jars of its various mayonnaise products. The book, with twelve recipes, could be obtained by calling a telephone number on the label. The jars themselves carry special edition labels with pictures encouraging consumers to use Hellmann's in different ways (*Promotions and Incentives*, 2002). This promotion integrates well with the theme of Hellmann's television advertising which also shows imaginative ways of using the product with a broad range of different foods and meal occasions.

Disseminate information. Sales promotions can be used effectively as a means of getting information across to consumers. Even a small sample pack distributed door to door, for example, not only lets the consumer experience the product, but also gives the manufacturer a chance to tell that consumer quite a lot about the product's features and benefits, where to buy it, and related products in the range. While advertising can do the same sort of information dissemination, it is easily ignored. If the consumer is tempted to try the sample, then they may take more notice of the information with it, and only then pay attention to the advertising.

Attract new customers. An established product may be striving to acquire new customers, either by converting non-users or by turning irregular customers or brand switchers into regular buyers. Advertising can only go so far in creating a positive image of the product, and sales promotion may be necessary to generate that first trial, or that repeat purchase. The kind of promotion that depends on collecting tokens over time to qualify for a mail-in offer might be sufficient, if it is backed up with strong advertising, to set up regular purchasing habits and brand preference.

Trade up. There are two facets to trading up. One is getting the consumer to trade up to a bigger size, and the other is to get them to trade up to the more expensive products further up the range. Trading up to bigger sizes is particularly useful where the manufacturer feels that the customer is vulnerable to aggressive competition. The bigger size will last longer and, therefore, that consumer is going to be exposed less frequently to competitive temptation at the point of sale. Any promotional effort that applies only to the bigger size rather than the smaller one might achieve that kind of trade-up objective. Persuading consumers to trade up to a product higher up the range benefits the manufacturer because such products are likely to earn higher margins. Car dealers and manufacturers often try to do this. Again, using promotions that are specific to one model or product in the range, or using increasingly valuable and attractive promotions as the range goes up, can help to focus the customer's mind on higher things. Price-based promotions are probably not a good idea in this case, because of the risk of cheapening the product's image.

Load up. Loading up is partly a defensive mechanism to protect your customers from the efforts of the competition. A customer who is collecting tokens or labels towards a mail-in offer with a tight deadline, or who finds a cut-price offer particularly seductive, might end up with far greater quantities of the product than can be used immediately. Effectively, that customer is now out of the market until those stocks are used up. This is a two-edged sword: the advantage is that they are less likely to listen to the competition; the disadvantage is that you will not be selling them any more for a while either, as you have effectively brought your sales to that customer forward. Of course, if that customer was originally a brand switcher, or a non-user, then you have gained considerably from loading them up.

Even out fluctuating sales. Evening out fluctuating sales links with the comments made above in relation to manufacturer–intermediary sales promotions. If seasonality is a problem, then sales promotion aimed at the consumer could help to even out the peaks and troughs a little.

Counter the competition. Again, the concept of countering or spoiling competitors' activities was introduced in the discussion of manufacturer–intermediary sales promotions. Diverting the consumer's attention through your own promotion can dampen the effects of the competitors' efforts, particularly if what they are doing is not particularly creative in its own right. Also, a well-chosen, regionally based sales promotion can seriously distort or introduce an element of doubt into the results of a competitor's test marketing.

Within these main categories of sales promotion, there are a number of possible techniques for achieving defined objectives. The techniques in each area are not mutually exclusive; ideas can be drawn from any one area and applied in another. The techniques selected will not only depend on the objectives and target audience of the sales promotion campaign, but also be influenced by a range of factors. These typically are market characteristics, competitive levels and activities, promotional objectives and the relevance of each technique to the product and its cost profile. The following sections outline a number of sales promotion methods, classified by target audience.

■ Methods of sales promotion to consumers

Money-based

Money-based sales promotions are a very popular group of techniques used by manufacturers or intermediaries. Sometimes they work on a 'cash-back' basis (collect a certain number of tokens, then send away for a cash rebate), but more often they are immediate price reductions, implemented in various ways, designed as a short-term measure either to gain competitive advantage or to defend against competitive actions. Such price reductions must be seen to be temporary or else the consumer will not view them as incentives. Furthermore, if money-based methods are used too often, consumers will begin to think of the promotional price as being the real price. They will then think of the product as being cheaper than it really is, and adjust their perceptions of positioning and quality accordingly (Gupta and Cooper, 1992).

Coupons (printed vouchers that the consumer takes to a retail outlet and uses to claim a set amount of money off a product) are a form of money-based sales promotion that do not look like a price cut, mainly because the price quoted on the shelf or on the product remains intact. The coupon is also a little more selective than a straight price cut, in that only those who collect a coupon and remember to redeem it qualify for the discount. However, to counter that, coupons are very common, and consumers are overexposed to them. Unless a coupon carries a significant discount on the product, or applies to something intrinsically new and exciting, it is difficult as a consumer to be enthusiastic about them.

Coupons are distributed using a variety of means. They are printed within advertisements, on leaflets delivered from door to door, on inserts within magazines and newspapers, through direct mail, at the point of sale and on packs. The technology is also now available to allow retailers to issue coupons at the checkout, as an integral part of the bill issued to the customer.

For manufacturers, coupons act as a kind of pull strategy, creating an upturn in consumer demand for the product, thus encouraging retailers to stock and prominently display the brand. By telling them what is available and by reducing the financial risks of purchase, coupons can help the consumer get round to trying a product, making a subsequent purchase, or trading up, either to larger sizes or to products further up the range. The main problem for manufacturers is misredemption. Some supermarkets, overtly or covertly, will accept any coupon at the checkout, regardless of whether the consumer has actually bought the coupon's product or not. Preventing this from happening is difficult.

A big drawback of money-based sales promotions is that because they are so common among consumer goods, it is very difficult to raise much enthusiasm about them in the market. The main problem is the lack of creativity that usually accompanies these methods. It is also far too easy for a competitor to copy or match a money-based promotion, and thus any competitive advantage may be short lived.

It is also important to remember that money-based promotion can be an expensive way of putting money back in the pockets of people who would have bought the product anyway. If an organisation offers 10p off a product, then that costs the organisation 10p per unit sold in addition to the overhead costs of implementing the offer. In other words, in most cases money-based sales promotions cost the organisation their full cash value, unlike many of the merchandise offers, yet the long-term effect (especially if the technique is over-used) may be to cheapen the value of the product in the consumer's eyes (Jones, 1990).

In their favour, however, money-based promotions are relatively easy to implement, they can be developed and mobilised quickly, and they are readily understood by the consumer. They appeal to many consumers' basic instincts about saving money, and the value of 10p off a price, or £1 cash back, is easy for the consumer to assess. If the objective of the exercise is to attract price-sensitive brand switchers, or to make a quick and easy response to a competitor's recent or imminent actions, then this group of methods has a part to play.

eg The major supermarket chains are keen to give the impression that they offer better value for money than their competitors, and short-term reduced price promotions are one way of reinforcing this stance. All the major chains have their generic ranges at the bottom of the price range and occasionally these are used to make attention-grabbing price statements. Thus at various times shoppers have found washing-up liquid at 7p per bottle, tins of beans at 3p per can and other products selling at approximately 10 per cent of the price of their premium branded competitors. These are in addition to a day-to-day selection of less drastic short-term price cuts on other own-label and premium brands. The voluntary chains too need to develop their own price cutting strategies in order to compete with the major multiples. Spar, for instance, has its ongoing X-tra Value initiative which offers three weekly promotions covering all product categories within store (**http://www.spar.co.uk**).

Rebates apply not only to manufacturer products. Look back to pp. 371 *et seq.*, where retailer cash rebate schemes aimed at increasing the value and frequency of purchasing were discussed.

Product-based

One of the risks of money-based promotions that was constantly reiterated in the previous sub-section was the ease with which consumers could relate the promotion to price cutting, and thus the image of the product could, in their eyes, be cheapened. One way of overcoming that problem is to opt for a promotion centred on the product itself. The 'extra free' technique involves offers such as an own-label can of tomatoes with '20% extra free' or a pack of own-label kitchen roll offering three rolls for the price of two, proclaiming 'ONE ROLL EXTRA FREE'.

A money-based promotion might put 20p back in the consumer's hand; a product-based promotion might give them 20p's worth of extra product free. To the manufacturer, either option rewards the buyer with 20p, but the buyer's perceptions of the two are very different. 20p in the hand is 'giving something back', whereas extra product free is clearly 'giving something in addition' and, in the consumer's mind, might be valued at a good deal more than 20p. These product-based promotions, therefore, break the link between promotion and price. This method may be especially attractive as a response to a competitor's price attack, as it can shape the value image of a product without a direct price war.

In contrast to offering extra free product within a single package, the BIGIF (Buy 1 Get 1 Free) or the BOGOFF (Buy One Get One For Free) offers centre on bigger rewards, and are aimed primarily at loading up the customer. Effectively, the offer is saying '100% EXTRA FREE'. Retailers are increasingly using a variation on this method, based around bulk purchasing, making the offer, 'Buy two and get a third one free' (B2G3F? – it doesn't quite have the same ring as BOGOFF, does it?).

These offers may need shorter lead times than the 20 per cent extra free type, because they do not involve significant changes to the packaging. Two ordinary packs can be banded together away from the main production line if necessary. In the case of the retailers' B2G3F offers, no banding is needed at all. The offer is made through notices at the shelf, and the computerised checkout is programmed to make the discount automatically when the required number of items have been scanned through.

Bringing the product to consumers – wherever they are

Sampling is a powerful promotional tool: a survey showed that over 70 per cent of consumers believed that free samples received through door-to-door distribution were 'very useful', and even people who claim they do not like unaddressed mail still welcome samples, coupons and special offers. Using the sophisticated techniques offered by geodemographic profiling systems (see pp. 119 et seq.), it is now possible to target door-to-door sampling and other drops to specific households. As one agency put it, 'Client companies know exactly who they want to target from their databases and they only want to deliver their message to those people. All the tools are there. We now have the potential to understand every postcode in the country' (as quoted by Miller, 2001). Door-to-door specialists TNT post (Doordrop Media) Ltd launched Personal Placement in 2000, a door-to-door service that delivers targeted messages to selected households, i.e. it only delivers to households that match specified profiles. According to TNT post, 'We can deliver to specific households based on a range of criteria – everything from whether they own a cat or have a home computer or have children between the ages of five and 16'. This cuts out wastage and reduces the cost of a door-to-door sampling exercise. One client was a large ISP that wanted to distribute CD-ROMs to households with a PC. TNT Post was able to deliver to 500,000 computer-owning addresses. 'It is a precise and low-cost method of placing a

A bright idea for distributing light bulb samples.

Source: © TNT Post (Doordrop Media) Ltd

tangible item directly into the hands of this hard-to-reach, but very valuable, audience'.

Even with this precision, door-to-door sampling has to work hard to grab attention and to ensure safe delivery of the sample, however. When Philips wanted to tell consumers about its Softone light bulbs, it dropped a bag through the door with a brochure about the product and a money-off voucher. If the consumer was interested, they left the bag outside the door the next day after ticking a box to say which colour bulb they wanted, and the sample was left in the bag for them. This allowed the company to deliver a fragile object safely and allowed consumers to opt out of the sampling exercise if they wanted to, thus making it more cost-effective and better targeted.

Home is not the only place where marketers can offer samples to consumers. An airport delivers a captive audience, often with time to kill while waiting for a flight, often in a spending frame of mind, and often looking to airport stores for new experiences. Nestlé offered

samples of its Polo Supermints to travellers at Gatwick airport and then directed them to the shops where they were on sale. Similarly, samples of alcoholic drinks can be offered just a short distance away from the duty-free stores that sell those brands. World Duty Free offers drink, cosmetic and fragrance samples in both departure and arrivals areas at airports near to its retail stores. The company has found that sampling is much more effective than money-off vouchers or gifts in stimulating sales.

Ferry terminals and railway station concourses can also be good places to carry out a sampling exercise. Concourse Initiatives, a company that markets and manages concourse space, claims that rail commuters tend to be affluent ABC1s aged under 45, and that 70 per cent of them are primary grocery buyers, in broad terms an attractive target group for many manufacturers. Around 2.4 million people pass through London Liverpool Street station every week, and outside London, stations in Birmingham, Leeds and Glasgow can deliver 0.5 million passengers or more per week. Given that passengers have, on average, seven minutes of 'dwell time' to kill while waiting for trains, stations offer a wonderful sampling opportunity. For one client, a walk-in freezer was built on a concourse and 25,000 ice-cream samples per day handed out. Over three years, Häagen Dazs handed out over 1 million samples in this way. Similarly, samples of draught Guinness have been handed out on a concourse, with a follow-up leaflet giving the consumer money off a Guinness four-pack as well as the opportunity to phone in for a free

Guinness glass. Interestingly, alcohol sampling is allowed in small measures on concourses but the drink cannot be handed out in bottles or in large quantities. It cannot be given to station staff or consumers aged under 18 and a security guard must be present at all times.

For many manufacturers, the numbers of consumers that concourses deliver are attractive, but there are potential problems. First, size isn't everything. It might be a large audience, but it is a broad one and it is difficult to identify and select a more specific sub-group out of it. Second, consumers on concourses, especially commuters, are often rushing to be somewhere else and, unless they have time to kill waiting for a train, are not likely to be receptive to messages, especially if they are stressed. Nevertheless, leaflets can be handed out quickly for consumers to look at later (on the train?), and incorporating competitions on them is a good way of generating responses and thus leads.

Sources: Fletcher (1999); Gray (1999); McLuhan (2000); Miller (2001); Wilson (2001); http://www.initgroup.com.

A variation on the 'free product' technique is sampling, used where the main objective is to persuade people to try a product. People can experience the product for themselves at little or no financial risk and decide on their own evidence whether to adopt the product and buy the full-sized pack or not. Samples are thus popular and effective. Seventy per cent of households claim to use the free samples that come through the letterbox. The added bonus, particularly with those samples distributed away from the point of sale, is that the sample's packaging can teach the consumer about the product's benefits, and through graphics that relate directly to the full-sized pack, aid brand recognition in the store.

eg Trojan adopted a somewhat more innovative stand when it decided to distribute more than 30,000 samples of its product in the back of taxis in Brighton. It was the first time that condoms had been distributed in that way. To avoid unnecessary embarrassment for the 'untargeted', however, the sampling was restricted to Thursday, Friday and Saturday nights after 10.30 p.m. to reach men and women coming out of nightclubs, pubs and bars. The condom was only available for those who asked and was available at the driver's discretion (*Marketing Week*, 2005d).

Gift, prize, or merchandise-based

A wide range of activities depend on the offer of prizes, low-cost goods or free gifts to stimulate the consumer's buying behaviour. Holidays, brand-related cookery books, mugs or clothing featuring product logos and small plastic novelty toys are among the vast range of incentives used to complement the main product sale.

eg Some care has to be taken with the type of free gifts offered. *Pokémon World* targets 10-year-old children. It was heavily criticised when it gave away a life-size plastic imitation kitchen knife complete with fake blood. It was originally targeted for Halloween as a 'trick or treat' accessory, but the magazine did not hit the shelves until a week later. The criticism and public reaction was a source of considerable embarrassment to *Pokémon World* (Hornby, 2005).

Gifts or merchandise. Self-liquidating offers invite the consumer to pay a small amount of money, and usually to submit specified proofs of purchase, in return for goods that are not necessarily directly related to the main product purchase. The money paid is usually just enough to cover the cost price of the goods and a contribution to postage and handling, and thus these promotions become self-financing if the expected number of customers take them up. Often, such a promotion is used to reinforce the brand name and identity of the products featuring the scheme.

eg A link-up between Disney and Britvic showed good synergy between the partners in the promotion, the premium offered and the target market. A promotion featured on bottles of Robinson's fruit juice concentrates offered a *Monsters, Inc.* alarm clock with a detachable cuddly Sully character. The twelve-week promotion was timed to coincide with the build-up to the release of the film in February 2002 and the period immediately after its release. To get the clock, consumers had to send in four bottle caps and £6.99. The number of caps required gives at least short-term brand loyalty, while the £6.99 covers the basic costs of providing the clock and administering the offer. The tie-in with the film ensures extra consumer excitement about the promotion as it benefits from synergy with the film's own marketing efforts. As well as featuring prominently on the packs, the promotion was supported with a £2m advertising campaign on children's television and in the press (*The Grocer*, 2002b). In the first month of the campaign the brand achieved its highest ever four-weekly volume share of 49 per cent, and highest ever household penetration of 54 per cent (Derrick, 2002).

In the case of a free mail-in, the consumer can claim a gift, free of charge, in return for proofs of purchase and perhaps the actual cost of postage (but not handling charges or the cost of the gift itself). The free goods attract the consumer and encourage a higher response rate, and the responses potentially provide the organisation with direct marketing opportunities. Of course, the promotion is only free to the consumer. The promoter has to consider carefully the merchandise costs, postage, packing, processing and even VAT. All of this has to be put into the context of the likely response rate, so that the total cost of the promotion can be forecast and an appropriate quantity of merchandise can be ordered and available when the promotion begins.

Offering free gifts contained inside or banded on to the outside of the pack can make a big impact at the point of sale because the reward is instant, and the purchaser does not have to make any special effort to claim it. One-off gifts are designed to bring the consumer's attention to a product and to encourage them to try it. The offer might shake them out of a routine response purchase and make them think about trying a different brand.

eg Kellogg's teamed up with Cartoon Network character Scooby-Doo for an in-pack promotion designed to build repeat buying with kids for its Rice Krispies and Coco Pops brands. A free DVD featuring two episodes and two games featured on each pack, and four different DVDs were available. The promotion was also linked with reduced membership fees for the Scooby-Doo club. This promotion thus offered the immediate incentive of a free gift featured prominently on the pack, but also had the link with collecting the whole set to ensure that the kids kept pestering mum to carry on buying those brands while the promotion was available. Kellogg's has for many years used links with children's favourite characters to promote some of its cereal brands.

'Free with product' is similar to an on-pack offer, except that the gift is not attached to the product but has to be claimed at the checkout. The consumer, for example, might be invited at the point of sale to buy a jar of coffee and claim a free packet of biscuits. The computerised checkout can tell whether the conditions of the promotion have been met and automatically deducts the price of the biscuits from the final total.

Customer loyalty schemes. Given the increasingly high cost of creating new customers, organisations have turned their attention to ways of retaining the loyalty of current customers. Major international airlines have their frequent flyer schemes, many different retail and service organisations give away air miles with purchases, and petrol stations and supermarkets issue swipe cards through which customers can accumulate points as mentioned earlier. All of these schemes are designed to encourage repeat buying, especially where switching is easy and generic brand loyalty is low.

Price promotions can be dangerous in that they encourage consumers to become price sensitive, and are easily copied by competitors. Tokens, points and stamps that can be traded in for other goods are all ways of adding value to a product, while avoiding costly price competition. They are thus known as alternative currencies.

One of the problems with loyalty schemes, however, is the sheer number of them. When every airline has a frequent flyer scheme and when every supermarket has a loyalty club, then the competitive edge is lost. Furthermore, there is evidence that the loyalty generated by such schemes is questionable, as will be seen in Case Study 11 (see pp. 408–10). Nevertheless, loyalty schemes are fast becoming an established part of the marketing scene.

> **eg** Over 86 per cent of consumers belong to at least one loyalty scheme. Schemes based on coupons and vouchers had tended to be regarded as downmarket compared with the plastic swipe card-based schemes such as those operated by Tesco and BA (Case Study 11). Coupons and vouchers had become associated with penny-pinching consumers who could be bothered to save scrappy bits of paper to get a few pennies off their next purchase! Through being linked with other loyalty schemes, however, coupons have regained some popularity in recent years. The modern coupon user is just as likely to be a young, urban, car-driving male as a 60-plus grandmother (*Marketing Week*, 2005c). High street retailers such as Boots, Tesco and a number of department stores have realised the strategic importance of having a mixed portfolio of coupons, vouchers and electronic points schemes built around their store loyalty cards. They all help lock the consumer into the brand and create another barrier to competition.

Contests and sweepstakes. Gifts given free to all purchasers of a product necessarily are limited to relatively cheap and cheerful items. Contests and sweepstakes, therefore, allow organisations to offer very attractive and valuable incentives, such as cars, holidays and large amounts of cash, to very small numbers of purchasers who happen to be lucky enough to win. Such promotions might be seen as rather boring by consumers, unless there is something really special about them.

Contests

Contests have to involve a demonstration of knowledge, or of analytical or creative skills, to produce a winner. Setting a number of multiple-choice questions, or requiring the competitor to uncover three matching symbols on a scratch card, or asking them to create a slogan, are all legitimate contest activities.

> **eg** 'Get there before the moles do' was the advertising slogan used by petrol company Texaco to support its Treasure Hunt sales promotion. The company buried five Mercedes SLK convertibles in secret locations across the UK, then gave out clues to their locations on cards given away with petrol purchases. Each site was marked with a Texaco hub cap under which was a spade, instructions and a flag. A hotline was also set up so that treasure hunters could check that they had indeed found the right site before they put in any digging effort. One vehicle was dug up in Kelso, Scotland, but the three people who found it said that they wouldn't be able to drive it because they couldn't afford the insurance! Around 3.6 million people took part in the hunt and 400,000 people called the hotline. The promotion was supported by broadcast, print, POS and poster advertising, and the PR coverage generated was estimated to be worth £3m (Brabbs, 2000; *Daily Record*, 2000; Middleton, 2002).

Sweepstakes do not involve skill, but offer every entrant an equal chance of winning through the luck of the draw. Additionally, they must ensure that entry is open to anyone, regardless of whether they have purchased a product or not. Thus *Reader's Digest* prize draws have to be equally open to those not taking up the organisation's kind offer of a subscription.

Such activities are popular with both consumers and organisations. The consumer gets the chance to win something really worthwhile, and the organisation can hope to generate many

Texaco customers were teased with clues as to the location of a buried car when they bought fuel. Large numbers were encouraged to choose Texaco for their next refuel in the hope of a further clue.

Source: © Texaco HACL & Partners

extra sales for a fixed outlay. With price or gift-based promotions, the more you sell, the more successful the promotion, the more it costs you because you have to pay out on every sale. With competitions and sweepstakes, the more successful the activity, the more entries it attracts, yet the prizes remain fixed. The only losers with a popular contest or sweepstake are the consumers, whose chances of winning become slimmer! However, at some stage consumers may become bored with such activities, especially if they do not think they have any reasonable chance of winning. At that point, a more immediate but less valuable incentive might be more appropriate.

 Müllerlight wanted to drive sales and maintain its market share. Market research indicated that typical consumers saw a connection between the values and brand statement

If you want to be young, fit and sexy like Bridget Jones, then eating Müllerlight yoghurt may help you to get your man.

Source: © Müllerlight, Müller Dairy UK Ltd (left); © Laurie Sparham/Universal Studies/Bures L.A. Collections/Corbis (right)

of the yoghurt brand and the Bridget Jones character. When the 'Edge of Reason' film was released, Müllerlight launched a large on-pack promotion offering 11,000 prizes on more than 70 million pots of Müllerlight yoghurt and 3.4 million packs of Müllerlight yogurt drink. Consumers were invited to have a Bridget Jones moment using a text and win competition. If they texted in the sell-by date on the pack, they would receive by return a Bridget Jones-style problem to solve. The instant-win prizes on the returned answers included luxury holidays to Thailand, champagne, boxes of chocolates and cinema tickets. For the unsuccessful, humorous messages were received telling them to try again to maintain repeat entries and a momentum for the campaign. The campaign generated 200,000 entries of which almost one-third were repeat entries, suggesting that brand loyalty had indeed been assisted by the scheme (*Promotions and Incentives*, 2005).

Store-based

This section looks more generally at what can be done within a retail outlet to stimulate consumer interest in products, leading perhaps to trial or purchase.

Sales promotion at the point of sale (POS) is critical in situations where the customer enters the store undecided or is prepared to switch brands fairly readily. Many different POS materials and methods can be used. These include posters, displays, dispensers, dump bins and other containers to display products. New technology has further changed POS promotion with flashing signs, videos, message screens and other such attention-seeking display material. Interactive POS systems can help customers to select the most appropriate offering for their needs, or can direct them to other promotional offers.

In-store demonstrations are a very powerful means of gaining interest and trial. Food product cooking demonstrations and tasters are used by retailer and manufacturer alike, especially if the product is a little unusual and would benefit from exposure (i.e. new cheeses, meats, drinks, etc.). Other demonstrations include cosmetic preparation and application, electrical appliances, especially if they are new and unusual, and cars. These demonstrations may take place within the retail environment, but the growth of shopping centre display areas provides a more flexible means for direct selling via a demonstration.

eg The challenges of promoting SPAM in the UK don't come much tougher. Many consumers are aware of the product, but a combination of the famous Monty Python SPAM sketch and SPAM's role in school dinners has created generations of consumers who feel they don't like it but have never actually tried it! The challenge fell to 12i Face to Face Marketing to organise a SPAM roadshow visiting 65 Sainsbury's, Tesco, ASDA and Somerfield stores in the Midlands and North of England, offering hot and cold SPAM samples in store. Incredibly, sales of SPAM increased significantly in the participating stores. By using field marketing, consumers were exposed to the taste and to serving variations all designed to tackle the stereotype. Lipton Ice Tea has a similar problem convincing British shoppers that ice tea is a tasty and refreshing drink rather than nasty cold tea. It remains to be seen whether in-store sampling will convince them otherwise (*Marketing Week*, 2005i).

■ Methods of promotion to the retail trade

Manufacturers of consumer goods are dependent on the retail trade to sell their product for them. Just as consumers sometimes need that extra incentive to try a product or to become committed to it, retailers too need encouragement to push a particular product into the distribution system and to facilitate its movement to the customer. Of course, many of the consumer-oriented activities considered in previous sections help that process through pull strategies. Some trade promotions are tightly linked with consumer promotions to create a synergy between push and pull strategies. The main push promotions are variations on price promotions and direct assistance with selling to the final customer. These will now be looked at in turn.

Allowances and discounts

Allowances and discounts aim to maintain or increase the volume of stock moving through the channel of distribution. The first priority is to get the stock into the retailer, and then to influence ordering patterns by the offer of a price advantage. All of the offers discussed here encourage retailers to increase the amount of stock held over a period, and thus might also encourage them to sell the product more aggressively. This may be especially important where there is severe competition between manufacturers' brands.

Retailers can thus be offered discounts on each case ordered or a bulk discount if they fulfil a condition relating to volume purchased. A version of BOGOFF (for example, buy ten cases and get another two free) is also commonly used. A more complex technique is the discount overrider, a longer-term, retrospective discount, awarded on a quarterly or annual basis, depending on the achievement of agreed volumes or sales targets. These may be applicable to an industrial distributor selling components as a retail outlet. Although the additional discount may be low, perhaps 0.5 per cent, on a turnover of £500,000 this would still be an attractive £2500.

Count and recount is also a retrospective method in that it offers a rebate for each case (or whatever the stock unit is) sold during a specified period. Thus on the first day of the period, all existing stock is counted and any inward shipments received during the period are added to that total. At the end of the period, all remaining unsold cases are deducted. The difference represents the amount of stock actually shifted, forming the basis on which a rebate is paid.

> **eg**
>
> Bendicks offered a free merchandise promotion to smaller retailers through special cases bought from selected wholesalers and cash and carries. The cases contained rolls of Werther's Original and Campino sweets and offered 120 rolls for the price of 98. The 22 free rolls, the equivalent of a 20 per cent discount on the price of the merchandise, were worth £6.60 at the recommended retail price, thus giving the retailer £6.60 extra profit. In addition, the case converted to a display unit to be put on the store's counter. The retailer had the choice of offering a further consumer-oriented promotion of 'buy any two for 49p' to encourage brisk sales, or could sell the rolls at the usual price of 30p each (*The Grocer*, 2002a).

Price-based promotions aimed at the trade are less risky than those aimed at consumers, as the organisational buyer will view them as legitimate competitive tactics rather than using them judgementally to make emotive evaluations of the product. Price promotions appeal to the trade because they make a direct and measurable impact on the retailer's cost structure, and the retailer has the flexibility to choose whether to keep those cost savings or to pass them on to the end consumer. However, in common with price promotions offered to the consumer, trade-oriented price promotions do have the disadvantage of being quickly and easily copied by the competition, leading to the risk of mutually destructive price wars.

Selling and marketing assistance

A number of manufacturer-supported sales and marketing activities assist the re-seller by means of promotion at both local and national level.

In cooperative advertising a manufacturer agrees to fund a percentage of a retailer's local advertising, as long as the manufacturer's products are featured in at least part of the advertisement. Cooperative advertising support can be very costly, and thus the manufacturer needs to think very carefully before offering it, as it can potentially put far greater pressure on the manufacturer's own promotional budget than some of the methods previously discussed.

Although in theory manufacturer support may result in better advertising, attempts by re-sellers to crowd a print advertisement with products, often with price promotions, tend to undermine the position and value of some goods – fmcg brands in particular. Rather than leaving the control of the advertisement in the hands of an individual re-seller, therefore, some manufacturers prefer to develop dealer listings. These are advertisements, controlled by the manufacturer, which feature the product and then list those re-sellers from whom it can be purchased. These are particularly common with cars, higher value household appliances, and top of the range designer clothing, for example.

Using money to provide merchandising allowances rather than for funding advertising may have a more direct benefit to the manufacturer. Payment is made to the retailer for special promotional efforts in terms of displays and in-store promotions such as sampling or demonstrations. This is especially attractive if the product moves quickly and can sustain additional promotional costs.

A manufacturer may wish to offer training or support for a retailer's sales representatives who deal directly with the public. Such assistance is most likely to be found in connection with higher-priced products of some complexity, for which the purchaser needs considerable assistance at the point of sale. Cars, hi-fi equipment and bigger kitchen appliances are obvious examples of products with substantial technical qualities that need to be explained.

Various prizes, such as cash, goods or holidays, may be used in sales contests to raise the profile of a product and create a short-term incentive. Unfortunately, the prizes often need to be significant and clearly within the reach of all sales assistants if they are to make any real difference to the selling effort. This is especially true when other competitors may adopt similar methods.

Other more direct incentives than those already mentioned are also possible. Additional bonuses, i.e. premium money, may be made available to sales assistants who achieve targets. These are useful where personal selling effort may make all the difference to whether or not a sale is made. However, the manufacturer needs to be sure that the cost is outweighed by the additional sales revenues generated.

■ Sales promotion to B2B markets

As the introduction to this chapter made clear, sales promotion in its strictest sense is inappropriate to many B2B markets. Discounts and incentives are applicable in situations where the buyer and seller are in direct contact and there is room for negotiation of supply conditions. Of course, where B2B marketing starts to resemble consumer marketing, for example in the case of a small business buying a range of standard supplies from a wholesaler, much of what has already been said about manufacturer–consumer or retailer–consumer sales promotions applies with a little adaptation.

Direct marketing

There are a number of reasons for the rapid growth of direct marketing, connected with the changing nature of the customer, the marketing environment and, in particular, technological development. Direct marketing is being used increasingly across a wide range of both consumer and B2B markets. Even in the relatively conservative financial services industry, there has been a marked increase in direct selling and direct marketing of a wide range of banking facilities and insurance. The next section of the chapter, therefore, looks more closely at what direct marketing is and how it is being used as an element of integrated marketing communications.

■ Definition, role, aims and use

The US Direct Marketing Association has defined direct marketing as:

An interactive system of marketing which uses one or more advertising media to effect a measurable response at any location.

This is quite a broad definition which does, however, capture some basic characteristics of direct marketing. Interactive implies two-way communication between buyer and seller, while *effect a measurable response* implies quantifiable objectives for the exercise. *At any location* implies the flexibility and pervasiveness of direct marketing, in that it is not inextricably linked with any one medium of communication, but can utilise anything (mail, phone, broadcast or print media) to reach anyone anywhere. What this definition does not do, however, is to emphasise the potential of direct marketing as a primary means of building and sustaining long-term buyer–seller relationships.

It is, therefore, proposed to extend this definition to form the basis of the content of the rest of this section:

> *An interactive system of marketing which uses one or more advertising media to effect a measurable response at any location, forming a basis for creating and further developing an ongoing direct relationship between an organisation and its customers.*

The key added value of this definition is the phrase *ongoing direct relationship*, which implies continuity and seems to contradict the impersonal approach traditionally offered by mass media advertising. Is it really possible to use mass media in a mass market to create a relationship with a single customer? Is it really possible to capitalise on the advantages of personal selling that arise from one-to-one dialogue to build and sustain that relationship without the need for face-to-face contact?

If the answer to those two questions is to be 'yes', then the problem becomes one of information gathering and management. To create and sustain *quality* relationships with hundreds, thousands or even millions of individual customers, an organisation needs to know as much as possible about each one, and needs to be able to access, manipulate and analyse that information. The database, therefore, is crucial to the process of building the relationship. We will look in some detail at the issues of creating, maintaining and exploiting the database at pp. 392 *et seq.*

Objectives

There are a number of tasks that direct marketing can perform, depending on whether it is used for direct selling or supporting product promotion. The tasks may be related to ongoing transactions and relationships with customers. At its most basic, therefore, direct marketing can fulfil the following objectives.

Direct ordering. Direct marketing aims to enable direct ordering, whether by telephone, by mail or, increasingly, by direct computer linkage. The use of credit cards, passwords and specific account numbers makes this possible. All kinds of direct marketing techniques can be used to achieve this, but the example of online ordering of CDs, mentioned earlier, is particularly interesting because sellers can both take the order and deliver the product immediately.

Information giving. Direct marketing aims to open a channel of communication to enable potential customers to ask for further information. Information may be given verbally by a salesperson, or through printed literature.

Visit generation. Direct marketing aims to invite a potential customer to call in and visit a store, show or event with or without prior notification. Nissan, for example, used direct mail-shots targeted at fleet buyers to encourage them to visit the Nissan stand at the UK Motor Show.

Trial generation. Direct marketing aims to enable a potential customer to request a demonstration or product trial in the home, office or factory.

Loyalty creation. Direct marketing offers organisations the opportunity to create loyal customers. If customers have entered into dialogue with an organisation, and have had their needs and wants met through a series of tailored offerings, then it is going to be quite difficult for the competition to poach those customers. Furthermore, using techniques such as direct mail, an organisation can communicate at length and in depth with its customers personally and privately (certainly when compared with advertising).

How and when to use direct marketing

Initiation. An important decision in direct marketing is how best to use it at various stages of the relationship with the customer. The earliest stage, *initiation*, can be very difficult, as it involves creating the initial contact and making the first sale. A combination of appealing advertising and sales promotion techniques may be used, for example, to overcome the potential customer's initial apprehension and risk aversion. Thus in its introductory offer, a book club may reduce the customer's perceived risk through drastic price reductions on the first order (any four books for 99p each), and further specifying a period within which the books may be returned and membership cancelled without obligation. Alternatively, a sale on credit or even a free trial may ease the customer's initial fears, despite the high administration costs. Any of these methods makes it easier for customers to part with their cash on the first order, thus opening the opportunity for a longer-term relationship.

Relationship building. Most direct marketing is in fact aimed at the *relationship stage* customer. This is when the seller has started to build a buying profile, supported by more widely available non-purchase specific data. This enables a steady flow of offers to be made, whether by telephone, mailshot or catalogue update. Customers are also likely to be more responsive at this stage, as they have established confidence in product quality and service performance.

Combination selling. Finally, combination selling results from using contacts gained from one medium, such as a trade exhibition, for regular contact by direct marketing means. This could be the mailing of special offers, price lists, catalogues or telephone calls to gain a face-to-face meeting, etc. The direct marketing activity is therefore used in combination with other methods.

The discussion so far has talked generally about the concept of direct marketing, with passing reference to specific areas such as direct mail and direct response, among others. The next section looks more closely at each of these areas and their individual characteristics. Figure 11.4 gives an overview of the range of direct marketing areas.

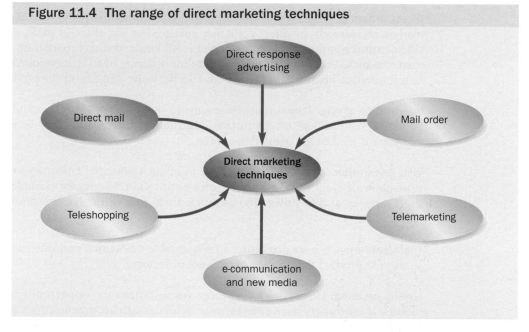

Figure 11.4 The range of direct marketing techniques

■ Techniques

The scope of direct marketing is very wide. It utilises what might be called the more traditional means of marketing communication, such as print and broadcast advertising media, but it has also developed its own media, through mail, telecommunications and modem. Each of the main techniques in direct marketing will now be considered in turn.

Direct mail

Direct mail is material distributed through the postal service to the recipients' home or business address to promote a product or service. What is mailed can vary from a simple letter introducing a company or product through to a comprehensive catalogue or sample. Many mailshots incorporate involvement devices to increase the chances of their being opened and read, through stimulating curiosity.

Most direct mail is unsolicited. Organisations compile or buy lists of names and addresses, and then send out the mailshot. The mailing list used may be cold, that is, where there has been no previous contact between the organisation and the addressee, or may reflect various selection criteria based on data held about previous or existing customers.

Direct mail has the problem that it has suffered from bad PR. All of us as consumers can probably think of a couple of examples of direct mail we have received that have been completely inappropriate, and misconceptions about direct mail's effectiveness are often based on such personal experiences of receiving 'junk'. Historically, this has arisen partly from the lack of flexibility and detail within databases, and partly from poor marketing thinking. Increasingly, though, marketers are using the information at their disposal more intelligently, and mailing smaller groups of well-defined prospective customers, using better-designed creative material. They are also keeping their databases more current, and so a household should not receive direct mail addressed to people who moved away or died over a year ago. In theory, then, an individual should be receiving less direct mail, but what they do receive should be of prime relevance and interest.

Although the information in Table 11.1 is heartening, it may not be enough. Think about the hierarchy of effects models shown in Figure 9.5, and how direct mail fits into those. Using the AIDA model as an example, opening the envelope begins the *awareness* stage, reading the content generates *interest* and *desire* and, finally, the mailshot clearly defines what subsequent *action* is expected. The main objective is to move the recipient quickly through all the stages from awareness to action. The key is not simply the opening of the envelope, but whether the content can pull the reader right through to the completion of action. As a consolation prize, if the recipient reads the content but chooses not to respond, there may still be an awareness or interest effect that may 'soften up' the customer for subsequent mailings or, in B2B markets, a sales visit.

Table 11.1 Some facts about direct mail in the UK

1 The average UK household receives 13.9 items of direct mail every four weeks (about 20.8 for the AB socioeconomic group).

2 Business managers are sent an average of 13 direct mail items per week.

3 5418 million items of direct mail were sent out in 2004.

4 Direct mail expenditure increased by 118 per cent between 1994 and 2004.

5 In 2004, nearly £2469m was spent on direct mail advertising.

6 On average, 60 per cent of B2C direct mail is opened and 40 per cent opened and read. 13 per cent is kept to be read later or passed on to someone else.

7 B2C direct mail generates nearly £27bn of business each year of which £11bn is spent on clothes, £2.8bn on books and £1.8bn on electrical goods.

8 The average consumer spent about £590 through direct mail in 2004.

9 Business managers open 70 per cent of their direct mail, 9 per cent is redirected to a colleague and 20 per cent is filed or responded to.

10 On average, business managers spent £8476 in response to direct mail.

Source: adapted from **http://www.dmis.co.uk**, Direct Mail Information Service (DMIS).

Plain brown envelope, please

The sex industry has a particular problem when developing mailing lists as few people want unsolicited approaches for exotic sex aids! Any mailing list has to be sound and discreet. Adult catalogue operations can even have trouble in distribution, such as the time when a German sex shop chain Beate Uhse had the doordrop of its catalogue refused by UK postal workers in the Midlands even though great care was taken in the development of the mailing list. On a previous occasion, it ran into trouble when it delivered a catalogue mistakenly to a four-year-old girl in Lincolnshire. The list contains 130,000 people of whom 25–35 per cent are women. The envelopes are labelled 'for over 18s only' and carry a message 'please do not open if you are easily offended'.

Subscribers to men's magazines such as *Maxim, Loaded* and *Premier* provide a useful list of potential targets for adult products, especially if the subscriber buys items by mail order off the page. Mail order video buyers and users of X-rated chat-lines are a further source, and so through a combination of methods a database can be built of people who may be generally reluctant to register their details. Adult Contacts has a list of potential customers and is often approached by companies wanting to rent the list to market lifestyle products as well as those selling adult-related products. It can, however, be difficult to convince list buyers that those on it are interested in anything other than adult products!

Some companies, such as Ann Summers, avoid direct marketing unless it is highly targeted and is related to previous customers. They do not want to damage the brand by sending unwanted material to poorly defined target customers, thus causing offence. Ann Summers ran a six-page insert in *Cosmopolitan* featuring lingerie to emphasise that it offered more than sex toys. Both the copy and images in the supplement were toned down so as not to offend. Using the responses to this feature, Ann Summers could further strengthen its database of interested customers. The company does, however, have a strong policy of never selling its customer lists to third parties and allowing customers to opt out at any time.

A final group of companies prefers not to use direct marketing at all. Durex does not want to cause offence and thinks that databases can be unreliable. It does not want to promote the virtues of condoms to badly targeted customers. Rather than expose its products to unwanted audiences, therefore, as in the case quoted above of the Lincolnshire girl, Durex considers that it is better to avoid the risk of doing significant damage to the brand altogether.

Source: Precision Marketing (2004).

Direct response advertising

Direct response advertising appears in the standard broadcast and print media. It differs from 'normal' advertising because it is designed to generate a direct response, whether an order, an enquiry for further information or a personal visit. The response mechanism may be a coupon to cut out in a print advertisement, or a phone number in any type of advertisement. This area has grown in popularity in recent years as advertisers seek to get their increasingly expensive advertising to work harder for them.

eg Slendertone UK became the market leader in the body-toning market within three years of its launch and much of this was attributed to its successful use of direct response media. Market share grew from 6 to 49 per cent. While sales went up sixteenfold, the cost per sale reduced by 40 per cent in just two years. How do they do it? After building a profile of target customers, the company is able to match it with the reader and viewer profiles of different media. The full range of direct response media are used, including television, press and radio as well as direct mail, catalogues and point-of-sale materials in selected retail outlets. Over 40 titles are used and each is tracked for the number and nature of responses. The campaigns are well integrated with the emphasis on creating impact. Potentially the world's largest bottom is featured on a billboard advertisement with the headline 'Does my bum look big on this?' at the junction of Oxford Street and Tottenham Court Road to announce the launch of the Slendertone Flex Bottom and Thigh System. Worth a trip to London to see it? (**http://www.slendertone.com**).

By using an eye-catching large bottom and making the viewer think of the common question 'Does my bum look big in this?', Slendertone managed to attract the attention of passers-by.

Source: © Slendertone from Bio-Medical Research Ltd

There is a range of types of direct response mechanisms that can be used in advertising. Advertisers can provide an address to write to, a coupon to fill in and send off for more information, telephone numbers or website addresses. Either the advertiser or the customer can pay for any postal or telephone charges. The ones who expect the consumer to pay for a phone call or postage, or who expect the consumer to compose a letter rather than filling in a coupon, are immediately putting up barriers to response. Why should consumers make any undue effort, or even pay directly, to give an organisation the privilege of trying to sell them something? In the light of that view, organisations either need to have incredibly compelling direct response advertising that makes any effort or cost worthwhile or, more realistically, they need to minimise the effort and cost to the potential customer. Schofield (1994) confirms that certainly in B2B markets, response should be as easy as possible. The easier the response, the greater the number of enquiries and the greater the conversion rate and revenue per enquiry.

eg Lunn Poly, the UK's largest travel agent, decided to launch its own television channel with a target of selling 100,000 new holidays a year. Screened for 18 hours a day and produced by the Travel Channel, all the TUI UK group's holidays are offered on the channel including Thomson Cruises and short breaks. Direct response can be via the telephone, the interactive button on the television, the internet or a good old-fashioned visit to one of the High Street shops, thus offering a multi-channel approach (Grimshaw, 2004). In the Netherlands, however, direct response television advertising has a poor reputation due to the dominance of cheap loan companies using it to encourage debt consolidation services. Of the total personal debt in the Netherlands, around one half is incurred through companies advertising by DRTV (*Precision Marketing*, 2003).

McAlevey (2001) identified a number of principles to follow to enable more effective direct response. Although generated in a North American cultural context, a number of them are relevant to European DR users seeking greater impact and higher response rates. The principles are as follows:

- The focus should always be on what sells.
- Don't always reinvent the wheel when designing campaigns.
- Make the 'offer' the central theme of the creative execution.
- Long copy can sell if the reader is engaged.
- Select creativity that sells, not that which just looks good.
- Always test and measure response.
- Select and retain media not on their ratings, but on their ability to sell for you.
- Always ask for the order or for further action. It must be loud, clear, easy to understand and easy to execute.

To McAlevey, success is 40 per cent the offer, 40 per cent the media/lists used and 20 per cent the message creativity. Perhaps that is why some of the hard-hitting direct response television advertisements for double glazing (no names!) are such a turn-off.

Telemarketing

While direct response advertising and direct mail both imply the use of an impersonal initial approach through some kind of written or visual material, telemarketing makes a direct personal, verbal approach to the potential customer. However, although this brings benefits from direct and interactive communication, it is seen by some as extremely intrusive. If the telephone rings, people feel obliged to answer it there and then, and tend to feel annoyed and disappointed if it turns out to be a sales pitch rather than a friend wanting a good gossip. The Henley Centre found that only 16 per cent of consumers actually welcome calls and the rest are basically not interested (McLuhan, 2001).

Telemarketing, therefore, can be defined as any planned and controlled activity that creates and exploits a direct relationship between customer and seller, using the telephone.

eg Hertz Lease is a leading vehicle leasing and management service provider in the UK and European B2B markets. Rather than the sales force using cold calling and prospecting techniques, Hertz Lease decided that it would prefer them to use their time more effectively by following up qualified sales leads. For over five years HSM, a telemarketing company, has been assigned to generate around 200 sales appointments per month for the sales force to follow up. As part of the exercise, HSM was contracted to build a database on company and fleet information for research purposes and to guide telemarketing campaign planning. Over time, the role of telemarketing has changed, and as the internal staff have become better trained and sufficiently experienced to take dialogue further with senior staff in the buying organisation, now all inbound enquiries are handled by the HSM team.

There have been a number of benefits from the relationship between Hertz Lease and HSM, not only by generating sales leads and databases, but also by helping to improve the productivity of the sales force. They can now concentrate on the hottest clients, with whom their higher-level sales and negotiation skills can be used to best advantage. In addition, regular contact can be maintained with the target prospect base using direct mail, telemarketing and e-mail marketing contact. This enables a more timely response, should a customer seriously consider changing or developing its vehicle management system. The sales team could not maintain such a presence cost-effectively (**http://www.hsm.co.uk**).

Hertz Lease is an example of outbound telemarketing, where the organisation contacts the potential customer. Inbound telemarketing, where the potential customer is encouraged to contact the organisation, is also popular. This is used not only in direct response advertising, but also for customer care lines, competitions and other sales promotions.

Telephone rental or ownership is high across Europe, averaging over 80 per cent of households, and thus if an appropriate role can be defined for telemarketing within the planned promotional mix, it represents a powerful communication tool. As with personal selling (see pp. 346 *et seq.*), there is direct contact and so dialogue problems can be addressed. Similarly, the customer's state of readiness to commit themselves to a course of action can be assessed and improved through personal persuasion, and efforts made to move towards a positive outcome. Telemarketing can also be used to support customer service initiatives. A carefully designed and managed inbound telemarketing operation can provide an important, sometimes 24-hour, point of contact for customers. This is an important part of maintaining an ongoing relationship with the customer.

Nevertheless, outbound telemarketing in particular is still not widely accepted by consumers and is often seen as intrusive. Where customers have an existing relationship with an organisation, however, and where the purpose of the call is not hard selling, they are less suspicious. Research by Datamonitor, reported by Bird (1998), found that 75 per cent of respondents like receiving calls that check their satisfaction with the product or service or that simply thank them for their custom. The figure drops to less than half if the call is linked to information gathering and a sales pitch. If the outbound calls are badly handled, research by Outbound Teleculture has indicated that 70 per cent of customers become annoyed and in some cases this damages the reputation and prospects for future business for that company.

eg PPP Healthcare uses inbound telemarketing to improve standards of customer care to its members. Initially the concept started as a customer helpline that was staffed by qualified professionals such as pharmacists, midwives and nurses who could dispense advice to the worried caller. The service was not just for those wishing to make a claim, but could handle even routine calls from policy holders such as how to treat an upset stomach or sunburn. Staff at its health information service, Health at Hand, have access to a large electronic library to provide members with the latest information on health topics. The service has evolved to provide advice not just on medical issues but on the organisations that can help, health scares, and where to locate mobile doctors, late-night chemists and other out-of-hours support. PPP, however, goes to some lengths to advise callers that Health at Hand is no substitute for a GP, that it will not provide a diagnosis and that the information it provides either verbally or via fact sheets should not be used for self-diagnosis (**http://www.ppphealthcare.co.uk**). The service has been so successful that some pharmaceutical companies have contracted the service to provide healthcare advice to their own clients, as part of raising their service levels. Pharmaceutical companies have an interest in ensuring compliance with the instructions on medicines to effect a cure and to reinforce brand loyalty as well as avoiding litigation. By printing helpline numbers on bottles or packs, the customer is free to call in and sort out usage problems such as side effects and drug combinations (Bashford, 2004).

Mail order, e-communication and teleshopping

E-communication. The rapidly growing area of e-communications and new media will be considered in depth in Chapter 14. It is probably too early to appreciate the full potential impact of some of the recent developments, but the growth of web and online marketing, texting and e-marketing gives marketers the ability to reach large audiences cost-effectively while retaining the targeting power of direct marketing. The challenge for planning an integrated marketing communications programme is to understand the potential of these relatively new and fast-changing areas, to consider how they will fit into the mix, and to execute them effectively. Whether it is web, WAP, SMS (and increasingly EMS) or e-mail communication, each information delivery gateway needs to be considered and exploited to its full advantage. In the previous sections of this chapter we have seen how some of these vehicles are already being used. At present, they are largely supplementing other communication elements, but as in the easyJet example, substitution over time is inevitable. What is certain, however, is that as bandwidth speeds improve dramatically, 3G generation technology becomes widely accepted, and users become fully adapted to new media, there will be many more creative opportunities open to the marketer.

Mail order. Mail order, as the name suggests, involves the purchase of products featured in advertising or selected from a catalogue. The goods are not examined before ordering, and thus the advertisement or the catalogue has to do a good sales job. Mail order companies promote themselves through any media, and receive orders through the mail, by telephone or via an agent. Direct selling through one-off, product-specific advertisements has largely been covered at pp. 388 *et seq.* under direct response advertising. This section will therefore concentrate on the mail order catalogue sector.

The home shopping market went through a period of rapid growth in the late 1990s, but there are now indications that future growth will be primarily in targeted direct catalogues rather than in the large agency-type catalogues such as those operated by GUS and Littlewoods. Society is changing, with greater use of credit cards and online shopping as well as increased variety on the high street. The internet and e-mail also provide an alternative approach to retaining customers and generating repeat sales. There are some exceptions. John

Lewis tested the market with small catalogues and online activity, before launching a giant 230-page catalogue focused on homeware. The challenge is to tailor offerings to the right target group. In addition to distributing its catalogues in store, John Lewis monitors online activity and analyses storecard data to segment and target customers profitably with direct mail. Not all retailers have not been so successful. Debenhams axed its loss-making catalogue to concentrate on its online operation (Wilkinson, 2004). Developments in database building techniques, customer acquisition, promotion, fulfilment, postal services and logistics have all helped the shift towards speciality catalogue selling.

eg Lands' End is an international mail order catalogue seller. Although it does have 16 stores in the US, two factory stores in the UK and a store in Japan, the bulk of its business is mail order and online selling. In 2001 in the US, it distributed 269 million catalogues, and on its website it claims that it gets between 40,000 and 50,000 calls on a typical day, but during the Christmas period this can rise to 100,000 calls a day on 1100 phone lines. Eight catalogues are available, although in Europe the catalogue choice is more limited. It has 6.7 million customers who have made at least one purchase in the previous year. Its US mailing list has 31 million names.

The catalogue came to the UK in 1991 and with a 24 × 7 × 52 operation, carefully selected merchandise and a full guarantee that merchandise can be returned at any time for any reason, the operation has grown to make Lands' End one of the dominant players in the mail order market. Although telephone ordering still predominates, the online ordering facility is rapidly growing in popularity. In addition, with the wider acceptance of websites, it is becoming much easier to enter markets than in the era when everything depended upon the catalogue.

The website increases the speed with which a database can be developed in a new market. From registrations on the web, it is far easier now to ensure that the catalogues reach people who are interested rather than having to rent a list of names. When Lands' End entered the French market, it used only PR and some limited media advertising to attract customers to its website. As the list builds, it plans to introduce a paper catalogue (Sliwa, 2001; **http://www.landsend.co.uk**).

This kind of catalogue is really a form of distribution channel, in that the operator performs the tasks of merchandise assembly, marketing and customer service. The important thing is to find the selection of merchandise appropriate to the market niche served, and to design an appealing kind of service package (in terms of ordering mechanisms, delivery, returns, etc.).

Table 11.2 shows the perceived advantages and disadvantages of mail order over retailing from the consumer's perspective.

Teleshopping. Developments in communications technology in telephone, cable and satellite television are enabling significant growth in home-based shopping or teleshopping, even before the impact of the internet is considered. Direct marketing through these media can vary from fairly standard one-off advertisements screened during a normal commercial break, to slots featured in dedicated home shopping programmes or channels, usually involving product demonstration, often to a live audience. The main problem with developments in this area is not the capability of the technology, but the willingness of consumers to participate. Digital television has, however, opened up further sales channels for companies such as QVC, which specialises in selling via the television and has 10,000 products on offer, There are also new opportunities for travel agencies and other retailers, a trend that is likely to continue.

Database creation and management

Any organisation with a serious intention of utilising direct marketing needs to think very carefully about how best to store, analyse and use the data captured about its customers. This means developing a database with as detailed a profile as possible about each customer in terms of geodemographics, lifestyle, purchase frequency and spend patterns. In B2B markets,

Table 11.2 Typical advantages and disadvantages of mail order compared with retail outlets

Advantages of shops over mail order	Advantages of mail order over shops
Can see/touch goods	Delay payment
Can try on/test goods	Choose at leisure
No delay in acquiring purchases	Choose at convenience
Easy to return goods	Easy to return goods
Easy to compare prices	Saves time
Cheaper	No pestering
Shopping is enjoyable	Shopping is not enjoyable
Advice/service available	Home delivery of purchases

information might also be held about decision-makers and buying centres. Whatever the kind of market, the deeper the understanding of the customer, the easier it is to create effective messages and products. However, if database usage goes wrong, it can cause some unfortunate errors, for example offering maternity wear or prams to pensioners. When the database works well, it can help to offer products that will appeal to the target audience and generate a response, enabling relationships to build and prosper.

This section looks at some of the issues connected with database creation and management, as summarised in Figure 11.5. Note that the end of the first cycle, customer recruitment and retention, is the start of a stronger second cycle, based on better, recorded information and subsequent targeting.

Customer information

The customer and sales database is a most valuable source of information for relationship management and campaign planning. Having the software to edit, sort, filter and retrieve data is essential (Lewis, 1999). Typical information contained in a database describes customer profiles. Through analysis and model building, its predictive potential can be exploited.

Keeping customers and re-selling to them

As with any marketing effort, the continuation of exchanges will depend on how well needs have been satisfied, service provided and value offered. However, the real challenge for direct marketing

Figure 11.5 Database creation and management

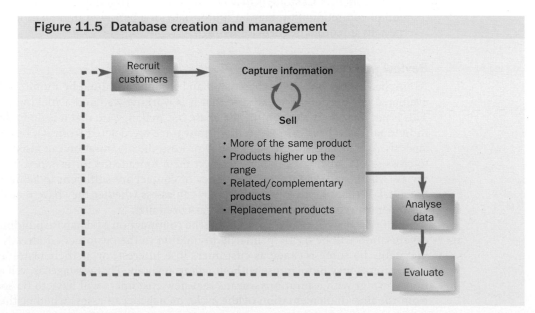

is to continue to communicate actively with the customer and win further orders after the initial contact has been made. It is always more cost-effective to retain customers than to win new ones, so careful use of direct marketing can assist the overall promotional programme.

eg Frequent flyers are an attractive source of business to airlines, as demonstrated in Case Study 11. With the opportunity to collect frequent flyer miles towards free flights, schemes such as BA's Executive Club with 1.7 million flyers and Singapore Airlines' Kris have proved very popular with regular travellers. By the end of 2004, almost 14 trillion frequent flyer miles had been accumulated to the potential value of $700bn, more than all the US dollar bills in circulation. Most of the airline clubs integrate offline and online activity and customers seem willing to provide e-mail addresses and opt in. BA uses e-mail to keep customers informed of special offers and updated information of relevance. Combined with actual journey information, class of travel and so on, a very useful and appropriate database has been developed to help BA nurture its valuable customers (Clark, 2005b).

There are five stages in a retention and customer development programme. These are considered in turn.

1 *Welcome.* The obvious first stage applies shortly after the customer has become active. An early contact can be reassuring, and assists in engendering receptivity to further communication. When *Next Directory* called new customers to welcome them after receiving their first orders, a much higher proportion of new customers were retained and they spent 30 per cent more than 'non-welcomed' customers.

2 *Selling up.* Apart from normal repeat business, such as occurs with customers of a book club, organisations should encourage the customer to adopt a better or higher-valued model. This approach would be appropriate for a wide range of products and services including cars, cameras and credit cards. American Express, for example, used direct mail to encourage green Amex cardholders to trade up to gold card status. The timing of contact will depend on the expected replacement period for the product.

3 *Selling across.* The selling across or cross-selling stage is where an organisation tries to sell a wider range of products than those in the area originally selected. A customer who purchases car insurance from a particular company might subsequently receive mailings about house insurance or private health cover, for example.

4 *Renewal.* With products that involve annual or regular renewal, such as motor insurance, the timing of appropriate and personalised communication around the renewal date can reinforce repeat purchases.

5 *Lapsed customers.* Customers may be temporarily dormant or permanently lost. A continuation of communication may be appropriate for a period of time so as not to lose contact, especially if reorder frequencies are high.

Review and recycle

As implied above, once a database is up and running it should be monitored, reviewed and evaluated periodically to make sure that it is working well and achieving its full potential. This is not just about 'cleaning' the database (i.e. making sure that it is up to date and that any individuals who have disappeared without trace are deleted from it), but also about data analysis. As part of the strategic planning process, the organisation can look for opportunities to cross-sell to existing customers or to get them to trade up, for instance. Managers can also review whether the nature and frequency of contact are sufficient to achieve full customer potential. Perhaps more importantly, they can assess whether they have recruited the kind of customer expected and whether targets have been met.

All of this analysis can be used to plan the continuation of database building. Although the organisation will be trying primarily to hold on to the customers it already has, there will inevitably be some wastage as customers lose interest, or as their tastes and aspirations change, or as they move house without telling anybody. That wastage, as well as the organisation's own growth aspirations, means that new customers will have to be sought. Learning from the first implementation of the cycle, managers can assess whether the 'right' kind of media were used to attract the 'right' kind of desired customer. They can refine their profiling and targeting in order to improve response rates and perhaps attract even more lucrative customers. They can review which promotional offers or which kinds of approach were most successful and repeat those with new customers, or try similar activities again.

Trade shows and exhibitions

Both B2B and consumer sellers may introduce trade shows and exhibitions into their promotional mixes. Such events range from small-scale local involvement, for example a specialist bookseller taking a stall at a model railway exhibition, to an annual national trade show serving a specific industry, such as the DIY and Home Improvement Show, or Pakex for the packaging industry. In either case, the exhibition may become an important element of the year's marketing activities, as this section will show. Even those who specialise in organising and supporting exhibitions have their own exhibitions!

eg From its humble UK beginnings in 1971, the London Book Fair has grown into a major international event for the book trade. It now has 1500 exhibiting companies and attracts over 15,000 trade visitors, including over 6500 from London and the south-east and 6000 of international origin. It provides an opportunity for publishers, booksellers and librarians as well as publishing logistics providers to network and generate business. Purchasing decisions are made, orders placed, rights bought and sold and new titles examined. It enables industry participants to keep up with events and trends in the industry and not least have a look at what the competitors are doing! Over 98 per cent of exhibitors were satisfied with the event, 79 per cent valued its role in generating new leads and 74 per cent indicated that it was important to them for maintaining their status and presence in the market (**http://www.libf.com**).

Exhibitions and shows can be of particular importance to the smaller business that may not have the resources to fund an expensive marketing communications programme. The exhibition can be used as a cost-effective means of building more 'presence' and reputation with the trade, and to generate potential sales leads.

For any sized organisation, international exhibitions can be particularly valuable because they bring together participants from all over the world who might otherwise never meet, and can thus lead to export deals. The Nürnberg International Toy Fair, for example, has been running for 50 years. It represents an opportunity for the trade to present new products to retail buyers from across Europe. New product launches are often planned to coincide with the fair to maximise both the impact to visitors and the subsequent coverage in the trade and hobby press.

For the manufacturer, attending exhibitions provides a formal opportunity to display the product range and to discuss applications and needs with prospective customers in a neutral environment. Depending on the type of show and the care that an organisation puts into planning its presence there, an exhibition provides a powerful and cost-effective way of getting the message across and making new contacts that may subsequently turn into sales.

eg Sharwoods, the Indian, Thai and Chinese food manufacturer, sells into both retail and wholesale channels and uses exhibitions as an integral part of its strategy. For each show, it sets specific, measurable targets and the main priority is to encourage tasting for retail and consumers, an experience that is difficult to achieve through any other medium. The chef demonstrations are very powerful for attracting visitors to the stand, as is free tasting. It attends fine food and ethnic food fairs as well as consumer events, with the aim of showcasing new products and generating new sales from the new trade contacts made (**http://www.exhibitionswork.co.uk**).

Public relations

■ Definitions

Stanley (1982, p. 40) defined public relations as:

A management function that determines the attitudes and opinions of the organisation's publics, identifies its policies with the interests of its publics, and formulates and executes a programme of action to earn the understanding and goodwill of its publics.

The Institute of Public Relations (IPR) is rather more succinct in its definition:

The deliberate, planned and sustained effort to institute and maintain mutual understanding between an organisation and its publics.

The latter is, nevertheless, a more useful definition that gets close to the core concern of PR, which is *mutual understanding*. The implication is that the organisation needs to understand how it is perceived in the wider world, and then work hard to make sure, through PR, that those perceptions match its desired image. Two-way communication is essential to this process. Another interesting element of this definition is the specific use of the word *publics*. Advertising, in its commonest usage, is usually about talking to customers or potential customers. Public relations defines a much broader range of target audiences, some of whom have no direct trading relationship with the organisation, and thus PR encompasses a wide variety of communication needs and objectives not necessarily geared towards an eventual sale. Finally, the definition emphasises that PR is *deliberate, planned and sustained*. This is important for two reasons. First, it implies that PR is just as much of a strategically thought-out, long-term commitment as any other marketing activity, and second, it counters any preconceptions about PR simply being the *ad hoc* seizing of any free publicity opportunity that happens to come along.

eg Whether affected by bombings, warfare or natural disasters, the tourism industry has to be adept at bouncing back and rebuilding brand confidence. The approach to recovery depends a lot on PR. First, it is important to demonstrate to readers and viewers that the problem has been tackled. Publicity given to terrorist captures, hotel rebuilding and security improvements is essential to rebuild confidence.

London had a difficult problem. The terrorist attacks on 7 July 2005, however tragic, were met with claims of 'business as usual' and a 'stiff upper lip'. The attempted attacks of 21 July, however, created the impression of a terrorist campaign rather than an isolated incident, and that is more difficult to counter with positive messages. Although bookings were not cancelled, forward bookings dropped by 20 per cent from the previous year and the longer-term impact is still being addressed. Hotel rates dropped to a 10-year low and research by CHH/Time showed that 25 per cent of adults in Britain, France and Germany would rather not visit the capital. Interestingly, it tends to be older people and women who are most sensitive to the risk (Skidmore and Demetriou, 2005). Visit London planned a large promotional campaign for events to be held in London in the autumn to rebuild visitor numbers. Overall, then, not long after any disaster, a PR strategy can play a central role in the recovery in a way that direct promotion cannot (Benady, 2005).

A public is any group, with some common characteristic, with which an organisation needs to communicate. Each public poses a different communication problem, as each has different information needs and a different kind of relationship with the organisation, and may start with different perceptions of what the organisation stands for (Marston, 1979).

eg A university has to develop relationships with a wide range of publics. Obviously, there are the students and potential students and the schools and colleges that provide them, both nationally and internationally. The university also has to consider, however, its staff and the wider academic community. Then there are the sources of funding, such as local authorities, the government, the EU and research bodies. Industry might also be a potential source of research funds, as well as commissioning training courses and providing jobs for graduates. It is also important for a university to foster good press relations. Local media help to establish the university as a part of its immediate community, national media help to publicise its wider status, while specialist publications such as the *Times Higher Education Supplement* reach those with a specific interest and perhaps even the decision-makers within the sector.

A number of different publics, which relate generally to any kind of organisation, are shown in Figure 11.6. It is, however, important to remember that any individual may be a member of more than one public. This means that although the slant and emphasis of messages may differ from public to public, the essential content and philosophy should be consistent. Appropriate techniques within PR for communicating with a range of different publics will be looked at later (see pp. 398 *et seq.*).

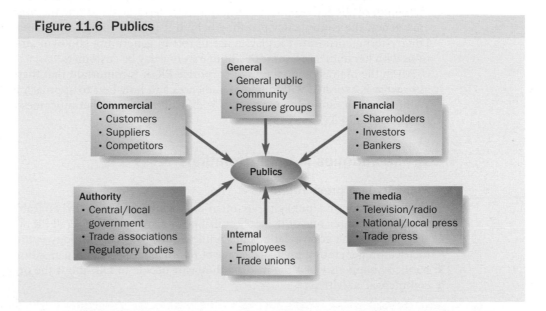

Figure 11.6 Publics

Not all publics will be regarded by an organisation as having equal importance. Some will be seen as critical, and be given priority in targeting PR activities, while others will just be left ticking over for the time being. As the organisation's situation changes, the priority given to each of the publics will have to be reassessed (Wilmshurst, 1993).

Even in the quietest and most stable of industries, the membership of each public will change over time, and their needs and priorities will also evolve. This process of change emphasises the need to monitor attitudes and opinions constantly, and thus to identify current and future pressure points early enough to be able to defuse or control them.

■ Role of PR

As with any marketing activity, managers must be sure that PR integrates with the rest of the organisation's promotional efforts, and that it is clearly related to wider company objectives. Cutlip *et al.* (1985) distinguish between marketing PR and corporate PR. Although the two are not mutually exclusive, there may be differences in their scope and objectives.

Marketing PR

Marketing PR may be used for long-term strategic image building, developing credibility and raising the organisation's profile, to enhance other marketing activities. When used in this way, it becomes a planned element of the wider promotional mix, working in synergy with the others. A new product launch, or the introduction of a big new innovative advertising campaign, for instance, might benefit from planned PR aimed at specific audiences through specific media to generate interest and awareness.

Corporate PR

It is possible to use corporate PR as part of a long-term relationship-building strategy with various publics or as a short-term tactical response to an unforeseen crisis. By definition, short-term circumstances are somewhat unpredictable, and therefore any organisation needs to have contingency plans ready so that a well-rehearsed crisis management team can swing into action as soon as disaster strikes. This means, for example, that everyone should know who will be responsible for collating information and feeding it to the media, and that senior management will be properly briefed and trained to face media interrogation. Such measures result in the organisation being seen to handle the crisis capably and efficiently, and also reduce the chances of different spokespersons innocently contradicting each other, or of the media being kept short of information because everyone thinks that someone else is dealing with that aspect. Although the duration of the crisis may be short, and thus the actual implementation of PR activities is technically a short-term tactic to tide the organisation over the emergency, the contingency planning behind it involves long-term management thinking. Longer-term, corporate PR plays a useful role in generating goodwill and positive associations with key audiences, some of whom may one day be customers.

Given the many potential uses of corporate PR, it is important that there is clear thinking as to what is expected with different audiences and how best to approach each target group. Without such a rationale for action, it is difficult to assess what outcomes and achievements have been realised (Stone, 1991).

■ Techniques in public relations

Publicity and press relations

Public relations and 'publicity' are often mistakenly used as interchangeable terms. Publicity is, however, simply one of the tools available for achieving the overall PR objective of creating and maintaining good relationships with various publics. Publicity is thus a subset of PR, focused on generating media coverage at minimal cost to the organisation. In other words, publicity happens when the media voluntarily decide to talk about the organisation and its commercial activities.

> **eg**
>
> Pillows are often taken for granted despite their importance for a good night's sleep. To create a bit of interest in pillows, the Duvet and Pillow Association organised a National Pillow Week to create awareness of the importance of washing and changing pillows on a regular basis. It felt that the more attention that was given to pillow hygiene and performance, the more sales could be generated for the pillow manufacturers. It used PR to help promote the week's activities but had to convince the media to cover the events in order to get through to the rest of us. Four press releases were developed tailored to business, family, women and the general media. It contained useful information on sleeping habits and pillows. One interesting fact may make you shudder – after 18 months 10 per cent of a pillow's weight is made up of dust, mites, sweat, mould and mildew!
>
> There were pillow tips from experts and case studies of the link between a good night's sleep and the suitability of the pillow. Of course no campaign would be complete without a pillow fight, and a Celebrity Wrestling Star and a former Miss UK duly obliged, wearing Tony Blair and Michael Howard masks (it was election time) along with scanty bikinis, just in case the media were losing interest. The campaign received much media coverage in the regional and national press, reaching 25 million people. The *Sun*

featured one of the photoshoot images in its online edition. Pillow sales also increased by 5 per cent in the period after the campaign compared with the previous year, but there were no recorded incidents of pillow fights that got out of hand (*PR Week*, 2005).

All areas of the mass media can be used for publicity purposes. Within the broadcast media, apart from news and current affairs programmes, a great deal of publicity is disseminated through chat shows (authors plugging their latest books, for instance), consumer shows (featuring dangerous products or publicising companies' questionable personal selling practices, for instance) and special interest programmes (motoring, books, clothing, etc.). Print media also offer wide scope for publicity. National and local newspapers cover general interest stories, but there are many special interest, trade and professional publications that give extensive coverage to stories of specific interest to particular publics. It must also be remembered that sections of the media feed each other. National newspapers and television stations may pick up stories from local media or the specialist media and present them to a much greater mass audience.

Publicity may be unsought, as when the media get the smell of scandal or malpractice and decide to publicise matters which perhaps the organisation would rather not have publicised. To reduce the risk of bad publicity, however, most organisations cultivate good press relations, and try to feed the media's voracious appetite with 'good news' stories that will benefit the organisation. This can be done through written press releases or verbal press conferences or briefings.

The media are obviously very powerful, not only as a public in their own right, but also as a third-party channel of communication with other publics. It may be argued that advertising can do just as good a communication job, in spreading good news to mass audiences, but publicity has a few advantages. Advertising is paid for, and therefore publics have a certain cynicism about the bias within the message. Publicity, on the other hand, is seen as free, coming from a neutral third party, and therefore has more credibility. Also, a good PR story that captures the imagination so that it gets wide coverage across both print and broadcast media can achieve an incredible level of reach (see p. 333) at a fraction of the cost, and might even make an impact on sections of the audience who wouldn't normally see or absorb advertising.

These advantages do, however, need to be balanced against the big disadvantage, *uncontrollability*. Whereas advertising gives the advertiser complete control over what is said, when it is said, how it is said and where it is said, the control of publicity is in the hands of the media. The organisation can feed material to the media, but cannot guarantee that the media will adopt the story or influence how they will present it (Fill, 2002). The outcome of this might be, at worst, no coverage at all, or patchy coverage that might not reach the desired target publics. Another potential risk is distortion of the story.

eg The US Grand Prix in Indianapolis turned into a fiasco when seven teams withdrew after the parade lap because of safety fears about Michelin tyres, due to adverse weather conditions. Bridgestone tyres were considered suitable for the conditions, so teams using those were able to compete, but the spectators were left with only a shadow of a race. This was not only bad news for F1 fans, but also left Michelin in a difficult negative PR position in the US market where it generates 30 per cent of its global sales. To minimise the damage, it offered to refund 120,000 tickets, but the compensation bill to the racers, advertisers, sponsors and media companies could stretch to £28m. It is always difficult to decide when to accept liability for a problem in order to minimise and short-cut any subsequent brand damage, yet without exposing the organisation to large compensation claims (Steiner, 2005b).

It is not true to say that there is no such thing as bad publicity. The risks of negative coverage can, however, be minimised by the maintenance of ongoing, good press relations, and by setting up a crisis management plan so that if disaster strikes, the damage from bad publicity can be limited and even turned to advantage.

Other external communication

Other forms of external communication are also used for PR. Advertising can be used as a tool of PR, although it is something of a grey area. The kind of advertising to which we are referring here is not the selling or promoting of a specific product or range of products, but the type that concentrates on the organisation's name and characteristics. As previously suggested, although this sort of advertising lacks the impartiality of publicity, it makes up for it in terms of controllability. As a means of helping to establish and reinforce corporate image, it is certainly effective, and as a mass medium will reach members of most publics.

An organisation can host or participate in various events for PR purposes. As well as press conferences, mentioned above, the organisation may host other social events. If it has just opened a new factory, for instance, it may hold a party on the premises for key shareholders, employees, customers and suppliers. Such one-off events will also, of course, create media interest.

An important public is the one with a financial interest in the organisation. The organisation's annual general meeting is an important forum for both shareholders and the financial media. Efficient administration and confident presentation can help to increase credibility (although none of that can disguise a poor financial position).

A well-presented annual report, distributed primarily to shareholders and the financial media, but often sent out to anyone who expresses an interest in the organisation, like the annual general meeting, is an opportunity to present the organisation in the best possible positive light and to make public statements about the organisation's achievements and its future directions.

Lobbying is a very specialised area, designed to develop and influence relationships with 'authority', particularly national and EU governmental bodies. Lobbying is a way of getting an organisation's views known to the decision-makers, and trying to influence the development and implementation of policy.

Internal communication

Although employees and other internal publics are exposed to much of the PR that is directed to the external world, they do need their own dedicated communication so that they know what is going on in more detail, and they know it before it hits the wider media (Bailey, 1991). This emphasis on keeping people informed rather than in the dark reflects quite a major change in employers' attitudes towards their employees. It is important for motivation, as well as being a means of preparing people for change and strengthening corporate culture.

The two main types of communication are written (house journals, intranet pages or newsletters) and verbal (management briefings, for instance). Few people would want to read a long working paper written by the managing director on quality management or production targets, but most would at least glance at a well-illustrated, short, clearly written summary of the important points presented in journalistic style. Briefings provide a good mechanism for face-to-face contact between management and staff, and for increasing staff involvement and empowerment. Frequent, regular departmental or section meetings can be used to thrash out operational problems and to pass communication downwards through the organisation. Less frequently, once a year perhaps, more senior management can address staff, presenting results and strategic plans, and directly answering questions.

Sponsorship

■ Definition and role

Sponsorship is defined by BDS Sponsorship (http://www.sponsorship.co.uk) as:

> ... a business relationship between a provider of funds, resources or services and an individual, event or organisation which offers in return some rights and association that may be used for commercial advantage.

While some sponsorship certainly does have altruistic motives behind it, its main purpose is to generate positive attitudes through associating the corporate name with sport, the arts, charitable enterprise or some other activity. That is why so many companies use sponsorship, including familiar names such as Coca-Cola, JVC, McEwan's lager, Carlsberg, Opel, Lloyds TSB and the Nationwide Building Society.

eg Vodafone takes sponsorship very seriously. It spends £250m per year globally on advertising and £100m on sponsorship deals such as those with Manchester United, Formula One team Vodafone McLaren Mercedes, the England cricket team and the Epsom Derby. Up until 2005, it also sponsored David Beckham to endorse its products as part of a deal with Manchester United but that went wrong when he moved to Real Madrid. He played the role of global brand ambassador and featured strongly in local advertising. The England cricket team's progress in world rankings has, however, proved advantageous to Vodafone (*Marketing Week*, 2005a, 2005f; Steiner, 2005a).

There are signs, however, that football sponsorship may be starting to lose its appeal to sponsors due to over-exposure and a free-for-all for any money-making opportunity (Carter, 2004b). That could be bad news for mobile companies as they have been particularly active in signing up sponsorship deals. Orange, Vodafone and T-mobile have struck large deals with over half the Premiership clubs. The agreements are based on a revenue share basis, with the clubs receiving a commission payment for club-relevant content, ringtones, wallpaper, goal alerts via text and services, while the operators are allowed numerous branding opportunities at the ground and on websites and exclusive handset deals and phone tariffs. This could be extended when 3G is widely accepted with video of goals shortly after the match (Hemsley, 2004). Vodafone, however, ended its £36m four-year sponsorship deal with Manchester United in November 2005, using a break clause half-way through the term of the contract. Little was being said by the parties involved, but it was thought that Vodafone wanted to focus more on its three-year sponsorship of the Champions League instead (Cohn, 2005). Even a big club like Manchester United cannot afford to lose £9m per year sponsorship money, and so a replacement sponsor is actively being sought, with names such as Etihan Airways, Google, Yahoo!, Sony and LG all rumoured to be interested in paying up to £12m per year for the privilege of sponsoring the club (Jacob *et al.*, 2005).

Vodafone and the other mobile brands want to connect with consumers' passions and to leverage those passions to alter what consumers think and do about their brand. Of course ultimately it is about product sales, and the emphasis on communication is an attraction to all the mobile operators, however crowded the market.

Sponsorship grew in popularity during the 1980s, partly because of its attractiveness as a supporting element in the promotional mix, and partly because of the growing cost of media advertising compared with the potentially greater coverage of various sports and arts activities (Meenaghan, 1998). Sponsorship has also become more global and has fitted well with the increased trend towards brand globalisation (Grimes and Meenaghan, 1998). Its growth was also helped by the tobacco companies using it as a means of achieving exposure in spite of the ban on television advertising.

■ Types of sponsorship

Sport

With the widespread appeal of sport across all ages, areas and lifestyles, it is perhaps not surprising that sports sponsorship has grown in popularity. This is especially true when it is linked to the televising of the events. The mass audiences possible through television, even for some minority sports, enable the widespread showing of the sponsor's name.

Flora has been sponsoring the London Marathon since the mid-1990s, as part of its commitment to a healthier Britain, as it claims. There is a clear link between the brand values and the nature of the event. As a bonus, television viewing figures often exceed 6 million, there is a website which clearly links the event to Flora and it has resulted in spontaneous awareness increasing to above 50 per cent. The 32,000 runners are therefore a small part of the multiplier for Flora by sponsoring the race.

Dressed as a sunflower from which Flora is produced, this runner guaranteed the attention of spectators and the media.

Source: © Dominic Burke/Alamy http://www.alamy.com

In 2005, it was decided to extend the impact of the sponsorship by appealing to those who were daunted by the thought of running in the marathon itself. It developed a Flora Family Marathon site to encourage families and groups of two to six friends to run 26.2 miles between them over five weeks but they all had to run one mile on the morning of the marathon itself. The targeting of families was thought appropriate for the brand and give-aways included personal training plans, a log of progress, a pedometer and baseball caps. When they finished the race the family received a piece of the marathon tape and a Flora Family Marathon medal. There were 20,000 sign-ups on the site and 100,000 unique views from click-throughs on the web. The brand health rating significantly improved during the campaign, showing the power of carefully matched sponsorship activities with the unique brand values (Rigby, 2005b; **http://www.london-marathon.co.uk**).

Many sports attract heavy television coverage and so although the typical sponsoring costs may be high, in comparison with the cost of direct television advertising, such sponsorship can actually be very cost effective. Sponsorship of sport has the added benefit that although people may ignore commercial breaks, they do pay attention when a 'real' programme is on, and therefore may be more likely to absorb the sponsor's name.

Sponsorship through Ellen high water!

Few would have rated the chances of Ellen MacArthur, from landlocked Derbyshire, being successful when she approached the Kingfisher group in 1998 to support her entry to the round the world Route du Rhum race. She was unknown, the race was little known and Kingfisher at that time was one of the giants of the retail trade with interests in such household names as Superdrug, Woolworths, and B&Q in the UK and Castorama in France. Fortunately for Ellen, the Chairman at that time was a keen sailor and the £50,000 to build Kingfisher 1 was forthcoming in return for a prime name location on her trimaran. She started the payback quickly, achieving strong positions in the early races, and became the fastest woman and youngest person to circumnavigate the world in a single-handed race.

In 2005, another 'repayment' was made by Ellen after she smashed the record for the fastest person to sail single-handed around the world non-stop in 71 days, 14 hours, 18 minutes and 33 seconds

precisely, beating the record by one day, eight hours, 35 minutes and 49 seconds! The sponsorship has been an outstanding success for Kingfisher and its B&Q and Castorama brands which featured most prominently. So far, Kingfisher has spent between £10m and £12m supporting Ellen, after a five-year deal was signed in 2002. Just what has Kingfisher got back in return?

The obvious answer is the corporate colours and logos all over the trimaran, surrounded by photographers and cameras. It was estimated that on the morning of her successful return to harbour there was £2m worth of free advertising, given the extensive television coverage. In the four days leading up to the return to port, media buyers estimated that print and television coverage was worth £75m and for the total 71-day voyage it rose above £100m. According to Kingfisher, between 1998 and 2001 it had nearly 10,000 mentions in 8,000 newspaper articles across 23 countries as a result of its association with Ellen. The cost of buying newspaper space to reach the same audience, some

4.85 billion people, would have been £15.4m. This is sports sponsorship at its best, in terms of the publicity spin-off and the creation of a long-term relationship. The cost is the annual sponsorship and support in building the trimaran along with support costs.

The other significant benefit is more subtle. Kingfisher is associated with MacArthur's determination, skill, professionalism, courage and success, none of which does a corporate reputation any harm at all. The B&Q theme is 'You can do it'. Ellen demonstrates that theme in action with her achievements, thus reinforcing the brand values. She makes regular appearances at store openings, top-performing staff are rewarded with a day's sailing with her, and she often appears at B&Q corporate events for staff. Ellen's next venture supports the B&Q market entry and development strategy in Asia. Yachting is less popular, so she is involved with the tea clipper challenge starting in Shanghai and finishing in London.

Sources: Milmo (2005); Rigby (2005a); Wheatley (2002).

Soccer has been one of the major sports to attract sponsorship because of its large-scale media coverage in all kinds of media. This has attracted sponsors at player, club, national league and international levels throughout the world.

Manchester United has been an attractive proposition for sponsors due to the club's large worldwide following. Nike has a 13-year shirt and equipment contract worth up to £130m over six years to Manchester United, and worth £303m to Nike. A myriad of other official partners are also linked to the club, such as Audi for cars, Air Asia for budget airlines, Pepsi for drinks and Budweiser for beer, for example. All are keen to be associated with the club through the website, live matches and so on (Klinger, 2005).

At league level, Barclays committed £57m to be the English Premier League sponsor for the period 2004–07. It took over in 2001 from Carling, which had backed the league for nine years. Initially called the Barclaycard Premiership, it became the Barclay's Premiership upon the renewal of the contract in 2004 (Davies, 2003; Szczepanik, 2003). Barclays is attracted to the sponsorship deal due to the huge following for the Premiership, not just in the UK but throughout the world. The FA Premier League is the most successful league in Europe when it comes to raising commercial revenue, and its television rights alone outside the UK generated £300m. The Premiership is now watched by 15.2 billion people on television every year, an increase of nearly 2 billion in three years. Sponsorship allows the game to flourish with the best players, the best clubs and the best leagues (Barrand, 2004, 2005; Britcher, 2004; Gillis, 2004a, 2004b, 2004c, 2005).

International soccer sponsorship is often too big a challenge for an individual organisation, however large it is. Even if it is part of a consortium, there is no guarantee of a successful outcome. A *Marketing Week* (2004b) survey revealed that more than half of UK adults failed to recognise any of the eight official sponsors of Euro 2004, with only Coca-Cola and McDonald's getting anywhere near value for money. Canon and JVC, despite being sponsors, hardly gained any recall as a number of other brands successfully ambushed the tournament – Nationwide, Barclays, Carling, Sainsbury's and Fuji were all thought by the public, incorrectly, to be official sponsors. The only hope for the forgotten sponsors is that the television ratings and exposure contributed to greater general awareness of the brands, provided that was the intention of the sponsorship in the first place. This may not be surprising considering the clutter. Perimeter boards, shirt sponsorship, big-screen commercials and programme advertising all are trying to gain the fans' attention.

If the sponsorship of tournaments does not appeal, then there is always the option of sponsoring individual athletes or players, or of sponsoring teams or leagues. Some sportsmen and women come at a high price. An Olympic medal winner should be able to net around £1m in sports endorsements and sponsorship. On a more limited basis, companies can sponsor match programmes, balls or even the corner flags. Smaller or non-league clubs are appealing for local businesses who want to reinforce their role in the community, and even large organisations can value this.

All of this works well as long as the sport and the individual clubs continue to maintain a 'clean' image. A riot in the stands or a punch-up on the pitch generates the kind of publicity and media coverage of the type 'What kind of depths has the game sunk to?' that sponsors will not want to be associated with. Every time a player is sent off for violent conduct with the sponsor's name on his chest, an F1 vehicle breaks down, or a player becomes embroiled in a scandal in his or her personal life, there is a risk to the sponsoring organisation. It has also been suggested that sponsors are becoming concerned over the commercial risks associated with ethical problems such as the drug testing that has featured in some high profile cases (O'Sullivan, 2001).

Broadcast sponsorship

Broadcast sponsorship, sponsoring programmes or series on television or the radio, is a relatively new area in the UK. Television sponsorship forms the largest part of broadcast sponsorship, but it still comprises a minor proportion of a channel's commercial income compared with advertising revenue.

eg Reckitt Benckiser decided to follow the lead of the long-running association between Cadbury and the soap *Coronation Street* when it agreed to support *Emmerdale* in a one-year deal thought to be worth £10m. The plan was to showcase brands on a rotational basis, again as Cadbury had done, so Mr Sheen, Finish, Dettol and Lemsip may all gain airtime. Reckitt took over from Heinz which used *Emmerdale* sponsorship to support the Salad Cream and Tomato Ketchup brands. The sponsorship deal covers all episodes of *Emmerdale* on all three ITV channels and online. It also extends to licensing and off-air promotions. It will also provide interactive television option. The soap attracts 10 million people six times a week, and so provides an ideal platform to reach the target audience for Reckitt products (*Marketing Week*, 2005g).

Television broadcasters have started to exploit the potential of gaining sponsorship for major sports coverage such as the soccer World Cup, league action and other major events. The broadcasters gain much-needed additional revenue and the sponsors are clearly linked to the show in all screenings and associated promotional coverage. Even within the current, fairly restrictive regulatory framework, broadcast sponsorship still has much to offer. As with advertising, of course, it is reaching potentially large audiences and creating product awareness. Further than that, however, it also has the potential to help enhance the product's image and message by association. Soft Lips, the lip protectant and sunscreen brand, sponsors the slightly raunchy ITV drama *Footballers Wives* and the spin-off drama *Footballers Wives Extra Time*. The sponsorship was thought to cost around £500,000 and the main reason for Soft Lips' decision was that it thought that the proposition for the brand and programme were the same – 'keeping millions of young women satisfied'! Its average audience is around 7 million (*Marketing Week*, 2005b). To get the best out of broadcast sponsorship, however, it should be integrated into a wider package of marketing and promotional activities.

The arts

Arts sponsorship is a growing area, second only to sport in terms of its value in the UK where in 2000 it was worth around £150m, more than double what it was worth five years before (Carter, 2004a). Over half of the money, however, went on projects in London. The art forms covered range widely from music, including rock, classical and opera, to festivals, theatre, film and literature.

To arts organisations, at a time of declining state funding, private sponsorship has become critical for survival. All over Europe, arts subsidies from government have been cut. Theatres, opera houses, orchestras and galleries are not, however, able to sit back and wait for the sponsorship income to roll in. They have to be proactive and approach potential sponsors and donors for money.

Arts sponsorship isn't just about trying to reach an audience that is older, more affluent and more highly educated than the typical sports audience, through opera, ballet and fine art exhibitions. A wider, if perhaps somewhat less discerning, youth audience can be reached through rock music. Various companies have become involved with sponsoring rock and pop events, such as the Lloyds TSB Live Tour of The Corrs and the Celine Dion tour sponsored by Avon Cosmetics (Finch, 2002; Kleinman, 2002).

eg High-profile events still attract a lot of attention. The various Live8 concerts for Africa in 2005 had considerable sponsorship support with stages branded with AOL and Nokia logos. Both were delighted to reach 16–34-year-old consumers worldwide with the extensive coverage by the BBC. It is believed that AOL paid £5m and Nokia £3m for that privilege. The BBC was itself thought to have parted with £2m for the broadcasting rights. The fit for Nokia was obvious as the concert was about people communicating around the world and working together for a good cause (*Marketing Week*, 2005e). Egg sponsored eight 'live' arts events at the Tate Modern gallery with a branded year-long festival called Tate & Egg Live. The exhibition was a festival of music, theatre and visual arts all mixed together in live performances. As a dotcom bank with no local presence to spread its logo on the High Street, the Tate Modern tie-up seemed a perfect way to appeal to Egg's target market of the young and media-savvy. Retailer French Connection also took up a cultural strategy when it backed an exhibition by Gilbert & George that combined graffiti swear words with images of urban living. The retailer, which is notorious for its irreverent FCUK campaign, sponsored the artists' 'The Dirty Words Pictures' exhibition at Hyde Park's Serpentine Gallery (Singh, 2004).

The important consideration for marketers in deciding whether to sponsor these events is understanding the link between the product and the music. To gain maximum value, it is necessary to ensure that the event features in all aspects of the communications mix, including packaging, advertising and sales promotion. This means exploiting the association before, during and after the music event.

With arts sponsorship there are a number of opportunities to present the sponsoring organisation, including on stage, in programmes, through associated merchandise including videos and CDs, around venues and even on tickets. There are also advantages in hosting key customers and suppliers at high-profile events, by offering the best seats and perhaps hosting a reception during the interval or after the show.

Cause-related marketing

Linkages between organisations and charities benefit both parties. If, for example, a company runs a sales promotion along the lines of 'We'll donate 10p to this charity for every token you send in', the charity gains from the cash raised and from an increased public profile. Consumers feel that their purchase has greater significance than simple self-gratification and feel good about having 'given', while the company benefits from the increased sales generated by the promotion and from the extra goodwill created from associating its brands with a good cause. Murphy (1999) argues that companies are taking a longer-term view of cause-related marketing because of the positive image associated with a good and caring cause.

eg Nivea, the skin care product from Beiersdorf, thought that it could exploit a close synergy with Cancer Research UK to inject some life into the brand. It was particularly attracted to sponsoring the annual Race for Life as it promoted a wholesome, healthy message for both parties. Fund raising came from runners being sponsored by their community. Linked marketing initiatives were designed to extend the full value of the relationship and joint publicity was organised through a series of radio interviews. Nivea teamed up with *Top Santé* – a national health and fitness publication – to highlight the fact that more funding is needed for cancer research, and that by taking part in the Race for Life and raising money, women can do their bit to help. Nivea planned to be a sponsor for the long term to build the relationship in the consumer's mind.

The relationship has not been without its problems, however. In 2004, both sides fell out over the Nivea suncare range. The rival suncare manufacturer Boots was approached to sponsor the annual Sun Smart campaign, and Cancer Research became edgy about its logo being used on products designed to allow people to spend more time sunbathing. Then, an independent research group examined a number of leading brands, including Nivea, and suggested that one-third of all products tested contained ingredients linked to cancer while 70 per cent may be contaminated with harmful impurities. The research results have been contested, but nevertheless this case is indicative of the challenges that can arise when good causes meet business (Edwards, 2005; *Marketing Week*, 2004a; Mortished, 2005).

Not all cause-related marketing is linked with sales promotions, however. Many large organisations set up charitable foundations or donate cash directly to community or charitable causes. Others might pay for advertising space for charities, whether on television, radio, press or posters. This is important at a time when consumers are becoming more conscious of the ethical and 'corporate citizenship' records of the companies they patronise.

Organisations clearly do not just take an altruistic view of their charity involvement. As with any other marketing activity, it should be planned with clear objectives and expected outcomes.

There are benefits in linking a brand to a good cause, especially if there is a direct synergy between values and aims, but if consumers feel it is just another means of gaining cash, it can backfire for both parties (Brennan, 2005). Cause-related marketing is now an established part of the marketing mix and when successful demonstrates brand values at a higher level than is possible in more traditional promotional marketing strategies. It is, therefore, important that care is taken before deciding the most appropriate charity, and lining up with a controversial social issue is often best avoided.

Chapter summary

■ Sales promotion is part of a planned integrated marketing communications strategy that is mainly used in a short-term tactical sense, but can also contribute something to longer-term strategic and image-building objectives. Sales promotions offer something over and above the normal product offering that can act as an incentive to stimulate the target audience into behaving in a certain way. Manufacturers use promotions to stimulate intermediaries and their sales staff, both manufacturers and retailers use them to stimulate individual consumers, and manufacturers might use them to stimulate other manufacturers. The methods of sales promotion are many and varied. In consumer markets they can be classed as money-based, product-based, or gift, prize or merchandise-based. Customer loyalty schemes in particular have become increasingly popular in the retail trade and in service industries. Manufacturers stimulate retailers and other intermediaries by offering money back, discounts, free goods and 'sale or return' schemes, among other methods. They also offer sales force incentives to encourage a more committed selling effort from the intermediary's staff.

■ Direct marketing is a means of creating and sustaining one-to-one, personalised, good quality relationships between organisations and customers. As well as direct ordering of goods, direct marketing can support the sales effort with information campaigns and after-sales customer care initiatives to help engender long-term loyalty. It can also pave the way towards sales by inviting potential customers to try out products or to make appointments to see sales representatives. Direct mail can be very effective in stimulating responses from tightly defined target audiences made up either of existing customers or of new ones. Direct response advertising uses broadcast and print media with the aim of stimulating some kind of response from the target audience. Telemarketing specifically covers the use of the telephone as a means of creating a direct link between organisation and customer. Mail order, e-communication and teleshopping similarly create selling opportunities and the means of building direct relationships.

■ Organisations reap the best benefits from direct marketing when they use responses to build databases so that any one campaign or offer becomes just one of a series of relationship-building dialogues. It is important, however, to create and maintain a database that can cope with a detailed profile of each customer and their purchasing habits and history.

■ Exhibitions and trade shows vary from small local events to major national or international shows. They bring together a wide range of key personnel in one place at one time, and can thus generate a great many potential sales leads cost-effectively.

■ Public relations is about the quality and nature of an organisation's relationships with various interested publics. Public relations performs an important supporting role, providing a platform of goodwill and credibility from which other marketing activities can develop and be enhanced. Public relations becomes particularly important in limiting the damage and repairing credibility when a crisis strikes an organisation. Publicity and press relations are important areas of PR. The media can be valuable in communicating messages to all kinds of publics and even in influencing opinion. There are, however, more controllable methods of PR. Advertising can be used to build corporate image and attitudes, and special events and publications can also target key publics.

■ Sponsorship is used by many organisations as a means of generating PR and enhancing both their image and their other marketing communications activities. Sponsorship might mean involvement with sport, the arts, broadcast media or charities or other good causes. Both parties should gain. The sponsor benefits from the PR spin-offs from the activities and the public profile of the organisations and/or events it supports, while those receiving the sponsorship benefit from cash or benefits in kind. Sponsorship might be corporate or brand-specific, and the sponsor's involvement might be plainly obvious or quite discreet.

■ CRM links PR, sponsorship and sales promotion activities with the aim of providing resources or publicity for charities and/or other non-profit organisations. This is important at a time when consumers are becoming more conscious of the ethical and 'corporate citizenship' records of the companies they patronise.

Questions for review and discussion

11.1 Research a recent new product launch by a manufacturer in a consumer market. What role did sales promotions play in that launch?

11.2 Explain the role that direct marketing can play in both creating and retaining customers.

11.3 Collect three pieces of direct mail and for each one assess:

(a) what you think it is trying to achieve;

(b) how that message has been communicated;

(c) what involvement devices have been used to encourage the recipient to read the mailshot; and

(d) how easy it is for the recipient to respond in the required way.

11.4 What is *PR* and in what ways does it differ from other elements of the promotional mix?

11.5 Find a corporate story that has made the news recently. It might be a 'crisis', a takeover battle, job losses or creation, new products or big contracts, for instance. Collect reports and press cuttings from a range of media on this story and compare the content. To what extent do you think that:
   (a) the media have used material provided by the organisation itself?
   (b) the story has developed beyond the control of the organisation?

   (c) Imagine yourself to be the organisation's PR manager. Write a brief report to the managing director outlining what you feel to be the benefits and disadvantages of the coverage your organisation has received, and what you think should be done next regarding this story.

11.6 Find out as much as you can about three different arts sponsorship projects. What role do you think the sponsorship plays in the sponsor's marketing strategy and what benefits do you think they derive from it?

case study 11

Whether it's £1 or £1000, they want your loyalty

Customer retention and loyalty are prizes worth having in many sectors, and no more so than in supermarket retailing and in the airline business. Neither of them just want one-off customers, but those who come back again and again. Sales promotion has an important role to play in encouraging greater loyalty and repeat business by providing an ongoing incentive to return.

Frequent flyer miles are one of the airlines' most important marketing weapons and most airlines have schemes whereby miles mean points, and points mean free miles and upgrades. Although the discount airlines such as easyJet and Ryanair have shunned loyalty schemes by letting the regular price do the talking, most of the larger carriers have their frequent flyer clubs such as BA's Executive Club with three grades of membership, and Singapore Airlines with its Kris flyer scheme.

Frequent flyer schemes took off in 1981 when American Airlines introduced the first mileage-based loyalty scheme *AA Advantage*. Now 120 million people belong to the various airline schemes, and there is one individual account holder who actually possesses 23 million miles (Clark, 2005a)! Ironically the more miles you accumulate, the less likely you are to want to redeem them, as the prospect of a further long-haul trip may not be that appealing! A standard BA account holder needs to make two economy flights to New York to earn a free one-way flight to Paris. Chalk up around 80,000 miles, and you can get a free trip to Australia. Some, however, have warned that this 'alternative cur-

rency' is running out of control: the more members who join schemes, the more miles the airlines must give away, and thus the less flexible they can be when it comes for them to be redeemed (Taylor, 2004).

Nevertheless, the advantage for the frequent flyer are clear and it's not just about free flights. The use of exclusive airport lounges, faster check-ins, pre-boarding and a better chance of an upgrade are all valued by the more frequent traveller. Each level of a loyalty scheme has different privileges that reward the most frequent flyers who travel in the higher cabin grades. If the scheme is managed properly the airline also gains. It has repeat business and some flyers deliberately take a slightly longer route where possible if it enables them to accumulate miles. Others book tickets with the favoured airline rather than the cheapest airline (Taylor, 2004). It also allows for relationship and database marketing to enable tracking of flyer behaviour, how they buy tickets, frequency of travel, and party size, for example. It can also enable a link with associated schemes, such as those provided by hotels and car hire companies. This all helps the airlines to decide on route schedules and services. Finally, with the formation of international airline alliances it is becoming much harder for non-aligned and smaller airlines to challenge the dominance of the larger airlines on long-haul routes (Whyte, 2004).

New types of frequent flyer schemes are now emerging. Some airlines target businesses rather than individual business travellers; SAS, for example, launched Payback which rewards SMEs that spend more than £10,000 per year with up to 20 economy return tickets, equivalent to a 15 per cent cash-back. Similarly airline alliance schemes where there are code-share and route-share arrangements have grown. Thus, for example, a traveller to Hong Kong can use the BA Executive Club for the long haul and accumulate Cathay Pacific miles as part of the OneWorld Alliance for onward flights to destinations such as Hanoi or Manila which BA does not serve. The OneWorld alliance includes BA, American Airlines, Qantas and Cathay Pacific, making it one of the strongest in the world, covering 135 countries (Bold, 2004). Its rival is the Star Alliance which includes Lufthansa, United Airlines, Air Canada and Singapore Airlines. With the price of long-haul travel and the perishability of airline seats (see Chapter 13), it is not surprising that air miles loyalty schemes based on membership have become important tools for marketers. That is also true, however, of the supermarket retail sector across Europe. The major UK supermarkets have long competed with each other using sales promotion techniques such as short-term price offers, BIGIFs and free recipe cards in store. It is, however, the permanent loyalty schemes that have made the difference since the launch of the Tesco Clubcard scheme.

Permanent loyalty schemes that allow the retailer to capture and analyse customer data on an ongoing basis began to emerge in the UK supermarket sector in 1995. The technology to handle the massive amounts of data about customers and the minutiae of their daily shopping habits existed, and Tesco, the first of the major multiples to develop such a scheme, decided that the time was right to do it. To participate, customers have to register, filling in a short form giving details about themselves and their domestic situation. They then receive a 'Clubcard' that is swiped through the checkout every time they shop so that points are accumulated electronically, with one point awarded for each pound spent. Every quarter, the customer receives a statement showing how many points have been collected, and turning them into money-off vouchers on the basis of one penny for each point collected.

Since its launch, Tesco's scheme has expanded and developed further. In June 1996, for example, Tesco launched Clubcard Plus. This is a combined loyalty and credit card, in that holders pay a fixed sum every month into their Clubcard Plus account and then can use the card to do their shopping and even to withdraw cash at the checkout. A credit facility, up to the same sum as the usual monthly payment, is also available on the card. Whenever the customer's Clubcard Plus account is in credit, however, interest is paid on the balance.

Ways of redeeming points have also evolved to try to keep the Clubcard scheme interesting and fresh for customers. The vouchers can be used in-store to get discounts against shopping, but they can also be used to 'buy' Air Miles or for Clubcard Deals. The Clubcard Deals are goods and services, such as family days out at visitor attractions, cinema tickets and even speciality weddings. According to Tesco there are 11 million active cardholders and they receive 80,000 different

The Tesco Clubcard is offered to all customers and they are encouraged to present it each time they shop. They benefit from targeted mailings, offers, vouchers and the possibility of saving for Air Miles.

Source: © Sue Williams

combinations of offers with each mailing. Around £50m in vouchers are offered every quarter and the redemption rates are as high as 90 per cent. It is claimed that Clubcard generates £100m in incremental sales every year and the scheme has been viewed as a central part of the tremendous growth of Tesco in the 10 years since the Clubcard's launch. It enables Tesco to be closely in touch with customer buying trends. Also, as Tesco has diversified into new product lines such as personal finance, insurance and telecoms the database of regular customers enables effective direct marketing campaigns to be implemented, building on the loyalty created (Mistry, 2005).

The schemes thus provide a flexible mechanism through which other promotional activities can take place. The retailer can, for instance, link with a brand and offer a double or treble points promotion very quickly. Through the Tesco Clubcard magazine, mailed out regularly to customers along with their vouchers, tailored offers relevant to the recipient's shopping habits can be made. Thus money-off coupons relating to specific brands or product categories can be used to reinforce brand loyalty or to increase the volume or frequency of purchase.

The biggest advantage of a loyalty card, however, is the quantity and quality of data it generates on customer purchasing preferences and habits, thus providing the basis for measuring the response to various types of promotional offer so that better targeted and better designed promotions can be developed in the future. The use of data is starting to go further than that, however, and what started off as a humble promotional tool is starting to play a pivotal role in retail strategy, and even in manufacturer strategy. Tesco is using its Clubcard data to determine the layout and product assortment carried by individual stores. The company sees this as a 'pull' strategy with customers essentially driving decisions. Tesco is extending this 'pull' up the distribution channel to manufacturers by sharing its knowledge with them, collaborating on promotional deals, and selling advertising space to them in its Clubcard magazine mailings.

Despite the impact of loyalty schemes, their future success cannot be taken for granted. Firstly there is the danger that they actually detract from loyalty, as opposed to repeat purchase behaviour. Around 86 per cent of consumers belong to a supermarket loyalty scheme, but a lot of them belong to more than one and so switch between supermarkets. Similarly Whyte (2004) found that there were doubts whether frequent flyer schemes actually generated sustained loyalty in terms of a feeling of there being a bond of trust and commitment. Loyalty is often low at the basic membership levels with airlines, and many travellers are attracted by the reward rather than the airline. Again, a number of travellers are members of several schemes and will switch depending upon the offers. The frequent flyer programmes may constrain the choice, but do not always generate a real commitment to fly with a particular airline.

Another problem with loyalty schemes is that they are easier to enter than get out of. Some airlines are worried about the rapid build of unredeemed points which represent a contingent liability, and as numbers grow so do the costs of managing and administering

the schemes. Whatever the costs and risks, it would be a very brave airline that decided to phase out its frequent flyer scheme.

Finally, the power of the databases behind loyalty schemes are of concern to a growing number of consumers. What you buy, when you buy, how you buy and so on are there for examination; an individual's and family's lifestyles are available for targeted and powerful marketing. The level of personal information held is growing, creating a risk of data being used for purposes other than that intended, leading to more intrusive marketing. Tesco guards its data and never sells it to partners and third-party organisations, a policy followed by the other large-scale loyalty scheme operators (Mistry, 2005). Consumers may not be so lucky, however, with the ever-increasing number of schemes offered in the retail sector, and once trust is shaken, the resistance to such data tracking might grow (*Marketing Week*, 2005h).

Sources: Bold (2004); Clark (2005a); Hemsley (2002); *Marketing Week* (2005h); Mistry (2005); Taylor (2004); Tomlinson (2001); Whyte (2004).

Questions

1 What factors have led the supermarkets towards these kinds of loyalty scheme and what do they hope to achieve from them?

2 What are the practical problems of setting up, managing and maintaining a promotion like this?

3 In what ways do you think suppliers could benefit from loyalty card schemes?

4 In the longer term, do you think that retailers such as ASDA and Morrisons are right to reject the loyalty card concept?

References for chapter 11

Bailey, J. (1991), 'Employee Publications', in P. Lesly (ed.), *The Handbook of Public Relations and Communication*, 4th edn, McGraw-Hill.

Barrand, D. (2004), 'Playing in the Major League', *Marketing*, 11 August, p. 18.

Barrand, D. (2005), 'Sponsorship Leagues', *Marketing*, 15 June, pp. 37–9.

Bashford, S. (2004), 'Customers Calling', *Marketing*, 8 September, pp. 42–3.

Benady, D. (2005), 'Wish You Were Still Here', *Marketing Week*, 4 August, p. 20.

Bird, J. (1998), 'Dial 0 for Opportunity', *Marketing*, 29 October, pp. 31–3.

Bold, B. (2004), ' OneWorld Goes After Star Alliance Flyers', *Marketing*, 15 September, p. 12.

Brabbs, C. (2000), 'Texaco Entombs Cars for Treasure Hunt Promotion', *Marketing*, 6 July, p. 4.

Brennan, J. (2005), 'Marketers Learn the Laws of Good Cause and Effect', *Sunday Times*, 3 April, p. 10.

Britcher, C. (2004), 'Football Risks Sponsor Overkill', *Marketing*, 22 September, p. 18.

Carter, B. (2004a), 'O₂ Sponsors Live Music to Boost Appeal to Youth', *Marketing*, 8 April, p. 1.

Carter, B. (2004b), ' Mobile Brands Play Tactical Game', *Marketing*, 10 November, p. 16.

Chesshyre, T. and Bryan-Brown, C. (2004), 'Eurotunnel Abandons its Loyalty Scheme', *The Times*, 20 November, p. 19.

Clark, A. (2005a), 'Redeeming Points', *The Guardian*, 8 January, p. 2.

Clark, A. (2005b), 'Which is the World's Favourite Currency?', *The Guardian*, 8 January, p. 2.

Cohn, L. (2005), 'You Wanted Manchester United, Malcolm. Did You Know How Much It Would Cost?', *The Independent on Sunday*, 4 December, p. 13.

Cutlip, S. *et al.* (1985), *Effective Public Relations*, Prentice Hall.

Daily Record (2000), 'Buried Merc Found by Trio', *Daily Record*, 18 July, p. 13.

Davies, C. (2003), 'Premier League Nets £57m Deal', *The Daily Telegraph*, 4 October, p. 3.

Davies, M. (1992), 'Sales Promotion as a Competitive Strategy', *Management Decision*, 30 (7), pp. 5–10.

Derrick, S. (2002), 'Making Money from Movies', accessed via **http://www.pandionline.com.**

Edwards, J. (2005), 'Caring Culture Comes to Fore', *Birmingham Post*, 13 June, p. 29.

Fill, C. (2002), *Marketing Communications: Contexts, Strategies and Applications*, 3rd edn, Financial Times Prentice Hall.

Finch, J. (2002), 'Trade off: Carling Takes its Brand to the Music Industry', *The Guardian*, 9 January, p. 1.20.

Fletcher, K. (1999), 'Getting the Most out of Mailshots', *Marketing*, 13 May, pp. 38–9.

Gander, P. (2005), 'See Me, Feel Me, Touch Me', *Marketing Week*, 10 November, pp. 39–40.

Gillis, R. (2004a), 'Cricket Moves up the Order', *Marketing*, 20 July, pp. 30–2.

Gillis, R. (2004b), 'Global Deal, Local Glory', *Marketing*, 11 August, pp. 36–7.

Gillis, R. (2004c), 'Giving Something Back', *Marketing*, 22 September, pp. 38–9.

Gillis, R. (2005), 'FIFA Turns the Screw', *Marketing*, 20 April, p. 17.

Gray, R. (1999), 'Targeting Results', *Marketing*, 13 May, p. 37.

Grimes, E. and Meenaghan, T. (1998), 'Focusing Commercial Sponsorship on the Internal Corporate Audience', *International Journal of Advertising*, 17 (1), pp. 51–74.

Grimshaw, C. (2004), 'Lunn Poly Introduces TV Shopping Channel', *Marketing*, 19 May, p. 9.

The Grocer (2002a), 'Bendicks Offers Savings to Retailers', *The Grocer*, 19 January, p. 65.

The Grocer (2002b), 'Robinsons Aims to Clock Up Monster Sales with Disney', *The Grocer*, 26 January, p. 64.

Gupta, S. and Cooper, L. (1992), 'The Discounting of Discount and Promotion Brands', *Journal of Consumer Research*, 19 (December), pp. 401–11.

Hemsley, S. (2002), 'Loyalty in the Aisles', *Promotions and Incentives* supplement to *Marketing Week*, 21 February, pp. 9–10.

Hemsley, S. (2004), 'You've Got to Know What the Goal Is', *Financial Times*, 29 June, p. 10.

Hornby, M. (2005), 'Fury at "Gory" Knives as Toys', *Liverpool Echo*, 17 November, p. 11.

Jacob, G., O'Connor, A. and Ducker, J. (2005), 'United Backers Line Up but Will the Price be Right?', *The Times*, 16 December, p. 90.

Jones, P. (1990), 'The Double Jeopardy of Sales Promotions', *Harvard Business Review*, September/October, pp. 141–52.

Kleinman, M. (2002), 'Safeway in Major Pop Concert Tie-up', *Marketing*, 31 January, p. 3.

Klinger, P. (2005), 'Man Utd Sponsors Lend Support from Touchline', *The Times*, 30 May, p. 41.

Lewis, M. (1999), 'Counting On It', *Database Marketing*, May, pp. 34–7.

Marketing (2001), 'Public Relations Agency of the Year: Cohn & Wolfe', *Marketing*, 13 December, pp. 17–18.

Marketing Week (2004a), 'Nivea Severs "Sun" Link with Cancer Charity', *Marketing Week*, 8 January, p. 5.

Marketing Week (2004b), 'Euro 2004's Sponsorship Own Goal', *Marketing Week*, 1 July, p. 10.

Marketing Week (2005a), 'Vodafone Boss Puts Emphasis on Brand Experience, Not Advertising', *Marketing Week*, 3 February, p. 7.

Marketing Week (2005b), 'Soft Lips Signs as Sponsor of New Footballers' Wives Series', *Marketing Week*, 24 March, p. 6.

Marketing Week (2005c), 'Vouchers: Coupons Can be Cutting-edge', *Marketing Week*, 23 June, p. 45.

Marketing Week (2005d), 'Trojan Plans Brighton Cabs Sampling Drive', *Marketing Week*, 30 June, p. 6.

Marketing Week (2005e), 'Analysis: Look Who Else has Benefited from the Concerts for Africa', *Marketing Week*, 7 July, p. 15.

Marketing Week (2005f), 'Vodafone Calls Off Beckham Deal', *Marketing Week*, 28 July, p. 6.

Marketing Week (2005g), 'Reckitt to Sponsor Emmerdale', *Marketing Week*, 28 July, p. 15.

Marketing Week (2005h), 'Ministering to the Faithful', *Marketing Week*, 4 August, p. 33.

Marketing Week (2005i), 'Taste of the Unexpected', *Marketing Week*, 22 September, p. 43.

Marketing Week (2005j), 'Scots Pubs Mull Action Over Happy Hour Ban', *Marketing Week*, 6 October, p. 9.

Marston, J. (1979), *Modern Public Relations*, McGraw-Hill.

McAlevey, T. (2001), 'The Principles of Effective Direct Response', *Direct Marketing*, April, pp. 44–7.

McLuhan, R. (2000), 'Promoting Sales in Departure Lounges', *Marketing*, 7 December, pp. 39–40.

McLuhan, R. (2001), 'How DM Can Build Consumer Loyalty', *Marketing*, 3 May, pp. 45–6.

Meenaghan, T. (1998), 'Current Developments and Future Directions in Sponsorship', *International Journal of Advertising*, 17(1), pp. 3–28.

Middleton, T. (2002), 'A Winning Formula', *Promotions and Incentives* supplement to *Marketing Week*, 21 February, pp. 3–6.

Miller, R. (2001), 'Marketers Pinpoint their Targets', *Marketing*, 18 January, pp. 40–1.

Milmo, C. (2005), 'Sail of the Century', *The Independent*, 9 February, p. 12.

Mistry, B. (2005), 'A Question of Loyalty', *Marketing*, 2 March, pp. 41–2.

Mortished, C. (2005), 'Cosmetics Firms Fear Crackdown on Safety of Products', *The Times*, 22 March, p. 40.

Murphy, C. (1999), 'Brand Values Can Build on Charity Ties', *Marketing*, 25 March, p. 41.

O'Sullivan, T. (2001), 'A Leap in the Dark for Sponsors Facing Drugs Tests', *Marketing Week*, 30 August, p. 25.

Precision Marketing (2003), 'Dutch Loan Firms Destroying DRTV', *Precision Marketing*, 22 August, p. 9.

Precision Marketing (2004), 'Is the Sex Industry Too Bashful to Go Direct?', *Precision Marketing*, 22 October, p. 11.

Precision Marketing (2005a), 'Orbis Eyes Over-55 Women in Mail Offensive', *Precision Marketing*, 15 April, p. 6.

Precision Marketing (2005b), 'Diabetes UK in Drive for Member Recruits', *Precision Marketing*, 1 July, p. 5.

Promotions and Incentives (2002), 'Hellmann's Runs Free Cook Book Recipe Incentive', accessed via **http://www.pandionline.com**.

Promotions and Incentives (2005), 'Promotion Works: Müllerlight', *Promotions and Incentives*, March, p. 6.

PR Week (2005), 'Research and Girls Give Pillow Sales a Boost', *PR Week*, 19 August, p. 23.

Rigby, E. (2005a), ' MacArthur Sponsorship Deal Proves Plain Sailing', *Financial Times*, 9 February, p. 3.

Rigby, E. (2005b), 'Campaign of the Month', *Revolution*, June, p. 69.

Schofield, A. (1994), 'Alternative Reply Vehicles in Direct Response Advertising', *Journal of Advertising Research*, 34 (5), pp. 28–34.

Singh, S. (2004), 'The Art of Sponsorship', *Marketing Week*, 24 June, p. 28.

Skidmore, J. and Demetriou, D. (2005), 'London Hotels Slash Room Rates', *Daily Telegraph*, 13 August, p. 4.

Sliwa, C. (2001), 'Clothing Retailer Finds Worldwide Business on the Web', *Computerworld*, 30 April, p. 40.

Stanley, R. (1982), *Promotion: Advertising, Publicity, Personal Selling, Sales Promotion*, Prentice Hall.

Steiner, R. (2005a), 'Owzat! England Clinch New £16m Vodafone Deal', *Sunday Business*, 3 July, p. C3.

Steiner, R. (2005b), 'F1 Steers Tyre Fiasco Bill at Michelin', *Sunday Business*, 3 July, p. C13.

Stone, N. (1991), *How to Manage Public Relations*, McGraw-Hill.

Szczepanik, N. (2003), 'Barclays Deal Means Small Change to Premiership Title', *The Times*, 4 October, p. 34.

Taylor, R. (2004), 'Business Solutions: Travel: Divided Loyalties', *The Guardian*, 25 March, p. 14.

Tomlinson, H. (2001), 'Yes, I Do Have a Card, But is There a Loo?', *The Independent*, 25 March, p. 5.

Wheatley, K. (2002), 'MacArthur on Speed Mission', *Financial Times*, 4 January, p. 11.

Whyte, R. (2004), 'Frequent Flyer Programmes: Is it a Relationship, or Do the Schemes Create Spurious Loyalty?', *Journal of Targeting, Measurement and Analysis for Marketing*, 12 (3), pp. 269–80.

Wilkinson, A. (2004), 'Mail Order Industry's Catalogue of Errors', *Marketing Week*, 15 April, p. 18.

Wilmshurst, J. (1993), *Below-the-line Promotion*, Butterworth-Heinemann.

Wilson, R. (2001), 'Tried and Tested', *Promotions and Incentives* supplement to *Marketing Week*, 6 September, pp. 15–18.

chapter 12

marketing planning, management and control

learning objectives

This chapter will help you to:

1 define marketing planning and the internal and external influences affecting it;

2 understand the different types of plan found within organisations and the importance of formal planning processes;

3 define the stages in the marketing planning process and their contribution to sound, integrated plans;

4 outline alternative ways of structuring a marketing department and their advantages and disadvantages; and

5 understand the need for evaluation and control of marketing plans and their implementation, and the ways in which this can be achieved.

Introduction

So far, this book has looked at the practical aspects of marketing, from identifying consumer needs and wants through to designing and delivering a product package that aims to meet those needs and wants, and maintains customer loyalty despite the efforts of the competition. The tools that make up the marketing mix are, of course, critical for implementing the marketing concept, but so far, the focus on the marketing mix elements has largely been operational and oriented to the short term. Managers must, however, think of their operational marketing mixes in the context of wider, more strategic questions, such as:

■ Which markets should we be in?
■ What does our organisation have that will give it a competitive edge? (This need not necessarily come directly from marketing.)
■ Do we have the resources, skills and assets within the organisation to enable planned objectives to be achieved?
■ Where do we want to be in five or even 25 years' time?
■ What will our competitors be doing in three or five years' time?
■ Can we assume that our current modus operandi will be good enough for the future?

These concerns are strategic, not operational, in that they affect the whole organisation and provide a framework for subsequent operational decisions. The focus is on the future, aligning the whole organisation to new opportunities and challenges within the changing marketing environment, as discussed in Chapter 2. The questions suggested above seem deceptively simple, but finding answers to them is, in fact, a highly skilled and demanding task. The future welfare of the whole organisation depends on finding the 'right' answers.

The need for a strategic perspective on marketing has never been greater. Industries are being transformed by fast-changing consumer attitudes and values, by disruptive technologies, and by the emergence of new powerful economies such as China and India. The large-scale increase in manufacturing capacity in technology-based industries in China combined with more effective approaches to branding is likely to play a major role in many sectors over the next five to ten years. A brief review of the major sectors affected starts to show just how big an influence China could be:

■ *Cars*: By 2008 capacity of the car manufacturing industry will be approaching 9 million vehicles per year, twice the number of expected buyers within the domestic Chinese market. Honda is already exporting cars from its Guangzhou plant and is finding that the quality is better than that produced in the US.

■ *Steel*: The Chinese steel industry became a net exporter in 2004. Although demand is still buoyant with the massive building programmes being undertaken, the market for foreign imported steels is on the decline.

■ *Chemicals*: There is a large increase in local capacity which will reduce China's import needs from 50 per cent to one-third by 2008. There are 50 projects underway involving $1bn of investment. Eventually again, China may become a net exporter in some specialist areas.

■ *Semi-conductors*: There is still much progress to be made in this area, although a number of factories are coming online that can produce basic chips for electrical appliances and consumer goods, rather than for advanced applications.

■ *Digital electronics*: China is already a giant in this area and will become stronger. It dominates the manufacture of colour televisions, mobile phones, desktop PCs and DVD players. The industry is now moving up market to the premium end. With the size of the potential market for many of these products, China will increasingly develop its own branded goods and set the specifications and standards for the world.

All these sectors are some way from the stereotype of China being the cheap producer of the world's shoes and clothing. With more sophisticated technology and massive home demand potential, economies of scale will enable cost advantages to become even more evident. To create an even greater threat, the Chinese are learning about the power of branding and how it can be used in both domestic and export markets. Brand awareness of Chinese products among Chinese and US consumers is at best patchy and largely non-existent beyond Tsingtao beer. Aggressive tariffs and import controls also provide some short-term protection. It took 20 years for the Koreans to build their international brands such as Samsung, LG and Hyundai, but China could learn from those examples and move more quickly, fuelled by a strong domestic market generating experience and revenues. TCL, Haier and SVA may be the brands of tomorrow, especially as most of them have gained experience from joint ventures to help them create appropriate quality standards in the first place.

So, how can Western brand manufacturers survive the potential onslaught? Many will be forced to go even further upmarket in design, technology and materials or they may face potential extinction (Bremner and Engardio, 2005; Roberts *et al.*, 2004).

This chapter first introduces strategic marketing issues by defining some of the commonly used terms and showing how they fit together. It examines some of the issues associated with designing a planning system for marketing and how it fits into the organisational planning process. Then, the various stages of the marketing planning process are discussed in detail. Although the implementation of the planning process may vary from situation to situation, the outline given here at least demonstrates the interrelated nature of many planning decisions.

The chapter then moves on to examine other managerial issues associated with managing marketing. Making sure that the organisational structure of the marketing function is appropriate, for example, is essential to the achievement of the tasks specified in the plans. Issues of marketing control and analysis are also considered because without adequate and timely control systems, even the best-laid plans may be blown off course without managers realising the seriousness of the situation until it is too late to do anything about it.

The role and importance of marketing planning and strategy

Planning can be defined as a systematic process of forecasting the future business environment, and then deciding on the most appropriate goals, objectives and positions for best exploiting that environment. All organisations need to plan, otherwise both strategic and operational activities would at best be uncoordinated, badly focused and poorly executed. At worst, the organisation would muddle through from crisis to crisis with little sense of purpose, until eventually competition would gain such an advantage and demand reach such a low level that continuation would just not be viable. The marketing plan provides a clear and unambiguous statement concerning which strategies and actions will be implemented, by whom, when and with what outcomes.

Marketing strategy cannot be formulated in isolation. It has to reflect the objectives of the organisation and be compatible with the strategies pursued elsewhere in the organisation. This means that marketers must refer back to corporate goals and objectives before formulating their own strategy, to ensure consistency, coherence and relevance. The two-way process between marketing and corporate strategy is shown in Figure 12.1.

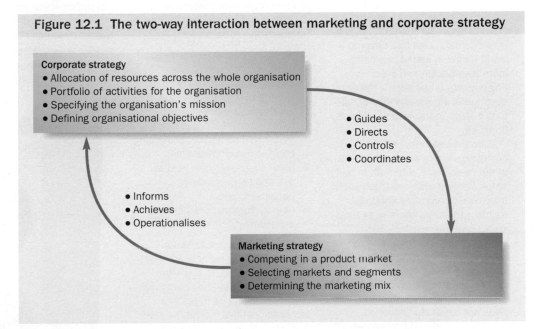

Figure 12.1 The two-way interaction between marketing and corporate strategy

Corporate strategy
- Allocation of resources across the whole organisation
- Portfolio of activities for the organisation
- Specifying the organisation's mission
- Defining organisational objectives

- Guides
- Directs
- Controls
- Coordinates

- Informs
- Achieves
- Operationalises

Marketing strategy
- Competing in a product market
- Selecting markets and segments
- Determining the marketing mix

To help to clarify the two-way interaction, the rest of this section is divided into two. First, we provide an overview of some of the different, and often overlapping, internal strategic perspectives, both corporate and marketing specific, that marketers have to consider in their strategic thinking. We then examine some of the broader factors that affect the formulation of marketing strategy in practice.

■ Definitions

This subsection outlines some of the strategic perspectives of the organisation, starting with the broad picture required by corporate strategy, then gradually focusing down towards the very specific detail of marketing programmes.

Corporate strategy

Corporate strategy concerns the allocation of resources within the organisation to achieve the business direction and scope specified within corporate objectives. Although the marketing department is primarily responsible for responding to perceived marketing opportunities and

A sound strategy

Linn Products is a Scottish manufacturer of high quality hi-fi equipment that targets the high-performance, top end of the European market. It made its mark with its first product in 1972, the Linn Sondek LP12, a transcription turntable that became the benchmark against which all the others were judged. The company applied the same standards and positioning to Linn speakers and the first solid state pitch accurate amplifiers. Linn now has over 50 products including CD players, tuners, amplifiers and speakers that it sells in 30 countries. In just over 30 years, Linn has become a world leader in sound technology, innovative design and precision engineering. It operates a policy of continuous improvement to ensure that it stays at the cutting edge of its niche.

Linn's mission is 'to thrill customers who want the most out of life from music, information and entertainment systems that benefit from quality sound by working together to supply them what they want when they want it'. Each product has the signature of the product builder. One product builder is responsible for the assembly, testing and packaging of an item. An old-fashioned attention to detail does not mean old-fashioned inefficient production processes, however. Linn claims to have one of the smallest plants in the world with automated materials handling right up to the assembly point. Within that, 'real-time' manufacturing is practised, meaning that each day's production is made to order for specific customers. The product designers too are close to the customer and are committed to continuous improvement. Such is the commitment to quality that due to difficulty in sourcing the top-of-the-range components for the multi-award winning Sondek CD12 CD player, Linn announced its premature withdrawal rather than compromise on its performance specification.

Linn's customer care philosophy extends from the manufacturing process through to the distribution channel. The company is selective about appointing dealers because it sees the key to selling its products as the expertise and product demonstration offered by the retailer. Linn is looking for those retailers that are the best in their area and have a quality reputation that fits with Linn's own. It wants retailers who want to sell quality products and are prepared to spend time with customers demonstrating and installing them. Retailers should be able to:

- work with customers to discover what kind of musical expectations and sound needs they have;
- appreciate the cost–value relationship inherent in Linn systems, if necessary comparing them with the competition;
- show customers how best to use and accommodate equipment; and
- help customers consider system expandability.

Linn is very reluctant to supply retailers who are not trained or are unable or unwilling to stock the range for demonstration purposes.

Linn Products operates in a highly competitive market, however, and by 2005 income was falling. The owner thought that the industry was becoming commoditised, in other words an excessive focus on price was making it increasingly difficult to retain profitability (Rogerson, 2005). The market was still very dynamic from a technological perspective, but the focus on price required Linn Products to concentrate even more on providing 'exceptional performance to discriminating customers'. That will be the competitive challenge for the years ahead.

Despite these challenges, Linn is an excellent example of how the vision and values of the leader have been translated into a competitive marketing strategy. Although one might expect the customer to be at the heart of a business from which a compact disc player could set you back £12,000 and to which a rock star paid £200,000 for a sound system for each room of his house, Mr Tiefenbrun, the owner, is controversially quoted as saying 'the customer comes third, the supplier comes first and the employee second. It was only by working with suppliers that the company got the components that worked in the way that customers wanted. Satisfied customers follow on from satisfied suppliers and employees' (as quoted by Murden, 2001).

Sources: Murden (2001); Rogerson (2005); **http://www.linn.co.uk.**

Linn speakers are quality products sold to customers by knowledgeable retailers with time to discuss individual needs.

Source: © Linn Products Limited
http://www.linn.co.uk

favourable competitive environments, it cannot act without the involvement of all other areas of the organisation too. Corporate strategy, therefore, helps to control and coordinate the different areas of the organisation – finance, marketing, production, R&D, etc. – to ensure that they are all working towards the same objectives, and that those objectives are consistent with the desired direction of the business as a whole. Typical issues of concern to corporate planners might thus be market expansion, product development priorities, acquisition, divestment, diversification and maintaining a competitive edge.

To help to make the corporate planning process more manageable, larger organisations often divide their activities into strategic business units (SBUs). An SBU is a part of the organisation that has become sufficiently significant to allow it to develop its own strategies and plans, although still within the context of the overall corporate picture. SBUs can be based on products, markets or operating divisions that are profit centres in their own right.

Competitive strategy

Competitive strategy determines how an organisation chooses to compete within a market, with particular regard to the relative positioning of competitors. Unless an organisation can create and maintain a competitive advantage, it is unlikely to achieve a strong market position. In any market, there tend to be those who dominate or lead, followed by a number of progressively smaller players, some of whom might be close enough to mount a serious challenge. Others, however, are content to follow or niche themselves (i.e. dominate a small, specialist corner of the market).

Marketing strategy

The marketing strategy defines target markets, what direction needs to be taken and what needs to be done in broad terms to create a defensible competitive position compatible with overall corporate strategy within those markets. Marketing mix programmes can then be designed to best match organisational capabilities with target market opportunities.

Marketing plan

It is in the marketing plan that the operational detail, turning strategies into implementable actions, is developed. The marketing plan is a detailed, written statement specifying target markets, marketing programmes, responsibilities, time scales and resources to be used, within defined budgets. Most marketing plans are annual, but their number and focus will vary with the type of organisation. The plan might be geographically based, product based, business unit based, or oriented towards specific segments. An overall corporate marketing plan in a large organisation might, therefore, bring together and integrate a number of plans specific to individual SBUs. Planning at SBU level and then consolidating all the plans ensures that the corporate picture has enough detail, and allows overall implementation and control to be managed.

Marketing programmes

Marketing programmes are actions, often of a tactical nature, involving the use of the marketing mix variables to gain an advantage within the target market. These programmes are normally detailed in the annual marketing plan, and are the means of implementing the chosen marketing strategy. Linn hi-fi systems, mentioned earlier in this chapter, found that an advertising campaign of £250,000 using quality journals, a direct mail programme, an annual brochure and a biannual magazine was appropriate for stimulating trial and maintaining customer relationships. Programmes provide clear guidelines, schedules and budgets for the range of actions proposed for achieving the overall objectives. These are determined within the framework of the overall marketing plan to ensure that activities are properly integrated and that appropriate resources are allocated to them.

■ Influences on planning and strategy

These are various influences on an organisation's marketing strategy, each of which is now discussed in turn.

Organisational objectives and resources

Marketing strategists need to be guided by what the organisation as a whole is striving for – what its objectives are and what resources it has to implement them. Some organisations might have very ambitious growth plans, while others might be content with fairly steady growth or even no growth at all, that is, consolidation. Clearly, each of these alternatives implies different approaches to marketing.

Resources are not only financial. They also include skills and expertise, in other words any area of the organisation that can help to add value and give a competitive edge. The exploitation, through marketing, of things that the organisation does well, such as manufacturing, technical innovation, product development or customer service, might help to create non-financial assets such as reputation and image, which are difficult for competitors to copy.

As the case of Holcim shows, marketing strategies do need to be compatible with corporate objectives and to capitalise on available resources.

eg Swiss Company Holcim is one of the world's largest suppliers of cement, aggregates and concrete with sales of CHF 7.87 bn in 2005. For any company of this nature to survive, there have to be economies of scale in production, consistent supplies of raw material and low transport costs. Holcim has established three fundamental strategic principles to guide its competitive position: cost leadership in its many overseas markets, market leadership to achieve volume sales, and strong vision and firm control over central strategy yet still allowing local autonomy.

When operating margins are down to around 25 per cent and price competition for a relatively undifferentiated product is severe, a focus on efficiency and keeping costs down is essential for survival. To achieve cost leadership, Holcim invests heavily in technology to reduce unit costs and often locates plants either near to raw materials or near to customers. Through a process of acquisition and new plant openings, it now has interests in cement plants in 70 countries, giving the company over 630 ready-mix concrete plants, many of which operate under different names. Wherever Holcim decides to expand, largely driven by construction opportunities because of demographic development or infrastructure renewal, the formula is the same: large volumes, efficient operations and local service. The strategic risk is spread by its involvement in many different markets, each at different stages of growth, decline and maturity, and this allows it to concentrate on its core business, to the point of divesting more marginal activities.

Although Europe is still its strongest market, it is also one of the toughest as Holcim vies with France's Lafarge for leadership. It is in emerging markets that the most severe competition is experienced, however. Asia and Latin America are especially important for future growth. In India, for example, the acquisition of Ambuja Cement Eastern and an increased shareholding in the market leader Associated Cement Companies are expected to strengthen the long-term competitive position. Holcim's long-term strategy is to build a truly global brand (*Financial Times*, 2001; Simonian, 2005).

Attitude to change and risk

The corporate view on change and risk often depends on the approach of top management. Risk tolerance varies widely from individual to individual, and from management team to management team. Managers will also, of course, be guided by the nature of the organisation and their interpretation of its business environment. The managing director of a small business may not want to take on high risk projects, feeling that the firm's size makes it more vulnerable to failure through its lack of resources. A larger firm might be able to absorb any losses, and therefore feel that the risk is worth taking.

eg

The biotechnology industry is a good example of the difficulties of managing risk and innovation in scientific fields. It was British scientists working in British universities who provided the intellectual foundation of the industry, but it has been US groups such as Amgen and Genentech that have been at the forefront of innovation and commercialisation rather than invention. Each is worth around four times the total UK sector. The academic culture in many British science universities favours spin-offs from the laboratory, but it is then that the strategic problems start.

It is not, therefore, the case that the biotechnology sector in the UK has a shortage of innovative ideas, indeed there has been a steady stream of technological breakthroughs, many coming from smaller companies. Being a smaller organisation can help to create a culture that encourages flexibility and inventiveness as long as there is sufficient capital to see it through the leaner start-up period. Venture capitalists do absorb some of the early risk on the promise of future returns. All too often in the UK, as soon as the product looks promising it is the large, well-financed organisations such as Amgen that move in to acquire the smaller companies. The announcement that Celltech, one of the UK's greatest hopes for market leadership to rival the Americans, was bought out by an American company is a case in point as it lacked the ability to build a sustainable long-term biotechnology business that could compete globally head-on.

A critical factor in the life of a biotechnology company is its ability to manage risk. The early period of development is concerned with the risk of sustaining the business at a time when the product has not been launched. Then there are risks associated with commercialisation, especially in a global industry, as not only does it drain resources further, but given the lead time for new product development, it often means that funds need to be diverted to the next generation of products. That is often too much for under-resourced smaller organisations when the shareholders may be prepared to take a risk, but institutional investors prefer to give in to the temptation of an early return when a buy-out offer comes along.

As with any new product, there is also the danger of product failure. The main cancer drug developed by British Biotech failed, and Scotia Holdings' diabetes drug was rejected by health regulators. In an industry characterised by high risks, long-term projects, and sometimes spectacular failures, it is not surprising that an appetite for risk is an important prerequisite for any strategic marketing plan. It's all about trading the risks of product development and the costs against the rewards of a successful and sustainable market entry. It sounds easy enough, but for many smaller biotechnology companies it is even easier to cooperate when the giants show an interest in acquisition.

The giant pharmaceutical companies, by contrast, invest far more heavily, perhaps two or three times the level of smaller biotech companies, as they need to record global product sales in the billions rather than millions to sustain growth. This can sometimes increase the development period and stifle some inventions that do not meet that criterion. Often, the large pharmaceutical companies could learn from the enterprise and drive of the smaller biotech companies, while the smaller companies could learn from the expertise of the big manufacturers in achieving success in getting ideas to the marketplace. Many of these larger organisations actively seek out smaller biotechnology companies for purchase, and Amgen holds a series of open days in cities around the US and Europe presenting its business and projects, and inviting potential biotech partners to meet with it to discuss cooperation options up to and including acquisition. All this suggests a 'feeding chain' in which universities invent, smaller firms launch, larger biotech firms commercialise, and then larger pharmaceutical firms capitalise through alliances and mergers. At each stage, however, the culture must be ambitious and risk-accepting if success is to be achieved (Dyer, 2001, 2004; Jack, 2005).

Market structure and opportunities

Markets vary considerably in their structure and dynamics. Some are fairly stable and not a great deal happens in them unless one of the major players decides to become aggressive and seeks to improve its competitive position. Some markets are simply too complacent. A good example would be the Dutch agriculture sector, which has been criticised for failing to keep up with market changes and increased levels of European competitiveness. Although competitiveness has been maintained in cut flowers and seeds, ground has been lost in the dairy, vegetable and pork sectors. The real problem has arisen from changes in the marketing environment, as consumers have sought a wider variety of products and higher product specifications, and European supermarket buyers have sought greater efficiency.

eg Mothercare (http://www.mothercare.com) is a retailer of specialist accessories and clothing for babies and children up to eight years old. In the UK, it is claimed that over 90 per cent of pregnant women visit one of its 245 stores before giving birth, generating a turnover of over £300m. From its launch in 1961, Mothercare worked hard to establish a reputation for quality, own-label brands, an attractive retail environment and a comprehensive range including maternity wear. Since 1984, export sales have been developed through direct retail outlets and franchises, resulting in operations in over 30 countries.

Despite its strong market presence, in recent years its performance has not lived up to expectations and market share has been lost. Particular difficulties have been experienced in the 4–8-year-old segment because children are developing fashion consciousness from an earlier age, but even apart from that, Mothercare has been under attack in all segments. Pregnancy is no longer an excuse for the removal of fashion clothing from the wardrobe, and Mothercare has had some difficulty in providing an acceptable variety of fashionable maternity clothing compared with more fashion-oriented stores. The trendier end of the children's clothing market has been driven by the likes of Baby Gap and Higsma Junior, while the value end of the market has been hit hard by ASDA, Tesco, and Hennes & Mauritz. Even the more upmarket niches have been targeted by retailers such as Gap, Next, and Tom and Daisy (Bashford, 2002; Kleinman, 2002). Boots has moved aggressively into the babywear segment, so in all areas the fight is on.

The challenge for Mothercare, therefore, is to plot its future corporate and marketing strategy. Should it concentrate on pregnancy and babies and toddlers, where margins tend to be higher and there is still a strong awareness and market penetration, rather than including the 4–8-year-old segment? Mothercare is still a respected and valued brand, but some of its clothes have failed to make an impact in a society where children have become a fashion statement. To restore its position, Mothercare embarked upon a recovery programme in 2002 to revitalise the business. It has focused on children's clothing with a determination to take on the more fashion-oriented competitors. Maternity wear has been revamped and occasional purchases such as cots and pushchairs have been de-emphasised, but new lines have been introduced such as space-efficient nursery equipment and ranges for premature babies. Distribution costs have been reduced through a new warehouse operation and a store refit programme is underway along with further store expansion, especially on out-of-town sites. This is all part of the strategic renewal necessary to respond to changing market opportunities (Buckley, 2005a, 2005b; Urquhart, 2004).

Competitor strategies

The competitive structure in different product markets will vary to create conditions of strong or weak competition. In markets such as computer chips, the dominant competitor has a major influence over the level and nature of competition. Challenges can still arise, but nevertheless, within constraints set by governmental competition policy and public pressure, a dominant competitor is effectively able to decide when and how to compete. The dominant competitor is likely to be confident that it has sufficient strength through its market position, its volume sales, and thus perhaps its cost base to fight any serious challenger successfully.

Types of plan

It is important to distinguish between *plans*, the outcomes of the planning process, and *planning*, the process from which plans are derived. While the process of planning is fairly standard and can be transferred across functions and organisations, there are often wide variations in the actual use of plans to guide strategy and operations. This is partly because there are several different types of plan that can emerge from a planning process. Plans may be differentiated in terms of a number of features. These are as follows.

Organisational level

Managers are involved with planning at all levels of an organisation. The concerns of managers, however, change at higher levels of the organisation, and the complexities affecting planning also change. The more senior the manager, the more long-term and strategic becomes the focus. At the highest level, the concern is for the whole organisation and how to allocate resources across its various functions or units. At lower levels, the focus is on implementation within a shorter-term horizon, and on operating within clearly specified parameters. The marketing director may thus have a particular concern with developing new innovative products and opening new segments, while the sales representative may have to focus on sales territory planning to achieve predetermined sales and call objectives.

Timescale

Plans may be short-, medium- or long-term in focus. *Short-term* normally means the shortest period of time appropriate to the operations of the organisation. Normally this is one year, or in some industries, such as fashion, one season. *Medium-term plans* are more likely to cover a one- to three-year period. The focus is not so much on day-to-day operations and detailed tactical achievement as on renewal. This could include the opening up of a new market, a new product innovation, or a strategic alliance to improve market position, for example. *Long-term* plans can be anything from three to 20 years, with the timescale often dictated by capital investment periods. Long-term plans are nearly always strategic in focus and concerned with resource allocation and return.

Regularity

Most longer-term plans have annual reviews to monitor progress. Shorter-term plans are often part of a hierarchy linking strategy with operations. Some plans, however, are not produced regularly as part of an annual cycle, but are campaign-, project- or situation-specific. A *campaign plan*, for example for a specific advertising campaign, might have a limited duration to achieve defined objectives. *Project plans* are specific to particular activities, perhaps a new product launch, a change in distribution channels, or a new packaging innovation. These activities are of fixed duration and are not necessarily repeated.

Focus

Plans will vary in their focus across the organisation. *Corporate plans* refer to the longer-term plans of the organisation, specifying the type of business scope desired and the strategies for achieving it across all areas of the business. The focus is on the technology, products, markets and resources that define the framework within which the individual parts of the organisation can develop more detailed strategies and plans. *Functional or operational plans* are, therefore, developed within the context of the organisational corporate plan but focus on the implementation of day-to-day or annual activities within the various parts of the organisation.

Organisational focus

Plans will vary according to the nature of the organisation itself. A number of alternative ways of organising marketing are considered later (see pp. 448 *et seq.*). If the organisational focus is on products, then plans will also take that focus, while if markets or functional areas are emphasised, plans will reflect that structure. For example, a functional organisational marketing plan will have distinct elements of pricing, advertising, distribution, etc. If SBUs are formed, then there is immediately a requirement for a two-tier planning structure:

(a) considering the portfolio of SBUs at a corporate level, and (b) for each SBU, looking at the more detailed organisational design. Similarly divisional, regional, branch or company plans may all be used in different circumstances.

There are several benefits to be gained from taking a more organised approach to planning marketing activity. In summary, the benefits can be classified as relating to the development, coordination or control of marketing activity, as shown in Figure 12.2.

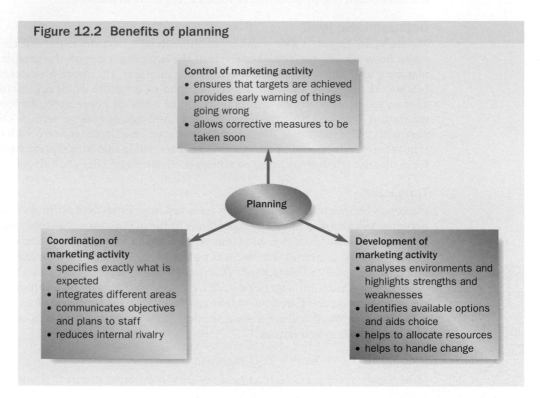

Figure 12.2 Benefits of planning

Despite the obvious benefits, we cannot assume that all organisations practise planning, and even those that do might not achieve all the results they expect. Planning in itself does not guarantee success. Much depends on the quality of the planning, its acceptance as a fundamental driving force within the organisation, and the perceived relevance of the resulting plans.

There is no room for a weak link in the chain, since the plans are only as good as the process that generated them, and the process is pointless if it does not result in acceptable, implementable plans.

The marketing planning process

The purpose of marketing planning has been defined as:

> to find a systematic way of identifying a range of options, to choose one or more of them, then to schedule and cost out what has to be done to achieve the objectives. (McDonald, 1989, p. 13)

Although the structure of a marketing plan will vary according to the complexity and variability of the organisation, and the emphasis may vary according to the turbulence in the environment and the resultant challenges facing the organisation, a number of broad phases in the planning process are likely to operate in any case. The main stages in the planning process are shown in Figure 12.3 and each stage is considered in turn.

Pilkington Glass, one of the world's largest manufacturers of glass and glazing products, developed long-term corporate strategies aiming to make it the number one or number two supplier in selected geographic markets. Essential to achieving this was a detailed review and restructuring of its marketing positioning and activities. The strategic plan, therefore, identified three sectors in which leadership was to be sought and retained: building, automotive and related technical markets. It also outlined the strategies for getting there, including product development and improving market coverage, while the operational marketing plans focused on any price promotions/changes, plans to improve service by online ordering in the automotive sector and developing the markets in China, India, the Middle East and Russia to combat sluggish growth in more traditional markets. This helps managers to put strategy into practice, however remote they are from corporate headquarters.

The role of any operational marketing plan is important when an organisation employs over 27,000 people worldwide with manufacturing in 25 countries and sales in 130 countries. During tough economic conditions, when the housing, construction and car markets are not buoyant on a global scale, uncoordinated local actions outside the overall policy and direction of the company, for example price cutting or positioning the products in an inappropriate manner, could have effects across the company (Foley, 2002). It is also important to take a unified approach to new product development. Pilkington is a market leader in 'added value', such as self-cleaning double glazing, and when it launches a new product, it rarely does it on a country-by-country basis, but in groups of countries in one go (**http://www.pilkington.com**).

Whether it is made in Poland or elsewhere, Pilkington produces glass that satisfies the customer's latest needs.

Source: © Sue Cunningham Photographic/Alamy
http://www.alamy.com

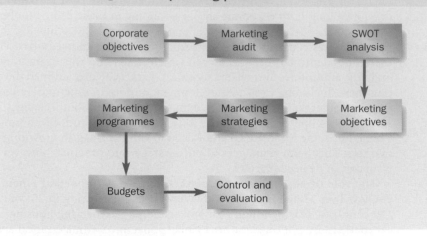

Figure 12.3 Stages in the planning process

Corporate objectives and values

Corporate objectives are at the heart of the planning process, since they describe the direction, priorities and relative position of the organisation in its market(s). Some objectives, such as market share (by value), sales, profit and ROI, are quantitative, while others, such as the philosophies reflected in mission and values statements, are more qualitative in nature.

Philosophical targets, often called vision and values statements, have grown in popularity in recent years as a more enduring and all-embracing perspective of where an organisation seeks to journey and how it intends to conduct itself on the way. McDonald's has the vision of providing the world's best quick-service restaurant experience, and to achieve that it seeks to provide a level of quality, good service, cleanliness and value that makes every customer in a restaurant smile. In contrast, Vivendi, the entertainment company, has the vision of being the world's preferred creator and provider of entertainment, education and personalised service to consumers anywhere, at any time and across all distribution platforms.

Qualitative targets also include items such as service levels, innovation and scope.

Whether quantitative or qualitative, these objectives help to create guidelines for marketing plans, since the output of the corporate planning process acts as an input into the marketing planning process. All objectives must be realistic, achievable within a specific time scale, and cited in order of priority. This will lead to a hierarchy of interlinking objectives.

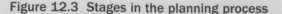

corporate social responsibility   in action

Cadbury Schweppes: walking the CSR talk

Cadbury has developed from a small family business established on Quaker values into an international company that still upholds the importance of taking a socially responsible approach to all facets of its work, despite being a commercial enterprise. Quakers have strong beliefs that are carried through into campaigns for justice, equality and social reform, reflected in Cadbury's original ideal of helping to end poverty and deprivation in Victorian

Britain. The foundations for a corporately socially responsible organisation were, therefore, laid over 100 years ago and have endured and been embodied in the social responsibility programme of today, despite the tremendous change, diversification and internationalisation that has happened in the company.

The overriding policy statement highlights the central importance of CSR to business strategy:

'Good ethics and good business go together naturally. We firmly

believe that our responsibility and reputation as a good corporate citizen plays an important role in our ability to achieve our objective of growing value for our shareowners.'

Keeping a watch over all aspects of the company's activities is a Corporate and Social Responsibility Committee at board level, chaired by a high-profile non-executive director, Baroness Wilcox, a former head of the National Consumer Council.

The CSR policy at Cadbury Schweppes is broken down into

eight areas, including the environment, human rights, corporate governance, employees, suppliers and community involvement. Not all these areas are examined in detail in this book, but each individually and collectively has helped to build a strong reputation, confidence and a record of achievement that could be considered a model. Each area is considered briefly in turn.

- *Corporate governance*. A corporate governance policy embraces the broad principles of business dealings and conduct with all Cadbury's publics in terms of ethics, openness and honesty. These reflect the enduring values inherited from the past. It also has a code of conduct approved by the board to which all employees are expected to adhere. This code embraces more practical issues such as legal and compliance issues, handling of conflicts of interests, gifts, dealing with competition, whistle blowing, confidentiality and political contributions. Each employee is provided with their own copy of the code and compliance to the code is enforced through the management process. To Cadbury, good ethics and good business go together.
- *Human rights*. Cadbury is particularly sensitive to the dangers of operating in cultures where different norms and practices may apply. The reports of slave child labour in the cocoa industry in West Africa were of particular concern. Although the allegations were made about the Ivory Coast where Cadbury does not buy, it is playing a full part in the industry, along with governments and NGOs, to ensure that such practices are stamped out. It fully contributes to surveys of child labour practices, independent monitoring and the certification of cocoa to ensure that all conditions have been met. Closer to home, the

company has also published its own human rights and ethical trading policy covering labour rights, dignity at work, health and safety, fair remuneration, diversity, a respect for differences and the need for personal development. Progress measurement in each of these areas is assessed by a working group reporting to the CSR Committee. This will increasingly also apply to the supply chains feeding into the company. A programme of education and implementation is now under way in all its businesses around the world.
- *Community and social investment*. Cadbury also recognises the role and responsibilities it has in the communities in which it operates. The policy is not about handouts and high-profile gift giving but takes a longer-term integrated approach as part of a 'managing for community value' programme. This means carefully selecting the initiatives to encourage and taking on a longer-term approach to achieving agreed objectives. It has a Foundation that makes grants to projects and partner organisations, especially in the fields of education and employment, focusing on social exclusion and deprivation in places such as Birmingham, Sheffield, Bristol and London. The concerns over obesity (see pp. 93–4) have placed companies like Cadbury's in the firing line of media criticism about chocolate calories, promotion to children, and confectionery's contribution to the so-called 'obesity epidemic'. Cadbury is, however, working closely with government and industry to find ways to tackle the problem, based on sound evidence, and is providing information and education to encourage consumers to eat sensibly and in moderation. This is especially important in targeting children. The CSR report gives detail of how

Cadbury Schweppes approaches and interacts with both children and parents.
- *Environment*. Sustainability is central to the policies in this area. The 'Environmental Report' outlines the programmes the company has undertaken in developing long-term sustainability, protecting the environment and assessing the environmental impact of its prime activities. The policy itself is still evolving to include transportation, supply chain management and raw material sourcing. The report also considers a number of areas such as waste management, water conservation and energy use to demonstrate the company's efforts to improve the environment. The beverages plant in Carcagente in Spain, for example, recycles all of its organic waste. Packaging is more problematic, but the PET, glass bottles and aluminium cans can all be reprocessed in-house or with specialist recyclers. Even broken pallets are repaired and reused. At a plant near Dijon in France, 90 per cent of all solid waste is recycled and only a small amount of water is sent for appropriate recycling. Global warming is also considered and Cadbury was recognised as being best in class in its approach to climate change in reducing CO_2 emissions.
- *Employment practices*. This area of CSR covers a variety of human resource issues such as personal development, the working environment and equal opportunities, all of which are beyond the scope of this text.

By adopting such a comprehensive approach to CSR, the values embodied within Cadbury and the business principles espoused are put into practice. Care has to be taken, however. One attempt to undertake cause-related marketing in Kenya led to a blurring of objectives. When sponsoring the Mediae Trust which produces radio programmes for rural communities focusing on social and environmental themes such as animal husbandry and child abuse, the distinction between education and advertising became confused. Cadbury paid for the air time for Mediae broadcasts in return for some advertising space, so although it helped product sales, it also contributed to broader rural social development policies. However, one audience member is quoted as saying, 'I like the show because it educates us, like what to do if your child is mistreated, it also teaches us how useful Cadbury's is; that it builds healthy bodies' (as quoted by Turner, 2002). Overall, though, Cadbury has 'walked the talk' and presents a good example to other companies.

Sources: Turner (2002); **http://www.cadburyschweppes.com.**

◼ The marketing audit

The marketing audit systematically takes stock of an organisation's marketing health, as the formal definition implies:

> *[The audit] is the means by which a company can understand how it relates to the environment in which it operates. It is the means by which a company can identify its own strengths and weaknesses as they relate to external opportunities and threats. It is thus a way of helping management to select a position in that environment based on known factors.*
> (McDonald, 1989, p. 21)

It is really the launching pad for the marketing plan, as it encourages management to reflect systematically on the environment and the organisation's ability to respond, given its actual and planned capabilities. The marketing audit is first and foremost about developing a shared, agreed and objective understanding of the organisation. Table 12.1 summarises the issues that a marketing audit should consider.

Table 12.1 Marketing audit issues

- Macro environment: STEP factors (see Chapter 2)
- Task environment: *competition, channels, customers* (see Chapters 3 and 4)
- Markets (see Chapter 12)
- Strategic issues: *segmentation, positioning, competitive advantage* (see Chapters 4 and 12)
- Marketing mix (see Chapters 6–11)
- Marketing organisational structure and organisation (see Chapter 12)

The audit should be undertaken as part of the planning cycle, usually on an annual basis, rather than as a desperate response to a problem. To help the audit process, it is critical to have a sound marketing information system covering the marketing environment, customers, competitors, etc., as well as detail on all areas of the internal organisational marketing effort. In order to complete an audit, managers thus have to look at both operational variables (i.e. an internal audit) and environmental variables (i.e. an external audit).

Internal audit

The internal audit focuses on many of the decision areas discussed in Chapters 3–11 and their effectiveness in achieving their specified objectives. It is not just, however, a post mortem on the 4Ps. Auditors will also be interested in how smoothly and synergistically the 4Ps fit together, and whether the marketing actions, organisation and allocated resources are appropriate to the environmental opportunities and constraints.

Portfolio analysis. In assessing the marketing health of the organisation, it is not enough to look simply at the performance of individual products. Although products may be managed as individual entities on an operational basis, strategically they should be viewed as a product portfolio, that is, a set of products, each of which makes a unique contribution to the corporate picture. The strategist needs to look at that corporate picture and decide whether, for example, there are enough strong products to support the weak ones, whether the weak ones have development potential or whether there are appropriate new products in development to take over from declining ones. The various portfolio models outlined below can be applied either to SBUs or to individual products, and thus the use of the word 'product' throughout the discussion should be taken to mean either.

The BCG matrix. Sometimes referred to as the Boston Box, or the BCG matrix, the Boston Consulting Group (BCG) market growth–relative market share model, shown in Figure 12.4, assesses products on two dimensions. The first dimension looks at the general level of growth in the product's market, while the second measures the product's market share relative to the largest competitor in the industry. This type of analysis provides a useful insight into the likely opportunities and problems associated with a particular product.

Market growth reflects opportunities and buoyancy in different markets. It also indicates the likely competitive atmosphere, because in high growth markets there is plenty of room for expansion and all players can make gains, while in low growth markets competition will be more intense, since growth can only be achieved by taking share away from the competition.

Market share position is measured on a logarithmic scale against the product's largest competitor. Thus a relative share figure of 0.2 means that the product achieves only 20 per cent of the market leader's sales volume, a potentially weak competitive position. Similarly, a share figure of 2 would mean that the product has twice the market share of its nearest rival. A share figure of 1 means roughly equal shares, and therefore joint leadership.

Figure 12.4(a) gives an example of the resultant matrix after all the products of an organisation have been thus analysed. The next stage is to plot the products within a simpler four-cell matrix that reflects the differing competitive positions, as shown in Figure 12.4(b). Each cell offers different types of business opportunities and imposes different resource demands. The general labelling of the cells as 'high' and 'low' gives an instant and sufficient feel for each product's situation, and the circle that represents each SBU's contribution to the organisation's total sales volume provides a further indication of the relative importance of different products. In Figure 12.4(b), for example, Product 2 can be seen to be the biggest contributor to overall sales volume, whereas Product 1 contributes very little. The 'ideal' model is one where the portfolio is reasonably balanced between existing strength and emerging opportunity. We now look in turn at each cell of the matrix.

Dog (low share, low growth): A dog holds a weak market share in a low growth market, and is likely to be making a loss, or a low profit at best. It is unlikely that its share can be increased at

Figure 12.4 BCG matrix

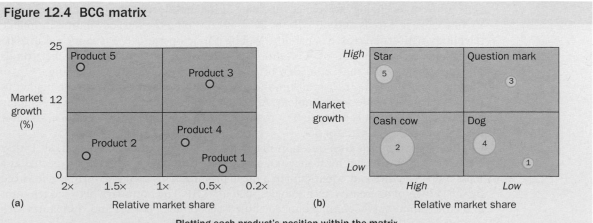

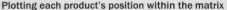

(a) Plotting each product's position within the matrix   (b)

a reasonable cost, because of the low market growth. A dog can be a drain on management time and resources.

eg Liptonice, a cold, fizzy, canned lemon tea, and other products like it had proved to be successful in continental Europe and its owners were confident that it could succeed in the UK market too. What they had not taken into account, however, was the nature of the British consumer's love affair with tea and the perception of it among younger consumers. In the British mind, tea should be drunk hot and milky – even drinking it hot and black with lemon is considered a bit risqué. The ritual of making tea 'properly' is also deeply culturally ingrained. Add to that the young person's view that tea is for grannies, and the prospects for canned, cold, fizzy lemon tea start to look less promising. A £6m product launch and later a £4m relaunch failed between them to achieve the product's target of £20m sales per year and the product quietly disappeared from UK stores. The initial failure has not, however, deterred further attempts. The fourth attempt was made in 2003 when it was decided to hit British attitudes head-on with the creative message 'Don't knock it until you've tried it', with the purpose of generating trial. Despite its disarming honesty, the public is still to be won over. In UK terms, the product remains a dog, and only buoyant sales elsewhere in Europe allow continued attempts to change British tastes (Gardner, 2003, 2004; *The Grocer*, 2002; *Marketing*, 2002).

The question, therefore, is whether or not to shoot the dog, that is, withdraw the product. Much depends on the strategic role that the dog is fulfilling and its future prospects. It may, for example, be blocking a competitor (a guard dog?), or it may be complementing the company's own activities, for example creating customers at the bottom of the range who will then trade up to one of the organisation's better products (a guide dog, or a sheep dog?).

Question mark (low share, high growth): The high market growth of a question mark is good news, but the low share is worrying. Why is relative market share so low? What is the organisation doing wrong, or what is the competition doing right? It may simply be that the question mark (also sometimes called a problem child or a wild cat) is a relatively new product that is still in the process of establishing its position in the market. If it is not a new product, then it might just need far more investment in plant, equipment and marketing to keep up with the market growth rate. There is also a risk, however, that a question mark with problems might absorb a great deal of cash just to retain its position.

eg The mobile phone market is now mature and penetration levels of 108 per cent in the UK and 111 per cent in Germany have already been achieved (Wray, 2005). The next generation of technology to change the shape of the mobile market is 3G, due to its ability to receive live feeds and broadcasts. 3G is meant to be the next revolution in mobile telephony with its increased capability. Mobile phone operator 3 was launched in 2003 to exploit the introduction of 3G technology and now has 3.2 million customers on its network, making it a market leader. It is, however, a long way behind Orange, O_2, T-Mobile and Vodafone in overall mobile market share terms and it has struggled to convert customers onto its technology. Although 3 has put a lot of effort into developing a brand personality, it is going to be a challenge to take on the larger operators, whatever the rate of market growth for 3G.

This raises the issue of a question mark's growth within the mobile market. Unless conversion improves, 3G itself may not achieve the penetration originally expected as a mass market service and could remain a niche product. This could be further reinforced by the launch of alternative technologies such as VOIP. The boundary between telecoms and entertainment is becoming blurred and attracts cable operators and companies such as Google into the arena. In the short term, much will depend upon whether users will regard advertising on their mobiles as a form of spam, and will quickly build up a resistance to, if not resentment of, one of the main sources of potential revenue for 3G operators. As a pioneer in this area, 3's position will be particularly adversely affected if the market itself does not take off as planned, without enabling the recovery of the considerable up-front investment (*Marketing Week*, 2005a).

Some of the alternatives for question marks, such as dropping or repositioning, are the same as for the dogs, but there are some more creative options. If the product is felt to have potential, then management might commit significant investment towards building market share, as mentioned above. Alternatively, if the organisation is cash rich, it might seek to take over competitors to strengthen its market position, effectively buying market share.

Star (high share, high growth): A star product is a market leader in a growth market. It needs a great deal of cash to retain its position, to support further growth and to maintain its lead. It does, however, also generate cash, because of its strength, and so it is likely to be self-sufficient. Stars could be the cash cows of the future.

eg Satellite navigation systems is one of the fastest growing areas of the car accessory market. TomTom is the market leader and its sales more than doubled in the first quarter of 2005 alone. Income is expected to treble over the year. Nevertheless, competition is becoming fierce and prices for satnav systems have tumbled from £1000 to £300 as the appeal broadens. Initially, the market was dominated by car audio manufacturers such as Pioneer and Kenwood, but specialist portable systems from new manufacturers have fuelled growth. Forecasts have suggested that growth will be 24 per cent per year over the next couple of years; saturation will take much longer as only 6 per cent of Europe's 200 million cars have navigation systems at present (Reid, 2005). TomTom is therefore in a strong position in the European market with a star product, and the challenge is to sustain that position against more recent rivals (*Euroweek*, 2005; Loades-Carter *et al.*, 2005; Reid, 2005).

Cash cow (high share, low growth): As market growth starts to tail off, stars can become cash cows. These products no longer need the same level of support as before since there are no new customers to be had, and there is less competitive pressure. Cash cows enjoy a dominant position generated from economies of scale, given their relative market share.

eg Wrigley's has a dominant position in the chewing gum market with annual sales of $2bn in the US alone and with sales in 180 countries. Just under half of all chewing gum sales are under the Wrigley's brand name. Wrigley's works hard to protect its position by pulling demand into the stores through strong branding and advertising and promotion, offering a wide appeal. Because of its market leadership position, it is able to out-promote and out-distribute its rivals, but because of its scale the cost per pack sold is actually much lower than that of its competitors, making it even more difficult for them to rival Wrigley's. It generates a lot of cash, $405m per year or 14 per cent of sales, which in part is used to refresh the product range and innovate within it (**http://www.wrigleys.com**).

The management focus here is on retention and maintenance, rather than on seeking growth. Management might be looking to keep price leadership, and any investment will be geared towards lowering costs rather than increasing volumes. Any excess cash can be diverted to new areas needing support, perhaps helping to develop dogs and question marks into stars.

Once the BCG matrix has been developed for an organisation, it can be used to assess the strength of the company and its product portfolio. Ideally, a strong mix of cash cows and stars is desirable, although there may be embryonic stars among the dogs and question marks. The situation and the portfolio become unbalanced where there are too many dogs and question marks and not enough cash cows to fund new developments to allow them to break out of those cells. There is also a risk dimension to all this. The organisation as a whole is vulnerable if there are too many products with an uncertain future (question marks).

Abell and Hammond (1979), however, identified a number of weaknesses in the BCG model and its assumptions, for instance that cash flow and cash richness are influenced by far more than market share and industry growth, and that return on investment (ROI) is a more widely used yardstick of investment attractiveness than cash flow. Although it is conceptually neat, the BCG matrix does not adequately assess alternative investment opportunities when there is competition for funds, as for example when it is necessary to decide whether it is better to support a star or a question mark.

Market attractiveness model: the GE matrix. Developed first by General Electric (GE), the market attractiveness–business position portfolio assessment model was designed to overcome some of the problems of models such as the BCG matrix.

The GE matrix adds more variables to aid investment decision appraisal. It uses two principal dimensions, as seen in Figure 12.5: *industry attractiveness* (the vertical axis) and *business strengths* (the horizontal axis). Within the matrix, the circle size represents the size of the market and the shaded part the share of the market held by the SBU.

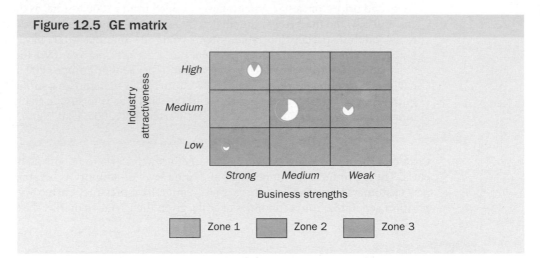

Figure 12.5 GE matrix

The first dimension, industry attractiveness, is a composite index determined by market size, rate of growth, degree of competition, pace of technological change, new legislation and profit margins achieved, among others. The second dimension, business position, is another composite index, comprising a range of factors that help to build stronger relative market share, such as relative product quality and performance, brand image, distribution strength, price competition, loyalty, production efficiency, etc. Both dimensions need to work positively together, since there is little point in having a strong position in an unattractive market, or a weak position in a strong market.

Within the matrix, there are three zones, each implying a different marketing and management strategy:

1 *Zone 1 (high attractiveness, strong position).* The strategy here should be investment for further growth.
2 *Zone 2 (medium attractiveness).* Because there is a weakness on one dimension, the strategy here should be one of selective investment, without over-committing.
3 *Zone 3 (least attractive).* Either make short-term gains or proceed to pull out.

The main areas of concern with this model are linked to methodology and the lack of clear guidelines for implementing strategies.

Shell's directional policy matrix. Shown in Figure 12.6, the Shell directional policy matrix has two dimensions: competitive capabilities and prospects for sector profitability. The nine cells of the matrix offer different opportunities and challenges, so that placing each product in an appropriate cell provides a guide to its strategic development.

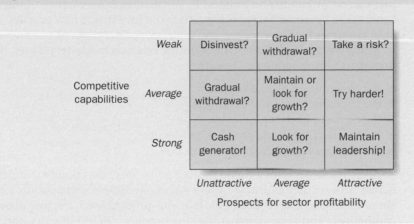

Figure 12.6 Shell directional policy matrix

Review of portfolio models. Portfolio models have been criticised, but they have, nevertheless, been useful in forcing managers, especially in large complex organisations, to think more strategically. Their great advantage is that they force managers to reflect on current and projected performance, and to ask important questions about the continued viability of products, their strategic role and the potential for performance improvement. These models do not, however, give solutions about what strategies should be adopted, and they need to be supported by clear action plans. Their main problem is the rather simplistic use of variables that contribute to the axes and the decision rules sought from the models. The preoccupation with market share is of particular concern, since it might be just as valid to consolidate and perform better as to pursue high-growth, high-share business. The models also fail to consider the synergies between businesses, where one may support another.

In some situations, it might be more appropriate to focus on a small number of areas and perform really well in these than to over-extend in the pursuit of market share or market growth. In many markets, a set of businesses survive with little reference to market share as niche operators. They might, therefore, develop attractive returns without necessarily seeking market share for its own sake or incurring the costs and risks associated with the pursuit of relative sales volume. This is also true in situations where technological change and obsolescence can quickly erode any significant advantage gained.

Although these models are commonly described in textbooks, they are not so widely used in practice. They are conceptually easy to design, but very difficult to implement effectively. They require considerable management skill and judgement, because of their focus on the identification of variables, weighting decisions and future changes, rather than just on present, tangible, measurable factors.

External audit

The external audit systematically looks at the kinds of issues covered extensively in Chapter 2 as the STEP factors. Sociocultural changes, such as in the demographic make-up of a market or in public concerns or attitudes, may well influence the future strategic direction of an organisation. The early identification of technological change might also change strategic direction, as the organisation plans ways of exploiting it to make cheaper, better or different products ahead of the competition. Economic and competitive factors are both, of course, very important. Low disposable incomes among target customers may force the organisation towards more rigorous cost control or into changing its product mix, while high interest rates on organisational borrowing might delay diversification or other expansion plans. Finally, the external audit should note what is happening in terms of the political and regulatory frameworks, whether national or European, that bind the organisation.

Competitor analysis. As part of the external audit, competition also has to be analysed very carefully on all aspects of its marketing activities, including its response to STEP factors and its choice of target markets. Competitors are an important factor that will influence the eventual success or failure of a business in any market. Ignore competition, and the likelihood of being taken by surprise or of being caught out by a strong new product or a major attack on a loyal customer base is very great and can create severe problems.

At the macro level, Porter (1979) in his Five Forces Model defined the competitive forces that operate in an industry. They are:

- the bargaining power of suppliers
- the bargaining power of customers
- the threat of new entrants
- the threat of substitute products and services
- the rivalry among current competitors.

Porter's five forces form a useful starting point for undertaking a competitive analysis, in particular because they encourage a very wide definition of competition. Competition is not just about established, direct competitors at end-product level, but also about indirect and future competitors and about competition for suppliers. Before the development of the Channel Tunnel, the cross-channel ferry companies felt little need to compete aggressively with each other. Once the concept of the tunnel became a reality, however, they were shaken into action because of the perceived competitive threat.

The Porter model gives a sound foundation, but there are still several areas that should be analysed, if there is to be a full appreciation of competitors.

Competitor identification. As the Porter model implies, the identification of competitors is often broader than it first appears. The exercise should look at potential competitors, focus on the extent to which market needs are being satisfied and look at the needs that are emerging, as well as evaluating the activities and capabilities of the obvious competition. Latent or new competitors can take a market by surprise. Any organisation should take a wide view of who it is competing with. Small local shops discovered the hard way that they were competing with the supermarket multiples.

In a large market, it might be possible to group them into clusters, depending on their focus and strategy. This can provide a useful framework for identifying opportunities, but remember that in order to implement the technique, the organisation needs detailed competitor information, not just on financial performance but also on segments served, marketing strategies, etc.

Competitive strengths and weaknesses. Examining a competitor's strengths and weaknesses provides a valuable insight into its strategic thinking and actions. A full range of areas should be examined, for example manufacturing, technical and financial strengths, relationships with suppliers and customers, and markets and segments served, as well as the usual gamut of marketing activity. It is particularly worth undertaking a detailed review of the product range, identifying where volume, profits and cash come from, where the competitor is the market leader, where it is weak and where it seems to be heading.

eg   India has developed competitive strength in call centres due to its pool of relatively low cost, English-speaking labour combined with a relatively sophisticated communications technology infrastructure. The sector now employs 350,000 people and is set to expand by 50 per cent per year for the foreseeable future. The main centres are in Bangalore,

Delhi and Mumbai, but each now suffers from the same problem that shifted call centres from Europe in the first place: the high turnover rate of staff, sometimes as high as 50 per cent per year. The difference is, however, that there is a large pool of willing replacements in a nation in which approximately 2.5 million young people graduate each year. Around 80 per cent of employees in call centres are in the 20–25-year-old age range and few consider it a long-term career option. In time, therefore, the competitive strength of Indian call centres may be eroded (Luce, 2004).

Competitors' objectives and strategies. It is important to understand what drives competitors, what makes them act as they do. Most firms have multiple objectives beyond the simple notion of profit. Objectives could relate to cash generation, market share, technological leadership, quality recognition or a host of other things. Sometimes developing an understanding of a competitor's product portfolio provides a valuable insight into likely competitive objectives. Once you understand their objectives, you have strong clues about how their strategy is likely to unfold in terms of their positioning, marketing mix and vulnerable points for attack, or your best means of defence.

eg Beans may Mean Heinz, but Premier Foods' Branston brand is about to challenge Heinz's dominance. To do so, it had to look at the situation from Heinz's perspective to establish the most appropriate attack strategy. With a market share of 67 per cent, Heinz's dominance has been barely scratched by Premier Foods' own Crosse & Blackwell brand and supermarket own-label brands. Its position looks unassailable, with its iconic brand reputation and huge customer loyalty in a market worth around £222m. Premier Foods believes that it can build a brand to £70–100m by 2007, which would make a serious dent in Heinz's position. A £10m promotional campaign is being planned for its launch, including £5m on national press, television, radio, sampling and PR. Around 750,000 consumer taste tests are planned in supermarket car parks to compare Branston beans with Heinz's. Premier Foods believes that Heinz has had it too easy, without any credible rivals, and prices have reflected the strong position. It also believes that the timing for an attack is good, as Heinz has frozen its above-the-line marketing as part of a strategic review of its European portfolio. If successful, Branston will be extending the brand into no-added-salt canned spaghetti and spaghetti hoops to challenge Heinz further. There is no intention in the short term to undercut the 44p charged by Heinz for its baked beans (*The Grocer*, 2005).

Competitive reaction. It is very important to be able to assess competitors' responses to general changes in the marketing environment and to moves in major battles within the market. These responses could range from matching a price cut or an increase in promotional spend, through to ignoring events or shifting the ground completely. An organisation can learn from experience how competitors are likely to behave. Some will always react swiftly and decisively to what is seen as a threat; others may be more selective depending on the perceived magnitude of the threat.

eg Following from the previous example, Premier Foods has to consider the kind of action Heinz will make when it finds itself under attack. There are no surprises in the food industry, and Heinz would have had time to consider if and when it should respond to the threat. Retaliation is probably inevitable as Heinz will not surrender its dominant share lightly. Premier Foods may have an idea as to how the retaliation will come and in what form. Price is an obvious weapon, but there is a risk that it could destroy value growth. There was a beans price war in the 1990s, and the history and role of Heinz in that could be studied. An increase in brand support promotion is likely and trade promotions could be increased to shift volume. Alternatively, Heinz could attack Premier Foods' own dominant position in other markets to undermine the support it is able to give to Branston beans.

Competitive information system. The above discussion of competitor analysis demonstrates the need for a well-organised and comprehensive competitor information system. This would be part of the MIS discussed in Chapter 5. Often, data need to be deliberately sourced on an ongoing basis, collated, analysed, disseminated and discussed. Then, management at all levels can learn what is happening. They may dispute the findings or the data may provide a basis for seeking further insights.

Market potential and sales forecasting

The extent to which plans can be successfully implemented depends not only on managers' abilities in setting and implementing strategies, but more fundamentally on their ability to predict the market accurately. This means two things: first, assessing the market potential, that is, working out how big the total cake is; and second, forecasting sales, that is, calculating how big a slice of that cake our organisation can get for itself. The following subsections will look at both of these areas.

Market and sales potential. The concept of market potential is very simple, but in practice it is very difficult to estimate. Market potential is the maximum level of demand available within the total market over a given period, assuming a certain level of competitive marketing activity and certain conditions and trends in the marketing environment. This definition immediately raises problems in calculating a figure for market potential, as it involves many assumptions about competitors and the environment, needs a precise definition of 'the market' and requires methods of quantifying the variables concerned.

eg There is a well-known story of the shoe sales representative arriving in a remote Amazon jungle community to find that none of the locals is wearing shoes. Is this a hopeless market with no potential, or a prime market for development? A similar problem faced Kooshies Baby Products from Canada when it sought to launch non-disposable nappies onto the Chinese market as part of a joint venture with a flannel cotton products company in China. Unlike Kooshies' other international markets, China was not used to non-disposable, flannel nappies, and has a preference for brushed cotton. Flannel is considered inferior and the Chinese are less interested in the environmental aspects of nappy use. Just 20 Kooshies non-disposable nappies can replace up to 7000 disposable ones. Other product adaptations were necessary: white waistbands were associated with funerals and animal patterns on nappies were not appreciated. So, just what is the Chinese market potential? Twenty million babies are born in China each year, but how many of those can be considered as representing real market potential given the environment described? What is the sales potential for Kooshies and is it worth the risk and the investment required to develop it (Gamble, 2001)?

Even after the potential has been estimated for the market as a whole, an organisation will then need to determine its own sales potential, that is, the share of the market that it could reasonably expect to capture. Obviously, sales potential is partly a result of the organisation's marketing effort and its success in attracting and holding customers. Although the level of total market potential will create a ceiling for an organisation's individual sales potential, in reality sales potential should be based on a clear understanding of the relative success of individual organisations' marketing efforts.

eg The Gambia Tourism Authority (GTA) was launched in 2002 as a public enterprise to promote tourism. After a period of rapid growth until the army takeover in 1994, visitor numbers grew to between 100,000 and 120,000 each year and full occupancy was often achieved in the peak season. After the military takeover and further political instability, however, many Western governments advised against their nationals travelling to the Gambia and occupancy levels plummeted to around 20 per cent. As tourism contributes around 12 per cent of GDP, any drop-off in visitor numbers seriously hurts the economy.

Fisherman on a Gambia river quayside selling freshly caught fish.

Source: © eyeubiquitous/hutchison
http://www.eyeubiquitous.com

The challenge for the GTA is to achieve its full sales potential as measured by visitor numbers to the Gambia. Forecasts have suggested that tourism to Africa will treble by 2020 and Gambia would like its share of that growth. The role of the GTA is to help fulfil that potential. It works with the airlines, the hotel sector and tourism operators to promote the Gambia as a destination both for the peak season and for the off-peak May to October period. Visitor numbers have almost recovered to pre-1994 levels. The target is to expand to 1 million by 2020, and to the GTA that represents the sales potential. Problems are already being experienced, however, that could delay progress. In addition to general worldwide threats to tourism, more local concerns include 'bumsters' pestering tourists for money, an influx of paedophiles undermining the country's reputation, and coastal erosion which threatens some popular beaches and even some hotels. Marketing challenges must also be met: in particular, promoting a relatively unknown destination to a wider range of tourists than just those from the UK, Germany and Scandinavia (*EIU ViewsWire*, 2003; Ford, 2003; Sonko, 2002).

Having a clear idea of market and sales potential provides a useful input to the marketing planning process. It is especially important for planning selling efforts and allocating resources. The allocation of sales force effort, and the establishment of distribution points and service support centres, for example, can reflect sales potential rather than actual sales, thus allowing scope for expansion. Similarly, sales potential can also be used to plan sales territories, quotas, sales force compensation and targets for prospecting.

Sales forecasting. Marketing often plays a central role in preparing and disseminating forecasts. This is perhaps one of its most important functions, as the sales and market forecasts provided are the basis of all subsequent planning and decision-making within most areas of the organisation. Get it wrong and the whole organisation can be caught out by major capacity or cash flow problems. In fashion markets, for example, it can be very difficult to forecast what styles are going to sell in what quantities, hence the popularity of 'end of season' sales as retailers try to sell off surplus stock. Holiday companies also find forecasting difficult, and again find themselves selling off surplus holidays at a discount right up to departure dates.

■ SWOT analysis

The marketing audit is a major exercise which ranges widely over all the internal and external factors influencing an organisation's marketing activity. It generates, therefore, a huge amount of material that has to be analysed and summarised to sift out the critical issues that will drive the marketing plan forward. The commonest mechanism for structuring audit information to provide a critical analysis is the SWOT analysis (strengths, weaknesses, opportunities, threats).

Strengths and weaknesses

Strengths and weaknesses tend to focus on the present and past, and on internally controlled factors, such as the 4Ps and the overall marketing package (including customer service) offered to the target market. The external environment is not totally ignored, however, and many strengths and weaknesses can be defined as such only in a competitive context. Thus, for example, our low prices may be seen as a strength if we are pricing well below our nearest competitor in a price-sensitive market. Low prices may, however, be a weakness if we have been forced into them by a price war and cannot really sustain them, or if the market is less price sensitive and our price is associated with inferior quality when compared with higher-priced competitors in the minds of the target market.

eg Teuscher (**http://www.teuscher.com**) truffle shops claim to offer a fairytale experience to all their visitors. Top quality chocolate surrounded by elaborate design in over 25 stores worldwide helps Teuscher to stand out from the crowd. The designs are deliberately themed and changed simultaneously in all shops four or five times per year. Examples have included autumn pheasants, pink flamingoes and bears, to name but a few, all set amid plants and flowers. Attention to detail also extends to the products themselves. The raw material is carefully selected couverture that has been specially tempered and has a high cocoa content and low melting point. Such delights as champagne truffles, chewy florentines, candied orange slices, hearts and fish shapes, golf balls, trains and pianos are all offered – in chocolate, of course. This attention to detail, a high level of creativity and an emphasis on premier class make Teuscher shops very special places.

Opportunities and threats

Opportunities and threats tend to focus on the present and the future, taking a more outward-looking, strategic view of likely developments and options. Thus the organisation that is the price leader in a price-sensitive market might see the opportunity to get its costs down even further as a means of maintaining its position and pressurising any challengers. The challenger's SWOT analysis would define that same scenario as a threat, but might see an opportunity in opening up a new, non-price-sensitive segment. Many opportunities and threats emerge from the marketing environment, when shifts in demographic and cultural factors are taken into account; when developments in emerging markets, such as China, are analysed; when, in fact, the implications of anything included in Chapter 2's STEP factors is considered.

Understanding the SWOT analysis

The SWOT analysis, therefore, helps to sort information systematically and to classify it, but still needs further creative analysis to make sense of it. The magnitude of opportunities and

If it's real quality and taste you are after, with the best ingredients, these chocolates should hit the spot.

Source: © Teuscher Chocolates of Switzerland
http://www.teuscher.com

threats, and the feasibility of the potential courses of action implied by them, can only really be understood in terms of the organisation's strengths and weaknesses. If strengths and weaknesses represent 'where we are now' and opportunities and threats represent 'where we want (or don't want) to be' or 'where we could be', then the gap, representing 'what we have to do to get there', has to be filled by managerial imagination, as justified and formalised in the body of the marketing plan.

eg Manufacturers of frozen pizza such as Green Isle (Goodfellas) and Schwan (Chicago Town) have to reflect widely in assessing changes in the environment. The pizza market is almost equally divided between chilled and frozen, by size, and by retailer and manufacturer brands. Then there is the choice of toppings just to finish it off! It is important for any marketing planning that the trends and issues in each area are well understood. Although the total market was worth £728m in 2004, subtrends could impact upon competitiveness.

A useful way of assessing changing consumer tastes is to find out the new variants offered in the fast food pizza chains, as that strongly influences preferences within the frozen and chilled market. The shift from deep-pan to thinner bases, for example, reflects the trend towards healthier eating and has stimulated innovation in the supermarket chiller and freezer aisles. There are still challenges facing pizza, with it being regarded as an unhealthy, fattening version of junk food according to a Mintel survey. Heavy price promotions also have to be taken into account in forecasting. Between 1999 and 2004, sales volume grew by 37 per cent but sales income by just 26 per cent.

Consumers are becoming more discerning and premium pizza ranges are being introduced to combat the junk food image. Goodfellas' La Bottega range is based on recipes from a Michelin-starred chef and uses a stone-baked ciabatta base. Supermarkets are essential for wide and mass distribution and as in many other food sectors they control distribution, both directly with their own-label products and less directly in terms of how much shelf space will be given to different brands. Sainsbury's is not allowing the manufacturers to have it all their own way in developing innovative tastes, as it has introduced toppings such as Pancetta with caramelised Pumpkin, and Chorizo with Cherry Bell Peppers under its Taste the Difference label.

By assessing these immediate market opportunities and threats, each brand manufacturer is better able to plan its product development strategy and its merchandising and promotional approaches (Bainbridge, 2005).

Marketing objectives

Objectives are essential for clearly defining what must be achieved through the marketing strategies implemented, and also to provide a benchmark against which to measure the extent of their success. Marketing objectives do, however, have to be wide ranging as well as precise, as they have to link closely with corporate objectives on a higher level but also descend to the fine detail of products, segments, etc. They must, therefore, be *consistent* with each other and with corporate goals, *attainable* in that they can be achieved in practice and their progress can be measured, and *compatible* with both the internal and external environments in which they are to be implemented. These criteria are generally applicable, despite the fact that marketing objectives can vary over time and between organisations.

Whatever the basis of the objectives, they cannot be left at such a descriptive level. It is not enough to say that our objective is to increase our market share. It is essential to quantify and make explicit precisely what is intended. Even when those questions have been answered, the objective is still quite general, and a number of detailed sub-objectives, which will perhaps relate to constraints or parameters within which the main objective is to be achieved, should also be defined. The main objective of increasing market share, for example, may have sub-objectives relating to pricing. Thus the marketing manager might have to find a way of increasing market share without compromising the organisation's premium price position.

Marketing strategies

A marketing strategy is the means by which an organisation sets out to achieve its marketing objectives. In reality, an organisation will be presented with a range of strategic options, relating to its defined objectives. Some will be related to increasing volume, while others relate to improving profitability and holding on to what the organisation already has (reducing costs, increasing prices, changing the product mix, streamlining operations, etc.).

This section examines a number of different strategies that organisations might adopt if their priority is growth. It is important to remember, however, that growth is not always a priority. In many small firms, for example, survival or sustaining the *status quo* might be the main objective. In other situations, standing still might be the right strategy if the market is starting to tighten up. The preoccupation with growth, therefore, should not be assumed to be relevant to all organisations all the time.

The Ansoff matrix

The product–market matrix proposed by Ansoff (1957) provides a useful framework for considering the relationship between strategic direction and marketing strategy. The four-cell matrix shown in Figure 12.7 considers various combinations of product–market options. Each cell in the Ansoff matrix presents distinct opportunities, threats, resource requirements, returns and risks, and will be discussed below.

Figure 12.7 Ansoff's growth matrix

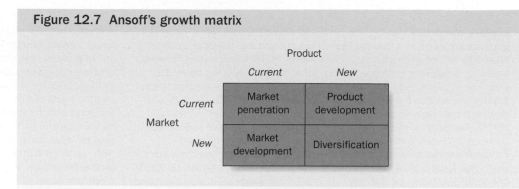

marketing in action

Console wars

By 2006 it has been estimated that the Sony PlayStation would have sold around 100 million consoles, with Xbox and GameCube selling between 25 and 35 million each, a long way behind, despite attempts to depose Sony (Lester, 2005).

A major battle has been taking place for the opportunity to entertain us. Sony with PlayStation 2, Microsoft with Xbox, and Nintendo with GameCube, are head-to-head in the global market for gamers. It's a highly competitive world too, with the global video game market said to be worth $25bn in 2005 and growing (Wingfield, 2005). In the UK alone, the market was estimated at £1.6bn in 2005. A 2004 survey by ChildWise, a market research company specialising in researching children, showed that 77 per cent of 5–16-year-olds in the UK have access to a games console at home and 54 per cent have their own consoles. It is hardly surprising, therefore, that Microsoft was tempted to enter this market, albeit as a late entrant against an established market leader.

When the Xbox was launched in 2001 in the US, and in 2002, in Europe with a $500m worldwide advertising campaign, the target was to sell 6m units within one year. It aimed to rival Sony within a short period of time. The Xbox was different from its competitors and has been described as being more like a cheap PC with a powerful graphics chip rather than a traditional console. At the time it was the only console with built-in broadband capability so that gamers could download new levels, characters and games, and participate in online multiplayer gaming.

The quality and desirability of the games are obviously important influences in selling a console. The Xbox launched with 20 games, costing about £45 each (claimed to be the strongest portfolio of games ever for a console launch), but 60 were planned within a short period after launch. Sales of games are also important financially as Microsoft earns approximately 30 per cent royalty on every game sold for the Xbox. In the US, nearly four games are being sold with every Xbox and around 2.5 per sale in Europe. Without a wide range of quality supporting games, users will not bother with the console (Chandiramani, 2003).

Although many argued that the Xbox was a superior model, Microsoft could not dislodge PlayStation 2 from the number one spot and remained a long way behind. Prices were slashed for the Xbox, from £299 to £129, which undercut Sony by £50. Instead of stimulating sales, it had the opposite effect, raising issues about the console and gaming quality compared with the market leader. The real edge for Xbox was expected to be the Play Live feature launched in 2003, as this took gaming into an even more competitive sphere; however, the take-up was not large enough to seriously dent PlayStation 2.

By 2004, it was estimated that Sony had sold 1.3 million units in the UK, according to *Screen Digest*. This put it well ahead of Microsoft, which sold 640,000 Xboxes, and Nintendo, which sold 250,000 GameCubes (Lester, 2005). Nintendo had suffered in the UK through the introduction of the Xbox. All three consoles, however, could claim some success over the previous couple of years, and although it was claimed that Microsoft had lost $4bn on the console up to that time, it had grown its market share from zero to 37 per cent worldwide (Dipert, 2005).

In 2005, Sony was still the champion and Microsoft the strong challenger. Whether that position will change will depend upon the next generation of consoles. Sony is about to release PlayStation 3. The Xbox 360 was launched at the end of 2005 just ahead of Sony, and Nintendo is about to launch its Revolution at some point in 2006. Sony spent four years developing the PS3 and it runs 10 times faster than home computers. Users can also access the internet through a wireless connection and the graphics are of cinema quality. The Xbox 360 still emphasises flexibility, by allowing the user to watch films, listen to music, view photos and access the internet, making it truly an entertainment centre. Microsoft aimed to sell between 2.75 and 3 million new consoles worldwide in the first 90 days after launch (Wingfield, 2005). The Xbox 360 launched with 18 titles, and can play about 200 of the 450-plus games developed for the original Xbox (Taylor, 2005). Both the PS3 and the Xbox have Bluetooth controllers and are backward compatible so that previously purchased games can still be used.

Both Sony and Microsoft argue that their console is better for gamers. The PS3 is certainly faster, allowing game flexibility and advanced features with its powerful processors and powerful graphic features. Microsoft argues, however, that the Xbox 360 has three 3.2 GHz Power PC cores compared with just one on the PS3, which gives greater games flexibility. This is important as the Xbox Live service now has 2 million members worldwide and they can play against each other on the internet. By 2006 Microsoft users could also download complete games, bypassing the retail stores (Nuttall, 2005b). Nintendo has its strength in the hand-held area, and by offering online access to classic games.

Interbrand believes there is room in a growing market for all three consoles as each one targets slightly different groups (Lester, 2005). Only internet usage is growing faster than game playing, and a survey suggested that the average American spends 75 hours a year playing games. This appears set to grow as new, more powerful and realistic games are released (Nuttall, 2005b). Although the PS3 has the most computing power, the full benefit of the graphics may only be experienced on high definition plasma televisions, while the Xbox 360, although a major improvement on the first model, will need yet more innovation to narrow the lead carved out by Sony. Overall, there may have been many battles between the three parties to date, but the war is far from over. That sounds like a cue for another game – but on which console?

Sources: Brand Strategy (2005); Chandiramani (2003); Dalby (2004); Dipert (2005); Lester (2005); Nuttall (2005b); Taylor (2005); Wingfield (2005); **http://www.childwise.co.uk**.

Intensive growth

Three cells of the Ansoff matrix offer opportunity for sustained growth, although each one has different potential according to the market situation.

Market penetration. The aim of market penetration is to increase sales volume in current markets, usually by more aggressive marketing. This means using the full range of the marketing mix to achieve greater leverage.

eg United Parcel Service (UPS) is a leading distribution and delivery company operating on a global scale. It has acquired a large portfolio of customers and a transportation and systems infrastructure to provide reliable and consistent service to customers. It seeks to maximise its competitive strengths by selling existing and new services to its current customer base, emphasising the technology-driven operation which all but the largest competitors find hard to emulate. It seeks to integrate its technical solutions into its customers' business processes, thereby providing timely information on parcel movements. UPS does not rule out other growth routes, however, including expanding its market position in the Middle East and Asia and making strategic acquisitions and global alliances to build on its market presence (**http://www.ups.com**).

Market development. Market development means selling more of the existing product to new markets, which could be based on new geographic segments or could be created by opening up other new segments (based, for example, on age, product usage, lifestyle or any other segmentation variable). Danish firms control nearly half of the world's market for wind turbine machines. Companies such as Vestas Wind Systems and Nordtank Energy Systems depend heavily on achieving growth by developing new markets.

eg Vestas Wind Systems (http://www.vestas.com) is the world's leading manufacturer of wind turbines. The world market for wind turbine systems is expected to continue growing over the next 10 years due to greater energy consumption, more environmental awareness and greater efficiency as technology continues to lower unit costs. From its origins in Scandinavia, Vestas now has 35 per cent of the world's market for wind power, twice that of its nearest competitor. European markets have been opened up, especially in Germany and Spain, and other markets being developed include Japan, the USA, China and Australia. In 2000, it agreed a new dealer-ship in Japan to form Vestech Japan Corporation, which is owned by a number of large Japanese corporations including Toyota and Kawasaki. This has enabled a fast entry into an otherwise difficult market. Additionally, contracts were signed for the first time in Costa Rica and Iran, while the less well-cultivated markets in Poland and Portugal showed positive signs. By opening up new markets, Vestas is able to retain and build its global position.

Part of the market development strategy is to establish local production facilities through acquisition or direct investment. In addition to Denmark, factories exist in Germany, Spain and India and sales offices are also being opened to support the development of a market, as it may take some time to achieve regulatory approval and to negotiate with power providers. Despite the international coverage, the success of Vestas has been built on the platform of product development, occupying 9 per cent of the workforce, quality, pre- and post-sales service, efficient production and competitive pricing. Although still primarily a wind turbine producer, Vestas' sales grew to €2.6bn in 2004 in a market with long-term growth prospects of between 10 and 20 per cent per year with the drive towards renewable energy sources. The market has, however, become more competitive with General Electric taking an interest with GE Energy, and Siemens which has purchased Danish rival Bonus.

Vestas has achieved success in China, which could be a huge market if the Chinese become very serious about renewable energy sources as opposed to conventional power. There are plans to start production in China to capture a bigger share of the energy market (Carey, 2004; *The Economist*, 2005; *Financial Times*, 2003; MacCarthy, 2005a, 2005b).

Product development. Product development means selling completely new or improved products into existing markets.

eg New Covent Garden Food has developed a strong reputation for wholesome soups with unusual flavours. A new range of ready-made chilled porridge represents a product development in the convenience market aimed at those who want breakfast on the run. When launched, it will be the UK's first branded fresh porridge, available in original, honey, maple syrup and citrus flavours, which can either be heated in the microwave or eaten straight from the container. Although it is a new food category, it is an alternative option for the breakfast market. Given that according to Datamonitor the British miss 114 breakfasts a year, the product could be just the thing on a cold winter's morning! (Hu, 2005).

Diversification

Diversification, the final cell in the Ansoff matrix, happens when an organisation decides to move beyond its current boundaries to exploit new opportunities. It means entering unfamiliar territory in both product and market terms. One of the main attractions of this option is that it spreads risk, moving the organisation away from being too reliant on one product or one market. It also allows expertise and resources to be allocated synergistically, for example theme parks diversifying into hotel accommodation, or airlines diversifying into tour packages. The danger is, of course, that the organisation spreads its effort too widely into areas of low expertise, and tries to position itself against more specialist providers.

There are two main types of growth through diversification, as follows.

Concentric diversification. Concentric diversification happens where there is a link, either technological or commercial, between the old and the new sets of activities. The benefit is, therefore, gained from a synergy with current activities. An organisation could, for example, add new, unrelated product lines to its portfolio, but still use the same sales and distribution network.

> **eg** The boundary between mobile and fixed line telephony, computing, digital photography and internet is blurring and this is leading to a lot of activity with mergers and alliances. Ericsson acquired the main part of Marconi's business. Ericsson is the world's biggest supplier of mobile networks and in buying Marconi was gaining access to a manufacturer of fixed line networks such as switches and optical multi-service platforms. This adds capability to an area in which Ericsson is weak and provides a solid base for moving forward with internet protocol technology and broadband transmission access. As broadband penetration continues to rise, there has to be enough transmission capacity and that's where the acquisition comes in. Other gains were associated with using Marconi's global distribution network and in obtaining greater leverage in purchasing (Odell, 2005).

Conglomerate diversification. The conglomerate diversification route is taken when an organisation undertakes new activities in markets that are also new. This involves risks in both the product development area and gaining acceptance in the marketplace.

> **eg** American Express decided to become a multi-product business, building on its image and experience with certain lifestyle segments gained through its credit cards. Not only was direct banking piloted in Germany, but consideration was also given to mobile phone services, travel products and private healthcare. The common thread for the diversification was the use of the Amex name.

'No growth' options

Not all strategies have to be growth-oriented. *Harvesting* is a deliberate strategy of not seeking growth, but looking for the best returns from the product, even if the action taken may actually speed up any decline or reinforce the no-growth situation. The objective is, however, to make short-term profit while it is possible. Typically, products subjected to harvesting are likely to be cash cows in the mature stage of their lifecycles (see pp. 204 *et seq.*), in a market that is stable or declining, as considered at pp. 427 *et seq.* Harvesting strategies could involve minimal promotional expenditure, premium pricing strategies where possible, reducing product variability and controlling costs rigidly. Implementing such strategies helps to ensure that maximum returns are made over a short period, despite the potential loss of longer-term future sales. Effectively, the company is relying on the short-term loyalty of customers to cushion the effect of declining sales.

In more extreme cases, where prospects really are poor or bleak, *entrenchment* or *withdrawal* might be the only option. A timetable for withdrawal or closure would be developed and every effort made to maximise returns on the remaining output, in the full knowledge that harm will be done to sales volume in the short term. Some care should, however, be exercised when considering withdrawal, as highlighted in our discussion of 'dogs' (see pp. 427–8). Although the profit potential may be poor and the costs of turnaround prohibitive, the loss of a product in a range may affect other parts of the range adversely. Thus entrenchment, protecting the product's position as best you can without wasting too many resources on it, might be the most appropriate course of action.

Competitive positions and postures

A final stage in the determination of a competitive strategy is to decide how to compete, given the market realities, and how to either defend or disturb that position. This means that the organisation has to consider its own behaviour in the context of how competitors are behaving, and select the most appropriate strategy that will enable overall objectives to be achieved. Two aspects need to be considered: competitive position and competitive posture. Competitive position refers to the impact of the organisation's market position on marketing strategies, whereas competitive postures are the strategies implemented by organisations in different positions who want to disturb the *status quo*.

Competitive positions. An organisation's competitive position usually falls into one of four categories, according to its relative market share. The four categories, and the kinds of marketing strategies that go with them, are shown in Figure 12.8 and are now considered in turn.

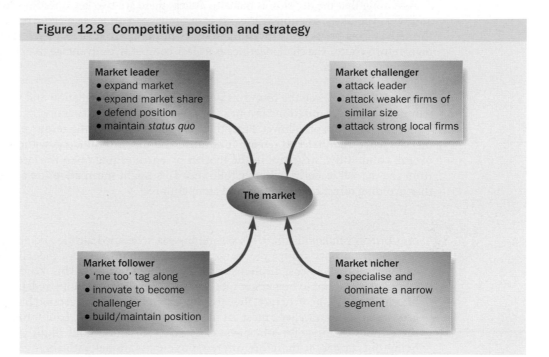

Figure 12.8 Competitive position and strategy

Market leader
- expand market
- expand market share
- defend position
- maintain *status quo*

Market challenger
- attack leader
- attack weaker firms of similar size
- attack strong local firms

The market

Market follower
- 'me too' tag along
- innovate to become challenger
- build/maintain position

Market nicher
- specialise and dominate a narrow segment

Market leader. In many industries, one organisation is recognised as being ahead of the rest in terms of market share. Its share might only be 20–25 per cent, but that could still give it a dominant position. The market leader tends to determine the pace and ways of competing in the market. It sets the price standard, the promotional intensity, the rate of product change and the quality and quantity of the distribution effort. Effectively, the market leader provides a benchmark for others to follow or emulate.

Market leadership can be at company, product group or brand level. Hellmann's claims over 50 per cent of the UK mayonnaise market, just ahead of a series of own-brand products. Chivers Hartley is the market leader in jams and marmalades, and Otto Versand is Germany's market leader in mail order. In each case there are a number of rivals, so the power associated with being a leader might not necessarily be very great, especially if markets are defined from a European rather than a domestic perspective.

Market challengers. Market challengers are organisations with a smaller market share, but who are close enough to pose a serious threat to the leader. However, an aggressive strategy can be costly, if the challenger is thinking of attacking where there is uncertainty over winning. Before making a concerted effort to steal share, therefore, the challenger needs to ask itself whether market share really matters so much, or whether there would be greater benefit from working on getting a good ROI from existing share.

eg   The growing challenge of AMD to Intel's supremacy of the memory chip market has led to a price war. In an effort to stem the progress of AMD, Intel is alleged to have initiated aggressive price cutting in the flash memory field to gain further market share at AMD's expense. Flash memory is widely used in mobile phones and games consoles, so volumes are high and a prolonged price cutting campaign is bound to affect overall profitability. AMD's market share dropped from 28 to 20 per cent as a result of the aggressive pricing. Overall, however, it indicates that AMD's challenge to the market leader is being taken seriously (Nuttall, 2005a).

Assuming that the decision is made to attack, there are two key questions: where to attack, and what the likely reaction will be. It is never easy to attack leaders, who tend to retaliate through cutting prices or by investing in heavy promotion, etc. It is, therefore, a high-risk but high-return route. The challenger needs a clear competitive advantage to exploit to be able to neutralise the leader.

Market followers. Given the resources needed, the threat of retaliation and the uncertainty of winning, many organisations favour a far less aggressive stance, acting as market followers. There are two types of follower. First, there are those who lack the resources to mount a serious challenge and prefer to remain innovative and forward thinking, without disturbing the overall competitive structure in the market by encouraging open warfare. Often, any lead from the market leader is willingly followed. This might mean adopting a 'me too' strategy, thus avoiding direct confrontation and competition.

eg   bmi British Midland is the UK's second biggest scheduled airline and as a result has to fight on two fronts: against the market leader, British Airways, for the scheduled market, and against the low-cost airlines such as Ryanair and easyJet. This is a dangerous territory as it can claim to be neither one nor the other. It is, therefore, redefining its service offering and pricing structure. Research indicated that whereas around half of its passengers are business travellers, most sat in economy seats for short-haul travel. Paying up to three times the price for a business class ticket for a one-hour flight was increasingly being questioned. It therefore offered a one-class model with three fare types: Tiny, Standard and Premium, based on the ticket flexibility required and the service level desired, such as access to airport business lounges. Other changes included lower catering costs, online check-in systems and fewer staff on flights, saving bmi around £30m a year if passenger numbers hold up. Effectively it means that bmi is chasing the economy sector. It remains to be seen whether bmi can retain its core values when going down into the budget sector for business travellers. The challenge will also be to distinguish it from the succesful offshoot bmibaby which carried 3.2 million passengers in 2004, 16 per cent up on the previous year, with a 78 per cent load factor (Britt, 2005; Jameson, 2005).

The second type of follower is the organisation that is simply not capable of challenging and is content just to survive, offering little competitive advantage. Often, smaller car rental firms operate in this category by being prepared to offer a lower price, but not offering the same standard of rental vehicle or even peace of mind should things go wrong. A recession can easily eliminate the weaker members of this category.

Market nichers. Some organisations, often small, specialise in areas of the market that are too small, too costly or too vulnerable for the larger organisation to contemplate. Niching is not exclusively a small organisation strategy, as some larger firms may have divisions that specialise. The key to niching is the close matching between the needs of the market and the capabilities and strengths of the company. The specialisation offered can relate to product type, customer group, geographic area or any aspect of product/service differentiation.

eg Raymond Connor spotted a niche when he formed the self-build home service, Buildstore. With high UK house prices, a niche was spotted to help those wanting to build their own houses by finding a plot of land, arranging finance, drawing up plans, gaining planning permission and even liaising with the builder where necessary. This built upon the conveyancing background of Raymond. Buildstore's website has a plot search tool, and the company has two visitor centres in Livingston and Swindon where visitors can see all aspects of self-build work in action. By making the whole process easier for the customer, Buildstore has found a niche not covered by the mainstream legal and building firms (Clark, 2005).

Competitive postures. The previous subsection considered the underlying rationale for defending, attacking or ignoring what is going on in the market from the point of view of an organisation's relative market position. This section examines *how to attack* or *how to defend* a position and the possibilities of alliances with competitors.

Aggressive strategies. Aggressive strategies are implemented when one or more players in a market decide to challenge the *status quo*. Again, the question of who to attack, when to attack and where to attack all need to be answered carefully in the context of the resources needed, the competitive reaction and the returns to be gained at what cost. Even in warfare, head-on assaults can be costly and do not always succeed.

eg ASDA wants to close the market share gap with Tesco and is not frightened to use price as an aggressive weapon. With Wal-Mart's backing and a reputation for being a low-price retail brand, ASDA promises to be a tough competitor. In order to be the lowest-priced place to shop, sourcing, distribution and store productivity have to be right. ASDA's market share has fallen to around 17 per cent, about half that enjoyed by Tesco, and Sainsbury's is challenging hard for the number two spot occupied by ASDA. With price deflation in grocery retailing already between 1 and 2 per cent, ASDA will have to cut prices hard to make any real impact (Finch, 2005).

Defensive strategies. Defensive strategies might be adopted by a market leader under attack, or by a market follower or nicher put under pressure by competitive activity. Even a challenger needs to reflect on likely competitive retaliation before committing itself to aggressive acts. One option is to sit tight and defend the current position. This can be risky, in that such defences might then be bypassed rather than attacked directly.

Selective withdrawal, to delay or even offset the attacking force, is also a form of defence. In commercial terms, that could mean withdrawing from marginal segments and areas where the presence is small and cannot be defended. This might mean that in areas where strengths do exist a better, more concentrated fight can take place.

The phrase 'the best form of defence is to attack' is now a recognised business strategy. If an organisation feels that it might soon be under attack, rather than wait for that to happen it takes deliberate aggressive actions. This might mean a particular marketing mix emphasis, for example advertising, dealer loaders or new products. Alternatively, signals can be sent that any attack would be vigorously defended.

Cooperation. It would be incorrect to assume that all competitive behaviour is challenging and confrontational. Many situations are characterised by peaceful coexistence and at times by cooperative alliances between competitors. Strategic alliances occur when organisations seek to work together on projects, pooling expertise and resources. This could include R&D, joint ventures or licensing arrangements, sometimes on a worldwide scale. Many large construction projects demand that different firms work together to provide a turnkey package. The alliance can be general, on many fronts or specific to a certain project (Gulati, 1998).

eg

Philips forged a strategic alliance with Dell to bring about collaboration on a range of electronics projects, including computer monitors. The arrangement includes cross-supply of components to be incorporated into each other's products, sharing knowledge and building joint computing architecture, for example for Philips' medical systems division. The deal also allowed Philips products to appear on the Dell website in the US, a market it had had trouble developing. The deal was anticipated to be worth $5bn over five years (Cramb, 2002). Meanwhile, Hino Motors, the Japanese lorry manufacturer, and Scania, the Swedish equivalent, also decided to form a strategic business alliance. Scania would provide heavy trucks for Hino to sell in Japan under its own brand name and dealer network. It was not an equity deal, but based on contractual agreement. In return, Hino would provide light and medium trucks to Scania. This enables both companies to enter markets that otherwise would be very difficult in terms of establishing brand awareness and dealer networks (Burt and Ibison, 2002).

There are many forms of alliance that can be created for mutual benefit. A number of non-competing organisations in the consumer goods area are forming marketing alliances to reduce costs and improve market impact. Coca-Cola uses marketing alliances to dominate the non-carbonated juice beverage market. It is working with Walt Disney to market its Minute Maid juices under the Disney brand, using containers featuring Mickey Mouse, Winnie the Pooh, etc. The alliance was expected to generate $200m over four years (Liu, 2001).

Finally, *collusion* is where firms come to an 'understanding' about how to compete in the market. Legislation prevents this from extending to deliberate price fixing: neither retailers nor manufacturers can openly collude to set retail or supply prices between them, although they can, of course, watch each other's pricing policies carefully and choose to match them if they wish.

eg

Three European companies were fined €75.9m for swapping market information and controlling the price of rubber chemicals used to make car tyres. Bayer AG, Chemtura and Repsol were all fined, but Flexsys NV was exempt as it blew the whistle on the practice in 2002. By seeking to control both the European and global markets, the companies were deemed to have breached anti-trust rules (*Wall Street Journal*, 2005). The services sector has not been immune from collusion claims either. A number of the top hotels in Paris were fined €708,000 by the French Competition Council for sharing information about occupancy levels and rates. Exchanging such information, even though it fell short of price fixing, did benefit planning. With a top room price of £10,000 in one hotel, the hotels argued that price comparisons hardly mattered anyway (Bremner and Tourres, 2005).

Although collusion is the unacceptable side of cooperation, the scale of investment and rate of change in technology, accompanied by increasingly global markets, are likely to generate more alliances and ventures in future.

■ Marketing programmes

Whereas the previous stage was about designing marketing strategies, this one is about their detailed implementation. The marketing programme will precisely specify actions, responsibilities and time scales. It is the detailed statement that managers have to follow if strategies are to be put into operation, as it outlines required actions by market segment, product and functional area. Within the marketing programme, each mix element is considered individually. This is in contrast to the marketing strategy itself, which stresses the interdependency between elements of the mix for achieving the best synergy between them. Now, the individual strands that make up that strategy can be picked out, and for each functional area, such as pricing, managers can go through planning processes, audits, objectives, strategies, programmes and controls.

On the basis of the overall marketing strategy, managers can emphasise those areas of comparative strength where a competitive edge can be gained, strengthen those areas where the organisation is comparable with its competition, and work to develop further or overcome those where the organisation is more vulnerable. The key challenge at the end of it all, however, is to ensure that the marketing mix is affordable, implementable and appropriate for the target segment. With that in mind, and given the dynamic nature of most markets, managers will also have to review the mix on a regular basis to make sure that it is still fresh and still serving the purposes intended.

■ Marketing budgets

The marketing plan must specify and schedule all financial and other resource requirements, otherwise managers might not be able to accomplish the tasks set. This is partly about costs, such as those of the sales force which include their associated expenditures, advertising campaigns, dealer support, market research, etc., and partly about forecasting expected revenues from products and markets. In determining budgets, managers need to balance precision against flexibility. A budget should be precise and detailed enough to justify the resources requested and to permit detailed control and evaluation of the cost effectiveness of various marketing activities, yet it also needs the flexibility to cope with changing circumstances.

eg When Cadbury Schweppes introduced its Managing For Value (MFV) programmes, it had far-reaching effects on marketing planning and budgeting. The underlying concept of MFV is that all existing and proposed products have to be profitable to survive. This means assessing a brand's impact, not just in terms of marketing returns, but also in terms of the total capital investment, such as in production machinery and logistics. To assess the return, marketing managers were expected to consider a variety of cost equations and schedules on different marketing and production options. The MFV also focused more attention on the effectiveness of the marketing budget and its contribution to market share, volume and earnings growth. The sponsorship of *Coronation Street* (see p. 404) was an outcome of the MFV drive, as it enabled a stronger focus on the master brand. It also allowed advertising expenditure on some individual brands to be reduced or redirected away from media advertising, although this was subsequently modified to allow individual brands also to be featured in the sponsorship (Murphy, 1999). Cadbury has a total marketing expenditure of over £1.1bn, representing nearly 20 per cent of sales revenue, which is steadily increasing year-on-year. The marketing plan must thus ensure that spend follows the various brands' strategic priorities and focuses appropriately on markets highlighted for development.

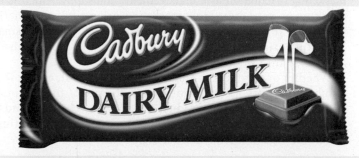

Wherever you buy a bar of Cadbury Dairy Milk, the packaging will be the same – only the language will be different. The slogan 'a glass and a half of full cream milk in every half pound' is one of the all-time greats of British advertising.

Source: © Cadbury Trebor Bassett http://www.cadbury.co.uk

We discussed budget setting, and some of the issues surrounding it, in Chapter 9 in a marketing communications context (see pp. 315 *et seq.*). Many of the points made there are more widely applicable, particularly the relative strengths and weaknesses of objective and task budgeting compared with methods based on historical performance (for example basing this year's budget on last year's with an arbitrary 5 per cent added on).

■ Marketing controls and evaluation

Control and evaluation are both essential if managers are to ensure that the plans are being implemented properly and that the outcomes are those expected. Although the defined marketing objectives provide the ultimate goals against which performance and success can be measured, waiting until the end of the planning period to assess whether they have been achieved is risky. Instead, managers should evaluate progress regularly throughout the period against a series of benchmarks reflecting expected performance to date. At that point, managers can then decide whether their strategies appear to be well on target for achieving objectives as planned or whether the deviation from expected performance is so great that alternative actions are called for.

Control and evaluation can take either a short- or a longer-term perspective. In the short term, control can be monitored on a daily basis through reviewing orders received, sales, stockturn or cash flow, for example. Longer-term strategic control focuses on monitoring wider issues, such as the emergence of trends and ambiguities in the marketing environment. This has strong links with the marketing audit, assessing the extent to which the organisation has matched its capabilities with the environment and indeed the extent to which it has correctly 'read' the environment.

This whole area of control and evaluation will be considered in greater detail at pp. 451 *et seq.*

Organising marketing activities

Effective marketing management does not happen by itself. It has to have the right kind of infrastructure and place within the organisation in order to develop and work efficiently and effectively. Central to the marketing philosophy is a focus on customer needs, and by understanding markets, customers' needs and wants and the ways in which they are changing and why, the marketer is providing essential information for planning corporate direction and the activities of other functions within the organisation.

It is important, however, to distinguish between a functional marketing department and marketing orientation as a management philosophy. Any organisation can have a marketing department, yet not be truly marketing-oriented. If that marketing department is isolated from other functional areas, if it is just there to 'do advertising', then its potential is wasted. Marketing orientation permeates the whole organisation and *requires* marketing's involvement in all areas of the organisation.

Whether or not there is a marketing department, and how it is structured, depends on a number of factors. These might include the size of the organisation, the size and complexity of the markets served, the product and process technology and the rate of change in the marketing environment. There are several ways of incorporating and structuring marketing within the organisation, and these are discussed below.

■ Organisational alternatives

There are four main choices for structuring marketing management within a department, focusing on function, products, regions or segments. The marketing department might also choose to develop a matrix structure, allowing an equal focus on both function and products, for example. These are all shown in Figure 12.9. The organisation might, of course, choose not to have a formal marketing department at all. Each of these choices is discussed below.

Figure 12.9 Forms of marketing organisation

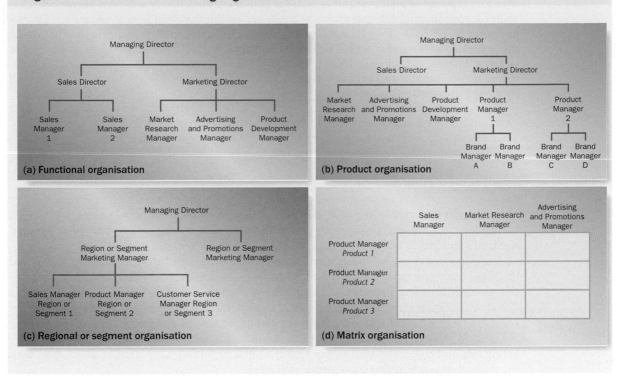

(a) Functional organisation

(b) Product organisation

(c) Regional or segment organisation

(d) Matrix organisation

Functional organisation

A functional department is structured along the lines of specific marketing activities. This means there are very specialised roles and responsibilities, and that individual managers have to build expertise. Such a department might have, for example, a market research manager, an advertising and promotions manager and a new product development manager, each of whom will report to the organisation's marketing director.

This system works well in organisations where the various business functions are centralised, but problems can arise where they are decentralised. Then, functional marketing tasks have to be coordinated across diverse areas, with greater or lesser degrees of cooperation and acceptance.

Product organisation

Giving managers responsibility for specific products, brands or categories of product might suit a larger company with major brands or with diverse and very different product interests. The manager, reporting to a product group manager or a marketing director, builds expertise around the product, and is responsible for all aspects of its development, its strategic and marketing mix planning and its day-to-day welfare. Other specialist staff, such as market researchers, might be involved as necessary to help the product manager.

The product, brand or category management approach is very popular in fmcg markets. It gives clear lines of management responsibility, but there is still a need for a central function to coordinate the overall portfolio. The main problem with product organisation is working with other functions, such as production, finance, etc., to get the resources, attention and effort that the product needs. There is also the risk that too many management layers will be introduced, hence the move towards category management (i.e. responsibility for a group of brands) rather than individual brand management.

Regional organisation

An organisation with its activities spread over a wide geographic area, or one operating in markets with distinct regional differences, might find regionally based marketing responsibility attractive. The regional marketing manager, along with a support team, will make all marketing decisions relevant to planning and operations in that territory. There will then be some mechanism for coordinating regional efforts at a national or international level to ensure consistency and strategic fit. As larger organisations become more international, this approach is becoming more common. The main benefit is that local managers develop the knowledge and expertise to know what is best for their region. They can then develop the most appropriate, fully integrated marketing mix package, as well as contributing intelligently to the organisation's overall strategic planning for that region.

Regionally based marketing departments are particularly attractive to organisations with a great emphasis on selling in the field, where close coordination and control are necessary. They are also appropriate for service industries, such as hospitality, where local conditions may differ and where, again, close control and coordination of service delivery are required.

Segmental organisation

An organisation that serves diverse groups of customers with very different needs might choose to develop marketing teams dedicated to each of those groups. This is because the marketing decision-making and the marketing mixes have to be tailored to the individual needs of segments in which the competitive threats may be very different.

A brewery, for example, will market to the licensed trade (for instance pubs and clubs) and the retail trade (for instance supermarkets and off-licences) very differently; a manufacturer of wound dressings will market differently to the hospital sector and to the pharmacist; a car dealer will market differently to the family motorist and to a fleet buyer. The volume purchased by individual customers within the same segment might create differences that are reflected in the marketing effort. An fmcg manufacturer will create a different kind of marketing mix and customer relationship with the top six multiple supermarket chains than with the many thousands of small independent grocers.

The marketing manager for a particular segment or customer group will have a range of specialist support staff and will report to a senior marketing manager or director with overall responsibility for all segments.

Matrix organisation

A matrix approach allows the marketing department to get the best of more than one of the previous methods of organisation. It can be particularly useful in large diverse organisations or where specialists and project teams have to work on major cross-functional activities, for example PR, new product development or marketing research programmes.

No department

Of course, another option is not to have a department at all. Small organisations might not be able to afford specialist marketing staff and thus perhaps the owner finds himself or herself performing a multi-functional role as sales representative, promotional decision-maker and strategist rolled into one. If a small organisation does decide to invest in marketing staff, the recruit might be put into an office-based administrative support role or into a sales role.

Sales-driven organisations

Some organisations are still driven by sales. They might have a few very large customers and be selling a complex technology. In such a case, the role of marketing is relegated to a support role that is largely concerned with PR and low-key promotional activity. Other organisations, particularly those currently or previously in the public sector, are still in the process of developing marketing departments. Universities, for example, are reappraising the role of marketing. Although they might have marketing departments, many of the key variables are beyond the control of their marketing managers. For example, academics, with or without the benefit of market research, develop and validate new courses; in another area, domestic full-time student fees and student numbers are agreed with the government. Often, universities see the marketing department's role as purely functional, handling student recruitment fairs, prospectuses, schools liaison and advertising. In short, there is no guarantee that having a department means that there will be a marketing orientation in the organisation.

Controlling marketing activities

Control is a vital aspect of implementing marketing plans, whether strategic or operational. It helps to ensure that activities happen as planned, with proper management. It also provides important feedback that enables managers to determine whether or not their decisions, actions and strategies are working appropriately in practice.

■ The marketing control process

The marketing control phase, shown in Figure 12.10, is not an afterthought to be bolted on to the end of the planning process, but should be designed as an important part of that process. In setting marketing objectives, it is important to define them in terms of detailed time-specific goals against which performance can be measured. This makes the task of control more manageable, since those areas where serious deviation is occurring can then be easily diagnosed. Management effort can thus be focused on areas of greatest need rather than being spread too thinly.

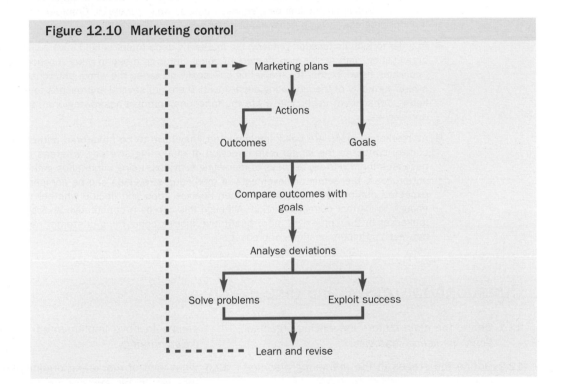

Figure 12.10 Marketing control

As soon as the control mechanism shows that a gap is opening between proposed targets and actual achievement, managers can start to look for reasons for this happening. Sometimes the reasons might be obvious, for example a stockout in a particular region or the loss of a major customer. In other situations, however, further research might have to be commissioned to support deeper analysis of the underlying causes. If, for example, a brand's market share continues to decline despite increased marketing effort, managers might start asking serious questions about customer responsiveness and the brand's competitive positioning. Failure to achieve targets does not, however, mean automatic condemnation of the marketing plan and its manager. It could be that targets were hopelessly optimistic, in the light of the emerging market conditions. Alternatively, other departments within the organisation, for example production or logistics, may have failed to achieve their targets.

Chapter summary

- Marketing planning is about developing the objectives, strategies and marketing mixes that best exploit the opportunities available to the organisation. Planning should itself be a planned and managed process. This process helps organisations to analyse themselves and their marketing environments more systematically and honestly. It also helps organisations to coordinate and control their marketing activities more effectively. Planning should be a flexible, dynamic activity that is fed with accurate, reliable and timely information, and is not divorced from the managers who have the day-to-day responsibility for implementing the plans. Marketing plans can be strategic or operational. The plans help to integrate activities, schedule resources, specify responsibilities and provide benchmarks for measuring progress.

- There are eight main stages in the planning process: corporate objectives, the marketing audit, marketing analysis, setting marketing objectives, marketing strategies, marketing programmes, controls and evaluation, and budgeting. Techniques such as product portfolio analysis and competitor analysis can be used to help compile the marketing audit, the key points of which can then be summarised in the SWOT analysis, a snapshot of 'where are we now?'. On the basis of the SWOT, objectives can be set and strategies defined with the help of tools such as the Ansoff matrix ('where do we want to be?' and 'how do we want to compete?'). These strategies are operationalised through marketing programmes ('how do we get there?'). Controls and evaluation help to monitor progress towards achieving objectives.

- In order to fulfil its function properly, the marketing department should have a central role within the organisation, with senior management of equal status to those in other functional areas. It is also important, however, that the marketing philosophy pervades the whole enterprise, regardless of the size or formality of the marketing department. There are several approaches to structuring the marketing department itself. These are the functional, product-based, regional, segmental or matrix approaches.

- As marketing plans are being implemented, they have to be monitored and controlled. Strategic control concerns the longer-term direction of marketing strategy, whereas operational control assesses the day-to-day success of marketing activities. Using information gathered in the monitoring process, the actual achievements of marketing strategies can be compared with planned or expected outcomes. Managers can then analyse gaps and decide whether they are significant enough to warrant corrective action. Although this can be a quantitative analysis, it should still be looked at in the context of more qualitative issues concerning customer needs and synergies between customers, markets or products.

Questions for review and discussion

12.1 Define the main factors influencing organisations' *marketing strategies*.

12.2 Define the stages in the *marketing planning process*.

12.3 What is a *product portfolio* and what are the problems of implementing portfolio models in practice?

12.4 Using whatever information you can find, develop a SWOT analysis for the organisation of your choice. What are the implications of your analysis for the organisation's short- and long-term priorities?

12.5 For each cell of the Ansoff matrix, find and discuss an example of an organisation that

seems to have implemented that particular growth strategy.

12.6 What kind of marketing organisational structure would be appropriate for each of the following situations and why?
(a) a small single product engineering company;
(b) a large fmcg manufacturer selling a wide range of products into several different European markets;
(c) a pharmaceutical company manufacturing both prescription and 'over the counter' medicines.

case study 12

Do you want something quick and thrashy?

Have you ever been overcome with the urge for something 'quick and thrashy'? If so you may have fallen victim to the 'Slag of all Snacks' campaign run for Unilever's instant hot snack brand Pot Noodle.

With that headline, Pot Noodle has come of age. Launched in 1979, Pot Noodle is now the 23rd biggest brand in the UK. Sales have grown from £70m to £120m in just seven years. The basic appeal behind the growth in demand for instant noodles stems from the trend towards snacking rather than traditional meal eating, with consumers seeking quick and easy gratification. Another helpful trend has been the desire for more variety and ethnic cuisine. It has been argued that the UK has the most developed snacking culture in Europe, accounting for a staggering 75 per cent of instant noodle sales (Benkouider, 2003).

Although an integral part of Asian diets, noodles are a new and relatively unestablished product in the rest of the world. In major European markets, the total market for noodles remains comparatively small. In Germany, for instance, sales of cup/bowl instant noodles have already reached a plateau. As a snack product, instant noodles face intense competition from alternative products which are better established in Europe, require no preparation at all and can be consumed on-the-go. Snack bars, biscuits and savoury snacks have been able to capitalise on the snacking trend to a greater extent, and manufacturers have furthermore adapted their products to serve snackers' needs better by offering mini or bite-size versions or through packaging innovation. Noodles are also up against pasta with its strong European heritage, especially in Italy. In the form of dry ready meals, pasta is far better positioned to exploit any trend towards more snacking.

So why have noodle-based snacks succeeded so well in the UK, when Western Europe as a whole represents just over 2 per cent of global noodle sales? Much of it is down to the popularity of one brand and its promotional strategy, namely Unilever's Pot Noodle. Although initially targeted at younger teenagers (the consumers) and their mums (the buyers), the focus has shifted as Pot Noodle sought greater appeal. The brand is now targeted at a 16–24-year-old, mainly male audience, and its appeal has been the humorous and mischievous personality created for the brand and established through a series of controversial advertising campaigns. The brand knows that its key market isn't just looking to enjoy a mildly saucy message but also wants to be entertained.

Pot Noodle has nearly 90 per cent share of the market for cup/bowl instant noodles in the UK due its highly successful use of marketing and in particular advertising, and it has been a driver of change in the product category. This has involved careful marketing strategy formulation and integrating that strategy with a series of tactical marketing plans to guide growth. Although any brand must have more than advertising appeal if it is to attract repeat purchase and survive, Pot Noodle is a fine example of how a market can be stirred into life through creative advertising. Unilever decided to re-launch the brand in 2002 after a period of fairly steady sales. It wanted to emphasise the 'subversive' personality of the brand when the target group wants something 'quick and thrashy' – in terms of

For some the importance of the Pot Noodle in all its various forms should be acknowledged in displays like this rather than being the guilty secret in your food cupboard.

Source: © Jeff Morgan/Alamy http://www.alamy.com

food, that is. The brand has no pretensions about what it is: it's artificial but capable of providing instant gratification. Building on the 'Slag of all Snacks' campaign was an important part of the re-launch and revised brand personality. An example of typical advertising dialogue between office workers in their twenties is 'have seen the way you look at my Pot Noodle', and the associated website gave a spoof narrative: 'Hello, I'm Ben and this is my site dedicated to Judy, the Office Bike at my work. She's amazing. I only started at my job two weeks ago but she's blown me away. I'd never done Pot Noodle at work before but I just couldn't resist Judy. I've done it with her at least eight times already! Judy says that I'm the best Noodling partner that she's ever had. I have just totally fallen for her gorgeous pots and this site is my way of showing my love. Judy I love you!!!'

Of course, phrases such as 'office bike' and 'slag' inevitably drew critics. In 2002 the Advertising Standards Authority upheld 400 complaints against a poster campaign using the word 'slag' due to its unrestricted access to view, but the ASA also ruled that the 'Slag of all Snacks' strapline was unlikely to cause widespread offence. The ITC, however, regulating the broadcast advertising, did ban the use of the strapline because of its use of the word slag, but the brand is still positioned as intended (Rogers, 2004). It would appear that smutty innuendo works. A subsequent television campaign designed to support Pot Noodle's Mexican fajita flavour reinforced the brand's appeal to twenty-something young men with its tongue-in-cheek references to 'backstreet' and dirty action.

Overall, the campaigns have worked using a variety of media, such as television, cinema, poster, radio and even kebab-wrappers, to drive home the message. During 2004, websites were launched for Pot Noodle as well as microsites for 'office bike' and 'natural noodling'. The sites are deliberately tacky and low budget yet still had 807,000 visitors in the first six months with no online advertising or other supporting activity. The integrated campaigns continue to be successful. A Millward Brown tracking study showed strong results: an awareness index of 20 (the average is four), with ad recognition at 74 per cent – all on a limited budget of £6m (*Marketing Week*, 2003). Market share grew 15 per cent in the four months after the campaign, the highest growth rate seen in the 10 years that Pot Noodle had been a youth brand (*Marketing*, 2003). Eventually, the message was toned down slightly, with the 'slags' campaign dropped in favour of the 'horn' campaign which was also filled with sexual innuendo.

Pot Noodle has not had it all its own way, however. Pot Noodle was involved in the Sudan 1 food scare and at the same time, healthier food options were also growing in popularity. Sales started to decline and this was not helped when new competition entered the market. Campbell's Batchelors launched the Super Noodle brand with a target audience in the 20–40 age range. The brand was designed to build upon the established brand name for instant food, soups and meals and was backed by a multi-million pound campaign including television, in-store promotion and point-of-sale material as well as radio and press ads. The price selected was similar to Pot Noodle's at around 79p, and four flavours were offered: roast chicken, chicken chow mein, sweet and sour, and curry. The positioning as a slightly older brand is designed to widen appeal, with the focus on a healthier alternative to Pot Noodle. However, given that Pot Noodle claims 90 per cent market share, any challenger will have to work overtime if it is to capture the imagination of the target market.

Sources: Benkouider (2003); *Campaign* (2004); Charles (2005); Coombs (1998); *Marketing* (2003); *Marketing Week* (2003, 2004, 2005b); McAllister (2004); *New Media Age* (2004); Rogers (2004).

Questions

1 What environmental influences are affecting Pot Noodle's performance? To what extent do you think they were predictable?

2 Why does advertising play such an important part in the marketing plan?

3 What factors are likely to be taken into account in creating market forecasts and sales forecasts for Pot Noodle?

4 Where do you think Pot Noodle should go from here? What kind of marketing objectives should it be aiming to achieve over the next few years?

References for chapter 12

Abell, D. and Hammond, J. (1979), *Strategic Market Planning*, Prentice Hall.

Ansoff, H.I. (1957), 'Strategies for Diversification', *Harvard Business Review*, 25 (5), pp. 113–25.

Bainbridge, J. (2005), 'King of Convenience', *Marketing*, 18 May, pp. 38–9.

Bashford, S. (2002), 'Why Are Modern Mums Deserting Mothercare?', *Marketing*, 24 January, p. 11.

Benkouider, C. (2003), 'Can Noodles Compete in Europe's Snack Food Market?', 8 May, accessed via **http://www. euromonitor.com.**

Brand Strategy (2005), 'Cyberspace Invaders', *Brand Strategy*, 5 December, p. 28.

Bremner, B. and Engardio, P. (2005), 'China Ramps Up', *Business Week*, 22 August, p. 118.

Bremner, C. and Tourres, M. (2005), 'Grandest of the Grand Paris Hotels Fined for Price-fixing', *The Times*, 30 November, p. 37.

Britt, B. (2005), 'bmi', *Marketing*, 2 June, p. 22.

Buckley, S. (2005a), 'Dividend Up and Focus Now on Growth', *Financial Times*, 20 May, p. 25.

Buckley, S. (2005b), 'Mothercare Looks Abroad for Growth', *Financial Times*, 18 November, p. 26.

Burt, T. and Ibison, D. (2002), 'Hino Motors Set for Alliance with Sweden's Scania', *Financial Times*, 19 March, p. 17.

Campaign (2004), 'Pot Noodle Unveils New Press Ad', *Campaign*, 23 April, p. 6.

Carey, J. (2004), 'Alternative Energy Gets Real', *Business Week*, 27 December, p. 106.

Chandiramani, R. (2003), 'Can Xbox Prevail Over Power of PlayStation?', *Marketing*, 15 May, p. 17.

Charles, G. (2005), 'Pot Noodle', *Marketing*, 24 August, p. 18.

Clark, M. (2005), 'Buildstore', *Marketing*, 20 April, p. 23.

Coombs, G. (1998), 'Reinforcing a Brand Ad Value: Pot Noodle', *Marketing Week*, 5 February, pp. 40–1.

Cramb, G. (2002), 'Philips and Dell Agree on Global Alliance', *Financial Times*, 28 March, p. 32.

Dalby, D. (2004), 'Console Giants Line Up to Win the Games War', *Sunday Times*, 14 November, p. 10.

Dipert, B. (2005), 'Got Game?', *EDN*, 16 December, pp. 51–8.

Dyer, G. (2001), 'The Power Shifts to Industry's Wunderkinds', *Financial Times*, 27 November, p. 5.

Dyer, G. (2004), 'Does the UK Biotech Sector Have the Culture to Make Science Pay?', *Financial Times*, 22 May, p. 11.

The Economist (2005), 'Business: Blowing a Big Opportunity?', *The Economist*, 9 April, p. 59.

EIU ViewsWire (2003), 'The Gambia: Tourism', *EIU ViewsWire*, 2 October.

Euroweek (2005), 'TomTom Satellite Navigation IPO to Fly on Growth Forecast', *Euroweek*, 20 May, p. 1.

Financial Times (2001), 'Holderbank Lays New Foundations', *Financial Times*, 30 March, p. 20.

Financial Times (2003), 'Wind Power', *Financial Times*, 13 December, p. 16.

Finch, J. (2005), 'Asda Chief Threatens New Price War in Move to Catch up Tesco', *The Guardian*, 14 December, p. 22.

Foley, S. (2002), 'Pilkington's Glass Markets Losing Shine', *The Independent*, 11 April, p. 25.

Ford, N. (2003), 'The Gambia: Reforms Reap Strong Growth', *African Business*, December, p. 50.

Gamble, J. (2001), 'The Struggle to Get Nappies off the Ground', *Financial Times*, 31 May, p. 14.

Gardner, R. (2003), Strategy of the Week: Lipton Ice Tea', *Campaign*, 13 June, p. 12.

Gardner, R. (2004), 'Lipton Continues "Don't Knock It" Idea', *Campaign*, 18 June, p. 10.

The Grocer (2002), 'An Ice Cuppa Tea is Tickling the Tastebuds of the Iced Beverage Sector', *The Grocer*, 4 May, p. 64.

The Grocer (2005), 'Is Heinz in a Pickle?', *The Grocer*, 29 October, p. 31.

Gulati, R. (1998), 'Alliances and Networks', *Strategic Management Journal*, 19 (4), pp. 293–317.

Hu, C. (2005), 'Time for Brits to Sow Oats', *The Grocer*, 29 October.

Jack, A. (2005), 'Amgen Works on the Formula for Profitable Science', *Financial Times*, 4 November, p. 11.

Jameson, A. (2005), 'BMI Returns to Profit on Success of Budget Baby', *The Times*, 3 March, p. 56.

Kleinman, M. (2002), 'Mothercare Aims for Warmer Look in Stores Revamp', *Marketing*, 4 April, p. 1.

Lester, R. (2005), 'Games Consoles: Real Fight for Virtual Victory', *Marketing Week*, 26 May, p. 26.

Liu, B. (2001), 'Coca-Cola and Disney Plan Drinks Venture', *Financial Times*, 1 March, p. 30.

Loades-Carter, J., Bickerton, I. and Leitner, S. (2005), 'TomTom Sets IPO Price at Top End of Range', *Financial Times*, 27 May, p. 1.

Luce, E. (2004), 'Call Centres Ring the Changes', *Financial Times*, 27 September, p. 4.

MacCarthy, C. (2005a), 'Vestas Profits Drive Calms Fears', *Financial Times*, 27 May, p. 26.

MacCarthy, C. (2005b), 'Ill Winds Blow Vestas to Forecast €100mn Loss', *Financial Times*, 25 November, p. 26.

Marketing (2002), 'Unilever Aims to Revamp Lipton Ice Tea for UK Market', *Marketing*, 14 March, p. 3.

Marketing (2003), 'Marketing Communications', The Marketing Society Awards supplement to *Marketing*, June, p. 16.

Marketing Week (2003), 'Effectiveness Awards 03: Campaign Of The Year Winner', *Marketing Week*, 16 October, p. S57.

Marketing Week (2004), 'Campbell's Launches Pot Noodle Challenge', *Marketing Week*, 24 June, p. 27.

Marketing Week (2005a), '3 Sets Sights on Big Four', *Marketing Week*, 27 October, p. 26.

Marketing Week (2005b), 'Unilever Approaches Agencies over £10mn Pot Noodle Campaign', *Marketing Week*, 24 November, p. 11.

McAllister, S. (2004), 'Super Noodles Takes Pot Shot', *The Grocer*, 24 July.

McDonald, M. (1989), *Marketing Plans*, Butterworth Heinemann.

Murden, T. (2001), 'Hi-fi Boss Who Strikes a Very Different Note', *Sunday Times*, 17 June, p. 7.

Murphy, C. (1999), 'Cadbury's Quiet Revolution', *Marketing*, 11 February, pp. 24–5.

New Media Age (2004), 'New Media Goes to Pot', *New Media Age*, 2 December, p. 18.

Nuttall, C. (2005a), 'AMD Warns as Price War with Intel Takes Toll', *Financial Times*, 12 January, p. 24.

Nuttall, C. (2005b), 'Microsoft to Launch Online Downloads for Xbox', *Financial Times*, 15 November, p. 21.

Odell, M. (2005), 'Convergence is the Key to Ericsson's Marconi Move', *Financial Times*, 26 October, p. 23.

Porter, M. (1979), 'How Competitive Forces Shape Strategy', *Harvard Business Review*, 57 (2), pp. 137–45.

Reid, S. (2005), 'Sony Follows TomTom's Lead on the Road to Riches', *Evening News*, 28 July, p. 6.

Roberts, D., Balfour, F., Einhorn, B. and Arndt, M. (2004), 'China's Power Brands', *Business Week*, 8 November, p. 50.

Rogers, E. (2004), 'Pot Noodle Moves to Calm Obesity Critics', *Marketing*, 4 August, p. 12.

Rogerson, P. (2005), 'Linn Sales Volume is Turned Down as Income Falls 8 Per Cent', *The Herald*, 3 September, p. 20.

Simonian, H. (2005), 'Holcim Expects Another Record Year', *Financial Times*, 26 August, p. 23.

Sonko, K. (2002),' "Bumsters" to Get the Bum Rush', *African Business*, April, pp. 46–7.

Taylor, P. (2005), 'The Xbox 360 is Ahead of the Game', *Financial Times*, 23 December, p. 12.

Turner, M. (2002), 'Cadbury's Clean Conscience', *Financial Times*, 18 February, p. 18.

Urquhart, L. (2004), 'Mothercare's Sales Uplift "Sustainable"', *Financial Times*, 16 July, p. 22.

Wall Street Journal (2005), 'Bayer AG: EU Regulators Issue Fines in Chemicals Price-Fixing Case', *Wall Street Journal*, 22 December, p. 1.

Wingfield, N. (2005), 'Xbox 360 Rollout from Microsoft Rattles Industry', *Wall Street Journal*, 24 December, p. A1.

Wray, R. (2005), 'Vodafone Shares Slide on Warning of Slow Sales', *The Guardian*, 16 November, p. 26.

chapter 13

services and non-profit marketing

learning objectives

This chapter will help you to:

1 define the characteristics that differentiate services from other products and outline their impact on marketing;

2 develop an extended marketing mix of 7Ps that takes the characteristics of services into account and allows comprehensive marketing strategies to be developed for services;

3 understand the importance and impact of service quality and productivity issues; and

4 understand the special characteristics of non-profit organisations within the service sector, and the implications for their marketing activities.

Introduction

The focus of this chapter is on the marketing of services, whether sold for profit or not. Service products cover a wide range of applications. In the profit-making sector, services marketing includes travel and tourism, banking and insurance, and personal and professional services ranging from accountancy, legal services and business consultancy through to hairdressing and garden planning and design. In the non-profit-making sector, services marketing applications include education, medicine and charities through to various aspects of government activity that need to be 'sold' to the public.

Marketing these kinds of services is somewhat different from marketing physical products. The major marketing principles discussed in this book – segmenting the market, the need for research, sensible design of the marketing mix and the need for creativity, strategic thinking and innovation – are, of course, universally applicable, regardless of the type of product involved. Where the difference arises is in the detailed design and implementation of the marketing mix. There are several special factors that provide additional challenges for the services marketer.

This chapter will, therefore, examine in detail the special aspects of services that differentiate them from physical products. It will then look at the issues involved in designing the services marketing mix and the marketing management challenges arising from its implementation. Finally, the whole area of marketing services in the non-profit sector will be considered.

Visitor demands are changing in the hotel industry. What would have been acceptable as an extra a few years ago is now considered as standard. Nowhere is this more true than in access to IT. Many business travellers consider the room as an extension of the office and expect full network broadband connectivity, fax and printing facilities. The hotel that cannot offer such service features will struggle to retain business customers. The recently opened Wynn hotel in Las Vegas takes the use of IT further. Of course, the $2.7bn luxury resort hotel has what you would expect in Las Vegas: over 2700 bedrooms, a 111,000 ft² casino, 22 food and beverage outlets, an 18-hole golf course, 76,000 ft² of retail space and even a Ferrari and Maserati dealership on site. It is in the use of the latest technology that the hotel takes service to a new level, however. At the heart it is the VOIP telephone connected to a USB printer so that it can be used as a fax machine. The phones are linked to the room management system and the services are set up and customised as soon as the guest checks in. The phone has become the portal for accessing all the hotel's services. The phone's built-in browser can show information about restaurants and services without any voice contact. The mini-bars are connected to the IP network and add purchases to the bill within 30 seconds. The flat-screen television offers streaming music services. The room key can be used not just to open the door, but to buy food and to play on the slot machines. Regardless of the time of day, the voice and data network keeps staff and guests linked. The staff consoles even show data about the caller's preferences. The Wynn is fast becoming a completely IT-driven hotel.

The growth of interactive databases means that the limits for hotels have yet to be reached. Your preferred room temperature, a television that knows your favourite programmes and music, a room in your preferred style and location, and communication in your native language are all possible, as the use of IT is harnessed to enhance customer service (Bisson, 2005).

Perspectives on service markets

Services are not a homogeneous group of products. There is wide variety within the services category, in terms of both the degree of service involved and the type of service product offered. Nevertheless, there are some general characteristics, common to many service products, that differentiate them as a genre from physical goods. This section, therefore, explores the criteria by which service products can be classified, and then goes on to look at the special characteristics of services and their implications for marketing.

■ Classifying services

There are few pure services. In reality, many product 'packages' involve a greater or lesser level of service. Products can be placed along a spectrum, with virtually pure personal service involving few, if any, props at one end, and pure product that involves little or no service at the other. Most products do have some combination of physical good and service, as shown in Figure 13.1. The purchase of a chocolate bar, for example, involves little or no service other than the involvement of a checkout or till operator. The purchase of a gas appliance will involve professional fitting, and thus is a combination of physical and service product. A new office computer system could similarly involve installation and initial training. A visit to a theme park or theatre could involve some limited support products, such as guides and gifts, while the main product purchased is the experience itself. Finally, a visit to a psychiatrist or a hairdresser may involve a couch, a chair and some minor allied props such as an interview checklist or a hair-dryer. The real product purchased here, however, is the personal service manufactured by the service deliverer, the psychiatrist or the hairdresser.

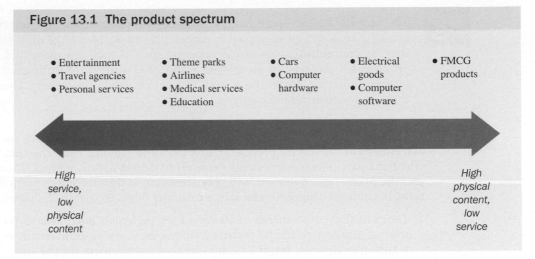

Figure 13.1 The product spectrum

Special characteristics of service markets

Five main characteristics have been identified as being unique to service markets (see, e.g., Sasser *et al.*, 1978; Cowell, 1984).

Lack of ownership

Perhaps the most obvious aspect of a service product is that no goods change hands, as such, and therefore there is no transfer of ownership of anything. A legal transaction does still take place; an insurance company agrees to provide certain benefits as long as the premiums are paid and the terms and conditions of the policy are met. A car rental company allows the customer full use of a vehicle for an agreed length of time, subject to some restraints on named drivers and type of usage, but the ownership of the vehicle remains with the rental company. A train seat can be reserved for a journey, but it is not owned. A subscription to the National Trust provides rights of access free of charge but no actual share in the ownership of its properties. The access, use or experience of the service is, therefore, often time-specific, usage-specific and subject to contractual terms and conditions.

The lack of ownership raises the issue of the transient nature of the purchase. Most service products involve some kind of 'experience' for the customer. This might be surrounded by props, for example a stage, lighting and sound systems, a lecture theatre, an insurance policy, a vehicle or a room, but these only serve to enhance or degrade the experience of the service. The faulty fuel gauge which means that the car hirer runs out of petrol in the most remote location, the hotel room next to the building site, the ineffective microphone at a concert all spoil the memory of the service consumed.

Intangibility

A visit to a retail store reveals an inviting display of products to purchase. These products can be examined, touched, tried on, sampled, smelt or listened to. All this can help the customer to examine what is on offer and to make choices between competing brands. The consumer regularly uses the whole range of senses to assist decision-making. This is especially important before the purchase is made, but even after the sale the product can be assessed in terms of its use, its durability and whether it lives up to general expectations. If there is a fault with a physical product, it can be returned or exchanged.

With service products, it is far more difficult to use the senses in the same way as a means of making a purchase decision because the actual service experience can only take place after that decision has been made. The heart of a service is the experience created for the customer, whether individually as with a personal service such as dentistry or hairdressing, or as a group experience, such as a lecture, a show or a flight. In many cases, once the purchase decision has been made, all the customer will receive is a ticket, a confirmation of booking or some promise of future benefit. The service experience itself is intangible, and is only delivered after the customer is committed to the purchase.

The Scottish Tourist Board ran a 'reawaken your senses' campaign to promote spring breaks. The campaign attempted to capture the intangible nature of the tourist experience by concentrating on visual imagery, such as fish, sea spray and scenery. The problem for this type of promotion is that it is difficult to distinguish the Scottish product offering from the many others available in equally scenic locations (http://www.visitscotland.com).

Despite the problem of intangibility, the potential customer can make some kind of prior assessment of the service product. Using available tangible cues, the customer can assess whether a particular service provider is likely to deliver what is wanted. The actual cues used and the priority given to them will vary according to the customer's particular needs at the time. In choosing a hotel, for example, a customer might look at the following:

1 *Location.* If the customer is on holiday, then perhaps a hotel near to the beach or other tourist attraction would be preferred, or one in a very peaceful scenic setting. A business traveller, in contrast, might look for one that is convenient for the airport or close to the client being visited.
2 *Appearance.* A customer's expectations about a hotel are likely to be affected by its appearance. Does it look shabby or well kept? Is it too big or too small? Does it look welcoming? What is the decor like, both internally and externally? Do the rooms seem spacious enough and well-appointed?
3 *Additional services.* The customer might be concerned about the peripheral aspects of the service on offer. The tourist who will be spending two weeks in a hotel might be interested in the variety of bars and restaurants provided, hairdressing, laundry or crèche facilities, shopping and postal services, or the nightlife. The business traveller might be more concerned about car parking, shuttle buses to the airport, or fax and telephone provision.
4 *Customer handling.* If the potential customer contacts the hotel for further information or to make a reservation, the quality of the handling they receive might affect the purchase decision. Courtesy and friendliness will make a good impression, as will a prompt and accurate response to the query. This kind of efficiency implies a commitment to staff training and good operating systems to assist easy access to relevant information and the speedy processing of bookings.

marketing in action

The multiplex: Oscar winner or turkey?

A visit to the cinema has been revolutionised over recent years, and further changes are still expected as efforts continue to be made to upgrade the customer experience. It is not very long ago that going to the cinema meant a choice of one main feature and a 'B' film and that was all. Stern-faced usherettes guided you with their torches towards a seat (usually the one you did not want), then they doubled up as ice-cream sellers during the interval (until they ran out of stock). Parking was usually non-existent, as cinemas were located in town centres, and queuing was the norm for more

popular shows as no advance booking was possible. The seating was not particularly comfortable, and the whole episode was not very customer friendly. It is perhaps not surprising that cinema audiences declined over many years as people switched to new leisure pursuits. In the late 1940s, around 1.6 billion tickets were sold each year, but this had shrunk to 54 million by 1984 (Rushe, 2001). Television and video were thought to be the culprits behind the dramatic decline.

Since the opening of the first multiplex in Milton Keynes in 1985, the decline has stopped as marketing strategies have become far more oriented towards the modern consumer's needs. Cinema entered a second golden

age that is still with us. This is very evident from a visit to a multiplex cinema, a format which has been a major influence in the rise in cinema attendances in the UK. A multiplex is a large building containing a number of small, individual cinemas around a central circulation area. A multiplex can thus show twelve or more different films at any one time and can seat up to 3500 customers in total. The size of the individual cinemas varies, so that, for example, blockbusting new releases can be put into bigger ones or even be shown in two cinemas at once, reflecting the expected popularity of the film. The seating in all the cinemas is invariably of a high standard.

For many film enthusiasts the multiplex is the only type of cinema they now visit.

Source: © VIEW Pictures Ltd/Alamy
http://www.alamy.com

Photographer: Hufton + Crow.

Despite the undoubted success of the multiplex format in offering choice and an experience that cannot be replicated on a small screen, there is growing concern over how long the rapid development of new sites can continue. Between 1988 and 1991 around fourteen sites per year were added, stopped by the recession in the early 1990s. The period 1992–95 saw growth again, but at a rate of six sites per year. Between 1996 and 2001, however, the number of new multiplexes rose to 25 per year (Dodona, 2001). Cineworld (formerly UGC), Cine UK and Warner Village added the most, followed by Odeon, UCI and Showcase. There are now ten UK cities with more than 50 multiplex screens within a 15–20 minute drive of the city centres, although many smaller towns still have no provision.

The impact of multiplex cinemas might not yet have been fully played out, as they have become part of the property development business. The concept has expanded into multi-leisure parks (MLPs) that are now taking prime edge-of-town sites with plenty of parking, with the multiplex as the anchor tenant, a bowling alley and a choice of restaurants making the sites 'one-stop shop entertainment experiences'. Following the US lead, more sites are planned. Star City outside Birmingham, for example, has a 36-screen cinema, twelve restaurants and shops. These sites are attracting leisure trade that previously used the city centre. Town centres can attract between 15 and 20 per cent of their income from the night-time economy, so a competitive response is likely, probably through efforts to create a café, pub and club culture to draw people back.

There is an alternative view, however, that suggests that significant growth in demand for multiplex cinemas may be over. Already, poorly located cinemas have closed. The cinema market is not in decline, but it may be oversupplied, thus affecting individual site viability. Estimates vary about how many seats are needed to make a profit, some suggesting that a seat must be sold between 300 and 400 times a year to make money. Some multiplexes are struggling to reach 200 times. As most of the costs are fixed, an empty seat is lost revenue for ever but with the same cost of providing it. Dodona (2001) estimated that by 2005 there would be nearly 3400 screens, a growth of 1400 on 2001 levels, so it is critical for the multiplex operators that audiences should continue to rise. The real victims could, however, be the remaining traditional cinemas and those multiplexes that are either poorly sited or not modernising further.

Marketing is therefore back on the agenda to build loyalty. Cinema audiences grew by 5 per cent in 2004 and box office revenues by 4 per cent, suggesting that despite the threats from DVD and other forms of entertainment, cinema-going remains a popular leisure pursuit. There were 175 million visits in 2004 and the prediction for 2008 is growth to 200 million. This perhaps reflects the fact that UK consumers, with an average of three visits per year per person, are attending the cinema a lot less often than their European counterparts and have some catching up to do.

The industry is still, however, heavily dependent upon the box office blockbusters. In 2004, the top ten film releases accounted for 40 per cent of box office revenues. What is needed is more creative marketing management to build upon an essentially undifferentiated cinema-going experience. Sophisticated service pricing systems could help, along with concepts borrowed from other sectors. For example, differentiation could be achieved through differential pricing, with earlier showings being cheaper, or pricing based on day of the week, month, location, seating position, service bundling (include meal), or even by specific film. Loyalty cards are also slowly being introduced, with UGC offering unlimited access to all of its 43 cinemas for a flat monthly fee. The idea has not been a great success to date.

Despite these challenges, service improvement has led to a trebling of cinema attendances at a time when many other visual media options are available, demonstrating the value of a strong customer focus in designing and delivering services.

Sources: Cox (2002); Dodona (2001); Kalsi and Napier (2005); *Marketing Week* (2005a); McCarthy (2002); Rushe (2001); **http://www.ukfilmcouncil.org.uk**.

In a wider sense, marketing and brand building are also important, of course. These help to raise awareness of a hotel chain's existence and positioning, and differentiate it from the competition. These communicate the key benefits on offer and thus help the customer to decide whether this is the kind of hotel they are looking for, developing their expectations. Advertising, glossy brochures and other marketing communications techniques can help to create and reinforce the potential customer's perception of location, appearance, additional services and customer handling, as well as the brand imagery. Strong marketing and branding also help to link a chain of hotels that might be spread worldwide, giving the customer some reassurance of consistency and familiarity. A business traveller in a strange city can seek out a known hotel name, such as Novotel, Holiday Inn, Sheraton, Campanile or Formule 1, and be fairly certain about what they are purchasing.

> **eg** Pizza Hut's menu, decor, servers, order processing, equipment, cooking procedures, etc., are all standardised (or allow minor variations and adaptations for local conditions), creating a consistent and familiar experience for the customer all over the world. Customers thus have a strong tangible impression of the character of Pizza Hut, what to expect of it, and what it delivers.

One of the greatest problems of intangibility is that it is difficult to assess quality both during and after the service has been experienced. Customers will use a combination of criteria, both objective and subjective, to judge their level of satisfaction, although it is often based on impressions, memories and expectations. Different customers attach significance to different things. The frequent business traveller might be extremely annoyed by check-in delays or the noise from the Friday night jazz cabaret, while the holidaymaker might grumble about the beach being 20 minutes' walk away rather than the five minutes promised in the brochure. Memories fade over time, but some bad ones, such as a major service breakdown or a confrontation with service staff, will remain.

Perishability

Services are manufactured at the same time as they are consumed. A lecturer paces the lecture theatre, creating a service experience that is immediately either consumed or slept through by the students. Manchester United, Ajax or AC Milan manufacture sporting entertainment that either thrills, bores or frustrates their fans as they watch the match live. Similarly, audiences at Covent Garden or La Scala absorb live opera as it unfolds before them. With both sport and entertainment, it is likely that the customer's enjoyment of the 'product' is heightened by the unpredictability of live performance and the audience's own emotional involvement in what is going on. This highlights another peculiarity of service products: customers are often directly involved in the production process and the synergy between them and the service provider affects the quality of the experience. A friend might tell you, 'Yes, it was a brilliant concert. The band were on top form and the atmosphere was great!' To create such a complete experience, the band and their equipment do have to perform to the expected standard, the lighting and sound crews have to get it right on the night, and the venue has to have adequate facilities and efficient customer handling processes. The atmosphere, however, is created by the interaction between performer and audience and can inspire the performer to deliver a better experience. The customer therefore has to be prepared to give as well as take, and make their own contribution to the quality of the service product.

Perishability thus means that a service cannot be manufactured and stored either before or after the experience. Manufacture and consumption are simultaneous. A hotel is, of course, a permanent structure with full-time staff, and exists regardless of whether it has customers or not on a particular night. The hotel's service product, however, is only being delivered when there is a customer present to purchase and receive it. The product is perishable in the sense that if a room is not taken on a particular night, then it is a completely lost opportunity. The same is true of most service products, such as airline seats, theatre tickets, management consultancy or dental appointments. If a dentist cannot fill the appointment book for a particular day, then that revenue-earning opportunity is lost for ever. In situations where demand is reasonably steady, it is relatively easy to plan capacity and adapt the organisation to meet the expected demand pattern.

Even where demand does fluctuate, as long as it is fairly predictable managers can plan to raise or reduce service capacity accordingly. A larger plane or an additional performance might be provided to cater for short-term demand increases. It can be more difficult, however, if there are very marked fluctuations in demand that might result in facilities lying idle

eg Attendance at soccer matches is a classic case of a perishable service. If missed, a match can never be experienced again, other than on film, and the revenue-earning capacity of the empty seat is lost for ever for that event. It has been argued that soccer clubs have become greedy when setting prices and that this is resulting in declining attendances at a number of clubs. Admission prices are so high that some of the traditional groups are being priced out of the market; the cheapest seat at a league match at Chelsea was £48 in August 2005. That's high compared with other forms of entertainment and staggeringly high compared to some of the low-cost airlines offering promotional fares. In 2003–04 occupancy levels at Premiership matches averaged 94.2 per cent. Many clubs have categories of fixtures according to their attractiveness, and categories are then priced in an attempt to avoid unfilled capacity (*Yorkshire Post*, 2005).

for a long time or in severe overcapacity. The profitability of companies servicing peak-hour transport demands can be severely affected because vehicles and rolling stock are unused for the rest of the day. Airlines too face seasonal fluctuations in demand.

eg The Kingdom Hotel in Zimbabwe is suffering from long-term decline, despite its great location at the Victoria Falls and catering for international tourists. This is just a part of the rapid decline of the tourism industry in Zimbabwe, caused largely by the policies of the Mugabe government. The revenue for tourism in Zimbabwe dropped from $700m in 1999 to just $60m in 2004. Meanwhile, the rooms remain empty, the facilities under-utilised, and the revenue lost for ever (Vasagar, 2005).

No matter how beautiful the setting, a hotel needs to promote itself to relevant customers in order to fill rooms and maintain revenue.

Source: © Kirk Pflaum http://www.sxc.hu

The concept of perishability means that a range of marketing strategies is needed to try to even out demand and bring capacity handling into line with it. These strategies might include pricing or product development to increase demand during quieter periods or to divert it from busier ones, or better scheduling and forecasting through the booking and reservation system.

Similarly, the capacity and service delivery system can be adapted to meet peaks or troughs in demand through such strategies as part-time workers, increased mechanisation or cooperation with other service providers. These will be considered in more detail later (see pp. 475 *et seq.*).

Inseparability

Many physical products are produced well in advance of purchase and consumption, and production staff rarely come into direct contact with the customer. Often, production and consumption are distanced in both space and time, connected only by the physical distribution system. Sales forecasts provide important guidelines for production schedules. If demand rises unexpectedly, opportunities might well exist to increase production or to reduce stockholding to meet customer needs.

As has already been said, with service products, however, the involvement of the customer in the service experience means that there can be no prior production and no storage and that consumption takes place simultaneously with production. The service delivery, therefore, cannot be separated from the service providers and thus the fourth characteristic of service products is inseparability. This means that the customer often comes into direct contact with the service provider(s), either individually, as with a doctor, or as part of a team of providers, as with air travel. The team includes reservations clerks, check-in staff, aircrew and perhaps transfer staff. In an airline, the staff team has a dual purpose. Clearly, they have to deliver their aspect of the service efficiently, but they also have to interact with the customer in the delivery of the service. An uncooperative check-in clerk might not provide the customer's desired seat, but in contrast, friendly and empathic cabin staff can alleviate the fear of a first-time flyer. The service provider can thus affect the quality of the service delivered and the manner in which it is delivered.

eg   British Airways trains its cabin staff to be aware of other cultures. It carries people from many different nationalities, so it believes that it is important for cabin crew to think about these cultures and be able to handle them with sensitivity. Sensitivity was apparently the last thing on an air stewardess's mind on a Thomson holiday flight from the Canary Islands to Gatwick. With a flight just two-thirds full and the passengers all seated at the rear of the plane, the captain decided to ask some of the passengers to move to create a more even distribution. Unfortunately, the stewardess allegedly asked for eight fat people to move to the front of the plane. Any volunteers? Was she looking at you? Thomson denied that the stewardess used the word fat, and said that all such announcements were scripted (Yaqoob, 2005).

While the delivery of a personal service can be controlled, since there are fewer opportunities for outside interference, the situation becomes more complex when other customers are experiencing service at the same time. The 'mass service experience' means that other customers can potentially affect the perceived quality of that experience, positively or negatively. As mentioned earlier, the enjoyment of the atmosphere at a sporting event or a concert, for example, depends on the emotional charge generated by a large number of like-minded individuals. In other situations, however, the presence of many other customers can negatively affect aspects of the service experience. If the facility or the staff do not have the capacity or the ability to handle larger numbers than forecast, queues, overcrowding and dissatisfaction can soon result. Although reservation or prebooking can reduce the risk, service providers can still be caught out. Airlines routinely overbook flights deliberately, on the basis that not all booked passengers will actually turn up. Sometimes, however, they miscalculate and end up with more passengers than the flight can actually accommodate and have to offer free air miles, cash or other benefits to encourage some passengers to switch to a later flight.

What the other customers are like also affects the quality of the experience. This reflects the segmentation policy of the service provider. If a relatively undifferentiated approach is offered, there are all sorts of potential conflicts (or benefits) from mixing customers who are perhaps looking for different benefits. A hotel, for example, might have problems if families with young children are mixed with guests on an over-50s holiday. Where possible, therefore, the marketer should carefully target segments to match the service product being offered.

Finally, the behaviour of other customers can be positive, leading to new friends, comradeship and enjoyable social interaction, or it can be negative if it is rowdy, disruptive or even threatening. Marketers prefer, of course, to try to develop the positive aspects. Social evenings for new package holiday arrivals, name badges on coach tours, and warm-up acts to build atmosphere at live shows all help to break the ice. To prevent disruptive behaviour, the service package might have to include security measures and clearly defined and enforced 'house rules' such as those found at soccer matches.

The implications of inseparability for marketing strategy will be considered at pp. 473 *et seq.*

Heterogeneity

With simultaneous production and consumption and the involvement of service staff and other customers, it can be difficult to standardise the service experience as planned. Heterogeneity means that each service experience is likely to be different, depending on the interaction between the customer and other customers, service staff, and other factors such as time, location and the operating procedures. The problems of standardising the desired service experience are greater when there is finite capacity and the service provided is especially labour intensive. The maxim 'when the heat is on the service is gone' reflects the risk of service breakdown when demand puts the system under pressure, especially if it is unexpected. This might mean no seats available on the train, delays in serving meals on a short-haul flight, or a queue in the bank on a Friday afternoon.

Some of the heterogeneity in the service cannot be planned for or avoided, but quality assurance procedures can minimise the worst excesses of service breakdown. This can be done by designing in 'failsafes', creating mechanisms to spot problems quickly and to resolve them early before they cause a major service breakdown. Universities, for example, have numerous quality assurance procedures to cover academic programmes, staffing and support procedures that involve self-assessment, student evaluation and external subject and quality assessment.

eg Mystery shoppers are widely used to monitor service levels and the service experience provided. They eat at restaurants to check food, service and facilities, stay in hotels, drink in pubs, travel on planes, and visit cinemas, health clubs and garages. The lucky ones even get to go on expensive foreign holidays. The feedback provides front-line commentary and, however revealing, often shows companies the difference between the service promise and the reality of what is delivered. Most of the time, the focus is on the overall experience rather than individual performance, although at times staff are also the focus of attention. Normally, the mystery shopper is given a checklist of points to watch out for, and they have to be skilled in classifying and memorising elements of the delivered service. To be effective, the mystery shopper must be believable and natural and thus cannot go round with a checklist on a clipboard (McLuhan, 2002). So next time you are in Burger King or Pret à Manger, to name but two, you could be next to a shopper on a mission.

Management therefore has to develop ways of reducing the impact of heterogeneity. To help in that process, they need to focus on operating systems, procedures and staff training in order to ensure consistency. New lecturers, for example, might be required to undertake a special induction programme to help them learn teaching skills, preparing materials and handling some of the difficulties associated with disruptive students. Managers have to indicate clearly what they expect of staff in terms of the desired level of service. This must cover not only compliance with procedures in accordance with training, but also staff attitudes and the manner in which they deal with customers.

The next section looks in more detail at the impact of the particular characteristics of service products on the design and implementation of the marketing programme.

Services marketing management

So far, this chapter has looked at the characteristics of service products in a very general way. This section looks further at the implications of those characteristics for marketers in terms of formulating strategy, developing and measuring quality in the service product and issues of training and productivity.

■ Services marketing strategy

The traditional marketing mix, consisting of the 4Ps, forms the basis of the structure of this book. For service products, however, additional elements of the marketing mix are necessary to reflect the special characteristics of services marketing. Shown in Figure 13.2, these are as follows:

■ *People*: whether service providers or customers who participate in the production and delivery of the service experience
■ *Physical evidence*: the tangible cues that support the main service product. These include facilities, the infrastructure and the products used to deliver the service
■ *Processes*: the operating processes that take the customer through from ordering to the manufacture and delivery of the service.

Any of these extra marketing mix elements can enhance or detract from the customer's overall experience when consuming the service. However, despite the special considerations, the purpose of designing an effective marketing mix remains the same whether for services or

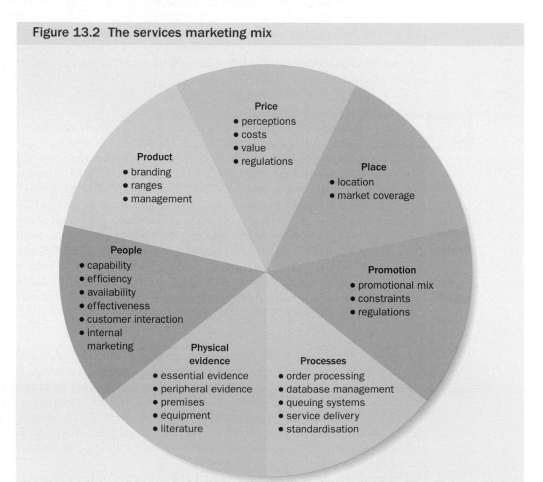

Figure 13.2 The services marketing mix

physical products. The marketer is still trying to create a differentiated, attractive proposition for customers, ensuring that whatever is offered meets their needs and expectations.

All seven of the services marketing mix elements will now be considered in turn.

Product

From a supplier's perspective, many services can be treated like any other physical product in a number of ways. The supplier develops a range of products, each of which represents profit-earning opportunities. A hotel company might treat each of its hotels as a separate product with its own unique product management requirements arising from its location, the state of the building and its facilities, local competition and its strengths and weaknesses compared with others in the area. These products might, of course, be grouped into product lines and SBUs based on similarities and differences between them, just as physical products can be.

corporate social responsibility   in action

What do the Prince of Wales, the Catholic Church and environmental protesters have in common?

The answer: unanimous opposition to a Dracula theme park that was planned in Transylvania, an area of Romania renowned for its beauty, ancient oak forests and cultural heritage. Better-informed readers will know, of course, that Dracula never existed as such, but the character created by Bram Stoker was based on Vlad Tepes, a fifteenth-century ruler who shot to fame for impaling over 1000 Turks after a particularly nasty battle. His real name was Vlad Dracul, Dracul meaning Devil in Romanian. The 'Tepes' (impaler) was added later for obvious reasons. Hollywood added the fangs, blood drinking and associated niceties. Vlad was born in the medieval fortress city of Sighisoara, a UNESCO world heritage site which the Romanian government has undertaken to protect.

The original proposed project planned to develop 40 hectares of land initially, expanding to 60 in phase 2. It would have cost around £30m and was due to be ready for tourists by 2004. Castle Dracula would have been the centrepiece, housing a judgement chamber, vampire den and alchemy laboratory. Included would have

been a mock torture room with stakes and knives, folk workshops for vampire protecting armour, a vampire fashion house, and rides with vampire themes, bringing a whole new meaning to 'The House of Horror'. The restaurants were going to offer such delicacies as 'blood pudding' and 'dish of brains' and for those who were brave enough, there would be motels on site. Linked to the park were a golf course, a campsite, a 700-bed hotel, souvenir shops, beer halls and a ballroom for 2000 dancers: something for everybody, but not eco-tourism (Moore Ede, 2002).

The park was expected to create around 3000 jobs and was planned to generate $21m per year from 1 million visitors. It is in a poor region in a poor country with a quality of life that has been likened to that of Namibia and Libya (Douglas-Home, 2001). The theme park offered jobs in an area with 17 per cent unemployment, and the chance to buy shares in the venture, with 100 shares costing about £20, one-third the average monthly wage. The company created to develop the park, Fondul Pentru Dezvoltare Turistica Sighisoara (FPDTS), was 99 per cent owned by the Sighisoara municipality but was intended as a profit-making enterprise. It was also argued that the city would be restored after many years of neglect.

From a government perspective, what better way for the Ministry of Tourism to start to rebuild the

brand image of Romania, which for many Europeans is off the tourism scale? Although the Transylvania region has much to offer, with fortified churches, castles, painted monasteries and unspoiled beauty, it is difficult to reach, about five hours by road from the capital Bucharest, it has little high-standard tourism infrastructure such as hotels and restaurants, no effective waste disposal system and no service tradition as a result of the Communist era. Dracula could have changed all that, however, even though Dracula films were not legal until 1989 and the Stoker book was not published in Romanian until 1992. A 1973 'Dracula: Truth and Legend' tour disappointed many foreigners as most of the time was spent tracing the life of Vlad, rather than the fangs and cape experience (George, 2002). The planned theme park would have addressed many of the issues of infrastructure and would have given the tourists what they really wanted.

There was a huge outcry across Europe and even from within Romania. Romania's Catholic and Orthodox bishops called for the abandonment of the park as they considered that it was an inappropriate symbol to offer visitors (Coppen, 2003). The Prince of Wales expressed concern (de Quetteville, 2004) and ecological protesters argued against the project on the grounds of the damage that it would do to the town of Sighisoara which was a world heritage site along with the surrounding natural environment. This wide variety of stakeholders formed a powerful and effective coalition (Jamal and Tanase, 2005). A stake was driven through the heart of the project and it was abandoned as being too controversial.

Within a year, however, the project was back, but this time bizarrely located nearer Bucharest at a farm once owned by executed dictator Nicolae Ceausescu. The connection between the new location at Snagov and Dracula is the claim that Vlad Tepes is buried nearby. Outside the Town Hall is a bust of the heavily armoured, thickly moustached Tepes. The park will include Disneyland style children's rides, a golf course, a horse racing circuit, and a housing development, and it is not likely to be opposed. The plan is to attract 1 million tourists annually with over 20 per cent coming from abroad, given the park's proximity to the international airport. It remains to be seen whether the development will be cheap and tacky or offer a true resort experience. The connection between evil and the glorification of death and happy family holidays appears to be regarded as incidental! Maybe Dracula should remain in Hollywood after all!

Sources: Coppen (2003); de Quetteville (2003, 2004); Douglas-Home (2001); George (2002); Jamal and Tanase (2005); Marinas (2004); Moore Ede (2002).

Many of the product concepts and the decisions concerning them that were discussed in Chapter 6 apply equally to services and physical products. Positioning, branding, developing a mix, designing new services and managing the product lifecycle are all relevant.

Product development. Product development in some service situations can be complex as it involves 'packaging' otherwise separate elements into a service product. Therefore a holiday company may need to work with airlines, hotels and local tour companies to blend a package for the target segment. From a consumer perspective, any failure in any part of the system will be regarded as a criticism of the holiday company, even though air traffic delays or faulty plumbing may not be directly under the company's control. At a regional and national level, government and private companies may work together to develop new attractions and infrastructure for tourists.

eg Hong Kong has adopted Disney in an effort to boost tourism. Although the smallest of the Disney theme parks, the Hong Kong park still has 1000 beds on site and hopes to attract 6 million visitors, one-third of whom will come from mainland China. An investment of that size and risk was only possible through a joint venture between Disney and the Hong Kong government. There will also be spin-off benefits for the whole economy, in terms of investment in infrastructure and employment in transportation, hospitality, catering and other related industries (Steiner, 2005).

Price

Because services are intangible, their pricing can be very difficult to set and to justify. The customer is not receiving anything that can be touched or otherwise physically experienced, so it can be hard for them to appreciate the benefits they have gained in return for their expenditure.

eg A solicitor's bill or the labour charges added to a repair bill can seem to be incredibly high to customers, because they do not stop to think about the training that has gone into developing professional skills nor of the peace of mind gained by having the job done 'properly'. As with any product, therefore, the customer's perception is central to assessing value for money.

The prices of some services are controlled by bodies other than the service provider. The amount that dentists charge for work under the National Health Service or that pharmacists charge to dispense a prescription is imposed by central government. Similarly, the BBC is funded by licence fees determined by government and charged to television owners. Other services price on a commission basis. An estate agent, for example, might charge the vendor a fee of 2 per cent of the selling price of the house, plus any expenses such as advertising.

Other service providers are completely free to decide their own prices, with due respect to competition and the needs, wants and perceptions of customers. In setting prices, however, service providers can find it very difficult to determine the true cost of provision, perhaps because of the difficulty of costing professional or specialist skills, or because the time and effort required to deliver a service vary widely between different customers, yet a standard price is needed. Perishability might also affect the pricing of professional services. A training provider, for example, who has little work on at the moment might agree to charge less than the normal daily rate, just to generate some income rather than none.

In service situations, price can play an important role in managing demand. By varying the price, depending on the time at which the service is delivered, service providers can try to discourage customers from purchasing at the busiest periods. Customers can also use price as a weapon. Passengers purchasing airline tickets shortly before the flight or visitors looking for a hotel room for the night might be able to negotiate a much lower price than that advertised. This is a result of the perishability of services: the airline would rather have a seat occupied and get something for it than let the flight take off with an empty one and, similarly, the hotel would rather have a room occupied than not.

---

eg The rail pricing system has changed considerably in the UK in recent years. Traditionally, the passenger bought a ticket, walked on to the train and found a seat. Few bothered to pay the additional charge for a seat reservation. The emphasis is now on encouraging advance booking so that capacity can be better planned. The price mechanism is used to achieve a spread of customers. Plans are now being considered, however, to introduce congestion charging on some overcrowded trains through the introduction of 'rail peak pricing' with passengers on the most popular services paying extra. With the use of smartcard technology it is becoming possible to charge by each train rather than generically by the time of day, although the main barrier is the difficulty of passengers knowing what price they have to pay before starting the journey. Something will have to be done on some of the commuter lines around London where on the one hand car passengers are being forced onto the trains because of road congestion charging, and yet rail investment is not keeping pace through more track, better carriages and better infrastructure. The conversion of the Waterloo to Reading trains from eight to ten carriages, for example, would increase passenger capacity by 25 per cent. Pricing is, however, one of the most powerful weapons for attracting customers to off-peak rather than peak-hour travel, provided work patterns allow it. The Great Anglia franchise, for example, offers passengers an early bird discount on their season ticket if they avoid arriving at Liverpool Street between 7.15 a.m. and 9.15 a.m. (*Modern Railways*, 2005; Webster, 2005).

Place

According to Cowell (1984), services are often supplied direct from the provider to the customer because production and consumption are simultaneous. Direct supply allows the provider to control what is going on, to differentiate through personal service, and to get direct feedback and interaction with the customer. Direct supply can take place from business premises, such as a hairdresser's salon, a solicitor's office or a university campus. Some services can also be supplied by telephone, such as insurance and banking services. Others are supplied by the service provider visiting the customer's home or premises, such as cleaning, repair of large appliances, equipment installation and servicing, or home hairdressing services.

Direct supply can cause problems for the service provider. It limits the number of customers that can be dealt with and the geographic coverage of the service. For sole traders or small businesses who particularly value the rapport and personal relationships built up with regular clients, this might be perfectly acceptable. Businesses that want to expand might find that direct supply involving the original proprietor of the business is no longer feasible. Professional service businesses, such as accountants or solicitors, might employ additional qualified staff to expand the customer base or to expand geographic coverage.

A fitness-oriented society coupled with rising levels of obesity has been a major factor behind the rapid growth of the health and fitness sector since the mid-1990s. Participation among the adult population grew from 3.8 per cent in 1996 to 8 per cent in 2005, with an expected rise around 13.5 per cent by 2007 (Urquhart, 2005). This is further encouraged by the government's increased focus on health and fitness issues generally and obesity in particular. In the short term, however, the number of new members coming forward may have dropped in 2005.

There are 2403 publicly run fitness clubs in the UK and 1982 private clubs (Stevenson, 2005). Holmes Place has 76 clubs (50 in the UK) with a membership retention rate of 60 per cent, which is high compared to the rest of the industry. Its rival Fitness First has 166 clubs in the UK, a further 173 in the rest of Europe, and a total of 434 clubs generating 1.2 million members worldwide. David Lloyd actually reported lower membership numbers in 2005 compared with 2004, as users switch centres to obtain the latest facilities or just lose interest in the treadmill. The premium clubs are especially vulnerable as they need to invest in more and varied facilities such as swimming pools and indoor tennis courts. It is expected that some rationalisation will take place as users become ever more demanding (Stevenson, 2005).

The main means of growth for most clubs has been to open branches in new locations offering the same standard range of facilities. David Lloyd is trimming back its expansion plans and its new venues will feature racquet sports centres rather than traditional gyms. The question is whether growth can then continue, as there are already signs that saturation has been reached for the time being. In 2004, there were 796 new gyms being planned, 15 per cent down on 2003. Other marketing activities also involve extending the reach with, for example, tie-ins with local sports associations, corporate membership drives and joint initiatives such as LA Fitness's 'Wellness Centres' operated in conjunction with BUPA.

Other service businesses such as fast food outlets, domestic cleaners or debt collection agencies might opt to expand by franchising, while others will decide to move towards indirect supply through intermediaries paid on a commission basis. Thus the local pharmacist might act as an agent for a company that develops photographic film, a village shop might collect dry cleaning, insurance brokers distribute policies, travel agencies distribute holidays and business travel, and tourist information offices deal with hotel and guest house bookings. In some of these cases, the main benefit of using an intermediary is convenience for the customer and spreading the coverage of the service. In others, such as the travel agency and the insurance broker, the service provider gains the added benefit of having its product sold by a specialist alongside the competition.

Promotion

Marketing communication objectives, implementation and management for services are largely the same as for any other product. There are a few specific issues to point out, however. As with pricing, some professional services are ethically constrained in what marketing communication they are allowed to do. Solicitors in the UK, for example, are allowed to use print advertising, but only if it is restrained and factual. An advertisement can tell the reader what areas of the law the practice specialises in, but it cannot make emotive promises about winning vast amounts of compensation for you, for example.

Service products face a particularly difficult communications task because of the intangibility of the product. They cannot show you pretty pack shots, they cannot whet your appetite with promises of strawberry and chocolate-flavoured variants, they cannot show you how much of this amazing product you are getting for your money. They can, however, show the physical evidence, they can show people like you apparently enjoying the service, they can emphasise the benefits of purchasing this service. Testimonials from satisfied customers can be an extremely effective tool, because they reassure the potential customer that the service works and that the outcomes will be positive. Linked with this, word-of-mouth communication is incredibly important, especially for the smaller business working in a limited geographic area.

Finally, it must be remembered that many service providers are small businesses that could not afford to invest in glossy advertising campaigns even if they could see the point of it. Many can generate enough work to keep them going through word-of-mouth recommendation, websites and advertisements in the *Yellow Pages*. Much depends on the level of competition and demand in the local market for the kind of service being offered. If the town's High Street supports four different restaurants, then perhaps a more concerted effort might be justified, including, for example, advertising in local newspapers, door-to-door leaflet drops and price promotions.

eg Ramada Jarvis Hotels (**http://www.ramadaJarvis.co.uk**) uses direct marketing to promote conference business in its 62 hotels in the UK. The information pack, which is targeted at potential business customers, includes a complete directory of locations, room configurations and prices along with a lot of visual imagery to show the standard of meeting rooms, food service and the range of staff who are employed to make the conference or meeting a success. The messages throughout stress quality and reliability.

It is important to remember, however, that customers are likely to use marketing communication messages to build their expectations of what the service is likely to deliver. This is true of any product but, as will be discussed at pp. 473 *et seq.*, because of intangibility, the judgement of service quality is much more subjective. It is based on a comparison of prior expectations with actual perceived outcomes. The wilder or more unrealistic the communication claims, therefore, the greater the chances of a mismatch that will lead to a dissatisfied customer in the end. The service provider does, of course, need to create a sufficiently alluring image to entice the customer, but not to the point where the customer undergoing the service experience begins to wonder if this is actually the same establishment as that advertised.

eg The Australian Tourist Commission also makes heavy use of imagery to portray the natural and cultural delights of Australia to European audiences. Whether it is kangaroos, Ayers Rock, the Great Barrier Reef or Sydney Opera House, the visual message is the same: vibrant, exciting and surprising. The media advertisements and PR usually reinforce these themes, making full use of holiday programmes and travel shows as well as supporting Australia-themed national supplements in some of the daily newspapers. 'Brand Australia' campaigns are, however, targeted to attract different audiences and a number of campaigns are run simultaneously in different geographic markets.

Images of Aboriginal people in traditional dress encourage tourists seeking alternative cultural experiences to visit the Australian outback.

Source: © eyeubiquitous/hutchison http://www.eyeubiquitous.com

The ATC has divided the 15 million potential visitors to Australia into five broad segments:

- Self challengers
- Comfort travellers
- Cocoon travellers
- Taste and try
- Pushing boundaries.

Each segment is distinguished by the travel experience sought, attitudes to travel, and the style of travel sought. For each segment, a media plan is developed to exploit the potential, and messages are tailor-made according to the attitudes held and benefits sought. There are unifying themes, however, such as overcoming the view that Australia is a remote, vast and 'once in a lifetime' destination to position it more as a 'liberating, civilised adventure' destination. A 'visiting journalist' programme, funded by the ATC, is especially important for stimulating more and better PR coverage, and around 1000 print and broadcast journalists are invited each year. It also helps to show Australia as being more than scenery and sun, with coverage of urban culture, food, wine, arts and cultural themes. An integrated campaign is important to overcome a concern, confirmed by research, that consumers are comfortable with Australia as a destination but lack an in-depth knowledge and sense of urgency to visit. The Brand Australia campaign aims to change that by strengthening the brand perception and presenting Australia as an experience destination for sophisticated travellers, not just a flop-on-the-beach paradise (Moldofsdky, 2005; **http://www.atc.australia.com; http://www.australia**).

People

Services depend on people and interaction between people, including the service provider's staff, the customer and other customers. As the customer is often a participant in the creation and delivery of the service product, there are implications for service product quality, productivity and staff training. The ability of staff to cope with customers, to deliver the service reliably to the required standard and to present an image consistent with what the organisation would want is of vital concern to the service provider. This is known as *internal marketing*, and will be discussed later at pp. 475 *et seq.* The role of the customer in the service is known as *interactive marketing*, and will be discussed at pp. 473 *et seq.*

Physical evidence

Physical evidence comprises the tangible elements that support the service delivery, and offer clues about the positioning of the service product or give the customer something solid to take away with them to symbolise the intangible benefits they have received. Shostack (1977) differentiates between *essential evidence* and *peripheral evidence*. Essential evidence is central to the service and is an important contributor to the customer's purchase decision. Examples of this might be the type and newness of aircraft operated by an airline or of the car fleet belonging to a car hire firm, the layout and facilities offered by a supermarket or a university's lecture theatres and their equipment as well as IT and library provision. Peripheral evidence is less central to the service delivery and is likely to consist of items that the customer can have to keep or use.

Processes

Because the creation and consumption of a service are usually simultaneous, the production of the service is an important part of its marketing as the customer either witnesses it or is directly involved in it. The service provider needs smooth, efficient customer-friendly procedures. Some processes work behind the scenes, for example administrative and data processing systems, processing paperwork and information relating to the service delivery and keeping track of customers.

Systems that allow the service provider to send a postcard to remind customers that the next dental check-up or car service is due certainly help to generate repeat business, but also help in a small way to strengthen the relationship with the customer. Other processes are also 'invisible' to the customer, but form an essential part of the service package. The organisation of the kitchens in a fast food outlet, for example, ensures a steady supply of freshly cooked burgers available for counter staff to draw on as customers order. Well-designed processes are also needed as the service is delivered to ensure that the customer gets through with minimum fuss and delay and that all elements of the service are properly delivered. This might involve, for example, the design of forms and the information requested, payment procedures, queuing systems or even task allocation. At a hairdressing salon, for instance, a junior might wash your hair while the stylist finishes off the previous customer, and the receptionist will handle the payment at the end.

eg Smartcards are revolutionising service delivery processes by cutting out human interaction, which can be slow, inconsistent and unreliable. Smartcards which are a similar size to a credit card have an embedded microprocessor and a memory that can be activated by either a reader or a signal-emitting device. The cards are especially popular with transport providers as a means of reducing queues at ticket offices and for travel authentication. The cards are not bound by travel zones and time restrictions as are normal season tickets and travel cards. The card reader at a station will automatically account for the journey time and distance, and the fare can be deducted from the previously topped-up card. Speed of processing is essential for keeping systems such as London Underground working. The Jubilee Line has the capacity to handle 39,000 people per hour and that's a lot of movement at its main stations in the peak periods.

Interactive marketing: service quality

Central to the delivery of any service product is the *service encounter* between the provider and the customer. This is also known as interactive marketing. This aspect of services is an important determinant of quality because it brings together all the elements of the services marketing mix and is the point at which the product itself is created and delivered. The challenge for the service marketer is to bring quality, customer service and marketing together to build and maintain customer satisfaction (Christopher *et al.*, 1994). Quality issues are just as important for service products as they are for a physical product, but service quality is much more difficult to define and to control. Authors such as Lovelock *et al.* (1999), Devlin and Dong (1994) and Zeithaml *et al.* (1990), for example, stress the importance of customer perceptions and use them as the basis for frameworks for measuring service quality.

eg Home delivery of pizzas is usually associated with supplier guarantees of free pizzas if delivered outside a certain period. This helps emphasise the speed of delivery and reinforces the convenience of home ordering services. A number of chains such as Domino's have added online ordering, with a central call centre directing orders to the nearest retail stores. The customer is then free to browse the menu at leisure and the site can be frequently updated with offers, etc. It has also gone further in ensuring improved service through the introduction of the Domino's Heat Wave hot bags with a patented electrically warmed heating mechanism. Once unplugged, it keeps the pizza hot during normal delivery times (**http://www.dominos.co.uk**).

Measuring service quality

Some aspects of the service product can, of course, be measured more objectively than others. Where tangible elements are involved, such as physical evidence and processes, quality can be defined and assessed more easily. In a fast food restaurant, for example, the cleanliness of the premises, the length of the queues, the consistency of the size of portions and their cooking, and the implementation and effectiveness of stock control systems can all be 'seen' and measured. Whether the customer *actually* enjoyed the burger, whether they *felt* that they had had to wait too long, or whether they *felt* that the premises were too busy, crowded or noisy are much more personal matters and thus far more difficult for managers to assess.

A particular group of researchers, Berry, Parasuraman and Zeithaml, have developed criteria for assessing service quality and a survey mechanism called SERVQUAL for collecting data relating to customer perceptions (see, e.g., Parasuraman *et al.*, 1985; Zeithaml *et al.*, 1988, 1990). They cite ten main criteria that, between them, cover the whole service experience from the customer's point of view:

1 *Access.* How easy is it for the customer to gain access to the service? Is there an outlet for the service close to the customer? Is there 24-hour access by telephone to a helpline?
2 *Reliability.* Are all the elements of the service performed and are they delivered to the expected standard? Does the repair engineer clean up after himself after mending the washing machine and does the machine then work properly? Does the supermarket that promises to open another checkout when the queues get too long actually do so?
3 *Credibility.* Is the service provider trustworthy and believable? Is the service provider a member of a reputable trade association? Does it give guarantees with its work? Does it seem to treat the customer fairly?
4 *Security.* Is the customer protected from risk or doubt? Is the customer safe while visiting and using a theme park? Does an insurance policy cover all eventualities? Will the bank respect the customer's confidentiality? Can the cellular telephone network provider prevent hackers from hijacking a customer's mobile phone number?
5 *Understanding the customer.* Does the service provider make an effort to understand and adapt to the customer's needs and wants? Will a repair engineer give a definite time of arrival? Will a financial adviser take the time to understand the customer's financial situation and needs and then plan a complete package? Do front-line service staff develop good relationships with regular customers?

These first five criteria influence the quality of the *outcome* of the service experience. The next five influence the quality of the *inputs* to the process to provide a solid foundation for the outputs.

6 *Responsiveness.* Is the service provider quick to respond to the customer and willing to help? Can a repair engineer visit within 24 hours? Will a bank manager explain in detail what the small print in a loan agreement means? Are customer problems dealt with quickly and efficiently?
7 *Courtesy.* Are service staff polite, friendly and considerate? Do they smile and greet customers? Are they pleasant? Do they show good manners? Do service staff who have to visit a customer's home treat it with proper respect and minimise the sense of intrusion?
8 *Competence.* Are service staff suitably trained and able to deliver the service properly? Does a financial adviser have extensive knowledge of available financial products and their appropriateness for the customer? Does a librarian know how to access and use information databases? Do theme park staff know where the nearest toilets are, what to do in a medical emergency or what to do about a lost child?
9 *Communication.* Do service staff listen to customers and take time to explain things to them understandably? Do staff seem sympathetic to customer problems and try to suggest appropriate solutions? Do medical, legal, financial or other professional staff explain things in plain language?
10 *Tangibles.* Are the tangible and visible aspects of the service suitably impressive or otherwise appropriate to the situation? Does the appearance of staff inspire confidence in the customer? Are hotel rooms clean, tidy and well appointed? Do lecture theatres have good acoustics and lighting, a full range of audiovisual equipment and good visibility from every seat? Does the repair engineer have all the appropriate equipment available to do the job quickly and properly? Are contracts and invoices easy to read and understand?

It is easy to appreciate just how difficult it is to create and maintain quality in all ten of these areas, integrating them into a coherent service package. In summary, Figure 13.3 shows the service experience and the factors that affect consumers' expectations of what they will receive. The criteria that influence their perception of what they actually did receive are also shown, as well as the reasons why there might be a mismatch between expectations and perceptions. This can have an important impact on the customer's perception of value and willingness to repeat purchase (Caruana *et al.*, 2000).

Figure 13.3 Service quality: expectations, perceptions and gaps

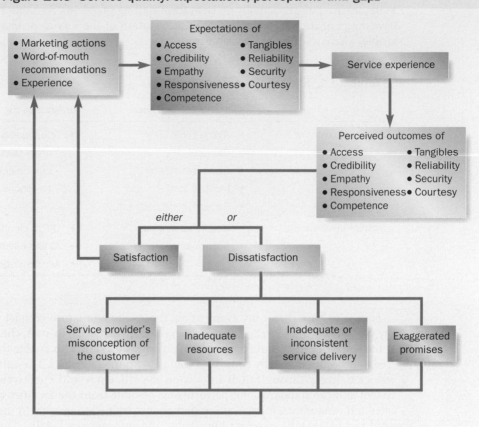

Internal marketing: training and productivity

Because of the interaction between customers and staff in the creation and delivery of a service, it is particularly important to focus on developing staff to deliver high levels of functional and service quality. The pay and rewards system employed can also help to boost staff morale and encourage them to take a positive approach to service delivery. Heskett *et al.* (1997) highlighted the connection between employee and customer satisfaction within services. The 'satisfaction mirror' can actually enhance the customer's experience if the service personnel are approaching service delivery in a positive way. They suggested that employees feeling enthusiastic about their job communicate this to customers both verbally and non-verbally and are also more eager to serve the customer. Similarly, employees who remain in the job longer reach higher capability levels and often a better understanding of customers, which again can enhance customers' feelings of satisfaction. Defining the ideal profile and right remuneration package for staff is not easy.

eg Research from MORI suggested that staff attitude was more important than quality or price in influencing consumer choice when buying a service. It would appear that the young (aged between 15 and 34) and the more affluent are especially sensitive. Whether it is poor advice, indifferent attitudes, a failure to keep promises or just poor attention to detail, the message is clear to service providers. Many readers will almost certainly recall situations where poor staff attitude has had a bearing on the quality of the experience. This creates pressure to ensure that staff are well trained, not just about the products but also in how to deal sensitively with customers. Faced with increased difficulty in attracting the right calibre of younger staff, retailers such as Sainsbury's and B&Q have scrapped the upper age limit for their workers and actively seek older staff. Carphone Warehouse and Eagle Star are also employing older sales staff to attract the 'grey market' (Buckley, 2002).

Staff training

Many service failures actually do stem from staffing problems. As Table 13.1 shows, some staff have direct or indirect involvement in the creation of the service product, and some staff are visible, whereas others are invisible to customers.

Table 13.1 Staff in the service function

	Visible to the customer	Invisible to the customer
Direct involvement	• Airline cabin crew • Cashiers • Sales assistants • Medical staff • Receptionists	• Telephone-based services: – order takers – customer helplines – telephone banking
Indirect involvement	• Hotel chambermaids • Supermarket shelf fillers	• Office cleaners • Airline caterers • Administrative staff

Staff who have direct involvement are those who come into contact with a customer as a key part of service delivery. In an airline, these might be cabin staff, check-in staff, and those at the enquiries desk. Indirect involvement covers all staff who enable the service to be delivered, but do not normally come into contact with the customer. They affect the quality of the service delivery through their impact on the efficiency and effectiveness of the operating system and the standards and performance possible from the facilities and infrastructure. In cafés and restaurants, many waiting staff are not trained to operate to their full potential: they need technical skills, product knowledge and interpersonal skills. These can be taught. In addition, the contribution of waiting staff to customer satisfaction must be emphasised (Pratten, 2004).

A hotel is judged by the quality of its staff and how well trained they are to deal with satisfying the needs of the customer.

Source: © eddy buttarelli/Alamy http://www.alamy.com

Ramada Jarvis Hotels (mentioned earlier on p. 471) places special emphasis on its staff training in its promotional material. Entitled 'Summit Quality Signature', its brochure outlines the various dimensions of training and the phased approach to awarding the quality signature to all members of staff. The first stage concentrates on core values and considers such issues as service delivery, clear merchandising, first impressions, introductions, cleanliness, freshness and how to encourage extra sales. The second stage is concerned with consistency. Quality standards are set for each core value and both self-checking and regular external 'flight tests' are organised to ensure that standards are being maintained and that, where necessary, corrective action is being taken (Ramada Jarvis Hotels corporate literature).

Visible staff (both those with direct involvement and those with indirect involvement with the customer) are in the front line of service delivery. Not only are they concerned with the practical aspects of service delivery to the required standards, but their appearance, interpersonal behaviour and mannerisms will also make an impression on the customer. Airlines, for example, will pay particular attention to a cabin attendant's personal grooming and dress standardisation to ensure a consistent visual impact. Dress is often used to help the customer identify visible staff, both those directly involved in the service, such as aircraft cabin crew, and those who are indirectly involved, such as stewards at soccer matches or security staff.

Indirect visible staff also include people such as the cleaners at McDonald's, chambermaids in hotels, or staff supporting the cashiers in banks. Invisible staff might or might not have direct contact with customers. Staff who take telephone bookings or those who deal with customer queries on the telephone are heard, but not seen. In some cases, these staff might be the only major point of contact for the customer, and thus although their visibility is limited, their ability to interact well with customers is still extremely important.

The organisation's strategy for internal marketing will vary, depending on the different categories of staff employed. Staff who are in the front line of service delivery, with a high level of customer contact, will have to be trained to deliver the standards expected. Staff who do not have direct contact still have to be motivated to perform their tasks effectively and efficiently. They have to understand that what they do affects the quality of the service delivered and the ability of the front-line staff to perform to expected standards. All of this strongly implies, however, that the different groups of staff have to work closely and efficiently together, and deliver a quality service to each other, which in turn will affect the quality of service delivered to the end customer (Mathews and Clark, 1996).

Staff productivity

Staff productivity within services is also a difficult issue for managers. According to Cowell (1984), there are several reasons for service productivity being difficult to measure. The main reason is that services are 'performed', not 'produced', and there are too many external factors influencing this live creation of a product. The service production process simply cannot be controlled and replicated as reliably and consistently as a mechanised factory line. Service productivity particularly suffers from the involvement of the customer. If customers do not fill forms in properly, if they are not familiar with procedures or they do not really know what they want, if they turn up late for appointments, if they want to spend time in idle chatter rather than getting on with the business in hand, then it will take service staff much longer to deliver the product. Where productivity is measured in terms of the number of transactions handled, the amount of revenue generated, or the number of customers processed, such delays essentially caused by the customer can reflect unfairly on service staff. This raises the whole question, however, of what constitutes appropriate and fair measures of service productivity. A customer who is given a great deal of individual help or who feels that service staff have taken time for a friendly chat with them might well feel that they have received a much better-quality service and appreciate not being treated with cold, bureaucratic efficiency. It might be worth tolerating a slightly longer queue if you feel that you will be treated with care, respect and humanity when you get to the front of it. Definitions and measures of productivity therefore need to be flexible and sympathetic, striking a fine balance between the customer's needs and the business's need to work efficiently.

None of this absolves managers from looking at ways in which service productivity can be improved. There are several possibilities for delivering services more efficiently without necessarily detracting too much from their quality.

Staff. Through improved recruitment and training, staff can be given better skills and knowledge for dealing with customers. A clerk in a travel agency, for example, can develop a better knowledge of which tour operators offer which resorts so that the key brochures can be immediately pulled out in response to a customer query. Library staff can be fully trained in the use and potential of databases and online search mechanisms so that customers can have their problems solved immediately without having to wait for a 'specialist' to return from a lunch break. Improving the staff profile might also allow more delegation or empowerment of front-line service staff. A customer does not want to be told 'I can't do that without checking with my supervisor' and then have to wait while this happens. Staff should be given the responsibility and flexibility to deal with the real needs of customers as they arise.

eg Nottingham City Council introduced a service training course for front-line construction staff in its building division. The course helped to bring about a 7 per cent increase in the number of day-to-day repairs completed on time, a 2 per cent rise in customer satisfaction, and a fall to zero in the number of allegations of racist or sexist behaviour in front-line employees. Nottingham is now devoid of the familiar builders' wolf-whistles, at least from public sector employees (Aaron, 2005)!

Systems and technology. The design of the service process and the introduction of more advanced technology can both help to improve service productivity and the service experience for the customer (Bitner *et al.*, 2000).

Technology combined with well-designed systems can be very powerful in creating market transactions where no interpersonal contact is required between buyer and seller (Rayport and Sviokla, 1994). Libraries, for example, have used technology to improve their productivity. Laser scanning barcodes in books make it far quicker to issue or receive returned items than with the old manual ticketing systems. This has also allowed them to improve the quality of their service. The librarian can immediately tell you, for instance, which books you have on loan, whether or not another reader has reserved a book you have, and which other reader has borrowed the book you want. Some technology means that the service provider need not provide human interaction at all. In the financial sector, 'hole in the wall' cash machines, for instance, give customers 24-hour, 7-day-a-week access to their bank accounts, usually without long queues, and because of the way these machines are networked they provide hundreds of convenient access points.

marketing **in action**

UPS: delivering the service package

Service efficiency and responsiveness have to be consistently at peak levels to handle 1.8 million customers sending 12.9 million packages and documents to 6 million receiving customers. Add that to the management of specialised transport and logistics on a worldwide scale, including 1713

operating facilities, 149,000 vehicles, and over 500 planes, and the complexity becomes daunting. That is the challenge that faces United Parcel Service (UPS), the express carrier and package delivery company (Alghalith, 2005). UPS has had to use systems and technology to a high degree to ensure that items can be tracked and processed on time, and delivered to the right place. This technology has become an important part of

the competitiveness of its service offering.

To manage all this activity, UPS has developed an integrated global IT network that coordinates the flow of goods, information and funds. Each package must be collected, shipped, tracked, and located at any time to provide customers with exact information on the whereabouts of their shipment. UPS has one of the largest Oracle databases in the world in its data warehouse, which is just as important as its physical goods warehouses in the provision of service. The drivers have handheld wireless computers to capture delivery information including signatures. Increasingly, these devices also include internet access and GPS.

Customers demand high performance levels in this competitive sector and UPS was one of the first to embrace the concept of e-commerce to deliver the goods that its customers order online quickly, reliably and securely. It provides all the account and shipping information in real time to offer a valued service benefit to its customers. With the UPS 'Time in Transit' package, customers can plan shipments and be confident of delivery dates and times without direct contact with UPS staff. The provision of such services is an important part of maintaining customer relationships and building loyalty.

Sources: Alghalith (2005); *Traffic World* (2005); Tyler (2005).

Reduce service levels. Reducing service levels to increase productivity can be dangerous if it leads to a perception of reduced quality in the customer's mind, especially if customers have become used to high levels of service. Reducing the number of staff available to deliver the service might lead to longer queues or undue pressure on the customer to move through the system more quickly.

If a busy doctor's surgery introduces a system that schedules appointments at five-minute intervals, one of two things might happen. A doctor who wants to maintain the schedule might hurry patients through consultations without listening to them properly or allowing them time to relax enough to be able to say what is really worrying them. Patients might then feel that they have not got what they came for and that the doctor does not actually care about them. Alternatively, the doctor may put the patient first, and regardless of the five-minute rule take as long as is needed to sort out the individual patient. The patient emerges satisfied, but those still in the waiting room whose appointments are up to half-an-hour late might not feel quite so happy.

Reducing service levels also opens up opportunities for competitors to create a new differential advantage. Discount supermarkets such as Aldi, Netto and Lidl keep their prices low partly through minimising service. Thus there are few checkout operators, no enquiries desk, and nobody to help customers pack their bags. The more mainstream supermarkets have been able to use this as a way of emphasising the quality of their service, and have deliberately invested in higher levels of service to differentiate themselves further. Thus Tesco, for example, promised its customers that if there were more than three people in a checkout queue, another checkout would be opened if possible. Tesco also announced that it was taking on extra staff in most of its branches, simply to help customers. These staff might help to unload your trolley on to the conveyor belt or pack your bags, or if you get to the checkout and realise that you have forgotten the milk, they will go and get it for you.

Customer interaction. Productivity might be improved by changing the way the customer interacts with the service provider and its staff. It might also mean developing or changing the role of the customer in the service delivery itself. The role of technology in assisting self-service through cash machines has already been mentioned. The whole philosophy of the supermarket is based on the idea of increasing the customer's involvement in the shopping process through self-service.

Customers might also have to get used to dealing with a range of different staff members, depending on their needs or the pressures on the service provider. Medical practices now commonly operate on a group basis, for example, and a patient might be asked to see any one of three or four doctors. If the patient only wants a repeat prescription then the receptionist might be able to handle it, or if a routine procedure is necessary, such as a blood test or a cervical smear, then the practice nurse might do it.

If any measures are taken that relate to the nature of customer involvement and interaction, the service provider might have a problem convincing customers that these are for their benefit and that they should cooperate. Careful use of marketing communications is needed, through both personal and non-personal media, to inform customers of the benefits, to persuade them of the value of what is being done and to reassure them that their cooperation will not make too many heavy demands on them.

Reduce mismatch between supply and demand. Sometimes demand exceeds supply. Productivity might well then be high, but it could be higher still if the excess demand could be accommodated. Some customers will not want to wait and might decide either to take their business to an alternative service provider or not to purchase at all. At other times, supply will exceed demand and productivity will be low because resources are lying idle. If the service provider can even out some of these fluctuations, then perhaps overall productivity can be improved.

The service provider might be able to control aspects of supply and demand through fairly simple measures. Pricing, for example, might help to divert demand away from busy periods or to create extra demand at quiet times. An appointment booking system might also help to ensure a steady trickle of customers at intervals that suit the service provider. The danger is, though, that if the customer cannot get the appointment slot that they want, they might not bother at all. Finding alternative uses for staff and facilities during quiet times can also create more demand and increase productivity. Universities, for instance, have long had the problem of facilities lying idle at weekends and during vacations. They have solved this by turning halls of residence into conference accommodation or cheap and cheerful holiday lets in the vacations, or hiring out their more attractive and historic buildings for weddings and other functions at weekends, with catering provided.

If the service provider cannot or does not wish to divert demand away from busy times, then the ability to supply the service to the maximum number of customers will have to be examined. If the peaks in demand are fairly predictable, then many service providers will bring in part-time staff to increase available supply. There might be limits to their ability to do so, however, which are imposed by constraints of physical space and facilities. A supermarket has only so many checkouts, a bank has only so many tills, a barber's shop has only so many chairs, a restaurant has only so many tables. Nevertheless, part-time staff can still be useful behind the scenes, easing the burden on front-line staff and speeding up the throughput of customers.

Non-profit marketing

The main focus of this section is the charities aspect of non-profit marketing, reflecting the growth of cause-related marketing (CRM) and the radical changes in the ways in which charities generate revenue, their attitudes to their 'businesses' and their increasingly professional approaches to marketing. Cause-related organisations form an important part of the non-profit sector. According to the Charity Commission, in 2005 in the UK, over £32bn was generated by over 190,000 charities (Opinion Leader Research, 2005). Mintel (2003) points out that many charities are relatively small with 88 per cent of them having income of less than £100,000 per year. Just 421 charities account for 44 per cent of all income. Increasingly, charities are becoming brands with attributes, emotive appeals and value statements that are designed to appeal to the population of interest. It works: Opinion Leader Research (2005) found that 85 per cent of people surveyed had given money to charities over the previous year, and over 30 per cent said that they had given more than £100.

Like many other organisations, charities have found that the environment within which they operate has changed. There are many more charities competing for attention and donations, and the attitudes of both individual and corporate donors have changed. Thus all sorts of organisations that have not traditionally seen themselves as 'being in business' have had to become more businesslike, fighting for and justifying resources and funding.

This section, therefore, discusses the characteristics that differentiate non-profit from profit-making organisations. Then, the implications for marketing will be explored.

eg The National Missing Persons Helpline (NMPH) was registered as a charity in the UK in 1993. It was set up because at any one time there are up to 250,000 people 'missing' in the UK, yet there was no central body to offer advice and support to missing persons' families, to coordinate information on missing people, or for missing people to contact for help. Although many people do 'go missing' on purpose and do not wish to be found, others disappear because they are distressed, ill or confused and need help and reassurance to solve their problems. A few are the victims of abduction.

The NMPH therefore offers a number of services, including:

■ a national 24-hour telephone helpline for families of missing people;
■ a confidential 'Free Call Message Home' 24-hour freefone telephone helpline so that missing people who do not want to be 'found' can at least leave a message to reassure their families that they are all right;
■ a national computerised database of missing people;
■ searching for missing people, using contacts among the homeless population, and advertising and publicity;
■ an image-enhancing 'age progression' computer that can create a photograph of what someone who has been missing for several years might look like now.

The charity's 'customers' are not just missing people and their families. The police find the NMPH and its database invaluable in assisting with identifying corpses and helping with missing persons cases generally.

In marketing terms, the NMPH's main problem is generating a steady and reliable flow of income. Despite relying on 200 unpaid staff, it has 80 paid staff and needs £4.1m each year to operate its services. NMPH does not charge commercial rates for its services, even to the police. It hopes, of course, that those who have benefited from the service will make a donation, but this is unlikely to cover the full cost. It thus relies heavily on cash donations, corporate donations of goods and services, fundraising and promotional events. The higher the profile of the event, the greater the opportunity to raise cash. In November 2005, a number of celebrities became DJs for the benefit of NMPH and featured on Magic Radio 105.4. It has also organised sponsored walks and celebrity events. It particularly welcomes 'donations in kind', for example television airtime or print advertising space, in order to carry on its work effectively. (NMPH literature; briefing given by Elaine Quigley at Buckinghamshire Chilterns University College; http://www.missingpersons.org.uk.)

■ Classifying non-profit organisations

As suggested above, non-profit organisations can exist in either the public or the private sector, although the distinction between them is rather blurred in some cases. A hospital that treats both National Health patients and private patients, for example, is involved in both sectors.

Characteristics of non-profit organisations

Clearly, all non-profit organisations operate in different types of market and face different challenges, but they do have a number of characteristics in common that differentiate them from ordinary commercial businesses (Lovelock and Weinberg, 1984; Kotler, 1982). These are as follows.

Multiple publics. Most profit-making organisations focus their attention on their target market. Although they do depend on shareholders to provide capital, most day-to-day cash flow is generated from sales revenue. Effectively, therefore, the recipient of the product or service and the source of income are one and the same. Non-profit organisations, however, have to divide their attention much more equally between two important groups, as shown in Figure 13.4. First, there are the customers or clients who receive the product or service. They do not necessarily pay the full cost of it. A charity, for example, might offer advice or help free to those in need, whereas a museum might charge a nominal entry fee that is heavily

Figure 13.4 Non-profit organisations: multiple publics

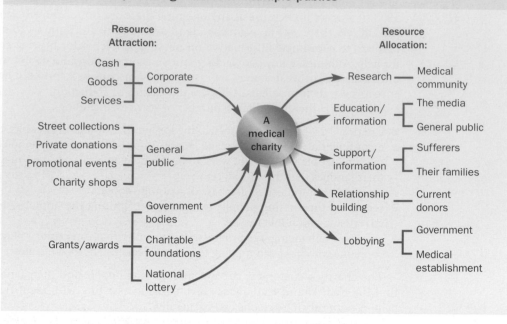

subsidised from other sources. Thus clients or customers concern the non-profit organisation largely from a *resource allocation* point of view. The second important group is the funders, those who provide the income to allow the organisation to do its work. A charity, for example, might depend mainly on individuals making donations and corporate sponsors, a medical practice on government funding and a museum on government grants, lottery cash, individual donations and corporate sponsorship as well as entrance fees. Thus funders concern the organisation from a *resource attraction* point of view.

eg Great Ormond Street Children's Hospital (**http://www.gosh.org.uk**) has the widest range of paediatric specialists in the UK, and welcomes over 22,000 inpatients and 78,000 outpatients every year, 50 per cent of whom are aged under two years. In order to provide care, to maintain its position at the frontier of medical research and to enhance its reputation for pioneering surgery, it needs to supplement the income it gets from the government via the National Health Service. GOSH aims to raise £150m over the next five years from individuals and organisations to fund pioneering research into childhood diseases, buy vital new medical equipment and offer improved support services to families. This will play an important role in the building of a new hospital, adding to the £75m already committed by the NHS. In 2004–05 it raised £26m from donations and legacies, including £1.5m from a Channel Island appeal in Jersey and Guernsey.

The hospital must therefore interact with a number of publics if it is to achieve its targets. Its core activities mean that it is working with patients, parents, local hospital consultants and doctors. Each has an interest in the paediatric care work of the hospital. The government and the National Health Service also have an interest in the hospital, given its role and profile and of course its prime funding source. However, the donor publics are critical to the future of GOSH and thus the hospital has an active fund-raising programme through GOSHCC. Schemes include sponsorship, advertisements on the website, private donations, payroll covenants and legacies, company giving and joint sales promotions such as one undertaken with Baby Bio, which raised £20,000. Zoom.com supported GOSHCC by contributing 5p per card for the first 50,000 e-cards sent from its site. That was good for Zoom in terms of viral marketing as well as being good for GOSHCC. Employee fund-raising through adopting GOSHCC for a month, for a year or for a special event provides a further source of funds as well as raising the profile.

Employees at Ford went on a two-year fund-raising programme to raise £100,000. Activities included a team of twelve cyclists undertaking a GOSHCC Anglo-Italian cycle challenge, eighteen employees taking part in the London Marathon, and a further team undertaking the Three Peaks Challenge in Yorkshire. All of these events and programmes mean that GOSHCC has to plan its activities carefully to maintain good relations with individuals and organisations to attract resources and in return to ensure that the gratitude and goodwill from the well-being of its patients is fed back to the supporters.

By encouraging younger people to enter the Flora Light 5km run, GOSHCC prompts charitable activity at an early age which hopefully will continue.

Source: © GOSHCC http://www.gosh.org

Multiple objectives. One definition of marketing offered earlier in this book is to create and hold a customer at a profit. As we have seen, there are many different ways of achieving this and many possible sub-objectives on the way, but in the end for most organisations it is all about profit. As a result, success criteria can be fairly easily defined and measured. In the non-profit sector, however, there might be multiple objectives, some of which could be difficult to define and quantify. They might concern fund raising, publicity generation, contacting customers or clients (or getting them to visit you), dispensing advice, increasing geographic coverage or giving grants to needy clients.

Service rather than physical goods orientation. Most non-profit organisations are delivering a service product of some sort rather than manufacturing and selling a physical product. Many of the services marketing concepts already covered in this chapter therefore apply to them. In some non-profit bodies, the emphasis is on generating awareness about a cause, perhaps to generate funds, and giving information to allow people to help themselves solve a problem. Particularly where charities are concerned in generating funds, donors as a target audience are not directly benefiting from their participation in the production of this service, other than from the warm glow of satisfying their social conscience. This contrasts with the more commercial sector, where the customer who pays gets a specific service performed for their benefit (a haircut, a washing machine repaired, a bank account managed for them, etc.).

eg Oxfam International is delivering not only a service product, but one that is often directed at beneficiaries many thousands of kilometres away. Its many programmes vary from very high-profile activities such as dealing with humanitarian crises in Sudan, Kashmir or as a result of the 2004 tsunami to, in comparison, its involvement in longer-term projects lasting many years. The River Basin Programme is one of Oxfam's largest projects, aimed at helping poor people along the Ganges and Brahmaputra rivers and their hundreds of tributaries in Bangladesh and India. Areas more than 1000 km wide are prone to severe flooding and Oxfam works on social and environmental aspects to help alleviate the worst effects.

Oxfam needs high-profile media coverage to make the suffering of people and the effective impact even of small donations more tangible. With natural disasters, much of the media coverage is done for Oxfam and the focus is on directing goodwill and sympathy to make donating easy. It was particularly effective at the time of the tsunami in raising corporate donations and rasing cash from the wider public (Woodward, 2005). It was also effective with its alternative Christmas gifts campaign, encouraging people to buy their friends and families a goat, a toilet, clean water, educational or medical services and equipment for communities in the developing world rather than spending money on cards and presents that have only fleeting value (Harvey, 2005).

In other cases, more subtle lobbying and influence are required to achieve the mission of 'saving lives and restoring hope'. Reports highlighting, for example, that in the world there are 870 million illiterate people, that 70 per cent of them are women, that 125 million children do not start school and that another 150 million drop out after four years are designed to stimulate debate. Reports and briefing papers are published and sent to politicians alongside lobbying for change. One campaign is concentrated on fair trade by seeking to help poor producers to access international export markets and offering a protected, fair trade market during transition while they acquire new skills and competencies. Over the last 20 years, although international trade has tripled, the 48 least-developed countries, containing 10 per cent of the world's population, have seen their share of world exports decline to just 0.4 per cent over the period. Central to Oxfam's campaign are informing consumers about trade-related causes of poverty, promoting a consumer movement in favour of fair and ethical trade, and lobbying for change in world trading systems where these cause poverty. The greater the publicity, the more tangible the problems and the more powerful the call for help. Oxfam has to be cautious in how it goes about managing its advertising and publicity, however. A story alleging the shelving of creative work for a direct marketing and advertising campaign that cost £240,000 hit the press after an internal dispute delayed its introduction (*Marketing Week*, 2005b; **http://www.oxfam.org**).

Public scrutiny and accountability. Where public money is concerned or where organisations rely on donations, there is greater public interest in the activities and efficiency of the organisation. To maintain the flow of donations, a charity has to be seen to be transparently honest and trustworthy and to be producing 'results'. The public wants to know how much money is going into administrative costs and how much into furthering the real work of the charity.

eg Greenpeace (**http://www.greenpeace.org**) relies exclusively on support from individuals and foundations. It makes a deliberate point in its publicity of stating that it does not seek funds from governments, corporations or political parties and will not take individual donations if they compromise its independence of action. It is proud to state that it has no permanent allies or enemies. Such a principled stand means that Greenpeace must be entirely transparent if it is to avoid criticism from parties who have suffered from its direct action, or even the wider publics that support its cause.

To achieve a policy of openness, Greenpeace must make public its campaigns, its governance arrangements and its financial affairs. The annual reports reveal detailed information in all areas. The campaigns in climate, toxins, nuclear, oceans, forests, ocean dumping and genetic engineering are all specified and details provided of the main achievements in each area. Two examples have already been mentioned in this book: the deforestation of the Amazon and the problems associated with over-fishing. An important part of retaining public support is highlighting successes. In 2005, for example, it highlighted success in stopping Xerox using fibre from the Sami Reindeer Forest in northern Finland, which is one of the last ancient forests in Europe. On a European scale it succeeded in lobbying the European parliament to ban six toxic chemicals, some of which had been used in popular toys such as Barbie dolls and Teletubbies. Greenpeace is still campaigning for all industries to stop using hazardous chemicals and to replace them with safe substances. These examples are but two of many campaigns run simultaneously and needing public support.

The financial breakdown and uses and sources of funds are all detailed in the Greenpeace annual reports and reassuringly demonstrate that around half of any donation goes into front-line activity. All of this is designed to retain the support of the 2.8 million members and to demonstrate Greenpeace's credibility to external groups.

■ Marketing implications

In general terms, the same principles of marketing apply equally to non-profit organisations as to any purely commercial concern (Sargeant, 1999). There are, however, a few specific points to note. A non-profit organisation might have quite a wide-ranging product portfolio, if the needs of both funders and customers or clients are taken into account. Their products might, for instance, vary from information, reassurance and advice to medical research and other practical help such as cash grants or equipment. Donors might be 'purchasing' association with a high-profile good cause or the knowledge that they have done a good deed by giving. Because the products vary so much, from the extremely intangible to the extremely tangible, and because there are so many different publics to serve, a strong corporate image and good marketing communication are particularly important to pull the whole organisation together.

If dispensing information and advice or increasing the profile of a cause are central objectives of the non-profit organisation, then marketing communication is an essential tool. This might mean using conventional advertising media, although that can be expensive for organisations such as smaller charities unless advertising agencies and media owners can be persuaded to offer their services cheap or free as a donation in kind.

Publicity can also be an invaluable tool for the non-profit organisation, not only because of its cost-effectiveness, but also because of its ability to reach a wide range of audiences. Publicity might encourage fund raising, help to educate people or generate clients or customers. Association with high-profile commercial sponsors can similarly help to spread the message, through publicity, sponsored fund-raising events or joint or sponsored promotions.

In sectors where a non-profit organisation offers a more clearly defined product to a specific target segment within a competitive market, then a more standard approach to marketing communication might be used. A university, for example, is offering degree courses to potential students. As discussed elsewhere in this book, it might use advertising media to tell potential students why this is the best place to study; printed material such as the prospectus, brochures and leaflets to give more detail about the institution, its location and the courses on offer; visits to schools and education fairs to meet potential recruits face to face; and publicity to increase awareness and improve its corporate image.

Pricing is applied somewhat differently in the non-profit sector than in the commercial world. As mentioned earlier, those providing income might be totally different from those receiving the product. It is accepted in most areas of the non-profit sector that the recipient might not have to bear the full cost of the service or product provided. In other words, the recipient's need comes first rather than the ability to pay. In the profit-making sector it is more likely to be the other way around: if you can pay for it, you can have it. Non-profit pricing, therefore, might be very flexible and varied. Some customers will not be asked to pay at all, others will be asked to make whatever donation they can afford for the service they have received, while others still will be charged a full market price.

Issues of distribution, process and physical evidence, where applicable, are similar for non-profit organisations to those of other types of organisation. The organisation has to ensure that the product or service is available when and where the customer or client can conveniently access it. This might or might not involve physical premises. Clearly, non-profit institutions such as universities, hospitals, museums and the like do operate from premises. They face the same issues as any other service provider of making sure that those premises are sufficiently well equipped to allow a service to be delivered and to deal with likely demand. They also have to realise that the premises are part of the marketing effort and contribute to the customer's or client's perception of quality. Prospective students visiting a university on an open day might not be able to judge the quality of the courses very well, but they can certainly tell whether the campus would be a good place for them to live and work, whether the teaching rooms are pleasant and well equipped, and how well-resourced the library and IT facilities seem to be.

Some non-profit organisations that focus mainly on giving information and advice by mail or by telephone do not, of course, need to invest in smart premises. Their priority is to ensure that customers or clients are aware of how to access the service and that enquiries are dealt with quickly, sympathetically and effectively.

eg The Samaritans (**http://www.samaritans.org.uk**) exists to provide a confidential counselling service to those in a desperate emotional state who are contemplating suicide. The service is offered 24 hours a day from 203 branches staffed by volunteers who answer the telephones and raise local donations. There is no move towards developing a central call centre as it would undermine the whole structure of the service. Volunteers are carefully selected and trained locally, and give of their time for no charge. In 2003, there were 17,600 volunteers across England on various shifts, normally giving no more than 180 hours per year each. Although the caller may not care where the Samaritan is located, the organisation insists that its volunteers should not have to travel more than 60 miles to an office. There were 4.8 million calls in 2003 in England and the operation had to be able to cope with that demand, especially during the recognised peaks between 10 p.m. and 2 a.m. Each volunteer takes over 250 calls per year, and some calls can last for a long time, depending on the needs of the caller. Each branch runs as an autonomous operation, generating its own funds to cover the *c.* £17,000 cost per phone line and office expenses.

Marketing in non-profit-making areas is rapidly evolving and the techniques used in commercial situations are being transferred, tested and evolved to cope better with the complexity of causes, ideas and attitude change in a wide range of situations. Marketing thinking is being applied to encouraging more 'users' and 'customers' to come forward to benefit from supportive contact for people or children at risk, such as that provided by the Samaritans and the NSPCC. It is also being applied backwards to attract resources into charitable organisations that often rely on voluntary staff and generous donations from individuals and corporations.

In addition, corporate sponsorship and affiliated programmes have been fast developing, as association with a number of the causes listed above does little harm to a corporate reputation. For example Tesco, Green Flag and Lindt all work with the RSPCA for their mutual benefit. Whether they take the form of joint promotions, supported advertising, or sponsored programmes and campaigns, the opportunities for cooperation are considerable.

Chapter summary

■ Although the variety of service products is very wide, all of them share some common characteristics that differentiate them from other types of product. With service products, for instance, there is often no transfer of ownership of anything, because a service is intangible. Services are also perishable, because they are generally performed at a particular time and are consumed as they are produced. This means that they cannot be stored in advance of demand, nor can they be kept in stock until a customer comes along. The customer is often directly involved in the production of the service product and thus the manufacture and delivery of the product cannot be separated. It also means that there is extensive interaction between the customer and the service provider's staff. Finally, because of the 'live' nature of the service experience and the central role of human interaction, it is very difficult to standardise the service experience.

■ The normal model of a marketing mix consisting of the 4Ps is useful but insufficient for describing services, and an additional 3Ps – people, processes and physical evidence – have been added to deal with the extra dimensions peculiar to services. *People* takes account of the human interactions involved in the service product; *physical evidence* looks at the tangible elements that contribute either directly or indirectly to the creation, delivery, quality or positioning of the service; and *processes* defines the systems that allow the service to be created and delivered efficiently, reliably and cost-effectively.

■ Service quality is hard to define and measure. Judgement of quality arises largely from customers' comparisons of what they expected from various facets of the service with what they think they actually received. Management can ensure that the service product is designed with the customer's real needs and wants in mind, that it is adequately resourced, that it is delivered properly, and that they try not to raise unrealistic expectations in the mind of the customer, but in the end, quality is a subjective issue. Staff are an important element of service and its delivery and must be fully qualified and trained to deal with customers and their needs, and to deliver the service reliably and consistently. The emphasis that is put on this will vary depending on whether staff have direct or indirect involvement with customers, and whether they are visible to customers or not. Like quality, productivity is a difficult management issue because of the live nature of services and the involvement of the customer in the process. Managers have to think and plan carefully in terms of staff recruitment and training, systems and technology, the service levels offered and the way in which customers interact with the service, to try to maintain control and efficiency in the service delivery system. Trying to manage supply and demand can also help to streamline productivity.

■ Non-profit organisations, which might be in the public or private sector, form a specialist area of services marketing. They differ because they are likely to serve multiple publics; they have multiple objectives that can often be difficult to quantify; they offer services, but the funder of the service is likely to be different from the recipient of it; and finally, they are subject to closer scrutiny and tighter accountability than many other organisations. It is also possible that where non-profit organisations are in receipt of government funding or where their existence or operation is subject to regulation, there will be limits placed on their freedom to use the marketing mix as they wish. Pricing or promotion, for example, might be prescribed or set within narrow constraints.

Questions for review and discussion

13.1 What are the main characteristics that distinguish *services* from physical products?

13.2 What are the ten criteria that affect customers' perceptions of service quality?

13.3 Design a short questionnaire for assessing the quality of service offered by a local dental practice.

13.4 In what ways might the following service organisations define and improve their productivity:
(a) a theme park;
(b) a university;
(c) a fast food outlet?

13.5 In what ways do *non-profit organisations* differ from other types of business?

13.6 What do you think might be the main sources of revenue for the following types of non-profit organisation and what revenue generation problems do you think each faces:
(a) a small local charity;
(b) a National Health Service hospital;
(c) a public museum?

case study 13

Full Stop

The NSPCC has one simple aim: to ensure that cruelty to children stops. However, it has to decide between many different, and sometimes conflicting, objectives to achieve its aim. The challenge is to ensure that the public is aware of the extent of the problem, when sometimes it is uncomfortable to think that such cruelty goes on in a modern society. The message has to be got across that, for example, every week in the UK one child dies at the hands of parents or carers and 600 children are added to the child protection registers.

The main objective of the charity is to end cruelty to children altogether, but as the figures above demonstrate, it is unfortunately a long way from that goal. It runs a series of programmes and campaigns to tackle child abuse, in the home, at work, at school, and in the community and in society. Since the campaign began, the NSPCC has been able to handle more calls on its National Child Protection Helpline, expand its schools service, produce parenting packs and work directly with over 10,000 children. To achieve its main objective, it must raise donations directly through fundraising and from individuals and corporate contributions. These sources provide 86 per cent of its income. It needs volunteers to raise funds, to campaign and to help with some of the core services. All of these contributors must believe they are doing a worthwhile thing in supporting the NSPCC rather than another charity. The NSPCC is therefore a prime lobbying and pressure group on child welfare issues. Campaigns have been run to influence government to raise such issues on the political agenda, to challenge government spending priorities and to influence law and policy making.

The NSPCC actually ran into trouble for being too hard-hitting with some advertisements as part of its Full Stop campaign. Overall, the campaign aimed to shake the reader out of complacency and to change public attitudes to enlist more support. The campaign's first stage was targeted at raising awareness of the brutality and types of child abuse that go on through a series of advertisements following a high-profile launch supported by Ewan McGregor and Madonna. The Prime Minister said at the launch, 'The private passion we feel for our own children should become a public passion we feel for all our children. I believe that ending cruelty is the right idea at the right time' (as quoted by Gray, 2001). The advertisements' imagery was very powerful and disturbing: 'Stop it, Daddy, stop it'. It featured well-known personalities such as pop group the Spice Girls, cartoon character Rupert Bear and foot-baller Alan Shearer covering their eyes as background voices focused on adults either physically abusing or just about to molest a child. Such an approach was considered necessary to shock readers and to bring home the reality of what sadly does go on for a small percentage of children. The first phase of the campaign was a great success, with independent research in 2001 confirming that the NSPCC generated the highest spontaneous awareness of any UK charity with a 12 per cent increase pre- and post-campaign. It also helped to raise over £90m from donations.

This was followed by equally powerful imagery in the 'Real Children Don't Bounce Back' campaign. It featured a cartoon boy being beaten up by a human father against a background of canned laughter. It ends with the cartoon boy falling down the stairs and then transforming into a real, but unconscious – possibly lifeless – child lying at the foot of the stairs. The television advertisements generated over 100 complaints to the ITC, but the NSPCC's intention was to bring home the reality of abuse, a reality that we are sometimes keen to ignore. The advertising made its point: it doubled the number of calls to the child protection helpline and enabled public awareness to be raised further as well as carrying the message that whatever the emotional stresses on parents, it should never turn to violence and child abuse. The television campaign, shown only after the 9 p.m. watershed, was designed to leave the viewer in no doubt that 'together we can stop abuse', and that the helpline could be used by anyone who suspects child cruelty. Further campaigns have focused on different target groups under the same overall Full Stop banner. The 'Someone to turn to' national press advertising campaign in 2004 featured teenage girls who were being abused but didn't know how to find help. The Full Stop campaign has proved very flexible to accommodate different priority groups with the same message.

The NSPCC has also entered into partnerships with companies to provide corporate support and assistance with fund raising. Mars (Masterfoods) supported the NSPCC with three major cause-related marketing promotions. The most recent focused on the launch of Kidsmix and for every pack sold, Masterfoods donated 10p to the NSPCC. Masterfoods has raised more than £100,000 for the NSPCC through various marketing and employee initiatives. The House of Fraser donates £2 for every toy sold in its Fraser Bear and Fraser Bunny ranges. The Yorkshire Building Society set up a Happy Kids Saver Account, aimed at parents or guardians who want to start a savings account for their child. YBS gave £1 to the NSPCC for every account opened and gave 10 per cent of the total gross that the accounts accrued each month. This promotion has raised £400,000 for the NSPCC. Microsoft has been especially supportive of the NSPCC over many years. It supported the design of a website, there4me, targeted at 12–16-year-olds who may be suffering from abuse and who can access the internet. Private 'inbox' facilities, confidential passwords and a chatline with a real counsellor supplement considerable information to enable young people to take matters further if appropriate. It also supports a team of educational advisors who work with teachers, schools and local education authorities to promote child protection.

A number of other more targeted campaigns are run by the NSPCC. A first disco experience of 2006 was organised for 3 January 2006 at the Savoy Hotel in London. The annual event raised £15,000 in 2004 and is targeted at 11–14-year-olds. Each ticket costs £35. In 2006, the NSPCC Lower Withington Horse Show is planned for Chelford and the entire proceeds are to be donated to the NSPCC Cheshire Child Protection Team for its work with children. Numerous events, such as the London Marathon, encourage NSPCC supporters to participate to raise funds.

Managing the media and PR is an important part of the marketing effort. The NSPCC actively lobbies Westminster, such as for the 'Tighten the Net' campaign which persuaded the Home Office to invest £1.5m in a public awareness campaign to show the dangers to children from chatlines and the internet. It also succeeded in arguing for the first Child Commissioner appointed in the UK, approved by the Welsh Assembly. Lobbying is still going on in the UK to improve the monitoring and supervision of child sex offenders and to prevent their early release. There has, however, been some criticism of the methods used by the NSPCC to educate the public on the plight of some children. Whereas nobody is soft on child abuse, most of the campaigns run by the NSPCC, it is argued, have no impact at all on the small number of serious cases of violent abuse and child killing. Instead they spread a message of mistrust, especially when training is being given to 250,000 school dinner ladies and playground supervisors to look out for signs of child abuse (Hume, 2005).

The Full Stop campaign had the objective to end child cruelty, but also had a financial objective: to raise £250m after its launch. Already £133m has been raised over and above normal fund raising. The NSPCC believes that it must sometimes use shocking promotional techniques to stir people out of their complacency. Celebrity ambassadors such as Catherine Zeta Jones, Kylie Minogue and Jonny Wilkinson have all declared support for the NSPCC by public endorsement and support. Through a variety of promotional methods and a conviction to act, to the NSPCC the ends justify the means and a safer, supportive cruelty-free environment is worth fighting for, however shocking the message execution!

Sources: Chandiramani (2002); Gray (2001); Hume (2005); http://www.nspcc.org.

Questions

1 In what ways do the special characteristics of services and the 7Ps of the services marketing mix apply to a charity?

2 List the multiple publics for both resource attraction and resource allocation that an organisation like the NSPCC might be targeting. What kind of problems do you think might arise from having such diverse target audiences?

3 What benefits does a charity get from a promotional tie-in, such as the one between the NSPCC and the Yorkshire Building Society?

4 To what extent can 'shock' campaigns such as those produced by the NSPCC be justified? What are the potential advantages and disadvantages of such a campaign?

References for chapter 13

Aaron, C. (2005), 'Nottingham City Council Builds the Skills of its Front-line Construction Workers', *Training & Management Development Methods*, 19 (1), pp. 307–12.

Alghalith, N. (2005), 'Competing with IT: The UPS Case', *Journal of the American Academy of Business*, 7 (2), pp. 7–16.

Bisson, S. (2005), 'Hotel with a Heart of IT', *The Guardian*, 26 May, p. 16.

Bitner, M., Brown, S. and Meuter, M. (2000), 'Technology Infusion in Service Encounters', *Journal of the Academy of Marketing Science*, 28 (1), pp. 138–49.

Buckley, C. (2002), 'Will Retirement Become a Thing of the Past?', *The Times*, 18 January, p. 26.

Caruana, A., Money, A. and Berthon, P. (2000), 'Service Quality and Satisfaction – The Moderating Role of Value', *European Journal of Marketing*, 34 (11/12), pp. 1338–53.

Chandiramani, R. (2002), 'Call to Action', *Marketing*, 28 March, p. 18.

Christopher, M. *et al.* (1994), *Relationship Marketing: Bringing Quality, Customer Service and Marketing Together* (2nd edn), Butterworth-Heinemann.

Coppen, L. (2003), 'Dracula Theme Park', *The Times*, 1 March, p. 50.

Cowell, D. (1984), *The Marketing of Services*, Butterworth-Heinemann.

Cox, J. (2002), 'Leisure Property Trends: Is It the End for Multiplex Anchors?', *Journal of Leisure Property*, 2 (1), pp. 83–93.

de Quetteville, H. (2003), 'The Dracula Project Lives Again', *Daily Telegraph*, 20 November, p. 18.

de Quetteville, H. (2004), 'Prince Joins Fight to Save Dracula's Old Villages', *Daily Telegraph*, 27 May, p. 16.

Devlin, S. and Dong, H. (1994), 'Service Quality from the Customers' Perspective', *Marketing Research*, 6 (1), pp. 5–13.

Dodona (2001), 'Cinemagoing 9', *Dodona Research*, Leicester.

Douglas-Home, J. (2001), 'Dracula Goes Disney', *The Times*, 6 November, p. 2.5.

George, R. (2002), 'Mickey Mouse with Fangs', *The Independent*, 27 January, pp. 18–21.

Gray, R. (2001), 'Partnerships for a Wider Awareness', *Marketing*, 3 May, pp. 31–2.

Harvey, F. (2005), 'Charities Afford Philanthropists Greater Respite from the Materialist World', *Financial Times*, 26 November, p. 4.

Heskett, J. *et al.* (1997), *The Service Profit Chain*, The Free Press.

Hume, M. (2005), 'Beyond Innocent Playground Chatter Lurks the Whisper of Propaganda', *The Times*, 7 October, p. 23.

Jamal, T. and Tanase, A. (2005), 'Impacts and Conflicts Surrounding Dracula Park, Romania: The Role of Sustainable Tourism Principles', *Journal of Sustainable Tourism*, 13 (5), pp. 440 *et seq.*

Kalsi, B. and Napier, D. (2005), 'Cinema Needs to Get the Marketing Picture', *Sunday Business*, 9 January, p. C12.

Kotler, P. (1982), *Marketing for Non-Profit Organisations* (2nd edn), Prentice Hall.

Lovelock, C. and Weinberg, C. (1984), *Marketing for Public and Non-Profit Managers*, John Wiley and Sons.

Lovelock, C., Vandermerwe, S. and Lewis, B. (1999), *Services Marketing*, Financial Times Prentice Hall.

Marinas, R. (2004), 'Banking on Count Dracula', *Amusement Business*, 29 March, p. 7.

Marketing Week (2005a), 'New Owner Rebrands UGC as Cineworld', *Marketing Week*, 10 February, p. 7.

Marketing Week (2005b), 'Oxfam "Will Still Use" Aborted Ad Campaign', *Marketing Week*, 10 November, p. 9.

Mathews, B. and Clark, M. (1996), 'Comparability of Quality Determinants in Internal and External Service Encounters', in *Proceedings: Workshop on Quality Management in Services VI*, Universidad Carlos III de Madrid: 15–16 April.

McCarthy, M. (2002), 'Multiplex Cinemas Pose Threat to Town Centres', *The Independent*, 5 January, p. 8.

McLuhan, R. (2002), 'Brands Put Service under the Spotlight', *Marketing*, 21 February, p. 33.

Mintel (2003), 'Charities UK', *Market Intelligence Essentials*, August, accessed via **http://www.mintel.com**.

Modern Railways (2005), 'Winning Capacity on the South Western', *Modern Railways*, December, pp. 56–9.

Moldofsdky, L. (2005), 'The Challenge is to Convert Enthusiasm into Increased Spending', *Financial Times*, 29 November, p. 4.

Moore Ede, P. (2002), 'Bloody Hell', *The Ecologist*, March, p. 47.

Opinion Leader Research (2005), *Report of Findings of a Survey of Public Trust and Confidence in Charities*, accessed via **http://www.charity-commission.gov.uk/Library/spr/pdfs/surveytrustrpt.pdf**.

Parasuraman, A. *et al.* (1985), 'A Conceptual Model of Service Quality and Its Implications for Future Research', *Journal of Marketing*, 49 (Fall), pp. 41–50.

Pratten, J. (2004), 'Customer Satisfaction and Waiting Staff', *International Journal of Contemporary Hospitality Management*, 16 (6), pp. 385 *et seq.*

Rayport, J. and Sviokla, J. (1994), 'Managing in the Marketspace', *Harvard Business Review*, 72 (November/December), pp. 2–11.

Rushe, D. (2001), 'Multiplex Cinemas Close Their Doors', *Sunday Times*, 25 March, p. 6.

Sargeant, A. (1999), *Marketing Management for Nonprofit Organizations*, Oxford University Press.

Sasser, W. *et al.* (1978), *Management of Service Operations: Text, Cases and Readings*, Allyn & Bacon.

Shostack, L. (1977), 'Breaking Free from Product Marketing', *Journal of Marketing*, 41 (April), pp. 73–80.

Steiner, R. (2005), 'Year of the Mouse Begins in Hong Kong', *Sunday Business*, 18 September, p. 1.

Stevenson, B. (2005), 'Gym Users Opt to Fight Their Debts Rather than the Flab', *The Independent*, 27 April, p. 63.

Traffic World (2005), 'UPS Drivers Receiving New Wireless Computers', *Traffic World*, 9 May.

Tyler, R. (2005), 'UPS Thinks Outside the Delivery Box', *Daily Telegraph*, 20 October, p. 3.

Urquhart, L. (2005), 'Pain Amid the Gain for Private Health Club', *Financial Times*, 19 July, p. 22.

Vasagar, J. (2005), 'Crocodiles Move In as the Tourists Move On', *The Guardian*, 29 March, p. 3.

Webster, B. (2005), 'Rail Commuters Face Congestion Charges', *The Times*, 21 June, p. 1.

Woodward, D. (2005), 'The Tsunami Effect', *Director*, March, pp. 45–6.

Yaqoob, T. (2005), 'Fatties to the Front', *Daily Mail*, 20 October, p. 33.

Yorkshire Post (2005), 'Price Hikes are Just the Ticket if You Want Empty Stadiums', *Yorkshire Post*, 25 August, p. 1.

Zeithaml, V. *et al.* (1988), 'SERVQUAL: A Multiple Item Scale for Measuring Consumer Perceptions of Service Quality', *Journal of Retailing*, 64 (1), pp. 13–37.

Zeithaml, V. *et al.* (1990), *Delivering Quality Service: Balancing Customer Perceptions and Expectations*, The Free Press.

chapter 14

e-marketing and new media

learning objectives

This chapter will help you to:

1 understand the nature of internet marketing;

2 appreciate the major trends in internet penetration and usage in both consumer and B2B markets;

3 gain insight into the marketing uses of the internet and its future development; and

4 appreciate the nature and usage of the three main elements of new media: e-mail marketing, wireless marketing and interactive television marketing.

Introduction

With the net, a new way of conducting business is available, but it doesn't change the laws of business or most of what really creates a competitive advantage. The fundamentals of competition remain unchanged.

Professor Michael Porter (quoted by Newing, 2002)

Porter is absolutely right: the internet does not change any of the fundamentals of doing 'good business' or 'good marketing'. Understanding the target customer's needs and wants and designing an integrated marketing package that delivers them remain critically important regardless of whether a company is a 'dotcom' or a 'traditional' organisation. Porter goes on to say that the companies that will succeed and benefit from the internet will be those that keep their core strategic objectives in view and then work out how to integrate, use and mould the internet to help achieve those objectives and to create and sustain competitive advantage. Those that fail will be those that adopt a 'me too' attitude, jumping on the internet bandwagon because 'our competitors are doing it', or that view internet applications as a diversification, parallel and almost completely separate from their core traditional business.

To a lesser extent, the same can be said of the new marketing communications media, such as viral marketing, SMS, and interactive television, that are emerging from technological innovation. Some companies are adopting them because they can see how they complement the use of traditional media within the context of the wider integrated communications strategy, and have defined a distinct 'fit' between the medium, the message and the target market (see, for instance, the 'Hey, Sexy!' Kiss 100 'Marketing in Action' vignette on pp. 516–17). Others, however, seem to be adopting them because they are the latest sexy thing that everyone else seems to be doing. No prizes for guessing which are likely to be the most successful campaigns!

Chelsea FC has become the fourth largest soccer club in the world in terms of income, after AC Milan, Real Madrid and Manchester United. Its plan is to become the biggest. New media are expected to play their part in that by bringing in revenues and membership to the club. It already has a joint venture with Sky to run television and interactive services so that fans can develop an ongoing relationship with the club. A website, the Chelsea digital television channel and the 'Chelsea mobile' service all provide sources of extra revenue and help to keep fans in contact with the club. The club now has over 1 million users monthly online and more subscriptions are being chased for the television channel and mobile service. It is expected that in the near future Chelsea will be able to stream games live online, perhaps using Chelsea broadband, a partnership with communications company Viatel. It can already stream live audio but the ability to see goals via the web or 3G mobile adds a new dimension for fans who can't make it to the match. This also adds greater value for sponsors such as Samsung as the logos on the shirts are seen in the digital and online environments. The emphasis is not just on the UK, as one of Chelsea's priorities is to widen its appeal with overseas fans. Thus each territory will have a local language site, since for the overseas fans the main point of contact with Chelsea is the website (Brooks, 2005b).

The purpose of this chapter is to examine the ways in which the internet and new media are providing new opportunities for marketers to get to know their customers better and to serve their needs and wants more effectively, and in some cases, a lot more engagingly. Throughout, we will be presenting examples and vignettes of organisations that are successfully using the internet and new media with clear strategic purposes relating to the creation of competitive advantage in mind.

The first part of the chapter looks at that relatively well-established tool: the internet. We examine its increasing penetration of both consumer and B2B markets and the ways in which markets are using it and might use it in the future. The chapter then turns to the less familiar world of new media, focusing particularly on e-mail marketing (including viral marketing), wireless marketing and interactive television. Again, we consider how these techniques are being used and their potential for the future.

Internet marketing

■ The nature of internet marketing

As more and more homes and businesses either get connected or develop their own websites, the internet has become an increasingly important tool of marketing. Smith and Chaffey (2001) and Smith and Taylor (2002) summarise the main benefits of investing in e-marketing as the 5Ss:

■ *Sell.* Selling goods and services online, potentially to a global market.
■ *Serve.* Using the website as a way of providing additional customer service or of streamlining service delivery.
■ *Save.* Saving money in terms of the overheads associated with more traditional forms of doing business.
■ *Speak.* Websites offer companies a chance to enter into one-to-one dialogue with customers more easily than ever before. As well as providing valuable feedback, with good database management, that dialogue can be the basis for fruitful customer relationship management.
■ *Sizzle.* A website that is well designed, in terms of both its content and its visual impact, can add an extra 'something' to a brand or corporate image through engaging, educating and/or

entertaining the visitor to the site. Increasingly, organisations are introducing an element of fun into their websites to grab and retain attention. Interactive games, webcam and video feeds, cartoons, free downloads and relaxed informality have all been introduced to keep the viewer's attention and to make company and product information more interesting.

Whatever its purpose, and however much is spent on it, a website should provide a powerful supplementary marketing tool. It should have all the creative flair of an advertisement, the style and information of a company brochure, and the personal touch and tailored presentation of face-to-face interaction and, not least, it should always leave the visitor clear as to what action should be taken next.

eg Selectadisc in Nottingham concentrates on the independent music scene, selling music on CDs, DVDs and vinyl, and also selling books. It focuses not just on the big sellers, as the High Street stores do, but also on stocking much harder-to-find and deleted titles. The site provides full search capability as well as customer wish lists, staff recommendations, and the latest news. The staff-driven, fully detailed album catalogue can be uploaded on a regular basis. Originally, the store had a paper-based stock control system but now it is all electronically controlled and linked to the online shopping catalogue. Specialist hardware was sourced not only to attach sample tracks to albums within the online catalogue but also to select and edit tracks from both CD and vinyl albums. Systems were introduced to upload products to the website and a full online web-based e-mail ordering system was developed to filter orders to the correct department so that they could be fulfilled quickly. Although Selectadisc is only a small business, it has used the internet to its full advantage in creating a profitable niche (**http://www.senior.co.uk**).

The dotcom boom and bust

While traditional companies have largely sought to integrate and use the internet and the 5Ss within the context of their existing businesses, the late 1990s also saw the rapid rise and equally rapid fall of many so-called dotcom businesses. These were businesses that came into being specifically to use the internet as a platform for delivering goods and/or services in an innovative way. Many potential investors were carried away by the enthusiasm of the dotcom entrepreneurs and promises of mega-profits, pouring money into these businesses. It soon became clear, however, that many dotcoms were running into problems. Some ran into technical problems that made it difficult to deliver on their promises and others simply found that paying customers were a lot thinner on the ground than forecast.

eg OnSpeed has been going for only 18 months but is generating £500,000 a month from its dotcom business. It offers a software download that enables users to experience broadband speeds without the need to pay for a broadband connection. It sells its products only online, so there are no packaging or delivery concerns. Most of its marketing spend is focused on pulling interested consumers to the website to get more information and make a purchase. It selects appropriate magazines to reach its target audience, and even used the Saga magazine when it found that over-50s wanted to surf the net but were unwilling to pay for broadband services. It claims to have generated 4500 customers from just one advertisement in that publication. Considerable effort also goes into generating positive editorial coverage in the IT and technology consumer press.

Rather than fight OnSpeed, the broadband giants such as BT and Wanadoo appear to have welcomed it. They have already agreed a deal to offer their narrow-band customers OnSpeed connection, and OnSpeed is now further extending its distribution through deals with Staples, PC World and WHSmith. The business is certainly growing nicely at present, but of course much will depend upon the continued take-up of broadband and the shrinking number of narrowband users (Carter, 2005).

Early growth doesn't guarantee anything, however. Sports website Sportal only just managed to survive the dotcom bust of the late 1990s. Sportal was set up in 1998 to offer action, information and links with sports clubs and events with a mission to 'create the first major sport brand of the 21st century'. It signed up for the internet rights of the top European football clubs, allowing it to show any action involving those clubs on the internet. Sportal earned revenue from showing football action and earned advertising revenue from running club websites. By 2000, however, it was clear that insufficient revenue was flowing in. Not enough people were willing to pay for the highlights being offered, and a number of alternative competing services became available. Sportal tumbled from being a company worth £270m at its peak to being sold for £1 (yes, that's £1 for the company itself, although its hardware was sold for £190,000) in November 2001 (Barr, 2002). The brand name has survived as part of the Teamtalk media group that offers multi-platform sports content delivery specifically for web, audio, iTV and mobile telephony. The group offers advertising opportunities to reach 6 million subscribers following a range of sports, and also provides online betting services (**http://www.sportal.com**).

The dotcom boom was followed by the dotcom bust as businesses collapsed or were taken over by their more astute competitors. Those that have survived and established themselves as leaders in their marketplaces, such as **lastminute.co.uk**, eBay and Amazon have done so not only by astute marketing and offering goods and services that people want and are prepared to pay for, but also by careful attention to defining and nurturing their competitive advantage along with some sober financial management. Investors have had to be patient, however: it took Amazon eight years before it was able to report its first small profits in January 2002.

marketing **in action**

Cashing in on the best days of our lives

Friends Reunited is a dotcom company with a difference. It is unashamedly in the nostalgia business and the number of users is growing at such a rapid rate that it is a challenge just to keep up with the necessary computer capacity to run it all. The site aims to link old school friends and work colleagues and has been responsible, if the press is to be believed, not just for reunions galore, but also marriages, divorces and even litigation from allegedly libelled teachers. Based on a similar idea in America (**http://www.classmates.com**), since its launch in October 2000 Friends Reunited has registered 12 million members, countless schools, universities and workplaces, and

has recorded 6.5 billion page impressions in total, which it proudly claims is the equivalent of reading the *Lord of the Rings* trilogy 4.2 million times! It also claims to register around 5000 new members every day. The website has become the eighth most popular in the UK (**http://www.friendsreunited.co.uk**).

Surprisingly, the business was built without the need for media advertising. The human interest angle means that a steady stream of reunion stories keeps the press coverage high and it could, in time, come to be regarded as one of the best word-of-mouth campaigns in promotional history. In one case a woman who had been searching 30 years for the son that she had put up for adoption found him very quickly in Australia (Pankhurst, 2005). Although accessing the site is free, it costs £7.50 to become a

registered member so that you can use the e-mail service. The other main source of revenue is banner advertising on the site. The service was extended to Australia and New Zealand, although interestingly the idea was less popular in Europe where social communities tend to be closer-knit. With such high traffic levels and minimal operating costs because the content is largely provided by the subscribers, it is not surprising that profits are around 60 per cent of sales income (*Marketing Week*, 2004). Sales are expected to have reached over £12m in 2005 and £18m in 2006 (**http://www.friendsreunited.co.uk**).

Brand extensions have also taken place based on the large database and the core concept of 'no customer exploitation'. The new sites include Genes, Dating and Jobs that operate in a similar way to the main Friends Reunited site.

The company never sold customer data from any of its sites to marketing houses and was selective about the type of banner advertising and pop-ups allowed. This philosophy could, however, be reconsidered. In 2005, Friends Reunited was bought by ITV for over £120m to create one of the largest online communities in the UK (White, 2005). For ITV, the takeover provides access to more UK internet advertising, provides a rich source of material for programming and not least enables it to acquire the largest independent online company in the UK in terms of revenue and growth (Edgecliffe-Johnson, 2005). The Friends Reunited customer base is an attractive one for internet advertisers with 53 per cent in the ABC1 sociodemographic group and 40 per cent in the 16–34 age range. Further brand extensions are expected to enable cross-promotion between ITV.com, ITV Local (broadband), and Friends Reunited.

Sources: Edgecliffe-Johnson (2005); Marketing Week (2004); Pankhurst (2005); White (2005); http://www.friendsreunited.co.uk.

Wanting to recapture the golden days of our individual pasts has proved a fertile ground for the Friends Reunited website, which now has a wide variety of different extensions to encourage you to sign up.

Source: © Friends Reunited http://www.friendsreunited.co.uk

The website

A US survey of 300 daily internet users found that two-thirds of people said that if a website did not meet their expectations, they would never return to it again. According to the survey, the four essential characteristics of a 'good' website are that it must be continually updated, be easy to navigate, have in-depth information on its subject and offer quick loading and response times (Gaudin, 2002).

The need for fast loading and response times is still a difficulty for marketers because of the technology driving website use. Once online, the quality of viewing can be reduced and the irritation level increased if graphics take a long time to load and in some cases crash the computer if they overload it. Better video plug-ins and ever more sophisticated browsers have enhanced quality and reduced loading times, but as yet for the average internet user the experience can still be frustrating.

A well-designed website with user-friendly pages is very important for capturing the user's attention. The user is not very patient, however. Nielsen//NetRatings' review of internet usage statistics for December 2005 (http://www.netratings.com) showed that people in the UK spend on average only 40 seconds on any single page. They visited on average 69 domains during the month and spent 25 hours online in total, but unless there is quick impact the viewer will soon move on. If images or pages are slow to download or if the checkout procedure is lengthy and complicated, there is always a risk that the customer will abandon their virtual shopping cart and run away before the transaction is complete.

eg *Apparel Industry Magazine* (2000) set up a focus group to explore and assess four fashion e-tail sites. The results give an interesting insight into what people are looking for in terms of website design and facilities/services offered. Complexity of navigation was raised as a problem. On one site, users found they had to do a tutorial to learn how to use the site and make purchases. Even then it was easy to make mistakes. The user could have up to 10 windows open at a time and closing the wrong one would mean exiting the site altogether and having to start again. As Kolesar and Galbraith (2000) said, the customer is an integral part of the e-tail service experience and the role they play has to be in keeping with their knowledge and abilities as well as their self-image.

Users did like having the facility to dress a virtual mannequin and get her to 'do a twirl' so that they could see the effect of putting different garments together as an outfit. They also liked being able to ask for recommendations, for example to find some shoes to match a garment already chosen. Detailed product descriptions, including fabric care, and the ability to zoom in on garments to see fabric and styling detail were also appreciated, but the quality of photographs and colour reproduction was generally thought to be poor and inconsistent. Uncluttered pages were preferred rather than those trying to show nine or more garments per page. Users were frustrated by missing product photographs and messages such as 'unavailable in the size/colour requested'. When sites offer a very large assortment of goods, users liked being able to use menus or search facilities to specify product types, size ranges or price bands that they were interested in to narrow down the number of products shown.

All the sites examined were e-tail stores bringing together a number of brand names and designer labels on the one site. The focus group best liked the sites that gave them an 'aggregated shopping cart' so that they could select goods from lots of different labels and pay for them in one transaction. The group was less impressed with the fashion e-tailers that simply acted as portals, so that clicking on a label name took them through to that label's own site. This means that the shopper cannot have the facility to see what one label's sweater would look like with another label's jeans, for example. It also means the inconvenience of having to undertake individual transactions with individual sites. Also on the processing side, users wanted clear information about shipping costs and times and returns policies.

Interestingly, researchers have also found that the industries that tend to deliver the good websites are the ones that have faced the fiercest dotcom competition. Thus Amazon, for instance, has set the benchmark for any online bookseller in terms of the quality of the website that customers expect to see. Cap Gemini Ernst & Young (CGE&Y) interviewed 6000 consumers across nine European countries to find out what online shoppers felt to be important about the e-tailers they dealt with. Honesty, respect and reliability were all rated a lot more highly than having the highest quality merchandise or the lowest prices. These are not necessarily easy virtues to communicate or 'prove' and companies face a difficult task in winning the trust of a fundamentally suspicious public.

eg Boots, the High Street pharmacy chain, has developed a website (**http://www.boots.com**) with dual objectives. One objective is to encourage visitors to buy online, by making it easy to search product categories, providing promotional offers to encourage visitors to act, making it easy to order and pay, and then providing the facility to track an order to the date of delivery. **Boots.com** outsells many of the High Street stores, especially at the busy times of year; and whereas a store might typically carry 15,000 lines, the website can offer up to 50,000 lines (Buxton, 2005). Increasingly, however, Boots is also seeking to use the website to drive customers into the High Street stores. IMRG (Interactive Media in Retail Group) predicted that by 2010 online shopping will represent 20 per cent of sales, and a further 40 per cent of sales will have been researched online before purchase (as reported by *Revolution*, 2005). The challenge then is to create a bridge between that research and a store visit. Increasingly, the integrated approach will be to attract potential buyers through PR and advertising. They then go online using a search engine to carry out their research on various websites, observing some advertising banners on the way, visit the websites or affiliated links for comparisons, and finally head for the chosen retail store for final confirmation and purchase. Boots wants to get the best of both worlds from its site (*Revolution*, 2005).

■ Consumer internet penetration and spending

Clearly, the opportunities for internet marketing are closely linked with a target market's ability to access the internet. The internet's penetration is still evolving and growing. In many EU countries the number of internet users more than doubled between 2000 and 2004, and in some of the countries that joined the EU more recently, such as the Czech Republic and Poland, the number of internet users has increased fourfold (Euromonitor, 2006). With so many more people having access to the internet at home, at school, college or university, at work, and at public libraries and cybercafés, its attraction to the marketer as a medium for communication, selling and other transactions is obvious.

Nevertheless, marketers need to exercise some caution. According to Euromonitor (2006), in some EU countries fewer than half of online users were actually using the internet to buy things. Even the best figures, 63.4 per cent in Germany, for example, show that marketers still have a long way to go in fully realising the internet's potential as a retail channel. Of course, the internet is not solely about e-tailing, but for many consumer goods companies it is a natural extension of their business, and it is important to them to see consumers becoming confident and accustomed to buying online to give them an opportunity to extend their customer base and generate extra revenues and economies of scale.

eg It is not just the youthful professional groups which have adopted the internet. Online travel has been booming, whether for air travel, hotel reservations or even complete packages. It is the over-50s who have been driving that growth. More than 86 per cent of the online over-50s had visited a travel website in the previous year, and in one month 1.5 million of them booked holidays online with Expedia as the most popular website. Travel is a particularly attractive topic of online browsing interest with research suggesting that up to 14 million people per month in the UK visit a travel website, spending on average 40 minutes per month looking at more than 70 website pages (Demetriou, 2005).

Booking your holiday or short break on the internet is a solution chosen by increasing numbers of people of all ages.

Source: Image courtesy of The Advertising Archives

The good news for marketers generally is that with increasing online penetration and greater familiarity, both the number of online shoppers and their average spend are expected to increase. Certainly, the UK buyer is spending much more on average than anyone else, perhaps because UK consumers are spending far more than anyone else in Europe on online grocery shopping. This reflects the proactive and very competitive approaches taken to online grocery shopping by the dominant supermarket chains who have invested a lot of money in setting up and refining the infrastructure to allow online shopping and home deliveries, as well as investing in marketing efforts to develop an online customer base.

■ B2B internet spending

According to the International Data Corporation, online B2B e-commerce was estimated to be worth $4.3 trillion by 2005 and still growing (**http://www.idc.com**). Much of the growth is being driven by companies recognising the advantages of moving to B2B e-commerce solutions, such as convenience, cost saving (up to 22 per cent in some supply chains), customer and competitor pressure as well as opportunities to generate new revenue.

Online procurement, pioneered by large, global organisations, represents a large part of B2B online commerce. A US survey found that 90 per cent of buyers surveyed regularly go online for product information with 50 per cent spending more than five hours a week looking. Around 70 per cent start their search with engines such as Yahoo!, with directories becoming less popular for online information (Burns, 2005). A further US survey showed that 73 per cent of organisations use the internet for indirect purchases and 54 per cent for purchases of direct material, with organisations with big purchasing budgets reporting the greatest involvement (Faloon, 2001). This could mean a lot of business. BA, for example, has used e-sourcing as a central part of its drive to lower cumulative running costs by £300m over a two-year period (**http://www.freemarkets.com**).

eg HP used the internet for B2B marketing aimed at smaller enterprises. Its research indicated that when IT professionals were evaluating IT vendors, they used the internet for researching specification and usage information even though they were buying offline. They researched widely and were heavily targeted by vendors, so it is important for a vendor to stand out from the crowd. A combination of techniques was thus used by HP to make an impact, including online banner advertising in local languages, and search engine marketing ensuring that key words linked through to HP. It also provided data feeds to price comparison engines such as Kelkoo where viewers often jump from a vendor's website to find the best price for an online purchase. HP has also created its own price comparison application so that potential buyers can compare prices for HP products through intermediaries without leaving the HP branded web space (Gates, 2005).

Some B2B online trading is being encouraged by the emergence of both independent and consortium-owned online 'marketplaces' or 'exchanges' that bring buyers and sellers together, facilitating transactions. They offer buyers access to a global network of suppliers and information on all aspects of their processes, practices and facilities and on their marketing focus. Acting as an intermediary, the marketplace helps would-be buyers to prepare their 'request for quotation' which advertises their needs to potential suppliers, and helps would-be suppliers to prepare their bids. FreeMarkets is one of the leading online exchanges, and any bids that are made through it include a cost breakdown so that the buyer can assess how realistic it is. FreeMarkets estimates that its clients save between 2 and 25 per cent on their purchases by using its service.

While online reverse auctions might be seen as a return to the bad old days of adversarial buyer–seller relationships, some companies and industries have thought in terms of 'e-collaboration' pooling information, data and resources online, often with direct competitors, and streamlining and integrating people, data and processes (Hewson, 2000). In October 2000, Covisint, an 'e-marketplace' or 'B2B exchange' serving the motor industry, started trading. Covisint was set up collaboratively by General Motors, Ford, DaimlerChrysler, Renault and Nissan at a cost of $270m with the intention of becoming the internet focal point for the global motor industry, a portal to which every buyer and supplier goes in order to find and

The buyer–supplier relationship under the hammer (or under the cosh?)

Through sites such as eBay, the idea of an internet auction has become well-established in consumer markets. The seller advertises the goods and the would-be buyer makes a bid. The highest bid made by the time the auction deadline passes gets to buy the goods. In B2B markets, the online reverse auction has started to become more common. The buyer advertises the specifications of what they want to buy and a starting price and then would-be suppliers make bids undercutting that price. All the bidders can see what others are bidding and can thus design their bids appropriately. Often, but by no means always, the lowest bid made by the close of the auction 'wins'. The lowest price does not always rule, however, unless the suppliers have been pre-selected on quality grounds (Carbone, 2005).

Understandably, buyers and suppliers have very different views on the benefits and usefulness of reverse auctions, as well as on the ethics underlying them. Some see it as a cynical way of frightening existing suppliers into reducing their prices. They find themselves pitched into an auction against both obvious well-known competitors and a few unknown companies, and although they don't make the lowest bid in the auction they still get to retain the business – but at a lower price than before. One existing supplier found that it did lose the business to an unknown competitor but later got a call asking it to continue to supply temporarily (at the new price, of course) because the auction winner had no experience of manufacturing that product and could not meet the delivery quantities required. Suppliers argue that if buyers were satisfied that all bidders could actually supply the quantities required to the specifications stated then the lowest price would

always win – but it doesn't. 'Auctions are not about getting the lowest price per se but getting the lowest price per supplier', as one manufacturer (as quoted by Watson, 2002b) put it. Indeed, price compression sometimes takes place resulting in a price no lower than that which could have been obtained by more traditional negotiation (Carbone, 2005).

Suppliers also feel that it is too impersonal a process with no room for old-fashioned face-to-face negotiation. There is too much emphasis on price and not enough on issues of collaboration and longer-term business development for the benefit of both parties. Suppliers feel that buyers are damaging relationships built up over years for the sake of short-term cost savings that are often not reflected in retail prices to the end consumer. Some buyers, such as Cisco and Dell, agree and have said that they will not subject their suppliers to this kind of process.

Most buyers who use auctions do not see it like this, however. They see it as a much more transparent process that can work in the supplier's favour as they can see exactly what rival bidders are offering and decide whether to undercut them (or not) and by how much, rather than going all-out for the lowest possible bid they can manage. Some suppliers are, however, cynical about just how genuine some of the bids are. One supplier, claiming to be number one in its field, said that the opening price on a relevant auction was 25 per cent lower than its best price. But as one buyer (quoted by Watson, 2002b) said, 'At the end of the day, it's a pain in the arse to change a supplier. We're not going to hold an auction unless there is a chance of a significant price reduction. And if we set a ridiculous price to open, we just shoot ourselves in the foot. After all, no one has to bid.' That may well be true, but it would be a brave supplier that would boycott an auction or would gamble on which rival bids should be taken seriously and which ignored.

Some big clothing retailers have introduced their suppliers to reverse internet auctions, often when sourcing large volumes for standard products with familiar and simple specifications. For clothing products such as shirts, the cost of materials can be between 60 and 75 per cent of the cost, so a 5 per cent saving can be significant. Reverse auctions have also been found to reduce negotiating times with manufacturers, but the emphasis is on a strategic partnership between the clothing manufacturer and its suppliers to ensure that the whole supply chain is competitive. In a typical auction, the opening bids are usually placed within 30 minutes and the whole auction is often over within two hours (Hirsch, 2005).

Buyers also claim that they do not use auctions in product areas where they have strategic relationships with suppliers as they do not wish to damage those relationships, but suppliers are claiming that buyers work on the principle that 'As long as you can define the product and more than one supplier can make it, you can auction it' (as quoted by Watson, 2002a).

Overall, the appropriateness of online reverse auctions and their impact on the long-term quality of buyer–supplier relationships is debatable. What seems clear is that their use in an industry seems to depend on the relative power balance between the parties and the nature of the goods and services being traded. High-tech companies such as Cisco and Dell operating in industries where there are few alternative suppliers, where suppliers hold the bargaining power, and where long-term innovation and collaboration are paramount may well see little point in risking relationships for the sake of short-term cost savings. Where the buyers are few and powerful, where switching costs are relatively low, and where there are many alternative suppliers, then it seems that the reverse auction is here to stay.

Sources: Anderson and Patel (2001); Carbone (2005); Hirsch (2005); Rosenthal (2002); Watson (2002a, 2002b).

place business. Covisint would conduct auctions and also be used to help run collaborative product development projects, taking products through from the drawing board to development and testing and into production.

Sadly, it seems that this particular e-collaboration was a Utopian dream and that the motor manufacturers had underestimated the level of mistrust and cynicism among the 7000 participating suppliers. The kind of objections outlined in the 'Corporate Social Responsibility in Action' vignette above began to be voiced. Suppliers felt that it was all just a mechanism to squeeze their prices down and did not like the idea of sensitive pricing information about their businesses being so readily available to competitors (Grant, 2002).

■ The marketing uses of a website

There are many reasons for an organisation to consider using the internet, but they tend to group into three broad categories: as a research and planning tool, as a distribution channel, and for communication and promotion, as seen in Table 14.1.

Table 14.1 Marketing uses of the internet

Research and planning tool

- Obtain market information
- Conduct primary research
- Analyse customer feedback and response

Distribution and customer service

- Take orders
- Update product offerings frequently
- Help the customer buy online
- Process payments securely
- Raise customer service levels
- Reduce marketing and distribution costs
- Distribute digital products

Communication and promotion

- Generate enquiries
- Enable low-cost direct communication
- Reinforce corporate identity
- Produce and display product catalogues
- Entertain, amuse and build goodwill
- Inform investors
- Detail current and old press releases
- Provide basic product and location information
- Present company in a favourable light – history, mission, achievements, views, etc.
- Educate customers on the products, processes, etc.
- Inform suppliers of developments
- Communicate with employees
- Attract new job recruits
- Answer questions about the company and its products

Research and planning tool

The internet provides direct access to a considerable amount of secondary marketing information. Some sources are free, but many can only be accessed through subscription.

Increasingly, the need to visit the library or purchase bulky directories and reports is decreasing as the power, convenience and flexibility of online searching become better known. Most organisations offering subscription services, such as Mintel, the *Financial Times* and the International Data Corporation, will update their sites frequently by adding new and updated information and reports. Many of the secondary data sources considered in Chapter 5 can also be accessed online.

As internet usage increases, the possibilities for primary research are also growing. Through online visitor books, feedback using structured questionnaires or via e-mail, web discussion groups and analysing visitor and online ordering traffic, useful information can be gathered for marketing planning purposes. It is also important to research the impact of the website itself, how the brand is perceived in an online environment, how the interaction proceeds, and how the site is used to create the desired viewer experience (Taylor, 2005).

Distribution channel

The growth of Amazon as an online retailer shows just how the power of the internet can have an impact on a conventional distribution channel. The impact will grow in the future as consumers gain more confidence in online purchasing. There are several advantages of online distribution:

■ The viewer is actively searching for products and services, and so every site hit could gain a potential customer if interest can be maintained. Regular and loyal customers can take short cuts and skip all the general background information. 'Shopping baskets' help the customer to keep track of what they have bought on this visit and help give the impression of a store just like any other. Books, music, DVDs, groceries, clothing and electrical goods, including PCs, have all become significant contributors to the e-tail economy. This is perhaps a sign that consumers are gaining enough confidence in online shopping to start making riskier purchases in terms of either financial risk (e.g. buying a high-priced PC or even a car and having sufficient faith that the online seller will deliver the goods in the first place and then be there to sort out any after-sales problems) or psychological risk (e.g. buying clothing on the basis of verbal descriptions and two-dimensional pictures).

■ Print and mailing costs are eliminated because no catalogue has to be produced and distributed each season. Although costs will be incurred in developing and maintaining an interesting website, they still represent a saving, especially because a website increases the seller's flexibility as it can be changed far more easily than the printed page with instant updates on prices, product availability and special offers. Amazon has well over 8 million users, yet the cost of communicating with them is a fraction of the cost that would have been incurred through direct mail or media advertising.

eg **Confetti.co.uk** dominates the online wedding market. It brings together information, advice, planning tools and purchasing opportunities (available on- and offline through its range of catalogues) and makes the organisation of weddings and other special occasions easier and much more fun for its customers. The site offers personalised opportunities for each user, be they bride, groom, best man, bridesmaid, family, guest or anyone else involved in a special occasion. There are twelve specialist channels: weddings, celebrations, gift lists, shopping, fashion, venues, men at weddings, café, supplier directory, travel, invitations, and health and beauty (http://www.confetti.co.uk).

It has proved very popular, and has become one of the leading women's websites for 18–24-year-olds. The website is a central part of the offering, because the content and online planning tools make wedding planning easier, more structured and more fun. It has been estimated that 90 per cent of would-be brides now research wedding details online before the big day, and Confetti makes it that much easier.

A natural extension of its wedding business is to go into anniversaries and special birthdays, building upon a formula that works and, in part, building upon relationships with previous customers. Confetti uses viral marketing (pp. 509–10) to target family and friends of existing customers, it uses e-mail newsletters, and it is considering setting up its own television channel, as the goods and services that it sells are high-involvement and benefit from display (Hargrave, 2005).

- Order processing and handling costs are reduced with online ordering as everything is already in electronic form and the customer is handling all the order entry without assistance. McNutt (1998), however, has argued that it is important for organisations to realise that opening the front door to customers with a website providing ordering capability means that they have to ensure that all the 'behind the scenes' logistics operations can cope with changes in ordering patterns. Linking back into the organisational systems for stock control and order fulfilment is essential if customer service levels are to be maintained.
- The IT systems have to be able to offer real-time information flows between the customer, customer support, distribution and the supply chain. Only then can realistic claims be made for cost-efficient and effective customer service, whether delivering a small parcel to Milan or Middlesbrough. Federal Express made a virtue of its integrated system by allowing customers to track the exact whereabouts of a particular parcel on the internet as a means of reassurance. It also turned this service into an effective selling tool to differentiate itself from competitors.
- Better after-sales service can be provided online, not only because of cheaper and easier communication, but also through feedback links, usage information, news flashes on any product changes and mechanisms for fault reporting.
- Digital products, in the form of magazines, music and video, are capable of being distributed via the internet, without the need even to send a parcel through the post. The distribution of music products that can be downloaded on to a computer is causing concern to CD manufacturers for copyright and piracy reasons.

eg Apple's iTunes website and download application grew by 241 per cent during 2005, thanks to over 20 million unique visitors. Teens aged between 12 and 17 are nearly twice as likely to visit the iTunes website as the average internet user, and 54 per cent of visitors are male. Despite the popularity of online file sharing and downloading individual tracks to build music libraries, CD purchases have not been seriously affected, as the downloaded material is often used as a sampler before the purchase of a complete CD by an artist. That CD itself could be purchased either as a download or as a CD bought online (**http://www.nielsen//netratings.com**).

- Manufacturers can get closer to the customer and potentially reduce costs through disintermediation, which simply means cutting one or more intermediaries out of the distribution channel (Rowley, 2002). Thus the package holiday company that sells online direct to the consumer rather than through a travel agent is bypassing an intermediary, as is the designer-label clothing manufacturer that sells direct rather than through a trendy Oxford Street retailer. There is a risk attached to this, however (quite apart from alienating the traditional intermediaries who are losing business). One of the roles of the intermediary is to bring assortments of products together and make them visible to the target market in one place. Online direct selling by a manufacturer loses this advantage and depends heavily on the consumer's ability to find the manufacturer's website. To overcome this, a new kind of intermediary, the cybermediary (Sarkar et al., 1996), has developed, including not only e-tail stores such as Amazon but also virtual shopping malls, online directories and search engines, among others, to help guide the consumer to relevant sites or to sell goods to them as a retailer would.
- In time, however, the growth of powerful ISPs and the emergence of customers in full control of what they will and will not search for and purchase could mean that the most powerful intermediaries in the twenty-first century will be the ISPs and search engine providers who build a wealth of information on individual customer preferences and requirements (Mitchell, 1999).

Communication and promotion

The internet is now as good as any other tool for communicating with customers and target audiences. Many of the principles discussed in Chapters 9–11 apply equally to the internet. As well as operating a dedicated website, companies are also taking advertising space on other companies' websites as joint or paid promotions. As can be seen from Table 14.1, extensive use is made of the internet for communications purposes. Many of the entries are self-explanatory. The main uses are as follows.

As an advertising medium. Table 14.2 shows the advantages and disadvantages of using the internet as an advertising medium (Pickton and Broderick, 2001).

Table 14.2 demonstrates that the internet is not a perfect advertising medium by any means. Its limitations and disadvantages are no more 'fatal' than those of any other medium, however, and simply emphasise the importance of incorporating internet activities fully into the wider marketing plan and using the medium within a coherent integrated communications strategy. It is also important, as we shall see with several examples within this section, to understand the target market and its internet usage patterns in order to identify the most appropriate use of the internet. Burns (2006) argues that strong visual design and careful web page construction are vital. Ease of navigation, straightforward checkout processes and helpful product descriptions are critical factors in easing the decision to purchase online. From research, she suggested that some of the main reasons for shoppers leaving a site are that they didn't want to register with the site (29 per cent), that they found it difficult to locate products (22 per cent), and that they went to other e-tailers because they didn't believe the site was trustworthy or secure (17 per cent).

Table 14.2 The principal characteristics of the internet as an advertising medium

Advantages	Disadvantages
• Message can be changed quickly and easily	• Limited visual presentation
• Interactivity possible	• Audience not guaranteed
• Can create own pages cheaply	• 'Hits' may not represent interest – casual browsers
• Can advertise on others' web pages	• Relies on browsers finding page
• Very low cost possible	• Can create irritation
• Very large audience potential	• Large numbers of target groups may not use internet yet
• Direct sales possible	• Creative limitations
• High information content possible on own web pages	

Source: Adapted from *Integrated Marketing Communications*, Pickton, D. and Broderick, A., Pearson Education Ltd. © 2001 David Pickton and Amanda Broderick

Advertising on the internet is thus similar to advertising through any other medium. The message should be communicated simply, clearly and by creating interest that will move the viewer through to further action, whether that is an enquiry, an order or just getting better informed about what is available. Many of the free internet access providers exploit this area to the full with comprehensive and sometimes intrusive display and banner advertising messages. Most of these messages are linked to the advertiser's website for further information and action. As the quality of information on web users improves, many of the ISPs have started to target advertising to their users, so for example a user with an interest in sport may receive banner advertisements on sports events and equipment. Amazon has gone further by creating a link with some search facilities, so if you want to know more about an organisation or market, you will be invited to allow Amazon to search for titles on that theme.

Choosing the right website upon which to advertise is obviously an important decision and there needs to be a close match between the brand's target audience and the profile of the audience delivered by the website. A number of brands targeting the 5–16-year-old age group have found the CiTV website (**http://www.citv.co.uk**) to be a successful medium for advertising and linked promotional activity. This website is connected with children's ITV and offers a fun, interactive environment with games, competitions, jokes, message boards, audio interviews, etc. Children are drawn to it not only because of its magazine-type content, but also because of its on-screen exposure during children's programming on the ITV channels and their desire to follow up links with specific programmes. Pontin's family holiday parks, for example, had a link with a crocodile game that also took the viewer with one more click into the full details of the parks' offerings. Lacoste, the fashion retailer, launched a data capture and sampling website for its limited edition fragrance Pop. On the site, visitors can request samples of four fragrances and the details they give could be used for future marketing campaigns. Targeted at the youth market, the online campaign sought to bring the fragrance to life through the proposition (*Precision Marketing*, 2005b).

Banner advertisements are still the main form of internet advertising, and normally appear either alongside a search engine on an ISP's pages while the customer is logging on to the internet, or as part of a joint promotion on another organisation's website. Most banner and other display advertisements enable the viewer to access the main information or booking page for the product or company with one click. Despite their power and convenience, there is some evidence from the US that banner advertisements are being ignored by viewers as wallpaper or background clutter, so their effect is wearing off, despite their intrusive capability. However, BMRB's Internet Monitor found that in spite of the fact that over half of internet users agreed that 'all web advertising annoys me', 40 per cent had clicked a banner in the previous month. Only 20 per cent of internet users agreed with positive statements such as 'I find web advertising interesting' and 'I find web advertising entertaining' (BMRB, 2000). Whatever the issues with online advertising, it continues to grow. In the first six months of 2005, online advertising in the UK alone was worth some £490m (Tiltman, 2005), more than in the whole of 2003. In Western Europe as a whole, online advertising was worth €3.2bn and this is expected to double by 2010 (Glover, 2005).

Loyalty reinforcement. The organisational website itself is also a powerful tool for increasing the level of interaction between the customer and the brand to reinforce loyalty. If the viewer can be entertained and informed, and enjoys coming back to the site, the brand values and image are enhanced.

Tesco has taken an interest in online grocery shopping for a number of years, but when it wanted to promote its clothing range further, it developed a dedicated website to showcase the range to existing Tesco.com customers. It offered £25 off garments upon registration and entered those signing up into a prize draw for money-off vouchers. Once registered to **www.clothingattesco.com**, customers receive regular e-mail newsletters on new clothing products, details of competitions and other promotions. An important part of the website was the store finder to tell customers where the clothing could be found, as currently it is not possible to buy the clothing online. The main role for the website is to build traffic to the stores and to keep customers informed of new ranges (*Precision Marketing*, 2005a).

Loyalty is clearly a big issue for e-tail sites too, trying to generate repeat business. As in any other form of marketing, it is cheaper and easier to sell to an existing online customer than to create a new one. Engendering loyalty through providing a trusted, quality product and service package is also important for e-tailers because it helps to deflect the consumer's attention away from pricing issues. One of the problems caused by the dotcom boom is that many e-tailers emphasised low price rather than service, product assortment or convenience as prime reasons to buy. This set up an unrealistic expectation in the minds of consumers that prices should be between 10 and 15 per cent lower on the internet than elsewhere. This is a dangerous strategy because if the e-tailer cannot deliver lower prices, then the consumer will not buy from them, and if the e-tailer does deliver low prices, it is vulnerable to making losses or to losing business to leaner, meaner competitors who can undercut. Thus in the wake of the dotcom shakeout, companies are perhaps taking a more sensible approach to pricing and trying to develop and emphasise less tangible and less vulnerable sources of competitive advantage and customer loyalty.

Corporate communications. The internet has been widely used by organisations to create goodwill and better understanding and to provide important information to shareholders and the community alike. Many organisations detail their financial reports on the web and often provide considerable coverage of their community relations programmes.

Often press releases are automatically placed on the web and so regular updating is necessary. Not only does this service help the media, but it also enables the organisation to get its message across to a wider audience in a more direct manner. Often press release archives can be accessed, going back several years. Even when full text is not available, contact details are provided to the press office for further enquiry.

eg Some web pages are designed to counter negative stories and views expressed by unofficial or even anti-lobbying group sites. Shell had to contend with a host of highly critical sites over its environmental record, particularly over its disposal of the Brent Spar oil rig, and its involvement in Nigeria. For example Bruno and Karliner (2002) contrast what they believe is a deliberate attempt to seemingly pursue a pro-environment and human rights strategy on the one hand, while still being engaged with destructive activity on the other. Shell, faced with such attacks, now uses both special web-based discussion lines and campaigns, along with a free flow of information, to counter some of the wilder allegations that are not actionable.

From its home page on **http://www.shell.com**, the visitor can click onto Tell Shell, a series of open discussion forums that are uncensored, other than for legal necessity. At the time of writing the most recent featured topics were 'How can we make transport systems more sustainable', a challenge to comments made by Friends of the Earth, and 'How can we meet the world's energy challenge'. Anyone can contribute anything, whether it is critical of Shell or not, although Shell will also put its own point of view, entering into the debate as it evolves. As Bowen (2002) describes it, it is 'a clever way of being transparent while getting its own views across'.

Sales promotion. Because of the relative ease of updating a web page and the flexibility it provides, it is possible to target offers on various products or over a defined period. Offers can be changed by the hour and the response of customers assessed (Wilson, 1999). Using price promotions, gifts and bonuses can all help increase short-term sales.

Personal selling. By its very nature, the web is impersonal and the internet is designed more for sales support and generating enquiries rather than for making direct sales. The cost per potential customer hit can be very low, and because people who do visit a site are likely to be interested in what it has to offer, the potential for increasing the level of enquiries is very great as net usage expands. Even in highly routine order-taking roles, the internet can be made more interactive if the customer database is able to personalise communication and relate it to offers that could appeal, based on a customer's previous enquiries and sales history.

Overall, the organisation should plan its use of the internet carefully and be sure that it is integrated into the rest of the marketing mix. Sumner (1999) argues that as much consideration should be given to the offline use of the website as to its online use. By featuring a web address in other advertising and promotional media, the overall site visibility is increased and additional site traffic could be generated. A glance at much poster, print and television advertising will often show a mention of an internet address for contact. It is important too that all of the internet budget should not be spent on highly interactive, fun websites at the expense of the more mundane, but critical, job of responding to e-mail enquiries.

■ Broadband

The wider adoption of broadband links, as opposed to the current dominance of narrow-band, is likely to revolutionise the potential for internet usage. In Western Europe, residential broadband usage has surged ahead and in the UK penetration is set to double within five years. Forrester Research (2004) predicts that 41 per cent of European households, i.e. some 72 million households, will have broadband access by 2010, and UK broadband penetration will eventually reach 42 per cent of all homes. As at 2005 in the UK only one-third of internet users have broadband, but price competition and a desire for faster transmission speeds is expected to see that rise to two-thirds within five years. Despite the rapid growth, the UK is just fourth in broadband density after Canada, Japan and France (Judge, 2005), but with growth in broadband usage of over 60 per cent across Western Europe, the revolution is still taking place (Macklin, 2005).

Broadband not only means faster internet connection, but because the bandwidth is greater it enables video and audio streaming rather than have the 'jerky' buffering and slower connections from normal line use. This means that live news and entertainment becomes a real possibility as a supplement, if not an alternative, to television. The rate of progress of broadband applications will depend upon the interaction of supply and demand. At present, there are not many streaming applications that merit the extra investment – after all why watch a film on a PC when there is top quality, high definition digital television available? Until revenues and penetration pick up, it is not worth the broadcasters' while to consider producing dedicated content for broadband. It soon becomes a vicious circle, slowing the rate of growth.

What are needed are new applications that can compete with television. Watching sports or business highlights from work or on the move, accessing specialist material such as DIY or gardening information, or browsing holiday brochures could all be enhanced by broadband. Such programmes are less likely to be mainstream broadcasting, even for the specialist satellite and cable television companies. The challenge for marketers, therefore, is to think through the applications where virtually real-time audio or visuals would enhance the proposition or support to the customer.

Tanner (2002) has suggested that people spend three times longer online each week (25 hours per week) when using broadband than narrowband. With increased time online, the broadband user is more likely to shop or bank online and be more actively engaged with internet services (*Financial Times*, 2005). It has been estimated that high-speed users view an average of 1144 pages per month, more than three times as many as narrowband users (Clawson, 2005).

eg As ISP providers increase the bandwidth for broadband services, new services such as video on demand, internet telephony and high definition TV over the web all become possibilities. This means that video can be used far more in web advertising to create impact (*New Media Age*, 2005a). BMW was an early pioneer in the use of internet short films when it ran a series 'The Hire', designed to offer high visual quality entertainment of car chases and high performance cars, between 2001 and 2005. During this time, the films received 100 million views between them (**http://www.bmwfilms.com**).

As broadband speeds grow, advertisers will increasingly regard the internet as not just equal to but better than television. Already, AOL believes that more people are logged on than viewing television, and when you accept that those online are active rather than passive viewers, the scope for providing a rich interactive experience with instant direct response mechanisms is a powerful attraction for marketers. This all helps to establish a powerful interaction with a brand that can lead to ordering and fulfilment (Clawson, 2005).

For broadband to achieve its full potential, technology, marketing and content need to be in line. A failure in any one can lead to delays and disappointment. As more material is compressed from video format, as new marketing applications are found and as broadband is installed, the power of the internet will be demonstrated to an even greater degree than in the first-wave revolution.

■ The future of internet marketing?

So what of the future of the internet in marketing? There are almost as many answers as there are pundits. What is certain is that more and more users will be attracted to the internet, bandwidth increases will enable more powerful applications and real-time communication, and finally the technologies will become more integrated, whether they are television-, PC- or mobile-based, and might even integrate some other home management systems such as hi-fi, security and climate control. To some, the internet will become part of television entertainment; others argue for more mobile media through 3G and even 4G, but most consider the future role of the PC for internet access to be limited in comparison.

For marketers this means not only greater opportunities for service provision, but also a more powerful medium for reaching consumers. It means more online research using chat-based focus groups, e-mail and internet-based surveys, more secure online buying, and more of a role for intermediaries to search, select and recommend buying options, as most organisations offer some form of electronic transaction facility.

Finally, in a mobile, last-minute society, wireless internet access will provide significant opportunities for attracting transient trade. Feather (2002) believes that there will be a move from 'www' to 'mmm' (mobile media mode), reflecting the increased use of access via mobiles. This will be considered later in this chapter. To Feather, the range of applications from mmm is very large indeed:

> Appliances will sense when food stocks need replenishing and order replacements to be delivered automatically to the home. Cars will call home, turning on appliances, setting room temperatures, filling the jacuzzi, and starting dinner. Even physical health will be automatically monitored and appropriate steps taken on your behalf. (Feather, 2002)

He then goes on to argue that by 2010, the internet will account for 31 per cent of all retail spending and most bricks and mortar retailers will be in trouble if they have not embraced e-tailing, largely due to the fully integrated nature of internet usage in individuals' lifestyles.

All of these exciting developments will depend less on technology, however; indeed in a number of cases the technology already exists. They will depend upon customer willingness to trust and participate with e-anything along with the suppliers of information and commerce services. With the service comes the loss of privacy when it is fully realised that virtually every click on the internet can be recorded and analysed. So the power will shift to the consumer for as long as the consumer is willing to use the low costs of switching and searching to full advantage. In part, that runs counter to many of the points mentioned earlier in this book about brand and company loyalty, buying inertia and risk aversion with some purchases.

Marketing and new media

Digitalisation has created new media opportunities to target messages better and to enable a far more effective personalised approach to acquiring and retaining customers. The advent of e-mail, wireless marketing and interactive television (iTV) has added a new dimension to integrated marketing communication and fragmented media usage to a degree not considered possible until a few years ago (Barwise, 2002). These new media opportunities have not replaced more traditional print and broadcast media, but are supplementing them as resources are reallocated to allow mass advertising and brand building and the more direct customer contact that is possible using new media.

This section examines the impact of three main elements of new media: e-mail marketing, wireless marketing and interactive television marketing.

■ E-mail marketing

More and more people use e-mail on a regular basis. A survey by Net Value estimated that in any one month we each send on average 12.3 e-mails and receive 39.1 from 13 million home computers. E-mail marketers, however, have to contend with an underlying scepticism about e-mail as a media vehicle. In 2004, it was reported that 19 out of 20 e-mails were spam; 10 per cent contained viruses, and 36 per cent phishing scams (*Precision Marketing*, 2005c). Brooks (2005a) reported that 63 per cent of people delete e-mail advertising without looking at it, while 56 per cent believe they receive too many e-mail promotions. Despite these difficulties, e-mail has emerged as a powerful means of communication that marketers are increasingly adopting as part of their promotional activity. We use e-mails primarily to keep in touch with friends, colleagues and contacts, and occasionally we use them to search for information or to place an online order. We may even welcome an incoming e-mail from a company that we have done business with previously or where we have declared an interest in what they are offering. What we do not want is to be bombarded with offers of cheap financing deals, special travel discounts, get-rich-quick schemes, herbal viagra or pornography. Many recipients are wary of receiving viruses via e-mails from unrecognised sources and therefore tend to delete 'cold calling' e-mails without opening them, just to be safe. Whereas e-mail marketers think that only 60 per cent of consumers would object to the receipt of unwanted e-mails, 80 per cent of consumers actually said that they objected (*Precision Marketing*, 2005c). Nearly half would rather not be contacted at all, whereas marketers thought it would be less than 20 per cent. The clock may well be ticking for unsolicited e-mail marketers.

Marketers are attracted to the potential of e-mail marketing as a communication tool that can target individuals rather than using mass media approaches. Carefully designed e-mail marketing can help to create initial contact as well as helping to develop an online relationship once transactions have taken place. The aim from a marketing perspective is primarily to encourage the reader to look at a website and to obtain permission to send more information to the recipient or to a third party. Typical uses of an e-mail marketing campaign are shown in Figure 14.1.

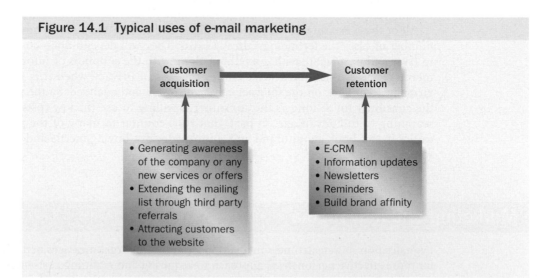

Figure 14.1 Typical uses of e-mail marketing

eg   Love it or hate it, Chelsea FC has a loyal following of fans, including 30,000 who are more than happy to be contacted by the soccer club. When Chelsea decided to launch a television channel with Sky, it used those fans as targets for an e-mail campaign. Research indicated that 56 per cent of the fans accessed the club's website on a daily basis and most would be highly receptive to a direct offer. The campaign, part of a wider promotional exercise, featured three e-mails highlighting Chelsea TV, giving details of a subscription hotline, and offering the incentive of a competition, along with further information. The campaign was a great success. The Chelsea TV call centre experienced three times the volume of calls in the period just after the e-mails were sent out and 91 per cent of subscribers were familiar with the campaign before the TV channel launch (**http://www.edesigns.co.uk**).

Rizzi (2001) argues that e-mail marketing has gone through three distinct phases since the first messages were sent through cyberspace in 1971, as shown in Figure 14.2. First there was the 'Broadcast/Spam Era' when e-mails were sent out indiscriminately, often with little attempt to target and tailor messages to the recipient. Consider sending out an e-mail message about Chelsea TV to an Arsenal supporter. Not only would response rates be very low, but it might actually generate (even more!) hostility to the sender. Some companies still operate this way, although European regulation is threatening to restrict spamming by moving from 'opt-out' to 'opt-in' schemes, thus assuming that people do not want to get e-mails unless they specifically request them. This has been prompted by the intrusive nature and sometimes dubious content of some spam e-mails.

Figure 14.2 E-mail marketing evolution

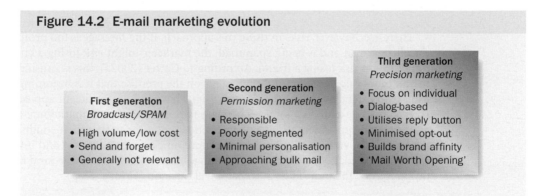

Source: Rizzi (2001). Copyright © 2002 e-Dialog, Inc.

The second generation represents the majority of e-mail marketers at present. Permission marketing offers the consumer the opportunity to volunteer to receive regular messages on special offers or new products (Dawe, 2002). Effectively it is an opt-in system but has been liable to some abuse, as the low cost and higher response rates from e-mail have been interpreted by some senders as permission to bulk e-mail rather than to select messages relevant to recognised customer needs and interests (Rizzi, 2001). Permission is the starting point, not the objective, of an e-mail campaign, so it is not surprising that e-mail marketing is moving into a third phase, 'Precision Marketing'. This combines the power of e-mail with the power of IT to record and analyse responses to ensure even greater targeting and almost individual CRM. In theory, each customer could receive slightly different mail.

Viral marketing

Viral marketing, or 'e-mail a friend', is word-of-mouth by e-mail. It is often deliberately stimulated by the marketer and is easy to achieve with use of a forwarding facility ('e-mail this page to a friend'). Alternatively, the customer could elect to provide details of friends who might like to receive information direct from the marketer. As considered in Chapter 10, word-of-mouth promotion and recommendation is often the most effective form of communication in terms of believability and trust.

Originally viral marketing was associated with youth brands to create a bit of excitement. If the material or the attachment is different and enjoyable, then there is more chance that it will be passed on. Lastminute.com, Budweiser and Levi's have all used viral marketing. Viral campaigns are not just the preserve of younger people, however. Age Concern used a viral campaign when it devised an e-mail quiz to test general knowledge of historical events. The quiz was scored and players were prompted to forward it to a friend so that they could compare scores. With a fun theme, people were happy to comply. Cause-related campaigns such as Comic Relief and Make Poverty History have also used viral marketing to solicit donor information (Reed, 2005).

eg Microsoft thought that it had an innovative creative theme when it launched a viral campaign for the Xbox 360 game Perfect Dark. US visitors to a game-related website were invited to provide the name and e-mail address of a friend who the female assassin Joanne Dark would 'take care of'. The friend then received an e-mail with a video attachment highlighting a body on a mortuary slab and a toe tag with their name on it (*Marketing Week*, 2005b)! Audi also used a viral campaign for the launch of its A3 Sportback. It wanted to generate requests for test drives and to reinforce the brand values. It sent an e-mail to 50,000 prospects with a film attached that had a story line that related the car's DNA with a human's, implying 'a perfect match'. Part of the response mechanism allowed the recipient to send a video clip to a friend in which the friend's name appeared. It generated a large number of click-throughs and forwarding because of the level of personalisation and the film's creativity (Rigby, 2005).

There are, however, risks in using this approach. If the message is too promotional, smacks of unsolicited mail and is being spammed, the marketer might risk losing a customer or the customer might risk losing a friend. According to Carter (2002a), this is causing marketers to seek to add more value to their viral campaigns on the premise that it is becoming harder to get customers to listen, let alone act. The campaigns have to have sufficient appeal and relevance for recipients to be bothered to act. There are two strands of viral marketing: the original strand aimed to get consumers to refer their friends to a website that then sought more details, but more recently, viral activity has focused more on generating interest and involvement through creativity (Reed, 2005). The more shocking, humorous or funny the viral campaign is, so the thinking goes, the more likely it is that it will catch on (Cridge, 2005).

Customer acquisition

Viral marketing is one way of building an e-mailing list, or a list can be purchased. Lists, whether they are purchased or rented, must be based on permission, a willingness to receive e-mails acknowledged by an opt-in mechanism. It is risky to use large, cheap lists of people to whom your communication may be most unwelcome. Some list owners are taking particular care about how their lists are used to avoid inappropriate or excessive use. Lifestyle data gatherers such as Claritas and Consolidata often record e-mail addresses as do online list builders such as Bananalotto and My Offers which sell permission-based lists. Some website operators now offer lists as a sideline, gathered from the users of their sites. TheMutual.net and Another.com, for example, have developed lists of relatively affluent young users who may be an attractive target for an e-mailing. Despite the attraction of these lists, the click-through rate may, however, be low, and rarely does it exceed 10 per cent for cold mailings (http://www.emailvision.com).

Online lists depend heavily on the sender's ability to track contacts from within its website. Sources can include online surveys, website registrations and responses to competitions and offers over the website. Web forms vary in the degree of information required beyond the e-mail details. Some seek data to enable customer profiling to take place and better-targeted messages to be sent before gathering the more specific information generated when or if clicks or orders are made. It is often advisable to seek only limited information at any one go, perhaps with three or four questions, rather than making the site visitor feel that they are being interrogated and delayed unnecessarily. If that happens, the visitor might lose patience or become uncomfortable about giving personal information away and fail to complete the registration process.

eg When Vodafone decided to adopt an e-mail marketing campaign to promote m-commerce in B2B markets, it established a list of existing and potential customers and then assessed them against predetermined qualifying criteria to ensure that they were appropriate decision-makers. At that stage Vodafone gathered the appropriate opt-in permission to enable it to e-mail only willing recipients confidently.

Customer retention

One of the greatest benefits for e-mail marketing is its ability to create and build a relationship with a customer on an individual basis. It can, therefore, play an important part in any customer relationship (CRM) programme. This requires a 'permission centre' (**http://www.emailvision.com**) comprising a list of opt-in respondents. Once the list has been developed, the response mechanism tracking can develop usable and powerful customer profiles. E-mails can be tracked for opening, clicks and purchases, so quite a detailed history, far superior to anything direct mail can achieve, can soon be built up. The more powerful and carefully designed the database, the easier it is to define small, well-focused sub-segments for targeting. The trend now is towards smaller and smaller segments, *micro segments*, perhaps comprising a list of just 100 people (Trollinger, 2002).

Although recording customer use of websites is a valuable tool for targeting offers and messages, some organisations now use e-mail newsletters to keep in touch with current and previous customers. These newsletters can play an important part of a more general CRM programme.

eg Flybe uses e-mail newsletters as an integral part of its marketing. It targets its e-mail content by sending out 11 different e-newsletters, each containing details of destinations served by the recipient's nearest airport (*Precision Marketing*, 2005c). Rainbow Flowers from Guernsey uses e-mail newsletters to promote its special offers on flowers, gifts and chocolates to subscribers, as a useful way of keeping in touch with both current and previous customers.

Personalisation is the aim of most marketers when building customer relationships. When successful, it combines all the benefits of personal selling with the cost-effectiveness of technology-driven marketing. Personalisation can take many forms, including:

- content
- offer proposition
- preferred frequency of contact
- transmission format (text, flash, etc.)
- subjects of interest
- personalisation by spend, product or interest.

The challenge for the e-mail marketer is to ensure that the database can facilitate data gathering and extraction to suit the particular purposes of a campaign.

Creative message design

Many of the principles of creative direct mail copy apply to e-mail messages. There is a need to make the right offer with a strong response-oriented copy (Friesen, 2002). This means careful targeting, a sound knowledge of customer clicking behaviour, personalisation wherever possible, and tailored rather than bland messages for mass e-mailing. The type of message will depend on the e-mail format – plain text, graphical html or rich media. Given the speed of response to campaigns, with 90 per cent of responses within a 48-hour period, adjustment can be made after piloting (Rizzi, 2001).

Viewlondon.co.uk is a web-based guide to 11,500 restaurants, bars, pubs and clubs in London. In order to attract a greater number of hits on the site, given that its ultimate success lies in its effectiveness as an advertising medium, it ran a competition entitled 'Are you Cockney or Mockney?', testing the visitor's knowledge of London. Although anyone could play, to have a chance of a prize, such as CDs, free drinks and free tickets, full registration was required. During the campaign, there were over 500,000 page clicks, the game was played 98,000 times and, most importantly for Viewlondon, 2500 new registrations were made. To keep people interested, there are new games and quizzes each month (Murphy, 2002). So if you know whether it's the Taj Mahal, Eiffel Tower or Statue of Liberty that is in Paris, your name, postcode and e-mail address are all you need to enter. All these traffic builders support its aim to become the first point of reference for Londoners searching for entertainment in London.

Even smaller organisations can, with creative design, use e-mail marketing effectively. For them it can be a very powerful promotional tool, given the often low level of resources available for promotion, but the emphasis must be on creativity, innovation and good execution (Sheehan, 2005).

eg The Fabulous Bakin' Boys from Witney near Oxford uses e-mail marketing. It created a database of jokes which could be downloaded from its website by registered users. The registration process asks basic questions such as gender, age, where you have seen the company's muffins for sale, and when you eat muffins. The prospect of some free samples is mentioned. It then introduced online games, and cheeky advertisements are regularly mailed out to previous website respondents (**http://www.bakinboys.co.uk**).

The Fabulous Bakin' Boys targets young adults who want good quality quick snacks delivered to their door or in their local shop. The website offers fun information to reduce any possibility of grumpiness.

Source: © The Fabulous Bakin' Boys
http://www.bakinboys.co.uk

The games, such as Muffin Munchin' and Cake Invaders, are designed to attract repeat traffic and each can be 'mailed to a mate' as part of a viral campaign. Online ordering is possible and look out for the golf game and the games graveyard. Alternatively, you could send a retro postcard showing a couple in swimwear sitting on the beach with the caption 'Percy was worried that Fanny's muffin would now be too sandy to eat'. Muffin munching will never be the same again.

As more organisations become familiar with using the internet as more than just a brochure supplement, the use of e-mail linked website activity will also grow for smaller businesses. The fragmentation of high cost, national media and the availability of targeted media that are within the reach of small business marketing budgets mean that there is likely to be much greater use of e-mail marketing in the next few years.

Response and review

One of the major advantages of e-mail campaigns is the speed of response. Ray (2001) described the situation at a holiday auction company where a newsletter issued between 4 p.m. and 5.50 p.m. will generate a significant number of responses by 6.30 p.m. and the bulk of the responses are in within two days. This means that considerable care must be taken to have a system in place to handle the response traffic generated. In part, the technology infrastructure can help to handle 'bounced' e-mails, undeliverable e-mails and routine enquiries, but in some cases, it may be necessary to have an inbound e-mail answering service.

eg In the Vodafone example mentioned earlier, a real-time reporting and tracking engine was employed that could list how many e-mails were sent, how many opened and how many clicked through. Normally, only 50 e-mails at a time were sent to allow for tracking, primarily over a six-hour period. Of the e-mails sent, over 50 per cent were opened and read and 21 per cent clicked through to the appropriate section of the website. Many of the latter were then converted into leads by the telemarketing team (http://www.inbox.co.uk).

Overall, targeted permission-based mailing campaigns generate an average response rate of 10–15 per cent, but this can drop to 2 per cent for bought-in prospect e-mail addresses (Murphy, 2002). After all responses are in, the analysis of campaign effectiveness can begin. This often requires careful pre-planning to cross-check unsubscribers, to assign codes to different target segments or different message types and to record the type of response generated, including where clicking has taken place but no formal response has followed. Data measured by campaign, customer or product on the number of openings and clicks, unsubscription rates, and bouncing, as well as responses, can be collected. This is an invaluable aid to updating records and further campaign planning.

■ Wireless marketing

If you are a Cahoot customer and about to go overdrawn you may receive a text message to warn you, and if you are on the Blue Arrow temps register you may be texted with information about vacancies as they become available. Text messaging is becoming an ever popular form of wireless marketing. Wireless marketing, sometimes called m-marketing or mobile marketing, has emerged as another major opportunity to target customers more closely, and as with e-mail marketing, its application is expected to grow significantly over the next few years. With over 2 billion mobiles in the world (Brodsky, 2005) and 76 per cent of the population in Europe subscribing to a mobile service, it is not surprising that marketers are attracted to the possibility of being able to reach consumers when and where they want (http://www.flytxt.com). It is predicted that spending on mobile marketing in Europe will increase from £75m in 2005 to £470m by 2010 (Brodsky, 2005).

M-marketing provides the means to carry voice messages, but is primarily used for sending text messages to targeted individuals at any time. Because of its intrusiveness and because different customers will be more receptive at different times of day, however, the m-marketer must fully appreciate consumer lifestyles and be careful in setting the right tone of the communication to avoid damaging any trust in the sender's brand (Carter, 2002b). Consider, for example, your receptivity to a text message received as you dash for an important meeting compared with one received over a relaxing lunchtime meal.

As in e-marketing, compiling target lists and profiles is an essential starting point. Consumers must be able to choose whether they want to receive information and there is a responsibility to ensure that any information is relevant. Irritation will soon grow if a torrent of mortgage deal messages are sent to students struggling to find next week's rent. It also follows that it must be easy to opt-out from receiving messages. Again, therefore, as with e-mail marketing, content selection should derive from customer profiling, but because of the medium, most text messages need to be short, alerting the individual to a special offer or promotion or engaging them with an interactive game that could direct them to a website.

eg Walls used SMS marketing to launch six Love Potion variants of its Cornetto brand. A 'teasecard' was given away free with every Love Potion purchase; it encouraged consumers to send a message with one of nine 'tease images' to a friend by SMS. The most original would win a £1000 prize for a dream date if the message was submitted. The target group was 18–24-year-olds, among whom there is a greater propensity to use text messaging (Rogers, 2004). Comic Relief also used a mobile link to run votes, competitions and alerts for a number of shows such as Celebrity Driving School and Celebrity Fame Academy. Mobile dominated the responses, and 70p of the £1 charged went to Comic Relief (http://www.flytext.com).

Most text messaging is currently SMS (short messaging service) which, as the name implies, usually means short, sharp messages to remind or inform. Marks & Spencer, for example, used e-mail and text messaging vouchers to encourage shoppers to visit a new branch in London with the offer of a free lunch, while Diageo ran trials targeting 16–24-year-olds with SMS text information and money-off vouchers if they provided their mobile numbers on entering some shopping centres (Carter, 2002b). Many campaigns, however, tend to be one-way communication, and fail to inspire or encourage interactivity. The next phase of development is likely to witness integration between voice and text, games, images and sounds to better entertain and engage the receiver (http://www.wirelessmarketing.org.uk).

eg Gossard wanted to eliminate sexist associations with G-strings and to reposition them as comfortable lingerie for the modern woman. It wanted to drive trial of the product and to build an opt-in database of its customers. The main campaign involved television and press, and this was followed by an invitation to text G4me in order to receive a £1 voucher for the G-strings range. After the initial text was submitted, the respondent was contacted back to ask them for their name, address and postcode so that they could be sent the £1 voucher. It also sought to build an opt-in mobile database for ongoing communication. The campaign was a great success. It achieved eight months' worth of sales within eight weeks; 1.5 per cent of the television audience responded, and 70 per cent submitted their name and address to receive their voucher. Through the database Gossard has regular contact with customers who account for 20 per cent of sales between them (http://www.flytxt.com).

The very strength of SMS could soon become its weakness, as more and more marketers are attracted to this new medium. One of the potential barriers to the development of text messaging is the continued bad practice of sending unsolicited text messages, along the lines of the earlier comments on e-mail spamming. One example that will surely become a classic was when an individual became alarmed at receiving a text message asking him to report to his local army recruitment centre after 11 September 2001 only to find that it was an advertisement for a computer war game. Some other activities are scams designed to encourage premium rate telephone calls. There are computer programs that will generate random mobile numbers and send out SMS messages to all of them, whether there has been an opt-in or not, thus constant vigilance is needed from the service providers.

All of that must be measured, however, against those who would welcome reminders or updates on something of relevance. How many garages contact their customers to remind them that their car is due for its annual service? Text messaging would enable low-cost reminders to be sent out along with a call for instant action to make a booking.

Users

The target market for wireless marketing campaigns tends to be younger and more willing to try new ways of communicating. Wireless marketing reaches virtually 100 per cent of the youth market, although there is some evidence of saturation in that segment with texting (http://www.flytxt.com). Mobile usage has become an important part of our lifestyles; witness the scenes in any High Street or, more annoyingly, in a crowded commuter train. It has moved from being a status symbol to an essential communication device, and fits well with the rushed, high-pressure, last-minute lifestyles of many younger people who leave decisions to the last minute and often make them 'on the run'. That plays into the hands of the m-marketers.

Happy Dog, a wireless marketing consultancy, proposed three broad categories of prime customers for targeting in its Moby Study (reported in Carter, 2002b):

- *Nomads*. Usually in the 18–24 age range, have few responsibilities, mainly live at home and tend towards last-minute decision-making rather than forward planning.
- *Gatherers*. Usually in the 25–40+ age range with the normal range of family responsibilities and career expectations. The mobile is used as an extension of the domestic phone as a matter of routine.
- *Hunters*. May be in the 20–35 age range, with few family responsibilities but enjoying to the full the stability and lifestyle that a career can bring.

These three groups may not represent all mobile users, but the profiles do suggest that the propensity to respond and the information sought will vary considerably between groups. This again highlights the importance of considering lifestyles as well as actual product usage behaviour when deciding on a particular campaign.

Systems and processes

Any successful wireless marketing campaign needs to be underpinned by an enabling technological infrastructure established either in-house or through the use of a specialist agency. The technological infrastructure enables reporting and tracking, personalisation and the interactivity interface, and must be capable of handling large numbers of outbound and inbound messages without crashing the system. Many organisations prefer to use established technology available from specialist agencies. Inbox (http://www.inbox.co.uk), for example, has a response management system that on receipt of an inbound message, sends a text message to the salesperson, orders a brochure to be sent to the sender by a fulfilment house, and e-mails an agent in a call centre. The priority then is to integrate the sophisticated technology that the specialist agency provides with the systems that individual marketers operate. MindMatics, for example, offers a 'Wireless Interactive Toolkit' that allows companies to start mobile marketing through standard applications without the need for any additional infrastructure. It uses a Windows-based application that connects directly with MindMatics' SMS gateway for sending and receiving.

The integration of these systems emphasises that it is dangerous to give too much attention to the creative and marketing application at the expense of the infrastructure that enables it to be adopted in the first place and to proceed effectively.

Next generation

SMS has limitations in that only relatively simple text messages can be sent, and it has been suggested that the number of text messages will soon start to plateau until the next generation of text services starts to become more widely available (Wray, 2002). The next innovation may incorporate wider use of EMS (enhanced messaging service), allowing small logos and icons to be sent over the air. A number of operators are, however, delaying major investment until MMS (multimedia messaging service) is introduced. MMS allows full-colour pictures to be sent over the air and in conjunction with video has the power to bring a handset to life. This will enable pictures, melodies, animation and styled text to be fully exploited in message design. This will make the handheld mobile the access point for a variety of entertainment, news and information services as well as the dominant e-commerce platform (Brodsky, 2005).

There are also issues about consumer acceptance of the new technology and their willingness to spend significantly more for the enhanced services because of the higher than expected cost of the handsets. Most text messaging takes place between friends and, although it might be convenient for marketers if enhanced MMS is adopted, the added value to the consumer is small unless there are significant changes in the desire for accessing information and entertainment on the move. It could be that the latest score from Wimbledon or the World Cup, or stock market prices, could be relevant to some, but that has to be related to increased rental or service charges. Marketers and consumers will have to be convinced of the financial rewards arising from those extra charges. MMS marketing can be five times as expensive as SMS but at present there are not enough capable MMS handsets to generate a return on that extra cost (*New Media Age*, 2005c). It is therefore not surprising that SMS still dominates mobile media budgets, but this will change as the capabilities of MMS, video and WAP-based content become better understood (*Marketing Week*, 2005a).

marketing in action

Hey, sexy!

Kiss 100 is London's youth radio station. It started life as a pirate station but was legalised in 1990. Its success has come from the central role it has played in popularising dance music and pioneering the growth of genres such as House, Garage, Hip Hop Jungle, Ambient and Breakbeat. It is recognised as being at the cutting edge of dance music and therefore attracts a loyal band of listeners. It seeks to generate ratings by day, and a reputation for being 'hot and sexy' by night, through its associated clubs. Every week, it reaches around 50 per cent of London's 15–24-year-olds who are among its 1.5 million listeners per week. It attracts a further 2 million viewers on its non-stop music channel on Sky Digital TV and the brand has been extended to holidays, clubs and network dance shows. Its Kiss CDs have sold 2 million.

Kiss is an experience brand that appeals to young people who enjoy fun and being sexy and has attracted an almost cult following. Kiss, therefore, wanted to use new media to create a strong customer relationship management

programme (CRM) for a generation that is unlikely to be responsive to direct mail and general mass media advertising. Kiss 100, with help from its retained creative agency, Angel Uplifting Marketing, and Flytxt, the wireless marketing expert, has thus used SMS effectively to promote greater listening and brand loyalty among its most loyal, committed listeners.

As part of a previous promotion, a database of 56,000 mobile phone numbers was created, called 'HeySexy' Club. This database of listeners who had opted-in to receive more information created a valuable marketing tool for maintaining regular contact with a willing audience, but it needed creativity and worthwhile ideas to keep them on the list and involved. Listeners initially registered by text message, via the website, or through a 0700HEYSEXY telephone line. Data captured included the registration medium, birth date and gender, as well as the obvious personal details. Two agencies, Flytxt (a mobile marketing specialist) and Angel Uplifting Marketing, were then able to design a campaign to improve loyalty through games,

competitions and promotions targeted primarily at the HeySexy members.

In all, over 20 different campaigns were designed to retain customer interest. These included:

- *The free 'Bamster' voicemail offer*, whereby listeners could phone an IVR line and download a free Bamster voicemail for their mobiles.
- The '*text to win*' competition that invited listeners to text in to the station while a particular track was being played, the track being repeated several times a day. Winners received a £100 prize, and there was evidence that listeners actually tuned in for longer periods to have a go at the competition.
- '*The Birthday Greeting*'. Every HeySexy member received a greeting from a Kiss DJ on their birthday, usually by the time the member woke up in the morning. The message is clear to the initiated: 'HeySexy! Bam Bam here. Happy damn birthday from me and every1else here@Kiss100-have a blinder & keep listening! TXT STP2 unsub.'
- '*The Anonymous Valentine Service*'. Listeners could send

anonymous Valentine's messages by texting a message along with the mobile number of loved ones to Kiss 100 for resending.

■ 'The Peach Party promotion' enabled listeners to sign up via text message for a £7 discount at the Peach Party guest list, a Kiss club at the Camden Palais.

The whole series of SMS promotions has been highly successful. Not only has the number of people on the HeySexy list grown, but an average of 13 per cent response rate for campaigns is normally achieved, which is well above what was expected. The response rate for the free Bamster voicemail was over 18 per cent. The Peach Party guest list contained over 16 per cent of all database members.

This example highlights the value of SMS in maintaining loyalty and developing a CRM campaign using a medium that this particular age group is very familiar with, and with content that is relevant to its lifestyle and language. Creating and retaining customer loyalty like this is very important to Kiss 100 as it seeks to attack Capital FM's dominant position among London's 15–24-year-olds (*Marketing*, 2001).

Sources: Marketing (2001); **http://www.kiss100.com**; and with grateful thanks to Lars Becker and Annabel Knight, Flytxt.

The 'Hey Sexy' campaign for Kiss 100 was an unqualified success in reaching its target market.

Source: © Flytxt Ltd http://www.flytxt.com

■ iTV marketing

Interactive television (iTV) marketing is still in its infancy, but does have the potential to revolutionise marketing communications by allowing the user, rather than the advertiser, to tailor information content and actions to individual needs. iTV is two-way communication between the consumer and the service provider who is responsible for delivering the communication to a television set-top box via satellite, cable or aerial and then creating the technology for a 'back service' to allow the user to interact. Normally the back service is provided via a normal telephone line, by wireless or, as in the case of NTL/Telewest, by special cable.

The problem with the development of iTV marketing relates to the overall take-up of digital television, a situation made worse by the demise of ITV Digital in the UK. According to e-marketer (2006), there are 16.5 million homes in the UK with digital television, well ahead of

France, Spain and Germany combined. However, the majority of applications tend to be linked with live television formats, such as quiz shows, voting, sports action (for example the player cam on Sky Sports), and only to a much lesser extent with interactive advertising. According to Two Way TV (**http://www.twowaytv.com**), gaming still dominates use. It found that:

- 10 per cent of households play Two Way TV games each month.
- 30 per cent of households play at least one game per month.
- 1.5 million games are played each month.
- Each player spends over £7.50 per month, with heavy users spending £30 per month.

The challenge is to convince advertising agencies and marketers that iTV offers a valuable addition to the media mix. Since the launch of interactive television on Sky in 2000, around 670 campaigns have been run for almost 200 clients. It took nearly three years to reach 200 and a further two years to get to around 500, suggesting that the medium is still in its infancy (Bonello, 2005).

eg When Ford launched the Ford Focus it devised a live 'advertainment' competition using ITV1 at peak times. Viewers were given a chance to win a Ford Focus estate and could respond by phoning, texting or pressing the red button. The purpose was to generate a response, to initiate customer contact and to build a database. The campaign generated 50,000 responses with one-third of interactive and phone entrants agreeing to receive updates on new offers. Pedigree pet foods also used iTV when it linked up with the This Morning programme. The interactive part allowed access to more editorial content for dog owners linked with an item from the show, and the opportunity to enter a quiz. The link between the brand and the programme was carefully researched to reveal the strong correlation with dog owners, presumably chilling out in front of the telly after the morning walk (Fry, 2005)!

From the marketer's perspective the main benefits of iTV advertising and marketing are perceived to be (in order of importance) targeting niche audiences, personalisation and one-to-one dialogue, providing a new channel to market, deepening the brand; and revenue generation (**http://www.emarketer.com**).

eg Nokia sponsors the highly successful talent show The X Factor. Although it was also interested in on-air exposure and the programme's dedicated website which linked to its microsite, Nokia was also interested in the way in which the programme used interactive television for extra content, voting and competitions. There were 1.5 million red button votes cast in a typical show and with such a high level of awareness Nokia was able to launch some new handsets on the back of the show. Citroën capitalised on its highly successful Happy Days campaign to relaunch the C3 by offering a red button facility. It allowed the viewer to go behind the scenes of the television campaign, enabled a further viewing of the 30-second commercial, and allowed the viewer to request a brochure or a test drive. The use of iTV was further extended to allow mobile phone users to download the Happy Days ringtone and to enter a competition for a jukebox (Fry, 2005; *New Media Age*, 2005b).

Targeting and personalisation are well ahead of the other perceived benefits. The set-top box is a source of considerable information to the service provider and enables it to build up a user profile just like any other media publisher. For on-screen interactivity, the growing number of specialist television channels covering everything from holidays to music, and from sport to motoring, allows careful targeting and the profiling of subsequent replies by the box. There is some concern that the power of tracking that is possible from the set-top box raises issues of privacy. Once this is addressed, it may curtail some monitoring (**http://www.broadbandbananas.com**).

Awareness of interactive advertisements is, however, growing only slowly, and many people who are aware claim to have seen an interactive advertisement but not to have interacted with it. Around 60 per cent of the Sky audience claims to have no knowledge of interactive advertisements (Gleave, 2005). There is also confusion over how interactive advertisements work, and given a reluctance to experiment, advertisers still have some way to go before the medium can be regarded as a powerful element of the promotional mix. Although the BBC, Sky and others have run campaigns explaining how the red button works, the interactive advertising industry has done little to promote its wider use. It is perhaps not surprising, therefore, that the average response rate from red button campaigns runs between just 0.5 per cent and 7 per cent (*New Media Age*, 2005d).

Despite some successes in the use of iTV, it is still early days for more widespread adoption. Even existing digital users regard the television as being for entertainment and the internet for information searching, so with current adopters the full range of interactive services are rarely activated. The service providers will have to promote the wider service benefits more positively, rather than focusing on the services at present that generate direct revenues. An advertising system that can show a standard car advertisement, for example, and with a press of the 'i button' can provide a menu of further information, show more footage, show the car in a selected colour and even allow a test drive to be organised, all from the comfort of an armchair, has many advantages over more conventional media that require telephone and mail responses. Its role for higher-involvement, high-priced, infrequently purchased items appears to be stronger than for more routine fmcg purchases.

All three forms of new media are still evolving, reflecting technological advances such as broadband, MMS messaging and two-way television. The opportunity to send personalised messages or to allow consumers opportunities to tailor the information they receive has been well received by marketers at a time of media fragmentation and greater difficulty in getting the message across. Coca-Cola, for example, has shifted some of its spend from television advertising into new media where it can target younger people with live music, sport and viral marketing (Day, 2002). As the technology improves, there will be more opportunities to create more complex campaigns to attract and retain attention, but only by encouraging interactivity will the real power of new media become evident.

There are still important issues to overcome in all areas, especially concerning privacy and data protection. Although privacy does not always appear to be a major topic for consumers, that may reflect the low level of understanding of just how companies collect and manage data about individuals (Barwise, 2002). With legislative trends and industry standards being imposed, the question remains whether the impact of controls on spamming and poor targeting can come quickly enough to avoid consumer resentment at being bombarded with a series of unwanted messages. The last thing genuine marketers want is to have their brands devalued by being regarded as 'pushy', or by association with spammers.

Chapter summary

■ Internet marketing has a wide variety of uses within an organisation, including information dissemination, PR, selling, CRM and market research, and is centred around the organisation's website which must be well designed to offer the user what they want in a form that is appealing and user-friendly. Internet marketing can be useful in any size and type of organisation, and can be very cost-effective in achieving marketing objectives when integrated with more traditional marketing tools and methods. The dotcom bust demonstrated that the 'traditional marketing values' of customer orientation, clear differential advantage and tightly controlled marketing planning and management and controls are still essential even for companies trading wholly on the internet. Generating and maintaining consumer trust are also seen as major factors in internet marketing success.

■ Internet marketing is increasing in importance as internet penetration among the general population rises. As individuals gain experience of using the internet and as their trust in it grows, they are likely to start spending more money via this channel on a much wider range of goods and services. The number of people buying via the internet and their average spend is already increasing rapidly. Businesses too are spending more on e-procurement. B2B exchanges or e-marketplaces run by independent organisations have emerged to help match buyers and sellers quickly and cost-effectively. Industry-specific exchanges, such as Covisint, dominated by large buyers have also arisen to streamline distribution chains and make them more cost-effective. E-collaboration on major projects is being experimented with, but so far has been disappointing.

■ The three main categories of internet use for organisations are for research and planning, as a distribution channel, and as a communications medium. The internet has opened up a vast wealth of information sources, both free and paid for, and has provided a new way of undertaking various types of market research. It has also become an additional cost-effective distribution channel with the emergence of e-tailers and cybermediaries alongside traditional companies using it in parallel with 'normal' retail channels. The internet has also become an advertising medium in its own right to complement other media and is also a means of delivering imaginative sales promotions and other incentives. It can add a lot of value to customer service and customer relationship programmes. In the future as the technology underpinning the internet improves (e.g. with the advent of broadband), its marketing uses are likely to become more sophisticated and consumers and businesses alike will come to regard it very much as a mainstream marketing tool.

■ The three main elements of the so-called 'new media' are e-mail marketing, wireless marketing and interactive television (iTV). E-mail marketing is primarily used as a means of CRM, to create and nurture relationships with customers through regular, targeted, relevant contact. Imaginative and well-designed messages can be used in viral marketing campaigns, encouraging the recipient to pass the message on to a friend to exploit word-of-mouth advantages. Wireless marketing (m-marketing or mobile marketing) harnesses the power of the mobile telephone and mainly involves text messaging as a form of marketing communication. As with the internet, advances in technology are likely to open up new applications for wireless marketing. iTV marketing provides the opportunity for two-way communication between the marketer and an individual via the television set. The consumer can use the interactive facility on the remote control to request further information about a product, or to interact in many ways as they would on the internet. The main problems, however, are the costs of creating the necessary digital networks to deliver the iTV service, and consumer acceptance and adoption of the full range of iTV capabilities.

Questions for review and discussion

14.1 What are the major advantages and disadvantages of *reverse auctions* from the B2B supplier's point of view?

14.2 Outline the three main categories of *website usage* for businesses.

14.3 What is *viral marketing* and why is it so useful to the marketer?

14.4 Compile a checklist of criteria against which a fashion e-tail website might be assessed. Visit three websites e-tailing clothing to a similar target audience. Compare and contrast those

sites in terms of their performance on those criteria. How could each of them improve its offering?

14.5 'New media have nothing more to offer the marketer than the more traditional forms of marketing communications.' Discuss.

14.6 Draw up a table listing the advantages and disadvantages of e-mail marketing compared with more traditional approaches to direct marketing. In what kind of situations do you think e-mail marketing might work best?

case study 14

E-loves me, e-loves me not

By Sylvia Rogan

In 1970, the twentieth 'Carry On' film featuring, of course, Sid James and Hattie Jacques was released. In 'Carry On Loving', Sid and Hattie run a dating agency called 'The Wedded Bliss Agency' which aims to bring together the lonely hearts of Much-Snogging-in-the-Green using a computer, which is completely bogus. To advertise the agency, the owner, Sid, produces a pamphlet called 'The Wit to Woo' and the strange collection of hopefuls desperate for romance leads to some outlandish matches and plenty of mayhem.

The technology might have evolved, and the marketing become more sophisticated, but the needs and the fears of the lonely hearts are the same as ever. As with The Wedded Bliss Agency, how can we be sure of the authenticity of any agency currently being advertised? There has been a tremendous growth in online dating agencies and chat rooms in the UK as they are easy to set up and require very little maintenance or manpower. No expertise, experience or even interest in the field of dating is required and they are cheap to set up, as the overheads in terms of offices, equipment and staffing are very low. Also, for those with little knowledge of computing, off-the-shelf software can be purchased.

Channel five screened a documentary (Channel five, 2005) examining the extraordinary rise of the dating agency in Britain. It reported that over the last 50 years, around 10 million people have used them, and that two out of every five singles trust them to help find their perfect partner. The first computer dating agency, Dateline, was established in 1966. The appliance of science to romance promised true love, and computer dating which matched up men and women with similar likes and dislikes was an instant hit. But, by the 1970s, the popularity of Dateline waned as it found it difficult to deliver on its promise (remember 'The Wedded Bliss Agency'!). Computer dating nevertheless continued, but was overtaken by a craze for video dating in the 1980s, followed by internet dating and international dating agencies in the 1990s, and finally speed dating.

In the last few years, mate-finding and courtship have seen further changes due to online dating services. Through the use of personal computers and the internet, these services help individuals, couples and groups to meet online and possibly develop social, romantic or sexual relationships. In a European sociocultural environment characterised by increasing affluence, with a tendency to establish a career before 'settling' down, and thus later marriage, with a greater propensity for divorce, and with a growing number of internet-savvy, geographically mobile young singles, it would seem that these services really are meeting a market need. Add to that the loss of many of the traditional mate-seeking social networks such as the church, closeknit extended families, and community dances, and it's not surprising that according to research quoted by Rowan (2006), there are over 800 dating sites in the UK alone, and in Europe as a whole the value of this market is forecast to rise from £115m in 2005 to £260m by 2010. Hoyle (2006) suggests that 65 per cent of the 5.4 million Britons seeking a partner used online dating services in 2005. As Mary Balfour, the founder of online dating agency Love and Friends, says, 'People work harder, settle down later and live more isolated lives. They're much more likely to end the day with a DVD and a can of beer than by going to a village dance' (as quoted by Hoyle, 2006).

Setting up as an online dating agency is very easy. The British dating service Dating Direct.com was set up for £250 using off-the-shelf software and is now the largest UK agency, with 3.2 million UK members and a turnover of over £10m, and yet just 13 employees. Marc Simoncini, founder of European dating agency meetic.com, says, 'As business models go, online-dating sites approach perfection. All we needed was two months of free services, and then word of mouth took over. Now our customers are our products, and they deliver themselves to each other' (as quoted by Tiplady, 2005).

The ease of start-up and lack of industry regulation has led to a proliferation of dating sites and there is now evidence that sites are starting to have to differentiate themselves in more sophisticated ways to attract customers. Some do it through the extent and quality of the profiling methods they use in order to match potential partners more closely, and many do it through focusing on a very specific niche segment, so there are dating agencies for various religions and dating agencies for tall people, short people, smokers, vegans, parents and gay people, as well as sites focusing on all sorts of activities and interests of a sporting, cultural or sexual nature. Then there's **http://www.seventy-thirty.com** whose membership fees for 'high net worth' individuals start at £10,000 per year. The aim of the specialist agency is to attract like-minded people so that a customer can be confident that their 'key characteristic' is accepted and thus there is no fear of rejection because of it. Customers can also be more confident that the agency and its other clients are used to working with any social and cultural consequences of that characteristic. A specialist Hindu agency, for example, would be capable of coping with the differences in

By using psychometric testing, nomorefrogs helps individuals to discover their perfect partner without having to kiss too many frogs, a none-too-subtle reference to childhood fairy stories.

Source: © nomorefrogs Ltd http://www.nomorefrogs.com

caste that would confuse non-Hindus, while a vegan agency would be aware of the wide implications for lifestyle that serious veganism can have.

One example of a specialist site is **BeautifulPeople.net** which is based on the premise that 'Beautiful people prefer to date other beautiful people. It's why Hollywood stars only go out with each other. Everyone knows that, but most would never dare to say it out loud. We just want to unite beautiful people. We're not interested in political correctness' (Greg Hodge, founder, as quoted by Chaudhuri, 2005). Potential clients have to submit a photograph and detailed personal profile which is then examined by existing members who then decide whether to accept or reject that application. Some people have been spending a lot of money on professional make-overs and photo-shoots just to get in! Once in, there is a sliding scale of charges for accessing all the facilities of the agency, from £5.00 for two days to £69.99 for a year. At the time of our visit to the UK site, there were 32,722 applications in process and 7822 members registered (all figures as at 28 January 2006).

On the face of it, **http://www.nomorefrogs.com**, based on the premise that you have to kiss a fair few frogs before you find your prince, might seem to share Beautiful People's core philosophy. It doesn't, however, focus on anything as shallow as 'looks'; rather it seeks to match people in terms of the compatibility of their personalities using detailed psychometric profiling.

It is free to register on the site, and then to become a full member it costs £38 for two months, £49 for three months and £72 for six months. Thereafter, renewal fees are £29 for two months and £40 for three months (all prices as at 28 January 2006). Let's hope it does help the princesses to find the right frogs!

For the lonely bikers among you, **bikerdating.co.uk** urges you to '*Join today and find other like minded bikers looking for love, friendship and expand your social life. Chat instantly to bikers worldwide via the Biker Chat room or message board. An important part of meeting the right partner is having shared interests, Biker Dating personals aims to provide an online forum for motorcyclists worldwide to chat, meet and socialise with people they know will share their passion for hot motorbikes*' (**http://www.bikerdating.co.uk**). It costs nothing to submit a profile, but a subscription is necessary to access the full range of services and facilities.

Going to a specialist agency does, therefore, give some reassurance that you'll find someone with whom you have something in common, but there are still some fundamental trust issues that have to be addressed, particularly about the honesty of the potential partners that you are being asked to consider. There are lots of stories, some funny, some frightening, about dates turning out to be something other than they claimed to be in their online profiles. The tall, dark, handsome, 35-year-old brain surgeon who turns out to a short, bald, 40-something year-old bus driver might be viewed as a sad, annoying waste of time (or indeed as very good company, once you get over the initial shock), but equally the deception could signal darker tendencies. Unfortunately, joining an agency which charges a higher fee is no guarantee that they will provide a better service or that security vetting of potential clients will be carried out. Most sites explicitly carry a disclaimer in the small print saying that they cannot guarantee that all their clients are trustworthy and honest, and in fact many agencies have pointed out that unless they have access to police records, they can never be entirely certain about the backgrounds of their clients. It is impossible to rule out all risks when using a dating agency or going on a blind date, but reputable agencies will give advice on commonsense safety rules for contacting and meeting potential partners, will never give out details such as surnames or addresses, and will carry out detailed electronic or personal interviewing to verify the identity and motivation of potential clients before accepting them.

Not all agencies are as reputable as they might be, however. It is not unknown for agencies to indulge in 'date-bait', i.e. sending out employees on dates to keep a client active and interested in the service when there are no suitable 'real' potential dates on the books. Similarly, some agencies have sent out false romantic e-mails to clients whose use of the service is declining to rekindle their interest, and if the pool of clients is looking just a bit jaded or limited, then why not create some interesting (but fictitious) new members? Care thus has to be taken. Although most agencies are honest and genuinely motivated to find a match for their members, some are set up purely as a lucrative sideline, or as an easy way to make money with a minimum of commitment to the people who use them.

So what is the future of the online dating industry? Some agencies are evolving into 'social networking' sites such as **http://www.friendster.com** where you can track the connections of people you already know to meet the friend of a friend of a friend. A further extension of this is 'mblogs', mobile community sites on which members can recommend partners to a network of friends via phone and internet. Perhaps meeting this way, via personal introductions, is a little safer than picking up relative strangers. Another interesting innovation from Dateline embraces 3G technology to provide a 'mobile dating' service. If you have a 3G mobile phone, you can record a one-minute video clip of yourself and submit it. Then, Dateline will send you a text when it has a potential partner for you and you can view that person's video profile to see whether you fancy them or not. If you do, then you can start exchanging messages over the system (which is designed to protect personal privacy and safety, of course) and take it from there.

So, the future seems to lie in SMS, MMS, camera phones and webcams. Whatever the technology, however, it's still all about good old-fashioned marketing values of convenience, service and giving the customer what they want. While no agency can guarantee to find you the love of your life, or even to weed out all of the frogs who aren't princes in disguise, if the testimonials and home page blurbs are to be believed, many lonely singles do indeed find true luurve on t'internet.

Sources: Channel five (2005); Chaudhuri (2005); Hoyle (2006); Hunt (2004); Marsh (2005); Rowan (2006); Sabbagh and Kirkham (2005); Tiplady (2005); **http://www.dating-agencies-uk.co.uk**; **http://theanswerback.co.uk**.

Questions

1 Summarise the sociocultural trends that have contributed to the success of online dating, and the ways in which online dating services have responded to those trends.

2 Visit four different online dating agency sites. Define their apparent target markets and compare and contrast their marketing mix approaches to assess their positioning.

3 Beyond the obvious use of the internet, what contribution can other new media make to dating agencies' marketing and their service delivery?

References for chapter 14

Anderson, J. and Patel, P. (2001), 'B2B Makes Seller Suffer', *The Times*, 12 July, p. 2.9.

Apparel Industry Magazine (2000), 'Who Will E-tail Your Products Best?', *Apparel Industry Magazine*, February, pp. 40–1.

Barr, D. (2002), 'Whatever Happened to These Likely Fads?', *Evening Standard*, 11 June, p. 14.

Barwise, P. (2002), 'Great Ideas. Now Make Them Work', *Financial Times*, 28 May, p. 4.

BMRB (2000), 'Users Ignore Banners, but Off-line Makes Up the Difference', accessed via **http://www.bmrb.co.uk**.

Bonello, D. (2005), 'The State of iTV', *Revolution*, September, pp. 50–2.

Bowen, D. (2002), 'Handling the Bad News', *Financial Times*, 25 January, p. 11.

Brodsky, I. (2005), 'Get Ready for Mobile Marketing', *Network World*, 7 November, p. 45.

Brooks, G. (2005a), 'Overcrowded Inbox', *Marketing*, 13 July, p. 13.

Brooks, G. (2005b), 'Strategic Play – Chelsea FC: Winning Streak', *New Media Age*, 28 July, p. 18.

Bruno, K. and Karliner, J. (2002), 'Shell Games at the Earth Summit', *CorpWatch*, 15 August, accessed via **http://www.corpwatch.org**.

Burns, E. (2005), 'IT Marketers Best Served by Being Straightforward', 19 September, accessed via **http://www.clickz.com**.

Burns, E. (2006), 'Web Design Key for Online Shoppers', 18 January, accessed via **http://www.clickz.com**.

Buxton, P. (2005), 'Web Helps Fuel Boots' Recovery', *Revolution*, September, pp. 30–2.

Carbone, J. (2005), 'Reverse Auctions Become More Strategic for Buyers', *Purchasing*, 8 December, pp. 42–3.

Carter, B. (2005), 'OnSpeed', *Marketing*, 8 June, p. 25.

Carter, M. (2002a), 'Branded "Viruses" Mutate to Entice Consumers', *Financial Times*, 7 January, p. 14.

Carter, M. (2002b), 'How to Hit a Moving Target', *The Guardian*, 27 May, p. 42.

Channel five (2005), *Secrets of the Dating Agency*, broadcast December, Channel five television.

Chaudhuri, A. (2005), 'Beautiful People Only', *The Sunday Times*, 17 April, p. 28.

Clawson, T. (2005), 'High-speed Shift', *Revolution*, July/August, pp. 48–50.

Cridge, M. (2005), 'Virtues of Viral', *Campaign*, 29 April, p. 13.

Dawe, A. (2002), 'Hitting the Target', *Director*, February, p. 17.

Day, J. (2002), 'Hard Sell in Your Hand', *The Guardian*, 19 March, p. 50.

Demetriou, D. (2005), 'Over-50s Log On Most', *Daily Telegraph*, 26 November, p. 4.

e-marketer (2006), 'UK TV Goes Digital', 4 January, accessed via **http://www.e-marketer.com**.

Edgecliffe-Johnson, A. (2005), 'Friends Are Not All ITV May Hope Them to Be', *Financial Times*, 8 November, p. 23.

Euromonitor (2006), *European Marketing Data and Statistics 2006*, Euromonitor (41st edn).

Faloon, K. (2001), 'B2B Adoption of Online Activities Expanding', *Supply House Times*, September, p. 30.

Feather, F. (2002), *FutureConsumer.Com: The Webolution of Shopping to 2010*, Warwick Publications.

Financial Times (2005), 'Broadband Surges Ahead', *Financial Times*, 20 April, p. 6.

Forrester Research (2004), *European Residential Broadband Forecast: 2004 to 2010*, Forrester Research, December 2004.

Friesen, P. (2002), 'How to Develop an Effective E-mail Creative Strategy', *Target Marketing*, February, pp. 46–50.

Fry, A. (2005), 'Interactive Opportunities', *Marketing*, 21 September, pp. 21–4.

Gates, D. (2005), 'Netting B2B Customers', *Brand Strategy*, 8 September, p. 54.

Gaudin, S. (2002), 'The Site of No Return', 28 May, accessed via **http://cyberatlas.internet.com**.

Gleave, S. (2005), 'iTV Data', *New Media Age*, 28 July, p. 28.

Glover, T. (2005), 'Google Sets Sights on Europe for Growth', *Sunday Business*, 13 November, p. 1.

Grant, J. (2002), 'Covisint Fails to Move Up into the Fast Lane', *Financial Times*, 4 July, p. 23.

Hargrave, S. (2005), 'Confetti.co.uk: Party Planners', *New Media Age*, 14 July, p. 18.

Hewson, D. (2000), 'Firms Reap Net Profits by Learning to Work Together', *e-business* supplement to *Sunday Times*, 26 November, p. 2.

Hirsch, S. (2005), 'Reverse Auctions Sharpen Competition', *International Trade Forum*, 3, pp. 14–15.

Hoyle, B. (2006), 'Why Today's Singles are Logging On in the search for Love at First Byte', *The Times*, 5 January, p. 6.

Hunt, J. (2004), 'Making the Perfect Match', *New Media Age*, 25 March, pp. 25–7.

Judge, E. (2005), 'Broadband Use in UK Surpasses US Levels', *The Times*, 22 September, p. 54.

Kolesar, M. and Galbraith, W. (2000), 'A Services Marketing Perspective on E-retailing: Implications for E-retailers and Directions for Further Research', *Internet Research*, 10(5), pp. 424–38.

Macklin, B. (2005), 'European Broadband Take-up Picks up Pace', *New Media Age*, 14 April, p. 7.

Marketing (2001), 'Best Use of Technology: Customer Loyalty', *The Marketing Awards: Connections 2001 supplement to Marketing*, November 2001.

Marketing Week (2004), 'Friends Extends its Circle of Reuniteds', *Marketing Week*, 18 November, p. 25.

Marketing Week (2005a), 'To Boldly Go Fully Mobile', *Marketing Week*, 8 September, p. 34.

Marketing Week (2005b), 'Microsoft Courts Trouble with Viral Marketing Push', *Marketing Week*, 20 October, p. 19.

Marsh, S. (2005), 'Wanted: Women Willing to Go Out with Strangers Who Lie ...', *The Times*, 4 August, p. 6.

McNutt, B. (1998), 'A Matter of Priority', *Precision Marketing*, 21 December, p. 16.

Mitchell, A. (1999), 'Online Markets Could See Brands Lose Control', *Marketing Week*, 15 April, pp. 24–5.

Murphy, D. (2002), 'Marketers Put E-mail to the Test', *Marketing*, 6 June, pp. 19–20.

New Media Age (2005a), 'Now Broadband's a Success, What Do We Do with It?', *New Media Age*, 25 August, p. 12.

New Media Age (2005b), 'Citroën Takes iTV Viewers Behind Happy Days Ad', *New Media Age*, 6 October, p. 2.

New Media Age (2005c), 'Why is Mobile Marketing Struggling to Get Beyond SMS?', *New Media Age*, 6 October, p. 28.

New Media Age (2005d), 'Will Viewers Buy into Shopping Via iTV Ads?', *New Media Age*, 13 October, p. 10.

Newing, R. (2002), 'Crucial Importance of Clear Business Goals', *Financial Times*, 5 June, p. 4.

Pankhurst, S. (2005), 'How We're Staying Connected in this Disconnected World', *Revolution*, September, p. 13.

Pickton, D. and Broderick, A. (2001), *Integrated Marketing Communications*, Financial Times Prentice Hall.

Precision Marketing (2005a), 'Tesco Launches Site to Promote Clothing Range', *Precision Marketing*, 1 July, p. 2.

Precision Marketing (2005b), 'Lacoste Offers Pop Perfume Samples Online', *Precision Marketing*, 1 July, p. 6.

Precision Marketing (2005c), 'A Sure Thing', *Precision Marketing*, 7 October, p. 17.

Ray, A. (2001), 'Profiting from the E-mail Grapevine', *Marketing*, 11 October, p. 27.

Reed, D. (2005), 'Too Much Information', *Precision Marketing*, 3 June, p. 25.

Revolution (2005), 'Time to Take the Web Out of its Box', *Revolution*, September, p. 25.

Rigby, E. (2005), 'Campaign of the Month', *Revolution*, April, p. 87.

Rizzi, D. (2001), 'Precision E-mail Marketing', *Direct Marketing*, November, pp. 56–60.

Rogers, E. (2004), 'Cornetto Backs Love Potions Line with SMS Push', *Marketing*, 19 May, p. 4.

Rosenthal, R. (2002), *Worldwide B2B Dynamic Pricing Forecast, 2002–2006: 'What Am I Bid for This…'*, March, Doc #26801 accessed via **http://www.idc.com**.

Rowan, D. (2006), 'Downloading Mr Right', *Sunday Times*, 8 January, p. 15.

Rowley, J. (2002), *E-business: Principles and Practice*, Palgrave.

Sabbagh, D. and Kirkham, S. (2005), 'Now Video Phone Answers Love's Call', *The Times*, 18 March, p. 16.

Sarkar, M., Butler, B. and Steinfield, C. (1996), 'Intermediaries and Cybermediaries: A Continuing Role for

Mediating Players in the Electronic Marketplace', *Journal of Computer Mediated Communication*, 1 (3).

Sheehan, D. (2005), 'Good Ideas Need Great Execution', *Revolution*, April, p. 73.

Smith, P. and Chaffey, D. (2001), *eMarketing eXcellence: At the Heart of e-Business*, Butterworth-Heinemann.

Smith, P. and Taylor, J. (2002), *Marketing Communications: An Integrated Approach* (3rd edn), Kogan Page.

Sumner, I. (1999), 'Web Site Novelties Can Bring PR Opportunities', *Marketing*, 17 June, p. 31.

Tanner, J. (2002), 'Broadband Vision', *America's Network*, 1 May.

Taylor, R. (2005), 'Time Spent on Site Design is Wasted Without User Research', *New Media Age*, 21 July, p. 17.

Tiltman, D. (2005), 'Digital Leagues', *Marketing*, 26 October, pp. 37–42.

Tiplady, R. (2005), 'Europe Falls in Love with e-dating', *Business Week Online*, 8 February.

Trollinger, S. (2002), 'The Role of E-mail in Micro-segmentation', *Target Marketing*, May, pp. 28–30.

Watson, E. (2002a), 'Online Auctions Come Under Fire', *The Grocer*, 29 July, p. 4.

Watson, E. (2002b), 'Hitting the Floor', *The Grocer*, 6 July, pp. 34–5.

White, D. (2005), 'ITV Chief Seeks Board's Blessing to Unite with Friends', *Daily Telegraph*, 3 December, p. 30.

Wilson, R. (1999), 'Discerning Habits', *Marketing Week*, 1 July, pp. 45–7.

Wray, R. (2002), 'Mobile Chiefs Get the Message', *The Guardian*, 14 May, p. 20.

index

index of company names